The Mythology of Eden

Arthur George and Elena George

Hamilton Books

A member of
Rowman & Littlefield
Lanham • Boulder • New York • Toronto • Plymouth, UK

Hamilton Books
4501 Forbes Boulevard, Suite 200, Lanham, Maryland 20706
Hamilton Books Aquisitions Department (301) 459-3366

10 Thornbury Road, Plymouth PL6 7PP, United Kingdom

Library of Congress Control Number: 2014933198
ISBN: 978-0-7618-6288-8 (paper   )—ISBN: 978-0-7618-6289-5 (electronic)

Myths are seldom simple, and never irresponsible.

Robert Graves

*Myth is the foundation of life. It is the timeless pattern,
the religious formula to which life shapes itself.*

Thomas Mann

Contents

Preface

For centuries the Bible has been the most influential and most read book in Western civilization, and in the Hebrew Bible[1] no story has been more profound and influential than the Adam and Eve story. As Stephen Langdon observed, this story "has influenced the beliefs and conduct of mankind more than any legend that has ever been conceived by the poets and priests of antiquity."[2] We all grow up with it as children, and it is in our blood, whether we are conscious of it or not.

The reasons for this are understandable. This story lies at the beginnings of the three great monotheistic religions, Judaism, Christianity and Islam.[3] It explains the origins and purpose of the universe and our place in it, as well as the nature and purpose of the human race. It has shaped our notions of God, and of how we should relate to God. It endeavors to explain the origins and nature of evil in our world, and later led to the concept of Satan (or the Devil). For Christians it provides a meaning for the life and death of Christ (to expiate humankind's original sin), and thus to a large degree for the origin and existence of Christianity.[4] It has guided Western culture's traditional view of women and their relationship to men. It has given snakes a bad name. The story has been portrayed countless times in our culture's greatest art and literature, not to mention pop culture.

And yet for something of such vast importance and influence, for the general public very little has been published to explain the origins and meaning of this story. Indeed, there is no generally accessible book dealing comprehensively with the whole Eden story. Our book is meant to help remedy this situation. From tradition many incorrect assumptions about the story persist and still need to be corrected. The story has been embellished well beyond its text and author's original intent, while some of what he intended has not gotten through or has been lost. Many elements of the story that our common understanding and traditions include in the story (e.g., an apple, Satan) are actually absent from it, or at least not specified in it. Some details in the story have been emphasized and become embedded in our culture to a degree that we do not generally realize, while others remain unappreciated, ignored and largely forgotten. Indeed, each time we read the story, even in translation, we notice and appreciate some detail, word or phrase that gives new meaning and provokes more questions.

The need for such a book at this juncture is particularly acute because in recent decades new knowledge has been gained—particularly in the fields of archeology, history, and mythological studies—that sheds new light on the story, corrects some misconceptions, and will enrich our understanding of it. Yet, this new information is generally unknown to the public, including to religious communities. Rather, it has largely remained within the province of academic specialists. Further, among scholarly disciplines there has been insufficient cross-fertilization of information and ideas, which means that the newer information and thinking has not been adequately synthesized. As a result, there has been no synthesis that can be presented to a public audience.

It is unfortunate that our culture lacks a modern, holistic interpretation of the Eden story, because the issues in question are important for people's individual religious and spiritual lives, our culture, our educational system, and the political life of our communities. For one thing, today fanaticisms that affect our national security, our politics, our personal safety and well-being are said to be based on books written by God, starting with the account of Adam and Eve. It is therefore timely to have a fresh look at the story that began it all, to do so using an interdisciplinary approach that synthesizes the work of specialists in various fields, and to explain it in a readable way that is accessible to any educated reader. This book endeavors to do so, drawing on the modern findings and ideas of biblical scholars, linguists, historians, mythologists, scholars of comparative religion, archeologists, anthropologists, psychologists, and philosophers, among others. Our analysis is rooted in mainstream scholarship and thinking but bridges the interdisciplinary gaps in order to attain a more holistic understanding of the story.

Since the subject matter of this book is both important and not simple, in order to make a contribution it must be detailed and substantive. It must go into details and refer the reader to the sources utilized in making particular points. In order to achieve this goal yet make the book readable for a broad audience, we have endeavored to keep the main text as simple as possible and free of technical terminology and transliterations, except when this is essential to the argument. We have added further explanations and supplemental information in the endnotes, which we encourage readers to consult as they read.

This book focuses on the meanings of the central mythological elements of the Eden story, which means that our discussion does not follow the story's plot in a linear way, and omits details tangential to our argument. Readers who desire a verse-by-verse explanation can consult the many annotated commentaries cited in the Bibliography. Because this book is written to be accessible to the general reader and useful to specialists in various disciplines, it contains a significant amount of explanatory material containing information that will be familiar to specialists.

Regarding technical matters, all dates are BC/BCE unless otherwise noted. Dates of reigns of kings of Israel and Judah follow the *Anchor Bible Dictionary* dates. We use an author-date style of citation keyed into the Bibliography and the list of abbreviations in the back of the book. The style of the endnotes, Bibliography, and abbreviations is a blend of the *Chicago Manual of Style* and Society of Biblical Literature styles, with some concessions to make them more understandable to the general reader. Credits for images in the Figures appear in their captions. Quotations of biblical texts are from the Revised Standard Version unless otherwise noted.

We wish to thank the many people, more than can be mentioned here, who have assisted us and made the book possible. We thank the staff and students of the Oriental Institute of the University of Chicago for their support in the research, in particular Foy Scalf, Head of its Research Archives (and Art's Egyptian teacher), for his research assistance and for reviewing portions of the manuscript pertaining to Egypt, and also Sam Boyd for assisting on biblical authorship/Pentateuch questions. We likewise thank the staff at Trinity International University for their assistance, in particular Neal Huddleston, Art's Hebrew teacher with whom we had many helpful discussions. Thanks also to Bernard and Fran Alpert, archaeologists who were helpful in discussing historical and archaeological questions and in reviewing Chapter 2. We have endeavored to avoid mistakes, but any which remain are solely our responsibility.

Introduction

Mythology and the Eden Story

A myth is the product of the unconscious mind; for this reason its full meaning goes beyond the present state of awareness not only of those who read the myth but of those who tell the myth. When the symbolism of the myth is understood, meanings that were hidden become conscious. . . . The story of Adam and Eve partakes of the genre of myth and so must be approached symbolically. But it is not pure myth because the [author] . . . had a conscious intention in mind when he used it. Therefore, to do justice to the story we must keep in mind not only its symbolic structure, but also the [author's] intention.

—Rev. John A. Sanford[1]

Narrative is a form of representation. Abraham in Genesis is not a real person any more than a painting of an apple is a real fruit. This is not a judgment on the existence of a historical Abraham any more than it is a statement about the existence of apples. . . . We must look not only for what the text says, but also how it says it.

—Adele Berlin[2]

To appreciate Genesis as myth is not to destroy that book but to discover again its spiritual vitality and relevance.

—Eugene Kennedy, Introduction to Joseph Campbell's *Thou Art That*[3]

People have always sought to understand where the Eden story came from and what it means, but we are not there yet. This book endeavors to improve our understanding of the story by analyzing it from a mythological perspective. Tying a biblical story to myth may seem odd and provocative, given that a common definition of myth is something that is false.[4] Here, however, we are concerned not with whether the details of the story are factually true, but with what truths the story tells. Quite apart from whether myths are accurate at the level of base facts, they still express important spiritual and psychological truths, which of course is their purpose. The mythologist Robert Segal stressed that such is the very nature of myth: "The subject matter is not literal but symbolic: not the external world but the human mind."[5] Among other things, this means that this book's analysis applies equally well regardless of whether the story is literally true and regardless of the reader's religious (or non-religious) persuasion.

We approach the Eden story from the standpoint of myth because that is *how* it is told; it belongs to the *genre* of myth.[6] That is, its truths are expressed through the art of mythological storytelling, using symbolic imagery, namely that available from myths in the ancient Near East.[7] Much as in modern literature, film, painting and other art forms, ancient myths communicated to and impressed their audiences through symbols recognizable to them, because symbols can best convey mysterious, hard-to-express sacred ideas, resonate with our psyches, and persuade.[8] The biblical scholar Millar Burrows understood this well, explaining that myth is

> a symbolic, approximate expression of truth which the human mind cannot perceive sharply and completely but can only glimpse vaguely, and therefore cannot adequately or accurately express. . . . It implies not falsehood, but truth; not primitive, naïve misunderstanding, but an insight more profound than scientific description and logical analysis can ever achieve. The language of myth in this sense is consciously inadequate, being simply the nearest we can come to a formulation of what we see very darkly. . . The procedure is quite legitimate if [we] understand what is being done.[9]

Scholars cannot agree upon a single definition of myth, but most would agree that myths usually have most of the following outward features:

- They are expressed in narrative form, as a story.
- The story is told using symbols or motifs familiar to and having particular meanings to the audience.
- They evoke feelings of the sacred and connect individuals with the sacred, in order to provide meaningful emotional, spiritual and other profoundly satisfying psychological experiences. They take the audience beyond their normal worldly ("profane") existence and experience into the sacred realm.
- They often concern the creation of the cosmos (including in particular humankind), and also the quest of a hero.
- They are often etiological, i.e., serving to explain how and why certain aspects of the world as we know it came to be the way they are.
- They are often connected with rituals and religious beliefs.

- On the one hand, they commonly function to promote or reinforce the socio-political structure and values within a particular collective, and therefore are relied upon and promoted by its establishment. On the other hand, they may be created and used by revolutionaries in support of their program.

As we shall see, in the Eden story all of these elements are present to some degree.

When a story is told as myth using symbols, it must be analyzed as such. As the biblical scholar James Charlesworth stressed regarding the Eden story, "The archetypal symbols are the story, not its embellishment."[10] This necessitates analyzing the Eden story by employing approaches from the field of mythological studies. Yet this field itself draws us into a plethora of human, literary, religious, and philosophical issues, meaning that several fields of study and academic disciplines are relevant.[11] Robert Graves noted, for example: "A proper study of myth demands a great store of abstruse geographical, historical and anthropological knowledge; also familiarity with the properties of plants and trees, and the habits of wild birds and beasts."[12] Understanding a myth to its fullest also requires knowledge of the language in which it was written and of the history and culture in which it arose and flourished. Thus, when studying any myth, an essential foundation for any interdisciplinary analysis must be the body of knowledge developed by specialists in the languages, history and culture of the location and time period (e.g., Classics, Egyptology, Native American, and Sanskrit studies). In the case of the Eden story we are truly blessed in this regard. Because the religions of the Bible have dominated Western civilization, the study of this single book, from Christian, Jewish, and secular perspectives, constitutes a discipline in itself. From this field a solid and essential body of knowledge has been accumulated. The analysis in this book is largely based upon and remains faithful to that body of mainstream knowledge, but also builds upon it by bringing in other relevant disciplines.

This raises a question of method, which must be considered from the perspectives of both mythological and biblical studies. The classical scholar G.S. Kirk emphasized the importance of a comparative and interdisciplinary approach in analyzing Greek myths:

> Greek myths must share our time and attention with others, because in the end more can be learned about them by an indirect approach, by considering the nature of myths in general, than by a frontal attack on problems that have proved hopelessly unyielding in the past. Moreover the general problem of the nature of myths is in itself at least as important and challenging as any narrowly classical application.[13]

What is true for analyzing Greek myths likewise applies to those in the Bible, especially to those questions which have proved "hopelessly unyielding." As the German biblical scholar Rainer Albertz observed, "Israel, which was a latecomer on the scene in the ancient Near East, did not enter a religious vacuum in which it had to create the religious world of symbols from scratch, but a sphere in which all fields of life had long been occupied by religious patterns of interpretation."[14] Therefore, the Eden story too must be interpreted in light of myths and symbols from throughout the biblical world, and therefore also from the perspective of mythology in general.

In our case, in order to conceptualize and follow a methodology we must be clear about the target within this field of comparison that we are endeavoring to analyze. In biblical studies an entire field of inquiry is devoted to when and to what extent we may consider a biblical text to have been derived from (or to allude to) an earlier non-biblical (or biblical) literary text.[15] The thinking on this is now well developed, and there is a rough consensus on the criteria justifying such "intertextual" comparisons, which include geographical proximity, chronological sequence, availability of the older texts to later writers, closeness in the genre of the texts, and closeness in the language of the two texts.[16] Having applied such criteria to the Eden story, biblical scholars do not believe that it is derived from any particular ancient Near Eastern myth(s) (although other biblical stories are, e.g., the flood). This result directs us to the key manner of comparison for our purposes, namely the author's use of mythological symbols as the main building blocks of the Eden story (e.g., the sacred garden sanctuary, the flow of water from the underworld, the sacred trees, the serpent, the four rivers, goddess symbolism, the opening of one's eyes, the cherubim, and the flaming sword). These same symbols appeared throughout ancient Near East in biblical times and indeed worldwide throughout history, and usually have similar meanings. Indeed, as the psychologist Erich Neumann concluded, "all studies and interpretations of culture are ultimately the study and interpretation of archetypes and their symbols."[17] This applies first and foremost to religion. As Professor Charlesworth maintains above, our target in studying the Eden story must be largely these symbols.

APPROACHES TO MYTHS

The study of myth has its own methodological questions and approaches, so we must be cognizant of them when analyzing the Eden story from the perspective of myth. Mythologists have differed over what elements of human experience best explain the origin and meaning of myths, and various schools of mythology have emerged. We cannot discuss them in detail, but it is important to summarize at least those methods which scholars have applied to the Eden story, so that the reader can be conscious of them and better understand the conceptual approach of this book and the reasons for our choice of content. We must begin with the approach that is most fundamental: attributing the origin, meaning and function of myths to the nature of the human psyche.

Psychology

Many scholars have emphasized the importance of analyzing a particular culture's myths in the context of myths in general and as socio-cultural phenomena including as a component of religion. This comparative and multidisciplinary approach, known as the "history of religions" school, was pioneered by the German scholar Albert Eichhorn in the late 19th century and was continued through the 20th century, most notably by Mircea Eliade.[18] Such research and analysis together with the results of anthropological research on native cultures has yielded an impressive body of knowledge showing uncanny similarities in mythical-religious symbolism and concepts across humankind, both over time and across disparate cultures which seem to have had little or no contact with each other. This is important here because many of the symbols in the Eden story are common to various civilizations in the ancient Near East.[19]

Scholars from various disciplines have sought to explain these similarities. One initial theory, that the symbols and concepts diffused from an original source,[20] could not be proved except in a few cases over limited geographies, so other explanations were sought. The German ethnographist and anthropologist Adolf Bastian (1826-1905), observed the uniformity of what he called certain "elementary ideas" *(Elementargedanke)* of humankind, which are never seen in their pure form but are manifested in each instance as particular "ethnic ideas" *(Völkergedanke),* which are based on elementary ideas but differ somewhat from case to case because they are affected by the local culture, environment and psychological milieu.[21]

Identifying common elementary ideas was important, but this still did not explain the *origin* of these common symbols or myths or *why* they are common to many societies.[22] Psychologists took up this problem, as they appreciated the role that human psychology plays in myth. Freud explained myths as stemming from childhood experiences, viewing them as a form of psychological imbalance, but this biographical, individual-specific interpretation could not explain the similarity of myths across communities and over time.

Focusing on the nature of the human psyche in general proved more productive. Already in the early 19th century the German philosopher Immanuel Kant had recognized that our mind is not a blank slate that passively and objectively perceives and interprets the outside world; rather, the structures of our mind are active in the knowing process, filtering and interpreting data via variety of *a priori* categories (patterns) already present in our brain at birth. Modern psychology built on that idea by focusing on the role of our unconscious. Carl Jung focused on what he called the "collective unconscious," by which he meant the deepest level of the psyche common to all humans. In contrast to our "personal" unconscious derived from personal experience, the collective unconscious features inherited organizational patterns called "archetypes,"[23] forms without content that in turn determine how content from our unconscious is expressed in particular conscious forms.[24] They are instinctual patterns which dispose us all to generate similar symbols.[25] A single archetype can project any number of similar images or symbols, using content from our outer world as the means of expression. Since the outer environment varies among cultures, the same basic symbol can take on local characteristics. For example, the archetype of wholeness, totality, and order (called the Self) has been symbolized by, among other things, the circle, square, quaternity, mandala, and the God-image.[26]

As generators of symbols, the archetypes likewise generate myths, which are their finest expression. They are projections (symbolizations, indeed "revelations") of archetypes which result from our confrontation with the mysterious unknown and sometimes uncomfortable reaches in our psyche. The characters, images, situations, and actions in myths (including the Eden story) are a symbolic portrait of the archetypal patterns of the psyche.[27] As Jung put it, "The whole of mythology could be taken as a sort of projection of the collective unconscious."[28] In that process, our minds project ideas onto the external world, selecting the most suitable things from that world (trees, the sun, water, particular animals, etc.) to populate the content of the symbols in myths.[29] The *kind* of experience that we have is determined by the archetypes, but *what* we experience depends more concretely on our culture and personal experience.[30] Myths arise to preserve our psychic health. In particular, "Myth originates and functions to satisfy the psychological need for contact with the unconscious."[31] Myths, especially creation myths, therefore convey psychological and spiritual truths important to the meaning of human experience.[32] The psychological understanding of myth thus refutes the earlier notion of some anthropologists that myth is simply a way for primitive peoples to explain the world,[33] and thereby affirms that the Eden story is still relevant to us in our modern world. As Joseph Campbell stressed, "the symbols of mythology are not manufactured; they cannot be ordered, invented, or permanently suppressed. They are spontaneous productions of the psyche, and each bears within it, undamaged, the germ power of its source."[34]

In light of their nature, myths must be read symbolically in order to be understood, hence the approach in this book. The fact that they are products of our collective unconscious accounts for the similarities of myths and their symbols across time, geography, and culture, despite local variations traceable to the culture and the outer environment that supply the particular content. "The archetype," Jung explained, "is a kind of readiness to produce over and over again the same or similar mythical ideas."[35] This enables us, for example, to validly compare a sacred tree in Mesopotamia (usually a date palm) with one in Egypt (typically the sycamore), and both with those in the Eden story. Since each particular myth appears and is expressed in its own socio-cultural context and is tailored to an audience in that context through language and symbols that it knows, however, analyzing any myth to its fullest necessitates understanding that context,[36] which is why we must draw on biblical and ancient Near Eastern studies in our case.

With this background, it is important to set forth and understand here at the outset a classic line of myth that is relevant to our inquiry.[37] The most fundamental myths trace an evolutionary process, beginning with the creation of the orderly cosmos from chaos and then focusing on rise and transformation of humankind from a primal state into a higher collectivized society. As this mythology ultimately concerns the creation and development of humanity, at bottom it is about the emergence of human consciousness.[38] As we shall see in Chapter 9, numerous biblical and other scholars have viewed the Eden story too as being about the rise to full human consciousness.

In the classic mythological motif, before the creation there exists only a formless unity, often termed "chaos," as order (forms), space, and time do not yet exist. Among psychologists and mythologists, this situation is commonly termed the "uroboros," after the image of a serpent forming a circle and biting its tail, because one connotation of the symbol is unity, totality, and perfection.[39] Primal humans first exist as innocents in this kind of perfect, unified paradisiacal world (as perceived by them),[40] which lovingly embraces them like a mother (deified as the Great Mother Goddess) and provides for all needs; all feels secure and pleasurable.[41] At this stage humans are aware only of their inner world, like small children, whose psychological development, as shown by developmental psychology, parallels that of the human race.[42] Eventually, as in childhood, consciousness grows to the point where humans can distinguish between themselves and the outside world (inner vs. outer), and thus begins our recognition of other opposites— chaos vs. order; light vs. darkness; male vs. female; life vs. death; good vs. evil—which appear in the foundational myths of Mesopotamia, Egypt, Greece and the Bible. Eventually humans must make a clean escape from the maternal uroboros in order to emerge as independent selves having ego consciousness, which in psychological terms is a masculine quality (in both men and women).[43] In myths, this act is undertaken by a hero figure, a man or god[44] who, transgressing the establishment's rules, ventures to overturn the status quo by confronting and doing battle with a dragon, serpent or similar monstrous beast (a goddess or her male satellite) that represents the uroboric state (e.g., Marduk vs. Tiamat; Indra vs. Vritra; Zeus vs. Typhon; Bellephron vs. the Chimera; Perseus vs. the Gorgon; and various biblical references to

Yahweh defeating the dragon (Leviathan, Rahab)). The vanquished beast is then dismembered (punished) in some literal or figurative way.[45] The victory is characterized by the enlightenment (elevation into higher consciousness) of the hero and an escape from the primal state, then leading to the building of civilization (e.g., marriage, the collective, law). Both historically and psychologically, this event is associated with the rise of patriarchy at the expense of the matriarchate (which for our purposes we need only view in psychological terms as a psychic stage from which humanity transitions, not necessarily as a historical socio-political institution).[46] From the psychological standpoint of the evolution of human consciousness, this "dragon fight" is a necessary and inevitable step in our development[47] (though it marks only the transition to the stage we are now in, from which we can and must evolve higher). The victor, however, is inevitably haunted by guilt over what he has destroyed in order to create the new, because what he has just vanquished (denied and repressed into the unconscious) was and remains a part of the psyche's total structure, and because consciousness reveals our vulnerability and gives us knowledge of suffering, sickness, death and finitude, which the ego interprets as condign punishment for its having been born.[48] Thus, upon leaving the containment of the paradisiacal comfort zone the ego initially finds itself in a state of loneliness, discord, guilt, and fear.[49] Ideally, this turbulent state is rectified when male ego consciousness then integrates with the feminine principle (good Great Goddess), as happened in medieval quests when the heroic knight would defeat the dragon and rescue the princess who becomes his mate, or (to some extent) when triumphant or aspiring father gods married goddesses (e.g., Zeus and Hera).[50] But the ego, fearing destruction, can reject its re-integration with the Feminine, which as we shall see has been a problem in our Western civilization that must be rectified in order for humans to evolve higher. The victorious ego also can go too far, become inflated and, wanting to be like God, commit hubris, like when Bellephron after his heroic victory over the Chimera tried to reach heaven on Pegasus, and like when Icarus ignored warnings not to fly too close to the sun and tumbled into the sea.[51]

We can readily see that the mythological substrate of the Eden story possibly includes much from this motif, which originated around that time in the ancient Near East and Greece.[52] On the other hand, the Eden story's author consciously altered aspects of this motif for his own purposes, reorienting the meanings of the symbols and omitting some details and adding others. Further, we can observe how the author himself and Israelite society fit into the evolutionary process that the motif reflects. In sum, the central meaning of the Eden story can be divined by analyzing its mythological substrate and what the author does with it, which we endeavor to do in this book.

Having reviewed this psychological basis of myth, we can turn to other schools of myth that may be relevant to the Eden story.

Functionalist and Ritual Schools of Myth

Another school of mythology takes what has become known as a "functionalist" approach, which studies how myths actually function for people and societies, which also may shed light on how they originate. Bronislaw Malinowski focused on how myths function in the lives of individuals, and as an anthropologist studied this in action among native peoples.[53] He concluded that culture and its myths arise as answers to man's organic (psychological and real-world) needs, as a means to an end.[54] Others such as A.R. Radcliffe-Brown focused instead on how myths have functioned in communities, at the social level, sometimes called structural (or social) functionalism. Thus, apart from being a means of spiritual satisfaction for individuals, myths serve to reinforce the existing social order and serve as a blueprint for desirable behavior, establishing and sanctifying the laws and mores of the community. This approach was inspired by the earlier work of the French sociologist Emile Durkheim, who had argued that myths and religion originate as social phenomena to meet the needs of society.[55] Indeed, in society myths and symbols are reinforced by influential individuals (rulers, religious leaders, writers and storytellers, artists and architects) and institutions that utilize, interpret and perpetuate the symbols. Importantly, the functionalist approach lends itself to comparing similarities in the myths and symbols among various peoples, an approach called "comparative functionalism" championed by the anthropologist Walter Goldschmidt.[56]

A related approach, known as the "ritual school" of mythology, focuses more specifically on the close connection between myths and ritual and argues that myths develop out of rituals.[57] The ritual approach, however, cannot explain all myths, and presents something of a "chicken and egg" problem because it fails to explain the origin of the rituals. As conscious enactments, rituals must first have some anterior content to enact. As discussed, psychology shows that the unconscious first generates symbols, which then become conscious content within the culture of a community in the form of its rituals and myths, at which point the two can develop hand in hand.[58]

Etiological Approach

The etiological approach focuses on how myths often provide explanations for how the world was created and came to acquire its characteristics. Especially important are the explanations for human qualities and things that trouble humans, such as the origin of evil, and social institutions and rules.

Such explanations are prominent in the Eden story, and we shall pay close attention to them.

Structuralist Approach

Finally, there is the "structuralist" approach developed by the anthropologist Claude Lévi-Strauss, based largely on his studies of South American native peoples.[59] Largely leaving aside the narrative and plot of myths, structuralism sees myths as mediating conflicts between pairs of opposites (e.g., man and nature, life and death) in a dialectical manner, thereby resolving problems for people and their communities. That approach was productive in explaining many myths and practices of the peoples that Lévi-Strauss studied, but has been criticized as purporting to explain more myths than it really can. Its critics argue that many myths do not fit into these categories, especially those from the literate civilizations (including Semitic) that gave rise to Western civilization.[60] Nevertheless, modern psychology holds that our psychic (including our spiritual) well-being does depend on balancing opposite tendencies within our psyche.[61]

THE APPROACH OF THIS BOOK

We must consider to what extent the above approaches to myth have explanatory value in the case of the Eden story. For this purpose, we must first return to the point stressed by John Sanford in the above epigraph, that the Eden story is not pure myth because of its conscious authorial aspect. Rather, it is myth transitioning into literature. Myth consists of symbols that have not been invented consciously,[62] but the symbols in the Eden story had already evolved long before the Eden story was composed and had acquired standard meanings in the conscious minds of ancient Near Eastern peoples. These symbols were ready-made and available in Israelite culture for the author to use, and they had a psychological impact and meaning for people. And he not only employed them, but altered their meaning to achieve his purposes, even though he almost certainly did not understand their earlier psychological origins.[63] Further, we have much more relevant information about the Eden story than about myths in more ancient cultures or pre-literate native cultures. Compared to many myths, in the case of the Eden story in important respects we are less dependent on theories and can apply real facts in our analysis. We know something about the author. We know where and approximately when he lived and wrote. As Professor Friedman stressed, the author of the Eden story was "tied to the life of that period, its major events, its politics, its religion, and its catastrophes."[64] And about that period we know a great deal, including the religious issues that were at stake in Palestine and with which the Eden story was concerned. Also, the Eden story is not an isolated, self-contained unit but is only the opening episode in a much longer text written by the same author and which formed a conceptual whole, so we can draw on the reminder of the story to understand its beginning. This epic story provided the conceptual underpinning of a vast social, political and religious project: the formation and rise of the Israelite nation and its religion. The culture of a nation is grounded by an archetypal canon which represents its highest and deepest values.[65] The biblical author portrayed the traditional in opposition to the new canon that he was endeavoring to construct.

The above makes functionalism relevant, but with an important qualification in this case: For most people of Palestine, the Eden story when composed was actually contrarian and revolutionary. As we shall see in Chapters 2 and 3, the author (the earliest of the biblical authors) was an innovator who wrote the story to *convert* people to Yahwism and *overturn* the old order. Thus, the Eden story *challenged the traditional meanings of the symbols.* Once the new belief took hold, however, the story could play a traditional functionalist role, which may help explain its retention in the Hebrew Bible along with the Genesis 1 creation account.

Likewise in the case of the psychological approach, we must recognize that the Eden story, though narrated in the manner of myth using symbols derived from the unconscious, is still a conscious, rational, polemical composition by a particular author, and that we are in a position to analyze his conscious intent. At the level of the audience, however, the psychological import and effect of the story's mythological symbols are extremely important for our purposes, because in telling the story the author utilized important symbols with which he knew his audience was familiar, and which we too must understand.[66] Examining these symbols is therefore a focus of this book, for which purpose the psychological approach is crucial.

The Eden story contains several binary pairs (opposites), which has attracted the interest of structuralists. These include: good and evil; man and woman; humans and gods; human and animal; immortality and mortality (or life and death); inside and outside the garden; we and they; divine and earthly; order and chaos; nature and civilization. When structuralism was in high vogue, some scholars sought to apply structuralism to the Eden story (and other Bible stories, including the primeval history as a unit).[67] While such analyses made useful contributions to our understanding of some aspects of the story, the results were modest.[68] Indeed, in light of the biblical author's conscious and groundbreaking intentions, the Eden story was not purely a myth and did not represent a settled tradition of how opposites had been resolved within Israelite culture. Rather, when and as compiled by a particular author, it presented a new idea challenging the old—an antithesis. In terms of the author's opposition to "Canaanite" religion, for example, there could be no true mediation and resolution of opposites. It was the author's way or the highway, and the story portrays his own position as triumphant.

Nevertheless, structuralism's attention to what we prefer to call "pairs of opposites" provides an important perspective for our purposes, because it is integral to our explanation of the nature and role of the knowledge of good and evil (discussed in Chapter 9). What the psychological approach (originally not incorporated into structuralism) says about pairs of opposites during the emergence of ego consciousness also sheds helpful light on the structuralist perspective. Finally, whereas structuralism in focusing on the pairs of opposites downplays both narrative and content, for the biblical author the content of the Eden story was paramount, and not just in terms of the symbols used. As a consummate storyteller the author made word choice, wordplay (puns), alliteration, assonance, and euphony important components of his tale, and he included poetry. This demands also a literary analysis with attention to the norms of narrative and drama. [69]

The ritual theory of myth is of marginal importance to us. Scholars generally have not argued that the Eden story arose from or was utilized in rituals, and we discuss this theory (in Chapter 6) only in relation to the Israelite New Year's Festival.

This book looks at the Eden story through the lens of a key stage in the development of humankind through historical, anthropological, archaeological, and psychological facts that are reflected in the story's underlying mythology. We interweave the story's mythological substrate with the author's conscious purposes. In doing so, it becomes clear that the Eden story manifests the new stage of human development that was emerging at the time. A paradox of the mythology of humankind as we shifted to this new patriarchal mindset of ego consciousness, however, was that the new mythology still had to make use of nature symbols originating in the (feminine) unconscious, where all symbols originate. [70] In this process driven by a hostile patriarchal spirit, the original symbols got distorted and perverted, resulting in unnatural images. [71] This is what happened when the biblical author produced the Eden story, Eve emerging from Adam being just one example. As, Peter Ellis, a specialist on the Yahwist author of the Eden story, observed, what the author did in Genesis 2-11 "for the most part is take pagan myths and mythological motifs and remove from them anything that might smack of polytheism and polytheistic theology." [72] Further, the author "is using symbolic presentations, easily understood by his audience, to communicate his intuitive theological insights. One should not confuse the reality of the truth perceived with its symbolic presentation." [73] That is, the author's message often did not fit the traditional meanings of the symbols used. John McKenzie pointed out that "what distinguishes these passages of the [Old Testament] from ancient myths is not the patterns of thought and language, which seem in every respect to be the same, but the Hebrew idea of God as known through His revelation of himself." [74] Both the Eden story's mythological substrate and its consciously constructed plot details and polemics must be understood against this background. This is why a mythological approach to the story combined with an analysis of author's conscious intentions is essential to understanding the story's meaning. When seen in this way, we can appreciate how the Eden story was a key to cementing within our civilization a new stage of human development, one which we are still in.

Chapters 1 and 2 of this book are concerned largely with putting the story and its composition into its proper historical and cultural setting. Chapter 1 reviews what we may know about the author of the story, when he lived and wrote, where he was from, the book that he wrote, and also compares his work to that of other authors of the Pentateuch. Chapter 2 puts the origins and composition of the Eden story in the historical context of ancient Israel and Judah through the author's time, in order to frame the religious issues of the day and to suggest to what questions and audience the Eden story was addressed. Chapter 3 then examines more specifically the religious environment of the time and traces the history of the god and dominant character in the Eden story, Yahweh, together with that of the goddess, Asherah, who scholars increasingly acknowledge was Yahweh's consort or wife, and whose figure lurks behind the story. In Chapters 4-8 we examine how the author employed the main figures and symbols in the Eden story. Chapter 9 then synthesizes the discussions in the prior chapters in order to analyze Adam and Eve's transgression and the meaning of their acquiring the knowledge of good and evil. The Epilogue discusses the applicability and meaning of the Eden story in the modern world.

Chapter One

Who Wrote the Eden Story?

When reading and studying great works of literature, we find it important to learn what we can about the biography and environment of the author. If we understand the author's family, upbringing and life, his time and environment, his aesthetic, political and religious views, health and other details that may bear on the author's writings, our understanding, appreciation, and enjoyment of the author's work is enhanced immeasurably. For example, in order to appreciate the work of Alexander Pushkin, it helps to understand high society in Imperial St. Petersburg in the early 19th century and to know that he lived within but was always an outsider to that society, that many men in that society had designs on his beautiful wife Natalia, that early in his career he was associated with disgraced political revolutionaries and almost arrested, and that he gambled and usually lost at cards and so was constantly in debt. Yet only a half century later we encounter Dostoevsky living in a transformed Petersburg, an age of industrial squalor and social and political unrest. When reading his writings, it is helpful to know that he was a former revolutionary who had been arrested and exiled to Siberia where he converted to a special kind of Christianity, that he was an epileptic, that he was addicted to gambling and lost much of his money, and that he both lived and spent much of his time in the poorer parts of St. Petersburg and knew the life of the downtrodden. Because of these differences, Pushkin's and Dostoevsky's writings and the two Petersburgs that they described were worlds apart, even though they lived in the same city in the same country in the same century.[1] The backgrounds of Dickens in England during the industrial revolution and James Joyce in turbulent early 20th century Dublin likewise shed light on their work. The same can be true of non-literary intellectual works. For instance, the memoirs of Carl Jung showed how many of his theories were inspired by deeply personal experiences.[2]

The situation is analogous with the authors of the Bible, including the author of the Eden story. While we do not know this author by name, to some extent scholars have identified relevant details about him that can enhance our understanding of his writings, so it is important that we explore this background.

THE AUTHORSHIP OF THE PENTATEUCH (TORAH)

According to both Judaic and many Christian traditions, the first five books of the Bible[3] were written down by Moses himself under God's guidance, but scholars long ago determined that they are a compilation of texts written or compiled by at least four principal authors.[4] According to this now-traditional analysis, the author of the Eden story and of much else in the Pentateuch is known as the Yahwist, or simply "J."[5] The other three are the "priestly" author (therefore known as P), the Elohist (E) (because he regularly calls God Elohim rather than Yahweh until the deity reveals himself to Moses as Yahweh at the burning bush), and the Deuteronomist (D). The four main texts, along with other material, were later combined by one or more redactors (known as R) during or after the Babylonian exile.[6] Although identifying which literary units and verses are from which sources is a never-ending process of refinement, by the mid to late 20th century, with minor exceptions, bible scholars who studied these sources (called source critics) had reached a fair consensus on which parts were written or compiled by whom.[7]

This approach to understanding the composition of the Pentateuch, known as the Documentary Hypothesis, took form as mainstream scholarship in the 19th century, and remained the dominant paradigm through the 20th century. Bible scholars, mainly in Germany, noticed that significant portions of the Pentateuch are incoherent, in that they contain contradictions, repetitions, and discontinuities.[8] For example, many stories in the Bible (including of the creation) are repeated (called doublets), while other parts of the text contradict each other in significant ways that would be inconceivable in the case of a single author,[9] especially if he were Moses guided by God. Examples include:

- The same places or individuals are given two different names. For example, The mountain of God is called Mt. Sinai by J[10] and P[11] but Mt. Horeb by E[12] and D.[13] Moses's father-in-law is called Reuel by J[14] but Jethro by E.[15]
- Contradictory numbers are given. Whereas P says Noah put one pair of each kind of animal (both clean and unclean) on the Ark,[16] J says it was seven pairs each of clean animals and birds, but only one pair each of

unclean animals.[17] J says the flood lasted 40 days and 40 nights and that Noah left the ark within a month afterwards,[18] while P says the flood was upon the earth 150 days and that in total Noah was in the ark over a year before he could disembark.[19]

- Significant details of the same episode do not match. For example, according to P, Noah released a raven from the ark as the flood receded,[20] but J says it was a dove.[21]
- In the Joseph story J says Judah (the founder of the tribe of that name) saved his brother Joseph from being killed by his other brothers,[22] whereas E claims that Reuben saved him;[23] J says the Ishmaelites sold Joseph to the Egyptians,[24] whereas E says that the Medanites (or Midianites) did this.[25]
- In some passages the Bible speaks favorably about particular individuals, groups, or nations, while other passages take a negative attitude toward them. Compared with J, E gave a more favorable account of the figure of Moses over Aaron, Shiloh over Jerusalem, the Tabernacle over the Temple, and Israel over Judah, among other things.[26] P emphasizes the prerogatives of Aaronid priests,[27] E and D focus on any Levite priests (so as to admit non-Aaronids), while J is not concerned with priests at all. P, E and D emphasize and compile formal law, J does not.

Finally, there are stark differences in language and style in the text which make it clear that different people penned different parts of the text. Thus, in explaining why scholars believe that a particular author (known as D) wrote most of Deuteronomy,[28] Friedman noted:

> Deuteronomy is written in an entirely different style from those of the other four books. The differences are obvious even in translation. The vocabulary is different. There are different recurring expressions and favorite phrases. There are doublets of whole sections of the first four books. There are blatant contradictions of detail between it and the others. Even part of the wording of the Ten Commandments is different.[29]

Taken individually, many of these differences could be plausibly explained by other reasons. For example, it is certainly possible that Noah released both a dove and a raven, either simultaneously or in sequence,[30] and indeed this may be what R intended to convey. But when there are so many differences that line up consistently with the authors that have been identified by the source critics and the resulting texts have an internally consistent continuity and point of view, the Documentary Hypothesis (at least in its updated current form, known as the neo-Documentary Hypothesis) becomes the most convincing explanation.[31]

Such differences are especially apparent in the creation stories of Genesis with which we are concerned and enable us to isolate J as the author of the

Eden story and other key related episodes. Genesis actually contains two separate accounts of the creation, including two creations of the first humans. The first is in Genesis 1 through 2:4a; then in Genesis 2:4b the Bible starts all over again with a second version of what happened, which duplicates the first version in some ways but contradicts it in others. For example, in the first version God creates plants first, then animals, and then man and woman simultaneously, but in the second version the sequence is man, plants, animals, and finally woman. Adam and Eve are not mentioned in the first version, in which the creation of humans (seemingly more than just an initial pair) is only one detail in a larger cosmogony; their tale is contained only in the second, which omits most details of the cosmogony in order to focus on the first humans. The two accounts use different words for God (see below). The first version contains the six days of creation and rest on the seventh, because its author wanted to stress the importance of keeping the Sabbath, whereas in the second the creation of the earth, heavens, and the first human occur in one day (Gen. 2:1-7). The two accounts (and the continuations of the texts of each author) evidence the differing concerns and interests of each author.

Before going further, we must caution that today the Documentary Hypothesis, at least in its classical form, is not universally accepted among biblical scholars, particularly in some parts of Europe where in recent decades a number of scholars have come to view the Pentateuch as having been formed more from a centuries-long incremental process of the formation of tradition through shorter, more fragmentary writings having a limited literary horizon than from four longer, discrete source documents (that is, real literary works by authors).[32] According to some, only P clearly stands out as a discrete author of a lengthy text.[33] In response, other scholars such as Joel Baden at Yale have exposed serious weaknesses in what he terms this alternative "European approach."[34] Israeli scholars also appear generally to support the Documentary approach.[35] Indeed, as the German biblical scholar Konrad Schmid (associated with the European approach) recently acknowledged, "it is not yet certain whether this [European] approach will prove enduring."[36] Any discussion of these complex issues is well beyond the scope of this book, but with Schmid's caution in mind, in this book we stick with the still-dominant neo-Documentary model, as no alternative model has yet clearly proven superior. Accordingly, we call our author J. Further, we note that the above debate focuses on material that comes after the biblical texts we are almost entirely concerned with, namely Genesis 2-3 and to some extent the remainder of the primeval history (Gen. 4:1-11:26).[37] There is little dispute that the Eden story was compiled generally as a literary unit by a single author (except for verses 2:10-14 perhaps being an insertion), and the still-dominant view is that he can be identified as J. Finally, from our mythological perspective, the material traditionally attributed to J does stand out as consistently having a more mythological character to it (as biblical scholars likewise have traditionally recognized), which also supports the traditional view that it is among the older material in the Pentateuch and the oldest of the four main sources. Our mythological analysis in this book would apply equally well even if the author were different or wrote at a later time than we suppose, including after the exile.

With these caveats, we may begin our investigation by focusing on the author of the Eden story and his agenda.

THE AUTHORS OF THE CREATION STORIES

The Eden story was written by someone whom scholars call the Yahwist (because he called God "Yahweh"), also known as the J source, or simply J. He wrote an integrated epic story covering virtually all biblical events from the creation through at least the designation of Joshua as Moses's successor. But in the Bible as it has come down to us J's book was edited, chopped up and interspersed among the texts of other biblical authors; possibly some portions were removed and have been lost, but the large majority of J's book seems to have been preserved.[38] Reading only J's text from beginning to end as an integrated work[39] is illuminating and enables one to understand what J was about, compare him to the other authors, and to better interpret his Eden story.

Who Was J?

What do we know about him? Regarding when he lived and wrote, tradition-ally biblical scholars placed him in the 10th century, during or just after Solomon's reign when Israel split from Judah. Virtually all scholars still believe that he wrote no earlier than Solomon's reign (ca. 970-931), almost certainly after Solomon's death (after the separation of Israel from Judah[40] was said to have taken place), and most probably in the mid to late 9th century.[41] Professor Friedman notes that J's emphasis on the importance of the Ark (which was in Jerusalem and particularly important for Judah) and Yahweh's command against molten gods (a characteristic of the kingdom of Israel), both point to a date after the separation of the two kingdoms (ca. 931).[42] According to Friedman, an objective marker of the oldest possible date for J is his story of Jacob and Esau (Gen. 27:39-40), which reflects an awareness that Edom (part of Solomon's empire) had broken away from Israel to become an independent kingdom (2 Kings 8:20-22). That occurred during the reign of the Israelite king Joram (851-42), which would place J after 851.[43] This could mean he was writing sometime during the tumultuous reign of Joram, the last king of the Omride dynasty, that of Jehu (842-14), or somewhat later. As we shall see in Chapter 2, such dating corroborates well with historical events taking place in Judah and Israel at that time and which touch on issues of concern to J, and so may have inspired him to write. This makes J the earliest of the biblical author-compilers, although he incorporates poems and other material from earlier times.

We are also confident that J was from Judah rather than the northern kingdom of Israel, because he is focused on the affairs of Judah and writes favorably about it, whereas he either writes unfavorably of or ignores other peoples. J was particularly critical of Israel, and consistently portrayed Judah favorably in relation to it. For example, in the Joseph story J says it is Judah (the founder of the tribe of that name which occupied Judah) who saves his brother Joseph from being killed by his other brothers (Gen. 37:26-27), whereas E claims that Reuben saved him (Gen.37:21-22). In the J account in which the dying Jacob blesses his 12 sons (who found the 12 tribes), the patriarch singles out Judah to receive the birthright and foresees that his tribe will be preeminent:

> *Judah, your brothers shall praise you;*
> *Your hand shall be on the neck of your enemies;*
> *Your father's sons shall bow down before you. . . .*
> *The scepter shall not depart from Judah. . .* (Gen. 49:8, 10)

In E's account, however, Jacob's grandson Ephriam, the ancestor of the tribe that will occupy central Israel and dominate that northern kingdom, receives the birthright, portending that tribe's ascendancy (Gen. 48:8-20).[44] According to E, when the Hebrews were in the wilderness of Sinai under Moses's leadership, Joshua, a hero also from the tribe of Ephriam, played an important role. He led the Hebrews into victorious battle, substituted for Moses in the Tent of the Meeting, and oddly was nowhere to be seen during the golden calf incident. J, on the other hand, never mentions Joshua.[45]

What is going on between these two authors? According to the traditional Documentary Hypothesis, E, who lived sometime after J, was from Israel, perhaps a priest from Shiloh, the traditional religious center in Israel.[46] According to one theory, E was aware of J's book and did not like the way J promoted Judah and denigrated Israel and its heroes, so he wrote his own account to set matters straight from Israel's perspective.[47] Alternatively, he may have been unaware of or not concerned with J, and simply wrote from his different Israelite perspective. According to the traditional theory, when Assyria conquered Israel in 722, E's text was taken to Jerusalem, where, as Israel's refugees were assimilated into Judah, J's and E's texts were combined into a compromise text that scholars call JE, which contained duplications and contradictions of the type described above.[48] As noted above, however, the existence of such a combined JE text is now in doubt;[49] but this question does not affect the analysis in this book.

J was also probably a member of or at least close to the royal court in Jerusalem, possibly a scribe. He does not seem to have been a priest because he displays no concern or interest with priestly affairs. His writings contain no detailed priestly law and he is not concerned with it, only with the most fundamental commands of Yahweh.[50] As a "layman," he has an earthy, populist, yet sophisticated literary style that differs from the more aloof writings of P and D. Much of J's book is devoted to family relations, and he views the Hebrew nation as one large family, originating with Abraham and growing into a nation with its own family problems. Almost all of the sex in the Hebrew Bible's prose is found in J. He includes tales of espionage, drunkenness and dreams, and is especially focused on the problems of humankind, and of humankind's relationship with Yahweh. And in particular, his key early stories are mythological in nature.

The Author of the Genesis 1 Creation Story: P

The author of the other version of creation (and much else in the Pentateuch) is known as the priestly writer ("P" for short). According to the traditional Documentary Hypothesis, P wrote his book as an alternative to J (and E, or JE) and to challenge it, and so contradicts it in many ways, including in the creation story; alternatively, he may have just been elaborating his own theological position, without being concerned about rebutting other authors. For some time, it was thought that P probably wrote from Babylon during the exile, because so much of his imagery and terminology seemed to be influenced by Babylon. Later scholarship generally held that P was pre-exilic[51] and probably wrote during the reign of the reformist king Hezekiah (ca. 727-698).[52] As we shall see in Chapter 2, Hezekiah introduced a program of religious reforms. It would have been natural for Hezekiah to rely on priestly talent to work out and memorialize laws, formulate religious doctrine and develop sacred texts, beginning with the creation story. P and Hezekiah seem to have been allies, a symbiotic pairing of prince and priesthood that enhanced and preserved the power of each.

Who was P? Biblical scholars believe he was an Aaronid priest in Judah. One of his principal purposes was to establish that only Aaronid priests in Jerusalem could be intermediaries between humans and Yahweh, and that worship of Yahweh and cult ceremonies must be centered in Jerusalem and performed by such priests according to strict religious laws. So unlike J, P's book was particularly concerned with technical laws and legal affairs, religious ritual, the prerogatives and powers of the priesthood, the importance of Aaron (at the expense of Moses), and the minutiae of dates, numbers and measurements. In particular, P is responsible for writing and compiling[53] the Book of Leviticus, which sets forth laws in great detail.

Differences between J and P

In light of the above, it is not surprising that P's and J's accounts of creation take different approaches to nature and man. P's God (Elohim) is cosmic, aloof, invisible, and does not interact with humans other than to tell them to be fruitful and multiply. So it is fitting that P's story starts with the heavens, J's with the earth.[54] J is not concerned with the details of cosmogony and how long the creation took. Instead, he simply recites that Yahweh created the earth and heavens in less than a day, and later that same day Yahweh gets right to the creation of the first human, initiating their relationship and issuing his first instructions. Yahweh gets personal with humans and he is a literary protagonist in the drama. He walks in the garden and interacts with humans; he even makes clothes for them. He meets Cain in the field. Later in Genesis Yahweh and two angels lounge, talk and dine with Abraham under a terebinth tree (Gen. 18:1-19), he or his angel wrestles with Jacob (Gen 32:22-32), he personally closes the door to Noah's ark (Gen. 7:16), and smells Noah's sacrifice after the flood (Gen. 8:21). He haggles with Abraham over whether to destroy Sodom and Gomorrah (Gen. 18:22-33), and is about to kill Moses until he is confronted by Moses's wife Zipporah (Exod. 4:24-26). And in the garden of Eden we have magic trees and fruit, a talking snake, cherubim, and a revolving, flaming sword; later in Genesis J writes of angels, and of the "sons of the gods" who copulate with mortal women who give birth to giants called the Nephilim. In contrast, P had no place for angels, cherubim, giants, and J's theophanies, anthropomorphisms and fantastic stories, an approach that scholars term "demythologized."

P and J also use different words for God. J in narration[55] uses *Yahweh,* which is singular, while P uses *Elohim* (a generic term for the male deity, like "God" in English).[56] *Elohim* is grammatically plural, but it can be either singular or plural depending on the context, and translators into English choose accordingly. Notably, J has Yahweh referring to supernatural beings other than himself (Gen. 3:22; 11:7). This is most often interpreted to refer to the group of deities in a divine council headed by Yahweh (as El did in Canaanite mythology).

Another important difference is that in P's creation story there is no hint that man will disobey God or commit any sin. On the contrary, P's account concludes: "God saw everything that he had made, and behold, it was very good" (Gen. 1:31). That "everything" obviously included humans. P's account is self-contained and lacks any need or premise for the events of the Eden story. But J viewed it as his task to explain why the world is the way it is, not entirely good. Even in the garden, something was out of joint. As we shall see, J viewed humans from their creation as imperfect creatures who inevitably will commit sins from time to time. In P's account, however, humans are created in God's image, initially perfect.

HOW KNOWING AUTHORSHIP HELPS TO UNDERSTAND THE EDEN STORY

Although our analysis of the mythological symbolism in the Eden story does not depend on the Documentary Hypothesis (or the dating of J), attention to authorship enriches our understanding of the story. First, recognizing which other parts of the Pentateuch were composed by J enables us to track his literary thread and ideas. We can then relate what we learn from the rest of J's work to his Eden story in order to better interpret it. Second, at least when focusing on Genesis 2-3, we can and should to some extent keep the works of others at some distance when analyzing the question of authorial intent. When interpreting J's Eden story, in many cases we have no need to reconcile it with the texts by later authors, and we can also avoid unfounded ideas which have built up over centuries due to assuming that a single author wrote the Pentateuch. This is especially important in relation to Genesis 1, because P wrote it long after the Eden story was written. We thus avoid the conflation and confusion of the two accounts that unfortunately taints much commentary about the Eden story, and in particular can avoid letting Genesis 1 unduly influence our interpretation of the Eden story. For one thing, we need not endeavor to resolve the contradictions. For example, there are often attempts to explain the existence of the two creation accounts by claiming that Genesis 1 sets forth the basic account while Genesis 2-3 then proceed to elaborate and "fill in the details." Nothing could be further from the truth, since Genesis 2-3 was written before Genesis 1.[57] There is no earlier account on which the Eden story could be elaborating. Further, if Genesis 2-3 were just "elaborating" on Genesis 1, then we would expect that it not contradict it in so many basic ways.

Another example is Lilith, sometimes said to be Adam's first wife before Eve. There are various colorful stories about her, including that she would not subordinate herself to Adam, would not have sex with him unless she was on top, and that eventually she abandoned him. When one turns to the Eden story, however, there is no hint of any of this, and many aspects of the story contradict the notion that there could have been a prior woman. Adam is lonely and feels incomplete, and so seeks a mate, but he (and even Yahweh) does not know what form his mate should take (whereas if he had a prior wife this would be known). The animals are therefore created as possible mates for him, and it is only after rejecting them and naming them that Yahweh creates the first woman, from Adam's side. Only then is this new being given a name ("woman," in Gen. 2:23), which in ancient Near Eastern mythology was an essential final step in the creation of the first example of a new kind of thing, as the process of naming confers upon the new creation its essential qualities and destiny. The whole narrative, logical and mythological structure of the story therefore excludes the possibility of any prior woman.

So whence Lilith? The stories of a biblical Lilith, which first appeared in medieval rabbinic writings, were made possible only because Genesis 1 already had mentioned the creation of at least one man and woman. This opens up room to argue that that there was an earlier woman from Genesis 1 who was Lilith and was gone before Eve appeared. But once we recognize that Genesis 1 was a separate story written by a different author much later and that it does not purport to dovetail into J's story, any such possible connection with the woman in Genesis 1 is lost. Therefore, there is no room for Lilith in our discussion of Adam and Eve.

A final example is the idea of man being created in the image of God. Unfortunately, this concept improperly colors much discussion of the Eden story, even in scholarly circles. The notion of man being in the image of God comes purely from P's account, in Genesis 1:26. There is nothing of the kind in J's Eden story. Rather, Adam is created from a mixture of dirt and water, and J writes that humans will return to dust after dying. J never says that the being formed from clay resembles Yahweh. To the contrary, J's position in the Eden story is that humans and the divine Yahweh are fundamentally different and that humans must respect this difference; but Adam and Eve did not and transgressed this boundary.

In light of such differences, the question thus arises why R chose to include both P's and J's creation stories in the Hebrew Bible. The short answer seems to be that both J's and P's books had been well known for centuries and hardly could be ignored. R's task was to unify the Israelite religion in the hope that this would help an Israelite state to rise again. So he opted for an inclusive approach. A more particular reason seems to be that since R was charged with restoring the Law to post-exilic Judea, it was important to have P's version emphasizing the importance of the Sabbath; J's Eden story and the remainder of his primeval history narrative also demonstrated the need for Yahweh's strictures to guide human behavior. Both P's and J's stories served his purpose. Despite the contradictions in the factual details of the two stories, the most essential truths that they convey about God and man's relationship to God are fairly consistent, so R and the Israelites were not concerned with the stories at the level of factual consistency.[58]

A final point on authorship that must be addressed is the integrity of the Eden story as a J text. Any inquiry into the body of scholarly exegesis of the Eden story reveals much debate and disagreement over a number of passages in it that were presumably J's but were rearranged, or which may not have been original to J's story but were added by editors.[59] Presumably some of J's original material was edited out as well and has been lost to us. In this book we cannot hope to resolve such editorial questions which have haunted biblical scholarship since the 19th century. Fortunately for our purposes, the main lines of the story including its principal mythological symbols are clear enough. Like the vast majority of commentators on the Eden story, we take the story as it has come down to us as an integral, albeit edited, whole and analyze that, recognizing that J's role in compiling it was central and that his essential views have been preserved.

Commentators on J's work have brought their own individual perspectives, some might say baggage. Of the four books dedicated solely to J's entire text, one, written by a theologian, views it primarily as a work of theology,[60] the second, written by a professor of literature, looks upon it principally as a literary work,[61] the third views it essentially as a socioeconomic tract,[62] while Professor Friedman is the only one of the four to analyze it primarily in terms of traditional biblical textual criticism, while incorporating the historical setting.[63] Such contributions show that there are many useful perspectives from which to analyze J's Eden story. Ours is that of mythology and religious and other history, using archaeology as evidence for both. Thus, it is important to place J into his historical and religious context, which provides clues to why and when the story was written.

Chapter Two

How the World of Palestine
Led to Eden

The Bible strikes root into every ancient Near-Eastern culture, and it cannot be historically understood until we can see its relationship to its sources in true perspective.

—William Foxwell Albright [1]

To appreciate what J is about, it is necessary to realize that J is not about the actual emergence of Israel.

—Robert Coote and David Ord [2]

Thus says the Lord God to Jerusalem: Your origin and your birth are of the land of the Canaanites; your father was an Amorite, and your mother a Hittite.

—Ezekiel 16:3

We have met the enemy, and he is us.

—Pogo

Like any writer, J wanted his story to resonate with his audience and be relevant to them. It had to be understandable, attractive, and persuasive. Therefore, he constructed it using traditional stories, symbols and language that would be familiar to his audience and best convey his meaning. Since these were rooted in the history and culture of the ancient Near East, we need to understand those components of Canaanite, Mesopotamian and Egyptian civilizations which both influenced and competed with J's ideas and accounted for the imagery that he used. We must also understand the burning social, political, and religious issues in Judah and in Israel during J's time that would have motivated him to write, and to do so in the way he did. We need to know who the Israelites were, where they came from, and how they developed in Palestine. Since J was champion of Judah, we must also be familiar with the contrasting histories of Israel and Judah and the complex relationship between them leading up to when J wrote.

Thanks to recent archaeological discoveries, our knowledge about these questions has improved dramatically. Our traditional notions of what transpired during Israel's formative period through J's time are increasingly at odds with this new knowledge. Understanding J requires us to compare the biblical accounts, including J's, with this new evidence. Therefore, in order to frame the key issues that we will be discussing in this book, we must provide here a more detailed historical background than usual in a book about a Bible story or myth.

The above point can be vividly illustrated by a passage from J's book containing one of his central messages, which as we shall see aligns perfectly with a major theme in the Eden story. The passage is at the beginning of the Ten Commandments,[3] according to which Yahweh's first and paramount command to Moses and the Hebrews is to occupy Canaan and destroy the Canaanites and their religion:

> Observe what I command you to this day. Behold, I will drive out before you the Amorites, the Canaanites, the Hittites, the Perizzites, the Hivites and the Jebusites. Take heed to yourself, lest you make a covenant with the inhabitants of the land whither you go, lest it become a snare in the midst of you. You shall tear down their altars, and break their pillars, and cut down their Asherim[4] (for Yahweh, whose name is Jealous, is a jealous God), lest you make a covenant with the inhabitants of the land, and when they play the harlot after their gods and sacrifice to their gods and one invites you to eat of his sacrifice, and you take of their daughters for your sons, and their daughters play the harlot after their gods and make your sons play the harlot after their gods.[5]

As we shall see, many leading scholars believe that major components of the Eden story constitute anti-Canaanite polemic,[6] so the question of what is the real history becomes central.

In the above passage, J is making at least four important historical claims:

- That prior to the emergence of Israel in Canaan, the Hebrews/Israelites[7] had their own ethnic identity separate from the peoples of Canaan
- That the Israelites were not originally from Canaan
- That the referenced cult objects and the deities associated with them are alien to the Israelites and their religion
- That Yahweh was the only deity of the Israelites[8]

But is any of this true? As we shall see, the evidence says mostly no. Rather, Israelite civilization developed *out of* that of Canaan, which itself was greatly influenced by the other, more powerful and developed civilizations in

Mesopotamia, Egypt, Anatolia, Syria and the Mediterranean. As a result, Israel's religion and mythology bore continuities with Canaanite and other ancient Near Eastern religion and mythology, including in the case of the Eden story.[9] The Eden story is built upon and cannot be properly understood apart from the mythology of earlier Canaanite and ancient Near Eastern culture. Therefore, we must begin our inquiry by examining this historical and cultural background, which will begin to reveal how the Eden story is richer in mythological symbolism than we had ever imagined.

OLD TESTAMENT PALESTINE

Since the Eden story sets the stage for the Bible's epic history of the Israelites (much of which also was authored by J), it is important first to review certain key aspects of the biblical account. We can then examine what the modern evidence says about these aspects and how that affects our interpretation of the Eden story.

The Biblical Account

The national epic of the Israelites begins with Abraham, a Mesopotamian who at Yahweh's behest abandoned his homeland to settle in Canaan and father, in the genealogical and broader senses, the Hebrew people. As the Bible relates, the Hebrews moved to Egypt to avoid famine and were eventually enslaved there. They resided in Egypt for over 400 years and greatly multiplied, so that when they left Egypt during the Exodus they had over 600,000 men able to carry arms, plus women and children (Exod. 12:37). When they escaped under Moses's leadership, rather than proceeding to Canaan by the direct coastal route (held by the Egyptians), they took a longer southerly route through the Sinai wilderness. Due to their transgressions against Yahweh en route, the generation that left Egypt, including Moses himself, was not allowed to set foot in the Promised Land and the people instead spent some 40 years in the wilderness of Sinai.

Yahweh ordered the Hebrews to exterminate all the inhabitants of Canaan, saying, "you shall save alive nothing that breathes, but you shall utterly destroy them . . . [so] that they may not teach you to do according to all their abominable practices" (Deut. 20:16-18). Further,

> You shall surely destroy all the places where the nations whom you shall dispossess served their gods upon the high mountains and upon the hills and under every green tree; you shall tear down their altars, and dash in pieces their pillars, and burn their Asherim with fire; you shall hew down the graven images of their gods, and destroy their name out of that place" (Deut. 12:2-3).

As just seen, this is also [10] what J had reported as Yahweh's prime commandment.

The Israelites invaded from the east, crossing the Jordan River near Jericho and conquering that city first, followed by the capture and destruction of Ai and dozens of other cities throughout Palestine, all in a matter of weeks. In some biblical passages, Joshua was credited with conquering a territory stretching from Arabah in the south to Baal-gad in Lebanon below Mount Hermon in the north, to the southeast in the land of Goshen near Egypt (Josh. 11:16; 12:7-8) and lands east of the Jordan river (Josh. 12:1-6). But Canaanites survived in some areas (e.g., Josh. 11:22) and "all of the regions of the Philistines" remained unconquered (Josh. 13:1-6); Judges 1:27-29 acknowledge that Beth-Shan, Megiddo, Taanach, Gezer, and certain other cities were not taken by the Israelites. As for Jerusalem, one passage reports that Joshua killed its king and presumably took control of the city (Josh. 10:3-5, 22-27, mentioning no destruction), but elsewhere Judah is credited with capturing and burning it shortly after Joshua's death; the Jebusite inhabitants were not killed and remained there (Judg. 1:8, 21), from whom David later captured it.

Notably, except for the Jebusites, the biblical portrayal of the Conquest says that the territory that would become Judah was completely conquered and its people exterminated as Yahweh had commanded. In contrast, to the north and southwest of Judah the Conquest was incomplete, thus allowing the Israelites in the north to be continually tempted by native paganism, which explains some of Yahweh's prohibitions, like marriage to Canaanite women and generally to remain apart from Canaanites (Josh. 23:7-12); these would have been unnecessary had the Canaanites been completely exterminated. The biblical picture of Judah, however, is that no such temptation initially existed there. Although Judges depicts rampant idolatry in the north, it depicts no idolatry in Judah before Solomon. [11] In fact, the Bible is curiously silent about *any* events in Judah between the Conquest and the rise of David.

Life in the North following the Conquest is depicted as chaotic, with each man doing "what was right in his own eyes" [12] and paganism running rampant. This is the period known as the time of the judges, where political, legal and religious functions were performed by the elders of clans and tribes. The tribes functioned largely independently, except when some of them entered into ad hoc military alliances.

In this formative period (and thereafter), most religious life was centered at the family and village level. Religion was practiced in the home or at small family shrines in a courtyard adjacent to it and concerned matters of importance to individuals and families such as crops, childbirth, and health. At the village or clan level religious observance took place at sanctuaries known as *bāmôt* (usually translated as "high places" in English language Bibles) located near villages, typically under or beside prominent trees or groves that were considered sacred, and usually on high ground. The Bible refers to several high places, and indeed many of them dating from early Israelite times have been discovered by archeologists, including at Hazor (11th century), Dan (9th-8th centuries), Taanach (10th century), and near Dothan (12th century).[13] Religion was practiced at high places both before and after the emergence of Israel, so the Israelites continued this tradition; at some point Yahweh was added to the deities venerated at them. Both before and during the Israelite period, all deities including El, Yahweh, and Baal were worshipped in their local variations and with local names, each answering to the concerns of the local community.[14]

At the high places stood cult objects, including altars for sacrifices and incense burning, stone pillars, and wooden poles (some perhaps carved with images) known as asherahs (from the name of the goddess Asherah). Pillars were thought to link heaven and earth and evoke the divine presence of the male deity (at first El, later also Yahweh), while the asherahs signified the female divine presence,[15] principally Asherah. After the time of the judges when temples began to be built, the pillars, altars, and asherahs were placed inside or immediately in front of the temple, as in the cases of Shechem, Samaria, Arad, and Jerusalem. Eventually various regional sanctuaries developed to service whole tribes or regions such as at Mt. Tabor (Deut. 33:19; Judg. 4:6). To the extent there was a religious center at which the tribes could consolidate religious understanding and cult practice, this was at Shiloh, where there was a sanctuary holding the tabernacle and ark, and a priesthood (1 Sam. 1:3; 2:12-36).

Government by tribal leaders had become unworkable in the face of the growing external threat, so Samuel, with the acclamation of the elders, anointed Saul as king with limited powers. Saul could not defeat the Philistines, and died (by suicide) in battle with them. His downfall was attributed to his violation of Yahweh's instructions (1 Sam. 15:10-18) and Yahweh's consequent rejection of this northern king (1 Sam. 16.1). Therefore, Yahweh instructed Samuel to go to Judah and seek a new king from the family of Jesse in Bethlehem, "for I have provided for myself a king among his sons" (1 Sam. 16:1). This was David, whom the elders of Israel duly anointed as king. Saul reigned at the end of the 11th century, David about 1005-970, and his son Solomon about 970-931.

David was originally a courtier of Saul, but rose as a war lord with his private army, giving him a base of support independent from any of the tribes. In short order, King David conquered virtually all of Palestine including most of the sea plain of the Philistines, and proceeded to build a large empire extending into what is now Jordan in the east, Syria in the north, and Sinai in the south. Thus was established what has traditionally been called the "United Monarchy" of Israel and Judah, comprised of the areas originally

allocated to the 12 tribes by Joshua; to that were annexed the outlying conquered territories to form David's empire.

In the course of his military campaigns, David captured the city sometimes called Jebus (from the Canaanite Jebusites), after which it became
known only as Jerusalem. He made it the capital of the United Monarchy, as
it was a neutral site independent from any of the tribal territories. He also
made Jerusalem Israel's religious center (though not the exclusive place of
worship), symbolized by his moving the ark of the covenant there. He placed
it in a tent shrine on what the Bible says was the site of the threshing floor of
a Jebusite named Araunah, who sold the place to David, but that high place
(soon to be known as Mt. Zion) was most likely already a religious sanctuary
of the Jebusites that David took over to preserve religious continuity[16] (much
like when Christian churches and cathedrals in Europe were erected over
sacred pagan sites).[17] This is where Solomon's Temple was later built. While
the Jebusites were dominated by the Israelites, they were not deported and
remained the majority of the city's population, and seem to have been treated
well.[18]

Despite this tolerance, in order to buttress the legitimacy and authority of
the king and the institution of kingship, it was important to promote Yahweh
as the chief god, who sanctioned the king. Thus, during David's and Solomon's reigns Yahweh was deemed to dwell in the city on Zion in its sanctuary, and to be closely associated with the king,[19] symbolized by moving the
ark there. In time the new establishment proclaimed Yahweh not merely the
god of the Israelites and Jerusalem but the supreme god over all peoples, for
which purpose Yahweh took on (from El) the role of creator of the world,
which he did not seem to have before then.[20] This role of Yahweh was
essential in order for J to write the Eden story, in which Yahweh created the
universe, the garden of Eden and the first humans (not Israelites).

The trends that began with David became more pronounced under the
more cosmopolitan Solomon. He is said to have expanded the empire and
entered into many judicious alliances with neighboring kingdoms, which
were sealed with marriages, including with the Pharaoh's daughter. He had
particularly good relations with the Phoenician king of Tyre, Hiram, whose
architects and builders constructed the Temple, and with whom he had sophisticated trading relations and partnered in overseas trading ventures; he
used Phoenician-built ships manned by Phoenician sailors. Such trade and
dynastic marriage relations inevitably led to foreign (especially Phoenician)
cultural and religious influence, with Solomon setting up religious sanctuaries to pagan gods to satisfy the needs of his foreign wives. The author of
Kings attributes the breakup of the United Monarchy to this sin of Solomon.[21] This came about through a revolt against forced labor, taxes and
conscription levied on the tribes. Feeling oppressed by the monarchy, the
northern tribes preferred to live according to the old religious and political

traditions. The eventually successful revolt by Jeroboam, king of the northern kingdom of Israel, came shortly after Solomon's death, helped by Egyptian manipulation. Jeroboam had fled to Egypt after unsuccessfully rebelling against Solomon, and returned essentially as an Egyptian puppet sent by the Pharaoh Shishak to lead a new, successful rebellion. This was followed quickly by a military campaign of Shishak against Judah, as a result of which its king Rehoboam had to pay tribute to avoid the destruction of Jerusalem. [22]

The northern kingdom of Israel now tried to function according to the old tribal traditions without a strong central authority, but this proved unworkable. Just like before Saul, Israel was politically unstable. Eventually, the usurper Omri seized the throne, became a powerful king, and established a new city, Samaria, as his capital. Much like the Bible's portrayal of Solomon, Omri and his successors centralized political and religious power and opened trade and political relations with other kingdoms, especially the Phoenician city-states, entering into dynastic marriages with these kingdoms, and establishing a more cosmopolitan culture including the incorporation of foreign religious cults, exemplified by Omri's son Ahab marrying the Sidonian princess Jezebel, who like Solomon's wives brought her own religion and clerics to the royal court. While these policies led to an economic and cultural boom, the Bible reports that later in the 9th century they triggered a religious backlash led by prophets such as Elijah and Elisha, highlighted by Elijah's holding the famous rainmaking contest between Baal and Yahweh at Mt. Carmel. The Bible portrays the Omrides as the worst religious offenders in Israelite history, resulting in grass roots opposition and a coup in 842 by the religious conservative Jehu, who sought to reestablish strict Yahwist religion, in the process demolishing a temple of Baal in Samaria (this will be important in Chapter 3). Subsequent Assyrian invasions resulted in the kingdom becoming an Assyrian vassal state by 738, [23] and following an unsuccessful revolt against Assyria in 722 the kingdom was annexed by Assyria. Much of the population was deported to northern Mesopotamia while many others fled south to Judah.

Eventually much the same happened in Judah, which had become a vassal state of Assyria in 734. When Assyria defeated Israel, Judah faced an influx of refugees from the north, many of whom held pagan religious beliefs which had developed further through contact with Phoenicia and Assyria. They also included non-Aaronid Levite priests (maybe E himself and the E document) bringing their own version of Yahwism. [24] A pro-Assyrian faction in Judah advocated accommodation with Assyria in political, economic and cultural spheres as the route to survival and prosperity.

The Yahwist establishment (or faction) in Jerusalem was horrified by this turn of events. The prophets too condemned the actions of the rich, the king and court as an affront to Yahwism, and their solution was to expatiate the nation's corruption and guilt by achieving social justice and putting the people's faith and fate in Yahweh (rather than through alliances with other nations). The fall of Israel was blamed on its religious sins.

In this environment, King Hezekiah (727-698) undertook comprehensive religious and social reforms designed to strengthen Judahite religion, morals, society and the state, while also preparing militarily and readying Jerusalem for the inevitable confrontation with Assyria. In the religious sphere, he sought to cleanse religion of Canaanite and foreign influences and practices and achieve exclusive Yahweh worship. In this endeavor Hezekiah was influenced by the Aaronid priesthood. Thus, he re-established Solomon's enfranchisement of Aaronid priests as the only legitimate priests and the centralization of worship at the Temple in Jerusalem. Worship elsewhere was forbidden, leading to the destruction of temples and sanctuaries elsewhere in Judah and its controlled territories. The reform also included the compilation of detailed law codes emphasizing the role of Aaronid priests. This may be when P lived and wrote.[25] His writings included not only his version of history from the beginning (as an alternative to the J and E accounts), but also the extensive laws that he compiled. But in military matters Hezekiah did not follow the prophets' advice to leave the nation's fate to Yahweh. Rather, he turned to Egypt for aid in revolting against Assyria after its king, Sargon, died in 705. But the revolt was crushed by Assyria in 701 and Judah was devastated. Hezekiah saved Judah as a kingdom only by remaining a vassal and paying a heavy tribute, which necessitated plundering the gold of the Temple.

The weakened Judah lasted about another century, mostly as a vassal state. There was a brief period of independence beginning about 630 under the reign of Josiah (639-609) thanks to the decay of Assyria that began mid-century and the rise of the neo-Babylonians, when Assyria lost control of its vassals and provinces in Palestine. Assur fell to the Babylonians in 614, Nineveh in 612 and the last outpost of the kingdom in Haran in 606. Suddenly Judah enjoyed a respite from Assyrian domination, and a power vacuum opened up in the territory of former Israel. So Josiah, apparently dreaming of reconstituting the United Monarchy, used this opportunity to occupy southern portions of former Israel. He also launched a wide ranging social, political, legal and religious reform movement, which went deeper than Hezekiah's.

The Deuteronomist religious movement was a cornerstone of Josiah's reforms. Whereas Hezekiah had been content just to reform cult practice, the Deuteronomists did not stop with cleansing the cult. They also modified religious doctrine, introduced new law, and extended the reforms beyond official religion down to the level of family religion. This was the first systematic theological conception of Yahwist religion.[26] J and E were not theologians, more storytellers than abstract thinkers, while P, though a priest, was more concerned with compiling laws, advancing the position of Aaronid priests, and centralizing worship at the Temple than in developing fine points of theology. According to the Documentary Hypothesis, the Deuteronomist program, including laws, was elaborated by a writer known as D, though the legal portion was based on a preexisting document.[27] Among other things, their program, like Hezekiah's, called for complete elimination of pagan worship and its associated sanctuaries (high places) and cult objects (pillars, asherim), as well as centralization of Yahweh worship at the Temple in Jerusalem; even Yahwist sanctuaries elsewhere were to be destroyed.

But D was not just a theologian. He also compiled a history of the Israelite people from Moses to Josiah[28] known as the Deuteronomistic History, consisting of Joshua, Judges, 1 and 2 Samuel, and 1 and 2 Kings. That account portrayed Judah's and Israel's kings as good or bad mainly according to whether they followed Deuteronomist law. D portrayed Josiah as the best king since David, and as endeavoring to restore the Golden Age of the United Monarchy; Josiah is also compared with Moses, as being the culmination of what Moses started, because he would fulfill the Mosaic covenant as never before.[29] As one might expect, this was a rewriting of history that served as propaganda to support and justify Josiah and his reforms.

But this dream was not fulfilled. Historically speaking, Josiah's revival was a brief, minor affair, as Egypt quickly moved into the power vacuum in northern Palestine left by Assyria. Josiah met his death fighting the Egyptians at Megiddo in 609, after which Judah became a vassal state of Egypt. The Deuteronomist movement collapsed. Soon King Nebuchadnezzar of Babylon drove Egypt out of Syria and Palestine. Babylon destroyed Jerusalem in 587 and ended Judah's existence as a kingdom. The next year most of Judah's upper classes, including the priests, were deported to Babylon, where they remained in exile until Babylon was conquered by Persia in 538 and they were allowed to return home.

During the exile Judah became depopulated, and afterwards it (now the Persian province of Yehud) recovered only slowly; not many exiles actually returned when given the opportunity. In this period Hebrew culture and religion sagged and were saved from possible oblivion by Ezra, who was driven by an extreme need to restore (and reconstitute) both history and the law. Ezra's efforts (perhaps as R) resulted in substantially the version of the Pentateuch that we have today, including the edited version of the Eden story.

The above biblical account of history was written largely from the Judahite point of view, another case of history being written by the victors (or survivors). As we shall see, the real historical legacy that came down to J was quite different.

INFLUENCES ON ANCIENT PALESTINE

The above biblical account paints a picture of an insular Israel in which the native Canaanites had been largely slaughtered by the Israelites, who already had their own religion and took up residence there. If the Canaanites were largely gone, there would have remained little or no foreign influence either. But this is far from the truth. In fact, the land that became known as Israel was a melting pot of various peoples, languages, cultures, mythologies and religious beliefs, and a central battleground for warring armies coming from all directions. Trade and conquest brought changes to the mythologies and religions of the peoples in this land, which was a crossroads for trade and migrations from all quarters: Egypt in the south, Mesopotamia in the East, Anatolia and Syria in the North, and the Mediterranean civilizations in the West (often via Phoenicia). Below we summarize these in order to set the environment in which Israel emerged and J lived, and then discuss relevant aspects of the actual history of Palestine.

Egypt

The Bible's Table of Nations (Gen. 10:6) considers both Canaanites and Egyptians to be Hamites (descendants of Noah's son Ham, the father of both Canaan and Egypt), which may be a recognition that Canaan historically lay within the Egyptian orbit.[30] Yet the Bible's narrative hardly acknowledges Egypt as playing any role in Palestine.[31] This is an astounding omission, because in fact Egypt was the controlling political and military force in both Sinai and Palestine during both the period usually assigned to the Exodus (about 1300) and the rise of Israel (1300-1000). Because the Bible never acknowledged this Egyptian dominance, our traditional perception of the Bible stories fails to take this history into account.

Egyptians viewed foreigners, in particular Canaanites, as inferior peoples, and Canaan as theirs to control and exploit. In the popular ancient Egyptian story *The Tale of Sinuhe,* the protagonist reminds Egypt's king that Canaan "belongs to you, a thing like your dogs." Egypt needed Canaan militarily as a buffer territory between Egypt and the great powers of Mesopotamia and Anatolia, and economically for trade and resources. Egypt first waged military campaigns there during the Old Kingdom, and hardly ever stopped. From about 1550 to until about 1150 (with brief gaps), Egypt thoroughly dominated southern Syria, Palestine, and Sinai.[32] Thereafter, until the Assyrians took over the region, Egypt regularly reasserted its power there, most notably in Shishak's 10th century campaign in which he claimed to conquer 154 Palestinian cities and set up a victory stele at Megiddo. Egyptian power faded in the early 9th century, which among other things left a power vacuum enabling the Phoenician city-states and Omride Israel to rise and prosper together.

Along the Mediterranean coast of Canaan, Egypt controlled the ports, Byblos being a prominent example. Egypt had highly developed trading relations with Mesopotamia, Asia Minor, Syria, and Palestine. While the region's major land trading route from Egypt to Damascus, known as the Way of Horus, ran right through Canaan and was protected by fortified way stations, sea trade flourished mainly through Byblos on the Canaanite seacoast. Originally it was Egypt's colony, but after the 19th century it was Egypt's vassal state. In the 14th century Amarna letters the vassal-kings of Byblos reminded Egypt's king that their city was as Egyptian as Memphis, Egypt's capital.[33]

Canaanites also went to Egypt and returned influenced by Egyptian culture, in particular during the Hyksos episode. As Egypt's Middle Kingdom (2040-1640) grew, it needed more labor, much of which was supplied by drafting Canaanites, who worked in the mining areas of Sinai and also came to make up much of the population of the Nile delta area. Typically they were not slaves as portrayed in the Bible, but simply a lower class that had to perform *corvée* labor as a tax payment, much like peasants in Medieval Europe. When the Middle Kingdom broke down, Egypt became vulnerable to military invasion and uncontrolled migration from the East. As a result, by the early 17th century, the leadership of these peoples, whom the Egyptians called the Hyksos ("foreign rulers"), ousted Egyptian power in the Nile delta and extended their control southward, establishing a Hyksos kingdom in Lower Egypt that lasted about a century (1630-1540).[34] Although in some ways the Hyksos rulers proudly maintained their ethnic identity, during their century of rule the Hyksos were influenced by Egyptian culture, religion and language (they did not yet have a written script so they used Egyptian hieroglyphs).[35] When the Hyksos were expelled and retreated back to Canaan, they brought that hybrid culture and religion with them and then reintegrated with the Canaanite population. The expulsion of the Hyksos inaugurated Egypt's New Kingdom (1550-1070), which soon reestablished Egyptian control over Canaan, where local rulers swore fealty to the Pharaoh as his vassals.[36]

Egyptian hegemony in Canaan lasted until the destructive turmoil across the Mediterranean caused by the Sea Peoples ended the Late Bronze Age (see below). But shortly before that, in about 1212, in response to revolts in Canaan, Egypt's King Merneptah conducted what he claimed was a successful military campaign there, which in about 1207 he memorialized in a famous stele erected in Thebes, which boasted:

> Canaan has been plundered into every sort of woe;
> Ashkelon has been overcome;

Gezer has been captured.
Yanoam was made nonexistent;
Israel is laid waste, his seed is not. [37]

Outside the Bible (which does not mention Merneptah's campaign), this is the first historical mention of Israel. From the morphology of the Egyptian hieroglyphs, we know that the stele is referring to Israel in ethnic terms as a foreign people, not as a land (territory) or political entity. This is understood to mean that a group already known as Israel was in Canaan, but that it had not yet formed a state that claimed a territory. [38]

Egypt's control over Palestine naturally influenced its civilization, and this was wide ranging. Archaeological sites from Syria to Sinai are littered with Egyptian or Egyptian-style artifacts. Egyptian influence appeared in art, architecture, language, literature (including the Bible), the numeric system, music, clothing, and most importantly for our inquiry, in mythology and religion. Egyptian deities became established in Phoenicia and Canaan, while local deities often acquired Egyptian characteristics. The Egyptian goddess Hathor was especially prominent in Canaan, where she was equated with the Canaanite goddess Asherah, [39] who will play a large role in our investigation.

An especially important Egyptian influence was the role of Egyptian hieroglyphs in the development of the Western Semitic and eventually Hebrew alphabet and hence ultimately the emergence of Hebrew writing and literature. As mentioned above, many Canaanites worked for the Egyptians in the mines of Sinai. They spoke their own language but did not have their own writing system or alphabet. Through interaction with literate Egyptians there, from hieroglyphs they developed their own hybrid script which became the world's first alphabet. [40] At first it was not widely used outside these mining camps, but in the late 13th-early 12th centuries the Sea Peoples destroyed in Canaan the cultures that had maintained literacy in the cuneiform and hieroglyphic scripts; this turmoil also shut down the Egyptian mines in Sinai, and the Canaanites returned home with their alphabet. Various peoples—Phoenicians, Moabites, Arameans, Edomites, and Israelites—began to write using this common script. [41] It took generations for a separate Hebrew script and language to develop. The first clear evidence of writing in the Hebrew language is from the mid to late 9th century. [42] This makes it problematic for J to have written before then.

In light of the evidence of Egypt's military and political control of all areas of Sinai and Canaan during the period assigned to the Exodus and Conquest, the biblical account of these events becomes most improbable. The biblical account of the Hebrews leaving the Egyptians behind drowning in the waters of the Reed Sea ignores the reality that the Hebrews would have been moving only from one part of the Egyptian empire into another, where more of the Egyptian military would have awaited, first in Sinai and then in

Canaan. Moreover, the notion that Moses authored these stories (or the Pentateuch as a whole) is impossible because there was not yet any Hebrew writing system. The archaeology of the region and Egyptian records instead paint a picture of continuous close interaction between Canaanites and Egyptians in Canaan, Sinai, and Egypt, which resulted in important cross-cultural influences including in religion. Later antipathy toward Egyptian culture and religion may be reflected in the Eden story.

Mesopotamia

J's narrative in the Bible's primeval history begins and ends in Mesopotamia (Eden and the tower of Babel). He then transitions to Abraham, a Mesopotamian who rejects his heritage and founds a new religion and nation in Canaan. These links with Mesopotamia are important in J's presentation.

From the earliest times Mesopotamia engaged in trade with the peoples of Canaan and Egypt. Some scholars believe that the stories of Abraham and other Patriarchs can be traced to this trading activity.[43] The Bible has Abraham coming from Ur, while his ancestors and family were said to be from the region around Haran ("caravan city"[44]) near the confluences of the Euphrates and Balikh rivers in upper Mesopotamia (now part of Turkey), where Abraham and his family settled for a while before migrating to Canaan. The Bible's story of Abraham as the patriarch of the Hebrews and initial shaper of their religion gives us an important clue to the background to the Eden story, because we encounter at once Mesopotamian culture and religion. Regardless of whether Abraham as a historical personage is included in that picture, Mesopotamian traditions, ways of thinking, and myths flowed into Palestine.

Mesopotamian influence in Syria-Palestine was massive and cannot be detailed here, but as one example we can take Mesopotamian writing and language. The international diplomatic language of the age, used even by the ruler of Jerusalem (Abdi-Heba) in the Amarna letters, was Babylonian written in cuneiform, reflecting what has become known as the "cuneiform culture" of the ancient Near East. It was the language of international commerce, diplomacy, learning, literature, and even within kingdoms often that of local law[45] and administration.[46] That language, through a strong scribal tradition, was the carrier of Mesopotamian culture, including its religion and mythology. Fragments of the *Epic of Gilgamesh* were discovered at Megiddo, and even at Amarna in Egypt. The Ugaritic language, which gave Palestine its myths of El, Baal and Asherah, was written in cuneiform script. Thus, Palestine was already permeated with Mesopotamian culture when Israel began to form within it.[47]

J wanted to deny influence from Mesopotamia and reject its civilization. Thus, Yahweh called upon Abraham to abandon his homeland and its religion and follow Yahweh. J portrayed the Hebrews as a family, essentially uncorrupted by foreign blood and influence, and developing their own culture and religion under Yahweh's guidance. J thus endeavored to cut off or at least minimize the Hebrews' connection with Mesopotamian civilization, gods and religious traditions. Notably, it was just before Abraham's appearance in the Bible that J placed his story of how Yahweh ruined man's attempt to build the tower of Babel, a Mesopotamian ziggurat (Gen. 11:1-9). A Mesopotamian origin for Abraham served J's purpose because the Hebrews were thereby established as ethnically separate from the Canaanites, having crossed over[48] to nationhood both geographically and in their religion.

Mediterranean Influence

Influence on Palestine also came from the Mediterranean, where advanced cultures had flourished since long before J's time. Prior to the Bronze Age Collapse around 1200 (see below), the Minoan and then Mycenaean civilizations dominated the Eastern Mediterranean, and their influence was felt in Cyprus, the Levant, and Palestine. Numerous Mycenaean and Cypriot artifacts have been found at archaeological sites throughout Palestine including in Jerusalem. These cultures featured, in their own forms, many of the same religious symbols that we will be examining: sacred trees, pillars, serpent symbolism and veneration, and prominent Goddess worship. The latter is especially important because Crete in particular was not impacted until a late stage by the sky god worship prevalent among patriarchal Indo-European and Semitic cultures from which Yahweh emerged, and thus offers something of a window into what religion was like when the Goddess was more prominent or even dominant.

The Phoenicians were the greatest traders in the world at the time, their ships plying the Mediterranean and bringing back goods to sell to Mesopotamia, Syria and Palestine, and with those goods came cultural influences from abroad. A particularly important early coastal city was Ugarit, discovered only in 1929. Ugarit produced epic literature, most notably the stories of Baal, Aqhat and Keret,[49] from which we have gained an understanding of the Canaanite deities El, Baal, and Asherah. The style and content of Ugaritic literature inspired parts of the Hebrew Bible. Ugarit was destroyed by the Sea Peoples, but Iron Age Phoenician cities such as Sidon and Tyre had a tremendous cultural influence on the northern kingdom of Israel, and to some extent on Judah as well.[50]

The Sea Peoples and the Bronze Age Collapse

At the end of the 13th and early in the 12th centuries large groups of confederated warriors who came to be known as the Sea Peoples descended upon the eastern Mediterranean. Historians and archeologists still debate exactly where they came from and what events sent them on their way, but it is at least clear what they did, which was to wreak destruction throughout Greece, the eastern Mediterranean and Anatolia, razing many cities and bringing to an end many civilizations: Mycenae, Ugarit, the Hittites, Canaanite city-states, and very nearly Egypt. Rameses III was able to fend them off around 1180 but Egypt was permanently weakened by them, which opened a power vacuum in Palestine and Syria. One group of Sea Peoples that became known as the Philistines[51] overran the seacoast and lowlands in southwest Palestine and settled there, including in the cities of Ashkelon, Ashdod, Ekron, Gath and Gaza.

The onslaught of the Sea Peoples resulted in the collapse of the Canaanite city-states' economic and political system. As Egyptian power faded, Canaan drifted into anarchy. Major building work ceased, maritime trade dwindled, culture declined, and cities became depopulated. The extremes of wealth and poverty grew; most people grew poorer. Many disaffected and displaced people wanted to break away and seek better fortune elsewhere. This was a Dark Age in Syria-Palestine which made the rise of Israel possible.

WHO WERE THE ISRAELITES?

Now that we have seen how the peoples surrounding Palestine influenced its civilization, we can address the question, "Who were the Israelites and where did they come from?" Even posing the question in this manner can be misleading, because it is so colored by our biblical tradition. According to the Bible, an "Israel" existed in a geographical, ethnic, religious, cultural, political and military sense beginning with Joshua's distribution of lands to the tribes. But is this an accurate picture?

Archaeological discoveries in recent decades, including some ancient extra-biblical texts, now afford us a better window into the past based on hard evidence, and this knowledge has radically transformed our understanding of this history. To summarize, this extra-biblical evidence shows that:

- The people that became known as the "Israelites" did not arrive in any large group from the outside and conquer Palestine, but mostly were indigenous to the land. In other words, they were mostly Canaanites.
- In the lands north of Jerusalem, the only significant political unit that could be called a state of "Israel" existed during the Omride dynasty, but that lasted only 42 years (884-42), and at its fullest extent it was limited to the biblical territories of Manasseh, Ephraim, some lands of Gilead across the Jordan, and perhaps part of the Jezreel valley. Before and after that,

Egyptian and Assyrian hegemony respectively prevented the formation of significant political units.

- David existed, and probably Solomon as well, but neither he nor Solomon had an empire. Judah was relatively poor, undeveloped, underpopulated, and did not exist as a significant independent state until after the fall of Omride Israel. The biblical United Monarchy of Judah and Israel dominated by Judah could not have existed. The first evidence of a king of Judah becoming involved in Israelite political and military affairs dates from the Omride period. Prior to the fall of the Omrides, Israel rather than Judah was the dominant party in the relationship.

- There is no sign of Yahweh or Yahweh worship in Israel or Judah until at least the 9th century.

Knowing the actual state of affairs is vital to understanding what may have motivated J to write, what he wanted to say, and how he said it. So we must review this history in some detail, beginning with the biblical accounts of the Exodus and Conquest.

The Exodus story does not hold up under the evidence. The Egyptians were meticulous record keepers, but there is no Egyptian evidence of any group of Hebrews having been present in Egypt, leaving Egypt, or of anyone named Moses[52] having existed. According to Exodus 12:37, the number of Hebrews leaving Egypt was about 600,000 men of fighting age, plus women and children" (which most conservatively would have yielded a total of about 2.5 million),[53] and accompanying that number were a "mixed multitude" of other rootless non-Hebrews together with their animals. Yet at the time the entire population of Egypt was only 3 to 4.5 million![54] The later tribal census from Numbers 1 yields a smaller total of 603,550 people. But just one-tenth of this figure would still be larger than the number to which the entire Israelite population had grown by the early 10th century (see below). Modern archaeology is able to detect even small, temporary encampments of ancient nomads, but even though archeologists have pored over Sinai for decades, they have found absolutely no evidence to suggest that any significant group of people was encamped along any of the potential routes of the Exodus or of the stay in the wilderness during the period in question.[55] In particular, the excavations at Kadesh-barnea, where the Hebrews were supposedly encamped for some 38 years, have yielded no evidence of activity there during the Late Bronze Age.[56] Nor could the Sinai desert support any such significant group.[57] As explained above, both Sinai and Canaan were Egyptian-controlled territories with numerous Egyptian forts and mines, through which Egyptian armies passed on regular campaigns reaching as far as northern Syria and Mesopotamia. The Hebrews in any Exodus would have been moving from one Egyptian territory into another. The idea that a large band hostile to Egypt which had escaped the clutches of an Egyptian force by

the Reed Sea could exist for 40 years in the Egyptian-controlled Sinai unde-
tected and unscathed is not credible.

And if there was no Exodus, then there was no one to undertake the
Conquest of Canaan. It is simply not possible that any group could invade,
conquer, destroy the cities, and exterminate most of the population of a
Canaan ruled by vassal kings of Egypt in a land full of Egyptian garrisons
and administered by Egyptian officials without any Egyptian response, and
without any Egyptian record being left of such events (as the Egyptians left
in the case of the attack of the Sea Peoples). [58] When Egypt's own vassal
kings in Canaan revolted, they were quickly put down; the Amarna letters tell
us that small units of a few dozen Egyptian soldiers were enough to pacify
unrest in Canaan when it erupted. [59] The archaeological excavations in Palestine provide no evidence of a Conquest of Canaan as described in Numbers
and Joshua, and so the scholarly consensus has abandoned the story. [60] Specifically, from the period in question there is no evidence of any military
invasion of Canaan, of any leader named Joshua, nor of even a peaceful mass
migration of any foreign or other ethnically distinct group. [61] Archeologists
have examined the sites of the 40 or so Canaanite cities that the Bible says
were conquered and destroyed, [62] and none save two or three (most notably
Hazor [63]) show any evidence of being destroyed during the time in question.
Many turned out to have been uninhabited at the time, most notably Joshua's
first two conquests, Jericho and Ai (its name means "ruin"), and the Gibeo-
nite cities. [64] Those which were inhabited at the time, contrary to the biblical
account, were not fortified with walls, because the Egyptians would not
allow it. [65] Some coastal cities were destroyed at or shortly after the time, but
by the Philistines or other Sea Peoples. [66]

So the question remains: Who were the Israelites and where did they
come from? Archaeologists were not able to make much progress on this
question until Israel occupied the West Bank in 1967. In the 1970s and 1980s
intensive surface surveys and excavations were conducted in that area. The
evidence revealed a pattern of settlements concentrated in the central Samar-
ian highlands stretching from the hills south of the Jezreel valley down
almost to Jerusalem, which area had been sparsely populated. The settlement
process began slowly in the 13th century, but starting around the turn of
12th-11th century the highland population grew quickly. Whereas only about
12,000 people inhabited that region in the 12th century, the population skyrocketed to approximately 40,000 in the 11th century. [67] Over that period, the
number of settlements in the hill country grew approximately tenfold from
about 30 to around 300; virtually all sites occupied in the 11th century were
new. [68] These were small villages with populations from a couple dozen to
perhaps 100 people.

Who were these new people, where were they from, and why did they
move there? Archaeologists and most scholars now agree that they were

Canaanites, from both sides of the Jordan. Several theories have been advanced to explain why they appeared.[69] Some scholars in the 1960s and 1970s argued that these people were refugees from disruptions in the coastal lowlands (peasant revolts or other social revolution against cruel Canaanite/ Egyptian overlords, or attacks by the Sea Peoples). But archaeologists quickly found holes in these theories, and they were abandoned. First, if the settlers had come from the lowlands, they would have brought that particular material culture (styles of pottery, other implements, and homes) with them, but none was discovered from that initial period in the new settlements.[70] Also, the lowland peasants had become impoverished and their numbers were already depleted much earlier (meaning also that they could not migrate in meaningful numbers), so the theory cannot explain the sudden settlement during the time in question.[71] Finally, the settlement pattern started in the *eastern* highlands nearer to the Jordan and moved *westward*. This pattern indicates that most of the settlers came from or through the Transjordan.[72] The eastern slopes were more suitable for the combination of farming and animal husbandry (sheep and goats) that the initial settlers practiced.[73]

An alternative explanation is that the settlers were nomadic or semi-nomadic pastoralists who peacefully infiltrated the area and settled down to practice both husbandry and farming. Indeed, the material culture of the earliest strata of these settlements suggests a pastoral origin of most settlers.[74] But such a process can take a long time and does not in itself explain the sudden wave of settlement that occurred. So although we know who most of these people were, the question remains, why did they settle there at that time?

The answer appears to come from how the interdependent trading relationship between pastoralists and the earlier lowland settlements was disrupted at that time. Pastoralists trade their animals or animal products (meat, dairy products, hides, wool, cloth) in exchange for grain for their livestock and other agricultural products. This was possible so long as the lowland settlements produced a surplus of grain and other products that they could trade. But in the wake of the Bronze Age Collapse the city-states could no longer produce enough to support this trade. Not being able to obtain grain for their herds and buy food, the pastoralists, or at least many of them, had to settle down and become self-sufficient by engaging in agriculture themselves.[75]

In summary, the real history is the reverse of the Bible's account: The Israelites were the *result* rather than the *cause* of the collapse of the Canaanite city-states.[76]

But what made these settlers "Israelites"? Was there anything distinctive about them in an anthropological sense that would justify that term? Not initially. At this point it is important to recognize that the settlement pattern just described was not unique to the central highlands of Palestine, nor was this the first time that it had happened.[77] The same process was occurring at the same time, and for the same reasons, in Ammon, Moab and Edom, where the archaeological (including linguistic) footprint left by the people in those new settlements was virtually the same as that in Palestine.[78] In this early period, "Israelite" material culture was hardly distinguishable from general Canaanite culture.[79] At that time the script and language in Israel was essentially the same as elsewhere in Canaan.[80] Nor is there any extra-biblical evidence of distinctive religious practices.[81] In fact, there is almost no evidence of any kind of cult practice: no ceremonial burials, no cemeteries, and no sanctuaries other than "high places" in a few larger settlements closer to the lowlands.[82] In particular, there was no indication yet of their having a deity called Yahweh.[83] Rather, their deities at the time were El, Baal, Asherah and possibly Anat, all of which are known from Ugaritic texts and elsewhere in Phoenicia/Canaan, and who in turn have roots in Mesopotamian deities.[84] The Yahwist movement emerged only later, during or after David's reign, and even then it was only the official state religion; family (folk) religion was relatively uninfluenced by it and remained essentially Canaanite.[85]

Nevertheless, over a few generations a more distinct Israelite culture evolved because the settlers lived self-sufficiently and largely in isolation from the lowlands.[86] Originally they did not trade with, make war with,[87] or otherwise interact with the lowlanders.[88] Eventually a distinctive building style and material culture appeared (e.g., no pigs[89]) that could be called "Israelite." The Merneptah stele shows that by around 1200 these Canaanites were already distinct enough to merit the ethnic label "Israel."

But in the end Israelite culture retained substantial continuities with the Canaanite culture from which it emerged; even Yahwism and the Hebrew Bible drew heavily upon Canaanite literature, religion, and other culture. In particular, the Israelites' religious cult terminology was essentially identical to or derived from the Ugaritic/Phoenician terms for the same.[90] The style and much of the content of Israelite literature (poetry, epic literature) and music have been shown to derive from and track Ugaritic/Phoenician antecedents.[91] Bible songs and poetry, including for example the Song of Miriam (Exod. 15), the Song of Deborah (Judg. 5), the Oracles of Balaam (Num. 24), and Psalms closely follow the Canaanite repetitive, parallel style of verse. The literary imagery of El and Baal was now applied to Yahweh.[92] In some cases the biblical writers simply quoted Canaanite verse, substituted "Yahweh" for "Baal," and inserted it in the Bible, such as in portions of the Song of Miriam (Exod. 15:17-18).[93] Many Psalms were of Canaanite origin and were adapted for Israelite use (e.g., Ps. 18, 29, 45).[94]

As the population increased and the society stabilized and grew more complex, Israelite settlements expanded westward toward the sea. On the western slopes the land and climate lent itself to viticulture and olive growing. As the lowlands in Canaan recovered from the Bronze Age Collapse, the Israelites developed a profitable trade in olives, olive oil and wine with the Canaanite cities and foreign traders, and they became quite well off. This interaction with other Canaanites and foreigners tended to dull whatever distinctive qualities the original "Israelite" highlanders had developed during their period of isolation. Contact with lowland city-states also inevitably brought the Israelites into conflict with some of them, particularly the Philistines.

So far, Judah and Jerusalem have not figured into the picture. Indeed, the Bible is tellingly silent about events in Judah during this formative period. Why? Because it lagged behind northern Israel and was an unimportant backwater.[95] The north where Israel emerged was located on trade routes with Mesopotamia and Anatolia and also could trade with the Phoenician port cities; Judah lay off those routes,[96] the Philistine cities held the southern coast, and Egypt controlled the southern lands. The north also had a more favorable climate that could support farming and a large population. Judah was relatively arid and not as good a place for pastoralists to settle down, so few did so there. Thus, by the 10th century, whereas the population in the central highlands in the north had grown to at least 40,000, in Judah the population was only about 5,000, many of the inhabitants still pastoral, scattered among Jerusalem, Hebron and about small 20 villages.[97]

This was still the situation when David and Solomon ruled.[98] Jerusalem's population was small (perhaps 2,000 people), and the city occupied only a few acres and, according to the archaeological evidence so far, lacked the monumental architecture or fortifications that are described in the Bible as Solomon's building projects.[99] There is no evidence of great wealth, literacy, or of any infrastructure or organization indicative of a developed state structure or significant military capabilities.[100] In short, David and Solomon could have been no more than local rulers controlling a relatively small territory. The archaeology does not support the biblical portrayal of David and Solomon ruling large empires or heading a United Monarchy of Judah and Israel.[101] According to the evidence obtained thus far, the manpower, military capability, wealth, and infrastructure needed to do so simply did not exist in Judah.[102]

In light of this evidence, many scholars (known as "minimalists") began questioning whether David and Solomon even existed, one of them claiming that David was no more a historical figure than King Arthur.[103] Indeed, despite the biblical account of David and Solomon's wars of expansion and alliances with foreign kings, neither David or Solomon are mentioned in any Egyptian or Mesopotamian records,[104] this despite the fact, as we have seen, that even tiny late 13th century kingless Israel (in the north) got a mention in the Merneptah stele. In 1993, however, excavations at Dan uncovered an inscription in Aramaic by Hazael, King of Aram-Damascus, who in 842 defeated an Israelite coalition that included a Judahite contingent. He boasted:

> I killed Joram son of Ahab king of Israel, and I killed Ahaziau [Ahaziah] son of Joram king of the House of David. And I set their towns into ruins and turned their land into desolation. [105]

This is not a flattering portrayal of either Israel or Judah and it contradicts the biblical account of these events (2 Kings 9:1-37; see below), but this inscription does evidence the existence of David and his being the founder of Judah's royal line. [106] But nothing in it indicates anything that he did, nor does it evidence a Davidic (or Solomonic) empire. Thus, although David (and, we may assume, Solomon) actually lived and ruled, the evidentiary record reveals little beyond that.

In the north, however, the 9th century saw a flowering of prosperity and the emergence of a fully developed state. This was made possible by the military campaign through Palestine of the Egyptian king Shishak in the late 10th century, in which he conquered and in many cases destroyed the lowland Canaanite cities as far north as the Jezreel valley (including Megiddo, where Shishak left a victory stele), resulting in the demise of reemerging Canaanite city-states. When Egyptian power in the area faded in the years after Shishak's campaign, a full-fledged kingdom of Israel was able to grow into the power vacuum and dominate the region. [107] King Omri (ruled 884-73) and his son Ahab (873-52) established what was for Israel a brief Golden Age lasting until 842. Trade flourished and the economy prospered, making possible the construction of the new Israelite capital city of Samaria with splendid architecture, and the rebuilding of cities that Shishak had destroyed. Economic and political ties between Omride Israel and Phoenicia were especially close, and Phoenician religious influence followed, all evidenced by the dynastic marriage between Ahab and the Sidonian-Tyrian princess Jezebel. In fact, the name Omri is unusual in Hebrew, he was a usurper of the throne, and, unlike in the case of other kings, the Bible gives no information about his ancestry (patronym, tribal origin). [108] In light of this, some scholars suggest that Omri was Phoenician. [109]

In this period Judah would have been the junior partner of Israel, as the above Dan inscription indicates. Eventually, however, the situation began to change in Judah's favor. After 842 Israel lacked a strong monarchy. Damascus and then Assyria came to dominate Israel, which became a vassal state to Assyria in 738. When Israel fell to Assyria in 722, Jerusalem and Judah were already on the rise. Earlier in the 8th century the prosperity of Israel had expanded southward, and a viable agricultural economy had started to develop in Judah. In mid-century, King Ahaz not only agreed to become Assyria's vassal but pursued a policy of integration with the Assyrian system, which in the economic sphere brought prosperity, better literacy, and population growth. In the wake of the fall of Israel, already in the reign of Hezekiah, tens of thousands of refugees fled south into Judah and the surrounding lands, giving rise to new farming settlements and real towns. The population of Judah skyrocketed to perhaps 120,000,[110] and "for the first time in Judean history, Jerusalem became a major metropolitan center."[111] In order to defend Jerusalem and Judah from Assyria, Hezekiah put the newly available manpower to work on an unprecedented program of monumental architecture, fortifications, and public works, including his famous tunnel to provide water to the city during times of siege. The city's population grew from perhaps two to about 15 thousand, and its area from about 10-12 acres to about 150 acres.[112] The economy diversified, including the first industries of olive and wine pressing and pottery workshops. Judah became a full-fledged state with a bureaucratic infrastructure; at this time we see the first strong evidence of broader literacy, seals, seal impressions and ostraca for royal administration, and monumental inscriptions.[113] Society became more stratified, with the emergence of a national elite, including apparently a religious elite, evidenced by the first elaborate tombs of wealthy Jerusalemites. This economic progress continued through the 7th century, largely due to the cooperation of Judah's kings with Assyria and integration into its imperial economic system.[114]

But as we have seen, Assyrian hegemony in Palestine ended in the late 7th century, enabling Josiah to exercise real sovereignty over Judah and expand its territory. He dreamed of extending Judah's power over the territory of former Israel, and began to do so. To support this endeavor his Deuteronomist supporters created a glorious, propagandistic national history of Judah that greatly magnified its importance. This effort was accorded divine sanction by portraying Yahweh as a national god who had given preference to Judah and David's royal line. History, including religious history, was drawn up so as to explicitly portray Josiah as another David, as the heir to a purported United Monarchy and destined to reestablish it. This edifice of national myth and official religion took shape at the expense of former Israel, which having disappeared a century before had no one who could bear witness against Judah's claims. Not only was Judah inaccurately portrayed as the dominant partner, but seems to have been given credit for some of Omride Israel's accomplishments.[115] The biblical stories of Phoenician influence in Solomonic Jerusalem may reflect that period.

In summary, the real history of Israel shows that the Israelites were actually the dreaded Canaanites themselves—their own worst enemy. Rather than coming new and ready-made from the Sinai desert, Israelite religion began as traditional Canaanite pagan religion, which itself was an amalgam of influences from Mesopotamia, Egypt, Anatolia and the Mediterranean. Canaanite religion was native, not foreign to the Israelites. As we shall see, it was Yahwism that was an alien creed probably imported by a relatively small but influential group, which its later proponents such as J were endeavoring to spread to the native Israelites. For purposes of J's message in the Eden story, the garden of Eden and the pagan temptations within it were not out of time and place, but right at home in contemporary times. J was endeavoring to wean the Israelites from their own religious traditions, so it helped to portray them as foreign. As we shall now discuss, we may be able to be more particular about how this dynamic was playing out in J's time, a special point in history, and his Eden story can be viewed in this context.

A SPECIAL TIME FOR J AND JUDAH

As a Judahite patriot, J wanted to tell from Judah's perspective the epic national story of the Israelites, from the perspective of his day. Traditionally Bible scholars have dated J to during or shortly after Solomon's reign, sensing that in the wake of the split with Israel he viewed the people's story as having its high point in the reigns of David and Solomon.[116] As we have seen, however, there seems to have been no United Monarchy, and David's and Solomon's reigns came nowhere near to the Golden Age depicted in the Bible. In that case, would J have had motivation to write immediately after Solomon? Probably not. What can our newly improved understanding of history tell us about J, his environment, and when and why he wrote? We can presume that J's choices of which issues to address and the symbols, allusions, vocabulary, and wordplay used to tell his story were tied to the religious and national issues of his day that were important to him. To investigate this, we must return to the mid-9th century, when a fundamental transition in Judah's history took place. Before then the situation in Judah was uneventful.

As seen above, in the first half of the 9th century Omride Israel was in its Golden Age, whereas Judah was a minor, less developed polity. Israel was a prosperous regional power, able to recruit Judah and other smaller kingdoms to join in fighting its battles against Damascus and Assyria. Omride Israel dominated Judah, which under Judah's King Jehoshaphat (870-46) was essentially Israel's vassal.[117] This relationship was cemented by a dynastic marriage between the Omride Princess Athaliah (the sister or daughter of Ahab) and Judah's king Joram (851-43), son of Jehoshaphat. This amounted to a takeover of Judah which effectively if not formally resulted in a united monarchy of Israel and Judah (probably for the first time), with Israel and its king in Samaria as the dominant party.[118] Athaliah's and Joram's son, Ahaziah, was the product of both the Israelite and Judahite royal lines, indeed a unity of the kingdoms.

With its close political and cultural ties to Phoenicia, the northern kingdom of Israel was not strictly Yahwist, but was a cosmopolitan polity that

tolerated many religions and deities, which we find reflected in the many
biblical condemnations of Israelites worshipping pagan deities at high places
and at Samaria, and in the biblical stories of King Ahab marrying the Sidonian princess Jezebel, her promotion of pagan deities, and the rainmaking
contest on Mt. Carmel. Israel's success ran counter to a principal tenet of
Yahwism, namely that Yahweh granted success to those rulers who were
strictly faithful to him.[119] Yet with the Omrides now dominant in Jerusalem,
they were able to introduce Phoenician and other forms of worship, probably
in the manner described in the Bible when Solomon was said to tolerate and
worship foreign deities and allowed sanctuaries to be built to them (1 Kings
11:1-11). This surely offended the Yahwistic party in Jerusalem, but they
were in no position to do anything about it. If J was there at the time, this
must have driven him crazy.

In mid-century the plot thickened. The rising power of Assyria now
threatened all of Syria and Palestine. In 878 King Ashurnasirpal had defeated
the Aramaean kingdom of Bit-Adini (the Beth Eden of the Bible),[120] which
paved the way for his successful invasion of Syria and the Phoenician coast
the next year.[121] His son, Shalmaneser III, again campaigned westward, defeating Bit-Adini in 856 and making it an important administrative center
and base for his six military campaigns in Syria between 853 and 838. In
about 842 at the Battle of Ramoth-Gilead, King Hazael of Damascus defeated the forces of Joram of Israel and his allies, including King Ahaziah of
Judah. As we have seen above, in the Dan inscription Hazael claimed to have
killed both Joram and Ahaziah. Joram's commander Jehu then became Israel's king. Shalmaneser III attacked again the next year. According to the
Assyrian records, in particular Shalmaneser's Black Obelisk, Shalmaneser
defeated Hazael of Damascus at Mt. Hermon and then subdued the Phoenician city-states as well as Jehu of Israel, collecting tribute from them all.[122]
Jehu is famously portrayed on the Black Obelisk bowing on his knees in
supplication before the Assyrian monarch. The caption reads: "The tribute of
Jehu, son of Omri: I received from him silver, gold, a golden *saplu*-bowl, a
golden vase with pointed bottom, golden tumblers, golden buckets, tin, a
staff for a king, [and] wooden *puruḫtu.*"[123]

Back in Judah, events now moved quickly. The biblical writers considered Joram a bad king because of his marriage to the Omride Princess Athaliah and his accommodation of her worship of Baal. He died in 843, and was
succeeded by Ahaziah, his son by Athaliah. But Ahaziah was soon killed
during or after the above-mentioned battle of Ramoth-Gilead (842). The
queen mother Athaliah, realizing her precarious position and unsure of support from Jehu's Israel, quickly seized power and sought to kill all potential
claimants from David's line. In an archetypal story of palace intrigue, the
Bible claims that quick-thinking loyalists were able to spirit away and hide
the last remaining descendant of David, Jehoash, son of Ahaziah. Seven

years into Athaliah's reign (836), the priest Jehoiada revealed Jehoash to the palace guards and had them swear an oath to him. Within days Jehoiada proclaimed Jehoash king and anointed him to the acclamation of the crowd, and the hated Athaliah was promptly seized and killed. The people then marched to the temple of Baal and tore it down, together with the altars and images of the god, and the priest of that temple was killed (2 Kings 11). Jehoash was said to be a righteous king who obeyed the priest Jehoiada's instructions, did what was right in the eyes of Yahweh, and ruled for 40 years (2 Kings 12:1-2).

For Judah and its Yahwistic party, this was an exhilarating turning point. After decades of domination by Israel, Judah now witnessed the downfall of the Omrides—the worst heretics in the Hebrew Bible—in Samaria, and the end of Omride control in Jerusalem. With Israel now weak, Judah, again allegedly under a Davidic king, was finally in control of its own destiny, at least for the moment. To J this seminal turn of events must have been most welcome and inspirational. Finally Yahwists could realistically hope to rid the kingdom of pagan worship. But the menace of Assyria loomed. Perceptive observers at the time must have understood that Assyria would be a greater threat than Israel, Damascus or the Phoenician states had ever been, both politically and perhaps also to Yahwist religion. For a Yahwist, it was a critical time of both opportunities and threats. If J was around then, he must have regarded this as a "do or die" period for Yahwism and Judah.

The new evidence thus suggests a new hypothesis. It makes eminent sense to date J during or soon after this crucial stage of history. The course of events described above provides a perfect motivation to write, which matches well with the anti-Israel and anti-pagan themes in his writings. As we have seen, historic turns of events inspired the composition of P in Hezekiah's time and D in Josiah's time, so why not J as well?[124] This was an optimal time for J and his sponsors to produce a national epic portraying Judah favorably and as better embracing the true creed of Yahwism, contrasting Judah with the more corrupt northern kingdom. The Eden story is the beginning of J's portrayal of this religious corruption, establishing it as a fundamental theme. The temptations portrayed by J as existing in the garden of Eden were those from the just-humbled northern kingdom of Israel, which might now be stamped out. For his audience, the story would have evoked recent memories. J writing at this time would also complement well the efforts of contemporary Yahwist prophets (Elijah, Elisha) who were likewise opposing the influence of Phoenician pagan religion.

Dating J as described above works better than the traditional dating from when Israel split from Judah, even though some similar factors would have been at work then and this book's analysis of J's work would still hold. But in our view this traditional explanation no longer works. First, the historical evidence now shows that there was no dominant Judah or United Monarchy

from which Israel could have broken, which would leave no clear basis for J
writing from a proud Judahite perspective shortly after Solomon, or even
during the period of Omride domination. Second, as discussed earlier,[125]
since J's story of Jacob and Esau (Gen. 27:39-40) reveals an awareness that
Edom had broken away from Israel, which occurred in Joram's reign (851-
42), J must have written after 851. Third, as discussed above, the epigraphic
evidence adduced so far shows that no Hebrew script in which J could have
written existed until at least the mid-9th century. It is hard to imagine that
this Judahite patriot could have written, for example, in Phoenician, but
Omride influence during his lifetime could have elevated literacy in Jerusalem. Fourth, since Omride rule in Israel provoked a wave of Yahwist pro-
phetic opposition there beginning in the mid-9th century and beyond, we can
presume that Omride dominance in Judah similarly provoked opposition
there, just as the Bible relates, so placing J within that scenario makes eminent sense. Fifth, assuming that E wrote before 722 while the northern kingdom of Israel still existed, then it is most sensible to place the two authors
somewhat closer in time (rather than two centuries apart) so that E's work
would be a truly relevant and meaningful alternative to (and, as some have
held, a reaction to) J's work. For these reasons, a reasonable hypothesis is
that J wrote sometime after 851, soon enough to have been inspired by these
critical events of the mid-9th century but probably no later than the early to
mid-8th century. We recognize that some scholars now date J even to the
post-exilic period. That would eliminate the coup against Athaliah as an
immediate inspiration for J writing, but in that case this book's analysis of
the Eden story's mythology and anti-Canaanite (and anti-northern kingdom/
anti-Omride) polemic would still apply equally well.

The discussion above makes the most fundamental commandment of Yahweh with which we began this chapter more understandable. The purposes
reflected in that passage pervade J's book, starting with the Eden story. J's
writings were in significant part polemic against both Canaanite (Israelite/
Phoenician) and other foreign religious beliefs, practices, symbols and cult
objects. In that effort, it was useful to portray them as foreign and not admit
that they had always been part of Israel's own religious heritage; therefore,
the Israelites were portrayed as coming to Canaan from the outside, already
having their own unique religion. It also helped to portray the northern kingdom of Israel as corrupted by pagan religion and Judah as separate and less
corrupted, and to cast Judah's own history in exaggerated, glorious terms.

It was in the Eden story that J began this polemic, and we should understand it in those terms. Thus, the Eden story contains or alludes to many of
the pagan deities, mythological symbols and cult objects of the religions of
Canaan and nearby civilizations, including sacred garden sanctuaries, sacred
trees, goddesses, serpents and serpent cults, cherubim, and myths about the

first humans being formed from clay. Below we examine each of these in turn. We begin in the next chapter with the origins, nature, and rise of the main character of the Eden story, Yahweh, together with his goddess wife, who also came from the Canaanite religious tradition.

Chapter Three

The Genesis of Yahweh and His Wife, and Their Divorce

Came Astoreth whom the Phoenicians called
Astarte, Queen of Heav'n, with crescent horns;
To whose bright image nightly by the moon
Sidonian virgins paid their vows and songs,
In Sion also not unsung, where stood
Her temple on th' offensive mountain, built
By that uxorious king, whose heart though large,
Beguiled by fair idolatresses, fell
To idols foul.

—Milton, *Paradise Lost* [1]

Come down and sit in the dust,
O virgin daughter of Babylon;
sit on the ground without a throne,
O daughter of the Chaldeans!
For you shall no longer be called
tender and delicate.
Take the millstones and grind meal,
put off your veil,
strip off your robe, uncover your legs,
pass through the rivers.
Your nakedness shall be uncovered,
and your shame shall be seen.
I will take vengeance,
and I will spare no man.
Our Redeemer—Yahweh of hosts
is his name—is the Holy One of Israel.

—Isaiah 47:1-4

41

At the very dawn of religion, God was a woman. Do you remember?
—Merlin Stone.[2]

The main character in the Eden story is Yahweh, the creator. So in order to understand the story we must first understand this god. As exemplified by Milton and Isaiah above, the story of the rise of Yahweh is that of the struggle against polytheism, in which goddesses were prominent. A growing number of Bible scholars interpret the biblical texts together with new extra-biblical evidence as demonstrating that the goddess Asherah (pronounced Ah-shei-RAH) was Yahweh's wife. Furthermore, numerous leading Bible scholars also believe that the Eden story alludes to and polemicizes against pagan religious practices, including the veneration of Asherah, sacred trees, and serpents.[3] Therefore, in order to fully understand the Eden story, we must understand the nature and rise of both Yahweh and Asherah, as well as the Yahwistic campaign against her and the relevant characteristics of the competing religion that J opposed. In this chapter we examine the nature of polytheism, the nature and role of the Goddess and Goddess veneration as seen in ancient Near Eastern myths, the rise of Yahweh, and the existence and role of Asherah and her symbols.

THE NATURE OF POLYTHEISM

Early humans experienced the world as wondrous and alive. The sun shines and gives warmth, and moves across the sky each day, as do the moon and stars at night. Water comes from the sky, flows in rivers and streams, and becomes a tempest at sea. Trees grow and flowers bloom. The wind wafts through waving trees. Clouds drift across the sky, and storms arise with thunder and flashing lightning. Animals and humans reproduce new life; all are born and die. The seasons come and go in an endless cycle of birth, death and regeneration. The patterns of the heavenly bodies are aligned with the seasons. Some aspects of nature are creative and associated with life, like the sun, rain, vegetation, and spring. Other aspects, like earthquakes, sea storms, volcanic eruptions, floods and tidal waves, are chaotic and destructive, and are associated with death. Some parts of nature are viewed as good, others as evil. Humans were awed by the powers of nature, most importantly by the heavens and the phenomenon of life.

Humans have always wondered what brought about the cosmos, what keeps it going each day, whether it will keep going, for what purpose (if any) is it here, and why do evil, pain and death have to be part of it. The ancients did not understand this, nor do we, although scientific progress has helped us understand the mechanics. The ancients naturally saw as inherent in the world supernatural, divine forces, energies, and beings that lay beyond their senses and understanding. Science, of course, has altered human thinking and brought us closer to the truth of such things. Nevertheless, the more recent theories of relativity (which equates energy and mass (i.e., matter)), quantum physics, and string and M-theory have shown that fundamental forces or energies do underlie and constitute all matter and the operation of the universe at all scales,[4] including even consciousness.[5] Thus, even according to science, a force or energy that is in some sense "divine" may lie at the source of everything. This realization brings us close to some longstanding Eastern spiritual traditions such as Taoism, Buddhism and yoga. In higher forms of Eastern spirituality, this force, energy, or "divinity" is not conceived of as a supernatural deity or deities "out there," and thus spiritual life is not a "religion" in our traditional Western sense. But in popular religion, including in the ancient Far and Near East, deities representing various aspects of divinity arose and proliferated.

Religion, much like science, is an effort to understand, classify, identify with and experience what we have traditionally experienced as the divine in a way that makes sense of the world and our part in it. Human religions at first were polytheistic. In polytheism, the world is conceived of and experienced as an emanation and manifestation of the divine in time and space. The divine is immanent in all things, whether "living" or not. In describing this consciousness of pre-Bronze Age humans, Joseph Campbell stressed, "it is not that the divine is *everywhere;* it is that the divine is *everything.* So that one does not require any outside reference, revelation, sacrament, or authorized community to return to it."[6] Early humans conceived of the cosmos in holistic terms, so that objects are not divided from one another but are united in a bond such that each participates in the other.[7] Originally the sun may not have been distinguished from the daytime sky (after all, it is still light on sunless days), or the moon and stars from the night sky.[8] Further, originally there was no sharp distinction between the sacred and the profane. Rather, as the British anthropologist Robert Marett noted in *The Threshold of Religion*, "the savage has no word for 'nature.' He does not abstractly distinguish between an order of uniform happenings and a higher order of miraculous happenings."[9] An ancient Egyptian poem dedicated to the god Amun-Ra illustrates this:

> He lives in what Shu uplifts [the clouds] to the end of the circuit of the sky. He enters into all trees and they become animated, with branches waving . . . He raises heaven to furor and the sea to revolt, and they become peaceful [again] when he comes to peace. He brings the divine Nile to a flood when his heart suggests it.[10]

Likewise, the Egyptian creator god Ptah arranged "so the god entered into their bodies of every kind of wood, of every kind of stone, of every kind of clay, of every kind of thing which grows upon him, in which they have taken form."[11]

The ancient polytheist held that in order to exist, any given thing—even a stone—must arise from and partake of some particular aspect of the divine. This principle applies equally to the nature of humans, who are likewise infused with the divine and in that sense godlike. The ancient Egyptians, for example, held that deities were formed from the sweat of Ra and humans from his tears,[12] thus implying that humans share in divinity. To the early polytheist, our modern Western distinctions between mind and matter, and body and soul—as if part of us was *not* divine—would be meaningless. Indeed, Canaanite religion too, being polytheistic, had no concept of the soul (as opposed to the body).[13]

Ancient humans attributed particularly meaningful manifestations in the cosmos to associated aspects of the divine, which determined their nature and actions. Since the divine is ultimately unfathomable, its various aspects became more understandable to humans symbolically in the form of deities. Human communities developed pantheons of deities representing various aspects of the divine: the wind, thunder and storm, the sea, crops, war, death, the sun, the moon, the underworld, and so on. In order for deities to be more understandable, humans gave them a humanlike (anthropomorphic) appearance, so that they related to each other and to us much as humans do.[14] Since an animated universe is best understood by humans in terms of human experience, having anthropomorphic deities is a valid approach to the divine, though only *an* approach. As one alternative, still later, in higher philosophy, the forms in our world were thought to correspond with particular divine principles, meaning that the material world is a reflection of a higher reality of prototypes or forms. There are two worlds, the visible and the invisible. In this view, the material world, though real, is a lower and lesser form of reality, so if one understands it as the only reality then one is living in an illusion, as in Plato's allegory of the cave or, in Buddhist thought, *maya*. Since the divine at its ultimate source is unknowable and has no multiplicity, humans, by approaching divinity through symbols, including anthropomorphic deities, can attain some level of understanding of it as well as spiritual satisfaction.[15]

This polytheistic symbolism is not only a system for *representing* the divine, but also for *experiencing* it, as a means for expressing human ideas, fears, desires, and emotions. Myths portray transcendent states of being through deities, demigods, heroes and symbols.[16] Connecting with the divine also was facilitated by those people considered closest and most sensitive to it, intermediaries such as shamans, priests, or kings (in some cultures considered divine). A more direct way was to eat or drink something thought to embody the deity, such as prepared cakes (often in the image of the goddess as with Astarte (Ashtoreth in Israel)), fruits of sacred trees, holy water, wine (which gave a seemingly transcendent experience) or other drinks that embodied the divine, so that one literally partakes of the substance of the deity. Christ's words at the Last Supper and the Catholic doctrine of transubstantiation and sacrament of the Eucharist are reflections of this tradition. As we shall see, this is in part the idea represented by eating the fruit from the tree of knowledge of good and evil in the garden of Eden.

We may now contrast the polytheistic world view to that of Yahwism:

> And behold, Yahweh passed by, and a great and strong wind rent the mountains, and broke in pieces the rocks before Yahweh, but Yahweh was not in the wind; and after the wind an earthquake, but Yahweh was not in the earthquake; and after the earthquake a fire, but Yahweh was not in the fire (1 Kings 19:11-12).

To J and the other biblical writers, nature was inert matter in Yahweh's hands. Yahwism, beginning with the Eden story, sought to demythologize nature by exorcizing divinity from it, arguing instead that all divinity resides in Yahweh, who should be the exclusive focus of spiritual life. As we shall shortly see, in the Bronze Age this demythologization of nature was a typical process, termed by Campbell the Great Reversal.[17]

The difference between the polytheistic and Yahwistic conceptions affects one's understanding of the origins and purpose of the universe. Whereas in Genesis only Yahweh is eternal and everything else was created by him and therefore had a beginning, in polytheism there need not and cannot be any ultimate beginning. This is because logically there cannot be anything anterior to or outside the ultimate divinity of which the universe is a manifestation, so there is no perceived need for a single creation. This understanding is epitomized by Indian philosophy, which visualizes an endless cycle of creation and destruction, with the divine, represented by the gods Vishnu and Shiva, accounting for this almost as if they are breathing in and out. In this vision, there is no ultimate purpose to the universe and thus no role for such a concept in spiritual life (aligning oneself with an outer purpose).[18] Spiritual life therefore takes another direction. The immanence of the divine in nature, of which we are a part, facilitates and demands an elemental correlation and alignment of human life and nature. In this understanding, our spiritual endeavors should be directed at approaching, understanding, experiencing, partaking of, drawing upon and achieving a form of unity with higher reality insofar as this is possible, and living in harmony with it.[19] In this way of thought, experiencing that harmony and unity, by breaking through the manifest to experience pure divinity, is the highest spiritual good to which humans can aspire.

An aspect of divinity can be experienced by various individuals and communities in diverse forms that are functionally close in that they yield comparable experiences. In this view, the more ways in which we can approach the divine, the better we can come to understand it. Therefore, the polytheist considers many approaches to representing the divine as valid.[20] Accordingly, the polytheist recognizes that the deities of other peoples represent the same aspects of nature and divinity that his/her own deities represent, and that they arise from the same divine source. Thus, when Caesar conquered the Gauls, he recognized in their gods those of the Roman pantheon.[21] In this understanding, no deity is right or wrong, and tolerance prevails. Unlike in biblical Palestine, Christian Europe, or what became the Islamic world, the wars of the ancient polytheistic peoples were not fought over religion, even while they invoked their own gods. When the warring parties concluded peace treaties, the deities of *both* sides were invoked,[22] and the victor did not impose religious conformity. In the polytheistic world, when peoples intermingled and assimilated as a result of trade or conquest, syncretism occurred, in which deities merged or one acquired the characteristics of another. Most famously, Lucius Apuleius, a Roman devotee of Egyptian goddess Isis, in a famous passage of his *Golden Ass* has Isis make this very point:

> I am she that is the natural mother of all things, mistress and governess of all the elements, the initial progeny of the worlds, chief of the powers divine, queen of all that are in hell, the principal of them that dwell in heaven, manifested alone and under one form of all the gods and goddesses. . . . [M]y name, my divinity is adored throughout the world, in divers manners, in variable customs, and by many names. For the Phrygians that are the first of all men call me the Mother of the gods of Pessinus; the Athenians, which are sprung from their own soil, Cecropian Minerva; the Cyprians, which are girt about by the sea, Paphian Venus; the Cretans which bear arrows, Dictynnian Diana; the Sicilians, which speak three tongues, infernal Proserpine; the Eleusians their ancient goddess Ceres; some Juno, other Bellona, other Hecate, others Rhamnusia, ... and the Egyptians, which are excellent in all kind of ancient Doctrine, and by their proper ceremonies accustomed to worship me, do call me by my true name, Queen Isis.[23]

To these could be added Inanna in Sumer; Ishtar in Assyria/Babylon; and Cybele in Anatolia (and Rome). And most importantly for our purposes, in biblical Syria-Palestine we must include Asherah, the consort of the chief Canaanite god, El, and subsequently of Yahweh once he had absorbed El. As such, Asherah represented aspects of divinity that Yahweh originally could not. So long as that was the case, Yahweh could not reign supreme and possess all aspects of divinity, which is why the biblical writers wanted to eliminate her from Israelite religion. This process began in the Eden story. Therefore, we must examine the backgrounds of this goddess and god, beginning with how goddesses and gods evolved generally in the ancient Near East.

THE WORLD OF THE GREAT MOTHER GODDESS

We use the word "matter" to describe what our universe is made of. This is no accident: It comes from the Latin *mater*, which means "mother,"[24] hence our expression "Mother Nature" to describe the natural world around us and its workings. This concept reflects how we originally perceived the divine, and it lurks behind the Eden story.

The workings of nature have always been a mystery to humans and still are. Through archeology, art history and the study of mythology we have been able to see how, beginning in the Upper Paleolithic (40,000 to 10,000), early humans developed their beliefs about the divine world and themselves. The earliest human representations of deities, from Paleolithic Europe, are almost exclusively goddesses.[25] They were relatively featureless except for their exaggerated breasts, belly, hips, and buttocks, pointing to the female role as lifegiver and vessel. Importantly, they were typically found at the entrances to the caves where males performed their pre-hunt rituals, meaning that the goddess was the primary divinity even in these early hunting groups.[26] Apparently, she was the provider of and even the living essence within the prey.

Early humans conceived of themselves as living and being enveloped in one big unity on which they were entirely dependent. At this stage of development, human consciousness was relatively undeveloped, like that of today's small child who does not yet clearly distinguish between one's self and the outer world, between subject and object, and cause and effect.[27] The pairs of opposites that a developed human consciousness perceives were only latent within what early humans experienced as a primal unity. Psychologists describe this relatively unconscious[28] state of being as the "uroboros," a non-dual unity symbolized by the circular serpent biting its tail, because the symbol connotes totality, unity, and perfection.[29] This environment has a womblike maternal feel, and in psychological terms is feminine for both men and women. Lacking opposites, this original world was experienced as a divine whole, a dreamy paradisiacal state of grace.[30] Even for modern humans, these forces of our unconscious continually try to draw us back into that more comfortable space, as when we struggle to wake and get up in the morning, against the urge to sleep and dream more, and when we tire and need to sleep.

As a result, early humans both experienced and conceived of their cosmos as a divine Great Mother.[31] As an archetype, she became the explanatory principle in relation to creation, the world, and life. Importantly, as the original unified totality of the cosmos, she encompassed what eventually became all three dimensions (tiers) of the cosmos: heaven, earth and the underworld.[32] She was the divine, creative force that gave existence and life to all things, and at the same time remained part of all things. She could generate all this on her own parthenogenically, with no need for gods.[33] (The notion of the Goddess as virgin derives from this concept.[34]) It was natural that humans' first conceptions and portrayals of this deity were rather vague and generalized, representing totality but without clear attributes, which could be seen as limiting. We see this in the very names for the earliest goddesses, such as Nammu (goddess of the primordial sea whose cuneiform ideogram was that for "sea"), Ninhursag ("lady of the (cosmic) mountain," which was the universe), and Ki ("earth") in Sumer and Gaia ("earth") in Greece. Later goddesses and gods emerged to symbolize more particular aspects of divinity.

Human notions of the divine evolved by observing nature herself: how the young of humans and animals are born of their mothers; the cycles of birth, life, and death of all living things; the cycles of the moon and the sun; the annual cycles of the seasons; how water from the sky and earth makes life grow and sustains it; and the nature and behavior of the various animals and plants. Pre-Bronze Age humans had no notion of time as a linear progression or of "progress." They viewed time as cyclical and conformed their thinking, myths, religion (including rituals and holidays), and life activity to the cycles of nature. For early humans the most important cycle was the lunar cycle, that of the waxing moon coming into being and growing to the full moon, waning and disappearing for three days, until the cycle began again. The lunar cycle took 28 days, which matched a woman's menstrual cycle, and pregnancy lasted 10 lunar cycles. For this and other reasons, the moon was often viewed as feminine and associated with a goddess rather than a god (though not in ancient Mesopotamia), often developing into a triple goddess (or goddesses) representing the maiden, the mother, and the crone, corresponding to the three phases of the moon. People used the lunar cycle to understand and represent the earthly cycles of life, death and rebirth, especially the seasonal cycle in which vegetation (later crops) came back to life in the spring, flowered and bore fruit and seeds in the high season (later the harvest), and then withered into barrenness (death) in the winter. The human life cycle came to be viewed in similar terms of birth, life, death, and rebirth. In this understanding, life itself never dies. Life, whether in humans or in the rest of nature, was conceived of as an indestructible and timeless divine force or energy. When through death it disappears in one form (or body), it must soon reappear in another.[35] Nature's cycles were understood in terms of the divine becoming manifest, then receding into invisibility, and reappearing. In his book *Dionysos: Archetypal Image of Indestructible Life,* the Classical scholar Carl Kerényi applied this concept to the Greek god by contrasting two Greek words for life, *zoe* and *bios,* which embody two complementary but contrasting dimensions of being.[36] *Zoe* is timeless, infinite and transcendent life and being and contains *bios,* whereas *bios* is the living and dying manifestation of *zoe* in the world and in time; "*zoe* is the thread upon which every individual *bios* is strung like a bead."[37] Significantly, Zoe is the name of Eve in the original Greek Bible, the Septuagint.

The above conceptions of the Great Mother gave women a special place in the earliest human communities, above and beyond their role in procreation. As the carriers of the power of life, the divinity of nature was most apparent in women, who were deemed to have mana; men had nothing comparable to offer.[38] Thus, in many cultures they were in charge of pottery making because it was made from earth and because pottery was a vessel like women themselves. The storing of food (including in pottery) was their domain, and eventually early agriculture, which they likely initiated (see below). So was tending the fire and hearth, as was the bed and the home as a whole. Control over fire, which is an agent of transformation (including in cooking and making ceramics), made women themselves a repository of transformation and center for the mysteries. Having the most natural insight into the operation of the divine, women were also originally the diviners and seers. In sum, women were instrumental in making humans sedentary and in generating early human culture.[39] Some commentators have gone further to posit an original historical matriarchy in a dominating political and overall social sense, but there is little evidence to support this.[40] For our purposes the important point lies elsewhere, in that there was indeed a "matriarchate" in psychological terms, a psychic stage in human development that produced our earliest conceptions of the world and generated the earliest myths, but from which humanity later transitioned during the Bronze Age (see below).[41]

Goddess worship seems not to have been prominent among nomadic peoples, who tended to worship sky gods, but the coming of agriculture and development of towns in the Neolithic age (10,000 to 3,500 in most of the Near East) elevated the position of goddesses. As Joseph Campbell observed, "Where you have agriculture as the base, the goddess is going to be the primary mythological figure."[42] Thus, the fact that Israel arose primarily as a result of agricultural resettlement within Canaan (Chapter 2 above) rather than in a nomadic environment as portrayed in the Bible helps account for the importance and staying power of the Goddess in its religion. Before agriculture, the Goddess alone gave rise to plants, and humans were passive observers; the sacred forces of the plant world were less of a human concern. The practice of agriculture, however, was proactive, a holy activity centered on unleashing the sacred powers of life, the divinity of the Goddess. Such activity required care, so it was filled with ritual, especially during sowing and reaping. Since the Goddess was the earth, humans sowed seeds into her, the act of plowing had sexual connotations, the crops were the epiphany of her presence, and the harvest was the substance of her body. Thanks were given to her for her bounty, often in the form of sacrifice; the first fruits of crops were dedicated to her. The harvest was literally a taking or killing of part of the divine body of the Goddess, which was thought to disrupt her unity, so an atonement was necessary to keep her goodwill and avoid her wrath and to restore the community's bond with the cosmos.[43] Consuming the first fruits of the harvest was a sacred act of imbibing her vital potency and connecting with the sacred order. The bounty of domesticated animals, particularly the sow, cow, and (especially in Palestine) goat, was also linked to the Goddess. As a result of these developments, specific goddesses emerged representing powers over agriculture, as well as other aspects of the divine, such as the moon, particular animals (such as the cow), trees, mountains, moisture, the sea, the watery abyss, and childbirth.

Similarly, humans saw a mystical connection between the fertility of the soil and the creative force of women.[44] Women took the lead in sowing, cultivating and harvesting field crops and fruit-bearing trees; they seem to have led the development of agriculture in the first place.[45] Their sexuality was important to agricultural rites. Thus, in some cultures married (therefore fertile) women sowed the seeds, in other cultures pregnant women did so, and yet in others only young girls—each practice having its own significance for fertility. In some cultures women sowed seeds naked. Sometimes the seeds themselves were brought to the fields in a cloth worn during menstruation, or by nubile girls. Furrows might be sprinkled with breast milk.[46]

Eventually the seasonal cycle of agriculture started to transform mythology. Human notions of time became focused on agricultural cycles. The lunar cycle took on agricultural connotations, becoming associated with seed coming to flower, bearing fruit, falling back into death, and regenerating, which became well represented in Neolithic art. The barren, infertile period of the year became associated with death, while the annual regeneration of life (in which agriculture and therefore humans now played an active part) supported an optimistic view of life in which death was not final but only a transition in which life recedes back into primal matter and then rejuvenates.[47] As before, the Goddess was thought of as a gateway through which living things enter and leave the world. But since the forms of life that live and die on earth are only temporary forms or manifestations of the Goddess (*bios*), the mythological expression of *bios* cannot be the Goddess herself but must be a form that emerges from her and returns to her after death. As a result, during the Bronze Age (ca. 3,500 to ca. 1,200) a mythological motif developed of the Goddess bearing a son-god, who would live on earth for a time, never reaching adulthood. As the year entered the barren season, he would die and enter the underworld (womb of the Goddess), after which he would be resurrected/ reborn. In this mythological cycle the son-god is taking an earthly form in time *(bios)*, so that upon "death" he can return into her, the invisible, eternal divine *(zoe)*.[48] His life-death-resurrection cycle paralleled the agricultural cycle.

Throughout the Near East and the Aegean, including in Mesopotamia, Crete, Greece and Canaan, the son-god was often represented as a young bull or calf, which was natural since the Great Mother was associated with the cow. The process of death and rebirth was reenacted in annual rituals in which the bull (son) was slain and sacrificed so it could return to the Great Mother for rebirth and so the growing season could successfully begin anew.[49] Another animal that acquired this meaning was the serpent, since serpents are chthonic creatures that hibernate in the winter and reappear in the spring when the plants come alive. Hence, the serpent too in one aspect symbolized the Goddess's consort.[50] The Goddess/son-god relationship was also symbolized by vegetation, with the Goddess being a tree or a grape vine (representing permanency), and the son-god being the fruit or grape clusters (which grow and die each year).[51]

As this motif evolved, the dying god (no longer necessarily the son) became the consort and lover of the Goddess. Such pairs included Inanna and Dumuzi in Sumer, Ishtar and Tammuz in Babylonia and Assyria, and Isis and Osiris in Egypt and Phoenicia, Aphrodite and Adonis in Phoenicia and Greece, and Cybele and Attis in Phrygia.[52] Thus originated the sacred marriage ritual. This important ceremony reunited *zoe* and *bios,* bringing the return of life through his fertilizing the Goddess, ensuring regeneration of the earth and well-being in the society.

The ancients developed symbols for various goddesses and their aspects using associated objects of nature, including the moon, the waters, various animals including serpents, birds and insects, eggs, trees, fruit, mounds and mountains, and in art through seemingly abstract patterns that may have been derived from nature (such as waves).[53] Caprids, especially ibexes and goats, were associated with the Goddess because they reproduced prodigiously and thus became a symbol of fertility, abundance, and regeneration.[54] In biblical Syria and Palestine, pairs of caprids were portrayed flanking the Goddess or one of her symbols, especially a sacred tree (Figs. 6 and 8), the idea being that the goddess is giving nourishment and succor to the animals. This motif will be important in our discussion of Asherah.

For our purposes water's association with the Goddess is also important. Water is all around us, and is nature's prime giver and sustainer of life. To the ancients water was the most fundamental thing imaginable, the absolute reality which had always existed. It was the formless (chaotic) primal substance, the source of existence from which all forms in the cosmos, in particular life, arose. Formless primordial waters therefore featured prominently in creation myths. Water was thus viewed a divine substance and symbolic of the primordial Great Mother.[55] An important example was the early Sumerian goddess Nammu, whose name meant "sea" and who represented (more correctly, *was*) the primeval ocean from which the creation emerged. In psychological terms, water represents the unconscious,[56] from which ego consciousness and the cosmos recognized by it emerges.

But water can also be chaotic and violent, a destroyer. Nature features violent, stormy seas, tsunamis, floods, and destructive rainstorms. Some sea creatures are monstrous and fearsome. It was therefore natural that water monsters featured prominently in myths of creation from chaotic primeval waters. An archetypal mythological motif involved a sea monster (serpent/ dragon) representing primordial watery chaos being vanquished by the creator deity, who represented victory over chaos so that the orderly forms of the cosmos could be created. But for this to happen there must arise a deity to do the vanquishing, always a sky god. Thus, in such mythology, the idea of creation (order) flowing naturally from the body of the primeval goddess was altered in favor of a sky god who ordered the cosmos. In this new mythology, creation became a transitive act by an outside agency, a supreme god transforming another substance. Whereas previously the Goddess had been the divine cosmos and creation grew organically from and as a divine manifestation of her, now the creator god stood outside the substance of the cosmos, which was not divine. As part of this process, in the ancient Near East during the Bronze Age, male deities (including El and Yahweh) came to control the freshwater and even seawater deeps. It was through water that the Great Mother lost her stature.

This new mythology marked a new stage in the development of humanity across the board, in politics, social life, religion, and psychology. J's writings not only reflected but actively promoted this new paradigm, beginning in the Eden story with its advocacy of Yahweh. Below we describe this historical change and how it related to the rise of Yahweh and his complicated relationship with the Goddess, ending in divorce.

THE DOWNFALL OF THE GODDESS

In the Bronze Age the position of goddesses deteriorated in favor of gods. The roles of goddesses in religious thought and rituals, public affairs, and even in the household diminished; goddesses assumed an increasingly mediatory function between the patriarchal human world and a masculinized divine realm.[57] This transformation of the mythology occurred due to several changes in ancient Near Eastern civilization.[58]

First, in Mesopotamia and Egypt astronomers and mathematicians developed our understanding of the orderly movements of the heavenly bodies and our images of the constellations, the knowledge of which was maintained by a growing class of male priests, which increased their power. This knowledge led to a vision of a perfect, rational celestial order that transcended the earthly order, traditionally the province of the Goddess. The idea developed that the superior heavenly order of the sky god governed the earthly one.[59] Creation came to be the work of the sky god and was modeled on the perfect, orderly forms of heaven overcoming formless chaos. Whereas in earlier religion earthly nature (as manifestation of the Goddess) was part of the divine, now a wedge was being driven between earthly nature on the one hand and the (heavenly) divine on the other. Indeed, creation literally became a process of separating heaven and earth, with the result that divinity and humanity were set apart as well.

A second development was urbanization. This was a result of specialization and technological developments creating food surpluses, as well as of the need to defend against invaders by constructing fortifications. City dwellers specialized into various non-agricultural professions, including traders, scribes, warriors, and priests. Society became more complex and stratified. As the range of human activities, concerns and interests proliferated, so did the number of deities reflecting these concerns. And whereas previously religious cult had been the concern of village chieftains, shamans, or priestesses of the Goddess, now a specialized and powerful priesthood developed, which was in charge of the temples and astronomical observations and predictions. The institution of kingship, together with a state bureaucracy, arose to govern this larger and more complex society. The king reported to the sky-god, and allied with the priests.

Third, into the developed areas of Mesopotamia, Anatolia and Canaan came continual waves (by a combination of invasion, migration, and infiltration) of Semites from the Arabian desert, Indo-Europeans and other Eurasians from the steppes above the Black and Caspian seas, and non-Indo-European Caucasian and Iranian peoples.[60] These newcomers each had a similar cultural impact, as they all came from nomadic or semi-nomadic warrior cultures. Their mythology and religion had developed into one where sky gods rather than goddesses reigned supreme, as is natural for desert and steppe peoples without agriculture or forests. Although they absorbed much of Mesopotamian and Canaanite religion, their own patriarchal religion influenced Mesopotamian civilization.

These three social and political developments impacted mythology and religion, causing the old Goddess-based cosmology and mythology to be reinterpreted, transformed and suppressed.[61] But there was a fourth factor at work that we must mention at this point. During this period the mentality of humans was undergoing an important evolutionary change into a higher level of consciousness, which was visible in the results. This change in mentality was partly[62] a result of the above-mentioned need to survive in a more complex world of greater celestial and other knowledge that one had to master, specialization, urban life, kings, and warfare, but it also itself contributed to and accelerated these changes. This is important because the climax of the Eden story is the acquisition of the knowledge of good and evil, which dramatized humankind's rise to a higher level of consciousness,[63] and because the results of both the above historical process and of the events in the

Eden story (as played out in the Hebrew Bible) are essentially the same: devaluation of the Goddess, the rise of a sky god, patriarchy, and the imposition of law as a means toward order. The Eden story can be viewed as a product of this historical and psychological revolution, and in this respect constituted a justification for it (functionalist myth). Campbell termed this revolution the Great Reversal[64] and it marks the stage of human cultural and psychological evolution that we are still in.[65] A description of the results of this revolution can sound negative, but we must recognize that this was an inevitable historical and psychological development, forming a necessary base from which humans could evolve further and higher.[66] This transformation has many dimensions, but for our purposes it is important to go into more detail on four of them, all blows to the Goddess.

First, our concept of time changed. In the new paradigm, the matriarchal conception of time and nature's workings as a cyclical birth and return to the Great Mother (birth-life-death-resurrection) no longer works. That mythology discouraged the development of ego consciousness; it was a treadmill that, as Campbell put it, was "getting absolutely nowhere."[67] In the new mythology, by contrast, creation by the sky god (who placed the keepers of time (the sun and moon) in the sky) gave the cosmos a beginning, so time became linear rather than cyclic. This implied that death is final, dark, and to be feared. Rather than being the womb of the Goddess where rebirth occurred, the underworld became fearsome, and various underworld manifestations of the Goddess (including serpents) took on sinister connotations. In the new mythology, the Great Mother was viewed as a chaotic force to be subdued and suppressed so that our orderly world could come into being and be maintained. The emergence of linear time also made possible the ideas of history and of a proactive role of humans in the cosmos. In particular, the notion of linear history made possible the Israelites' national historical epic in the Hebrew Bible, in which history Yahweh intervened, calling upon man to renovate the world in Yahweh's name, which J commenced with the Eden story as its necessary conceptual prologue.

Second, in consequence of the new creation myths in which sky gods created the cosmos as inert material, divinity was exorcized from nature, including from humans, and appropriated principally to the sky-god, though also to other gods and goddesses. Campbell therefore described the Great Reversal as

> when the sense of holiness departed from [humans'] experience both of the universe and of their own nature, and a yearning for release from what was felt to be an insufferable state of sin, exile, or delusion supervened. . . . In the West, . . . the agony was read as a divorce from God, largely in terms of guilt, punishment and atonement.[68]

As we shall see, this is the situation reflected in the Eden story. Yahwists obeyed a divine principle outside of nature.

Third, society as a whole was patriarchalized. Kingship arose, along with a male priesthood, as in Israel. Kings were the lieutenants of sky-gods, fulfilling their principles of civilization. Sky-gods and kings imposed order, as lawgivers. Being linked to the Great Mother, women (like Eve) were viewed as carriers of chaos and disorder, so had to be subordinated. Operating according to the egoic masculine principle, society, in theory, was oriented toward the avoidance of chaos and maintenance of order, although the result was often war.[69]

Fourth, the Goddess's stature, functions and roles were fundamentally changed. Whereas originally the Great Mother literally was the entire cosmos (heaven, earth, and underworld), the sky god took over the heavens and atmosphere (including the weather), while the goddess was relegated primarily to earth and to the underworld. An example was the sky-weather-fecundator gods (e.g., Sabazios, Min, Baal, Hadad, Teshub and Yahweh) fertilizing the earth with rains, in response to which the earth somewhat passively bore crops. This was portrayed in sexual terms, with the rains conceived of as semen.[70] Thus, in a fragment from one of his lost tragedies, *The Danaids,* Aeschylus wrote, "The holy sky is drunk with penetrating the body of Earth,"[71] while one Sumerian poem read:

> *The holy Earth, the pure Earth, beautified herself for holy Heaven,*
> *Heaven, the noble god, inserted his sex into the wide Earth,*
> *Let flow the semen of the heroes, Trees and Reed, into her womb.*
> *The Earthly Orb, the trusty cow, was impregnated with the good semen of*
> *Heaven.*[72]

This motif explains the imagery of the sky god as a bull and the Goddess as a cow that became prevalent throughout the ancient Near East, Mediterranean and India.[73] More generally, once the Great Mother (or more precisely her chaotic, dark side) was defeated in myths and psychologically suppressed or repressed, there remained mainly "good" aspects of the Great Mother, which were still valued.[74] The preservation of this Good Mother is a natural psychological necessity that explained the continued vitality of goddesses such as Asherah into the Iron Age and beyond. In psychological terms, this was a "fragmentation" of the uroboric Great Mother archetype into that of the Good Mother whereby the feminine principle (the anima) broke free of the uroboric dragon so that it can (potentially) exist as a healthy component of the personality.[75] As we will discuss in the Epilogue, this would become important, and still is, as the Good Mother embodies the spiritual and creative aspects of the Great Mother which humans can tap in order to further elevate their consciousness and spiritual lives.[76]

The above also explains why it was natural to unite the sky-god and Good Mother as spouses or consorts.[77] In fact, all major deities in the ancient Near East had consorts.[78] Such a relationship is not limited crudely to fertility and sex. At their best, a divine pair will represent the cosmos and spirituality as balanced unions of opposites,[79] in particular the male and female principles. These opposites can take largely abstract form, as in China in the case of the yin and yang principles, but more commonly they are manifested concretely as male and female deities which are ultimately derived from the divine unity. Thus, the Indian pair of Shiva and Shakti are commonly pictured as entwined, while Shiva and Kali are sometimes portrayed as a single being;[80] in China the unity of the creator goddess Nuwa with her (mortal) consort Fu Xi were typically represented with their serpent tails being twined around each other.

Such marriages took a different turn in the Bronze Age Near East and Mediterranean, however. Marriage became a device for a god dominating a goddess and usurping her powers. The Goddess had gone from being the unified divinity to the superior partner in the son-lover relationship, and now was the subordinate consort of a sky-god. For example, Zeus married Hera, and Poseidon married the sea nymph/goddess Amphitrite and assumed sovereignty over the sea. The best example of this in Syria and Palestine was the pair of El (whose identity Yahweh later assumed) and his goddess-wife Asherah. El was the father god of heaven said to have created the world, and together the pair engendered all other deities. Then, after Yahweh merged with El and acquired Asherah from him, J and the other biblical authors sought to eliminate her, so that Yahweh could assume her divine functions and appropriate all aspects of divinity, and then jettison her. The old mythology was entirely reversed: According to J, the sky-father god Yahweh, having no consort (no goddess exists), creates the world, then man, and finally creates woman out of man. Asherah was exorcized.

The Great Reversal produced important ancient Near Eastern myths, especially creation myths, which shaped the world views of peoples. These myths were then reflected and even referred to in the Hebrew Bible. Importantly, J took much issue with them and sought to refute them, starting in the Eden story. It is therefore important to review more specifically how this mythology developed, focusing on Mesopotamia. The sequence should sound very familiar in light of our discussion above.

THE GREAT REVERSAL AS REFLECTED
IN ANCIENT NEAR EASTERN MYTHOLOGY

In Sumerian mythology, originally there was only the primordial ocean personified by the goddess Nammu. From her body-waters rose the cosmic mountain, a unity known as An-Ki ("heaven-earth"), the Sumerian word for the universe. An-Ki embraced all of creation, reaching up through heaven as well as downward into the watery abyss; thus, even heaven was an emanation of the Great Mother.[81] Nammu was therefore known as "the mother who gave birth to heaven and earth."[82] The mountain itself was identified with the goddess Ninhursag ("lady of the (cosmic) mountain"). She was venerated as early as the Ubaid period (5300-4000), from which a temple to her has been found,[83] in the Uruk Period (4000-3100), and beyond.

But at some point this mythological concept began to change, due to the factors described above. Now An and Ki (already deities of heaven and earth) bore Enlil ("lord of the airspace"), representing the airspace (sky) between heaven and earth.[84] Enlil as creator thus split heaven from earth (i.e., inserted himself (the atmosphere) between them), and carried off earth (Ki) to be his bride, while An retained heaven.[85] The union of Enlil and Ki led to the creation of all other gods and of all living things on earth including humans, and eventually civilization, all of which he performed through utterances of words.[86] He became known as both "father of the gods" and "king of heaven and earth."[87] This is the first known instance in the ancient Near East of a god usurping much of the role of the Great Mother, separating heaven and earth in an act of creation, and marrying her in order to subordinate her.

Still, in Sumerian mythology goddesses held onto many functions and powers. An example was the myth known as *Enki and Inanna,* which has biblical parallels. In that myth, Inanna, tutelary deity of Uruk, and Enki ("lord earth"), tutelary deity of Eridu, fought for possession of tablets engraved with the *Me* (pronounced "may"), which were the fundamental laws of the universe and civilization as decreed by the gods, possession of which gave their holder great powers. Interestingly in this case, it was the goddess, Inanna, who was victorious, taking the *Me* from Enki through trickery, bringing glory to Uruk. But this is obviously Uruk's side of the story, designed to justify Uruk's domination in Sumer.[88] Another example of the hold of the Goddess tradition mixed with newer mythology was the ziggurat and the religious ceremonies relating to it. The ziggurat was microcosm of the original cosmic mountain representing the three planes of heaven, earth, and the underworld. Derived from earlier, smaller structures in sanctuaries of the Goddess (see Chapter 4), it originally represented, was inhabited by, and constituted the body of the Great Mother. It was thought that deities (now mainly in heaven) descended to the ziggurat so as to be available to humans.[89] Thus, the ziggurat at Borsippa was called *Etemenanki,* meaning "the house of the bond between heaven and earth."[90] That was where earth and heaven, the visible and invisible, the earthly and divine, *bios* and *zoe,* met. This bond was realized most clearly during the New Year in the sacred marriage rite, where the king and a priestess had sexual union in a temple at the base of the structure, while the god and goddess were thought to do the same at its summit, thereby assuring through sympathetic magic the fertility of the land and well-being of the kingdom over the next year.[91]

The Goddess suffered a further blow when Semitic peoples (Akkadians and then Amorites) established the Old Babylonian empire, centered in Babylon. Babylon's tutelary deity was the king of all deities Marduk, the son of Enki (Akkadian Ea)[92] and Damkina. The rise of Marduk resulted in the Great Mother's fall, most famously depicted in the creation myth known as *Enuma Elish,* which must be treated in detail.

Enuma Elish was derived from Sumerian dragon myths in which the dragon, named Kur, represented the underworld below the cosmic mountain, just above the waters of the abyss (*apsu*), which Kur controlled.[93] In one version, right after Enlil separated heaven and earth, the goddess Ereshkigal ("Lady of the Great Below [or Earth]") was carried off by Kur to become goddess of the netherworld, and Enki set sail in a boat to save her. He fought Kur while the primeval waters attacked his boat.[94] Unfortunately the text ends before we learn the outcome, but since Enki was known as lord of the watery abyss *(apsu)* in Sumer and Ereshkigal as goddess of the underworld, presumably he was victorious and made Ereshkigal queen of the netherworld. In a similar myth, known as *The Feats and Exploits of Ninurta,* the god Ninurta, son of Enlil, wages an epic battle against and destroys the dragon of the *apsu,* but this releases upon the earth the chaotic salt waters of the primeval ocean (which Kur had previously held in check), which flood the land and render it barren. Ninurta overcomes chaos by building a hill of stones in the underworld to hold back the primeval ocean, and gathers the floodwaters and directs them into the Tigris, restoring order to the land so that farming may be renewed. His feats so impress the earth goddess Ninmah that she falls in love with him and wants to visit (or live with) him in the underworld. Touched by her love, he names the (now cosmic) hill Hursag ("mountain"), blesses it so that it will yield all kinds of useful plants and animals, makes the goddess (now apparently called Ninhursag) its queen.[95] It is a charming story, but the result is the subordination of the Goddess, both as primeval ocean and as Earth Goddess, and a God's assumption of jurisdiction and control over her functions. This process is reflected in a mid-second millennium seal from Mari in northern Mesopotamia that depicts a vegetation or fertility goddess rising from the waters of the *apsu,* in order to pay homage to a supreme god who reigns atop the cosmic mountain at the source of two waters, offering him vegetation, her bounty (Fig. 1). As she does so another god stands behind her, with one foot planted on the waters that form the train of her gown, and points, pierces, or thrusts into the waters (the train of her robe) with his spear, guarding her and the waters and keeping them under control.[96] The god of that mountain could be an early form of El, uniting characteristics of both Anu and Enki/Ea.[97] Here too, the gods were taking control of realms formerly governed by the Great Mother.

The later *Enuma Elish* begins with Apsu (now personalized as a god) and Tiamat[98] as the primal father and mother. Apsu was the fresh (sweet) water deep, Tiamat the sea water deep, represented as a female sea serpent or dragon. Their waters "mingled" (note the new male role in creation) and they produced the first generations of gods and goddesses, who became unruly and noisy (representing chaos), which was depicted as a stirring of evil in Tiamat's belly (note the female-vessel imagery). Apsu wanted to destroy them, but when he proposed this to Tiamat she became enraged and refused to disturb this status quo (i.e., chaos): "How could we allow what we ourselves created to perish?" But Apsu plotted to destroy the gods nevertheless. Ea learned of the plot, took charge of protecting the younger gods, and put Apsu to sleep through a spell and killed him, thus becoming ruler of the *apsu*. He then established his dwelling atop the *apsu,* and with his wife, Damkina, produced Marduk,[99] who was perfect and above all other deities.

Tiamat, distraught by Apsu's murder, plotted revenge, for which purpose she bore giant snakes as an unfaceable weapon as well as other monsters. She appointed one of this brood, Qingu, who had become her son-god lover, as their head, enthroned him, and gave him the *Me* tablets and affixed them to his breast. For his part, Marduk was enthroned by the gods, given the scepter and ring of power, as well as his own invincible weapon, the thunderbolt. A fierce battle between Marduk and Tiamat ensued:

> *Face to face they came, Tiamat and Marduk, sage of the gods.*
> *They engaged in combat, they closed for battle.*
> *The Lord spread his net and made it encircle her,*
> *To her face he dispatched the evil-wind, which had been behind:*
> *Tiamat opened her mouth to swallow it,*
> *And he forced in the evil-wind so that she could not close her lips.*
> *Fierce winds distended her belly;*
> *Her insides were constipated and she stretched her mouth wide.*
> *He shot an arrow which pierced her belly,*
> *Split her down the middle and slit her heart,*
> *Vanquished her and extinguished her life.*
> *He threw down her corpse and stood on top of her.*[100]

Marduk then kills Tiamat's monsters including Qingu, wrests the *Me* tablets from him, seals them with his seal and affixes them to his breast. Now he has the power to create the universe. He begins the process by dealing with Tiamat's corpse:

> *And to Tiamat, whom he had ensnared, he turned back.*
> *The Lord trampled the lower part of Tiamat,*
> *With his unsparing mace smashed her skull,*

Severed the arteries of her blood,
And made the North Wind carry it off as good news.
His fathers saw it and were jubilant: they rejoiced,
Arranged to greet him with presents, greetings gifts.
The Lord rested, and inspected her corpse.
He divided the monstrous shape and created marvels (from it).
He sliced her in half like a fish for drying:
Half of her he put up to roof the sky. [101]

From the other half he made the earth. He created the sun, moon and other heavenly bodies and set them on their paths. He created the stars, giving the pole star its position, designed the constellations corresponding to the gods, and established the 12-month year. He used Qingu's blood (and clay) to have Ea create man. He leveled Ea's home Apsu, built a new temple called Eshar-ra, and founded cult centers in other cities for the other gods, who were now liberated from Tiamat. He gave his own city its name, Babylon (derived from *babili,* which meant "gate of the gods"), and made it the center of the religious cult. The doors of Marduk's palace were said to have been decorated with images of the various monsters that had been Tiamat's cohort and which he vanquished or took prisoner. [102] One of them, the snake-dragon known as the *mushussu,* became Marduk's symbolic animal depicted in miniature at his feet, perhaps as a reminder of his victory and of his subordination of the chaotic deep.

This is the first known myth in which god establishes creation as something separate from the divine, vanquishing the Great Mother and replacing her as the creator of life. [103] Her body still comprises the universe, but only because Marduk had killed her and used her lifeless corpse as inert building material, no longer divine. The unity of creator and creation as divine embodied in the matriarchal mythology was now erased, replaced by a dualism between the divine and the natural world, including humanity. The Great Mother, represented as a serpent, now embodied only chaos, destruction and evil (i.e., only her dark side), while the god represented the good, having brought order out of that chaos.

These developments brought ancient Near Eastern mythology closer to that of the Eden story. The motif of an upstart sky-god vanquishing a sea serpent or terrestrial dragon/serpent representing the Mother Goddess (or her proxy son-god) became typical in the Near East and Mediterranean, and beyond. In early Indian mythology, according to the Rig Veda Indra defeats and kills Vritra, dragon-son of the earth mother goddess Danu (whom Indra also kills), which enables him (like Ninurta above) to release the imprisoned waters and make the barren land fertile. [104] In Greece, the earth goddess Gaia creates as her proxy the monster Typhon to destroy the sky-god Zeus, but it is killed by Zeus's thunderbolt, "by which deed," remarks Campbell, "the reign of the patriarchal gods of Mount Olympus was secured over the earlier Titan broods of the great goddess mother."[105] At Delphi, where Gaia originally presided, the goddess appointed the Pythoness Delphyne as guardian of the oracle there, which was regarded as the navel *(omphalos)* of the earth, but she was killed by Apollo, who then assumed control of Delphi. A sea dragon combat myth also appeared at Ugarit, known as the Baal epic. In it El's and Asherah's son Baal defeats her other son, the sea monster Yam representing the forces of chaos, thus reestablishing order and his dominance over nature.[106]

The Hebrew Bible utilizes the same motif of vanquishing the sea monster and controlling the waters, appropriating Baal's and Marduk's deeds and imagery to achieve supremacy over other deities and over nature. We will discuss this in more detail in Chapter 4 when we cover the creation, but for now it is important to focus on certain biblical references to Yahweh stilling the waters of the underworld (the deep, *tehôm*) (e.g., Psalm 65:7; 107:24, 29) or which otherwise convey the idea of Yahweh's dominance and control over the *tehôm,* as dramatized in Psalm 104:6-7:

> Thou didst cover it [the earth] with the deep [tehôm] as with a garment;
> The waters stood above the mountains.
> At thy rebuke they fled.[107]

Yahweh likewise reminds Job (38:8), "Who shut in the sea with doors, when it burst forth from the womb"? As such, the waters must be overcome at the creation, kept under control thereafter, and affirmatively utilized as a tool when appropriate. Thus, in the Exodus Yahweh splits the waters of the Reed Sea to allow the Hebrews to cross and then releases them to engulf and drown the pursuing Egyptians, and similarly he holds back the waters of the Jordan to allow the Hebrews to cross into the Promised Land on dry ground. And most importantly for our purposes, in J's Eden Yahweh causes a mist to erupt from inside the earth, from the *tehôm,* to water the ground and enable the creation of plants and man (Gen. 2:6). This motif had Mesopotamian antecedents.[108] The *tehôm* is seemingly personalized. Indeed, Patai points out that in Hebrew *tehôm* never takes the definite article, which indicates that a form of the word once was proper name for a deity representing the primordial deep, most likely Tiamat since the words are etymologically related.[109]

For J, therefore, Yahweh stands superior to and controls the *tehôm.* Thus, in the Blessing of Jacob, an old text that J included in his account, Jacob can bless his people

> with the blessings of heaven above,
> the blessings of the deep [tehôm] that couches beneath,
> blessings of the breasts and of the womb.[110]

The reference in the above passage to the blessings of the deep couching beneath with the blessings of the breasts and womb (Gen. 49:25) is probably an allusion to Asherah;[111] as El's consort in Ugarit, she was known as "the one of the womb."[112]

THE ORIGINS AND RISE OF YAHWEH

As seen in Chapter 2, Israel and the Israelites arose in Palestine principally from Canaanite civilization. As a result, at first "Israelite" religion was indistinguishable from Canaanite religion and had the same deities.[113] Yahweh was not native to Canaan, but once he arrived in Israel, native deities were to some extent absorbed by him, and he appropriated their key characteristics, powers and functions.[114] This included endeavoring to usurp the functions of Canaanite goddesses, chiefly Asherah and Astarte (Ashtoreth).

At the top of the Canaanite pantheon stood the divine couple, El and his wife, Asherah. Together they were the parents of all other deities; hence El was known as the father and Asherah as the mother, creatress, or progenitress of the gods.[115] They were said to have 70 sons[116] as well as a few daughters such as the warrior goddess Anat.

El originated in Mesopotamia, most directly from the Amorite god Amurru,[117] but he also shared traits of the earlier Anu (An) and Ea (Enki).[118] For example, Ea was said to live enthroned at the mouth of the two rivers (Tigris and Euphrates), El on or at the base of a mountain located at the sources of two rivers, the "double deep" (or "two oceans"), referring to the freshwater and seawater deeps.[119] There El lived in a tent, or tabernacle, as did Yahweh before Solomon built the Temple. He is depicted as an aged, fatherly, bearded god, enthroned and presiding over his divine council of deities. He was considered wise, compassionate, and strong and virile despite his age, hence his epithet "Bull El" and the bull imagery associated with him. Although his acts of creation are nowhere detailed in any discovered texts, he was clearly considered the creator-god. Thus, in one text he is called Elkunirsa, which means "El creator of the earth," a title which survives in Genesis 14:19;[120] he was also called 'ab 'adm, which means "father of humanity," and bny bnwt, "creator of creatures."[121]

The other major Canaanite god was El's son, Baal. Having his origin in third millennium Mesopotamia,[122] his real name in Ugarit was Hadad, Baal simply being an epithet meaning "lord" or "master" that was applied to a variety of deities in Canaan. In Syria-Palestine Baal was a storm (rain) god, especially important in a region dependent on the autumn rains, as well as a warrior god, often being depicted in a smiting posture wielding a mace. It was because of Baal's role as a weather god that the prophets of Yahweh felt it necessary to challenge Baal for supremacy in this sphere at Mt. Carmel.

Initially (in Ugarit) both Anat and Astarte seem to have been Baal's consorts,[123] but as Anat's importance faded and Astarte's status and popularity grew during the first millennium, she emerged as his consort.[124]

In Ugarit, Baal upstaged El and became the more dominant and popular deity, as reflected in the Baal epic where he defeats Yam and goes on to have a palace built for him by the other gods, whereas El remained in his tent. Much the same happened when Enlil supplanted An, Marduk supplanted Anu, and Zeus supplanted Ouranos as the dominant deity.[125] It is worth pausing to consider this common dynamic, as it helps explain the rise of Yahweh. Supreme heavenly creator gods are not only literally aloof, but also largely aloof from human concerns and affairs. Representing totality, it was difficult for them to take on particular attributes because they would tend to limit their totality and omnipotence. That is why the most pure conceptions of divinity representing totality in philosophy and religion, from the Tao to the Neoplatonist One, are abstract. But it is the particular attributes relevant to human affairs, and a belief that the deity has a personality and actively takes an interest in human affairs and can be a "personal" god, that can endear deities to humans. This explains the panoply of deities in polytheism, each representing an area of human concern. Thus, in dry regions such as the ancient Near East, weather and water gods were most important; as were the corresponding earth fertility goddesses who were typically their consorts. As a pair, they reinforced each other. Thus, the heavenly creator gods like An, Ouranos and El declined in popularity; this was also a problem with featureless goddesses such as Nammu and Gaia, who yielded their places not only to gods but to particular goddesses (of childbirth, fertility, etc.) who more directly resonated with human needs. Let us now examine how Yahweh navigated this minefield in his effort to become supreme, and whether he, as an ineffable and imageless deity, could do so without the help of a consort by his side.

Yahweh's start was inauspicious. There is no extra-biblical record of Yahweh in Palestine until the monarchy. Traditional Canaanite religious practices seem not to have been widely opposed until the 9th century, when Baal and his prophets competed with Yahweh.[126] In the Bible Yahwistic theophoric names are almost entirely absent prior to the monarchy, while many were derived from El, including Isra*el* (Jacob) himself.[127]

If Yahweh was not from Canaan, where did he come from? Actually, the Bible points the way, in describing how Moses discovered and introduced Yahweh to the Hebrews. The Bible states several times that Yahweh originated in Seir (or Teman) in the Midian,[128] which spans the east and west sides of the Arabah running between the Dead Sea and the Gulf of Aqaba along the border with Sinai. That is where Moses fled after killing the Egyptian taskmaster, met a priest of the Kenites, Jethro, married his daughter, Zipporah, and lived there for years (Exod. 2:15-25). It was there that Moses was introduced to Yahweh at the burning bush by the sacred mountain of God, Mt. Horeb,[129] and was commissioned by Yahweh for his life's mission. The Bible then says that the Hebrews passed through this region on their way to Canaan, and took on Jethro's son Hobab (Moses's brother-in-law) as their guide in the wilderness (Num. 10:29-32). Hobab and his priestly family eventually migrated to Judah and served as priests at a sanctuary in the region of Arad.[130] Kenites accompanied the Israelites into Canaan and they lived there together, including during the time of King Saul (Judg. 1:16; 4:11). Hobab's descendant, Heber the Kenite, and his priestess-wife Jael were said to have helped the Israelites defeat the Canaanites of Hazor (Judg. 4:11-23). The Kenites were eventually incorporated into Judah under David (1 Sam. 30:29). This family alliance between the priestly descendants of Moses and those of Jethro was preserved not only at Arad, but also at other sanctuaries, including those at Shiloh, Dan and Kadesh-Naphtali.[131] Given the later hostile relations between Israel and the Midianites, the above tradition may reflect an undeniable history rather than being invented.[132]

This portrayal of Midianites mingling with the Israelites in this region south of Palestine is corroborated by archeological evidence, to the point where most Bible scholars now agree that Yahweh originated in the Midian,[133] where he seems to have been primarily a warrior god but also a sky-weather god. Early 8th century inscriptions on walls and pottery found nearby at Kuntillet Ajrûd in the southeastern Sinai refer to "Yahweh of Teman," where both Habakkuk (3:3, 7) and Zechariah (9:14) also indicate Yahweh originated.[134] The Kenites were known as coppersmiths/metalworkers,[135] a trade supported by copper mines in the region, including at Timna in the Arabah (where Judah once pastured his flocks (Gen. 38:12-14)), which supplied copper and copper articles to Egypt, Israel, and elsewhere. Snakes seem to have been part of the religious cult in the Midian, evidenced by a 13th-century copper votive serpent found at a Hathor[136] temple at Timna (Fig. 45). This may help explain the origin of the story of Moses's staff (obtained while living with Jethro) turning into a snake through Yahweh's mediation (Exod. 4:2-3), the Hebrews being attacked by "fiery" serpents while encamped in the region, and Moses making his bronze serpent there for protection (Num. 21:1-9).

Going further back in time, 15th century Egyptian inscriptions refer to *"Yhw* in the land of the Shasu," which most specialists now agree refers to Yahweh, meaning that Yahweh was venerated in that land by that time.[137] The Shasu (meaning "moving on foot") had their homeland in the east Arabah in Edom (Seir) and Moab. Archeologists have traced movements of some Shasu north into Transjordan and from there into the highlands of Canaan.[138] The Egyptologist Donald Redford believes that they entered Canaan and adapted to Canaanite material culture for the most part, but left some distinctive marks on the highland culture which differ from traditional

Canaanite culture and became features of Yahwism, such as an aversion to images of the deity.[139] It is difficult to attribute Yahweh worship to a particular group in the Midian such as Kenites or the Shasu, but the evidence that Yahweh emerged from the Midian is strong. In light of the biblical and extra-biblical evidence, it is logical to posit that a chieftain, priest or charismatic or influential figure(s) from the Midian (who later became known as Moses, Aaron, Hobab, etc.) migrated with his/their clans from this traditionally Egyptian territory into Palestine, either as Israel was forming during the time of the judges or early in the monarchy, bringing Yahweh along and instituting his cult among the native Israelites.[140] Another hypothesis is that a migrant group from Sinai became established as the Levites, as only they had Egyptian names, which might account for why they were not accorded any territory in Israel.[141]

The extra-biblical record does not indicate how and why Yahweh came to be accepted as the god of the Israelites and became associated with the drive to unite them and carve out a national identity.[142] For this purpose having one's unique non-native patron deity is useful. The polytheistic nature of Canaanite religion enabled Yahweh to be accepted into El's pantheon,[143] from which position he could contend for superiority (as Baal had done). Several biblical passages indeed portray Yahweh as being in El's pantheon and assuming a leading role in it, much as Baal had done in Ugarit;[144] indeed, part of the idea may have been to usurp Baal's role. Eventually, El and Yahweh could be merged, with Yahweh as the survivor.[145] Like El, Yahweh was portrayed as wise, compassionate, aged (sometimes), was associated with mountains, and chaired a council of other divine beings, the sons of God.[146] Like El, Yahweh resided in a tent, the tabernacle.[147] El made covenants, as did Yahweh. El was associated with the young bull (calf), and it seems that at least in the northern kingdom of Israel so was Yahweh,[148] but ultimately, at least in Judah, this symbol for Yahweh did not stick, perhaps because Baal had also taken on bull imagery, and Yahweh was competing with Baal as well. Instead, Yahweh became associated with cherubim, as on the Ark of the Covenant, in the Holy of Holies in Solomon's Temple, and in the Eden story. The Bible also portrays Yahweh as assuming functions of Baal, especially his role as a weather/storm god, achieved in the competition between the prophets of Baal and Yahweh at Mt. Carmel (1 Kings 18:19-46). Baal's deeds in defeating the sea monster of chaos were also claimed by Yahweh.[149] And just as the victorious Baal had to have a fitting palace built for him, Solomon built a glorious Temple for Yahweh.

This process of merging El and Yahweh is reflected in the patriarchal narratives, which say that the Hebrews first knew their god as El, the god of Abraham and the other patriarchs.[150] Indeed, when the Israelites formed their nation, they called it Isra*el*, which was the name assigned to Jacob after his struggle with a divine being and probably means "God [El] strives (or rules)" but is also taken to mean "he strives with God [El]."[151] Jacob then proceeded to establish an altar to his god at Beth*el,* which means "house of God [El]," while hiding the cult objects of "foreign" gods under an oak near Shechem (Gen. 35:1-8). Indeed, El was venerated at the shrine of Shechem. In the patriarchal narratives he became known there as "the god of Israel," and El's religious lore and cult practice was adopted by the Yahwistic priesthood.[152] Yahweh revealed himself to the Hebrews through Moses far to the south, at the burning bush in the land of Midian (Exod. 3:1-6, by E). He announced, "I am the God of your father, the God of Abraham, the God of Isaac, and the God of Jacob." Then he tells Moses (Exod. 3:15, also E), "Say this to the people of Israel, 'Yahweh, the god of your fathers, the god of Abraham, the god of Isaac, and the god of Jacob sent me to you'; this is my name forever, and thus I am to be remembered always."[153] Later, back in Egypt when Moses was in the process of convincing Pharaoh to let the Hebrews leave Egypt (Exod.: 6:2-3, by P), God told Moses, "I am Yahweh, I appeared to Abraham, to Isaac and to Jacob, as El Almighty, but by my name Yahweh I did not make myself known to them." This means that Yahweh was unknown to the Patriarchs, who worshipped El.[154] Indeed, E calls God "El" or "Elohim" before the incident at the burning bush, but "Yahweh" afterwards. By feeling the need to come up with these explanations, E and P betray that the old god from before Moses and the new god being promoted by the authors are historically distinct; they are trying to paper this over by saying they are really the same. This is a typical case of one deity absorbing or merging with another. The above biblical texts appear to reflect a compromise where religious and political leaders (in Israel and Judah) agreed that Yahweh and El were the same God rather than fighting over whose was the true or predominant god.[155]

J, however, seems to have lived before this resolution was reached, because he proffered a different solution which would have eliminated El from the picture. First, as we have seen, he makes Yahweh, not El, the deity in the Eden story. Eve then invokes Yahweh's name in Genesis 4:1 (by J). Then, in Genesis 4:26, J claimed that people began calling God Yahweh almost from the beginning of humankind, from the time of Adam's grandson through Seth, Enosh. But in the end J's position did not prevail. The El traditions were undeniable and strong, particularly in the northern kingdom of Israel, where E was from.

The biblical account of the struggle between Yahweh and paganism makes it appear that Yahweh was generally regarded as the national god but that the people and many kings strayed into worshipping "foreign" deities. In fact, it was the other way around. Yahweh was the outsider god being imposed on the native people by certain kings and the priesthood. The Israelite people and most kings were simply preserving local deities and religious practices that they had observed for centuries. Although the Bible's more overt and extreme anti-Canaanite polemic came after J's time, that was a consistent and logical extension of J's thinking, and he can be said to have inspired and initiated the process, beginning in the Eden story.

Thus, in Exodus 34:11-16 and Deuteronomy 12:2 Yahweh commanded the Hebrews to destroy Canaanite sanctuaries at high places and "under every green tree," tear down their altars and pillars, and hew down and burn the asherahs and other graven images. There is no record of anyone obeying these commands for a long time, however. Thus, under Solomon's son Rehoboam (ruled 931-14) the people are said to have "built for themselves high places, and pillars, and Asherim on every high hill and under every green tree" (1 Kings 14:23). Similarly, king Ahaz (743-27) was said to have "walked in the way of the kings of Israel" and "sacrificed and burned incense on the high places, and on the hills, and under every green tree" (2 Kings 16:4). The first true Yahwist king was Ahaz's son Hezekiah (727-698), who "removed the high places, and broke the pillars, and cut down the Asherah [156] [before the Temple]. And he broke in pieces the bronze serpent that Moses had made, for until those days the people of Israel had burned incense to it; it was called Nehushtan" (2 Kings 18:4).

After Hezekiah, the rulers and the people are said to have reverted to traditional Canaanite religious practices until the reign of king Josiah, who took even stronger measures to eradicate them. He commanded the priests in Jerusalem

> to bring out of the temple of the Lord all the vessels made for Baal, for Asherah, and for all the host of heaven; he burned them outside Jerusalem in the fields of the Kidron, and carried their ashes to Bethel. And he deposed the idolatrous priests whom the kings of Judah had ordained to burn incense in the high places. . . . And he brought out the Asherah from the house of the Lord, outside Jerusalem, to the brook Kidron and burned it at the brook Kidron, and beat it to dust and cast the dust of it upon the graves of the common people. And he broke down the houses . . . where the women wove hangings for the Asherah (2 Kings 23:4-7).

He likewise purged cities and shrines elsewhere, in Geba, Beersheba, Bethel, and Samaria, destroying high places, shrines and altars, burning the cult objects, and slaying priests, mediums, and wizards. But after him kings reverted to Canaanite practices.

Any religion depends on its pantheon of deities, rituals, and symbols. In order for Yahwism to triumph, all competing deities, symbols, and rituals had to be eliminated and their functions absorbed by Yahweh, hence the biblical passages calling for the destruction of high places, pillars, altars, asherahs, and the condemnation of incense burning, divination, wizardry, and "foreign" deities. In the Bible, J was the father of this process, beginning in the Eden story. The symbols used in his Eden story must be viewed from this perspective. Below we show, first, that the trees of life and of knowledge of good and evil, the forbidden fruit, the serpent, and Eve herself are all associated with Canaanite religious beliefs and ritual, and often are Goddess symbols. Second, in the Eden story J was seeking to divorce Asherah from Yahweh and drive her into oblivion. Third, J elevated Yahweh to supremacy not only by eliminating other deities and transferring their divine characteristics to Yahweh, but also by exorcizing all divinity from nature and accumulating it in Yahweh. With this in mind, we can now discuss Asherah and her role in Israelite religion and as Yahweh's consort, and their divorce.

THE HEBREW GODDESS

Asherah was the chief Canaanite and Israelite goddess, but we must first acknowledge the importance of another goddess in Canaan and Israel, Astarte, the biblical Ashtoreth. She and her name are derived from the Babylonian and Assyrian goddess Ishtar.[157] In Ugarit she was the daughter of El and Asherah, so her brother was Baal, and apparently she (and also Anat)[158] was his consort. She then became established as Astarte along the Phoenician coast in cities such as Byblos, Tyre and Sidon, surpassing Asherah as the chief goddess there during the first millennium.[159] Like Inanna and Ishtar before her, Astarte was associated with the heavens, her images including the moon and Venus. Thus, she was probably the "Queen of Heaven" condemned in the Bible (e.g., Jer. 7:17-18).[160] As the main consort of Baal, she was a fertility goddess. Women burned incense, poured libations and baked cakes to her, which were made in her image (or in the form of a star) in molds and eaten so as to partake of her divinity, all practices condemned in the Bible.[161] In art she was portrayed similarly to Asherah: usually naked, sometimes in a bouffant Hathor headdress, sometimes standing atop a lion (although Asherah was more consistently associated with lions), and holding lotus flowers or serpents, also sometimes with horns (like Hathor, Isis and Ishtar) in association with bovines or sheep.[162] Her cult spread across the Mediterranean, in particular to Cyprus and Greece, where she became Aphrodite. In Israel, her cult was popular only after J's time, beginning in the latter half of the monarchy.[163] Nevertheless, since J aimed broadly at any form of goddess worship, some aspects of Astarte's cult are relevant to the Eden story, and we mention them where applicable.

As the epigraph to this chapter from Milton illustrates, Europe traditionally was aware of Ashtoreth/Astarte as an important goddess in the Holy Land, but for about two millennia was largely unaware of Asherah. There are several reasons for this. First, for centuries Asherah lay hidden in our European and American Bible because her name was mistranslated as a grove of trees, for which reason she was simply outside our religious awareness. This mistake occurred in both the Greek Septuagint[164] and the Latin Vulgate,[165] which were the two Bibles used in Europe until Martin Luther's translation into the vernacular in 1534. The mistake was carried over to the King James Version published in 1611, so that despite the some 40 occurrences of asherah/Asherah in the Hebrew Bible, this goddess did not become known to a wide Western audience until other translations of the Hebrew Bible became widespread in the mid-20th century. Second, until the discovery of Ugarit in 1929, even biblical scholars and archeologists had no adequate context (even in Hebrew) for understanding the biblical references to asherim/Asherah.[166] Ugarit, however, yielded a rich body of literature describing Asherah and other deities in the Canaanite pantheon, which finally enabled us to understand that Asherah was traditionally the chief Canaanite goddess.[167] Finally, in recent decades archeology has provided important new information about the goddesses of the Hebrew Bible and about Canaanite and Israelite religion that is still not well known to the public or even to the clerics who preach to the public. If we are to understand the Eden story, we must bring these discoveries to the fore.

Like El, Asherah had her origins in Mesopotamia. By 2000 she had emerged as an Amorite goddess known as Ashratu, and was the consort of the chief Amorite deity, Amurru, he being lord of the mountains but (like El and Enki/Ea) with ties to the watery deep, and she—"Lady of the steppe."[168] Later, in one of the Amarna letters an Amorite prince is named Abdu-Ashirta ("servant of Asherah"), signifying the importance of his being a devotee of Asherah's cult.[169] She later came to be venerated in Ugarit, Byblos, Sidon and Tyre as a sea goddess—all seaports dependent on the bounty of the sea, which she came to represent. Thus, in Ugaritic texts she was known as "lady Athirat [Asherah] of the sea,"[170] and her servant was a fisherman. Her shift from being lady of the steppe to lady of the sea is a result of her migration to a port. Further, as Baruch Margalit observed, "with El thus cast in the role of Ea and successor of the primeval Apsu, it is easy to understand how Athirat becomes a Canaanite Tiamat, consort of Apsu."[171] Later, as the Phoenician goddess Tannit, Asherah's cult extended westward across the Punic world of seafaring Phoenicians.[172] Another of Asherah's epithets was *Elat* (simply the "Goddess," the feminine form of the name of her husband El, "God").[173] The port city Elath at the northern tip of the Gulf of Aqaba at the south end of the Arabah in the Midian (the area of Yahweh's origin) seems to have been named after her.[174] Similarly, her association with sacred trees is seen in the word for the Bible's term for the sacred terebinth tree *(ēlāh)* at Shechem.[175] The terebinth was deified and was planted in the high places,[176] making it likely that the asherah was originally thought of as a living tree and later was simplified into a wooden pole.[177] Hence, Isaiah (1:29-30) and Hosea (4:13) condemn such trees.[178] Most scholars agree that Asherah in the Hebrew

Bible is the same as Asherah in Ugarit, [179] which is also to say that she is
recognized as a goddess (not just the asherah pole) in the Hebrew Bible.

In Late Bronze Age Canaan Asherah was represented sometimes as a
nurturing, nursing mother (Fig. 2), representing reproductive powers and
human fertility. Indeed, she was sometimes called "womb." [180] Another of
her epithets in late Bronze Age Canaan during the Egyptian domination was
Qudshu or Qedesh ("Holiness" or "the Holy One"), [181] as in the *Keret* epic
when the king was about to make his vow to Asherah:

> *He approached Qedesh*
> *Asherah of Tyre*
> *And Elat of Sidon.* [182]

In this capacity, on terracotta plaques she was often portrayed in frontal
nudity (including a prominent pubic triangle) and with a hairdo and ears
characteristic of Hathor (with whom she was equated), often standing atop
her lion, and holding plants or serpents in her hands to show her as providing
fertility to the land (Fig. 3). She was portrayed similarly in pendants that
women wore around their necks (Fig. 4).

The origin and underlying meaning of Asherah's name are still a matter
of debate. [183] Some specialists believe that the name comes from the Akkadian word *asirtu* ("temple") or a Semitic root for "place" such that asherah
meant "sanctuary" or "holy place." [184] This is consistent with her veneration
in sacred groves of trees at high places, which could explain the above-
mentioned mistranslation of her name. Another theory is that her name is
based on the Hebrew root *'ašr* meaning "happiness," "blessedness," or "good
fortune." [185] This comes from the episode in Genesis when Jacob's aging wife
Leah gave her maid Zilpah to him as a wife to bear children. When Zilpah
bore the second of two sons, Leah exclaimed, "Happy am I! For the women
will call me happy"; so she called his name Asher (Gen. 30:13). While this
explanation would be consistent with Asherah's veneration in association
with childbirth, most scholars are skeptical of it. [186] A third theory is that her
name comes from the root *yšr* meaning "to be upright," [187] echoing her association with the upright wooden poles known as asherahs (the cult objects
symbolizing her) or possibly trees. [188] A final theory, offered by Margalit, is
that it derives from Akkadian and Ugaritic words reflected in Hebrew meaning both footstep and consort/wife, as one who follows in her husband's
footsteps. [189] In the case of a goddess, etymologically Asherah would therefore mean something like "goddess-wife-follower," which as we shall see
may be a key to understanding Asherah's relationship to Yahweh.

In the Hebrew Bible asherahs appear in two contexts. In some cases,
several stand under a tree or otherwise at high places (e.g., Jer. 17:2; 1 Kings
14:23; 2 Kings 17:10), whereas a single asherah stands next to an altar of a

god (e.g., Deut. 16:21; Judg. 6:25-26).[190] Only single asherahs are described as an image or graven image, apparently having features that evoke if not portray the goddess. For example, king Manasseh was said to have made and erected a "graven image of Asherah" (2 Kings 21:7), and king Asa's mother Maacah "had an abominable image made for Asherah; and Asa cut down her image" (1 Kings 15:13; also 2 Chr. 15:16).

Asherah was venerated throughout Israel, from its beginnings right through the Babylonian conquest.[191] She was a natural carryover from Canaanite religion, which explains how she became Yahweh's consort: She was El's consort, so when Yahweh was identified with El, she naturally came along with him.[192] No ancient Near Eastern culture could do without one or more goddesses associated with life, fertility, and childbirth, and Israel was no exception. With few exceptions, all major gods and goddesses in the ancient Near East had consorts.[193]

Asherah was worshipped at high places among sacred trees, where devotees set up altars, stone pillars and asherahs, which at least in some cases seem to have been carved to some extent to evoke or perhaps actually represent her. She had her own priests, wizards and diviners, and she was a patroness of diviners.[194] Devotees burned incense to her on small incense altars,[195] and women wove hangings (probably clothes) and hung them on the asherah that stood before the Jerusalem Temple (2 Kings 23:7).[196] This means that these women had dedicated themselves to the goddess, probably through taking an oath, and were part of official Temple ritual.[197] In private folk worship, which was largely unaffected by official Yahweh religion,[198] Asherah was a patroness of mothers and was portrayed in small figurines kept at home, which were invoked in her name for fertility and successful childbirth.[199] Their base was in the shape of the trunk of a tree, like an asherah itself (Fig. 5).[200]

Archeologists have found numerous inscriptions invoking Asherah and portrayals of her or symbols of her dating from the earliest times of Israel right through the monarchy. An early example comes from Lachish, southwest of Jerusalem, where archeologists discovered a temple, near to which was found a famous ewer dating from the late 13th century (ca. 1220).[201] It was apparently presented to the temple, for it bore the dedication, "Mattan. An offering to my Lady Elat" (an epithet of Asherah).[202] Importantly, this inscription is accompanied by an image of a sacred tree flanked by ibexes (the word "Elat" appears directly above the tree), which confirms that the tree is associated with Asherah (Fig. 6).[203] This is brought home by four identical images around the shoulder of a goblet found at the same temple depicting ibexes flanking a pubic triangle (Fig. 7) symbolizing a goddess as in the pendants discussed below (Fig. 23). Importantly, therefore, *here the goddess and her tree symbol are portrayed together and equated, and are interchangeable in the iconography.*[204] Another example comes from Taanach just south of Megiddo. A 15th century letter from a resident Egyptian official to the local prince, Rewassa, on a cuneiform tablet found there reads in part, "if there is wizard of Asherah, let him tell our fortunes, and let me hear quickly; and the [oracular] sign and interpretation send to me."[205] This means that Asherah was venerated in Palestine when or even before Ugarit was flourishing, that she had diviners there,[206] and that the resident Egyptians accepted her.

Asherah's cult became central to both popular and official Israelite religion, including at the Temple itself. In Judah it was practiced without incident or interruption except during the reigns of the reforming Yahwist kings Hezekiah and Josiah.[207] As we saw in Chapter 1, Deuteronomy was written, and its law code first read in Jerusalem, only during and shortly after Josiah's reign (639-609). This means that its prohibitions against Asherah worship and related pagan practices were not generally known to Judah's population until a century after the northern kingdom of Israel fell to the Assyrians.[208] Prior to then, in Judah we are left only with above-mentioned command in J's text (Exod. 34:11-16) as prohibiting Asherah veneration. In the northern kingdom of Israel, the 9th century prophets Elijah and Elisha campaigned against Asherah worship, and the priests at Shiloh (who produced E) composed the Deuteronomic law code prohibiting Asherah worship sometime before 722,[209] but we do not know how widely the code was disseminated there. In summary, before J's time we see no formal prohibitions against Asherah worship. He was the earliest visible source of opposition to her.

With no actual strictures against Asherah until a late period, it is not surprising that the Bible reports her popularity, right from Israel's beginnings during the time of the judges. Judges 3:7 reports that the people then served the Asherahs.[210] as illustrated by the story of Gideon, whom the biblical authors regard as a savior of Israel. Gideon's father Joash, the local chieftain of the village of Ophrah, respected the old ways, but after being visited by an angel of Yahweh Gideon introduced Yahwism to the village by, among other things, destroying the local asherah pole secretly at night and then making a burnt offering to Yahweh, the fire being made using the wood from the asherah (Judg. 6:25-30). This act incurred the wrath of the villagers, who wanted to kill him, and he was saved only by the intervention of his father (Judg. 6:30-32).

When we move to the monarchy in Judah, we see that David accommodated Jebusite religion, and we are told that Solomon's heart was "not wholly true" to Yahweh, that he did "not wholly" follow Yahweh, and thus "did what was evil in the sight" of Yahweh (1 Kings 11:4-6). Namely, he married foreign wives who brought with them their goddesses and turned Solomon's head to them (1 Kings 11:4-5), and he "sacrificed and burnt incense at the high places" (1 Kings 3:3). Most probably this included worship of Asherah,[211] although the Bible mentions only the Phoenician Ashtoreth (Astarte) rather than Asherah as a goddess worshipped by Solomon (1 Kings 11:5, 33; 2 Kings 23:13). In any event, his son, king Rehoboam, or his queen Maacah made and erected by the Temple altar an image of Asherah (1 Kings 15:13), most likely the "image of jealousy" later referenced by Ezekiel (8:1-18),[212] which suggests that another one still stood there after Josiah's reign.[213] Indeed, according to Patai's calculation based on the Bible's rendering, it remained at the Temple (with gaps) for about two-thirds of the period of the monarchy (236 of 370 years) until the Babylonian conquest, being removed for short periods only by the Yahwist reforming kings Asa, Hezekiah and Josiah, and being restored by their successors.[214] There were vessels[215] for Asherah inside the Temple (2 Kings 23:4), and Jerusalem's women wove hangings for the Asherah at the Temple (2 Kings 23:7). Asherah worship was spread across the high places and sanctuaries in Judah and Benjamin (1 Kings 14:23; 2 Chr. 31:1; 34:3-5; Jer. 17:2), and Judah's kings ordained priests to burn incense in the high places (2 Kings 23:5). Clearly Asherah's cult was understood, accepted and practiced as a legitimate and mainstream element of the official religious cult in Judah.[216]

Asherah worship was even more popular in the northern kingdom of Israel, which the Bible says was spread across at least the tribes of Manasseh, Ephriam, Simeon, and Naphtali (2 Chr. 34:6-7), and at Bethel (2 Kings 23:15). Asherah's cult was practiced beginning with Israel's first king, Jeroboam (1 Kings 14:15), and the Bible attributes the fall of Israel to such pagan practices (1 Kings 14:16; 2 Kings 17:7-18). King Ahab (873-852), under the influence of his Sidonian queen, Jezebel, installed an Asherah at a sanctuary in Israel's capital, Samaria (1 Kings 16:33). He was also said to have hosted 400 of Asherah's prophets at his court who attended Elijah's rain making contest between the 450 prophets of Baal and those of Yahweh at Mt. Carmel (1 Kings 18:19). Interestingly, while the defeated prophets of Baal are said to have been put to death, nothing was mentioned about the fate of Asherah's prophets. Most commentators conclude that no action was taken against them, otherwise the Bible would have exulted in that fact.[217] Nor was the Asherah at Samaria removed, because we are informed that, although the radical Yahwist reformer king Jehu (842-814) massacred the remaining prophets of Baal and destroyed Baal's temple and pillar at Samaria (2 Kings 10:19-27), the Asherah was still standing during the reign of Jehu's son, Jehoahaz (817-800) (2 Kings 13:6). Since these zealous Yahwists who acted to destroy Baal worship took no action against Asherah worship and since no other northern (or Judahite) prophets up through that time (reign of Ahab)[218] ever mention Asherah, it seems that in the North either Asherah worship was too well entrenched to challenge or, more likely, was not considered inconsistent with the worship of Yahweh and indeed was closely associated with it.[219] Asherah's being Yahweh's consort would help explain this.

Importantly in this regard, it appears that the sanctuary in Samaria where the Asherah stood was *Yahweh's* sanctuary (not Baal's),[220] which would parallel the Asherah that stood at the Temple in Jerusalem. The biblical passage describing Ahab's construction of Baal's temple and the erection of the Asherah (1 Kings 16:32-33) does not actually say that the Asherah was in that temple. Rather, it says, "He erected an altar for Baal in the House of Baal, which he built in Samaria. And Ahab made an Asherah," leaving unsaid where it was located. In Deuteronomist polemic against Baal, Asherah was often linked with Baal (implying that they were consorts) in order to discredit her, but in fact there is no evidence that they were consorts either in Ugarit or Israel; rather, Baal's consorts were either his sister Anat or Astarte, with the rising Astarte predominating in Iron Age Canaan/Israel.[221] If the Asherah at Samaria were really in Baal's temple and associated with Baal worship, surely Jehu (if he was a strict Yahwist) would have destroyed it. Deuteronomy, however, indicates that an asherah was commonly placed alongside an altar of Yahweh (and prohibits this),[222] as in Jerusalem. As Saul Olyan observed, "There would be no need for such a prohibition if this were not a common practice."[223] This practice means that in the minds of both the populace and priests the two deities were worshipped in tandem, which supports the conclusion that they were consorts.[224]

Archeology cannot directly prove that wooden asherahs stood beside Yahweh altars because they would have rotted away long ago, but many archeological findings do point to a strong link between Yahweh and Asherah. At the site of Khirbet el-Qom southwest of Jerusalem, an inscription from the mid-8th century was discovered describing the good fortune of its governor (or simply a rich man), Uriah (or Uriyahu), which reads:

> *Uriah the rich wrote it.*
> *Blessed be Uriah by Yahweh,*
> *yea from his enemies by his* [Yahweh's] *Asherah he* [Yahweh] *has saved him*
> *by Oniah*
> *by his Asherah*
> *and by his Asherah*[225]

Similar 8th century inscriptions were made in Sinai at a caravanserai now known as Kuntillet Ajrûd, which served as a place for travelers to worship and pray for a safe journey. There one wall inscription reads, "To Yahweh of Teman [Edom] and to his asherah [or Asherah]." Another inscription on a large store jar known as Pithos B similarly refers to "Yahweh of Teman and his asherah [or Asherah]." On another store jar (Pithos A) appears a longer inscription that ends, "I blessed you by Yahweh of Samaria and by his asherah [or Asherah]."[226] Pithos A also features next to this inscription a drawing of a sacred tree atop the usual lion of the Goddess and flanked by her usual caprids (Fig. 8), which many specialists believe symbolizes the goddess Asherah and illustrates the inscription.[227]

The inscriptions at Khirbet el-Qom and Kuntillet Ajrûd have sparked intense interest and debate, but some basic points are clear. First, in them Yahweh is closely connected with either an asherah pole or the goddess Asherah. Second, Yahweh and an asherah/Asherah are connected specifically in regard to Samaria, where as we have seen an Asherah stood in Yahweh's sanctuary. Presumably this is the Asherah referenced in Pithos A,[228] which connects Asherah with Yahweh (not Baal) at Samaria and thus corroborates our conclusion that such Asherah stood at Yahweh's (not Baal's) sanctuary in Samaria. Importantly in this regard, the Kuntillet Ajrûd and Khirbet el-Qom inscriptions referring to this Asherah are from well *after* Jehu's anti-Baal reform in which Baal's sanctuary in Samaria was destroyed, meaning that the inscriber knew that the Asherah still stood there at the remaining sanctuary—Yahweh's.

The main scholarly debate concerning the Kuntillet Ajrûd and Khirbet el-Qom inscriptions revolves around whether they refer to the wooden cult object called the asherah or to the goddess Asherah herself as Yahweh's consort. The main positions in this debate fall into three categories, which we must consider.

The first (minimalist) position is that only the wooden cult object is referenced.[229] This is based in part on a linguistic argument that in biblical Hebrew a possessive suffix (here meaning "his") is never used with a proper name, meaning that the inscriptions cannot be referring to a goddess named Asherah and therefore must refer to an asherah.[230] The scholars believing that only the asherah is referenced, however, then subdivide into two camps. One camp, based largely on the notion that Asherah had faded away as a goddess by the date of these inscriptions, thinks that only the cult object as Yahweh's instrument is meant, as a mediating entity to confer blessings and save people.[231] Thus, a supplicant would have prayed to Yahweh in front of (and through) the asherah at a sanctuary/shrine.[232] The other camp, however, believes that Asherah was still alive and well as a goddess and that the cult object bearing her name remained her vital symbol, meaning that even though "his" refers to the cult object, the goddess is ultimately intended.[233] Indeed, the evidence discussed in this chapter shows that Asherah still flourished at this time and beyond, as the Bible itself says.[234] Some scholars have also criticized the notion of a blessing through a mere cult object as awkward and strained, because it would run contrary to the parallelism so typical in Hebrew writings (which would require here that Yahweh be paired with a deity and not a piece of wood).[235] Further, it is argued, based on attested usage, that only a divinity can be the agency in such a blessing formula *(brk l-)*.[236] One indeed wonders: If Yahweh himself is the ultimate source of the blessing and of all divinity, then why would he need a tree-like instrument to assist him?[237] On the other hand, were Yahweh simply using a cult instrument unrelated to a goddess (just like the many other cult objects associated with his veneration), then why would the biblical authors oppose the asherah so vehemently? One must conclude that the instrument was perceived as a threat because it did symbolize the goddess. Thus, any distinction between the asherah as a symbol and the goddess herself would be one without a difference. In the ancient Near East the idol (or similar symbol or cult object) represented and symbolized the deity itself.[238] As Olyan, pointed out, "The deity and his or her symbol are inseparable. . . . [N]aming the cult symbol of the deity is synonymous with naming the deity herself."[239] In the minds of devotees the symbol was the same as the deity so that, as Hadley pointed out, "offering something to the statue of a deity would be the same as offering it to the deity itself, and vice versa."[240] This understanding is reflected in the Bible itself, which refers to idols themselves as gods (e.g., Gen. 35:4). The ancient Near East was replete with symbols representing deities. Examples include Inanna being symbolized by a stylized reed post; Ishtar and Astarte by a star in a circle; Sin by a crescent moon with two tassels; Shamash by the winged sun disc; Resheph by a star; Isis by a throne; the Cretan Mother Goddess by a sacred knot; Maat by an ostrich feather; and El by the bull.[241] The most prominent modern example is the Christian cross, which we all understand to symbolize Christ and his crucifixion. So, for example, when the rich man Uriah said he was saved by the asherah/Asherah, he had the goddess herself (and her powers) in mind.

The second (maximalist) position is that the inscriptions directly refer to the goddess Asherah.[242] This position is based on the context of other evidence that Asherah was Yahweh's consort, the above-mentioned attestation of such blessing formulas only having deities as the agent of blessings, and the accompanying drawings on Pithos A.[243] This camp does not view the grammatical argument against possessives on proper nouns as decisive, arguing variously that the ending in question is not a "possessive suffix" but an alternative feminine ending on Asherah's name,[244] that we should not expect perfect grammar in such inscriptions,[245] and that possessive suffixes on proper nouns do appear in related Semitic languages, meaning that just because they are not attested in the Bible does not mean that there is an actual rule against this.[246]

In light of the above, one is faced with well-grounded arguments from context pointing to a goddess together with two opposing linguistic arguments, one claiming that such blessing formulas can only refer to divinities and another maintaining that there cannot be a divinity because a divinity's name cannot take a possessive suffix. An emerging third camp of scholars has offered a solution that elegantly reconciles the various positions. They argue that in these inscriptions, as in some biblical passages, Asherah is being used as a title of the goddess, which would be a common rather than proper noun so it could take the possessive suffix, meaning that "Yhwh's asherah is indeed the goddess."[247] This theory is based on the fact that when the word asherah/Asherah in the Bible clearly refers to a goddess (especially Judg. 3:7; 1 Kings 15:13 (duplicated in 2 Chr. 16:13); 1 Kings 18:19; 2 Kings 21:7), it is preceded by the definite article, thus implying that the deity is being referenced by her title (just as she was in Ugarit under the general titles of Elat and Qedesh/Qudshu).[248] The inscriptions would therefore specify via her title the goddess known as Yahweh's consort. Margalit then takes this theory further to specify what this title etymologically means. As noted earlier, he concludes that Asherah denotes a subordinate wife following in her husband's footsteps, which would also explain why there was no need in either Ugarit or Israel to redundantly specify that Asherah was El's/Yahweh's wife.[249] This makes better sense of passages like Judges 3:7 referring to a collection of deities, where "the Baals" are the husbands and "the Asheroth" are their subordinate consorts in their train ("baal" itself means "master" or "lord"). It is therefore significant that Adam's one fault for which he was rebuked by Yahweh was that he listened to and followed the lead of Eve, a Goddess figure.

In summary, regardless of which of the three above approaches one adopts to the Khirbet el-Qom and Kuntillet Ajrûd inscriptions, the result is that the goddess Asherah is directly or indirectly intended. This explains why Yahwists were so afraid of the asherahs and demanded that they be destroyed:[250] Asherah as a goddess was alive and well at the time. That accounts for why the Bible says she had prophets (poles don't have prophets), and vessels in Solomon's Temple, and that women made hangings to place on the Asherah by the Temple. One doesn't battle opponents that don't exist. If the asherah were merely an instrument of Yahweh rather than a symbol of another deity, it would not have been objectionable and there would have been no battle. The above inscriptions thus serve well to frame the polemics of J and later biblical authors.[251]

At least three other archeological sites have yielded other important evidence connecting Yahweh and Asherah.[252] The first is the small temple found at the Judahite royal fortress at Arad, east of Beersheba near the border with the Negev desert. It dates to the late 8th century, shortly before or during the reign of Hezekiah. One inscription on a pottery sherd found there refers to the "temple of Yahweh."[253] At its entrance were two small horned altars, one smaller than the other, bearing traces of burned organic material, while at the back were two apparently matching undressed stone pillars. Also found there were an offering stand with a removable bowl, an oil lamp, and a small statue of a crouching lion. The presence of the paired altars and pillars suggests that two deities were venerated there, one of whom we know was Yahweh. The lion statue together with the fact that one of the altars was smaller than the other, suggests that the smaller altar was for Asherah and

evidences their being consorts.[254] This fits the similar pattern at Samaria and
Jerusalem where Yahweh and Asherah were likewise venerated together in
the same sanctuaries. It is hard to imagine any other second deity here.

The second site is Tel Miqne (biblical Ekron), which among other things
was a center for olive oil production. There 7th-century inscriptions on fragments of two pithoi that contained olive oil were found in a cultic context,
one of them containing an offering dedication, "sacred to [the?] Asherah."[255]
Most scholars, including the excavator, agree that this refers to the goddess
herself and not to an asherah pole or the sanctuary at the site.[256] As Halpern
commented,

> it is all but inconceivable that one should have agricultural goods "dedicated to
> the pole": such a notion regresses to the level of taking literally prophetic
> polemic against idolatry—assuming that the worshippers being accused of it
> could not distinguish *at all* between the sublime deity and the concrete repre-
> sentation standing in front of them. Indeed, in biblical usage, "sacred to..." can
> be completed only with the name of Yhwh . . . . "Asherah" in the Miqne
> inscriptions therefore almost certainly functions as a name for or soubriquet of
> a goddess.[257]

Also discovered there were several chalices in the form of a tree trunk with
lotus petals for branches, which the excavator believes also relate to Asherah,
symbolized by the sacred tree, as in the Kuntillet Ajrûd drawings.[258]

The third and most fascinating discovery is a late 10th century cult offering stand at Taanach (Fig. 9). It is immensely important because it appears to
portray Yahweh and Asherah together,[259] and also because "the asherah as a
cult symbol occurs right alongside a portrait of the goddess herself [meaning]
that the goddess had *not* been separated from the cult symbol that bore her
name."[260] So we must cover this in detail.

The stand is about 60 centimeters high and consists of four registers
(tiers), each with different imagery, which should be viewed from the bottom
up. The bottom register depicts a naked goddess figure flanked by lionesses,
which the goddess holds by the ears. The second register shows two cheru-
bim-like sphinxes, between which is an open space rather than a divinity.
Rather, it appears that the opening was to enable the lighting and viewing of
a flame inside. The third register depicts two lionesses virtually identical to
those on the first register, only this time instead of the naked anthropomorphic goddess we have the familiar image of ibexes flanking a sacred tree, just
as in Pithos A from Kuntillet Ajrûd (compare Figs. 8 and 9).[261] The top
register is framed by two column-like objects with volutes that spiral on top.
Between the columns stands a bull or horse[262] bearing a sun disk; on the
sides, but not visible from the front, are griffin-like figures with bird's heads.
Thus, the stand features alternating pairs of lions as well as of sphinxlike
figures.

In the stand the lionesses, cherubim and pillars all frame deities. Scholars generally agree that the goddess on the bottom register and the tree flanked by ibexes on the third, each framed by identical lions, are both representations of Asherah.[263] The identity of the deity or deities on the second and top registers is less clear. The scene on the second register seems to indicate Yahweh, since he was generally conceived of as enthroned invisibly between cherubim and also was associated with fire, which a flame visible through the opening would symbolize,[264] and which would coincide with the sun on the top register. Given the representation of Asherah on tiers one and three, it would make sense that only one deity, Yahweh, is represented on tiers two and four.[265] In that case the top tier with the sun and the quadruped would symbolize Yahweh, so we must consider this.

Some extra-biblical evidence of a sun cult in biblical Palestine exists.[266] In particular, archeologists have unearthed throughout Israel and Judah (Hazor, Lachish, and Jerusalem) figures of animals bearing sun disks, including figurines of horses bearing sun disks between their ears.[267] The question then becomes whether Yahweh was associated with the sun. The Bible does contain such associations, in particular Psalm 84:11 which says that Yahweh "is a sun and shield"; Deuteronomy 33:2 describing Yahweh as dawning and shining upon the Israelites from Seir; and the blessing for Moses in Numbers 6:25, "Yahweh make his face to shine upon you," which is also found on two 7th century plaques discovered in Jerusalem.[268] In this kind of reference, Yahweh is not a sun god, nor is the sun worshipped; rather, the sun is a motif for "seeing" Yahweh, experiencing his divine presence, and receiving blessings and bounty.[269] This could very well be the idea in the top register of the Taanach stand. The voluted pillar-like objects suggest a temple scene,[270] and in fact there are some associations between the sun and Solomon's Temple.[271] In 2 Kings 23:5 we read that priests burned incense to the sun at the Temple, and in 2 Kings 23:11 that at the Temple stood a statue of *horses* dedicated to the sun (apparently pulling a chariot bearing the sun), which Josiah removed. Ezekiel 8:16 includes a vision of 25 men at the Temple worshipping the sun as one of the many abominations there. A corroborating example of this may be Pithos B from Kuntillet Ajrûd, which in addition to the above-mentioned inscription mentioning Yahweh in conjunction with Asherah depicts a procession of worshippers (presumably of Yahweh) gazing upwards, apparently at the sun (Fig. 10).[272] It thus seems that until Josiah and the Deuteronomist movement such solar imagery was not viewed as inconsistent with the worship of Yahweh.[273]

In the end, since Asherah appears on the Taanach stand and she was not associated with Baal or any deity other than Yahweh, we are left with no other choice but Yahweh. The number of specialists who now accept their pairing on this stand is growing.[274] Hadley concludes that the Taanach stand "not only indicates that Asherah was worshipped at this Israelite site, but that she was also closely associated with Yahweh and his cult," and that the stand "provides the clearest picture so far discovered of the worship of both Yahweh and Asherah together."[275]

In conclusion, both the biblical text and extra-biblical evidence shows that Asherah the goddess was alive and well in J's time. J needed to portray Yahweh as supreme and as controlling the beneficent and destructive elements of nature traditionally associated with the Goddess. This explains why Canaanite pagan symbols appeared in the Eden story. According to J, Yahweh created and controlled (in the end) everything in the garden of Eden, especially the elements of water and life traditionally associated with the Goddess: the sacred trees and other vegetation and their fruit, the animals (including the serpent), the *tehôm* which he caused to rise up and water the ground so that vegetation and other life could be created, and the four rivers that supported life outside the garden. And as we shall see, Eve was a Goddess figure, portrayed in a negative light. In this way, J sought to demolish in people's minds the image of the Goddess as the source of benevolence, life, succor and wisdom, and eliminate Asherah. In the following chapters we explain how this tactic appeared in the Eden story.

Chapter Four

The Creation, the Garden in Eden, and Its Restoration

The cosmos is born from chaos, taught the ancients. A son may not resemble his father except for one hidden trait, but that is what makes them alike. The world order is uneasy: It is the child of chaos and may not coincide with our ideas about what is good and bad.

—Alexander Blok[1]

Well directed are men, the cattle of god.
He made heaven and earth according to their desire,
And he repelled the water monster.
He made the breath of life for their nostrils.
They who have issued from his body are his images . . . .
—The Instruction for Merikare (Ancient Egyptian Wisdom Text)[2]

The story of Adam and Eve transpires in a world that Yahweh had not quite finished creating, and in a distinctive setting: the garden of Eden. It was important to the story's meaning that it be connected with the creation of the cosmos and that it transpire in such a special place. This chapter explores why.

THE FRAMEWORK OF CREATION IN THE BIBLICAL WORLD

The ancient Near East had a seemingly bewildering variety of creation myths. We are already familiar with *Enuma Elish,* in which Marduk vanquished the sea monster Tiamat and created the universe from her corpse. According to one Egyptian creation myth, the cosmos self-developed from a serpent coil within primeval waters as a monad which was Atum, the first god, from whom then emerged the main components of the universe and the

81

deities representing them; in another, the god Ptah created the elements of the cosmos simply by conceiving and uttering their names; in yet another, the creator god Amun was an uncaused "first cause" above and separate from the created world.[3] And in the Bible there is P's wondrous story of God accomplishing the creation in six days and resting on the seventh. Underlying all these stories, as well as J's Eden story, are important cosmological concepts and assumptions that all peoples of the ancient Near East shared and which resulted in fundamental similarities in their creation myths. P and J lived and wrote within this framework of beliefs, and their creation stories reflect it. Therefore, in order to understand the Eden story we must first become familiar with the ancient Near Eastern pattern of creation and the "cosmic geography" of the ancient universe.

The creation myths in the ancient Near East present a different concept from what we moderns conceive of as the creation. Today when we seek to understand the creation of the universe, we tend to ask questions such as whether there was a point when nothing existed at all, how the substance of the universe came into being, what this substance is made of, and how the cosmos has evolved to the present day and (consequently) what is in store for the future. The ancient myths are not concerned with any of this. In those myths there is never nothing, nor is there any discussion of what the underlying cosmic substance is, except that it is likened to water when in a chaotic state. Further, the universe was fairly static; except for human activities and their effects, it did not evolve further,[4] although it could unravel. Finally, the concept of creation was not limited to the physical world, but extended into the establishment of ordered human society after the physical world is established.[5] For our purposes, this means that creation of humans is still going on in Genesis 3 and beyond. Indeed, the society concerned is not fully created until the Israelites are in the Promised Land, governed by wise kings (David and Solomon), and Yahweh's temple is built and consecrated.

In physical terms, in the ancient myths land rose from the primeval waters (it could be seen forming in the deltas of the Tigris, Euphrates and Nile) while at the same time it reached down into and was anchored in the netherworld; the highest land, mountains, rose toward the heavens, thus linking heaven, earth and the underworld. Surrounding all land and stretching indefinitely to the horizon was the sea. Water also rose from underground and was accessed through wells, while rain fell from the sky, so there must be water up there too. Since rain falls only some of the time, however, something (a deity or a solid physical structure) must be holding it back and occasionally letting it fall through in droplets.[6] The formlessness of water was also meaningful to the ancients. It could become agitated, chaotic, fearsome, and dangerous. Ships and sailors would perish in great storms at sea, the ocean was home to terrifying "sea monsters" (giant squid, whales) that stirred the sea to violence; rivers flooded and destroyed fields and settlements, and the sky would break forth with violent storms. In contrast, solid things have regular forms and behave in predictable ways; they seemed to have been given an inherent order at the creation, and therefore enjoyed a higher level of existence than water. In particular, iron was considered a heavenly substance, since it fell from the skies in the form of meteorites, hence the idea that the firmament was made of metal, which allowed it to hold back the celestial waters and for the heavenly bodies to be affixed to it. [7] The ancients therefore viewed the pre-creation state of affairs as a dark watery chaos, a formless substance in a resting state that would last indefinitely, until a creation process was initiated by a divine force. But even the notion of this state of affairs lasting "indefinitely" is somewhat misleading, however, because at that stage time itself did not exist either; it too is a form of order that had to be created. Earthly time was created when the heavenly bodies that mark time were created. [8]

Thus, in the ancient Near East, the process of creation involved not the creation of any material, but rather *giving form to preexisting formless (chaotic) material* in order to *establish order* so that the resulting cosmos [9] will *function in a divinely decreed manner*. This entailed a process of *separation into multiplicity* whereby one thing became differentiated from another, *in particular into pairs of opposites,* so that each thing in the cosmos has its own characteristics, function, and name. [10] For the ancients, a thing could not fully exist until it had acquired a form and been given a function (its destiny decreed) and a name. [11] This need is illustrated in the famous opening lines of *Enuma Elish* describing the situation just before the creation:

> *When on high the heaven had not been named,*
> *Firm ground below had not been called by name,*
> *Naught but primordial Apsu, their begetter,*
> *[And] Mummu-Tiamat, she who bore them all,*
> *Their waters commingling as a single body;*
> *No reed hut had been matted, no marsh land had appeared,*
> *When no gods whatever had been brought into being,*
> *Uncalled by name, their destinies undetermined,*
> *Then it was that the gods were formed within them.* [12]

This passage also touches upon the question of what caused the creation process to begin, since seemingly there were not even any deities yet. For the ancients, however, this was not a problem. Originally the creation had been understood as the *self-development* and expansion of the eternally existing divine into multiplicity, into concrete things (forms). It was thought of in terms of generation, analogous to the birthing process. In Chapter 3 we discussed the ancient notion of the Mother Goddess self-generating the cosmos, which remained part of her; when there was no creator deity, there was only the creative primordial divine force symbolized by her. This idea was reflected in the self-generation of the cosmos from the primeval waters. In Sumer the primordial waters were identified with the goddess Nammu, whose name meant "sea."[13] She self-generated the initial universe in the form of An-Ki ("heaven-earth," theretofore undifferentiated) by causing it to rise from the sea (i.e., out of herself), with heaven and earth then being identified respectively by a god (An) and a goddess (Ki). Ancient Egyptian cosmogonies also featured self-generation of the universe from the primordial waters (Nun). Thus, Egyptian creator gods such as Atum, Shu, and Ra, claimed to have self-generated themselves before embarking on the creation of other deities and the cosmos.[14] But even in these cases there was an underlying divine force, which enabled the gods to be self-generating and manifest themselves, and which they then harnessed in order to do their creative work. This force, which naturally moves toward existence and life (and rebirth) is most often associated with goddesses and serpents (and therefore was often thought of as serpent power), will be discussed in Chapter 7. For the moment, the important point is that eventually the idea developed that for creation to occur this force must be harnessed by (and eventually embodied in) a sky god so as to produce order (the cosmos). Without such guidance the divine force itself would remain chaotic rather than being creative. Such guidance and control had to be based on principles of order, balance, justice, truth, and cosmic law *(maat)*. In Egypt, such ordering principles were embodied in the goddess Maat,[15] while a god handled the actual creation. Thus, Ptah, a god of craftsmen, created by first conceiving in his heart (mind) the order that he would create and then uttering the corresponding effective words. Hathor (who represented the underlying "fiery" serpent force or impulse) and Maat were thus complementary deities essential to the creation and maintenance of the universe. Thus, for example, they were portrayed together on the prow of Ra's solar bark as it passed through the chaos of the night to protect him and prepare him to emerge into a new day (a new creation) in which Hathor's energy compels the sun to rise, hence the common depiction of her carrying the sun disk between her cow horns.[16] Mesopotamians likewise recognized that the creation, as well as the maintenance of the cosmos against the forces of primordial (evil) chaos which still surrounded the cosmos, required the application of ordering principles. This idea is reflected in the Mesopotamian concept of the *Me* (discussed above), the divine principles or laws governing the operation of the cosmos. They were inscribed on tablets of that name which the chief deity possessed and had to keep safe so that cosmic order and justice would be preserved; but in times of social or political upheaval (a manifestation of chaos), the *Me* were said to have been dispersed, lost, forgotten, or gathered and put away in a corner, hence the problems.[17] The Decalogue, Yahweh's commandments inscribed on stone given into the possession of Moses and kept in the Ark, seem to be derived from this tradition. From that emerged Yahweh's Law

(Torah), which likewise was designed to provide ordering principles to guide humans, so that order, good and justice rather than evil (a form of chaos) will prevail in human society and in the cosmos as a whole (discussed in Chapter 9).

In the ordering and differentiating process of the creation, roles (destinies) and names were assigned to the components of the universe. The starting point had to be the separation of heaven and earth and fixing the heavenly bodies in heaven, because that is what enabled light to appear and time to begin. In Egyptian mythology the air god Shu separated earth (the god Geb) and the sky (the goddess Nut). In Sumerian mythology, An-Ki was physically undifferentiated until Enlil separated heaven and earth, leaving heaven to An and usurping earth from Ki. Similarly, in *Enuma Elish,* Marduk made heaven and earth out of the two halves of Tiamat's corpse. He then created other parts of the cosmos and their associated deities, decreeing their functions and destinies and giving them names. As multiplicity developed in the creation process, corresponding deities took their places as components of the cosmos (e.g., Shamash as the sun and Sin as the moon) and actively participated in cosmic events.

P's creation account was similar, but there are also important differences. The same primordial watery chaos and cosmic geography are present. God differentiated light and darkness (Gen 1:4-5), then separated the upper and lower primeval waters by making and placing a firmament between them, and finally separated land and sea (Gen. 1:6-10). But importantly God created no other deities and was thought to embody and embrace all of divinity; there was no separate divine force which he utilized, nor did any of the things he created have a divine nature; they were purely material. In the ancient Near East, this was a newer and revolutionary concept, and eventually it made monotheism possible.

After the initial creation (and any re-creation), the creator god maintained a presence, but typically retired to his palace-temple (or had one built for him), from where he could oversee and control the operation of the cosmos. Examples include Marduk in *Enuma Elish,* Baal after defeating the sea serpent Yam, and P's creation account when God "rests" on the seventh day.[18] These gods were not really resting from fatigue. Rather, this signified that, having created and ordered a perfect cosmos so that it could function, the creator could assume his position in a cosmic "temple" in which he could survey his work and take leisure, a divine prerogative.[19] This idea is later reflected in the account of Yahweh ceremonially taking up occupation of his Temple built by Solomon atop the Temple Mount, which among other things symbolized the culmination of the divinely-led creation of the United Monarchy of Israel and Judah.[20]

Following the creation of humans, the establishment of civilization was a process of the gods giving further order to the world, thus continuing the creation. Humans for their part were expected to preserve the creation (order), and to some degree extend the creation process. This required living a life in harmony with the (good) order of the cosmos. Thus, according to Egyptian funerary texts, a deceased person's heart was weighed on a scale against a feather representing *maat*. The idea here was not whether the heart was physically as light as a feather, but rather to determine whether the heart (in the ancient Near East considered the repository of human thought and will) was in balance with the principles of *maat* (cosmic order and justice), which would be the case if the deceased had lived a good, just life.

But left to their own devices humans were incapable of living according to cosmic order. They needed divine guidance and discipline. Therefore, religious thought and ritual developed as a means of preserving and protecting the natural order of creation and civilization itself, viewed principally as that of the community concerned (Sumerian, Egyptian, Israelite, or other), from which developed the concepts of law and kingship. Thus, in Mesopotamian myths, the gods devised the institution of kingship (which had "descended from heaven"), under which the king was the gods' vicar responsible for preserving and furthering the divinely decreed order,[21] embodied in the *Me*. As such, kingship was considered the pinnacle and perfect ordering principle of humanity, without which its creation was incomplete and order in civilization could not be maintained. Only under kingship do humans rise above their savage *(lullu)* state mired in chaos.[22] Such growth is portrayed in the *Epic of Gilgamesh,* where the primal man Enkidu, originally living in a *lullu* state, begins his transformation into full humanity through consort with a priestess-courtesan and completes the process by traveling to Gilgamesh's city of Uruk and there embracing his kingship.[23] In Egypt the king played the same kind of role. He was identified with and obligated to maintain *maat*.[24]

As we shall see, much the same theory underlies J's and P's accounts of humans in the primeval history and the subsequent epic story of the evolution of the Israelite nation, culminating in the kingships of David and Solomon. In the Hebrew Bible the natural proclivity *(yeṣer)* of humans is to sin and do violence to each other, which threatens the divinely ordained, created order.[25] Prior to the monarchy, each Israelite "did what was right in his own eyes" (Judg. 21:25), a manifestation of chaos. Hence the need for the Law *(Torah)* and a pious king to enforce it and lead the nation. Under such a king's rule, his subjects live in accordance with the divinely created order (part of which is the Law), which serves to maintain that order.[26] Adam's assignment from Yahweh to tend and keep the garden of Eden (keep it perfect) coincides with the above notions.

THE COSMIC GEOGRAPHY IN THE ANCIENT NEAR EAST

The above framework for creation reflected a common "cosmic geography" held by peoples throughout the ancient Near East, including in biblical Palestine. As depicted (in only two dimensions) in Diagram 4.1, the cosmos is "tiered," consisting principally of heaven, earth, and the underworld, all of which is surrounded by the primeval waters. The cosmos arose from a point and expanded within this ocean, like a bubble. This is the meaning of Genesis 1:6-7, in which God says:

> Let there be a firmament in the midst of the waters, and let it separate the waters from the waters. And God made the firmament, and it separated the waters which were under the firmament from the waters which were above the firmament. And it was so. And God called the firmament Heaven.

In this understanding, the cosmos is created and exists somewhere *within* the formless primeval waters, which continue their entropic existence outside the borders of the created cosmos. As a result, chaos, often in the form of

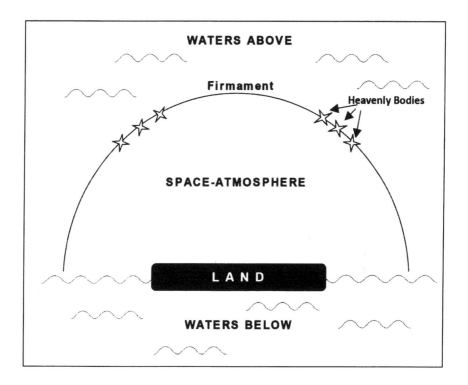

Diagram 4.1.

primeval waters (represented by a sea monster), inevitably and constantly threatens to and does permeate into the cosmos and damage it. When this happens and so long as chaos prevails, the creation (or part of it) is literally undone and ceases to exist. In fact, as the Egyptians recognized, chaos (non-existence) has penetrated all of creation to some degree.[27] As a result, there is a perennial tension and ebb and flow between order and chaos, existence and non-existence, creation and un-creation, time and timelessness.[28] Our world exists and we live within this unstable dynamic.

Chaos has many manifestations, however, not simply as primordial waters. The appearance of any form of corruption or malaise on earth—plague, sickness, death, darkness, earthquakes, floods, desert sandstorms, civil and political strife, the rise of and attacks by enemies, *as well as evil and sin*—was deemed *a manifestation of chaos* intruding into the cosmos. Order is good, as God calls his creations in Genesis 1, while chaos is identified with evil. According to an Egyptian Coffin text, Ra's creative acts were undertaken "out of my desire to quell evil."[29] The cosmos when first formed by the wise creator god was *necessarily* perfect and good. The appearance of chaos in the world is a corruption of the ideal forms of the world decreed at the creation. When chaos appears, this evil cancer must be eliminated or at least kept in check, by humans with the guidance and help of the gods.

Any such eruption of chaos followed by the restoration of order could be understood quite literally as a partial or full repetition of the creation. In the ancient Near East, the creation (re-creation) process can recur any number of times, with the world emerging anew each time.[30] This explains why, for example, in Egypt each night the sun was deemed to descend into the dark chaos of the netherworld, represented by the serpent Apep, the personification of chaos *(nesfet)* and evil, which had to be killed by Seth so that the sun (Ra) could again rise (be reborn) and stability could be restored.[31] The morning of each day was a kind of new creation. In Mesopotamia the world was considered to be recreated during each annual New Year's festival. In many native cultures, when sickness (a form of chaos) infects a member of the community, the treatment involves the ritual burial of the patient, so that curing the illness is viewed as a rebirth (re-creation) of the individual.[32] (If the patient dies, chaos has prevailed, into which the deceased dissolves.) The ancient flood myths of Mesopotamia, Egypt (associated with the annual inundation of the Nile),[33] and the Bible similarly represent a dissolution of the earth into chaos followed by a restoration of order, a new creation.[34]

In the ancient Near East, the watery primeval chaos often was personified by a sea monster (serpent or dragon). In Chapter 3 we discussed several myths concerning this archetypal monster: the Sumerian myth in which the dragon of the *apsu,* Kur, was destroyed, *Enuma Elish* in which Marduk vanquished the sea dragon Tiamat, the Ugaritic myth in which Baal destroyed the sea serpent Yam, and various Greek myths in which a dragon was killed. This mythological motif, often called "creation by combat" or the "dragon fight," represented an important new stage in cosmogonic thinking: Instead of the Goddess peacefully self-generating the universe from herself, chaos-monster (a goddess or her male proxy) now poses an obstacle to orderly creation and must be overcome by a sky god so that he can create the cosmos. Dramatized as a conflict of wills,[35] fundamentally it is the contest between chaos and order, which both in the myths themselves and in modern scholarly analysis is sexualized: chaos-feminine-unconscious vs. order-masculine-ego consciousness. The sky-father god vanquishes the monster, which reflects the rise of patriarchy, kingship, and the imposition of laws.

This combat motif recurs throughout the Hebrew Bible,[36] where the monster is sometimes called Leviathan (Ps. 74:13-14; Job 41:1; Isa. 27:1), sometimes Rahab (Job 26:12-13; Ps. 89:9-10; Isa. 51:9), and sometimes is simply an unnamed dragon or sea monster.[37] This imagery is used in two separate but related ways. In some cases it refers to Yahweh vanquishing the primeval sea monster during the creation of the cosmos.[38] Thus, in Job 26:12-13:

> *By his power he stilled the Sea;*
> *by his understanding he struck down Rahab.*
> *By his wind[39] the heavens were made fair;*
> *his hand pierced the fleeing serpent.*

And likewise in Psalm 89:9-10:

> *You rule the raging of the sea;*
> *when its waves rise, you still them;*
> *You crushed Rahab like a carcass;*
> *You scattered your enemies[40] with your mighty arm.*

In other instances the sea monster is an image identified rhetorically with enemy foreign peoples and lands and their kings: Egypt, Assyria and Babylon (e.g., Ps. 87:4; Isa. 27:1; 30:7; 59:9-11). This imagery reflects common mythological thinking in ancient cultures, according to which a people identifies its homeland to the ordered cosmos consecrated by the creator god, while the relatively unknown places and peoples outside it represent an indeterminate space associated with primordial chaos and non-existence, and are therefore demonized.[41] In ancient Egypt, for example, foreign peoples (such as Canaanites) were considered uncivilized and inferior, and rebellions in foreign lands were viewed as manifestations of chaos that the king was charged with eliminating.[42] The Egyptians considered that attacking enemies or rebelling subjects were transgressing against the divine order. Preventing this, or at least eliminating this when it happened, was a royal duty. Thus, Ramesses II, often considered the Pharaoh of the Exodus, enjoyed the epi-

thet, "he who makes rebellious foreign lands nonexistent."[43] The mythological idea behind the Israelite Conquest of Canaan was much the same.

The Exodus tradition reflects this concept but turns it around on the
Egyptians, so that the splitting of the Reed Sea and destruction of the Egyptians by chaotic waters brought on by Yahweh replicated primeval events and
was mythologized as a creation in historical terms,[44] namely the emergence
of the nation. The drying up of the Reed Sea so the Hebrews may cross
parallels the emergence of land from the primeval sea during creation. This
imagery is later repeated to like purpose when Yahweh blocks the flow of the
Jordan so that the people can cross into the Promised Land on the dry riverbed. This tradition was invoked in exilic times in Isaiah 51:9:[45]

Awake, awake, put on strength, o arm of the Lord;
Awake as in the days of old, the generations of long ago.
Was it not thou that didst cut Rahab into pieces,
that didst pierce the dragon?
Was it not thou that didst dry up the sea,
The waters of the great deep;
That didst make the depths of the sea a way
for the redeemed to pass over?

This passage likens Egypt to the evil chaos monster that Yahweh had van-
quished at creation, and entreats Yahweh to vanquish the monster (now the
Babylonians) once more to restore the proper order of things, so that the
Israelites will be liberated, their Law can operate in the land, and worship can
be resumed in a new temple in Jerusalem. A late biblical variation on the
dragon theme appears in the story of Bel and the Dragon.[46] When the prophet
Daniel was in Babylon, its king urged him to worship the dragon that the
Babylonians venerated. This was none other than the *mushussu* snake-dragon
that had been part of Tiamat's cohort and was later adopted by Marduk (Bel)
as his symbol.[47] But Daniel, seeking to emulate and outdo Marduk's feat and
demonstrate the superiority of his religion, claimed he could kill the dragon,
which the king dared him to attempt. Daniel made a concoction of pitch, fat
and hair and boiled it into cakes, which the dragon ate.[48] It distended the
dragon's insides, causing the dragon to burst open and die, much as Marduk
had killed Tiamat by bursting her insides (with winds and an arrow).

THE CAUSES OF CHAOS ON EARTH
AND REMEDIES AGAINST IT

We can now turn to other key questions arising from the above dynamic:
What causes chaos (evil) to visit the earth and human civilization? Why do
the gods allow this? Who or what is at fault? The answer in the ancient Near

East was usually that humans bring this on themselves and are to blame.[49] The struggle against chaos was not just the responsibility of the gods. Although humans are supposed to maintain and even extend the creation, through improper conduct they also could bring on chaos and undo it. Humans had a sacred duty to avoid this, and to remedy the consequences if it occurred.

To illustrate this, it is useful to recount the ancient Mesopotamian flood myth known as *Atrahasis,* which dates at least from Old Babylonian times.[50] The story begins with the lesser *(igigi)* gods having to perform manual labor on earth, since only the higher gods enjoyed the divine prerogative of leisure. Growing tired and angry, and aspiring to higher status, the lesser gods went on strike and proposed creating humans to do the work instead. The high gods agreed, and had Enki and the birth goddess Nintu create a primitive humankind. The humans multiplied rapidly and eventually raised a din, which constituted a rebellion similar to the earlier rebellion of the lesser gods;[51] in seeking to avoid toil, humans too aspired to be godlike.[52] This noise made Enlil sleepless, thus denying him leisure and infringing upon his divinity. In response, the gods sent plagues on humans to kill them off, but, thanks to humankind's friend Enki, the plagues did not work. Finally, the gods in council decided to destroy humankind with a flood. But Enki resolved to preserve humankind by saving his pure, pious devotee Atrahasis ("Very Wise"), a model of what humans should be. Enki warned him of the upcoming flood and told him to build a large boat on which to put his household and representative animals to ride out the deluge. After the flood, Enlil made peace with humankind, but only through ordering Enki and Nintu to modify humans by amending the "human regulations" (originally issued at their creation) so as to prevent a recurrence of such rebellion.[53] Thus, humankind's aspiration to be like gods was frustrated.[54]

The Bible's treatment of such questions begins with the Eden story and continues as a unified narrative through the remainder of the primeval history, in which as in *Atrahasis* the flood is key. It is a story of a world originally given perfect form (deemed "good" in P's creation account; mythologically equivalent to the garden of Eden in J's) which becomes increasingly corrupted through a series of human transgressions, of which Adam and Eve's was only the first. They continued through Cain's murder of Abel, Lemech's murder of a man and a boy (Gen. 4:23-24),[55] and eventually women marrying the "sons of the Gods" giving rise to the Nephilim (Gen. 6:1-8), a race of super-humans that had some divine qualities, possibly including near-immortality, similar to the primitive humans in *Atrahasis* who were produced in part from divine blood. And as in *Atrahasis,* the sins of primeval humans condemned them to death by deluge. Human sins, themselves a form of chaos, eventually led to complete chaos overtaking the Earth in the form of Noah's flood. Importantly, the flood occurred by means of God allowing onto the Earth the primeval waters of chaos that surround it and are always pressing at the doors: He let open both[56] the fountains of the deep and the windows of the heavens (Gen. 7:11), and to end the flood he closed them (Gen. 8:2). During the flood, except for the ark and its occupants, the Earth was destroyed (Gen. 9:11), meaning that there was a return to pre-creation chaos.[57]

The outcome of the flood was understood as a new creation and a new beginning for mankind. In P's part of the flood story, this is signified by God repeating the same blessing on humankind[58] together with the command to be fruitful and multiply and rule the earth that he gave to humans in Genesis 1 (compare Gen. 1:28 with Gen. 9:1-2). In J's text, the same idea is signified by the sacrifice that Noah makes to Yahweh as his first act after emerging from the Ark, which was the first whole burnt sacrifice, and on the first altar, in the Bible (Gen. 8:20). This serves as a final expatiation of the sins of antediluvian humans and to give thanks to and propitiate Yahweh. And it was effective, as it moved Yahweh to promise never again to send a flood to destroy the earth, which established a new relationship between Yahweh and humans. To mark this covenant he set his bow (a rainbow, signifying the end of a storm) in the cloud[59] (Gen. 9:13-17, by P). As in *Atrahasis,* the end of the flood and restoration of the cosmos was marked by new rules.[60] In both the *Atrahasis* and Genesis flood stories, the primeval period ended with the reestablishment of the world and the redefinition of humankind, so the world as we know it could begin.[61] Importantly, this re-creation meant that the sins and other abominations of the past were wiped out, because they were literally part of the chaos that had been eliminated by the flood; the cosmos had been purified.[62] The world having been restored, humans again had a sacred responsibility to avoid misbehavior that could bring on chaos and also to conduct the rituals necessary to satisfy the gods and ensure the continuation of order in the world. As explained in Chapter 9, the Christian doctrine of original sin, in which Adam and Eve's sin haunted humanity until the crucifixion and resurrection of Christ, contradicts this mythological meaning of this primeval history, in which the flood eliminated forever any consequences of Adam's and Eve's transgression.

Humans then, like today, also wanted to experience the divine, in sacred time. For these purposes, the creation held central significance, because that was when the gods decreed the fundamental order and workings of the world, in sacred time, when the divine and cosmic realms were most intimately linked. So when humans aspired to experience the divine, they looked back to the creation. Therefore, in their mythology and religious rituals people sought to recreate and repeat the events of creation, both to restore and reaffirm order in the world and as a means of spiritual renewal and purification, enabling them to venture out into the new world with a clean slate. Mircea Eliade called this the Myth of the Eternal Return.[63] This is, for example, the fundamental meaning of the New Year's holiday in all cultures, [64] and it held a central position in Mesopotamian religious life. In Babylon, during each New Year's festival, *Enuma Elish* was publicly recited in order to reenact Marduk's battle with Tiamat, his creation of the cosmos, and his acquisition of the *Me* (Tablets of Destiny). [65] During this ritual the gods were deemed to descend from heaven to the ziggurat complex (where the earthly and the divine came together), the sacred marriage rite was performed, and the destinies for the new year were decreed by the priests. This ceremony was not merely a retelling of the creation. In an important sense the creation was actually recurring and the people were experiencing it in sacred time: The new year was created by the process of reverting to formlessness in order to destroy the prior year and any of its chaos, thereby creating new forms and destinies and reaffirming the reign of the king as god's vicar on earth charged with maintaining order. [66] *Enuma Elish* thus culminates by recognizing that the cosmic struggle never really ends—Tiamat can resurrect anytime—and so the myth looks forward: [67]

> *May he* [Marduk] *vanquish Tiamat; may her life be strait and short!*
> *Into the future of mankind, when days have grown old,*
> *May she recede without cease and stay away forever.* [68]

CREATION AND CHAOS IN GENESIS

In order to understand how the above concepts of creation apply in J's creation story, it is useful to contrast it with some aspects of P's account. Scholars have long recognized that many fundamental aspects of P's creation story, though not necessarily its creative details, are derived from ancient Near Eastern creation myths. [69] While P's story is often considered "demythologized" because its narrative lacks characters and violence (e.g., God creates rather than defeats the sea monsters), it still fits well within the above-mentioned mythological archetype of a wise deity giving form to primordial chaos. The "beginning" is viewed not in chronological but functional terms, as being that moment when God begins to give form to the cosmos by applying his wisdom, symbolized by lifting the veil of darkness associated with chaos and creating through utterance a special divine light, which allows the creative process of differentiation to begin. [70] Earthly light and time begin only on the fourth day, when the sun and moon that mark time are created. ·

In describing this process P draws on the motifs discussed earlier, especially those from Mesopotamia. It begins with a pre-creation state of dark, unformed, chaotic primeval waters. P calls them the *tehôm* (Gen. 1:2; then not yet in the underworld since there was no land), which, as we have seen, is etymologically related to Tiamat. In Genesis 1:21 P alludes to the sea dragon myths in mentioning that God "created the sea monsters," implying that God was in supreme control of them.[71] God causing the waters to bring forth water creatures and the earth to bring forth plants and living creatures (Gen. Gen. 1:11-12, 20-25) likewise places God in firm control of that part of creation. In the older ancient Near Eastern mythology, as we have seen, the earth as Goddess had generated these, but now the Hebrew God has appropriated that function. The divine wind moving across the primeval waters in P's story just before God declares, "Let there be light" (Gen. 1:2) recalls Enlil as "lord of the air," or "wind" separating earth from heaven (by inserting himself between them) to initiate the creation, resulting in the familiar tiered cosmos,[72] and Shu doing the same in Egyptian myth. Elohim, Enlil, and Enki all created in part by utterance (naming their creations).[73] In all these cases, rather than the world arising from and being part of divinity, creator gods overcome primeval chaos and transitively *create* the cosmos, which is not divine.

J's creation story at first seems strikingly different, because an account of Yahweh's creation of the cosmos as a whole is virtually absent. As Professor Brandon observed, "it scarcely merits the designation 'cosmogony.'"[74] The cosmogony consists entirely of a passing reference in the introductory clause[75] of the first sentence of his story (Gen. 2:4b), the main purpose of the passage being to describe how Yahweh created the first human. Already in the second sentence the man is living in the garden of Eden, which indicates how focused J was on beginning his human tale. Still, given J's fondness for writing colorful episodes of Yahweh's interventions in the world, together with the presence of the sea monster motif throughout the rest of the Bible, many scholars believe that J's original text probably contained more about the creation of the world, possibly including a version of the traditional battle with the sea monster.[76]

But even in its extant form, J's story includes many elements of the traditional Mesopotamian cosmogony and cosmic geography, including the primeval deep, decreeing the destiny of humans, and having things named as part of the creation process. But in one telling respect he reversed the Mesopotamian imagery. Whereas P says that God created "the heavens and the earth" (Gen. 1:1), J states that Yahweh created "the earth and the heavens" (Gen. 2:4b). As we have seen, the words "heaven and earth," in that order, were a set phrase in Mesopotamian myths etymologically related to the names of the deities.[77] Thus, to create the universe was to create "heaven-earth." P continued the Mesopotamian phraseology, whereas J's reversal of the terms accentuates his anthropocentric approach.[78] To the extent J cared about the cosmogony and the created cosmology, he altered its symbolism to his own purposes.

Thus, J omitted the primordial stage of a formless ocean, but he utilized an analogous primordial motif linked more closely to humanity. Specifically,

J's story begins with a dry, barren, lifeless wasteland on earth called Eden. [79] In mythology, including in the ancient Near East and throughout the Bible, such a wild, uncultivated, desert wasteland commonly signifies chaos, the void and nonexistence—the formless modality of pre-creation—and thus parallels in meaning the primordial waters. [80] Thus, the barren Eden is analogous to the primordial formless void described by P in Genesis 1:2, and similarly has been translated as "desert and a wasteland" or like terms. [81] As Professor Thompson stated it succinctly, in Genesis 1 "Chaos is pictured as a sea, in the latter [Genesis 2] as a desert." [82] It is in this void of nonexistence that creation occurs: Yahweh begins to form all things on earth, first by bringing up the primordial waters from the deep *(tehôm)* to irrigate and moisten the ground [83] so that it could support plants and so the first human could be molded, and then by creating the garden in Eden: planting trees there, placing the first human there, and creating other living things there. Mythologically speaking, it was just as important to J to portray creation out of formlessness as it was for P, the Mesopotamians and the Egyptians; they just chose different but related mythological symbols to portray it.

Having begun in the garden, the creation then spreads to the rest of the earth. This is symbolized by the four rivers flowing out of the garden to the four corners of the earth, which as we shall see is similarly represented in other world myths involving four rivers flowing from a center of creation, such as a cosmic mountain. Such symbolism is not limited to the most literal meaning of waters of life bringing fertility to the land, but more broadly signifies the extension of the elements of creation from its Center. In the Hebrew Bible, the creative process is briefly continued by humans tending and keeping the garden of Eden, and after their expulsion by multiplying and by cultivating the earth, especially after the flood, once Yahweh lifted the curse on the ground. By cultivating the soil that was formerly barren, humans are repeating and extending the acts of the creator and therefore the creation itself. [84] But the creation process can be reversed, with cosmos degenerating into chaos, most notably in Israel's own history.

CREATION AND CHAOS IN ISRAELITE HISTORY

The mythological symbolism of creation vs. chaos was utilized by J and the other biblical authors to narrate their epic history of the Israelites. But it is important to realize that this imagery is not just a literary device. [85] Much as the Babylonians really thought their world was recreated each New Year, the biblical authors genuinely thought that the cosmological dynamic of creation vs. chaos played a real role in their nation's history. Israel's history had cosmic dimensions. In that story sinful behavior (a form of chaos) led to (greater) chaos, while good behavior according to the Law kept order and maintained and extended the creation. From this perspective, it is important to review this dynamic as told in the national epic because it sheds light on what J was getting at in the Eden story.

We have already reviewed the cosmogonic imagery in the Exodus, but it continues soon afterward, when the Hebrews disobey Yahweh on several occasions. As a result, Yahweh relegated that generation of Hebrews to nearly 40 years of a kind of exile in the barren, chaotic wilderness of Sinai, enabling them to survive only thanks to his various acts of grace.[86] Out of this uroboric modality a new, purer generation grew up (i.e., was created) which was too young to have participated in the above-mentioned sins (i.e., who did not yet know good and evil at the time),[87] pure people worthy of participating in a new creation in the Promised Land.

The imagery of chaos and its elimination continues in the Conquest of Canaan. Immediately after restoration of the cosmos after Noah's flood, Canaan, as represented by Ham's son of that name, had been cursed in connection with nakedness (Gen. 9:22-27, a J text), a characteristic of Canaanite religion and society likened to chaos that was continually brought up and was said to result in the eventual subjugation of Canaan by Israel.[88] Canaan was thus set off from the world as a place of chaos, and it was Israel's duty and destiny to eliminate this chaos, establish order (though Yahweh's Law) in that part of the cosmos, and build the chosen people's Center in that land, in Jerusalem. Mythologically speaking, this explains the need (on Yahweh's orders) to completely eliminate the sinful Canaanite population and portray the Israelites as a divinely led force of order from the outside. The slate in that land had to be wiped clean, much as had been done for the whole world in the flood. This is reflected in Yahweh's first commandment to the Hebrews discussed in Chapter 2 as well as in Yahweh's instructions for invading Canaan, namely that "in the cities of these peoples that the Lord your God gives you for an inheritance, you shall save alive nothing that breathes, but you shall utterly destroy them, . . . that they may not teach you to do according to all their abominable practices" (i.e., let chaos back in) (Deut. 20:16-18). Israel will be a new creation, not just in a political sense but also in a sacred cosmic sense. Thus, as Joshua leads the people into Canaan, Yahweh holds back the waters of the Jordan and the people cross the dry riverbed, echoing the above-mentioned cosmic symbolism from the crossing of the Reed Sea and of the creation itself.[89] At Gibeon the sun stands still. At Jericho the walls tumble down in response to a shout.[90] Divine, cosmic forces are at work.

But the goal of cleansing the land was not initially fulfilled. As seen in Chapter 2, in the North some important cities remained in Canaanite hands, meaning that elements of chaos remained and the land was still tarnished, and as a result the Israelites could be tempted and ensnared by pagan ways. But this goal initially was more completely achieved in Judah through David's conquest of the last Canaanite holdout, Jebusite Jerusalem, after which David completed the process in the North as well. When David died, Solomon was coronated at the Gihon spring (1 Kings 1:33), a link to the Gihon river of Eden and therefore back to the original creation.[91] Under David and the early Solomon, the lands of Israel and Judah were said to be united and at peace, and Yahwism was made the official religion; the forces of chaos that the Israelites had been fighting since Joshua's time seemingly had been repelled. Mythologically speaking, in a divinely-led process, creation (by definition perfection), that of the nation, had been achieved. Historical or not, the United Monarchy was a mythological necessity. This achievement was symbolized by the ceremonial dedication of the Temple and the enthronement of Yahweh in it, a mythological parallel to Elohim resting on the seventh day to survey his creation. That day, after Solomon said his prayer and made an offering to Yahweh, "fire came down from heaven and consumed the burnt offering and the sacrifices, and the glory of the Lord filled the temple" (2 Chr. 7:1).

But, as seen above, the creation can unravel into chaos. When the Temple was consecrated, Yahweh told Solomon that the well-being of the nation, its continued existence in the Promised Land, and the continuation of the Davidic line depended on the king keeping Yahweh's statutes and ordinances (1 Kings 9:4-9). But Solomon proceeded to disobey Yahweh by inviting in paganism, which caused the separation of Israel from Judah (1 Kings 11:30-33); there followed the long, slow decline of Israel and Judah into nonexistence. The final force of chaos, Babylon, overcame the Israelites, who were exiled right into its midst. Isaiah (51:3) likened the Israelites' exile in Babylon to being in a desert chaos, although Yahweh could offer some comfort:

> For the Lord will comfort Zion;
> he will comfort all her waste places,
> and will make her wilderness like Eden,
> her desert like the garden of the Lord . . . .

The human story had now come full circle: It began with Adam and Eve being exiled to the surrounding Mesopotamian wasteland (Eden) for their transgression, and due to their sins the Israelites too were be exiled from their Promised Land to what they considered a Mesopotamian wasteland. If this situation were not remedied, The End would come. Indeed, Jeremiah, writing on the eve of Jerusalem's downfall to Babylon, wrote that in such case the cosmos would revert to formless, dark chaos (4:23-28):[92]

> I looked on the earth, and lo, it was waste and void;[93]
> and to the heavens, and they had no light.
> I looked on the mountains, and lo, they were quaking
> and all the hills moved to and fro.

I looked and lo, there was no one at all,
and all the birds of the air had fled.
I looked, and lo, the fruitful land was a desert,
and all its cities were laid in ruins
before the Lord, before his fierce anger.
For thus says the Lord: The whole land shall be a desolation; yet I will not
make a full end.
For this the earth shall mourn,
and the heavens above grow black.

So much for the national story. Now let us consider the individual.

THE CREATION AND THE INDIVIDUAL HUMAN

J's and P's creation stories together with *Enuma Elish* share an important difference with earlier creation accounts. According to the earlier polytheistic creation myths, *the material world emanated from the divine,* which means that the created world still partakes of the divine. This earlier idea is most classically exemplified in the myths in which a Mother Goddess self-generates the universe, but it is not restricted to that scenario. In an Egyptian creation myth, Atum self-generated himself from the primeval waters as a concrete deity, and then generated, again as his own physical substance, other deities which in turn *were* the components of the cosmos. Creation consisted of "Atum's self-realization of his own physical substance," so that there was a "continuity of matter from the original [divine] mass to the differentiated elements of the world."[94] Atum himself described the process: "See, the Flood is subtracted from me: see, I am the remainder."[95] Similarly, in another Egyptian text, the gods were created from Re's sweat and humans from his tears,[96] which again implies that humans like gods partake of divinity. Similarly, in India, according to the *Brihadaranyaka Upanishad,* the divinity divides itself to become the cosmos, including humans; everything is a manifestation of the single divine substance.[97] In that account, first there was nothing but the divine Self, which had the form of a man but was "as large as a man and woman embracing." The Self lacked delight and (like Adam) wanted a second, and so divided into man and woman. When they embraced, the human race was born. Then they took the form of animals, which also united, creating their populations as well. In the end, the man realized that, being divine, he was a creator:

"I, actually, am [the whole of] creation; for I have poured forth all this."
Whence arose the concept "Creation." Anyone understanding this becomes,
truly, himself a creator in this creation.[98]

In the garden of Eden, humans, upon their creation, are said to have "fallen" when they aspired to the divine and be like God, but in India creation in a sense is a fall of God—his fragmentation into the divine cosmos, including humanity, rendering humans' godlike aspirations unnecessary, because metaphysically the divine is already within humans.[99]

As already noted in Chapter 3, however, the vision of the divine and the universe in Genesis is fundamentally different, akin to that in *Enuma Elish* and conceptually an evolution from it. In the Hebrew Bible, God and the created cosmos are separate, the cosmos being in the realm of what Professor Westermann calls "not God."[100] As Professor Cassuto likewise observed, the Hebrew god is

> not a deity associated with nature and identified with it wholly or in part, but a God who stands absolutely above nature, and outside of it, and nature and all its constituent elements, even the sun and all the other entities, be they ever so exalted, are only His creatures, made according to His will.[101]

In creating both man and the animals from dirt, J's Yahweh[102] acted transitively on material existing outside the sphere of divinity; and both humans and animals will return to dust when they die (Gen. 3:19). To J, humans are by nature *objects* of creation. According to J, the world is not infused with the divine, and people should not take any religious attitude toward it.[103] By comparison, in polytheism the cycle of birth, living and dying is understood as a passage through different modalities of the divine: We live as a manifest form of the divine, and after earthly "death" we return to the divine realm in non-manifest form. Unlike in polytheism, for J, to understand the world is not to see the divine in all things,[104] because it does not reside there, nor is man at one with the other things in the universe by sharing a divine spark.[105] Humans and divinity are intrinsically different. Accordingly, the goal in religion is not to achieve identity with or directly experience or know the divine (as in Canaanite polytheism)—that is prohibited. The transgression in the Garden occurs precisely because, in defiance of Yahweh's command, Adam and Eve seek to know or partake of the transcendent. For J, Yahweh must be humankind's exclusive channel for relating to the divine. If humans seek to come to know, partake of or encroach upon the divine in any other manner—even if the initiative comes from divine beings—Yahweh will punish them. Yahweh thus draws boundaries and tells humans where they must stand in relation to them. J makes this point not only in the Eden story, but also in his tower of Babel story and his story in Genesis 6:1-4 about improper interbreeding between the "sons of the Gods" and human women.[106]

Since, according to J, humans and the divine are separate by nature, this gap is unbridgeable; instead, a *relationship* must be formed between them.[107] In the Hebrew Bible, Yahweh and humans establish this relationship by making covenants with each other. Human interaction with the divine is by contract.[108] Among other things, the notion of covenant was a way of shunting aside human aspirations to the divine. Further, the relationship is unequal: Humans must serve, love, worship, have unconditional faith in and obey Yahweh and his Law; and for the Israelites, in return, Yahweh would enable his chosen people to conquer and prosper in the Promised Land. J does not talk about individual salvation or an afterlife; he was quite clear that, at least as of the expulsion from the garden of Eden, man is mortal and death is final, upon which humans return to dust. In J's view, the good that comes from the proper relationship with the divine (Yahweh) concerns man's life on earth. This is in significant part a social and political good, relating not so much to individual spiritual life as to the national and religious community. Contrary to the traditional Western understanding of the Eden story, the story, in J's mind, ultimately is less about individual spiritual life and more about the religious challenges faced by the Israelites. In the ancient Israelite mind, as throughout the ancient Near East, the interests of community (social groups of family, clan, tribe, and nation) were paramount and the individual was secondary.

Now that we have discussed the nature of the creation and the cosmos, including their relationship to religious life and the story of the Israelite nation, we can address how the creation relates to the garden of Eden.

THE GARDEN OF EDEN AND THE SYMBOLISM OF THE CENTER

J's concept of the garden of Eden being created by Yahweh within a barren wasteland devoid of the usual forms of creation, symbolic of formless primeval chaos, fits into a classic mythological motif that mythologists such as Eliade and Campbell call the symbolism of the Center.[109] People and communities need their own Centers to fulfill psychological needs and establish their position in the world. Thus, the ancient Chinese called their land the Middle Kingdom because they considered themselves the center of all civilization; the Egyptian and great Mesopotamian civilizations thought the same of themselves,[110] as did the Israelites. For millennia humankind insisted that the earth and humans were at the center of the universe, which revolved around us. Importantly, this psychology works not simply because it makes us feel more secure and important, but because the concept of the Center has explanatory power. Being at the Center has spiritual significance: It helps explain the origin and nature of the cosmos and facilitates humans experiencing the sacred.

In world mythology, the Center archetypically is the heart of reality, the locus in mythic geography where all essential modes of being come together and can be accessed and experienced.[111] On earth, it is the place where the tiers or planes of the cosmos (heaven, earth and the underworld) intersect, and so it is often described as the navel of the earth or the world axis (*axis mundi*). Therefore, it offers humans (or at least select humans) access to the other tiers, and therefore the opportunity to experience and know the sacred, divine aspects of reality. The Center is a sacred place connected with the presence of divinities, where humans can invoke and interact with them, so naturally a sacred sanctuary is found there. Finally, the Center is where the creation of the cosmos, including the creation of humankind, is considered to have begun.[112] From there the creation spreads,[113] as in the case of the four rivers of Eden flowing outward.[114]

The cosmos at the moment of creation at the Center is considered perfect, reflecting the perfection of divinity.[115] In order for the first humans also to be considered perfect, they too must be created contemporaneously with and as part of the cosmogony, at the Center.[116] Our endeavor to experience the sacred inevitably begins with how we believe the world as we know it came to exist. The notion of a perfect creation of the cosmos and humans together at the Center implies an ideal existence there. It is thus easy to see how the notion of an original paradise developed in myth, and also to understand the original meaning of that concept. The original "paradise" was not primarily a garden of earthly delights and pleasure, although it might be that too. More importantly, it is an ideal of perfection that among other things enables humans there to experience an ideal spiritual life, however that might be conceived.

As the space where the creation occurs, the Center is where chaos is turned into order, a place of transformation and becoming. The Center thus partakes of both uroboric chaos and the dynamic of creation.[117] It is both a place of unity where latent opposites are initially at rest and the place where opposites first spring into being. Psychologically speaking, it is where consciousness emerges from unconsciousness. Our unconscious experiences the unity of the uroboros as pleasurable, paradisiacal, and as perfection, while our consciousness beholds the order of the initial creation as perfection. The drama in the garden of Eden traces this process of initial unity changing into opposites: male and female, death and life, mortality and immortality, good and evil, divine and human. Once these essential opposites of the real world have come into existence, humans are fully conscious (having the knowledge of good and evil) and it is time to leave the garden. Indeed, at that point the garden, an uroboric modality, no longer exists. The transformation was within, as we shall discuss in Chapter 9.

The fact that such initial perfection existed inevitably necessitates a mythological explanation of how humans have deteriorated to their present state. In the myths of many cultures an initial ideal age of humankind, followed by subsequent stages (ages) of degradation, is usually attributed to the fault of humans. A famous example comes from Greek mythology, which describes an original golden age, followed by a silver age, two bronze ages and an iron age.[118] As we have seen above, the Hebrew Bible also follows this pattern, not only in the deterioration of humankind depicted in the primeval history, but also in the deterioration of the Israelite nation following the culmination of its creation, which had been marked by the dedication of the Temple in Jerusalem, its Center.

Having once been in the Center in an ideal state enables people to recreate and experience it to some extent. Humans want to be in sacred space and time, at least on occasion. Hence our mythologies and religious rituals often revolve around the idea of the Center, including many holiday celebrations, especially the New Year. We also build sanctuaries, temples, and holy cities on the spots considered Centers (or in other locations considered to evoke this idea)[119] using designs that represent the same. As we shall see below, humans often do this when designing their dwellings, in order to "cosmicize" them.[120] Our myths, rituals and holy sanctuaries evoke the idea of a return to and reenactment of the primordial act of creation at the Center as a means of expiation of the tarnished past, rebirth, and spiritual renewal, called by Eliade the Myth of the Eternal Return.[121]

The Center can be symbolized by various images, separately or in combination. Several archetypal motifs of the Center appear in the Eden story, making it the ultimate Center of the earth: the garden as a place of creation; the Center as symbolized by a sacred tree; the Center in connection with the number four; the association of water (or some other nutritious liquid) with the Center; and the Center emanating radiance, in the form of celestial light, through glistening precious stones.

The motif of the sacred tree, mountain or *omphalos* as the Center appears in many cultures. In Ezekiel 28:14-16, the garden of Eden is said to be located on the holy mountain of God; Mt. Zion was eventually considered Israel's Center. A sacred tree or mountain are interchangeable[122] symbols of the Center because they reach into the sky and down into the depths of the earth, thus spanning the planes of heaven, earth and the underworld. (Thus, one can venture into a mountain's depths (as via a cave) and symbolically enter Earth, the Mother Goddess.) Examples include Mount Meru in India, Mount Kailash in Tibet, Maraberezaiti (Elburz) in Iran, Mount Zaphor in Ugaritic Syria, and in Palestine Mount Tabor and Mount Gerzim.[123] According to Egyptian cosmology (the Heliopolis creation myth), the cosmos emerged from the primal waters of chaos as a primal mound, which concept later developed into the mastaba tomb design, step pyramids and later the true pyramids.[124] The motif of the cosmic mountain also appears in ancient Mesopotamia, both in mythology and in the form of the ziggurat,[125] as do the Center motifs of the sacred tree, garden-sanctuary, watery deep, and the notion of an initial paradise at the Center (all discussed below).

The Center is also typically associated with the number four, manifested as a confluence of four symbolic images of like kind, such as the four rivers flowing from the garden of Eden. People conceptualize the extent of the earth in terms of four points: front-back and side-to-side; on a map, it is the four points of the compass. The number four and compositions of four like images signify totality and completeness, thus embracing all of the created cosmos.[126] The spatial confluence of four images of like kind at a Center connotes a place of emergence, of creation.

This symbolism is especially well developed in ancient East Asia. Mt. Kailash in southwestern Tibet was sacred to several religions. According to the Hindu *Vishnu Purana,* it had four faces made of crystal, ruby, gold, and lapis lazuli; from it four rivers flowed to the four quarters of the world, dividing it into four regions. The *Vishnu Purana* also spoke of another cosmic mountain, Mt. Meru (this one situated in heaven), being buttressed by four mountains from which four mountain ranges extended in the four directions; adjacent were four lakes, the waters of which the gods partook, and from there the celestial Ganges divided into four mighty rivers to irrigate the four quarters of the earth.[127] In the ancient Tibetan Bon religion, the paradisiacal Center of Tagzig Olmo Lung Ring had a pyramid-shaped cosmic mountain called Yungdrung Gutsek. The Bons held that four rivers flowed from the four corners of the mountain's base from formations in the shape of heads of animals: the snow lion of the east; the horse of the north; the peacock of the west; and the elephant of the south.[128] According to Vedic religion, from the soma tree that links earth and heaven four springs (turning into rivers) gushed forth ambrosia.[129] According to early Buddhist mythology, at the center of the world stands Mt. Sumeru,[130] viewed as a pillar, half above the surface and half in the underworld. It is made of four treasures on each of its four faces in the cardinal directions: gold on its northern face; silver on the eastern face; lapis lazuli on the southern face; and crystal on the western face.[131] Around it is a sea in which lie four land masses in the four cardinal directions. That mass which includes India and Tibet, called Jambudvīpa, has its own Center, a lake in Tibet north of the Himalayas called Anavatapta ("no heat or fever"), beside which stand sacred Jambu trees (from which the name Jambudvīpa originates), and from which flow four great rivers (Ganges, Indus, Oxus and Sītā).[132]

A similar concept is found in other ancient and indigenous cultures. In ancient Mesopotamia, both Sumerian and later Akkadian texts divide the earth into four quadrants according to the cardinal directions.[133] Mesopotamian kings held the title "King of the Four Quarters [of the World]."[134] In ancient Egypt the Nile was considered to have originated from four sources, sometimes symbolized by four serpent heads, also by a goddess holding a vase from which four streams of water flow.[135] In Homer's *Odyssey* the island of Ogygia where Calypso held Odysseus and offered him immortality was located at the "navel of the sea," and her home was situated in a vineyard garden from which four crystal streams flowed. [136] The mythology of the Kalmucks tells of a sacred Zambu tree rising from the Marvo Sea, which is as deep as it is broad and contains water of eight separate elements; from this sea four rivers flow to the points of the compass. [137] The *Prose Edda* (Norse myth) speaks of four rivers of milk flowing from the udder of the primeval cow, Audhumla. [138] Navajo art portrays a place of emergence marked by a ladder from which rivers flow in the four cardinal directions. In Mesoamerican mythology, four gods including Quetzalcoatl, together with four men that they created, were said to have made four roads that crossed through the center of the earth, in order to enter it and raise the sky. To do so, Quetzalcoatl and another god transformed themselves into sacred trees; then the trees, the remaining gods, and the four men raised the sky with the stars, after which the gods gave life to the earth. [139] According to Mayan myth the world has four quadrants extending out from a Center, with the sky supported by Atlantean gods called "water sprinklers." [140]

We cited numerous examples above because they also illustrate another important archetypal characteristic of any Center, which is that water lies within it or close by, in the form of a river, lake, or spring above or below ground, or simply the primeval watery deep. This is natural, given that in myths the cosmos so often emerges from the primeval waters and since water is associated with generating life. That is, in order for a Center to be true to its nature and function as such, it must be associated with such waters. Thus, in Egypt the sanctuaries at Heliopolis and elsewhere included a sacred well and pond representing the primeval waters. Similarly, many Centers in Asia such as Angkor Wat have one or more large moats surrounding them, again representing the primeval waters from which creation, and first and foremost the Center, arose. In Mesopotamia, Eridu, and in particular its temple, was considered to lie over the *apsu* of creation, and was presided over by Enki, the water god. [141] According to the *Kausitaki Upanishad,* the miraculous Tree of Life (Ilya) at the Center grew beside an "ageless" river (Vigarâ). [142] In ancient Greece the most ancient shrines of Dodona and Delphi featured holy springs. In Norse myth, the Norns lived beside Urdar's fountain that watered the roots of the cosmic tree Yggdrasil. [143] In Ireland, the Neolithic sanctuary complex of Newgrange and Knowth was built on a hill rising inside a dramatic loop of the Boyne River. In Colombia the Barasana Indian people endeavored to build their Center, the *maloca* house in which a kinship group lived, on land between two rivers set in a garden. [144] Similarly, Central Asian and Iranian myths about mountains and sacred trees normally depict underneath them a spring containing the water of life. [145] In ancient Persian literature the sacred tree grew on the sacred mountain Hara Berezaiti, under which flowed the spring of the water of life, Ardvisura, while in the mythology of the Ostiaks of Siberia the sacred tree grew by "the watery sea of the heaven-center."[146] A Minusinsk Tatar poem beautifully incorporates this and other Center motifs:

> *Piercing twelve heavens*
> *On the summit of a mountain*
> *A birch in the misty depths of air.*
> *Golden are the birch's leaves,*
> *Golden its bark,*
> *In the ground at its foot a basin*
> *Full of the water of life,*
> *In the basin a golden ladle. . . .*[147]

Such golden bark on the Center's sacred tree exemplifies another archetypal motif of the Center, that of a radiance, which can be manifested by gleaming precious metals or stones, whiteness (including on snow-capped sacred mountains), or fire. Such manifestations are associated with the heavens (shining stars, the sun, moon, and Milky Way) and divine energies and powers, which can be accessed at the Center. Thus, for the Aztecs, whose myth of origins, like that of the Israelites, was a migration story, their blissful place of origin was a great hill-island in the midst of primeval waters, Aztlan, which means "whiteness," so they recognized their Promised Land (the lake of Mexico) by signs reminiscent of Aztlan: white cypresses, willows and reeds, white rushes and white aquatic creatures.[148] Greek texts describe Mt. Olympus, home of the gods, as being snow-capped or having a radiant whiteness over it.[149] Mt. Meru was covered with glowing herbs that illuminated the darkness, resembling a flame without smoke.[150]

Related to this is the archetypal motif of the presence of precious, radiant stones on or around symbols of the Center (mountains, temples, sacred trees, groves and gardens). Ezekiel 28:13-14 mentions many precious stones and metals as being in the garden of Eden, which he calls "stones of fire." Mount Kailash (meaning "crystal" in Sanskrit) with its four jeweled sides is another example; as are the four streams of crystal flowing from Calypso's vineyard. Another example comes from the *Epic of Gilgamesh,* which describes the goddess Siduri's vineyard (garden) with bunches of grapes appearing as jewels beautiful to behold, which is reminiscent of the attractive fruit on the tree of knowledge of good and evil:

> *Carnelian bore fruit*
> *Hanging in clusters lovely to look at,*
> *Lapis lazuli bore foliage;*
> *Bore fruit, and was delightful to view.*[151]

Such precious stones are not simply adornment designed to convey glory and power, or the presence of the divine. Mythologically, the idea also is that the jewels, when at the Center, like the other objects associated with the Center, represent and mediate between the three main tiers of the cosmos: They originate from within the earth, appear to us on the earth, and shine like the heavenly bodies, perhaps also like the light of dawn.[152] This is illustrated by sacred *kiskanu* tree in Eridu, which had lapis lazuli (a consummate stellar symbol) as foliage and a crystal root extending down into the *apsu*.[153]

Such imagery of radiance is present in the Eden story in both the precious metals and stones associated with the Pishon river flowing from the Center and also possibly the flaming sword that guards the tree of life and the forbidden fruit that is a delight to Eve's eyes. In doing this J was utilizing traditional imagery of the Center. Let us now look at how these symbols of the Center were developed and exemplified in Mesopotamia and then adapted by J in the Eden story.

THE CENTER AS A SACRED GARDEN IN MESOPOTAMIA

The mythological motifs discussed above and which appear in the Eden story first developed in and can be traced principally to Mesopotamia, some of them dating to Neolithic and Chalcolithic times before Sumerian civilization arose in the late 4th millennium. Originally religion in that early society of small agricultural communities seems to have been largely Goddess-based, with the things most important to people—the earth, crops, other living things and the waters—being viewed as manifestations of the Goddess.[154] Religious life was led by priestesses of the Goddess and her attendants, and it was centered around a sanctuary with a reed enclosure, which had developed from the cow-byre and sheepfold. The sacred enclosure featured a temple mound (or reed hut-temple in the shape of and representing a mountain) conceived of as the cosmic mountain representing earth, heaven and the underworld. (It was this mound which later developed into the ziggurat.) The inside of the mound was thought of as the underworld and the womb of the Goddess, where regeneration occurred. The human settlement that grew up around the sacred precinct was thus grounded in the eternal order, a model that was retained when temples and cities were built.[155] The earliest evidence of these sanctuaries associates them with the goddess Inanna. Her sanctuary is illustrated in the famous late 4th millennium (3300-3000) "Uruk Trough" now at the British Museum (Fig. 11), which depicts her reed hut in the shape of a mountain with plants growing from the roof, and lambs surrounding it.

In this sanctuary was a garden representing the Goddess's bounty. From it were taken the first fruits of the yearly harvest, which were ritually consumed as her body. According to Stephen Langdon, originally the plant earliest associated with the Goddess and her garden was the grape vine, meaning that her garden was a vineyard. Therefore, in Sumer the Goddess was originally known as *Gestin,* which means "Mother Goddess of the (Grape) Vine." After the Goddess became the consort of An, the god of heaven, she became known as *Gestinanna* ("Heavenly Mother Goddess of the Vine"), also Ninanna ("Queen of Heaven"), and eventually Inanna, reflecting the increasing importance of the heavens and sky gods. Thus, her temple precinct in Uruk dating from the late 4th millennium was called "House of Heaven" (*Eanna*).[156] As Albright observed, goddesses such as Gestin/Inanna and Siduri presided over this garden/vineyard as "her rightful estate as goddess of the vine."[157] Other examples from ancient Greece include Calypso's vineyard in *The Odyssey,* the garden of the Hesperides (belonging to Hera), the Earth Goddess's sanctuary at Dodona, and Hebe's cypress grove sanctuary.

Being a Center, the garden sanctuary of the Goddess featured a sacred tree or vine. Thus, in the *Epic of Gilgamesh* the hero beholds the goddess Siduri ensconced in her sanctuary/vineyard that is "fair to behold" and where the grape clusters hang as precious stones (see quotation above). A variation appears in Greek mythology, where Mother Earth gave to Hera the sacred garden of the Hesperides, with its sacred apple tree with immortality giving[158] golden apples, tended by the three Hesperides (the triple-goddess) and guarded by the serpent-dragon Ladon.

Closely associated with the Goddess and the garden sanctuary was the sacred water of life, another archetypal feature of a Center noted above. In Mesopotamia as elsewhere, water was regarded as the fundamental substance from which everything else was created and as generative of life,[159] in particular the crops on which the community depended. Water therefore featured prominently at the sanctuary and in Mesopotamian mythology, religious ritual and art. This meant that there had to be one or more water deities. Originally the goddess Nammu (or later another local goddess) was viewed as the personification and source of the waters and as the creatrix, but over time this changed. In Eridu the priests had a favorite local god, whom they wanted to be lord over earth, the underworld and its waters (instead of any goddesses or Enlil, who had usurped Ki's powers), and therefore named him *En-ki* ("lord of the earth"). Enlil remained supreme, however, so a resolution was reached whereby Enlil made Enki his steward on earth to execute his will. In this way Enki succeeded in assuming some earth powers and functions of the Goddess, most importantly as the water god (see Fig. 12).[160] Nevertheless, various goddesses continued to represent the earth itself. In Eridu, Gestin assumed a role complementing Enki's. She retained her role as patroness of sheep and cattle, but also became important in incantations related to water. As a result, she became known as Nina ("Queen of the Waters") and bore the epithet "Lady of Incantations." She had her own temple located in the quarter of the city named Nina after her.[161]

As described in Chapter 3, the initial archetypal conception of the cosmos as a manifestation of the Goddess began to erode and male deities began to

usurp her province and functions. Previously the Goddess embodied everything, including heaven. But in accordance with the rise of masculine ego
consciousness, sky gods became viewed as the creators of the initially perfect
cosmic order, represented most clearly by the regular, seemingly ideal, workings of the heavens. Consequently, heaven became principally the realm of
the sky god, while the Goddess remained associated with the earth, birth, life
and underworld.

As a result, in Mesopotamia religious life became structured around the
link between heaven and earth, as expressed in the form of sanctuaries,
rituals, myths and mythological symbols. Indeed, as we have seen, the Sumerian word for the universe itself was *an-ki,* which meant "heaven-earth,"
and thus embodied this link. This unity was exemplified by the cosmic or
sacred mountain, where heaven, earth, and the underworld converge, at the
Center of the world, the *axis mundi.* The mountain was begotten by the
primeval sea goddess Nammu, who caused it to emerge from the sea, which
was her body. The mountain was surrounded by the sea, and inside it the
underworld extended down toward the primeval ocean below. It was called
Khursag (or simply Kur);[162] hence a version or aspect of the Mother Earth
Goddess was known as Ninhursag ("lady of the (cosmic) mountain," or "lady
of the land").[163] Under the earth-mountain, but above the primeval ocean,
was also a freshwater deep called the *apsu,* which could rise up and flow onto
the earth; it too originally had feminine connotations.

Mesopotamians thus conceived of the cosmos as having tiered levels of
reality stretching along the *axis mundi* from heaven through the atmosphere
and earth down into the netherworld and the watery abyss. Where a religion
conceives of reality in tiers, it is important for at least some people (shamans,
prophets, heroes, kings, priests) to be able to pass from one tier to another,
which is reflected in myths involving Centers (e.g., Jacob's ladder, Mo-
hammed's Night Journey). These people undergo transformations (enlightenment, rebirth, transcendence) as they move between the tiers (as in initiation
rituals, dreams, and shamanic flights).

Archeology provides clues to how ancient peoples tiered their universes
and how they connected with and moved between the tiers, to the sacred. In
the Paleolithic era humans penetrated the netherworld by entering into caves
and performing rituals there. This was a passive approach in that humans
used what nature afforded. In the Neolithic era, when humans began to build
permanent structures, however, people proactively created sacred space by
building sanctuaries or even their homes as microcosms of the tiered cosmos.
Thus, in the Neolithic Near Eastern settlement of Catalhöyük (in present-day
southeast Turkey) people buried their dead under the floors of their homes,
representing the underworld; they also constructed an *axis mundi* within their
homes, as the entrance (through the roof) looked onto heaven and was accessed by a ladder.[164]

Bronze Age Mesopotamians recreated the cosmic mountain in the form of the ziggurat and its surrounding temple complex, which was viewed as a cosmic lynchpin: the meeting point of the higher and lower orders, between the sacred and the profane, and between man and gods. A ziggurat was built at a holy Center where heaven and earth met (and above the *apsu),* which was called a *Dur-an-ki,* meaning "Bond of Heaven and Earth." This term is not merely figurative, but is derived from critical mythological events. In the Sumerian myth known to us as *The Song of the Hoe* about the origins of the Sumerians, Enlil separated An-Ki into An and Ki, and the cosmic space (atmosphere), which was Enlil, appeared between them, which marked the initiation of creation (analogous to Gen. 1:3-8). Here Enlil installed the axis (pillar) of the world, which was the *Duranki* that connected the now-separated earth and heaven. On this spot Enlil also fashioned and used his hoe to break the ground so that humans, (the Sumerians) could then be generated, growing like plants from the soil (Mother Earth) rather than being created by a god. The place (in this case the site of Inanna's temple in Nippur) became sacred, because humankind emerged from the womb of the earth, so it was called the place "where the flesh sprouts."[165] This was an obvious effort to reconcile the earlier Goddess religion with the emerging notion of Enlil as creator god. The myth presumes that, in order for people to exist fully as humans, they must have access to the divine, for which a *Duranki* is needed. The myth also closely connects the creation of the cosmos to that of humans, as in the Eden story.

In Mesopotamia there were many *Duranki,* including at Eridu, Nippur, Larsa, Sippara and, later, Babylon. Each was conceived of as a cosmic mountain, represented by a ziggurat. This follows an archetypal worldwide pattern of temples representing the Center as a cosmic mountain, famous examples being the temples of Borobudur in Java and Angkor Wat in Cambodia (representing Mt. Meru). In cases where the temple itself did not take the form of a mountain, the same symbolism could be achieved by locating it on a high place, like the Acropolis in Athens. The Temple Mount in Jerusalem also fits this scheme, set atop or near the rock which was thought to reach into the *tehôm* below.

But at the moment of creation there were no cities, temples, kings or priests, so the question for Mesopotamian theologians and mythmakers was how to portray the nature and appearance of the sacred Center of creation at the time. For this purpose they developed several symbolic motifs, the most important of which were the sacred waters, the sacred garden and the sacred tree, which were then incorporated into sanctuary design. These motifs are reflected in the Eden story.

The creation, including the creation of the first humans, had to occur in the place where chaos was originally overcome, which was the spot within the primeval ocean where the cosmos emerged. There is a link between chaos and cosmos (think of the modern cosmological wormhole), and on the earth-ly side this link is the central spot on earth from which the creation arose and spread, the Center. This spot lay over the underwater deep (*apsu*), which rose to the surface and enabled the creation of life on earth, like the rising of the *tehôm* in the Eden story (Gen. 2:6). In early mythology the creation of the earth came from below rather than above, and the place whence it emerged was the holiest place on earth. Naturally any *Duranki* was deemed to be located over the *apsu*. Only from there, and by linking to heaven as well, could the three tiers of the cosmos be united along the *axis mundi*, so that humans could access the divine, both above and below. This unity of the tiers at the *Duranki* is illustrated by the Babylonians' Center, Babylon. It was built upon *bab apsi*, the "gate of the *apsu*," and the city's name meant "gate of the gods."[166] The early name for the city was Tintirki (or Dintira), meaning "the place of the Tree [or Grove] of Life,"[167] which can have the same connota-tion.

The cosmic geography and mythology of such a Center is well illustrated by the original Center of the Sumerians, Eridu, located in the marshes where the Tigris and Euphrates met and mixed with the sea waters of the Arabian (now Persian) Gulf.[168] In a tiered cosmos, marshes are seen as transitional between land and water and therefore are imbued with the sacred, even more so when positioned in an intertidal zone or at the seashore, where the bitter salt water ocean and sweet fresh waters derived from the *apsu* meet and mingle.[169] The earth seemingly rose from the water like the cosmic mountain as silt from the rivers was deposited there, while the luxuriant growth of reeds and other plants in the marshes of the delta gave the impression of life rising spontaneously from the watery deep. (The Nile delta inspired similar Egyptian mythology.) We have already seen this image in *Enuma Elish*, in which Apsu (freshwater deep) and Tiamat (sea waters), viewed as the primal father and mother, "mingled" and set off the process of creation. *Enuma Elish* was modeled on the earlier Sumerian mythology of Eridu, which has many parallels with the Eden story, so it needs to be explained in some detail.

The Sumerians believed that Eridu was some 250,000 years old. It was where the first humans and human civilization arose, the first city in the world, and the residence of humankind's first kings. The opening lines of the Sumerian King List read:

> *When kingship was lowered from heaven,*
> *Kingship was* [first] *in Eridu.*[170]

In the Sumerian flood myth, Eridu is described as one of five antediluvian cities founded by the gods in "pure places" to be "cult centers," and it was given to Enki.[171] Eridu may indeed have been Mesopotamia's first city, with the first settlement dating from around 5400 in the early Ubaid period, some two millennia before the rise of Sumerian civilization proper. A temple to Enki was built there soon after the arrival of the Sumerians. Archeologists also found an uncompleted ziggurat there, which could be an inspiration for the tower of Babel story. In one myth, *Enmerkar and the Lord of Aratta,* when Enki was unable to supplant Enlil as chief deity, he took out his frustration on humankind by confusing its tongues:

> *Harmony-tongued Sumer, the great land of the me of prince-ship, . . .*
> *The whole universe, the people well cared for,*
> *To Enlil in one tongue gave speech.*
> *[But then Enki], the lord defiant, . . .*
> *The lord of Eridu, endowed with wisdom,*
> *Changed the speech in their mouths, put contention into it,*
> *Into the speech of man that [until then] had been one.* [172]

J's story differed in that the confusion of tongues was the result not of a rivalry among gods, but was a punishment for humans overstepping their proper boundaries. [173]

Enlil made Enki steward over the earth, including its waters. For this purpose, Enlil entrusted Enki with the Tablets of Destiny (the *Me*) containing the principles and rules ordering the cosmos and civilized life. Because the center of the world was at the meeting of the waters at the delta of the Persian Gulf, Enki lived there, for which purpose he built in the *apsu* his magnificent silver and lapis lazuli palace, *E-apsu* ("house of the watery deep," also known as the "house of wisdom"). Having done that, Enki created and raised the city Eridu from the *apsu* and made it float over the water like a lofty mountain. [174] The waters below Eridu were thus the substance out of which the earth was created and given its generative potentialities. [175] Enki then filled its fruit-bearing gardens with birds, and the waters abundantly with fish. As the Center of creation, Eridu was also where the first humans were made by the gods, from clay. In an old Sumerian account, Enki calls upon his mother, Nammu (the primeval sea) to "mix the heart of the clay that is over the *apsu*," and recites that "Ninmah [the earth-mother goddess] will work above thee" and that birth goddesses "will stand by thee at thy fashioning." [176]

With the rise of Eridu and other cities together with the institution of kingship, the king was viewed as the earthly builder and guardian of this sacred garden and its sacred tree, and in such sacral role he acquired the title of "gardener," specifically An's (Anu's) gardener. [177] The king was responsible for seeing that water was abundant and that the crops were watered and flourished. In fulfillment of his role, the king-gardener exercised a priestly function, and among the rituals that he (and his priests) performed was pouring libations of the water of life, including over the sacred tree in the garden. [178] Thus, much Mesopotamian iconography depicts kings and/or deities together with imagery of water flowing from the deities or vases, and sprouting vegetation (see Figs. 12, 13, and 14). In the *Adapa* myth, Enki designated the sage Adapa as gardener at Eridu. Among his duties was acting as a priest to carry out religious rites in Eridu's sacred sanctuary, and attending to it daily.[179]

Another important Mesopotamian Center of creation was Dilmun,[180] described in the myth known as *Enki and Ninhursag, a Paradise Myth*.[181] The story begins by portraying Dilmun in idyllic terms:

> *The land Dilmun is pure, the land Dilmun is clean;...*
> *In Dilmun the raven utters no cries,*
> *The ittidu-bird*[182] *utters not the cry of the ittidu-bird,*
> *The lion kills not*
> *The wolf snatches not the lamb,*
> *Unknown is the kid-devouring wild dog,*
> *Unknown is the grain devouring [. . .]*
> *[Unknown] is the . . . widow; . . .*
> *The dove droops not the head,*
> *The sick-eyed says not "I am sick eyed,"*
> *The sick-headed [says] not "I am sick-headed,"*
> *Its old woman [says] not "I am an old woman,"*
> *Its old man [says] not "I am an old man,"*
> *The wailing priest walks not around him,*
> *The singer utters no wail,*
> *By the side of the city he [utters] no lament.*[183]

But like in Eden, initially water was lacking, so the goddess of Dilmun, Ninsikil, pleads with Enki for water, who has the sun god Utu cause it to spring forth from the earth. Enki then fertilizes the land (impregnates goddesses including Ninhursag) with his semen, after which the marshland becomes sacred and Enki swears by the life of Anu, "Let no one walk in the marshland." Dilmun thus becomes a divine garden with fruit-laden trees, vines and other plants, and which has a "gardener." Enki presents fruits to goddesses as he woos and impregnates them. Eventually Ninhursag makes eight plants grow forth, and the curious Enki decides that he must know their fate and their heart, so he eats of each. Ninhursag considers this a mortal sin, so she curses Enki's name and looks upon him with the eye of death. As Enki lies dying, Enlil takes up his cause and with the help of a fox brings Ninhursag back to remove the curse and heal Enki. She places the seated Enki in or by her vulva, and as she inquires about his eight ailing body parts corresponding to the eight plants, she brings into existence eight deities, each of which heals one body part. In each case, the name of the deity sounds like the word for the affected part of Enki's body.[184] They include a goddess who heals his rib, Ninti, meaning both "lady of the rib" and "lady who makes live."[185]

Dilmun is also described as "the place where the sun rises," a sacred mountain abode of the gods which is the final dwelling place of the only mortals that the gods ever let attain immortality, the Noah-like hero of the Sumerian flood myth, Ziusudra (Utnapishtim ("he who saw life") in the Babylonian version) and his wife.[186] In the flood story in the *Epic of Gilgamesh,* after the flood, Enlil, who had brought on the deluge, placed his hands on the foreheads of Utnapishtim and his wife, blessing them after they passed through their seven-day trial, and proclaimed something that Yahweh would never allow:

> *Hitherto Utnapishtim has been but human.*
> *Henceforth Utnapishtim and his wife shall be like unto us gods.*
> *Utnapishtim and his wife shall reside far away, at the mouth of the rivers!*[187]

Gilgamesh aspires to the same and goes on a quest for immortality. He seeks out Utnapishtim, who tells him the secret of a magic plant growing in the watery deep, which when eaten confers eternal life. Gilgamesh dives into the deep and obtains it, but soon afterwards it is snatched away from him by a serpent, which then departs to shed its slough (signifying rejuvenation, suggesting that the serpent ate it). Gilgamesh is left weeping, condemned to mortality.[188]

The above Mesopotamian myths have many motifs in common with those in the Eden Story, including:

- Creation from chaos at a Center
- A lush garden sanctuary at the Center
- An initially dry and infertile earth from which the creation and Center (sanctuary with garden) arise
- The association of precious stones/radiance with the garden's features
- The number four in association with a Center, including directions of the compass, four lands, and four waters
- The association of a goddess with the garden sanctuary and its sacred trees, which are her province (later becoming the province of a male deity)
- A watery deep that rises up in the Center (later the garden sanctuary) and waters the earth, originally associated with a goddess and later with a god
- The formation of the first human(s) from the earth/clay
- The assignment of humans to tend the garden sanctuary as gardeners
- Sacred trees or other plants of abundant fertility in the sanctuary that are attractive to the eyes and which are eaten, with some giving life or even immortality, and at least one connected with the desire for knowledge, which was a sin
- A serpent who deprives the protagonist of eternal life
- A rib story, identified with "the lady who makes live"

We do not argue that J specifically utilized or even knew of all the above-mentioned myths when composing the Eden story, but it is apparent that these motifs existed throughout the biblical world; much of it was archetypal. Therefore, we must explore them in relation to the garden of Eden in order to understand what J was doing.

THE GARDEN OF EDEN AS A CENTER

In order for J's human drama to begin, Yahweh must first create the setting—the garden—so we must begin there, starting with the garden's name. In J's story the name Eden is not restricted to the garden itself, nor does the word "Eden" itself have anything to do with gardens. Rather, J specifies that Yahweh planted the garden *"in"* Eden (Gen. 2:8). Scholars agree that Eden refers to the geographical region where the garden is located rather than to the garden itself.[189]

But what does "Eden" mean? Theories abound. We consider four possibilities, each of which would confer its own shade of meaning on the story. Since J uses Eden as a geographical term, we may begin with a geographical approach, which yields the first two possibilities.

Outside Genesis, the Hebrew Bible refers several times to an actual historical city or region in Mesopotamia called (in English) Eden. Amos 1:5 mentions a place called "Beth Eden,"[190] while both 2 Kings 19:12 and Isaiah 37:12 mention "the people of Eden who were in Tel-assar."[191] Scholars believe that all these references are to Bit-Adini, which was an Aramaean/Neo-Hittite kingdom (city-state) in the 10th and 9th centuries located along the east bank of the Euphrates in northern Mesopotamia. Bit-Adini means "House of Eden," so Adini refers to the unknown Aramaean founder of the royal house that gave its name to the territory. It was a strategic point commanding passage along the Euphrates,[192] and therefore became an object of conquest. It was defeated by Assyria in 878 and again in 856 (more or less when J may have lived, as we have postulated), and later became known as Tel-assar ("Assyrian hill").[193] Bit-Adini then became a launching point for the frequent and ultimately successful Assyrian military campaigns in Syria-Palestine, which brought Assyrian culture and religion in its train. But as seen in Chapter 2, Assyrian power ebbed and flowed, and when it ebbed the Aramaean states (including Bit-Adini) led by Damascus fought the Israelites. Bit-Adini became associated with the threat of *both* Aramaean and Assyrian military power and pagan civilization, which may account for Amos denouncing it:

> *"I will break the bar of Damascus,*
> *and cut off the inhabitants from the Valley of Aven,* [194]
> *and him that holds the scepter from Beth-eden;*

and the people of Syria shall go into exile to Kir," says the Lord.[195]

Thus, the image in the Eden story of a perfect garden of Yahweh arising in the middle of a hostile pagan land fits the idea of Israel being established in pagan Canaan, as well as the historical situation at J's time, since Israel at the time was exposed to military and religious threat from Bit-Adini.[196]

According to a second geographical theory that in the past had been supported by numerous biblical scholars, the name "Eden" is derived from the often-used Sumerian noun *eden/edin,* which in Akkadian became *edinu.*[197] A well-known Sumerian-Akkadian vocabulary (dictionary) equates these Sumerian and Akkadian terms, showing the latter as a loan word from Sumerian.[198] Both words mean an arid "plain" or "steppe," or even "desert,"[199] especially one between two rivers.[200] In Sumer *edin* was commonly used to denote such geographies. J too portrayed Eden as a dry, barren, undeveloped region (a form of chaos), so deriving Eden from the Mesopotamian terms describing such geography would be apt. This certainly fits the mythological image of the garden of Eden as a Center of creation that arose in the middle of formless chaos (the desert).[201]

There is a major difficulty in linking *edin/edinu* with Eden, however, because in Akkadian, the language of Assyria and Babylon, the only attested mention of *edinu* is in the above-mentioned Sumerian-Akkadian dictionary.[202] In all Akkadian texts discovered so far, the real Akkadian word for steppe *(tseru)* is always used rather than the loan word *edinu* (though for *tseru* the Sumerian cuneiform logogram for *edin* is employed). Because *edinu* is not attested in Akkadian texts, there is a large gap in time and geography between the Sumerian *edin* and the biblical Eden that is hard to bridge. Scribal traditions did keep knowledge of Sumerian (and therefore of Sumerian texts)[203] alive in Mesopotamia and Syria at least through the Late Bronze Age,[204] but this trail of evidence so far does not extend into Iron Age Palestine.[205] Thus, we cannot assume that J was aware of either *edin* or *edinu.* For these reasons, more recently scholars have tended to shy away from the earlier idea that Eden is derived from *edin/edinu.*[206] Therefore, while the earlier theory fits well conceptually and is intriguing, the present state of the evidence does not allow us to reach any conclusions one way or the other.

In addition to the two geographical explanations for the meaning of Eden, there are two linguistic explanations, which in our view are related.

According to the first explanation, embraced by an increasing number of scholars, the word Eden denotes a place that is well watered and therefore lush,[207] which is consistent with the idea of perfection at the Center and J's description of the garden, though not with his description of Eden itself. This interpretation is based in part on Ugaritic texts in which a word with the same consonants as the Hebrew *(dn)* denoting moisture, watering the ground, and refreshment, matches the root used in some biblical passages denoting the same.[208] This theory recently received further support by the discovery at Tell Fakherye in Syria of a statue to the Aramaean god Hadad (equivalent of the Canaanite Baal) containing an inscription dedicated to him. It contains the epithet of Hadad, "he who makes the whole world luxuriant," using the verb *'dn* meaning to "make luxuriant."[209] This indeed corresponds to the description in the Eden story where a mist, *'ēd,* comes up from the ground to water it and support the garden's lush vegetation, and from which the four rivers originate to water the world, first and foremost the formerly dry steppe of Eden. Further, since *ēd,* is pronounced virtually the same as the "Ed" *(ēd)* in "Eden," J could have been engaging in wordplay based on assonance.[210] J's giving credit to Yahweh for making the garden and entire earth luxuriant and fertile is key, because it enables Yahweh to assume powers and functions associated with fertility held by competing deities such as Baal and goddesses.

The second and more traditional linguistic explanation of the meaning of "Eden" is that it is a play on words with a Hebrew root signifying delight, enjoyment, pleasure, or wonder, meaning that J had in mind a garden of paradise in that sense.[211] Indeed, it does have a homonymous if not etymological relationship with a West Semitic (Ugaritic) root connoting "delight."[212] Other scholars, however, disagree that Eden was intended to connote delight.[213] But since it seems that J's audience would have recognized the above-mentioned similarity with roots connoting delight, it is clear enough that J made such an allusion. The interesting question is, "Delight in what sense?"

In our view, Eden cannot mean simply a pleasure garden for enjoyment or a paradise in the common meaning of the term; the idea would have been understood in a narrower sense. First, J's portrayal of the life in the garden focuses not on enjoyment or a carefree existence. Rather, Adam, like Adapa, in accordance with the usual Mesopotamian purpose for humans, was tasked to *work* as gardener to till and guard the garden. Second, it would not be in keeping with J's solemn purpose (which included opposing erotic pagan fertility rites) for the Garden in its initial state to be seen primarily as a place for enjoyment.

In light of this, we are left with perhaps three senses in which delight fits the mythology and could have been intended here. The first arises from the fundamental meaning of a Center such as the garden as being an initial state of perfection arising out of chaos (the surrounding Eden) at creation. This can be pleasing and a delight, in a most elevated sense. Second, the notion of delight (or at least pleasantness) may correspond with the above-mentioned idea that Eden connotes a well-watered, luxuriant place, which is how J describes the garden's vegetation (Gen. 2:9). Thus, the name Eden, though originally the arid wasteland (in the Sumerian meaning) in which the garden arose, might have been used to *anticipate* the watering process, much as Eve was called the mother of all the living before she conceived and bore any children. Third, the delight in question could be more focused, referring to the crucial moment in the story when Eve finds the tree of knowledge of good and evil to be a "delight to the eyes" (Gen. 3:6). This aspect would indeed fit with J's opposition to Canaanite veneration of sacred trees and his general focus on the human drama in the story.

THE LOCATION AND SYMBOLISM OF THE GARDEN OF EDEN

Over the years many attempts have been made to identify the location of the garden of Eden, none of them successful.[214] Commentators have sought to locate Eden in places as disparate as the Arabian Peninsula, Iran, Egypt, Missouri and the North Pole. Another leading candidate often advanced is southern Turkey/Armenia, mainly on the basis that the headwaters of the Tigris and Euphrates are located there, although contrary to J's description they do not have the same source.[215]

Such confusion should not be surprising: Endeavors to interpret mythological cosmography in terms of actual earthly geography are conceptually flawed[216] and doomed from the start.[217] As Professor Victor Horowitz once quipped, "I doubt we'll ever find Eden outside the pages of the Bible."[218] Psychologists and mythologists add that we will never find it outside of our mind, because a myth by nature is outside normal reality.[219] Campbell thus explained: "There was no Garden of Eden as a concrete place. To believe so is to misunderstand and misconstrue the metaphoric language of religion. . . . The Garden is a metaphor for the following: our minds."[220] To approach a myth as if it were meant to be realistic is generally unsound; one must look instead at the characteristics and meaning of the mythological imagery itself, utilizing what we have learned from mythological studies, human psychology, and the specifics of the civilization that produced the story. Insofar as J had any geographical message in mind, it was limited to the idea that the fertility of all lands of the earth originated with the rivers of the garden, as a blessing of Yahweh.[221] Further, as noted above, J might have been alluding to Beth Eden as a concern, but this would be a separate, contemporary non-mythological meaning.

Although for such reasons we cannot expect to pinpoint a particular location for the Garden, there is still much in the story's geographical description that sheds light on the possible origin, symbolism and meaning of the story, so it is important to explore the description at least from this perspective. We can begin with J's[222] description in Genesis 2:10-14:

> A river rises in Eden to water the garden, and there it divided and became four rivers. The name of the first is Pishon; it is the one which flows around the whole land of Havilah, where there is gold; and the gold of that land is good;

bdellium and onyx stone are there. The name of the second river is Gihon; it is
the one which flows around the whole land of Cush. And the name of the third
river is Tigris, which flows east of Assyria. And the fourth river is the Euphrates. [223]

J names at least two well-known rivers, the Tigris and Euphrates, as
originating in and flowing through the Garden; he gives other geographic
details indicating a large territory, some of which are familiar to us, and he
associates one river, the Pishon, with sources of precious metals and stones.
From this description, J's use of the word "Eden," and the Mesopotamian
mythology described above and below, the Garden is probably associated
with and is located somewhere in Mesopotamia, but it is perilous to try to be
more specific. [224] Specifying the location with further accuracy is not important to the meaning of the story. It is better to focus on the mythological
symbolism in this description rather than dwell on the location.

From this perspective, it is most useful to examine the waters of the
Garden in connection with the symbolism of the Center. According to the
story, since there had not yet been any rain in the world (Gen. 2:5), the only
possible source of water for the river that divides into four rivers is the only
water yet in existence, namely that rising from within the earth and watering
the surface of the ground generally (Gen. 2:6) and the garden itself (Gen
2:10). [225] In light of that fact, scholars agree that the reference in Genesis 2:10
to the "river" that flows from Eden and divides into four is a reference back
to the flow that rises up from the earth as described in Genesis 2:6. [226] Both
references are understood to refer to the subterranean deep *(tehôm)* rising up
and in some fashion watering the ground, [227] which as we have seen was a
longstanding image in Mesopotamia in association with a Center where the
holy sanctuaries stood.

The water that comes onto the surface of the earth in Genesis 2:6 is
described in Hebrew as an *ēd,* which connotes any flowing water. This word
is derived from the Semitic root *id* or Akkadian *edû,* which in turn comes
from the Sumerian word *id* meaning "river." [228] In Assyria and Babylon *edû*
means the flooding of a river or simply flood, [229] while one Akkadian vocabulary defines the word as "watering of the field." [230] The word *id* was also
used in upper Mesopotamia (Mari and Assyria) as the name of the river god
and guardian of the waters of the deep, Id, who played a cosmogonic role. [231]
The imagery of a deity bringing such waters forth from the earth in order to
water previously barren ground is traditional in Mesopotamia. In *Enki and
Ninhursag,* at Enki's command the moon-god Nanna brought "sweet water
from the earth" to water the fields and provide drink to the inhabitants of
Dilmun, which theretofore had been barren. [232] Recall also the above-mentioned *Feats and Exploits of Ninurta,* in which Ninurta goes to the under-

world to release the waters of the deep so that the barren Tigris valley can become fertile.

The division of this flow of water into four rivers reflects the archetypal symbolism of the Center discussed above and Mesopotamian thinking in particular. In the case of Mesopotamia, the Sumerians divided the world into four regions, which they called *ubdas,* corresponding roughly to the four points of the compass, which were marked off at the time of creation.[233] Likewise, a common Akkadian expression for the world or the whole of Mesopotamia was *kibrat erbetti,* meaning "the borders of the four."[234] The beginning of the *Etana* myth refers to the gods creating the four corners of the world.[235] According to a Sumerian poem, "The four corners of the world grow for Enlil *as a garden.*"[236] Mesopotamian deities are often portrayed showing four streams of water emanating from them (or from vessels that they hold, importantly, at their navel), symbolizing the centrality and completeness of their lordship over the earth and in particular over the waters of the earth. This imagery is captured magnificently in an early second millennium palace mural from the royal palace in Mari. It depicts two standing goddesses surrounded by a paradisiacal garden featuring sacred trees guarded by cherubim. Each goddess holds a vase, from each of which flow four streams of water, from which in turn a tree sprouts (Fig. 13).[237] From Assyria comes a similar image of a god with a skirt symbolizing the cosmic mountain holding a vase from which four streams of water flow (Fig. 14). J meant to convey the same ideas by placing the garden of Eden at the source of the four rivers and by placing the sacred trees in the garden.

The main point here is not that J's description has a Mesopotamian background but to illustrate the fundamental nature of such a sacred garden. The garden of Eden is not simply a paradise in terms of enjoyment or satisfying human needs. Rather, as in Mesopotamia, it is a Center that represents the perfection of the creation and a link with the divine. J brings this point home by contrasting the lush fertility of the Garden with the barrenness of the earth outside it, symbolizing the realm of chaos.[238] Before the Garden was created, there had been no rain, and only some wild shrubs and herbs grew on earth (Gen. 2:5); correspondingly, after the expulsion from the Garden the ground sprouts thorns and thistles and Adam is relegated to eating plants of the field, because Yahweh has cursed the ground (Gen. 3:18). This connotes hardship and pain in the ordinary world,[239] as well as a more profane existence compared to that in the garden. To some extent the perfect creation has been rolled back into chaos. Understanding this symbolism also makes it easier to accept the view of some commentators that the Gihon and Pishon are simply mythological, perhaps included in the narrative in order to bring the number of rivers to four to accord with the usual motif.[240] Indeed, their inclusion allows J more opportunity for wordplay, on the rivers' names. Professor Friedman has observed that Pishon has same three root letters used by J to

refer to the first human becoming "a living being" *(nepeš),* while the name
Gihon may be a play on the Hebrew word for "belly" *(gĕḥōn),* given that as a
result of Yahweh's curse the serpent must go on its belly and that a river's
course is snakelike.[241] The Gihon, of course, is also the name of Jerusalem's
main spring not far from the Temple Mount, a link that would strike J's
audience and present to them an image of the river running (underground)
from the original Garden to Jerusalem and rising up there as the spring. This
(quite literal) connection would have been important because, as discussed
below, the Israelites idealized Jerusalem as a Center and a kind of restoration
of the original paradise.

J's description also echoes the above-mentioned quality of a Center being
associated with radiance and precious stones and metals. J associates the
Pishon with precious stones and gold (Gen. 2:11-12). Later Ezekiel (28:13-
14) associates them with the garden of Eden even more directly:

> *You were in Eden, the garden of God;*
> *every precious stone was your covering,*
> *carnelian, topaz and jasper,*
> *chrysolite, peril and onyx,*
> *sapphire, carbuncle, and emerald;*
> *and wrought in gold were your settings*
> *and your engravings.*
> *On the day you were created*
> *they were prepared.*
> *With an anointed guardian cherub*
> *I placed you;*
> *You were on the holy mountain of God;*
> *in the midst of the stones of fire you walked.*

J utilized the symbolism of the Center, but in his own way to suit his
purposes. He kept most of the Center motifs, including the Center as the
place of creation, as a place of connection with the divine, as the link between chaos and creation, and as where humans can achieve a higher consciousness. Whereas in traditional Canaanite religion humans directly connected with divinity at a Center and most commonly the Goddess represented
that divinity, now Yahweh stood above all the traditional imagery of the
Center and was portrayed as having created it. Humans were not to experience divinity directly via the Center in the traditional way, but instead should
recognize Yahweh as the ultimate source of divinity and enter into a relationship with him. According to the usual symbolism of the Center (and as the
serpent claimed), the tree of knowledge of good and evil represented the *axis
mundi* and as such the link for humans to access divinity. But in the story
Yahweh himself had created this tree, so he (not the Goddess) was associated
with the tree. In the story humans are depicted as being able to communicate

with Yahweh quite apart from any sacred trees. But it is a *relationship* between the deity and humans, not their direct experience of divinity. Thus, in J's story the sacred tree in the garden is only partially functioning according to the archetype. In another key respect, the motif of the Center as mediating between primordial chaos (uroboros) and creation (order), the garden of Eden suited J's purposes very well. Here in the story was cosmos vs. chaos in microcosm, on the human scale: The chaos of Eden outside the garden was intruding into it, represented by the serpent, similar to the demons of the surrounding desert wasteland (chaos) attacking a sanctuary as found in ancient Near Eastern mythology.[242] In the garden appeared various pagan snares[243] for the pious man: a sacred tree, a serpent, and a goddess— just as they appeared in Israel itself, to which J was surely alluding. He focused on how the perfection of the original creation can be lost, namely through humans utilizing traditional ancient Near Eastern elements of the Center that had served as the path to the divine. J knew his audience, and understood that such associations would be familiar and hopefully convincing.

We can now explore how the symbolism of the garden of Eden as the Center was used in the Hebrew Bible in connection with the center of Israelite religion, Jerusalem.

THE EDEN STORY AND JERUSALEM AS A NEW CENTER

The Hebrew Bible tells of how Abraham, from Mesopotamia, at Yahweh's behest rejected his homeland and its religion in order to build a new religion and a homeland for his progeny, the Hebrews. J and the other authors of the Hebrew Bible opposed Mesopotamian culture and religion and portrayed them in a negative light. The Hebrew Bible traces the rise of the new nation and its peculiar religion centered in Jerusalem. J, a Judahite and advocate of Judah's interests, was the ideal person to initiate this epic, and his Eden story serves this purpose well. The original Center, the garden of Eden, was in Mesopotamia, but the first sinners, Mesopotamians, were driven from it and due to their transgression the original Center was lost to humanity. The cosmos reverted to chaos during Noah's flood, but was restored thereafter. A new Center had to be established, through a new type of creation, that of Yahweh's chosen nation.

Except for the garden of Eden, in the Hebrew Bible a Center was symbolized primarily by a sacred cosmic mountain rather than by a garden and sacred trees. Sacred trees reeked of the Mesopotamian and Egyptian sanctuaries and Canaanite high places and were too connected with pagan worship and goddesses. But a mountain as a sacred place to interact with God was both traditional and acceptable. In Ugaritic mythology in particular, El resided and had his tabernacle on the cosmic mountain of the gods (Mt. Zaphon in coastal north Syria), hence his epithet *El-Shaddai* ("El the mountain one"). El's mountain sat atop the "double deep" representing the fresh and salt waters, much as Eridu and any *Duranki* with its mountainous ziggurat was situated above the *apsu*.[244] In the Ugaritic myth where Baal rose to prominence, he too had his palace on Mt. Zaphon.[245] Yahweh simply usurped that cosmic mountain from El/Baal (Isa. 14:13-14).

In the Hebrew Bible, the Center in Canaan including for the Israelites, originally was located in the North rather than in what would become Judah. When Abraham traveled to Canaan to start a new religion, his first stop was its religious center, Shechem, which was located in a mountain pass at the foot of the sacred Mt. Gerizim, which the locals considered the navel of the earth (Judg. 9:36-37). Mt. Tabor, located about 10 miles west of the southern tip of the Sea of Galilee, is mentioned in several places in the Hebrew Bible as a sacred mountain (possibly also a navel of the earth), and there seems to have been a sanctuary there (Deut. 33:19; Judg. 4:6; Ps. 89:13; Jer. 46:18; Hos. 5:1). Similar sacred mountains included Mt. Hermon, the highest point in the entire Levant located in the Lebanon mountains east of Damascus, sometimes called in the Hebrew Bible Mt. Baal Hermon (Judg. 3:3; 1 Chr. 5:23), and Mt. Bashan in the Golan Heights, which Psalm 68:15-16 portrays Yahweh as taking over and dwelling upon, much as he had usurped Mt. Zaphon from El/Baal.[246] As we know, Moses ascended Mount Sinai/Horeb to meet Yahweh there. This imagery recalls the Mesopotamians meeting their deities at ziggurats, but is perhaps more directly traceable to the El/Baal traditions of the North and their sacred mountains (Zaphon and Baal Hermon).

Since J and many later biblical authors were Judahites who sought to elevate the status of Judah and its capital, Jerusalem, it was inevitable that in the Hebrew Bible the Center eventually would shift from the north to Mt. Zion in Jerusalem (particularly after the fall of the North in 722). Various traditions developed associating it with Eden and the Center of the world. Jewish tradition eventually held that Adam and Eve were buried there.[247] It was also there that Abraham was traditionally said to have taken Isaac for sacrifice and encountered the angel who stopped him.[248] Presumably that spot had enjoyed sacred status as a "high place" even before patriarchal times; hence Yahweh was said to have appeared to David there, and David bought the site from the Jebusites (2 Chr. 3:1). 1 Enoch (e.g., Chs. 17, 24-26, 32) also utilized the familiar language and imagery of the Center in reference to both heaven and Jerusalem (precious stones, a sacred tree of wisdom (stated as being the forbidden tree in Genesis), the highest mountain reaching to heaven, mouth of the deep, mouth of the rivers of the earth, cornerstone of the earth, the four winds, etc.).[249] J's making one of the rivers of Eden the Gihon recalls the Gihon spring in Jerusalem at the foot of the Mount, an association that J's audience surely would have made. [250] The Gihon spring served as Jerusalem's main source of water and was where Solomon was proclaimed king and anointed (1 Kings 1:32-46). The Bible refers in many places to the life-giving waters of Zion (Ezek. 47:1-12; Joel 3:18; Zech. 14:8; Isa. 33:20-22). The Gihon was considered to rise from the subterranean deep *(tehôm);* thus, Zion stood over the *tehôm,* down to which its rock reached. [251] Since the *tehôm* was traditionally linked to primordial sea monsters, it would have been under Mt. Zion that Yahweh defeated the sea monster at creation, [252] implying that the cosmos was created there. Yahweh is depicted as enthroned atop the flood (Ps. 29:10). Yahweh's tabernacle is also associated with the Center. Its construction was revealed to Moses on a mountain, and it was eventually placed on Mt. Zion by David. The tabernacle's successor, Solomon's temple complex, also features usual imagery of the Center. [253] The Temple structure itself, like temples in Mesopotamia and elsewhere, evoked the tiered cosmos, a connection between the netherworld through earth up to heaven. [254] It was also decorated with garden imagery (date palms) and cherubim associated with the Center, which could have been intended to evoke the garden of Eden. [255] The large water basin in front of the Temple known as the Bronze Sea replicated the similar basins at Mesopotamian temples that had represented the *apsu*[256] and honored Enki/Ea. [257]

J and later writers consciously linked Jerusalem, Zion and the Temple complex with the garden of Eden. [258] In their minds, Jerusalem as the Center was the replacement of the original, lost paradise, [259] which, of course, is a Myth of the Eternal Return. Therefore, Zion was viewed as having become the most important and fundamental cosmic mountain (Ps. 68:15-16), shunting all other pretenders aside:

> *O mighty mountain, mountain of Bashan;* [260]
> *O many-peaked mountain, mountain of Bashan!*
> *Why look you with envy, O many-peaked mountain,*
> *at the mount which God desired for his abode,*
> *yea, where the Lord will dwell forever?*

Christians then added their own Myth of the Eternal Return to Jerusalem. Since Christ through his death and resurrection was deemed to have redeemed humankind's original sin in Eden, Golgotha, the traditional site of the crucifixion, correspondingly was considered (beginning in the 4th century CE) to have been the site of the garden of Eden, for which reason so many paintings portray Christ on the cross with his blood spilling on Adam's skull. [261] That imagery symbolizes the reversal of original sin at the very place where (in traditional Christian thinking) sin came into the world. [262] Christ's ascension to heaven in Jerusalem, symbolizing the possibility for anyone to reach heaven, cements the place in Christian minds as a Center, from which heaven can be accessed.

For Muslims Jerusalem carries a similar symbolism of the Center. The lives of several Prophets of Islam—Abraham, David, Solomon and Jesus— were associated with the city, for which reason Jerusalem was initially the direction of prayer for Muslims until this was changed to Mecca in 623 CE. Most symbolically, the climax of Muhammad's Night Journey is also associated with Jerusalem, because it is from there than he ascended to the heavenly garden paradise *(Jannat)*, which had seven levels through which Muhammad passed. The eighth and ultimate level, called *Firdaws,* is normally forbidden to anything that has been created, symbolized by its gate being guarded by a sacred lotus tree, the *Sitrat al-Muntaha.* [263] But Muhammad was allowed to pass, and, once inside, he met with earlier prophets including Abraham, Moses and Jesus, and then was escorted by Gabriel to Allah, after which he returned to earth. The Masjid Al-Aqsa mosque on the Mount is the third holiest site in Islam (after Mecca and Medina), and, of course, the Dome of the Rock (the site of the Night Journey) is located at and symbolizes a Center.

THE END OF CREATION

Creation accounts must come to an endpoint, which can only be the world as we know it. By definition, a creation story cannot end with humans still living in an ideal mode of unreality, in a sacred Center. There is inevitably some disappointment, because our world is imperfect. The story must culminate in and explain the profane real world, where people are mortal and must procreate, where giving birth is painful, where evil exists, where unhappy and tragic events occur seemingly for no just reason, and where life is unfair. It was thus inevitable that the humans would leave the garden of Eden. For our purposes, the important questions are how this transition occurs, what reasons are given for its cause, and how thereafter humans should experience the sacred. In the following chapters we trace how J handled these questions from the perspective of the symbols that he utilized in his story: the first human (Adam), the sacred trees, the serpent, and Eve (the Goddess), as well as more minor symbols such as the cherubim and flaming sword, all coming together in the story's climax, the acquisition of the knowledge of good and evil.

Figure 1. Tree goddess emerging from waters to present offering to king of the gods enthroned on the cosmic mountain at the source of two subterranian waters, which flow from under the mountain through serpent or bird heads. Cylinder seal from Mari, ca. 2250-2150. Keel 1998, fig. 7.

Figure 2. Figurine of nurturing goddess, sometimes identified as Asherah as patroness of mothers, with caprids and trees on her thighs and nursing twins. Late Bronze Age, from near Revadim, Israel. Keel 1998, fig. 52.

Figure 3. "Winchester plaque" separately identifying Anat, Astarte, and Qudshu ("The Holy One," an epithet of Asherah). Goddess has Hathor "wig" and holds serpent in her left hand and lotus stem in right. Egyptian, probably 20th Dynasty. Winter 1983, fig. 37.

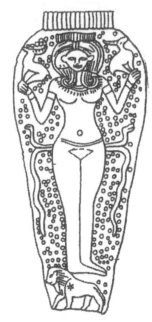

Figure 4. Gold pendant of Asherah with Hathor 'wig," holding caprids and with serpents running behind or through her reproductive area. Minet el-Beida (port of Ugarit), Late Bronze. Negbi 1976, fig. 119.

Figure 5. Palestinian pillar figurines, often identified as Asherah, in tree trunk style. 9th-7th centuries. BibleLandPictures.

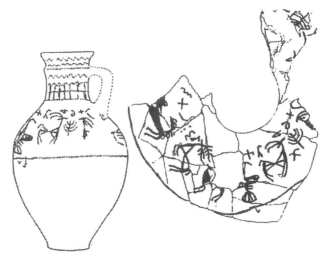

Figure 6. Lachish ewer image of sacred tree representing Asherah flanked by caprids. The word "Elat" ("the Goddess"), an epithet of Asherah, appears over the tree. Lachish, ca. 1220. Keel 1998, fig. 49.

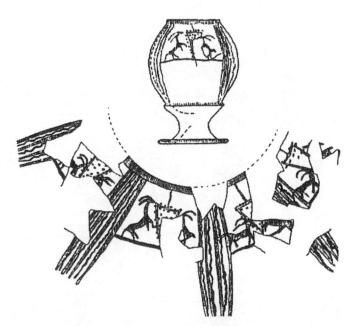

Figure 7. Lachish goblet (found together with ewer in Fig. 6) showing caprids flanking pubic triangle of goddess (Asherah). Lachish, ca. 1220. Keel 1998, fig. 50.

Figure 8. Drawing on Pithos A from Kuntillet Ajrûd showing sacred tree (representing Asherah) on lion and flanked by ibexes. 8th century. Keel 1998, fig. 77.

Figure 9. Taanach cult stand, late 10th century. Asherah appears to be represented on bottom and 3rd levels, most likely Yahweh on 2nd and top levels. Zevit 2001, fig. 4.9.

Figure 10. Drawing on Pithos B from Kuntillet Ajrûd showing procession of worshippers looking skyward, perhaps at the sun. 8th century. Dever 2005, p. 164.

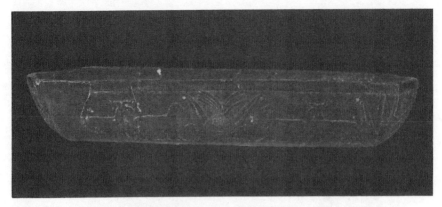

Figure 11. "Uruk trough" depicting Inanna's sanctuary. Late Uruk Period, ca. 3300-3100. © The Trustees of the British Museum.

Figure 12. Detail from cylinder seal depicting Ea/Enki as water god. Akkadian Period, ca. 2300-2200. Black and Green 2003, fig. 60.

Figure 13. Mural from Simri-Lim's palace at Mari showing 4 rivers and sacred trees with cherubs. Ca. 1750. Keel 1998, fig. 8.

Figure 14. Ivory from Assur depicting god with clothing representing cosmic mountain holding vase from which 4 streams emerge and flow in the 4 directions of the compass. Ca. 1500. Keel 1997, fig. 153a.

Figure 15. Mycenaean ring portraying fruit-laden sacred tree atop pillared shrine with sacred pillar inside, with Goddess in center. Her attendant bends the tree toward her, perhaps to partake of the fruit. Evans 1901, fig. 53.

Figure 16. Hellenistic Greek carving from temple of Athena at Priene, Ionian coast, depicting stylized combination of pillar and sacred tree between flanking animals. Meehan 1995, fig. 8.

Figure 17. Scarab portraying "Branch Goddess" with Egyptian headdress holding small trees or branches and with branches in pubic area. Gezer, Middle Bronze IIA. Keel 1998, fig. 26.

Figure 18. Sumerian cylinder seal of Dunghi, King of Ur, holding sacred tree branch caduceus in right hand and serpent staff in left. Ward 1910, fig. 436.

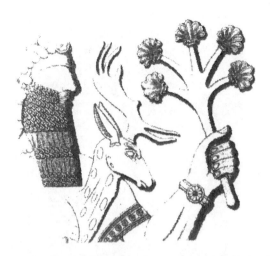

Figure 19. Drawing of detail of relief from throne room of Assyrian King Ashurna-sirpal II (883-859) in Nimrud, depicting genie with palmette of Assyrian sacred tree. Giovino 2007, fig. 52.

Figure 20. Archangel with flowering rod from Book of Kells. Meehan 1995, fig. 15.

Figure 21. Image of sacred tree atop cosmic mountain. Third Dynasty of Ur, ca. 2100-2000. Louvre. © RMN-Grand Palais/Art Resource, NY.

Figure 22. Goddess Artemis in the fork of a tree. Roman coin from Myra. Philpot 1897, fig. 24.

Figure 23. Pendant depicting Hathorlike goddess, probably Asherah, with tree growing from pubic triangle. Ugarit, Late Bronze. Keel 1998, fig. 18.

Figure 24. New Kingdom ushabti box depicting Nut as tree goddess nourishing the deceased and deceased's ba. Note upraised serpent as general guardian of goddess and sacred tree (not against the deceased). Billing 2002, fig. F.3.

Figure 25. Typical Assyrian sacred tree, from Ashurnasirpal II's palace at Nimrud, ca. 865. British Museum. © Werner Forman/Art Resource, NY.

Figure 26. Proto-Aeolic Capital from Megiddo. 10th-8th centuries. Courtesy of the Oriental Institute of the University of Chicago.

Figure 27. Greco-Roman amulet of Yahweh with serpent legs, bearing a shield and the whip of Helios. The combination of bird and serpent symbolizes his encompassing heaven and earth. 2nd-1st century. Goodenough 1953, fig. 1083.

Figure 28. Osiris rising from serpent coil as his enemies disappear. Tomb of Rameses VI, Valley of the Kings, mid-12th century. Piankoff 1954, fig. 27.

Figure 29. Goddess in serpent form holding child also in serpent form. Ur, ca. 4000. National Museum, Baghdad. © Scala/Art Resource, NY.

Figure 30. Libation vase of Sumerian King Gudea from Lagash portraying the god Ningiszida as two serpents twined around a pole or column and inscribed, "Lord of the Tree of Truth." 22nd century. Ward 1910, fig. 368c.

Figure 31. Mesopotamian cylinder seal depicting Ishtar holding serpent caduceus in right hand, serpent scimitar in left, foot resting on lion. Ward 1910, fig. 414.

Figure 32. Scarab from Jericho portraying Egyptian-style uraei as branches and foliage of sacred tree. Ca. 1750-1550. Kenyon 1965, fig. 298.4.

Figure 33. Prometheus and Athena creating man, with serpent and tree behind the goddess. Decharme 1886, fig. 82.

Figure 34. Front view of Figure 35.

Figure 35. Head of shaman depicting serpent rising up top of spine, neck, and head. Pan-shan, China, ca. 3000. Courtesy of Östasiatiska Museum, Stockholm.

Figure 36. Babylonian serpent box shrine with serpents in appliqué on outside and 3 serpents aligned before the deity's (probably Inanna's or Ishtar's) stepped throne. Ca. 2700 Courtesy of Yale Babylonian Collection.

Figure 37. Mesopotamian cylinder seal depicting god and goddess by sacred tree with erect serpent behind goddess. Provenance and date unknown. Ward 1910, fig. 388.

Figure 38. Sumerian cylinder seal depicting Inanna with Dumuzi emerging from under bowed tree. Girsu, ca. 2330-2150. Ward 1910, fig. 399.

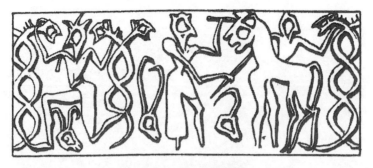

Figure 39. Mesopotamian cylinder seal depicting pairs of serpents entwined around themselves. Ca. 2800-2600. Goff 1963, fig. 703.

Figure 40. Cult standard depicting serpent goddess flanked by 2 serpents, possibly holding them as in the Qedesh/Qudshu models. Hazor, 14th-13th centuries. BibleLandPictures.

Figure 41. Scarab of sacred tree flanked by two Egyptian-style women posed like uraei, with 2 uraei and head of Hathor over treetop, with Egyptian hieroglyph for gold in between. Shechem, Middle Bronze IIB. Keel and Uehlinger 1998, fig. 14a.

Figure 42. Scarab of Hathor head flanked by uraei. Lachish, Late Bronze. Keel and Uehlinger 1998, fig. 75b.

Figure 43. Cult stand with serpents and doves. Beth-Shan, Late Bronze. Courtesy of Penn Museum, image #150820.

Figure 44. Cult stand with serpent and naked man. Beth-Shan, Late Bronze. Courtesy of Penn Museum, image #150175.

Figure 45. Bronze votive serpent with remains of gold leaf on head. Timna, ca. 13th-12th century. BibleLandPictures.

Figure 46. Pottery with serpents in appliqué on and near handle. Late Bronze Palestine. Photo © The Israel Museum, Jerusalem.

Chapter Five

The Creation of Adam

We now reach the centerpiece of Yahweh's creative work, his creation of humanity, at the garden Center, which testifies to the central importance and role that J envisioned for humans and for their relationship with their creator. In this chapter we explore the nature and characteristics of humans as envisioned by J, beginning with Adam.

WAS "ADAM" REALLY IN THE STORY?

A traditional image from the Eden story is that of the first human named Adam. But was this so? It turns out that one of the interesting questions is whether in the garden of Eden (as opposed to after the expulsion) we really have a first man[1] with the proper name Adam. And what does this name mean?

The Hebrew word used for the first human in the Eden story is the masculine noun *ādām,* preceded by the definite article, which means that it is not being used as a proper name. The word simply refers to a member of the human species and means "human," "earthling" or "person." While *ādām* is often translated as "man," actually it can include both men and women and at least until the end of the Eden story represents humanity in general.[2] Only when *ādām* is not preceded by the definite article can it be a proper name,[3] which is the case only in a few places in Genesis. The word is unambiguously first used as a proper name in Genesis 4:25, by R, and not by P until Genesis 5:3,[4] that is, not until after the transgression, just as the name Eve also is not used until after the transgression (before then she is the "woman" or "wife"). As a result, modern scholarly translations of the Eden story tend to use *ādām* as a proper name sparingly, if at all.[5]

125

Where did this name come from and why did J choose it? Here J was engaging in wordplay. Yahweh created the first human from the ground (soil, dust, or clay) and the Hebrew (feminine) noun ădāmâ means "ground,"[6] specifically arable ground. Thus, in a classic example of mythological naming, the 'ādām was named after what he was made from and what would be his divinely decreed destiny, to till the ground as its gardener. This is like saying in English that Yahweh created the "human from humus" or the "earthling from earth."[7] This origin also serves J's point that humans are earthly rather than divine beings. The 'ādām was created from dust and in the end will return to dust (Gen. 3:19).

But there may be further refinements. Some commentators have suggested additional wordplay on the biblical Hebrew word 'ādōm, meaning as a noun "red" and as a verb "to be red," because the soil from which man was made (particularly if clay) typically has a red (or reddish brown) color.[8] The color red is also associated with life-giving blood, as in Aramaic where ădām meant blood.[9] In creation myths blood is often the life-giving agent, as in *Enuma Elish* where humans were formed in part from the blood of the vanquished god Qingu, which animated them. In the burial practices of many cultures, graves are colored with red ochre to evoke the renewal of the life force and rebirth.[10] It has also been suggested that the association with red arises from the reddish color of human skin.[11]

As for the origin of Adam as a proper name, it was not a common Hebrew name in J's time, but it is Semitic. The first and most prominent appearance of the name[12] was as *Adamu* in the Assyrian Khorsabad King List, as the second Assyrian king, who would have ruled late in the third millennium.[13] As seen in Chapter 4, the most likely location for the garden of Eden was in Mesopotamia, where Assyria was located. As also discussed earlier, J was anti-Mesopotamian and was using the Eden story in part as polemic against various Mesopotamian (including Assyrian) religious beliefs, and during J's time Assyria was the main threat to Israel. Adam is often viewed as having a kingly role as the steward of the garden of Eden.[14] One might therefore speculate that J utilized an Assyrian regal name for the first human, who transgressed against Yahweh by embracing religious ideas originating in Mesopotamia.[15]

WHAT HUMANS WERE MADE OF

In the ancient Near East creating humans was a two-stage process: forming the human form from some primal substance and then animating it by imparting some vivifying quality or element (blood, breath of life, etc.),[16] as in *Enuma Elish*. Similarly, in a leading Egyptian myth about the creation of humans, the god Khnum shaped man (also gods, animals, and indeed everything) on a potter's wheel, while a goddess (commonly Hathor, Isis, or Heket (birth goddess and consort of Khnum)) animated the figures by holding an ankh (the symbol of life) to the nostrils or mouth so that the breath of life is inhaled.[17] J's Eden story conformed to this paradigm, whereas P's later account did not. In P's creation story Elohim created by utterance, not by physical manipulation, and all was accomplished in a flash. In P's story both plants and land animals were brought forth from the ground, but humans were not. P did not explain what substance humans are made of, and instead emphasized that we were created in God's image. According to J, however, Yahweh created both man and animals by giving form to preexisting material, and then breathing life into them. Below we investigate the origin and mythological meaning of the first human having been created from the ground, and also the significance of the breath of life.

Creation from Earth

In the Eden story, the ground from which Adam was created was called *ădāmâ*. This meant not dust or dry soil but rather clods of earth[18] which had just been watered by the upflow *(ēd)* from the *tehôm* in the garden and therefore were damp enough to be pressed into a form. Indeed, the Hebrew verb that J uses for this formation process *(yāṣar)* is the one used elsewhere in the Bible to refer to a potter molding clay.[19] J appears to have followed the ancient Near Eastern myths in which deities sculpted the first humans from clay.[20] This motif indeed has a rich history, which sheds important light on what Yahweh was doing when creating Adam.

J's account of humans being made from earth (and into which they will return at death) recalls the earlier mythological tradition of all life, including humans, deriving from Mother Earth.[21] Indeed, in saying that plants likewise came from the watered earth, J effectively accords them the same substance as man and the beasts. Earth has been associated with human birth (and death) in both the ancient world and contemporary pre-literate cultures. Since the human mother was an extension of the Earth Mother, mothers the world over would give birth on the ground.[22] Further, it was common, in many civilizations to lay newborn infants on the ground once they were bathed and swaddled, only after which the father could lift the child from the ground and show his gratitude.[23] When people fell sick, they were placed upon or sometimes buried in the ground; in this way the patient was regenerated free of illness as if reborn, much as in water rituals such as baptism.[24] Likewise, in initiation rituals a candidate is often placed literally or symbolically in the ground in darkness, so that he is resurrected as a new man, via the cosmic Mother. Here we are reminded, for example, of many ancient mysteries (in which initiates are spiritually reborn) being conducted underground (e.g., in the Mithraeum in Mithraic initiations), also of the crucified Christ being placed in the cave tomb and then resurrecting. And of course at death, as seen in Chapter 3, people were returned to the earth, as a means of returning to the mother, into eternal life *(zoe)* in order to be reborn. World mythology has normally connected humans with the earth in the cycle of birth, death, and rebirth.[25]

Creation from moistened earth is an extension of such thinking and a natural deduction. Earth, when watered, gives rise to life, which Yahweh effected by moistening the dirt in the garden, and then sculpting and animating it into life. Myths of creation of man from clay are ubiquitous across cultures around the world.[26] In China the creator goddess Nuwa fashioned the first humans out of clay as the earth emerged from the chaos of a primeval flood.[27] For their part, humans too molded clay figurines of themselves and of anthropomorphic deities, most often in connection with birth and fertility; the archeological record of the ancient Near East and elsewhere is replete with them.

Greece provides many examples of the creation of humans from earth. Plato's *Menexenus* recites how the people of Attica had grown from the ground, associated with the goddess Athena, which gave the Athenians special merit.[28] According to the Pelasgian creation myth, the first man, Pelasgus, sprang spontaneously from the soil of Arcadia.[29] Another Greek myth has the first man spring spontaneously from the soil of Boeotia; his fictitious name, Alalcomeneus, is simply the masculine form of a title of the goddess Athena as guardian of Boeotia.[30] He and others who sprung from the soil were said to be among the first (golden) race of men, subjects of Cronus, who lived before Deucalion's flood in an ideal state without labor, not growing old, and eating only fruits, honey and milk from goats and sheep.[31] In another Greek creation story, known as the Cadmean myth, Cadmus,[32] on the advice of the oracle of Delphi, followed a cow in order to found a town where she lay down. When she did so (in the future Thebes), he intended to sacrifice her but when preparing for that (seeking water) he encountered a dragon guarding the spring, slew it, and sowed its teeth in the soil, from which men grew up, warriors known as the Spartoi ("sown men").[33] Finally and most famously, Prometheus, much like Yahweh, was said to have formed men out of clay, yet it was the goddess, Athena, who breathed life into them.[34] As in J's case, the idea of Prometheus making humans from clay was probably borrowed from Mesopotamia,[35] to which we now turn.

Numerous Mesopotamian myths relate how man rose from earth or was formed from clay, but there was no standard version and each myth had its own twists. One so-called "cosmic" Sumerian account from the city-state of Nippur, describes the original state of the earth much as J did in Genesis 2:4b-5 prior to the upflow *(ēd)* from the deep *(tehôm)* in Eden:

An, Bel, made the heaven resplendent,

Earth was in darkness, the lower world was invisible,
The waters did not flow through the opening [in the earth],
Nothing was produced, on the vast earth the furrow had not been made. [36]

Life, including humans, springs from the earth herself (Ki), usually after being impregnated by heaven (An), her husband. [37] In this way, human creation relates back to the sacred cosmic marriage, some texts stating that humans sprouted on that occasion. Thus, one hymn recites:

When the destinies had been fixed for all that had been engendered [by An],
When An had engendered the year of abundance,
When humans broke through earth's surface like plants, . . . [38]

And in the Sumerian myth *The Song of the Hoe,* Enlil, operating at the Center *(Duranki)* where a pillar connects heaven and earth, digs into the earth with his golden pickax and places in the hole a brick mold (a womb) for humans which contains their seed. The humans then emerge from Mother Earth. Enlil then gives the pickaxe to the human race to enable them to better tend life (crops) in the fields, to serve the gods as gardeners. [39]

A different line of so-called "chthonic" Sumerian myths, from Eridu, has Enki creating man from the clay of the *apsu,* at the Center. Enki, as water god, moistens the clay with the life-giving waters of the *apsu,* which in Sumerian texts concerning fertility is equated with his semen, thus fertilizing the earth much as in the cosmic Nippur accounts. In the Eden story J has Yahweh do much the same by watering the theretofore barren earth with the upflow *(ēd)* from the deep *(tehôm)* at the Center, producing the moist clods of soil from which the first human was formed. In an Eridu myth known as *Enki and Ninmah,* Enki's mother, the primeval sea goddess Nammu, asks Enki to fashion man from "the clay over the abyss [*apsu*]" [40] to serve the gods and free them from laboring for their sustenance. He then has the birth goddess Ninmah fashion several humans from the clay, but they are all defective in one way or another; yet Enki finds roles (destinies) for them. Enki then tries his own hand at creating a human but also produces a defective creature. Unfortunately, we do not know the end of the story because the tablet on which it was written is broken off. [41]

This Eridu line of myths dominates in the later and more famous Akkadian myths such as the *Epic of Gilgamesh,* the Noah-like flood story *Atrahasis,* [42] and *Enuma Elish.* In *Atrahasis* the minor gods revolt under the burden of their labors in serving the higher gods, so they create primitive humans (*lullu*-man) to bear the yoke instead, for which purpose they summon the mother goddess Mami (a version of Ninhursag) to assist Enki/Ea. [43] In a process reminiscent of the birth rituals associated with the ground discussed above, she assembles 14 mother wombs to tread on clay before her, recites an incantation, and then pinches off 14 pieces of clay, laying 7 to her left and 7

to her right with a brick between them. After further operations over 7 days,
7 of the mother wombs bear men and the other 7 women; they are created in
pairs. The humans were animated with life by the blood of one of the rebelling gods, Geshtu-e.[44] Similarly, in *Gilgamesh* the prototype savage *(lullu)*
human, Enkidu, is created by the mother goddess Aruru by pinching off clay
and casting it on the steppe; mankind then returns to clay during the flood.[45]
In *Enuma Elish,* the soil or clay element is nominally skipped over and
everything on earth, including animals and humans, is made from the body of
Tiamat; which is still to say that the substance in question is really the
Mother Goddess, just as in creation from the earth. And as in *Atrahasis,*
humans are animated with life by mixing the substance with blood from the
body of a slain god, in this case Qingu, Tiamat's cohort and consort.

Surely J was aware of the traditional association of soil/clay with the
Earth Goddess, and in typical form he turned it to Yahweh's advantage.[46] He
depicted Yahweh as being in control of the Goddess's functions and usurping
her role, first controlling the flow of the *tehôm* to water the ground and then
manipulating Earth herself (now an inert substance) to create man and other
life. This reflects the Great Reversal, which reversed the earlier mythology
where the Goddess could generate life on her own. In these newer myths, the
earth initially is barren and lifeless, as in Genesis 2:4b-5. It is an object to be
brought under the high god's control so that he can create life. In each case a
god supplies to the earth an animating agent that gives the earth life so it can
become a living human or other form of life: semen, water, blood of a
vanquished god, or, in the case of Yahweh and Adam, the breath of life.[47]
Instead of a goddess animating life on her own or with the help of a god, J
credits Yahweh with the entire process. Yahweh was assuming the function
of the Goddess.

The Breath of Life: Did Adam Have a Soul?

In the ancient Near East the breath of life was often the animating agent of
life for man, animals, and sometimes the land and plants. The Egyptian
Instruction for Merikare (epigraph to Chapter 4) says of humans that god
"made the breath of life for their nostrils." In one Egyptian myth, the god
Amun, the wind, was also, as breath, the source of life for both man and
animals;[48] and as noted above goddesses animated clay humans by holding
an ankh to their nostrils or mouths to confer the breath of life. And Sinuhe
hyperbolically writes to his divine king, "Men live on the breath of your
giving."[49] In the Sumerian myth known as *Cattle and Grain,* deities bring
both humankind and the land itself to life by conferring "breath" upon
them.[50]

In the West we have traditionally thought of this breath of life as our soul,
something of a divine nature that transcends our physical bodies and endures

after our physical death, perhaps giving us an afterlife and rebirth. This notion was encouraged by the KJV, which reads that upon being given the breath of life "man became a living soul" (Gen. 2:7). But the RSV and NRSV do not use that term, preferring instead "living being," nor do other modern scholarly translations refer to a soul. So what exactly did J have Yahweh confer on humans? Was it a real soul or merely an animating force that brings us (and other living beings) physically alive?

Actually, on this question the Old Testament is quite clear, and scholarly opinion too is united: The breath of life is not a divine quality, and in ancient Israelite religion man was not endowed with a soul and had no afterlife in the sense that modern humans understand it. [51] In the Eden story, the Hebrew term for what the KJV called a "living soul" is *nepeš ḥayyâ,* and exists in both humans (Gen. 2:7) and animals (2:19); a dead person was merely a dead *nepeš.* [52] Like humans, animals were formed from the ground *(ădāmâ)* (2:19), and animals too had the breath of life (Gen. 7:22 (J); also 6:17 (P); 7:15 (P)). Thus, in J's mind, particularly since Yahweh thought that an animal might be a suitable mate for Adam, humans and animals did not differ much in their essential natures (at least before humans acquired the knowledge of good and evil), which among other things implies that humans were not originally immortal and makes more problematic the notion of a tragic "fall" in the Eden story. [53]

The Eden story in all aspects reflects this understanding of the human constitution. This is indeed the general view in Israelite religion, according to which the dead did not ascend to heaven but descended to the gloom of a netherworld called *Sheol.* The Israelite view of death is well summarized in Job 7:7-10:

> *Remember that my life is a breath;*
> *my eye will never again see good.*
> *The eye of him who sees me will behold me no more;*
> *While thy eyes are upon me, I shall be gone.*
> *As the cloud fades and vanishes,*
> *So he who goes down to Sheol does not come up;*
> *He returns no more to his house,*
> *Nor does his place know him any more.*

Ecclesiastes 3:19-20 acknowledges that humans desire an afterlife, but rejects the notion:

> For the fate of the sons of men and the fate of beasts is the same; as one dies, so dies the other. They all have the same breath, and man has no advantage over the beasts; for all is vanity. All go to one place; all are from the dust, and all turn to dust again.

When J had Yahweh tell Adam that he was created from dust and to dust he shall return, he meant it literally.

As mentioned in Ecclesiastes above, humans are on par with the animals in sharing the breath of life. In the Eden story, animals too are made from the ground; J does not specify that Yahweh gave them the breath of life but this can be assumed.[54] Later, in the flood story (Gen. 7:21-22), J confirms this, however, stating that man and animals are equally endowed with the breath of life: "And all flesh died that moved upon the earth, birds, cattle, beasts, all swarming creatures that swarm upon the earth, and every man; everything on the dry land in whose nostrils was the breath of life died." This follows logically from the Eden story: Since the animals are also formed from the ground, it is fitting that they too be brought to life with the same animating agent. Similarly, in his creation story (Gen. 1:30), P says that both animals and humans have the breath of life, although he does not describe how they acquired it.

This understanding is in line with traditional Mesopotamian and Canaanite beliefs about the nature of human life. For example, in the Sumerian deluge myth the hero Zisudra is granted eternal life via the "breath eternal," but apparently not a soul or full divinity.[55] In *Gilgamesh,* the plant that will rejuvenate Gilgamesh (but not make him immortal) is described as the plant "whereby a man may regain his life's breath."[56] In light of this common understanding of humans having no soul, it is not surprising that Israelite funerary practices were essentially the same as elsewhere in Canaan.[57]

Why did Israelite religion not conceive of an immortal soul? To begin with, we must realize that except in Egypt[58] no one had yet conceived of such an idea, so in J's time there was no competing idea to deny. The idea of a soul in our traditional understanding first arose only much later, under Greek influence.[59] Thus, in the Bible it is first hinted at in Daniel 12:1-3 (written in the Hellenistic era around 165) and in the (also Hellenistic) apocryphal Wisdom of Solomon (3:1-3; 9:15). The idea was later embraced by Christianity, beginning in some New Testament passages (e.g., Luke 12:4; 1 Peter 1:9). Second, having a soul would have entailed a divine quality that brought humans too close to the gods, which J too did not want. Instead, as stated in Psalm 115:16-17 in the epigraph to this chapter, heaven was exclusively the realm of Yahweh, while man was confined to earth.[60] Indeed, the absence of divinity in humans may actually help explain Adam and Eve's godlike aspirations and the nature of their transgression. Lacking divinity, they want some. Third, in order to claim the all-encompassing supremacy of Yahweh in all matters divine, it was necessary to suppress the popular cults of the dead in folk religion.[61]

Although humans enjoy no divine status simply by being endowed with the breath of life, it is nevertheless clear from the Eden story that humans enjoy a more elevated status than the animals. This can be seen from Adam not finding a suitable companion from among the animals and from the fact that Adam is given the power to name things, including the animals, and is assigned the destiny of tending the garden. Let us now focus on these differentiating qualities.

THE POWER TO NAME

In the ancient Near East, naming creations was a power and privilege of creator-gods. Naming was an essential part of the creation process that assigned functions to earthly creations and decreed their destinies. Until something was named, its creation was incomplete and it did not fully exist. J followed this traditional approach in the Eden story. Yahweh's calling the first human the "earthling" signified the ground from which he was formed and to which he will return upon death, Adam's role as a gardener, and humankind's close connection with the soil and agriculture.

To some extent the gods accorded humans powers of creation, including the power to name certain things. Thus, in the Mesopotamian *Adapa* myth, the first model of man, Adapa, was given wisdom and the power to name, and was credited with originating all nouns in human speech. In the Eden story too, Yahweh gave Adam the authority to name his potential partners (Gen. 2:19), first the animals and then the female human. At first he named the female simply "woman" *(iššâ)* because she was derived from the man *(iš)* (Gen. 2:23). After the transgression, Adam named her a second time, as Eve, because she would be mother of all the living (Gen. 3:20), to signify the fertility that she was about to be granted by Yahweh and a woman's role as mother. To this extent he had a divine prerogative and participated in creation. The power to name these particular creatures also accorded Adam dominion over them.[62]

ADAM AS THE GARDENER

Yahweh put the first human in the garden of Eden "to till and keep it." In this way, the human was given his destiny and function, according to the usual ancient Near Eastern formula. This was all J had to say in the story about the purpose of this human's life. One may wonder why, in such a spiritual book as the Bible, the human was given such a menial existence, especially in a paradisiacal Center,[63] and where this idea came from. For the answer we must once again look to Mesopotamian mythological traditions.[64]

According to Mesopotamian religion (particularly once gods became dominant over the Goddess) humans were created to serve the gods, to relieve them of the menial tasks necessary to provide food, shelter, clothing, and other necessities. Before that, the greater gods had created lesser gods to do this. Most of the work, and the hardest, involved digging ditches and canals to irrigate the fields, and other agricultural work.[65] Eventually the lower gods complained to the greater gods, and the solution was to create humans to perform these tasks instead. According to the *Atrahasis* myth, the lower gods revolted in order to effect this change.[66] Similarly, according to the Sumerian *Cattle and Grain* myth, the higher gods (the Annunaki[67]) had created lesser gods of cattle and of grain and charged them with providing food, but the higher gods found their products unusable, so man was created to produce them instead:[68]

> *The Anunnaki of the Dulkug[69] eat, but remain unsated;*
> *In their pure sheepfolds milk, . . . and good things,*
> *The Anunnaki of the Dulkug drink, but remain unsated;*
> *For the sake of the good things in their pure sheepfolds,*
> *Man was given breath.[70]*

In ancient Mesopotamia, one important way to serve the deities was by attending to their holy sanctuaries. As seen in Chapter 4, these sanctuaries, originally those of the Goddess, first arose in sheepfolds and had sacred gardens around them, the first fruits of which were dedicated to the Goddess. In sacred marriage ceremonies at the sanctuaries, the term "gardener" was the epithet given to males (eventually kings) who played the role of the son-lover.[71] A possible example was Sargon I, who was said to be the son of a high priestess and a gardener,[72] and became a royal gardener himself before becoming king, in which role, he said, "Ishtar granted me her love."[73] In the Sumerian myth known as *Enki and Ninhursag, a Paradise Myth,* when Enki brings water to Dilmun, a gardener, who until then had suffered in the dust, burst into joy and embraced Enki, and at Enki's request brought to Enki the resulting crops (apples, cucumbers, and grapes). Thus supplied, Enki himself courted the goddess Uttu, claiming to be a gardener himself, giving her the produce, and then taking his joy of her.[74] And in the *Adapa* myth, the first man, Adapa, tended the holy sanctuary (including its garden with sacred tree) in Eridu and had a priestly role. But unlike the earlier gardeners he served not the Goddess but Enki and other the gods. The king was regarded as the chief tenant farmer, meaning only that he was chief in serving the gods and charged with organizing his people (essentially slaves) to do the same.[75]

J's placing Adam in Yahweh's garden sanctuary to till and keep the garden derives from this long tradition.[76] But, as usual, J changed the traditional motif for his own purposes. Whereas in Mesopotamia the cosmos functioned for the benefit of the gods, in J's story (as well as P's) the cosmos functions for and in relation to human. J portrays Yahweh as self-sufficient, so unlike in Mesopotamia humans are not needed to provide necessities to the gods. In J there are no images of lesser deities or humans digging irrigation canals; to the contrary, Yahweh himself provides water from the *tehom* to make the land lush. And the garden provides food for humans rather than humans providing its harvest to the gods.

But the Eden story resembles the Mesopotamian myths in that agricultural activity is divinely assigned to humans from the moment of creation.[77] Here too, in order for the creation to be satisfactory, complete, and perfect there had to be humans to till the ground.[78] That the purpose of humans is to engage in agriculture and eat its produce becomes clearer as Adam and Eve are expelled from the garden. Adam, named after the soil, is sent forth from the garden of Eden "to till the ground from which he was taken" and is to eat the plants of the field and bread all of the days of his life (Gen. 3:17-19, 23). Doing so now will simply be more difficult than in the garden.[79]

J is not claiming, however, that agriculture is humankind's only legitimate activity. His story is consistent with the broader idea that humans must perform some work or other, and that what matters is their attitude toward their work and how this places humans in their relationship to Yahweh.[80] This becomes evident in J's story of Cain and Abel, in which Yahweh prefers Abel's offering of the choicest parts of his lambs to Cain's offering of the fruits of the ground. In that story J is not saying that farming and the fruits of the ground are inherently inferior to animal husbandry; rather, Cain rebelled against Yahweh in his attitude toward his work and to God.[81] Unlike in the Eden story, here Yahweh is defending rather than cursing the ground, and it is the ground that curses Cain (Gen. 4:10-12): "The voice of your brother's blood is crying to me from the ground. And now you are cursed *from the ground,* which has opened its mouth to receive your brother's blood. When you till the ground, it shall no longer yield to you its strength." Cain then grieves to Yahweh (Gen. 4:14), "Behold, thou hast driven me this day away from the ground." Instead of continuing to farm, he becomes a wanderer and his descendants learn other, non-agricultural professions (Gen. 4:12-22).

Adam's assignment to till and keep the garden, however, should not be thought of simply as agricultural activity; there is a deeper meaning here that goes back to earlier myths. As seen in Chapter 4, to settle and till new (especially desert) soil, and especially to irrigate it, was a new act of creation, establishing order from something formless and then maintaining it against threats of chaos. In this case, Yahweh set up the garden (order) in the middle of a desert (chaos) and handed off to humans the task of tending and keeping it. This task was farming only at a superficial level. Mythologically speaking, the task of gardening signified maintaining the perfect creation, preserving order and not letting chaos into that ideal world, a heavy responsibility similar to God's charge to humans in Genesis 1:28. To an important degree this repeats the deity's acts of creation.[82] Understanding "tending the garden" as a metaphor for maintaining the orderly creation thus sets up the climax of the story, because this is precisely where the humans failed, letting in chaos symbolized by the serpent, who gained their ear, rather than obeying Yahweh's command. When they were expelled into a more chaotic world, humans continually failed to obey Yahweh, leading ultimately to the flood. When the future flood hero was born, his father Lemech indicated his destiny by naming him Noah (connoting rest, respite, comfort), saying, "This one will console us from our labor and from our hands' suffering from the ground, which Yahweh has cursed."[83] When the flood was over, Yahweh removed the curse from the ground, and Noah settled down as a tiller of the soil, planting a vineyard (Gen. 8:21; 9:20).

This relationship between humans and the earth and their destiny to practice agriculture become important in the epic history of Yahweh's chosen people. In the Eden story, Yahweh curses the ground and makes the earth outside the garden difficult to farm. Then in the Cain and Abel story the ground curses Cain the farmer, who becomes a wanderer and whose descendants establish other professions. Human alienation from earth reaches a climax in the flood story. In the Hebrew Bible, the Hebrews are essentially nomads until they arrive in the Promised Land, where Yahweh has made the land friendly and fertile and the people can settle down to farming.

J'S HUMANS AND THE DIVINE

We can now synthesize and summarize several of the ideas from ancient Near Eastern mythology which we have been discussing and which underlie J's thinking and his story. Before the rise of kingship in Mesopotamian civilization, time was viewed as cyclical, in keeping with the lunar and solar cycles, the rhythm of seasons, and the cycle of life, death and rebirth in all living things. When time was cyclical there was no need for a fundamental creation or a creator god separate from nature. The world was as it always had been, divine in and of itself. Humans were an emanation of the divine, *bios* during in earthly life, and in death returning to eternal life *(zoe)* in Mother Earth, the source of rebirth. The rise of the high god, linear time, and the institution of kingship changed all this. Now there was an initial creation in which earthly time began, typified as bringing order and form out of chaos, all of which occurred at the Center. Under this conception, the creation was typically a violent affair with the high god emerging victorious over chaos (typically represented by a female deity or force), after which the earth remained a stage for ongoing tension between chaos and order, the divine and the human (material). The created world was not divine, including humans, who were not immortal in any sense. Living things were made of inert substance though animated by the gods. Humans were created from the ground as the high god's tenant farmers, to serve and provide for him in unremitting toil. The king, not divine either, was only chief of the human servants, directly accountable to the high god. In official Bronze Age religion the idea was no longer human *identity* with and *partaking* of the divine, but a *relationship* with the divine, now represented as the high god, and that relationship consisted in serving and obeying that god.

J's conception of humans as reflected in the Eden story fits largely within this newer framework. There was a beginning to time and a creation by the high god, in which he brought order out of chaos at the Center. Humans are created by the high god from the ground, which contrary to older tradition had no life until Yahweh conferred it upon them. Humans are to till the soil, maintain and further other aspects of the creation, and obey the high god's commands, entering into a covenant relationship with the high god. Of course, the initial existence of humans in the garden of Eden is more cheerful than the dreary human condition depicted in Mesopotamian myths. On the other hand, in the Mesopotamian myths human yearnings for divinity were only frustrated rather than punished.[84] J turned this motif into an etiological myth in which humans were condemned to a more dreary existence in the real world precisely because they sought to connect with divinity when Yahweh had commanded not to do so. The story's ending clearly established the boundary between humans and the divine, as J desired. As Professor Wright observed, "ever since the expulsion of Adam and Eve from the garden of Eden, God and humans have been separated: the divine retreated to the heavens and humans scattered across the face of the earth."[85] We must bear this very point of J in mind when considering any putative "alienation" of humans from God arising from the transgression.

The divine powers at stake in the Eden story were represented by the sacred trees in the garden as well as by the serpent, so let us now turn to these important symbols.

Chapter Six

The Sacred Trees, the Cherubim, and the Flaming Sword

Which is the tree, which is the forest, from which they have fashioned Heaven and Earth, stationary, undecaying, and giving protection to the deities?
—The Rig Veda [1]

I am the vine, you are the branches. He who abides in me, and I in him, he it is that bears much fruit, for apart from me you can do nothing.
—Jesus Christ, John 15:5

Here feel we but the penalty of Adam,
The seasons' difference, as the icy fang
And churlish chiding of the winter's wind,
Which, when it bites and blows upon my body,
Even till I shrink with cold, I smile and say
"This is no flattery: these are counsellors
That feelingly persuade me what I am."
—Shakespeare, *As You Like It*, [2] of the trees in the Arden Forest

Student: What is the meaning of Zen?
Master: The oak tree in the garden.

—Zen Dialogue

The opening and climactic scenes of the Eden story are framed by sacred trees with extraordinary powers that are keys to the story's meaning. One tree, by or in which the serpent lurks, confers godlike knowledge of good and evil; Yahweh forbids Adam and Eve to eat from it, yet it gives Adam and Eve wisdom. The other tree represents the unattainable goal of godlike immortality, becomes a symbol of Yahweh, and is guarded by his trademark cherubim and a flaming sword. These symbols must have been familiar to J's

139

audience, which is why they are in the story. In order to understand how J utilized and reworked this symbolism, we must first examine what such trees generally symbolized in the biblical world.

THE SYMBOLISM OF SACRED TREES AND PILLARS

In the ancient polytheistic world, where humans viewed nature as charged with the divine, trees held a special place, and naturally so. They are the largest and tallest living things on earth. Their branches rise through the air toward the heavens, while their roots reach into the earth towards the under-world. In the wind their limbs sway and leaves rustle, as if animated by divinity and communicating its oracles. They attract lightning, channeling the fire and power of the Thunderer to earth. Their wood burns, turning into fire—divine energy, as in the burning bush of Moses. We build from them our homes, holy sanctuaries and coffins (or burn our dead on pyres of their wood). Unlike most plants and animals, they outlive humans and seem eternal, wise, and venerable. In step with the seasons, they wither in the cold months when life retreats but eternally renew themselves in the spring, when their sap rises and runs like water, milk, or blood;[3] evergreens remain green in the winter, always retaining life. Trees embody the cyclical regeneration of transient life (*bios*) from eternal life (*zoe*). Indeed, trees teem with life; birds and animals make their homes in them. Many bear fruit and nuts for us to eat, and thus nourish us, thought the ancients, with the body of the divine.

So it was only natural that trees have been considered sacred, have been venerated, and became an important part of mythology and religion the world over. Connecting earth, heaven and the underworld, and encompassing the traditional elements (earth, air, fire and water), trees have represented life, renewal, rebirth, immortality, and unity in the cosmos, and have served as a connection with the divine above and below. As such, the tree symbolizes the *mode of being* of the cosmos.[4] "The idea of referring to the form of a tree the apparent conformation of the universe," wrote Count d'Alviella, "is one of the most natural methods of reasoning which can occur."[5] Referring to the numerous myths worldwide in which sacred trees mean similar things, he observed that "there is not, in all these tales, a single peculiarity whose presence cannot be connected with the most ordinary processes of mythical reasoning."[6] Trees became stylized as, morphed into, or were equated with a multitude of similar symbols, including columns/pillars, obelisks, ladders, stairways, Maypoles, asherahs, branches, scepters, the caduceus and other staffs, the *omphalos*, the umbilical cord, cones, cosmic mountains, the meno-rah, and the cross.[7]

It is no accident that J placed the sacred trees in the *middle* of the garden (Gen. 2:9). This was inevitable, as it is archetypal symbolism of sacred trees.[8] The sacred tree was the most essential and central feature of a holy sanctuary or garden at a Center, the garden or sanctuary being its precinct.[9] As such, it represents the *axis mundi* that links people with divinity, both above and below. It does so by spanning the three planes of the cosmos (heaven, earth and the underworld),[10] as in the case of the Norse World Tree, Yggdrasil.[11] The planes above and below a sacred tree are often symbolized respectively by an eagle or other bird perched on its crown and a serpent coiled at its base.[12] The image of a bird atop a pole or pillar was also common and carried the same association with the heavenly realm.[13]

In respect of the heavenly plane, the ancients observed that the celestial bodies revolved around a central axis passing through the Pole Star,[14] which came to be symbolized as a tree or pillar. This idea comes from the ancients' experience that axial motion requires a shaft, such as an axle of a wheel, the shaft on a potter's wheel, or the distaff on a spindle whorl.[15] Thus, some peoples, including the Phoenicians, envisioned the cosmos as a kind of tent with a central pole, around which the heavenly bodies embroidered on the fabric revolved.[16] A sacred tree was often depicted with a star or sun-disk (often winged) above or atop it;[17] hence the star atop our Christmas tree. Some peoples built their homes (sometimes just tents or yurts) with poles or tree trunks in their center oriented toward the Pole Star.[18] In fact, our words for oak tree and the Pole Star have a common etymology.[19]

Because of these meanings, sacred trees and their derivative form of the pillar/column had an "architectural" function in cosmic geography, serving to hold up the heavens.[20] Thus, the Egyptians thought that the heavens were held up by four pillars located at the four directions of the compass, represented by four deities known as the "sons of Horus"; heaven itself was sometimes called the place of the four pillars.[21] Homer wrote in the *Odyssey* that Atlas held the pillars which kept the earth and the sky apart.[22] According to 1 Samuel 2:8, pillars in the underworld support the earth:

> *For the pillars of the earth are the Lord's,*
> *and on them he has set the world.*[23]

The original sanctity of the tree trunk from which the pillars in temples were actually or figuratively hewn[24] enhanced the holiness of the sanctuary.[25] As stylized trees, pillars and columns likewise symbolize the *axis mundi* and facilitate access to the divine, which explains why ancient temples featured columns/pillars so prominently in their architecture, so as to represent the temple as a Center. As seen in Chapter 4, the major Mesopotamian temples were located at a *Duranki* ("bond between heaven and earth"). Eric Burrows explained that such a temple was "a lofty column, stretching up to heaven and down to the underworld—the vertical bond of the world."[26] Thus, in the Mesopotamian creation poem *The Song of the Hoe* (quoted in

Chapter 4), Enlil first separated heaven and earth and then set up the *Duranki* connecting them. In the architecture of the ancient Near East this idea was embodied through columns, which connected the base of the temple building, conceived of as the earth and standing over the underworld,[27] to its ceiling, representing the heavens, the realm of the gods.[28] The columns of Jachin and Boaz before the Jerusalem Temple and similar columns before other temples in Syria seem to have embodied the same idea.[29] To emphasize the connection with heaven, in some ancient (especially Greek) temples, the cella was open to the sky. This was naturally the case at sanctuaries at Palestinian high places, where the effect of reaching toward heaven was enhanced by pillars and asherahs.

In such architecture the symbolism was often accented by including foliage on the capitals of columns, as in the Egyptian lotus and papyrus capitals, the flowering *djed* pillar in Egypt symbolizing resurrection (after that of Osiris), the proto-Aeolian capitals that flourished in Syria and Palestine during J's time, and in Greek Corinthian capitals. A more direct variation, in iconography rather than architecture, was to mix pillar and tree, as in Mycenaean seals portraying sacred trees growing from pillared shrines (Fig. 15), and in Celtic art depicting pillars bursting into foliage. A variation was to have the pillar both grow out of foliage and sprout foliage at its top, as in an ancient Greek carving from Priene (Fig. 16). A miniature version of the tree was hand-held, in the form of a branch or branching scepter or wand having life or other powers, as in Sumerian seals (Fig. 18), Assyrian art (Fig. 19),[30] and later in Celtic art,[31] most famously in the Irish *Book of Kells* (Fig. 20). Here one is reminded of the asherah's mediating function.

In comparison to trees and wooden poles, which eventually rot, stone pillars add an element of permanence and indestructibility, symbolizing the eternal in the face of change, *zoe* vs. *bios*. Perhaps that is the significance of the small trees growing from atop stone pillars in Mycenaean art. The combination of pillars and asherahs at Syro-Palestinian high places may have had a similar complimentary meaning, expressing eternal life in which humans during their lifetimes can partake.[32] The permanency symbolized by stone is also why a stone stele or pillar was used to memorialize important events, including in the Hebrew Bible. Thus, Joshua set up a great stone to mark the covenant and statutes made with the people at Shechem (Josh. 24:25-26) and a stone circle to commemorate the crossing of the Jordan (Josh. 4); Jacob set up a pillar at Bethel after his dream (Gen. 28:18-22); and Samuel set up the pillar Ebenezer ("Stone of Help") to commemorate a victory over the Philistines (1 Sam. 7:12).

The World Tree or pillar is associated with the Cosmic Mountain and symbolically is identical to it, both representing all planes of the cosmic axis,[33] so the two are often combined or interchanged in myth and iconography. Thus, a Mesopotamian vase from about 2300 depicts a sacred tree atop the cosmic mountain (Fig. 21), while Prometheus was depicted interchange-ably as bound to a pillar or a mountain.[34] In India the paradisiacal garden of Indra was said to be located atop Mt. Meru. That garden had magical trees, the chief of which was the paridjata, which had a flower that preserved its freshness all year, except in the hands of the sinful when it would lose its splendor;[35] like J's forbidden tree, it was a test of virtue. The *omphalos*, meaning "navel" (of the earth, or sea), carried a similar meaning. An *ompha-los* was a cone-shaped mound commonly located on graves or, as in the case of Delphi, at oracles, or at temples, such as at Eleusis and at Aphrodite's temple at Paphos. Originally it was associated with a goddess,[36] and marked an axis through which the spirit of the deceased, a priest/priestess or worship-per, or (at Delphi) the Pythoness could connect to a different cosmic plane. Since the *omphalos* was a navel, the axis was often conceived of as an umbilical cord (or string, or rope) that connects the planes and along which one would travel.[37] The omphalos serves a function similar to trees and pillars, and is often linked with them.[38] Thus, adjacent to the cleft and om-phalos at Delphi stood a laurel tree;[39] other ancient omphali (or cones) are also depicted together with sacred trees, amongst columns, or within col-umned temples.[40] For this reason the Greek poet Pindar called the Delphic oracle "the central navel [*omphalos*] of the fair tree-clad mother," meaning Gaia, Earth.[41]

As we saw in Chapter 4, the Center is archetypically associated with a water source that brings life. Since the sacred tree is the centerpiece of the Center, it too has an essential association with water, which of course enables it to live.[42] Thus, in Mesopotamia sacred trees were located at the Center over the *apsu* and were watered with its waters of life, while in ancient Egypt, similarly the sacred *ished* tree grew from or by a spring or pool representing the primeval waters. All three roots of Yggdrasil reached down to separate springs, providing it sustenance.[43] This and other motifs of sacred trees are elegantly combined in a Minusinsk Tatar poem:

> *Piercing twelve heavens*
> *On the summit of a mountain*
> *A birch in the misty depths of air.*
> *Golden are the birch's leaves,*
> *Golden its bark,*
> *In the ground at its foot a basin*
> *Full of the water of life.*[44]

This motif is seen in the garden of Eden as well, where the water from the deep *(tehôm)* made its vegetation (including the sacred trees) and Adam himself possible, all of which was generally lacking in the barren steppe of Eden outside the garden.

Sacred trees were not merely infused with the divine like the rest of nature but had a special transcendental status: They were regarded as more highly and permanently charged with divinity.[45] The ideas that trees connect with the divine and that humans and the deity can communicate (both ways) through trees were often taken a step further, such that the sacred tree (or equivalent symbol) was regarded as the abode (momentary or permanent) of an indwelling deity. This idea also makes the tree an ideal medium for a theophany, as in the case of the burning bush of Moses and the appearance of Yahweh to Abraham under the venerable oak at Mamre (Gen. 18:1-33). Trees were also thought to draw on the divine through their roots, which connected to the underworld where departed spirits resided and wisdom and knowledge of the future were vested.[46] Sometimes the trees themselves were deified. The Celtic Druids took such veneration to the fullest extent we know of.

Special trees were therefore regarded as oracles through which a divinity communicated, as vehicles of divine knowledge and wisdom. Priests, priestesses, and other adept diviners read the meanings and messages hidden in the wind rustling through their leaves, birds roosting in their limbs, or hangings placed on them. Thus, in the story of Jason and the Argonauts, Jason incorporated into his ship the *Argos* a piece of the oracular oak at Dodona to ensure that he and the other Argonauts would receive wise divine counsel.[47] And under the second root of Yggdrasil was the well of the wise sage Mimer where knowledge and wisdom were concealed, and which he gained by drinking from the well.[48]

Indeed, given that trees embodied and symbolized divinity and were oracles for communication with the divine, naturally they were associated with wisdom and were looked upon as a means for enlightenment and revelation. J was confronting this wisdom motif when he brought into his story the issue of attaining wisdom through the tree of knowledge of good and evil, so it is important that we focus on this aspect of sacred tree symbolism. An archetypal way to experience a revelation is to connect with the divine by traveling along the axis to a different plane, either upward to the heavens or downward to the underworld. This is what shamans do, with those traveling to the heavens being known as "white" shamans and those traveling to the underworld being called "black" shamans.[49] The initiation rites of shamans often require the candidate to climb a tree, pole, or ladder; [50] to reach the top is to reach divinity (the center of the universe) and experience an ecstatic vision.[51] Likewise, in many "ascent" myths the protagonist reaches heaven and experiences the divine by ascending a tree, pole, ladder, or stairway, or by crossing a bridge. In an Indian holy text, the initiate upon reaching the top of the pole cried out, "I have attained to heaven, to the gods: I have become immortal!"[52] In the famous culminating episode of Plato's *Republic,* Er, in recounting his ecstatic vision, reports that he reached a spot where he "discerned, extended from above throughout the heaven and earth, a straight light like a pillar, most nearly resembling the rainbow, but brighter and purer," around which the heavens revolved, which he and his companions followed in their journey of realization.[53] In the biblical story of Jacob's ladder, Jacob falls asleep at Luz, his head resting on a stone, and dreams: "And here was a ladder, set up on the earth, and its top reaching to the skies. And here were angels of God, going up and going down by it. And here was Yahweh standing over him," who in oracular fashion told of Jacob's and Israel's future. When Jacob awoke, he exclaimed, "Yahweh is actually in this place, and I didn't know!"[54] So he erected as a pillar the stone on which he had dreamed and re-named the place Bethel ("house of God," referring to the pillar). Correspondingly, at the entrance to or in the center of heaven there is often a sacred tree. In Islamic belief, in the center of seventh heaven stands the sacred Tuba (lotus) tree from which the rivers of paradise flow, which Muhammad encountered on his Night Journey.[55] In Mesopotamian mythology twin trees, the tree of life and the tree of truth, stood at the entrance to Anu's heavenly palace. In other myths, the axis-pole protrudes through a hole in the celestial "tent," functioning as a door that opens the way into heaven for the traveler.[56] The route to the divine is typically depicted as difficult and dangerous, accessible only to suitably prepared initiates of pure mind and spirit.[57]

As in the cases of Plato's shaft of light and the white Yggdrasil, sacred trees and pillars as channels for accessing the divine are often themselves depicted as white, luminous, on fire, or as having gleaming jewels on their branches.[58] Light symbolizes life and the illumination of divinity,[59] and in psychological terms connotes the appearance of consciousness.[60] In the Hebrew Bible, the burning bush of Moses is the most obvious example; also, the Hebrews during the Exodus followed a "pillar of fire" which was Yahweh,[61] and Yahweh instructed Moses to create the menorah, known as the tree of light and which evoked Yahweh.[62] A classic example from Egypt is the Phoenix *(benu)* bird at Heliopolis, the Center of the earth, typically shown perched atop a sacred pillar, pole or obelisk capped by the sacred *benben*[63] stone, where during each creation it appears in a flash of fire as the manifestation of the sun-god Re, and at the end of each cosmos is consumed by fire, only to resurrect in the next cycle.[64] A later example comes from the poet Nonnos of Panopolis in Egypt (ca. 4th-5th century CE), who in his *Dionysiaca* drew on earlier myth in describing the foundation of the island-city of Tyre. On a primeval rock floating in the sea grows a "self-rooted" olive tree. The tree is engulfed in flames but (like Moses's burning bush) is not consumed by them. At its top sits an eagle, while a serpent curls around its base, neither of which attacked or harmed the other, maintaining the status quo. But the eagle had to be caught and sacrificed so that the rock would attach to the immovable foundations of earth and Tyre could be built upon it.[65] The divinity of fire also underlies the myth of Prometheus (god of wisdom) giving humankind the gift of fire, for which he was punished like Adam and Eve and for much the same reason. As we shall see, the flaming sword placed beside the tree of life similarly symbolized divine power, that of Yahweh.

When a divine revelation or enlightenment is experienced, the traveler himself often becomes hot, luminous or white (whence our terms "en*light*en-ment" and "illumination" to describe the experience), since fire (or the sun) represents the divine energy. Thus, Buddha (meaning "the enlightened one") was described as becoming luminous after his enlightenment.[66] Likewise, after Moses ascended Mount Sinai and spoke with Yahweh, the skin of his face "shone" because he had been talking with God, and he had to wear a veil (Exod. 34:29-35). When Christ ascended a high mountain (a Center) to con-verse with Moses and Elijah (the only others in the Bible who had journeyed to the divine[67]) he became transfigured, "and his garments became glisten-ing, intensely white, as no fuller on earth could bleach them" (Mark 9:2-3). Likewise, Christian saints have halos, reflecting their special connection with the divine. A similar modern example comes from Tolkien's *Lord of the Rings,* in which the wizard Gandalf the Grey undergoes a death-and-rebirth initiation and reappears as Gandalf the White.

The most famous example of someone gaining high wisdom in associa-tion with a sacred tree is Buddha attaining enlightenment while sitting on the immovable spot at the base of the Bodhi tree, an *axis mundi* both symboliz-ing and actually facilitating Buddha's connection with the divine. The idea here is similar to the ascent motif just discussed, but adds that the channel of ascent also includes the yogi's own body, namely the spinal column. The spine is not merely *symbolically associated* with the cosmic sacred tree axis, but rather is conceived of as *literally yoked*[68] *to and becoming one with that axis* during meditation, enabling the adept to connect with divinity, the con-cept being that divine energy flows through the cosmos connecting each thing with everything else, so that one may directly experience divinity lying "outside" one's body. Buddha connected so completely with the axis that he *became* it (or one with it), and was liberated. Similarly, the *Taittirīya Samhitā* says, "In truth, the sacrifice makes *himself* a ladder and a bridge to reach the celestial world."[69] The meaning is similar in the myth of Brahma coming into being from a lotus in Vishnu's navel (the Center) at creation, and even in the thinking of the romantic poet Coleridge, who wrote, "What the plant *is,* by an act not its own and unconsciously—*that* must thou *make* thyself to become!"[70]

In both the human and cosmic examples, divinity is manifested and expe-rienced through the form of the tree/axis/navel, into which humans are physiologically equipped to tap. In Indian thought, within the human body divine energy known as Kundalini, conceived of as a coiled serpent located at the base of the spine, rises up the spine through a series of energy centers called chakras, all the way to the top chakra located at the crown of the head. Much like the fire associated with sacred trees, kundalini serpent energy is considered hot and fiery,[71] which is why Buddha was portrayed as luminous. Sacred trees or pillars are sometimes depicted in the form of the spinal column, the most famous ancient example being the *djed* pillar symbolizing Osiris, who was encased in a wooden pillar/tree before being reborn. In other myths, worthy mortals who underwent a special spiritual experience were actually transformed into trees. Thus, in Ovid's *Metamorphoses* the peasant couple Baucis and Philemon offered gracious hospitality to the gods Zeus and Hermes when the latter were in their "mortal guise" of ordinary travelers and a thousand other people had refused them food and shelter. The gods rewarded the pair by transforming their humble cottage into a holy temple (archetypically, columns sprang up), making them its priest and priestess, and granting their wish to end their lives together. At their final moment they were transformed into oak and lime trees:

> *Guardians of the shrine*
> *They were while life was left, until one day,*
> *Undone by years and age, standing before*
> *The sacred steps and talking of old times,*
> *Philemon saw old Baucis sprouting leaves*
> *And green with leaves she saw Philemon too,*
> *And as the foliage o'er their faces formed*
> *They said, while still they might, in mutual words*
> *"Goodbye, dear love" together, and together*
> *The hiding bark covered their lips. Today*
> *The peasants in those parts point out with pride*
> *Two trees from one twin trunk grown side by side....*
> *And said: "They now are gods, who served the Gods;*
> *To them who worship gave is worship given."* [72]

The deity most associated with trees was the Earth Goddess.[73] A fine example comes from a Yakut myth, in which the first man was created by the high god and birth goddess and set on earth, fully grown, by a tree. Unaware of his origins, the man said to the milk-breasted goddess of the tree: "Be my mother, as though thou hadst given birth to me; be my creator, as though thou hadst created me. . . . Thou hast brought up me, an orphan, to man's estate, thou hast suffered me, the little one, to grow up."[74] This link between trees and the Goddess arises from their common connection to the life principle, fecundity, and regeneration. Trees sprout from the earth and after dying decompose back into the earth from which they came; thus, they grow from and return to the womb of the Goddess.[75] The death-and-rebirth cycle also occurs annually, when trees wither in the cold months only to be reborn (from Mother Earth) and bear fruit each spring as their sap rises. Evergreens such as the cedars prominent in ancient Near Eastern myths remain green and "alive" in the barren months when everything else seems to die (from which comes the symbolism of the Christmas tree, always an evergreen). Trees as the Goddess thus symbolize life and rebirth, the eternal cycle of *zoe* and *bios*.

Sacred trees often bear fruit or nuts, which typically represent the offering and body of the Goddess. To partake of the fruit of a sacred tree, or the milk of the Goddess within it, was to imbibe and thereby acquire some qualities of divinity. The Yakuts, for example, believe that at the "golden navel of the earth" stands a tree where the first human was born, who feeds on the milk of a goddess who emerges from the trunk of the tree.[76] In higher symbolism of this kind, eating the fruit or foliage of a sacred tree (or other plant) could confer knowledge, wisdom, immortality, rebirth after death or at least renewed youth, as in the *Gilgamesh* myth (see below) and the sacred trees in the Eden story. At a simpler level, sacred trees were associated with fertility in the vegetable and human world (female reproductive power). Therefore, they or their symbols were used in fertility rites to foster bountiful crops and human procreation. In Mesopotamia deities were often shown holding a branch of a tree with fruit, a stalk of grain, or a staff or trunk with dots representing fruit, in all cases representing life and bounty.[77]

The identification of sacred trees with the Goddess was depicted in various ways in the ancient Near East and Mediterranean. Numerous goddesses, including Isis, Nut, Asherah, and Ishtar, were portrayed as trees or in association with trees or their branches, but the tree (or pillar) as the embodiment of the Goddess was most prominent in Crete and Mycenae.[78] A gold ring found by Schliemann at Mycenae depicts her seated at the base of a cosmic, fruit-bearing tree growing from a stylized cosmic mountain.[79] Later, in Greece itself, an olive tree sacred to Athena stood by the Erechtheion on the Acropolis in Athens.[80] A Sumerian cylinder seal depicts a forked tree decorated with fillets next to which stands a worshipper pointing to it, who in the inscription invokes the Goddess and proclaims himself her servant.[81] A Roman coin from Myra similarly depicts a figure of the goddess Artemis in the fork of a tree (Fig. 22).[82] It was common to portray both the Goddess and trees interchangeably between two rearing caprids, as we have seen in the cases of the Lachish ewer, the depictions on the Kuntillet Ajrûd pithoi, and Asherah on the Taanach stand (Figs. 6, 8, and 9). In all such cases the symbolism of life and the earth's fecundity was essentially the same.

But tree symbolism was not limited to goddesses. They were also associated with gods, especially the dying and rising god, who represented the cycle of the seasons. Thus, the Mesopotamian gods Tammuz and Ningiszida were portrayed as trees, as was Dionysus. The dead Osiris was enveloped by a tree (often depicted as a djed pillar) and was resurrected from it as it burst into foliage upon Isis's passing footfall. Many Greek deities were either born or brought up at the foot of a tree. Pausanias wrote that Hermes was raised under a tree, [83] while Leto gave birth to both Apollo and Artemis while clasping two trees. [84] In Rome, Romulus and Remus were found under a fig tree by the Tiber. [85] In India, Vishnu was born under the shade of the banyan tree, Brahma appeared from a lotus growing from Vishnu's navel at the creation, while Buddha was said to have been born and died under a sâl-tree. The manner of depiction of the dying and rising god depends on which aspect of the birth-death-rebirth cycle is being represented. Thus the dying and rising god Adonis was born from a tree, Tammuz inhered in one, while the dead Osiris was interred and resurrected in one.

Eventually, when sky gods usurped the powers and symbols of goddesses, they also usurped the goddesses' association with trees. As seen in Chapters 3 and 4, in Mesopotamia male deities gradually appropriated the position of the Goddess as the sovereign of the garden and its waters and plants, including the sacred trees. Another famous example comes from Dodona, the oldest oracle in ancient Greece, where there was a sacred oak tree (the oracle) associated with the dove, [86] with a shrine and spring alongside. Originally the oracle belonged to the Pelasgian mother goddess, [87] but when the cult of Zeus rose, he married her, the site became his, and a temple was built to him there. [88] At Delphi, when the earth goddess Rhea still presided over it, a sacred laurel tree grew by the oracle, and it figured in Apollo's usurpation of the holy site, as the prior existence and meaning of the tree was not directly acknowledged in Olympian mythology. Instead, in the Olympian version, Apollo at Delphi became enamored with Rhea's daughter, the priestess-nymph Daphne (meaning "laurel"), and made unwelcome advances. Daphne, fleeing from him, entreated her mother [89] to save her. In response, Daphne was transformed into a laurel tree just as Apollo was about to embrace and kiss her, a moment beautifully captured by the Renaissance painter Antonio Pollaiolo. Apollo cried out,

> *My bride, since you can never be,*
> *At least, sweet laurel, you shall be my tree.* [90]

He vowed to tend her as his own tree and used his powers over immortality and eternal youth to keep her ever green. He crowned his head and lyre with its leaves (so too the heads of victorious athletes at the Pythian Games) and claimed the laurel as a symbol of his Delphic sanctuary. An analogous usurpation later occurred in Christianity. Saint Boniface, famous for converting pagans, was said to have felled the sacred oak dedicated to Thor, having in mind the example of Elijah defeating the prophets of Asherah and Baal at Mt. Carmel. He was then commonly portrayed with his foot stepping on an oak, symbolizing the overcoming of paganism, especially Druidism.

As we shall see, the same kind of appropriation of sacred trees and tree symbolism by sky gods was at work in the Eden story. In order to understand that, we must first review tree symbolism in the ancient Near East and the Bible.

SACRED TREES IN THE BIBLICAL WORLD

Since sacred tree imagery and veneration prevailed throughout Egypt, Mesopotamia, and the Mediterranean, it is important to review these influences on Syria-Palestine.

Egypt

Egypt was not rich in trees. Except along the Nile, the country even in ancient dynastic times was mostly desert, while in the Nile floodplain the annual inundation prevented forests from forming. Instead, the river landscape was dominated by lotus and papyrus plants, which became the prominent sacred plants in Egyptian art and mythology. Thus, in one myth the sun god Ra (like Brahma) was born out of a lotus plant.[91] And as we have seen, the iconography of these plants made its way to Syria and Palestine, as in the Qedesh/Qudshu plaques and in a 9th-8th century ivory from Arslan Tash portraying a god on a lotus flanked by two winged anthropomorphic cherubs.[92]

The Egyptians generally viewed their sacred plants and trees not as themselves divine, and they were not venerated as such.[93] Rather, particular divinities were thought to be present in certain trees, which were vehicles or mediums of divinity. One Pyramid Text refers to a "tall sycamore in the east of the sky, quivering of leaves, on which the gods sit."[94] By the sacred springs or pools at the temples one or more sacred trees was planted, in which a deity was thought to dwell. These were most often sycamores, but also acacias and date palms.[95] Such a sacred pool was an essential component of any major Egyptian temple complex, representing the primeval waters from which life originally arose.

The Egyptians had a sophisticated understanding and iconography of pillars. At their most basic level pillars were derived from trees, and in Egypt as elsewhere their capitals took the form of vegetation, in this case lotus or papyrus plants (the lotus symbolized resurrection, while the papyrus was associated with the primeval marsh where the creation occurred);[96] one hieroglyph for "column" is a stylized papyrus stem.[97] It is possible that the four pillars which upheld heaven were symbolized by the four capitals in many depictions of the *djed* pillar (sometimes reduced to four bars), making it four pillars in one.

The *djed* pillar carries other connotations as well. First and foremost, it represents the tree in which Osiris was enclosed (which became a pillar in the king's palace) before being reborn. Similarly, because of the qualities of trees, the wooden coffin became preferable to the stone sarcophagus as the encasement of the dead in Egypt because being buried in wooden coffins symbolized one's return to the womb of the mother tree-goddess (most commonly Nut), from which one could be reborn.[98] It was inside such coffins that the famous Coffin Texts were written. Because of this significance, sycamores were often planted by tombs, and funerary amulets were made in the form of their leaves.[99]

At the onset of the sowing season a ceremony was performed called the "Raising of the Djed," in which the pillar was raised, symbolizing the resurrection of Osiris and the return of fertility to the land.[100] As such, the *djed* pillar is comparable to the tree of life.[101] It was thought to represent (among other things) the backbone of Osiris,[102] an intriguing comparison in light of the sophisticated meaning given to the spine in yogic schools of thought. There are some hints that in certain contexts the Egyptians had a similar symbolism, such as in one Pyramid Text referring to the Pharaoh ascending to the sky along the backbone of Osiris,[103] but no organized system of thought along these lines seems to have emerged (unlike in India). For the most part, the spine (and so the *djed*) seems to have signified, like pillars elsewhere, stability, duration, and support, for which the *djed* was the hieroglyph.[104] Similarly, Nut, as a sycamore tree, "shielded"[105] the dead Osiris and rejuvenated his soul from among her branches.[106]

Rebirth was also symbolized by two "sycamores of turquoise" standing at the eastern gate of heaven and which represented the goddess Nut, who each morning gave birth to Ra, who emerged from between the two trees.[107] The sacred *ished* tree growing at the temple at Heliopolis similarly represented rebirth. Ra was said to have split its trunk in the morning after defeating his nocturnal enemies, a metaphor for opening the horizon for sunrise. Ra is often depicted as inhabiting this tree, or as a cat protecting it from (and indeed slaying) the evil chaos serpent Apep, so as to keep order in the cosmos and enable the sun (Ra himself) to rise.

Egypt's goddesses, especially Nut, Hathor (called "Lady of the Sycamore") and Isis, were depicted as trees or as residing in them (Fig. 24). In many cases the point was taken further and the goddess-tree was shown as offering (by hand, breast) waters or milk of life, fruit or other food (i.e., her body) to humans in order to provide divine sustenance, just as in the above example of the Yakut tree. In such depictions, most often the human recipients were recently deceased and the food was being provided so that they could be sustained and reborn. In other cases, the goddess-tree nourishes living humans. The parallels with the sacred trees and fruit of the Garden of Eden are obvious.

Mesopotamia

In Mesopotamian symbolism of the Center, sacred trees held a special place both in iconography and in myths. These must be explored in detail, because, as Professor Wensinck observed, "the trees mentioned in the Biblical narrative have the same cosmological meaning as those in Babylonian literature."[108]

Mesopotamian sacred tree iconography displays many of the archetypal characteristics of sacred trees already discussed. Thus, Mesopotamian sacred trees are often paired with other sacred images symbolizing a Center such as sacred mountains, *omphaloi*, pillars, and water of life; they are often luminous, often by means of a sun disk but also (as seen below) by having jewels as fruit; a bird symbolizing heaven is often on top (often combined with the sun as a winged solar disk); and they are associated with and typically flanked by a pair of hybrid beasts, and sometimes have a serpent at the roots. Importantly for our purposes, the sacred trees (or pillars, or stylized mountains) themselves are often paired, framing a central symbol of divinity (omphalos, a deity), thus rendering the two trees a gateway to divinity or heaven.

Out of this background evolved the most developed, stylized and ubiquitous representation of the sacred tree in ancient Mesopotamia, that of the Assyrians, of which we have hundreds of examples and which became known distinctively as the Assyrian sacred tree.[109] Its design conformed to well-established rules that made the tree symmetrical, yet no two examples are alike. In its most developed form, it was in a bell shape suggestive of an omphalos, with a metal-banded column in the middle standing on a base that sometimes portrayed the cosmic mountain, while the outer bell shape consisted of garlands of foliage in the form of palmettes and fruit or cones, all connected by intersecting lines (Fig. 25). On top was usually a winged sun-disk. The tree was always flanked by two figures, which were sometimes humans, sometimes beasts, including hybrid creatures, genies or deities. As an evolution of the Sumerian theme of the king as guardian of the temple and sacred garden and tree, the Assyrian sacred tree developed mainly as a royal symbol, depicting the king as duly maintaining the divine world order and even identifying the king with the tree, thereby characterizing him as the perfect man and an image of God.[110] When Assyria came to dominate Palestine, this tree became known there.

Turning to sacred trees in Mesopotamian texts, it is important to begin with the sacred tree of Eridu, which in Chapter 4 we identified as a Center. As such, the city had its sacred tree in the garden of Enki's temple, and so its roots stretched down toward the waters of the *apsu* where Enki had his abode. Called the *kiskanu* tree, it was described in a consecration incantation of king Nur-Adad:

In Eridu there is a black Kiskanu tree,
growing in a pure place.
Its appearance is that of lapis-lazuli,
erected on the Apsu.
Enki, when walking there, filleth Eridu with abundance.
In the foundation thereof is the place of the underworld,
in the resting place is the chamber of Nammu.
In its holy temple there is a grove, casting its shadow,
therein no man goeth to enter.
In the midst are the Sun-god and the Sovereign of heaven, [111]
between the two mouths of the river. [112]

A hymn of Eridu elaborates on this tree:

Its root was of white crystal stretched towards the deep [apsu]*;*
Before Ea was its course in Eridu, teeming with fertility;
Its seat was the central place of the earth;
Its foliage was the couch of Zikum the primeval mother.
Into the heart of its holy house which spread its shade like a forest hath no
man entered; There is the home of the mighty mother who passes across the
sky.
In the midst of it was Tammuz.
There is the shrine of the two gods. [113]

Here we encounter the archetypal sacred tree symbolism discussed above and seen in the Eden story. The *kiskanu* was the Cosmic Tree, rooted in the navel of the earth and spanning three cosmic planes. [114] It derived its vitalizing power from Eridu's waters of life, which made the *kiskanu* a tree of life. [115] Around it was a sacred precinct off limits to mortals. There stood Enki's temple, known as the "house of wisdom," [116] situated on the sacred underworld chamber of Nammu. In another inscription, the goddess of the *kiskanu* tree and garden precinct was called both the "divine goddess of the tree of life" and "the lady of the steppe." [117]

It seems that each Mesopotamian city-state's temple had its sacred garden sanctuary with its own sacred tree (or other plant), each thought to be located over the *apsu*. [118] For example, Warad-Sin, king of Larsa (ruled 1770-1758), left an inscription reciting that he built a temple for the goddess Nininsina, which was her house:

The House of the Plant of Life, the holy dwelling . . .
her secure making place, her house . . .
for my life and the life of Kurdur Mabug, the father who begat me,
I built for her. [119]

Earlier, Sumu-ilu, king of Ur at the end of the 2nd millennium, had done likewise for the same goddess:

Unto Nin-Isin . . . the fine garden,
Where a plant is growing, the Plant of Life, he gave. [120]

This seems to be a carryover from the earlier Goddess religion tradition before there were kings, where the sanctuary with garden and sacred tree were under the jurisdiction of the Goddess's priestesses, as was the case with Inanna's sacred garden. [121]

Sacred trees or plants and their produce appear in a number of Mesopotamian myths which contain as well other elements found in the garden of Eden. First, in the *Epic of Gilgamesh,* following the death of his dear companion Enkidu, the hero Gilgamesh, two-thirds god and one-third human, laments his and man's mortality. "Unbridled [in] his arrogance," he resolves to escape death, and embarks on a heroic quest for immortality, which he pursues doggedly even while being warned along the way that he is pursuing a "puff of wind." [122] He embarks upon a pilgrimage to meet Utnapishtim, the Mesopotamian "Noah" who had survived the primeval flood and for which reason he was the sole human to be granted immortality by the gods; Gilgamesh wants to ask him about death and life. [123] He first travels to the Cosmic Mountain in the range of Mashu (said to span heaven and the underworld) along a mountain path called the "road of the sun" which no human had traversed. After trekking many leagues in darkness, at the end of the path a bright dawn breaks to reveal a Center in the form of a group of stones in the midst of which a fruit-laden sacred tree grew:

Malachite grew as its fruit;
A grapevine hung down, fair to behold;
Lapis-lazuli grew as clusters of grapes;
Fruit grew, dazzling to see. [124]

This sacred tree is essentially the same as the *kiskanu* tree of Eridu, [125] and its attractiveness recalls that of the tree of knowledge of good and evil.

At this Center Gilgamesh encounters the goddess of the vineyard sanctuary, Siduri, the keeper of life. He inquires about or perhaps entreats her for the gift of eternal life, but she demurs and addresses him:

Gilgamesh, whither rovest thou?
The life thou pursuest thou shall not find.
When the gods created mankind,
Death for mankind they set aside,
Life in their own hands retaining.
Thou, Gilgamesh, let full be thy belly,
Make thou merry by day and by night.
Of each day make thou a feast of rejoicing,
Day and night dance thou and play!
Let thy garments be sparkling fresh,

Thy head be washed; bathe thou in water.
Pay heed to the little one that holds on to thy hand,
Let thy spouse delight in thy bosom!
For this is the task of mankind! [126]

But Gilgamesh does not heed her words and insists on seeing Utanapishtim. Siduri reluctantly arranges for Utanapishtim's boatman to take him across the "Waters of Death" for the meeting.

When they meet, Utanapishtim reveals the secret story (heretofore kept between himself and the gods) about how he was warned by Ea (Enki) of the coming flood ordered by Enlil, and built a boat on which to place his family and "the seed of all living things" in order to survive it. Gilgamesh is then stripped naked and cleansed in lustral waters, the band on his head is renewed and he is given new clothes to cover his nakedness. Utnapishtim then reveals another secret of the gods, the existence of a plant of life located in the deep *(apsu)*:

"Its thorns will prick thy hands just as does the rose.
If thy hands obtain the plant, thou will find new life."
No sooner had Gilgamesh heard this, than he opened the water-pipe.
He tied heavy stones to his feet.
They pulled him down into the deep, and he saw the plant.
He took the plant, though it pricked his hands.
He cut the heavy stones from his feet.
The sea cast him upon its shore. [127]

Gilgamesh embarks on his return to Uruk, intending to eat of the plant and proclaiming that its name shall be "Man Becomes Young in Old Age." As evening falls Gilgamesh bathes in a pool, leaving the plant at the water's edge. But then a serpent smells the plant's fragrance, comes up and carries it off. It then sheds its slough, showing that it has eaten of the plant and renewed its youth. Gilgamesh's quest thus thwarted, he laments that he has given a boon to the serpent. [128]

The Mesopotamian *Etana* myth contains an interesting variation on the theme. Instead of a plant that prevents old age or death, we have a "plant of birth" that confers fertility. In this story, the gods will establish the institution of kingship in Kish only if the designated king, Etana, produces an heir. But he is childless and needs the plant of birth in order to father an heir. As instructed by the sun-god Shamash, he frees an eagle imprisoned in a pit, and the eagle carries him up to the gods in heaven, where Ishtar can give him the plant of birth. [129]

Such sacred plants also have the power to resurrect, such as in the *Descent of Inanna* myth where the goddess is resurrected with the help of the water of life and plant-food of life. She tells her messenger, Ninsubur:

Father, Enki, the lord of wisdom,
Who knows the Plant of Life, who knows the Water of Life,
He will surely bring me back to life.

And her confidence is not misplaced. Enki commands:

Sixty times the Plant of Life, sixty times the Water of Life communicate to it.
Verily, Inanna will arise. [130]

In the Sumerian myth known as *Enki and Ninhursag* already discussed in Chapter 4, Enki himself was the protagonist.[131] There Enki, in paradise, offended Ninhursag by eating forbidden sacred plants, was cursed by her, and narrowly avoided death by reconciling with her and then being cured by Ninti, a goddess of life and of the rib.

Finally, we have the *Adapa* myth. Adapa was a wise antediluvian sage assigned by Enki to tend his temple and sacred garden compound, a priestly endeavor through which Adapa introduced religious rituals to mankind and established other elements of civilization.[132] While fishing one day he was hindered by the south wind, so he broke its wing, which upset the gods, before whom he then had to appear at Anu's palace in heaven to account for himself. Enki coached Adapa on how to behave before the gods. He advised Adapa to accept the gods' hospitality, with one exception: Enki warned that Anu would offer Adapa the bread and water of eternal life, but that he should refuse and not partake of it because actually they are the bread and water of death. Adapa duly refused them, but it turned out that they were indeed the bread and water of eternal life, and he lost his chance for immortality.[133] Enki had tricked Adapa so that he would remain mortal and resume his duties on earth. Thus, here as in *Gilgamesh* the Mesopotamian mind accepted man's mortality as the divine will. J, in contrast, would not portray Yahweh as having decreed such an original divine order of things; instead, he shifted the blame for human mortality (and other worldly problems) onto humans.

These Mesopotamian myths share a number of motifs, objects, and ideas in common with the Eden story, including:

- sacred trees and plants, located at a Center, in a holy sanctuary garden
- their association with precious stones; that they are lovely to behold
- their ability to confer, save, and resurrect life, and to confer immortality yearned for by humans
- the idea that a serpent can thwart obtaining these benefits
- the idea that eating the sacred plant can be an infraction resulting in a punishment of death
- their association with goddesses

It is hard, however, to say that J directly borrowed from any particular myth. It is best to view Palestine as sharing a common menu of motifs with Mesopotamian thinking and mythology, the traditional meanings of which J found objectionable but which he could use for his purposes.

Mediterranean Influences

Mediterranean influence on sacred tree imagery is seen in a wide variety of archaeological finds in Palestine of Mycenaean and Cypriot artifacts. In Mycenaean culture both sacred trees and pillars were central religious symbols, and in sanctuaries and in art were paired or combined, sometimes within the same object (Fig. 15).[134] One example of the combination of pillar and tree is the proto-Aeolic capitals in architecture, which developed originally in Syria-Palestine in the 10th century, based on influences that scholars have traced to the Minoan/Mycenaean civilizations, Egypt, Mesopotamia, and Anatolia.[135] This style developed from designs of sacred trees and symbolizes them.[136] Through the filter of Phoenicia this style flowered into high fashion across Palestine (including Jerusalem) during the 9th century, being particularly favored by the Omride rulers and featured in their complexes in Samaria and Megiddo (Fig. 26); the columns of Jachin and Boaz before Solomon's Temple also may have had such capitals.[137] These capitals are important because, like the lotus and papyrus pillars in Egypt, their design is a stylized form of plant and so turns the pillar more obviously into a symbol of a tree. This architecture demonstrates that sacred tree and pillar symbolism was prominent not only in the high places but also in the royal palaces and possibly temples of the rulers whose religious policies J opposed.

SACRED TREES AND PILLARS IN PALESTINE

Sacred tree motifs flowed into Palestine from Mesopotamia, Egypt and the Mediterranean, which led to a rich mix of sacred tree symbolism. The Bible provides insight into sacred trees and pillars in Palestine, but we have no extra-biblical texts from Palestine describing them. Archaeology, however, has yielded evidence of sacred tree veneration and symbolism in art, sanctuary design, and cult objects.

We must begin by recalling from Chapter 3 the close connection between sacred trees and Syro-Palestinian goddesses, especially Asherah. Asherah was characteristically symbolized as a sacred tree, as in the Lachish ewer, Pithos A from Kuntillet Ajrûd, and the Taanach cult stand. Such iconography connecting the goddess and trees has a long history in Syria and Palestine, consistent with that described above for Mesopotamia, Egypt and the Mediterranean. In Middle Bronze Age Canaan the close bond between the Goddess and trees was portrayed ubiquitously in metal pendants and scarabs

depicting the Goddess, commonly called the "Branch Goddess," either standing between tree branches or small trees or holding them in both hands (Fig.
17), while in other instances the branch or tree is depicted in her navel, as
part of her pubic triangle, or between them (Fig. 23).[138] In another common
motif lasting into the Iron Age, Goddess and tree were interchangeably portrayed as the central figures of veneration flanked on each side by real animals (most commonly caprids) or hybrid creatures, as in the cases of the
above-mentioned artifacts from Lachish, Kuntillet Ajrûd, and Taanach (Figs.
6, 8, and 9). As noted in Chapter 3, in Iron Age Palestine Asherah seems not
to have been directly depicted, perhaps due to the prohibition against depicting her husband Yahweh, meaning that she could not be depicted either. As a
result, we have only her symbols, and then only those few not made of her
characteristic material, wood. Thus, we are left with depictions of trees on
pottery, cult stands, plaques and other artifacts.

Asherah's ubiquitous identification with sacred trees in Palestine suggests
that the sacred trees in the garden of Eden may allude to her. In order to
understand this potential association, it is helpful to review where sacred tree
and pillar veneration took place in Palestine, namely at the high places
(bāmôt).

Mountaintops, hilltops, or other high points naturally lend themselves to
serving as sacred places. There one is closest to the heavens, can survey
creation from on high, be close to the forces of nature, and think profound
thoughts, all of which generates a numinous experience and a connection
with the divine. Such was the idea behind the Mesopotamian ziggurat, the
pyramids in Mayan and Aztec civilizations, and many of the temples in the
ancient Far East such as Angkor Wat, each an artificial high place representing the Cosmic Mountain as the Center.

Where a venerable old or large tree or grove of trees is situated at or
near[139] a prominent high point it is naturally considered sacred, and the
sacredness of the site is enhanced; likewise, the spring or well commonly
associated with the site (as in Eden), was thought to provide (from the underworld) the holy water of life. Thus, the high place sanctuary typically featured the traditional combination of the sacred tree and sacred waters of
life.[140] Instead of or in addition to natural trees, a connection to the divine
was also achieved by erecting stone pillars and asherahs. The Bible states in
several places that asherahs stood beside altars in high places and other
sanctuaries (Deut. 16:21; Judg. 6:25, 28, 30), as did sacred trees (Josh. 24:26-
27). At such sanctuaries also stood an altar, often on a platform near the
center, and at the larger and more developed sanctuaries there were temples,
halls for feasting, and storage areas for cult paraphernalia.[141]

In the case of pillars, as seen above, in some cultures such as in the
Mediterranean the pillars were identified with both the Goddess and sacred
trees; in Palestine too pillars sometimes may have been connected with god-

dess worship. Given that religion in Palestine was more patriarchal than in the Mediterranean and the fact that Syro-Palestinian deities had consorts, however, scholars generally believe that in Palestine pillars most likely represented the god and the male principle, while the tree or wooden trunk or pole represented the god's consort and the female principle.[142] Thus, Yahweh would be represented by a pillar, Asherah by an asherah.

The Hebrew Bible's descriptions of sacred trees and pillars in Palestine match their archetypal characteristics described above. To begin with, theophanies tended to occur at sacred trees. Abraham's first stop when he arrived in Canaan from Mesopotamia was at the sacred oak (or terebinth) of Moreh at Shechem (Canaan's religious center at the time), where Yahweh appeared to Abraham to proclaim that Canaan shall belong to his descendants (Gen. 12:6-7, a J text). Soon afterwards, Yahweh appeared to Abraham at the oaks of Mamre to announce that Sarah will bear a son; there they also discussed whether to destroy Sodom and Gomorrah (Gen. 18:1-33, a J text). Later, of course, Yahweh appeared to Moses in the burning bush.

In Palestine sacred trees were also used as oracles and for divination. The oak of Moreh mentioned above means "Oak of Oracles."[143] It was probably this same (or successor) oak tree in Shechem that is later referred to as the "Diviner's Oak" and as being at the center of the earth (Judg. 9:37). Deborah would sit under a palm tree in order to do her judging and prophesying (Judg. 4:5). Yahweh instructs David that when he hears the rustling of leaves ("the sound of marching") in the tops of balsam trees he should set forth against the Philistines (2 Sam. 5:4).

Sacred trees were also chosen as burial sites. Saul and his sons were buried under an oak at Jabesh (1 Sam. 31:13; 1 Chr. 10:12). Rebekah's nurse was buried by an oak at Bethel (Gen. 35:8). When Jacob's wife Rachel died, he set up a pillar over her grave (Gen. 35:20). This conforms to the archetypal practice of locating graves at Centers (marked by omphali or sacred trees) so that the spirit of the deceased may travel between the planes of the cosmos.

Events important to the community took place or were commemorated at sacred trees or pillars, lending divine sanction to the occasion. Shortly before his death, Joshua gathered all the tribes of Israel to Shechem, and by its sacred oak tree made his covenant with the people and issued laws, and then set up a stone there to mark the occasion (Josh. 24:25-27). Abimelech was proclaimed king by that tree, now termed the "oak of the pillar" (Judg. 9:6). Saul held council under a tamarisk (1 Sam. 22:6). In Jerusalem, the king would stand by the pillars before the Temple (perhaps to invoke Yahweh's presence in the pillars) when making important announcements (2 Kings 11:14; 23:3; 2 Chr. 34:31).

The above sacred tree sites were at Canaanite religious centers where Canaanite deities were venerated. The stories of patriarchs in the Hebrew

Bible highlight these ancient Canaanite sanctuaries as being appropriated by
Israelite religion. At this early stage in the development of Yahwism,[144] a
problem arose only when trees and pillars were taken to symbolize or embody deities other than Yahweh (including Asherah) and were worshipped as
their idols. Thus, the struggle was not against trees and pillars as such, but
over which deities inhabited or were associated with them.[145] This is vividly
illustrated by the biblical account of the events following King Ambilech's
coronation at the sacred oak in Shechem, which Abraham had previously
visited and connected with his god (see above). Abimelech was a Baal worshipper, so when he became king, the oak reverted to being associated with
Baal. With Yahweh's help, Jotham then overthrew Abimelech (Judg. 9:7-
57), after which presumably the tree again became associated with Yahweh.
Thus, when the narrative tells of Abraham or his descendants visiting one of
these sacred sites and erecting an altar or pillar near its sacred tree,[146] the tree
and the entire site was being claimed in the name of the Hebrew god. This is
illustrated by the story of Gideon at Ophrah (Judg. 6:11-32), already recounted in Chapter 3, who narrowly escaped death at the hands of irate
villagers after he destroyed the village asherah. Jacob, after dreaming of the
ladder to heaven, erected as a pillar the stone on which he had slept, anointed
it with oil, invoked Yahweh, and renamed the town Bethel, all of which
symbolized Yahweh's appropriation of this ancient sacred site. Later, when
Jacob returned from Haran with his family, God appeared to him at Shechem
and told him to erect also an altar at Bethel to the god who had appeared to
him in the dream. Before embarking on such a sacred task, he gathered his
family and had them surrender to him the Mesopotamian gods that they had
brought with them, and he buried them under the sacred oak of Shechem
(Gen. 35:1-4). (This was one very busy tree!) Finally, after the well digging
episode at Beer-Sheba, Abraham planted a tamarisk there, calling it El Olam
("El the everlasting"), thereby claiming the site for his god (Gen. 21:33).
Later, Isaac travels there but it is *Yahweh* who appears to him, presumably by
the tree, and promises to multiply his descendants; Isaac then built an altar
and dug a well there, invoking Yahweh's name (Gen. 26:23-25).

Later the Hebrew Bible adopts a more negative attitude toward high
places, trees and pillars in themselves, and especially against asherahs and
therefore Asherah herself: All were roundly condemned and had to be destroyed.[147] The biblical polemic against these ancient traditions is of course
biased, but it nevertheless provides useful descriptions of the religious practices taking place by sacred trees at the high places that J was targeting in the
Eden story, as follows:

- The most fundamental and frequent observation is that Israelites worshipped "under every green tree" at the high places.[148] This indicates that

the sacred tree itself was deemed to have divine qualities and played a role in rituals.

- Numerous passages call for destruction of the asherahs,[149] in which context it is sometimes mentioned that they stand under or next to sacred trees.[150] The biblical texts thus associate Asherah with sacred trees, while the wooden asherah manifested this connection.

- Pillars and asherahs stood together at high places.[151] This makes sense in light of our conclusion that the asherah (or tree) and pillar respectively represent the female and male principles, and therefore male and female deities as consorts. Pillars are condemned,[152] one passage stating that Yahweh hates them.[153] Other idols are also mentioned as standing at high places.[154]

- Fertility rites (not clearly described) were conducted at high places under the sacred trees.[155] These might include formal sacred marriage rites or more general Dionysian-style fertility rites involving sexual abandon. Thus, Isaiah rails against "the children of transgression, the offspring of deceit, you who burn with lust among the oaks, under every green tree."[156] Some passages portray Israel itself as "playing the harlot" under every green tree.[157]

- Some passages object to the practice of divination through both sacred trees[158] and asherahs,[159] which presumably was practiced at high places.

- Several other objectionable practices are described as taking place at high places, including burning incense,[160] making various kinds of offerings to deities,[161] making sacrifices,[162] and taking an oath by an asherah.[163]

- The high places always had an altar, which numerous biblical passages demanded be destroyed.[164] Asherahs stood beside altars at high places and other sanctuaries, as did sacred trees.[165] Some passages prohibit setting up an asherah next to an altar of Yahweh, which means that this practice was occurring.[166] In so commanding, the authors clearly wanted to separate Yahweh from Asherah.

- As will be discussed in Chapter 7, serpents were venerated in the sacred marriage rite and other rituals at the high places.

These descriptions of high places have been borne out by archaeological excavations conducted at Shechem, Hazor, Dan and elsewhere.[167]

Separately from the high places, Ezekiel in his famous vision of idolatry at the Temple describes people putting a tree branch to their nose, the "image of jealousy" (probably a replacement statue of Asherah[168]), together with a number of other sins (Ezek. 8:7-18). The objectionable tree branch recalls the older Canaanite "Branch Goddess" discussed in Chapter 3, the Mesopotamian seals depicting fruit-laden tree branches held by deities, images of kings holding tree branches,[169] Assyrian sacred tree imagery, and also the

Egyptian imagery of holding an ankh to the nose, all of which connote life, fecundity and prosperity.

But perhaps not only the activities transpiring at Solomon's Temple complex were of concern, but also some of its physical features. The Temple was, after all, on a high place like most other sanctuaries, and it had many features found both at high places and in the garden of Eden. The entire interior walls and ceiling of the Temple were said to be lined with Phoenician cedar wood from the mountains of Lebanon; the floor boards were made of cypress wood and the doors of olivewood, meaning that it was all wood (though overlaid with gold) inside, even the altar in the holy of holies (cedar) and the cherubim (olivewood); "no stone was seen" (1 Kings 6:14-36). The walls and doors were decorated with complex tree and garden imagery, including carvings of palm trees, blossoming flowers, and gourds (1 Kings 6:18). Cherubim not only guarded the Ark, but also were depicted on the Temple walls (1 Kings 6:29) and on the veil of the Holy of Holies (2 Chr. 3:14). Outside the entrance stood the two pillars of Jachin and Boaz, the capitals of which were said to feature lily work and were adorned with pomegranates (1 Kings 7:18-22). Along with the Sea of Bronze, they also could have constituted the archetypal combination of sacred trees and the water of life (not simply lustral waters of purification). And lastly, in front of the Temple, together with the Asherah, stood the bronze serpent of Moses twined around a pole (see Chapter 7), which the people venerated and used for healing.

The chief occasion for pagan rites involving trees (and vines) was the autumn New Year's festival, known as the Feast of the Ingathering. It was celebrated after the first fruits of the harvest were gathered and the grapes and olives were pressed, making it a feast of plenty in which thanks were given to the deities responsible for fertility. It was well established in Canaan before the emergence of Israel; in fact, such a harvest festival was the norm throughout the ancient Near East and Mediterranean.[170] The Canaanite model at first was continued in Israel but eventually took another course under Yahwist influence.[171]

The traditional Canaanite feast was celebrated over seven days, mainly in the vineyards but culminating in the sanctuary/temple, where a ritual meal (apparently only for men) was held.[172] As in the case of the Dionysian festivals of ancient Greece, in Canaan vineyards, grapes and wine lent themselves to this type of festival. Cultivating grapevines requires a great deal of effort, but the reward is great. Canaan exported its wines (also olive oil) and winemakers to Mesopotamia, Egypt and the Mediterranean, so its vineyards were a source of prosperity and well-being.[173] The vineyard represented life and fertility, and having a successful vineyard was considered a divine blessing.[174]

The festival was celebrated right in the vineyards. There the people built and stayed in booths made of freshly cut leafy branches, to symbolize life and fertility—booths of life. [175] While the festival included solemn ritual and prayer, it also featured ecstatic merrymaking thought to achieve union with the divine, including dances by young women (Judg. 21:21), intoxication from wine, feasting, nakedness, and sex. The intoxication from imbibing wine was seen as divine inspiration and a divine experience. [176] (We still refer to alcoholic beverages as "spirits.") A key part of the festival, in traditional Canaanite practice and at least in the early Israelite period, was the sacred marriage rite involving ritual intercourse, thought to connect the participants and the community with the divine and ensure fertility in the coming year. [177]

Only at a late stage did the Yahwist establishment associate the holiday with Exodus ideology, (re)naming it the Feast of Booths (or Tabernacles), or Sukkot, which now was supposed to be celebrated only in Jerusalem. It became associated with the consecration of the Tabernacle; indeed, Solomon consecrated his Temple at the time of this festival. The festival's culmination became the enthronement of Yahweh in the Temple. The theology changed so that instead of New Year being an agricultural festival, it celebrated the Exodus and sojourn in the wilderness. [178] The booths were now taken to symbolize the tents in which the Hebrews lived in the desert wilderness before entering Canaan, and living in the booths during the festival was meant to inspire people to reflect on that legendary past. The sacred marriage ritual was also not part of the official version of the festival, [179] which obviously means that the Goddess was not part of it.

Since the festival celebrated the New Year, naturally it was associated with creation, so a mythological account of creation (or re-creation) would be recited or perhaps reenacted on the occasion. As we have seen, in the ancient Near East this meant a ritual combat of purgation in which the sins and chaos from the last year were defeated and a new, pure order was established. [180] In later Israelite religion, this purging ritual occurred during the Day of Atonement shortly before the Feast of Booths, a day of fasting and prayer in which a scapegoat bearing the community's accumulated sins of the past year was expelled into the wilderness (i.e., out of order into chaos). [181] Originally in the Canaanite festival, however, the mythological combat utilized was probably the traditional myth of Baal defeating the sea monster (vestiges of which appear in the Hebrew Bible), although there is no clear proof of this. [182] Some scholars believe that, as the holiday took on Yahwistic overtones, J's own creation account including the Adam and Eve story was probably recited on the occasion, [183] which would have served to oppose the original form of the holiday and turn it in a Yahwist direction. Indeed, the pair's expulsion from the garden sanctuary of Yahweh following their offense, punishing the serpent, and Yahweh establishing himself with his cherubim there, would serve to eliminate chaos from and purify the garden, and thus has intriguing parallels to the traditional New Year's ritual and even the above-mentioned purgation and scapegoat rite. Similarly, scholars have also suggested that P's

seven-day creation account reflects and may be derived from the later Yahwist liturgy for this holiday.[184] If by that time reciting J's Eden story was
already a fixed tradition in the rites of this holiday, it would be difficult to
dislodge it, which could help explain why in Genesis it was retained along
with P's newer account.

In many of J's Bible stories, grapes, vineyards and wine play a key
role.[185] He authored the part of the story of the spies dispatched to Canaan
where Moses told them to bring back some of the land's fruit. They went to
the vinicultural region near Hebron during the time of the harvest of first
grapes (i.e., the very time of the Canaanite New Year's festival) and brought
back a huge cluster of grapes (two men carried it on a pole) as the prime
evidence of the fertility of Canaan, and named the region Wadi Eshcol ("Valley of the Cluster").[186] J also authored the episode of Noah's nakedness/
drunkenness (Gen. 9:20-27). After the flood receded and Yahweh lifted the
curse on the ground that he had imposed in response to Adam and Eve's sin,
Noah, a "man of the ground" *(ĩš hā ădāmâ)* planted a vineyard and, much
like Adam, worked it, thus evoking the original planting of the garden of
Eden. But one day he gets drunk from his wine and lay naked in his tent. His
son Ham, the father of Canaan,[187] sees Noah naked and commits some unclear offense.[188] In response, Noah curses Canaan, and by implication that
land and its future inhabitants, so that later it would be subservient to the
Israelites. Since J linked the conduct in question to Canaan and given that the
Canaanite (and Israelite) New Year's Festival was the prime example of
nakedness and sexual abandon, many Bible scholars believe that in this story
J was polemicizing against these Canaanite vices at that religious festival,[189]
though not necessarily being critical of the righteous Noah.[190] Such polemic
was later taken up by Isaiah and others specifically in reference to the New
Year's feast,[191] evidencing that such practices continued into the late 8th
century. Hosea too wrote that Yahweh, who is the true source of the grain,
the wine and the oil, will punish Israel for celebrating her pagan feasts (2:9-
13):

> *I will take back*
> *My grain in its time,*
> *And my wine in its season . . .*
> *And I will put an end to all her mirth,*
> *Her feasts, her new moons, her sabbaths,*
> *And all her appointed feasts.*
> *And I will lay waste her vines and her fig trees*
> *Of which she said,*
> *"These are my hire, of which my lovers have given me." . . .*
> *And I will punish her for the feast days of the Baals . . .*

THE SACRED TREES OF EDEN

In his Eden story J utilized many of the above meanings of sacred trees, but in doing so he added details which raise new questions. Why did J introduce two trees, from both of which the first humans could potentially eat? What was the forbidden fruit? Why place the cherubim and the flaming sword by one of the trees? We explore these and other questions below.

Why Two Trees?

Unlike most mythological descriptions of sacred trees, in which there is only a single tree, the Eden story mentions two sacred trees: the tree of life (Gen. 2:9; 3:22) and the tree of knowledge of good and evil (Gen. 2:9; 3:3). Why did J depart from the usual motif? This was one of J's main innovations in the story.

Scholars have struggled for centuries to understand why there are two sacred trees in the garden, sometimes differing over what the trees mean, which one is more important, and even over whether there are two or only one.[192] Many such efforts focus on textual analysis, given that the text in relation to the two trees is rather convoluted and may reflect lifting material from other sources, bad editing, or both. But in the end such textual exegesis has not enabled us to see the forest for the trees. In order to understand why there are two trees and what are their roles, we must step back and examine this aspect of the Eden story in relation to ancient Near Eastern mythology and symbolism. When so viewed, this actually becomes one of the easier dimensions of the story to understand. As Professor Engnell concluded, *"both* trees are from the very beginning organically at home in the narrative."[193]

In the ancient Near East, being divine (like a god) consisted of having two classic attributes: immortality and wisdom (or knowledge).[194] The tree of life and the tree of knowledge of good and evil symbolize these two prongs of divinity.[195] As Gunkel observed in this regard, "We should not be surprised to encounter both in the garden of God for they embody characteristically divine properties."[196] These two qualities are precisely what Adam and Eve sought. But in any etiological myth of the origins of the world as we know it, *such a quest must inevitably founder on the question of immortality,* because in our real world humans are not immortal. Etiological myths simply provide one or another explanation for this inevitable result, so J had to develop his. In light of his agenda, for this purpose he utilized primarily the other prong of divinity, knowledge or wisdom, which placed the narrative's focus on the tree of knowledge of good and evil. In such etiological myths humans, before failing to attain immortality, often do attain a degree of wisdom that differentiates them from animals and brings them closer to the gods. Thus, in *Gilga-*

mesh the primitive Enkidu attained this state after his encounter with the priestess, who exclaimed, "Thou art wise, Enkidu, art become like a god!"[197] But he ends up dying, which so distressed Gilgamesh that he embarked on his quest for eternal life. Gilgamesh too was wise, but his quest was thwarted by a serpent. In the *Adapa* myth, Adapa was a wise sage but likewise failed to attain divinity because he could not attain immortality, tricked by his god Enki who did not want this. Adam and Eve's fate falls within this mythological tradition.

There was some precedent in the ancient Near East for a pair of sacred trees, of which J may have known and which may have inspired him to adopt this motif. According to Mesopotamian inscriptions from Gudea there stood at the east gate of heaven (Anu's palace) two trees, the Tree of Life *(gisti)* and the Tree of Truth *(giszida)*.[198] As in the *Adapa* myth, these could take the form of Tammuz/Dumuzi and Ningiszida, who as we have seen are closely associated with trees, the former as inhabiting a tree and Ningiszida being "god of the tree of truth." As also mentioned earlier, in Mesopotamian and Egyptian iconography two trees, pillars or mountains commonly frame a deity or other symbol of the divine (such as an *omphalos*, or the sun), thus rendering the pair of trees a visible gateway to the divine,[199] in accordance with the usual function of sacred trees. The Egyptian *Book of the Dead* similarly describes two sycamores of turquoise at the eastern gate of heaven, which Re passed through each morning.[200] J accentuated this idea by identifying his two trees with the two prongs of divinity.

But at the same time we must recognize the underlying unity of the two trees in that they represent complimentary aspects of divinity, while sharing fundamental properties of sacred trees.[201] For example, the mythology of Hawaii features two trees similar to those in Eden, only they are called the tree of eternal life and the tree which brings knowledge of death; but they are visualized as a single tree with different physical characteristics on either side, one side being alive and verdant, the other dead, dry and brittle.[202] Mythologically speaking, the differences among sacred trees can be viewed as two aspects of the same sacred tree,[203] just as in polytheism various deities represent particular aspects of the divine that is ultimately one. This is apparent from the various names of the sacred trees discussed above. Thus, calling it a Cosmic Tree or World Tree emphasizes the aspect of the tree as the *axis mundi* connecting the three planes of the cosmos. As a "tree of life," it emphasizes the life-giving and regenerative qualities of the divine force present in the tree. When having an oracular function to communicate divine information and knowledge, it may be called a tree of knowledge or wisdom.

What Kind of Trees and Fruit?

When describing sacred trees, the Bible normally specifies their type: the oak (or terebinth) at Shechem, Abraham's tamarisk at Beer-Sheba, Deborah's palm, and so on. But not so with the sacred trees in the garden of Eden, even though they are the most important trees in the entire Bible. One might expect that for literary purposes J would have used the opportunity to enrich the meaning by identifying the trees. Did he not do so because he assumed his audience would understand from tradition what trees are involved, or did he deliberately leave this vague for some reason?

All J tells us is that Adam and Eve could potentially eat from both trees, meaning that they must bear fruit or nuts. We may also infer that they are two different kinds of trees, because one is forbidden and the other is not (initially) and since eating of them is said to have different effects. The tree of life enables one to live eternally, whereas the tree of knowledge of good and evil confers some form of divine knowledge or wisdom; it is also pleasing to look at, which attracts Eve. Adam and Eve cover themselves with fig leaves, but these could have come from any tree in the garden. J thus provides no hint regarding the species of the sacred trees. Therefore, we must examine the possibilities from among the sacred trees common in the biblical world, and see how each fits or doesn't fit the story.

We can exclude from the outset the Christian tradition of an apple tree.[204] In the ancient Near East, apple trees were not common and they did not feature in the mythology or iconography of the time; when humans were pictured partaking of the bounty of sacred trees, the fruit was never an apple. The tradition that Eve ate an apple arose in medieval Europe from a pun in Latin (which, of course, did not exist in J's time), based on the similarity between the Latin words for apple *(malum)* and bad or evil *(malus)*.[205] That has nothing to do with J's story.

J specifies that "fruit" *(peri)* grew on the tree of knowledge of good and evil and other trees in the garden (Gen. 3:3, 6), but does not clearly specify a fruit on the tree of life. Although we tend to assume that J had in mind primarily an actual fruit since he says that the tree was pleasing to look at, we must consider the possibility of nut-bearing trees, at least in the case of the tree of life. Such trees appear frequently as sacred trees in the Bible and elsewhere. Oaks, which bear acorns, are one biblical example, but probably more important in this respect are almond trees, to which the Bible many times attributes sacred qualities.[206] In the ancient Near East the almond was the first tree of spring, blossoming in radiant white, and was the last to shed its leaves.[207] Edible "fruit" and its seed share an identity, which Philo observed made the almond both a beginning and an end, "a beginning in that it springs from no other power but itself, an end in that it is the aspiration of the life which follows nature."[208] Its ancient Semitic name, Amygdala, may

mean Great Mother, in reference to a Mesopotamian goddess.[209] Bethel's
original name of Luz before Jacob renamed it in Genesis 28:19 meant almond (making the place "City of the Almond Tree"), probably in reference
to a sacred almond tree there;[210] later Jacob used poles from an almond tree
to encourage the sheep in his flock to mate (Gen. 30:37-43). Aaron's magical
serpent-rod blossomed and bore ripe almonds (Num. 17:8). In Jeremiah 1:11-
12, another Hebrew word for almond is used to associate it with Yahweh and
his watchfulness. Jeremiah has a vision and Yahweh asks him what he sees,
and he replies, "I see a rod of almond [*šāqēd*]," to which the deity replies,
"You have seen well, for I am watching [*šōqēd*] over my word to perform it."
Yahweh instructed Moses to make the branches of the menorah (a form of
sacred tree, as discussed below) end in almond-shaped cups (Exod. 25:33-34;
37:19-20), which represent the almond tree's blossom while the fire-lights
within them symbolize the sacred fruit.[211] The Hebrew word for fruit in
question (*perî*), however, never appears in the Hebrew Bible in reference to
nuts,[212] which seems to exclude any nut from being the forbidden fruit
though not from growing on the tree of life. Even if J did not have an almond
tree in mind, he might have meant to embrace within his broad symbolism
any sacred or magical qualities associated with the almond and other nut-
bearing trees.

Among trees bearing fruit with seeds, the leading candidates seem to be
the date palm, sycamore fig, pomegranate, olive, and grape. In Mesopotamia
the date palm was the tree most frequently portrayed as a sacred tree and the
tree of the Goddess (Fig. 37), while in Egypt the sycamore fig (associated
with Hathor and Isis) filled this role. The fig, however, did not grow in
Mesopotamia,[213] where Eden was located, which may make the date palm
the better candidate to the extent the story is faithfully derived from Mesopotamian mythology.[214] Since J mentioned fig leaves in the story and *perî* is
used to refer to a fig in Proverbs 27:18, however, this remains a possibility.
Pomegranates were popular in Palestine as emblems of fertility (due to their
hundreds of seeds), and so were featured in the garden imagery of the Temple and its pillars[215] and on Aaron's priestly robes (Exod. 28:33). An inscription on an 8th century priestly scepter head in the form of a pomegranate
references Yahweh and is probably from Jerusalem Temple.[216] Given that J
was concerned with religious imagery and practices within Palestine, the
pomegranate is a possibility. Finally, the olive is a candidate because it is
sacred, as evidenced in the sacred trees of Nonnos and Philostratus; the later
apocryphal *Life of Adam and Eve* identifies the tree of life as an olive.[217] The
olive tree itself is durable and can sustain itself in dry, rocky soil, lives
seemingly eternally, and is able to regenerate itself from its roots, even after
being burnt. These qualities made it a symbol of life and fertility, which is
why it became a tree of life in ancient Greece and Rome and an emblem of
Athena and her gift to humankind. Also, olive oil burns (and so lit lamps in

ancient homes and temples, as well as those of the menorah in the Tabernacle[218]), which evidenced its divine qualities. Accordingly, it was used in religious rituals and for anointing people and holy objects, as when Jacob anointed the sacred pillar of Bethel.[219] Significantly, in Genesis 8:11 J himself used the olive to convey precisely the above ideas, in recounting that the dove which Noah released from the ark returned with a freshly plucked[220] olive leaf (or branch) in its mouth. J used it here to symbolize the restoration of the cosmos and of life after their dissolution during the flood and the subsequent restoration of harmony between the earthly and the divine. There is nothing inherent in the ideas behind or actual effects of eating these types of fruit which would make them a target for J's polemic, however, other than the mere idea that people imbibe them as part of the divine. The grape, however, has greater explanatory power.

We suspect that J had in mind the grape, and that his audience would have recognized this, because this best fits into the cultural context and aligns best with the arguments and characterizations that J was making in the Eden story. A grape makes most sense in light of our earlier discussion of the Canaanite New Year's festival and J's polemic against it. Not intending a grape here would be to lose a golden literary opportunity. When Moses sent the spies to Canaan, he told them to bring back "fruit" *(perî)* of that land, and they returned primarily with the grape cluster, so J indeed associated Canaan with grapes and viniculture. The same Hebrew word for fruit is used to refer to grapes throughout the Hebrew Bible.[221] Indeed, some scholars have argued that in the biblical description of that land as one of "milk and honey," honey is actually grape syrup or sweet wine.[222] In Judges 9:7-15, grapevines were chosen by the other plants in that land to reign over them. The grape also fits well with certain details of the Eden story. The attractiveness of the fruit to Eve recalls the attractive crystalline grapes on the sacred tree/vine in the Siduri episode in *Gilgamesh*. The effect of eating it on Eve and Adam also parallels the inebriating effects of grapes and wine and the ancient concept that this embodies a connection with the divine. The grape seemed magic to people because it did not need added yeast for fermentation (it already being present on the grape skin), and so itself produced the physical effects that were thought to be an experience of the divine.[223] The apocryphal 3 Baruch (ca. 1st century CE) identified the tree of knowledge of good and evil as a grapevine and the forbidden fruit as a grape, because it was capable of such "trickery" and (with Eve) thus functioned in tandem with the serpent; the fruit of the tree itself deceived Adam.[224]

In the end, we cannot be certain regarding the species of the sacred trees in the garden, which may have its own significance; J may have so intended it. If such a talented writer considered the species of tree to be symbolically important for his story, he could have specified this, but instead he named each tree after its main attribute and function. As d'Alviella observed, "it is not the identity of the species of plants which constitutes the essential feature of the symbol through all its local modifications, but rather the constant reappearance of its hieratic accessories."[225] Indeed, as we have just seen, the varying specific characteristics of sacred trees (and pillars and mountains) often still symbolize the same things. Thus, J may have intended a purely symbolic kind of tree or an amalgam, for which there was ample precedent in the conventionalized sacred trees in ancient Near Eastern mythology and iconography, especially the Assyrian sacred tree.[226] Conventionalizing the trees would focus attention on the names that he *did* give to the trees, which described their *essence,* namely the two prongs of divinity. This accords with the ancient Near Eastern tradition, described earlier, of naming things to establish their character, function and destiny, a practice occurring elsewhere in the Eden story itself when Adam named the animals and Eve.

YAHWEH'S COMPLEMENTS:
THE CHERUBIM AND THE FLAMING SWORD

The cherubim and the flaming sword appear only in the last verse of the Eden story (Gen. 3:24). But last is not least. These symbols are central to the message that J sought to convey, so we must consider them in detail.

The Cherubim

Deities are commonly symbolized by particular animals, either singly or in pairs. Marduk was associated with his *mushussu* dragon, Cybele and other goddesses with lions, Aphrodite with the dove, swan and goose. In iconography deities were often portrayed as dominating their animals, as when standing on the animal's back, by placing one foot upon it, or by being guarded or venerated by animals (Figs. 3, 4, 8, 12, and 31). In order to understand the cherubim of Eden, we must review this symbolism in more detail.

The Hebrew word for cherubim *(kerûb)* comes from Mesopotamia, most directly from the Akkadian *karibu/kuribu* (from *karabu,* "to bless"),[227] which refers to an intermediary between humans and gods that, among other things, carries human prayers to the deities.[228] Their conceptual origin may have been as the winds which carry fructifying pollen,[229] particularly to fertilize female date palms, for which purposes they were represented as winged genii of fecundity and eventually became the guardians of the sacred tree (in Mesopotamia most often a date palm).[230] Yahweh was indeed commonly depicted as riding cherubim on the winds through the sky.[231] The iconographic origin of Yahweh's cherubim is most clearly Mesopotamian, although similar representations are seen in Egypt (including Egyptian-controlled Palestine and Syria), Anatolia and in the Mediterranean.[232] From an early date two hybrid figures—cherubim, genies, or sphinxlike creatures, often with wings—as in heraldry flank a central image, which is sometimes a tree or pole, sometimes a deity (usually a goddess), guarding it and in some cases venerating it as well (Figs. 6, 8, 16, 25, and 30). The imagery spread to Syria and Palestine. Yahweh enjoyed the epithet *yôšēb kerûbîm,* meaning "[he who is] enthroned on the cherubim," previously an El epithet.[233] When Yahweh absorbed El, the cherubim (like Asherah) came as well.

J does not actually say what the cherubim of Eden looked like. The Hebrew Bible mentions cherubim 91 times and the descriptions, when given, often differ.[234] Their one consistent characteristic is that they are hybrid creatures with wings, which associate them with heaven/sky and divinity. Such creatures with wings, ophidian features, and sometimes webbed feet symbolize an ability to traverse different planes (or elements) of the tiered cosmos and thus connect with divinity, in some cases with a particular divinity. This type of creature thus complements the sacred tree, which likewise spans these realms. When flanking a central image, they symbolize the presence of the divine and are venerating it, in J's story Yahweh.[235]

By placing Yahweh's characteristic guardian cherubim by the tree of life, J rendered the tree a symbol of Yahweh. As we have seen, in ancient Near Eastern art sacred trees were typically guarded by animals associated with the Goddess (caprids, lionesses), including in the case of Asherah. In these cases, the tree that the animals were guarding or venerating was considered a symbol of the Goddess. J turned this symbolism around. In Judah the cherubim were Yahweh's trademark animals. They were his guardians and formed his throne platform.[236] Thus, on the Ark the cherubim flanked the "mercy seat" of Yahweh where he was thought to be present, and similarly in the Holy of Holies in the Temple cherubim flanked the Ark itself and therefore also Yahweh.[237] When depicting Yahweh as the giver of life and therefore as associated with the tree of life, it was natural that the guardians of this tree be those associated with Yahweh. By becoming the venerated object of the tree's guardians, Yahweh usurped Asherah's position as the divinity of the sacred tree.

By identifying Yahweh rather than Asherah with the tree of life, J was arguing that veneration of Yahweh was the only legitimate approach to the divine and the only way to obtain those benefits traditionally represented by sacred trees and the Goddess. Juxtaposed to the tree of life (which in the story was not forbidden until the expulsion) is the tree of knowledge of good and evil and its forbidden fruit, representing the traditional and wrong approach to the sacred. This contrast is enhanced by the different guardians by each tree: the serpent by the tree of knowledge of good and evil, the cherubim by the tree of life. The idea that Yahweh himself (rather than a sacred tree) represents divinity was advanced in later biblical passages associating Yahweh symbolically with trees, fruit and wisdom, but nowhere more eloquently than in Hosea 14:8-9:

O Ephraim, [238] *what have I to do with idols?*
It is I who answer and look after you. [239]
I am like an evergreen cypress,
from me comes your fruit.

Whoever is wise, let him understand these things.
Whoever is discerning, let him know them.
For the ways of the Lord are right,
And the upright walk in them,
But transgressors stumble [240] *in them.*

As seen in the epigraph to this chapter, Christ later made much the same claim.

Bible scholars understand the above passage from Hosea to be polemicizing against sacred tree veneration and symbolism in Canaanite/Israelite religion, [241] which as we have seen includes in particular asherahs (and therefore Asherah herself). The author of the Apocalypse of Isaiah, written after Hosea, seems to have interpreted Hosea this way. Specifically, Isaiah 26:13 through 27:11 consist of eight consecutive passages that closely track Hosea 13:4 through 14:9. [242] One of them, Isaiah 27:9, specifically mentions and condemns the asherim, saying that their abolition will be the "full fruit" of the removal of Israel's sinful idolatry, [243] just as the corresponding Hosea 14:8 claims that Israel's fruit comes from Yahweh rather than the idols (most likely asherim). In fact, some scholars beginning with Wellhausen himself have argued that the above phrase in Hosea 14:8, "It is I who answer and look after him," which in Hebrew reads *'ă nî ānîtî wa 'ăshûrennû,* was mistaken and should be emended to read, *'ănî 'ă nātô wa 'ăshērātô,* "I am his [Israel's] Anat and Asherah." [244] Most contemporary scholars disagree that such a correction is sound or necessary. More likely Hosea was engaging in wordplay, at least in respect of asherahs and possibly Asherah, by using a similarly sounding word when the goddess and her symbol were already in context. [245] The idea would have been to portray Yahweh, a luxuriant tree, as a more effective source of life and fertility than an asherah or Asherah. [246] Yahweh was appropriating the asherah's/Asherah's function.

Thus, in the Eden story, J expressly associated one tree with life by naming it as such, but he told the story so that the Goddess was nowhere to be found in connection with this tree. Rather, the tree is the creation of Yahweh, it is under his control, and it is guarded by his cherubim. The tree and life are now associated with him, not the Goddess. Notably, J says that Yahweh created the sacred trees and other plants of the Garden *after* he created Adam but *before* Eve (who as we shall see in Chapter 8 was in part a goddess figure), much as Adam was created before the female, who emerged from him. In this way, the creation of life was structured so that it had none of its traditional connections with the Goddess or the female principle,[247] connections which would have been in the minds of J's audience.

But this is still not all. Placing the cherubim by the tree also symbolized *Judah's* particular understanding and portrayal of Yahweh, as opposed to that in the northern kingdom of Israel. As discussed earlier, in the northern kingdom of Israel the molten calves (young bulls) were the preferred throne platform for Yahweh, as they had been for El whom Yahweh absorbed; like the cherubim and Asherah, the calves came to Yahweh as El's baggage. Originally this seems not to have been a problem, but it became a flashpoint of religious conflict between Israel and Judah after, according to the Bible, Israel split from Judah and Israel's and Judah's kings each sought to create (or preserve) their own religious identity within Yahwism, which included Israel using the calves rather than cherubim as Yahweh's throne platform. This was probably a major point at issue in the golden calf incident in Exodus, which, importantly, occurred right after Yahweh had instructed Moses to use cherubim as his throne platform (on the Ark).[248] In Chapter 2 we saw that Yahwists from Judah, especially upon being freed from Omride domination, sought to emphasize Judah's separate identity by fostering their separate cult practices and cult articles, in which connection it was important to promote the cherubim rather than the calf as Yahweh's symbol. This was the period when J wrote, and stamping the culmination of the Eden story with his cherubim can be seen in part as an idealized realization of that goal.

The Flaming Sword

The cherubim were complemented by a single flaming sword which revolved, whirled, turned, or moved every which way. What is its origin and significance? Here we must be attentive to J's description, which specifies that "at the east of the garden of Eden [Yahweh] placed the cherubim, and a flaming sword which turned every way, to guard the way to the tree of life." Importantly, there are two cherubim but only one sword. J does not say that one of the cherubim holds the sword; indeed, it would be odd for only one of them to wield a sword and the other to be without a weapon. Indeed, in the relevant ancient Near Eastern iconography cherubim or analogous figures generally do not wield swords or other weapons but instead are shown facing and venerating the central figure in the composition (tree, pillar, deity, etc.). Further, the sword moves as if it is either animate or driven by a divine power. This has led commentators to conclude that the sword stood independently and functioned autonomously;[249] some have suggested that it is an animate demonic being.[250] In our view, once we understand that Yahweh is invisibly present between the cherubim (just as on the ark and in the Temple), it is logical to deduce that it is Yahweh who wields the sword.

Scholars have offered various theories for the origin and nature of the flaming sword. Yahweh himself is associated with fire (e.g., the column of fire in Exodus/Numbers, the burning bush), so the flame connotes his presence and divine power.[251] Many scholars consider Yahweh to be (among other things) a solar deity. Thus, Albright thought the fire imagery was derived from the winged solar disk, which originally shone over the Assyrian sacred tree (between the flanking genii) to ensure maturity of the crop.[252] Indeed, in one 8th century tableau, the tree and winged sun-disk are together replaced by a revolving sun wheel between the genii.[253] Another possibility sometimes suggested is that the flame represents lightning,[254] which in addition to being a weapon is a fertility motif. Thus, Hadad/Baal (like Zeus) were storm gods who, in order to bring fertilizing rains, brandished lightning, which Yahweh also famously wielded[255] and which could be doubly meaningful to the extent that in the Eden story Yahweh was symbolically appropriating Baal's powers.

Whatever the origin of this super sword, the clear purpose is to demonstrate and magnify Yahweh's strength, vitality, and power, a classic meaning of the sword as a symbol.[256] In mythology the sword is the classic weapon used by gods and heroes when vanquishing dragons, serpents or other monsters.[257] Thus, Yahweh's flaming sword seems to hark back to the wonder weapons that Marduk used against Tiamat and Baal against Yam. J could not have Yahweh appear any less mighty. Indeed, Isaiah 27:1 later uses this very imagery:

> In that day the Lord with his hard and great and strong sword will punish Leviathan the fleeing serpent, Leviathan the twisting serpent, and he will slay the dragon that is in the sea.

In the Hebrew Bible Yahweh wields both a sword and fire (and lightning), and in the Eden story they are combined.

The image at the end of the story therefore may be that of Yahweh positioned invisibly between the cherubim (as on the ark of the covenant and in the Holy of Holies at the Temple), identified with the tree of life, between his trademark cherubim and brandishing the flaming sword in his right hand. This would explain why it seemingly floats in the air and moves back and forth or revolves. Given that Yahweh often used, and probably held in his hand, an asherah as a mediating entity, we can also speculate that, in this story where Asherah's presence loomed but had to be replaced, the sword in Yahweh's hand may have replaced the asherah.

But why use a sword rather than some other weapon to symbolize strength? Because of its long sharp edge (sometimes double edge) and the manner in which it is wielded (to cut, slice, separate, dismember), the sword symbolizes delineation, definition, and clarity between alternatives and opposites, as well as finality in the results of the sword's action; fire enhances this and also may connote purification.[258] This is why the flaming sword appears only at the culmination of the story, when the story's binary opposites have been established and all matters are settled. At that point, the serpent has been vanquished, humans have been made mortal, and the creation has been completed; earthly existence has been separated from paradise, the profane (material) from the divine; and the garden has been cleansed of evil. As the humans exit the garden, the tree of life, winged cherubim, and fire—all now symbols of Yahweh's divinity, remain.

In summary, the cherubim and the sword are separate but complimentary symbols, the cherubim symbolizing Yahweh's presence and association with the tree of life (by his substitution of Asherah), and the flaming sword representing again his presence but additionally his power. Yahweh's fearsome power was likewise memorably symbolized by both cherubim and fire in David's account of Yahweh delivering him from the hands of his enemies (2 Sam. 22:9-15):

> *Smoke went up from his nostrils,*
> *and devouring fire from his mouth;*
> *glowing coals flamed forth from him.*
> *He bowed the heavens, and came down;*
> *thick darkness was under his feet.*
> *He rode on a cherub, and flew;*
> *he was seen on the wings of the wind.*
> *He made darkness around him his canopy,*
> *thick clouds, a gathering of water.*
> *Out of the brightness before him coals of fire* [lightning] *flamed forth.*
> *The Lord thundered from heaven,*
> *And the Most High uttered his voice.*
> *And he sent out arrows* [lightning], *and scattered them;*
> *Lightning, and routed them.*

EPILOGUE: THE RESURRECTION OF THE SACRED TREE (AND ASHERAH)

Mythological traditions and symbols die hard and often never do, based as they are on human needs and archetypal psychology. As we know from passages in the Hebrew Bible written well after J's time, people continued venerating trees, asherahs/Asherah, and pillars. But Yahwist religion did more than simply oppose tree (and Goddess) veneration on the one hand and on the other identify Yahweh instead with their divine qualities. Rather, as has often happened in the case of Christianity, the objectionable pagan image was sublimated into an acceptable alternative form which over time became a partial substitute meeting much the same needs. In this case the sacred tree (and possibly asherah) was transformed into a new cult article, the menorah,[259] which helped Yahweh appropriate the symbolism and qualities of sacred trees in the struggle against tree veneration and asherahs/Asherahs.[260]

Already in early Mesopotamian civilization there were images of a sacred tree having seven branches and often bearing fruit, which appears to have been linked with the Mesopotamian mysticism of the number seven. In one Mesopotamian depiction a seven-branched tree grows out of the top of the Cosmic Mountain (Fig. 21). The seven-branch motif began to appear in Syria and Palestine as well. Most notably, in the 13th century Lachish ewer the tree between the caprids that symbolized Asherah had this motif (Fig. 6), so the association of the seven-branched tree with the Goddess was well established.

Over time, the imagery evolved so that the fruit on the seven branches (now only on their ends) became balls representing fire-lights from olive oil; sometimes the tree itself was flaming (recall Moses's burning bush and Tyre's flaming olive tree). These on the one hand represented life, but they also could symbolize the seven heavenly bodies which hovered above the tree as it reached toward heaven. From this symbolism it was only a short step to a lampstand tree.[261] This is what Yahweh was said to command Moses to make as part of the Tabernacle cult paraphernalia (Exod. 25:31-40), and it remained with the religion thereafter. But in its origin it was a sacred tree and carried connotations of the trees of the ancient sanctuaries and the Goddess inhabiting them.

Chapter Seven

The Serpent Whose Powers Yahweh Usurped

And as Moses lifted up the serpent in the wilderness, so must the Son of man be lifted up, that whoever believes in him may have eternal life.

—Jesus Christ, John 3:14-15

Be wise as serpents and innocent as doves.

—Jesus Christ, Matthew 10:16

Today, at least in the Western world, the serpent does not enjoy a good reputation. But it hasn't always been this way. In the biblical world, before, during, and after J's time the serpent was venerated as noble and divine.[1] Gods and goddesses were often depicted with or as serpents. Serpents were kept in temples, as well as private homes, as guardians and symbols of divinity, and they were invoked to provide fertility and good health. In the ancient world no one would have been surprised to see a serpent in paradise.[2] According to the biblical scholar Alberto Soggin, the Eden story "doubtless arose with a people to whom the serpent was sacred, and who were impressed with its wisdom."[3] We must approach the Eden story with this in mind, because in it the serpent's fate was altered and, along with it, that of Western civilization. As a result of this story, the serpent's reputation and position deteriorated, until the serpent became the Devil himself, the personification of evil. And it was J who initiated this process. Why? To answer this, we must examine the serpent as it has appeared in the art, myths, religious beliefs and rituals of the biblical world.

The serpent is the most ubiquitous, mysterious and complex symbol in world mythology. Mythological symbols often have many meanings, but the serpent outdoes them all. A serpent can be portrayed as male or female, chthonic or celestial, lunar or solar; it can represent healing or poison, life or death, and it can assume related forms like dragons, sea monsters, hydras, and crocodiles. In his comprehensive study of serpent symbolism in the ancient Near East, James Charlesworth identified 16 negative and 29 positive symbolic meanings of serpents, as well as 32 symbolic meanings deriving from just its physical characteristics, and so concluded that J "inherited diverse and conflicted meanings of serpent symbolism."[4]

Why is serpent symbolism so universal and why does it have such a bewildering variety? As mentioned in the Introduction, according to modern psychology, symbols become universal because they are projections from the archetypes of our collective unconscious, meaning that there is an intrinsic relationship between the symbol and the corresponding underlying pattern in our psyche which is common across humanity.[5] Having so arisen, a basic symbol of the unconscious (here, for example, the uroboros or primordial serpent coil as a power) then gets processed by our consciousness (by perceiving, discriminating, dividing, registering from a distance) into particular contents of consciousness, a phenomenon known as the "fragmentation of the archetypes," because the pure archetype is too amorphous to be comprehended by the ego.[6] The ego only registers and understands things that are more ordered, so it creates this order through concrete symbols having their beginning in the unconscious. In this process, a single symbol can acquire various meanings because it can resonate with our varying experiences, so different aspects of the same symbol become associated with different experiences (fears, desires, ideas, etc.). As we shall see, the serpent has a variety of distinguishing physical characteristics and behaviors that can either cause or align with various kinds of experiences, each of which over history has been processed into meanings. Further, differences in natural environmental conditions and human culture in different places and civilizations will influence the content of the symbol in each particular case, yielding various "dialects" of the same general symbol across time and geography.[7] The multiplicity of meanings and variations in images thus corresponds to the many possible attitudes and reactions of our consciousness.[8] Thus, water can be a positive symbol of life because we associate it with life-giving rain and the process of birth (bursting of the amniotic sac), but because it is associated with storms, floods, and tidal waves it can also symbolize chaos and destruction. Fire likewise can symbolize life, comfort and positive energy on the one hand, but destruction and terror on the other. Similarly, serpents can be associated with life and healing, but also with death because their chthonic character associates them with the underworld realm of the dead and their deadly venom can cause death within minutes. And as we have already seen in the creation stories, since serpents can also be associated with water, these two symbols combine to yield the sea serpent of chaos that must be vanquished in order to create an ordered cosmos. These varying meanings should not be thought of as contradictory or problematic. They are all equally valid because they all authentically derive from how symbols are generated and function in our psyches.

When investigating what symbolic meaning(s) J and his audience associated with the serpent in the garden of Eden, we can be guided by what we know about J's purposes, especially his desire to portray Yahweh as the sole repository of divinity. His goal collided directly with the fact that in the biblical world, serpents were held to have divine qualities and powers and were venerated by rulers, priests, priestesses, and common people, particularly women. J and later biblical authors sought to exterminate such beliefs and practices on the one hand, while on the other hand endeavoring to attribute to Yahweh the divine qualities and powers traditionally associated with serpents,[9] which proved to be a difficult balancing act.

In the Eden story Yahweh created the serpent and placed it in the garden of Eden, thus asserting that it was under his jurisdiction and control. Then, after it misbehaved together with the humans, Yahweh proceeded to punish and humiliate it, and changed it into its final earthly physical form and even altered its diet, rendering it the lowest of the ordinary animals, below the other wild and domesticated animals (Gen. 3:14). He also set the serpent in conflict with women from that point forward. Thus, starting with the Eden story, Yahweh began appropriating the serpent powers, just as he appropriated the divine powers of Asherah and sacred trees. He soon exercised them in the episode of Moses and the bronze serpent (Num. 21:6-9) and subsequently for centuries at the Temple itself, where that bronze serpent on a staff stood until it was taken down and destroyed by King Hezekiah (2 Kings 18:4). So it is not surprising that, when Yahweh was eventually represented iconographically, he had serpent legs (Fig. 27).

Recognizing that J portrayed Yahweh as assuming the serpent's powers is the easy part. The greater challenge is to identify what divine characteristics and powers the serpent had which posed a challenge to Yahwism and therefore were at stake in the Eden story. Given the manifold aspects of serpent power and symbolism in Palestine and beyond, J's task was formidable. He had to target various meanings rather than one, and we must understand the serpent imagery in the story accordingly. In order to do so we must examine the background of serpents in the mythology, religion and iconography of the biblical world, for which purpose we must first explore the more general characteristics and meanings of serpents as symbols in mythology.

SERPENT SYMBOLISM IN MYTHOLOGY

Of all earthly creatures, serpents are the most unique and mysterious in the way they look, the way they move, how they behave, and where they live.

Over the centuries and all over the world, serpents have evoked a wide variety of strong associations and emotions, and it is easy to see why they inspired notions of the divine among the ancients, and modern humans too. Serpents have been widely portrayed in art, used as symbols by rulers, played important roles in myths, and became ubiquitous images and cult objects in religious practice. So it is only natural that serpents featured prominently in the Bible, especially at the creation in Eden.

In order to avoid getting lost among the manifold symbolic meanings of the serpent, it is important not simply to list these meanings but to analyze them from a conceptual mythological standpoint, proceeding from the most fundamental meaning to more particular meanings. When approached in this manner, the interrelated meanings will hold together conceptually better than a mere listing would suggest.

As discussed in Chapter 3, the ancients believed that the world was infused with the divine. The various deities in polytheism were imbued with and represented particular *aspects* of divine energy or power (i.e., were vehicles of such power), and were portrayed through corresponding symbols. The serpent, on the other hand, *represents the underlying divine cosmic energy, force or power itself,* which is *one* and pervades the entire universe, [10] though it has many aspects and manifestations in deities and otherwise. In modern popular terms, think of The Force in *Star Wars*. Modern physics too has equated mass with energy, meaning that the solid matter in the universe originated as pure energy and is still composed of it (being structured energy), and can be transformed back into pure energy. In mythology, the ultimate manifestation of pure divine serpent power was primordial, as the eternal force behind the creation of the cosmos. Therefore, as we shall now see, in creation myths serpents commonly symbolize that divine primordial force which either in itself generates the cosmos or is manipulated by a creator-god (who inevitably claims such power as inhering in him).

Serpents appear in numerous creation accounts besides J's. Most typically, the creation process begins with the serpent power in a latent, dormant state, not yet awakened, representing potentiality. This is well illustrated in Hindu mythology. The creator god Vishnu, the inner cause and power by which the forms of the manifest world were created and continue to be held together, is classically depicted as resting on the coiled serpent Shesha who floats on the primeval waters prior to Vishnu's creating the world, at which stage Vishnu was called Narayana ("moving on the waters"[11] —compare Gen. 1:2). Shesha thus represents *both* primordial chaos *and* the underlying force causing ordered creation that will be manifested through Vishnu. In the myth, the awakening of this creative power is symbolized by a lotus growing from Vishnu's navel that holds within it the god Brahma, the active agency from whose body the substantial forms of the universe then emanate. [12] After the creation, Shesha lies below the netherworld holding together the three realms of the universe (heaven, earth, netherworld), "wearing them like a tiara on his head."[13] The idea of serpent power awakening to create the world appeared in Sumer as well, where as we have seen Nammu, the serpent goddess, engendered heaven and earth out of the primeval waters (herself).

The same concept appears in the ancient Egyptian Heliopolitan creation myth, in which a coiled primeval serpent emerged from the darkness of the watery abyss before anything existed, taking the form of the creator god, Atum. Then, following the usual cosmogonic formula of creating order from chaos and assigning names, he created the many forms of things (multiplicity) and assigned to everything its essence *(ka)*. But Atum, the High God, takes inspiration, direction, and knowledge from the serpent, which enables creation by the word. Thus, in a Coffin Text the High God explains that he delivered the laws of creation while "still in the midst of the serpent coil,"[14] while in a Pyramid Text the serpent boasts:

> *I am the outflow of the Primeval Flood,*
> *he who emerged from the waters.*
> *I am the "Provider of Attributes" serpent with its many coils,*
> *I am the Scribe of the Divine Book*
> *which says what has been and effects what is yet to be.*[15]

At the end of creation, the chaos-serpent aspect of the creator god separates and recedes into the underworld, while the celestial (creative) aspect takes up residence in the sky. This separation (emergence of opposites) is symbolized by Atum taking the form of a mongoose, a snake-killing animal. Thus ended the time of the serpent and a new age dawned, that of the ordered cosmos. In Eden the serpent suffered a similar but worse fate. At the end of the creation, Yahweh condemned the serpent to crawl in the dust on earth rather than to an otherworldly existence, thus denying it any divine qualities. Only Yahweh remained as the incarnation of this power.

The serpent thus first exists latently within primordial chaos, but its power eventually rises as a creative force (in the form of deities—Atum, Vishnu). After the creation, the chaotic aspect of this force can threaten to damage or destroy the cosmos, and in many mythologies it inevitably does. In Chapter 4 we discussed the eternal dynamic between creation and chaos. This is serpent power at work, in both opposites. In these mythologies, the creative and destructive aspects of serpent power are parts of a conceptual whole, often featuring cycles of creation and destruction of the cosmos; thus, the cosmos, by virtue of the pre-creation state, contains, as serpent power, the seeds of its own destruction (and, in the interim within the cosmos, evil). In Hindu mythology, the cosmos is inevitably destroyed, only to be recreated again, with Shesha as its creator, sustainer, and destroyer.[16] In fact, the name Shesha means "remainder," because after the destruction of a cosmos he is what

remains as inchoate divine energy; he also carries the epithet Ananta, meaning "endless."[17] In pre-Columbian Mesoamerica the serpent was similarly
involved in catalyzing (through fire) each new cosmic cycle in the calendar.
A figure from the Aztec culture of Mexico depicts the rekindling of fire on
the body of the fire-serpent Xiuhocoatl in order to inaugurate the new cycle
of the cosmos.[18] In Egyptian myth, at the end of earthly time Atum again
becomes a serpent as the cosmos reverts to chaos and is engulfed by the
primeval waters.[19]

In the sophisticated understanding of such cyclical mythologies, no nor-
mative judgment is made about the serpent as a force of chaos. This is just
how the cosmos works. Reducing everything back to its original uroboric
state of "oneness" is not necessarily bad. Nevertheless, much of the negative
symbolism of serpents is traceable to this part of the dynamic. The serpent in
Eden lies at this end of the spectrum, and as discussed in Chapter 4 it is clear
that J was portraying it negatively as an agent or manifestation of chaos and
evil. Thus, when the serpent makes its appearance in the middle of the newly
created, perfect garden in Eden, there is an immediate sense of foreboding; it
is clear which aspect of the serpent is being represented, and that something
bad (chaotic) is about to happen.

Following creation, at any moment (or periodically) during the existence
of the cosmos, chaos could appear as represented by a serpent or similar
creature, and would have to be vanquished by a deity. Thus, the Egyptians
believed that each night appeared Apep, the chaos serpent, through whose
body in the underworld darkness (chaos) the sun (embodied by Ra) must
travel to the east on a boat and who is vanquished before dawn by the
boatman Seth so that the sun may rise.[20] Likewise, Osiris in his death mode
in the underworld was envisioned as being enfolded in the coils of the serpent Nehaher, from which he was released to rise again.[21] Figure 28 shows
Osiris midway through this process, rising as the serpent opens up and his
enemies disappear.

Since serpents are born from eggs, they are also associated with creation
accounts in which the cosmos emerges from a primeval egg, which is sometimes depicted as wrapped in a serpent representing the creative force and
totality. One such account was the Hermopolitan creation myth in Egypt. In
that myth four beings—Nothing, Inertness, Infinity and Invisibility (or Darkness)—emerged from the primeval waters together with their female counter-
parts, the eight being known as the Ogdoad. They were represented as serpents (all four female members had snake heads[22]) and frogs, who swam
together and formed the invisible primeval egg. From the egg emerged light
(in the form of bird) followed by the other elements of the cosmos, including
all forms of life.[23] There again the serpent symbolized both the creative force
and the primal unity of the earth's elements and creatures, whose existence
was underpinned by that force.

In earlier mythologies lacking a male creator-god, the serpent was associated with the elemental Great Mother, as in the case of the Sumerian goddess Nammu, who took serpent form. Several statues of a Goddess with a serpent head were found in Ur dating from the 4th millennium; some portray her holding her child *(bios),* also with a serpent head (Fig. 29).[24] Inanna, Ishtar, Asherah and other goddesses were associated and depicted with serpents, sometimes having serpents (often together with fruits) rising out of their shoulders.[25] Egyptian goddesses were also generally associated with serpents. In fact, a hieroglyph (determinative) for "goddess" in Egypt was an upraised cobra.[26] Goddesses outside the ancient Near East were also associated with serpents: in Greece—the goddess of wisdom Athena, and Hera, the sister and wife of Zeus; the Aztec goddess Coatlicue; and the Hindu Kali, to name a few. In Irish Celtic religion the serpent was the emblem of Brighid, goddess of fire and wisdom, at whose Imbolc festival the serpent was venerated; she later became the Christian St. Bridgit.[27] The serpent could also be depicted as the son-god of the Goddess, the earthly manifestation of her creative power. Thus, the Python at Delphi was the child of Gaia, as was Typhon. There are also numerous male serpent deities, including Atum, Zeus, Poseidon, Shiva, Enki, Ningiszida, and Quetzalcoatl. In the end, what made one a goddess or a god was her or his divine (serpent) power. As Campbell explained, generally "the gods are agents, manifestations, or imagined functionaries of an energy that transcends all conceptualization. They are not the source of the energy but rather are the agents of it."[28] *In that sense, all gods and goddesses can be considered serpents,* which is why they were so often depicted as such. Thus, according to one scholar, the serpent was "looked at as the primary 'body' of any autochthonic deity in historical times."[29] Similarly, the ancient Greek diviner of dreams Artemidorus wrote that "serpents . . . stand for all the gods who are sacred. These are Zeus, Sabazius, Helios, Demeter, Kore, Hecate, Asclepius, [and] the Heroes."[30] Yahweh too claimed this power. Indeed, it was increasingly claimed that this ineffable and undepictable deity *was* the power.

From these accounts it is apparent how the serpent also came to represent the ideas of totality, unity, eternity/eternal return, and perfection.[31] This symbolism takes concrete form by combining the serpent with the circle, which itself symbolizes such ideas.[32] In ancient Egypt, the symbol and hieroglyph (determinative) for totality/eternity was a string/rope tied to form a circle, known as the shen ring, which is the origin of the cartouche surrounding the names of Egyptian kings.[33] Egypt and other civilizations also developed the archetypal symbol of a serpent forming a circle and biting its own tail, representing totality and oneness. In Greece this symbol was known as the uroboros and often carried the inscription, "all is one."[34] In many cultures this circular serpent was represented as surrounding the cosmos, embracing its totality. Given the serpent's association with water and the primeval deep,

in cultures where the cosmic geography featured primeval waters surrounding the cosmos, the uroboros serpent represented the undifferentiated (chaotic) primeval waters as well. Thus, in Norse mythology the giant serpent
Jörmungandr encircles the earth (Midgard), biting its tail, symbolizing the
sea that envelops the earth.[35] The notion of totality in the cosmos is similarly
symbolized by the fire-breathing dragon, a composite beast, whose features
represent the four traditional elements of the cosmos. Thus, it has wings
representing air, its body represents earth, its webbed feet—water, and it
breathes fire, symbolizing the divine energy that animates the other elements.
A less comprehensive common figure is the winged serpent (dragon), representing the span from earth (the earthly) to the heavens (spirit).[36] This is also
the symbolism behind the Mexican deity Quetzalcoatl (Kukulcan among the
Mayans), the "plumed serpent," because serpents paired with birds often
represent a harmonization of the three planes of heaven, earth and the underworld. This idea is also commonly symbolized by a serpent at the base of a
sacred tree together with a bird perched on its crown.

   Thus, while the uroboros can represent the primordial chaotic totality
before the emergence of opposites, and also the border where the cosmos
ends and the surrounding chaos begins, it also has been taken to represent the
ultimate union of opposites in the sense of transcending them into a higher
whole, just as in China the union of Yin and Yang formed a circle having a
similar connotation. As Campbell observed, serpents "incarnate the elementary mystery of life, wherein apparent opposites are conjoined."[37] Two entwined serpents can have the same meaning. Thus, in Chinese mythology,
Nuwa, the creator serpent goddess is commonly represented together with
her consort/brother Fu Xi as two serpents entwined to symbolize the union of
heaven and earth and of the male and female principles.[38] In ancient
Mesopotamia the image of two entwined serpents was common, the most
celebrated example being the steatite libation vase of king Gudea of Lagash
from the 21st century, now at the Louvre (Fig. 30). Dedicated to the serpent
god Ningiszida, it depicts two entwined (according to some, copulating)
serpents around a pole, whose tails are actually joined at the bottom, symbolizing the union of male and female principles[39] and in a larger sense—
totality and unity in the cosmos. Over time, in Mesopotamia, the image of
entwined serpents became simplified into various forms of a caduceus, which
was used widely in seals and other art (Fig. 31).[40] Hermes's caduceus, which
carries the same symbolism, may have evolved from these Mesopotamian
precedents;[41] a serpent twined on a single pole could have a similar meaning.[42] In Egypt, where the cosmos was viewed generally in terms of pairs of
opposites, separate serpents represented the poles of concern. Thus, creator
gods such as Atum and Amun represented the "positive" creative aspect of
serpent power, while Apep represented the "negative" destructive aspect.[43]

The union of opposites entails the harmonious assimilation of everything in between, the concept of merism.[44] Thus, an uroboros was sometimes inscribed with an alpha and omega, the first and last letters of the Greek alphabet.[45] This is why Christ could be likened to a serpent as in the epigraph to this chapter (John 3:14-15), because he too embodied merism, being viewed as the alpha and omega, the beginning and the end, the first and the last.[46] As seen above, this idea of serpents being at the poles has a temporal and cosmological meaning as well, where primeval serpents figure at the beginning and end of time and of the cosmos itself. The uroboros thus became the symbol of the Aeon, the life span of the cosmos, as well as of the universe renewing itself.[47] Accordingly, the expression "all things are one" encompasses not simply unity, but also the idea that all things arose from the One and will return to the One, so that the Aeon extends from One to One,[48] which is to say from primeval serpent to primeval serpent, symbolized by the uroboros. As we shall see in Chapter 9, merism is important to the meaning of the Eden story.

Having reviewed the most fundamental symbolism of the serpent, we can now discuss its more particular manifestations, associations and characteristics. Since these are numerous, we touch only on those which are important to the Eden story.

The most basic is the serpent's association with the earth, which is related to its association with the Goddess. Serpents live on the ground, slither across it, and inhabit holes under its surface, which are regarded as doors to the mysterious underworld, the domain of a deity.[49] In the annual cycle of death and rebirth, they hibernate underground during the barren months and emerge in the spring, much like the various son-gods/dying gods of the Goddess with whom serpents are associated, overcoming death to be reborn. In this way, serpents are among the few creatures that span two planes of the cosmos, the earth and the underworld. This renders them messengers between the planes for purposes of revelation, instruction, and judgment.[50] Hence, Hermes, the messenger god, is associated with serpents, which appear on his caduceus, and he was probably once a serpent himself, most likely a double-entwined, two-sexed[51] serpent.[52] In myths he escorts visitors to the underworld, summoning the dead with his caduceus, and also frequents heaven, hence his winged feet, symbolic of birds who span the planes of earth and heaven.

Serpents are also connected with water, which comes from the underworld and generates life, as in the Eden story (Gen. 2:6). Many serpents live in water, which made it easy to associate them with the mythic sea monsters of chaos that dwelled in the primordial deep and had to be vanquished in the process of the creation.

Serpents are associated with trees and their roots, which likewise span the planes of earth and the underworld. Both the serpent and the sap of trees rise

up in the spring, together signifying life and renewal.[53] Serpents are archetypically portrayed as twined around a sacred tree or as positioned at its base
or among its roots. In Sumer, where vineyards grew in the holy sanctuary of
the Goddess and the ascending vines (coiled around a tree) resembled serpents, the words for serpent and tree sounded the same, which fostered their
association.[54] Thus, in the Sumerian story of Inanna known as *The Huluppu
Tree,* a serpent "who could not be charmed" made its nest in the roots of the
tree.[55] Gilgamesh, the hero of Uruk, where Inanna was tutelary goddess,
intervened and struck the serpent, loosened the roots of the tree and made the
tree into articles for the Goddess, a creative act.[56] Likewise, in the Mesopotamian *Etana* myth, the serpent resided in its nest at the base of a tree.[57] In the
Greek mythology of Heracles, the tree with the golden apples of immortality
and youth in the Garden of the Hesperides was guarded by the serpent Ladon.
In the story of Jason and the Golden Fleece, the Fleece hung on a tree
guarded at its base by a serpent-dragon.

   The combination of a sacred tree and a serpent symbolizes a Center where
something special and sacred occurs. In this symbolism the tree is the passive
axis mundi, while the serpent is the active messenger and energy that travels
along the axis; indeed, in ancient iconography the tree trunk or pillar is styled
as a serpent helix, or serpents are portrayed as the branches (Fig. 32). As
such, the serpent and tree in combination can be viewed as different aspects
of the symbolism of divinity traversing the three planes, as well as the combination of the energizing, fructifying force and the passive bearer and vehicle
of life (fruit).[58] Figure 33 from ancient Greece depicts this concept in a
creation scenario. There Prometheus is modeling the first human from clay
with the aid of the serpent-goddess Athena, who stands by a sacred tree with
a serpent emerging from its base. That the serpent and sacred tree similarly
appear together in the garden of Eden in connection with the final creation of
the first humans is thus no surprise because it fits this mythological motif.

   As in the above examples, an archetypal role of the serpent is that of a
guardian.[59] This is in part because a snake has no eyelids and thus always
appears to be awake; therefore, some deception or formula must be devised
to put a guardian serpent to sleep. The serpent Ladon that guarded the apples
of the Hesperides was said to never sleep, and the Kholkian serpent-dragon
guarding the Golden Fleece at the oak in a sacred grove was ever-wakeful
and had to be put to sleep by Medea's spell. In ancient Egypt, the upraised
cobra *(uraeus)* was the quintessential figure of a divine guardian[60] and so
protected kings, as represented by the *uraeus* on their foreheads. There, as
well as in Mesopotamia, the gates of cities and doorways of palaces and
temples were guarded by live serpents or by images of serpents or dragons
for apotropaic purposes (i.e., to ward off evil or other trouble), as in the case
of the Ishtar Gate in Babylon. In India and southeast Asia, live serpents
guarded temples, homes and even protected young children, while images of

mythical serpents known as Nagas likewise protected both sanctuaries and ordinary buildings. Throughout ancient Syria-Palestine, figures of serpents were appliquéd or painted around the rims or on the handles of pottery jars, pitchers and bowls, in order to both guard and consecrate their contents (Fig. 46).[61] A serpent guarded Athena's temple in Athens, and one kept watch over Apollo's gold in Scythia. The many later European tales in which a dragon guards a treasure derive from this old motif. We see the same in Ecclesiastes 10:8, which says that anyone who breaks through a wall (hedge) shall be bitten by a serpent. In light of this common symbolism, it seems that in the Eden story the serpent was guarding the tree of knowledge of good and evil, its fruit, and more broadly the knowledge to be gained through it.

As chthonic creatures, serpents are associated with the death aspects of the underworld, where the dead reside. Since serpents also represented the vital life principle, life was said to leave the deceased in the form of a serpent[62] (ghosts were thought of as serpents) and stay in the underworld as the embodiment of the deceased or bearer of his/her spirit,[63] thus also having the potential to facilitate rebirth, meaning that every human in a sense has serpent ancestry.[64] Serpents were thus important for communicating with the dead, not simply as intermediaries (messengers) *between* the living and the dead, but more accurately as manifestations of the dead *themselves*.[65] In much of the ancient world, particularly in Crete, Greece and Rome, house serpents were kept as pets and could represent the blessings of departed ancestors, and also avenge any slights against the departed.[66] Hence, images of serpents were often placed on tombs, as in ancient Greece, where they appeared on an *omphalos* atop or around a grave mound. The *omphalos* at Delphi (marking the grave of the Python which Apollo had killed) symbolized the Center of the cosmos and was portrayed with the Python coiled around it.[67] Therefore, the *omphalos* was not simply a decoration, marker or a memorial to the deceased, but was designed to render the site a Center to act as an axis to transmit divine or magic forces or the spirits of the dead (symbolized by the serpent) to and from the underworld.[68] (That is why our gravestones traditionally are vertically oriented.) In visualizing a Center *(axis mundi)*, one must look down as well as up.

Ultimately, however, in Palestine as elsewhere the significance of serpents as symbols of life dominated; their associations with death were normally paired with (and limited to) the ideas of regeneration and renewal (cycles), even immortality. Serpents do not appear to age, and they regularly (up to four times a year) slough their old skin to sport a new one. Thus, in the *Epic of Gilgamesh*, when the serpent steals the plant that confers eternal life, it shed its slough.[69] Their own apparent capability for renewal substantiates their above-mentioned use as symbols for the never-ending cycle of creation and destruction of the cosmos and for eternity.

The serpent's association with life and renewal also derives from the fact that in the winter it descends into the lower world unknown to humans, and rises up and emerges from there each spring. Therefore, it was thought of as the source of life that generates the plants each spring.[70] Thus, in spring festivals serpents were lifted up as a symbol of the earth's rejuvenation.[71] It was also believed that serpents could transmit this life force/energy to people, hence the serpent's association with human fertility. So it was natural that serpents could take on quasi-sexual[72] significance, either as directly fertilizing the earth and females or at least conferring fertility.[73] This fertilizing quality of serpents is also illustrated by the Greek myth of Cadmus, who sowed the teeth of a serpent-dragon he had killed, which sprouted from the ground into a race of men.[74] In India stones called *nagakals* ("snake-stones") are engraved with figures of entwined serpents, placed in ponds for about six months to become imbued with the earth's generative energies (serpent power), and then set up under sacred trees as votive gifts by women desiring offspring.[75] In the ancient Near East the serpent played a role in sacred marriage rituals, functioning as a mediator between the man and woman to stimulate the divine life force and ensure conception.[76] The serpent unified the spouses, and symbolically the male and female principles.[77] Thus, in an Ugaritic text describing the sacred marriage ceremony, the goddess requests:

> *Give as the marriage price serpents!*
> *An adder give as my marriage price,*
> *And sons of asp as my love gift!* [78]

And the god complies. In the Eden story Eve becomes fertile only after her encounter with the serpent. This may allude to traditional serpent fertility symbolism, but J turns that symbolism around to claim that it is Yahweh, the source of serpent power, who confers fertility. Thus, upon bearing Cain, Eve proclaims, "I have gotten a man with the help of Yahweh" (Gen. 4:1).

Given the serpent's connection with life and renewal, it also archetypically represents health and healing.[79] Indeed, snakes never seem to be ill or in pain, or to age. This linkage is apparent in the biblical story of the Israelites in the wilderness being bitten and dying from fiery serpents and Moses putting a bronze serpent on a pole so that anyone gazing at it after being bitten would be healed (Num. 21:6-9). But the most famous example of the association of the serpent with healing in the ancient world is Asklepios, the Greek god of physicians, medicine, and healing, and his daughter Hygieia,[80] the goddess of healing. Asklepios is typically depicted holding a staff, around which a single serpent is coiled; Hygieia too is commonly depicted with a serpent though without a staff. People afflicted with ailments would sleep in a temple or sanctuary called an Asklepion, where serpents would be present, and dream; the dream would either itself heal the patient or reveal the means for the cure.[81] This dream and the cure were thought to derive from the serpent power arising from within the patient, the physician being merely a facilitator.[82] This power was represented by Asklepios, who may have once been a serpent.[83] His staff with a serpent twined about it became the emblem of today's medical profession. Asklepios is important to us because, together with his Semitic (Phoenician) incarnation Eshmun, he seems to have evolved in Phoenicia during J's time and very likely influenced serpent veneration in Palestine, including in Jerusalem (see below).

Importantly, renewal and transformation through serpent power were thought to occur not simply in a biological sense, but in a spiritual sense as well. The most famous example, from India, is the awakening of Kundalini—a spiritual energy or life force depicted as serpent power, as a coiled serpent resting initially at the base of the spine. The Kundalini energy is the divine cosmic energy, or energy of the Self, present in a dormant (primordial) state in every human being. This serpent (also referred to as a goddess) can be awakened through yogic exercise and spiritual practices, although spontaneous awakenings of Kundalini also are reported. When awakened, the serpent power rises up the spine to the crown of the head, leading to enlightenment, expansion of consciousness, bliss and Self-realization—a creative process. This experience is most famously represented in the image of Buddha meditating under the Bodhi tree in a yogic posture on a coiled cobra (the serpent goddess Mucalinda), from which he received both energy and protection. In the ancient Near East and Greece the serpent had similar associations in the context of mysteries and initiations. The idea is similar with the ecstatic flights of shamans to another plane of the cosmos (into divinity),[84] achieved by tapping into serpent energy. This phenomenon is depicted elegantly by an ancient Chinese pottery figure of a shaman (or perhaps deity) with an appliquéd serpent rising from his spine along the back of his head (Fig. 35).

Serpents were also believed to possess and control magic. This belief derives from several of their characteristics: their mysterious chthonic life; their apparent ability to renew life and not to age; their open eyes and apparent sleeplessness; their ability to live for long periods without food; their being imperceptible; and their unique means of seemingly effortless and mysterious locomotion. The classic biblical episode associating serpents with magic was when the staff of Moses was turned into a serpent and a contest ensued between Egypt's magicians on the one hand and Moses and Aaron on the other, in which the participants on both sides turned their staffs into serpents, but Moses's and Aaron's serpents devoured those of Egypt's magicians (Exod. 4:2-5; 7:8-12). Serpents were also used in incantations and sacred rituals, and appeared on amulets. Ophiomancy (the practice of divination through serpents) was widespread in the ancient Near East,[85] in which serpents were used as oracles to foretell the future and decide upon future actions. In the Greek world the Python at Delphi was the best example until it was killed by Apollo, whereby Apollo usurped the serpent's power. Another example of the magical powers of the serpent is the legend of princess Cassandra of Troy (and her twin sister Helenus) acquiring the power of prophecy by being licked on the ear by a serpent's tongue in a temple of Apollo;[86] Melampus and the blind seer Teiresias acquired their powers of prophecy in the same way.[87]

It is therefore natural that the serpent was thought to be wise and came to symbolize wisdom. Since it has no ears, it is attuned to the spiritual world without the need for hearing speech or other sounds, and its open-eyed, silent, constant stare led to the snake's eye (particularly cobra's) symbolizing wisdom.[88] In India Naga serpents were assigned to guard the holy Wisdom Sutras, books containing knowledge deemed too powerful for a world that was not ready for such teachings, until the sage Nagarjuna (ca. 150-250 CE) was deemed worthy to see them, after which he propagated them to the world. The Greek goddess of wisdom, Athena, as we have seen, was also associated with serpents. J somewhat acknowledges this tradition in the Eden story, where he describes the serpent as the subtlest of creatures and places it in its familiar role of a guardian of knowledge. In the story, although the serpent is an animal created by Yahweh, it possesses certain knowledge that no other being but Yahweh has. The serpent's biblical associations with wisdom do not stop in Eden, but carry through to the words of Christ, who tells his followers to "be wise as serpents and innocent as doves" (Matt. 10:16).

The symbolism of serpents discussed above is mainly positive, but it is well known that serpents also have negative connotations.[89] For one thing, their venomous bite causes death. They also represent chaos and darkness. The serpent's bifid tongue and apparent slipperiness (and sliminess) gave it the image of being a deceiver, corrupter and tempter. As such, it can be God's (and humankind's) antagonist. These qualities, combined with a snake's independence, cold-bloodedness and ability to appear suddenly, have made it a logical symbol of evil, already available in the biblical world for J to use. The fact that serpents can have such dual (opposite) aspects makes them an ideal mythological subject and enriches their symbolism.

Having reviewed the general symbolism of serpents, we can now focus on what the serpent meant in ancient Palestine and in the Eden story, based on the archeological record and ancient texts.

THE SERPENT IN THE BIBLICAL WORLD

Serpent symbolism and ritual filtered into Syria-Palestine mainly from Mesopotamia and Egypt, each contributing different myths, concepts, iconography, and rites. In order to understand serpent symbolism in Syria-Palestine, we must see what it meant in those civilizations.

Serpent Symbolism in Mesopotamia

Serpents are fundamental figures in Mesopotamian mythology, beginning with creation myths. As we have seen, the Mother Goddess Nammu, from whom emerged both heaven and earth (the cosmos), was portrayed as a serpent. As elsewhere, in Mesopotamia serpents symbolized the fundamental cosmic energy that generated the creation and lay at its essence. Already in the pre-dynastic period, serpents took on the meanings discussed above. Thus, a serpent as a fertility symbol was depicted beside or between copulating animals (antelope, lions) in seals from about 3500 from Tepe Gawra (near modern Mosul, Iraq).[90] In another object from the Gawra period (3500-2900) a serpent was depicted next to a copulating human couple.[91] An even older depiction from the Ubaid period was found at Tepe Gawra showing copulating serpents next to a naked woman.[92] Fragments of pottery bowls or jars having cultic use at Tepe Gawra from as early as the Jemdet Nasr period (3100-2900) feature appliquéd serpents at their rims and spouts and on lids.[93] These serpents were guardians of the contents of the vessel (holy liquid or food), and perhaps also consecrated the contents.[94] Also at Tepe Gawra numerous bronze serpents, possibly votive, have been found.[95] At the lowest levels of excavations in Ur (from the Ubaid Period—5300-4000) clay statues of a goddess with a serpent head were discovered in graves. In some of them, to emphasize her life-giving qualities she holds a child also having a serpent head (Fig. 29). Later, from Babylon ca. 2700 came a portable shrine in the form of an open serpent box (Fig. 36).[96] It had entwined serpents in appliqué on the outside, while inside three serpents approach the stepped throne of a seated deity, probably a goddess.

In Mesopotamia serpents were normally portrayed in an upraised position, not like the *uraeus* in Egypt, but standing erect on their tails, without feet. This occurs both in the case of single serpents (Fig. 37)[97] and when two serpents are entwined, either around themselves or around a pole or tree (Figs. 30 and 39). At its most essential, the upraised serpent, whether as depicted in Mesopotamia or in Egyptian *uraeus* form, represents the action (rising) of the fundamental life-giving energy of nature, whether earthly or heavenly (the source is the same[98]); it is the energy flowing up that enables the serpent to rise and yields the symbolism, much as in the case of Kundalini. In the case of a coiled serpent the energy is simply more latent, either not yet or only partially released. Depending on the context, particular aspects of this force can predominate, such as in giving life to new vegetation in the spring or in the procreation of humans or animals. This same serpent power, or particular manifestations of it, was embodied in Mesopotamian deities.

Thus, Inanna was called the Great Mother Serpent of Heaven, while Ningis-zida and Tammuz/Dumuzi were also conceived of and represented as ser-pents.[99]

Another important Mesopotamian serpent motif was in connection with trees, especially sacred trees. Indeed, sometimes the helix of stylized en-twined serpents formed the trunk of the tree (or pole), or were coiled around it.[100] A famous example is a Sumerian cylinder seal from Sumer dated to 2500, now in the British Museum (Fig. 37),[101] known as the "temptation seal." It depicts a god and goddess seated on either side of a sacred tree (a date palm), with an upraised serpent behind the goddess; a gardenlike setting may be presumed. The pair are gesturing, apparently encouraging each other to partake of the fruit of the sacred tree. Many early commentators thought this seal was a forerunner of the temptation scene in Eden, positing that a similar myth must have existed in Mesopotamia,[102] but so far no such paral-lel Mesopotamian myth has been discovered.[103] Even without such a direct link, however, the image is important for our purposes because it still evi-dences the natural relationship between the serpent, the goddess, and the sacred tree and its fruit, all of which appear in the Eden story. In this seal, the serpent symbolism is entirely positive, probably representing the life force and bounty.

Scholars have not reached agreement on which deities are depicted in the above seal, but a strong possibility is Inanna and her consort, Tammuz/Dumuzi,[104] whose center of worship in Sumer was at the temple of Inanna in Uruk.[105] Inanna, who became the principal goddess in Sumer, was originally considered a serpent, evidenced by her cuneiform logogram, a staff with a serpent twined about it.[106] Her Babylonian and Assyrian successor, Ishtar (later Astarte in Syria-Palestine), was likewise associated with serpents. Ish-tar was depicted in her fertility aspect with serpents crawling up her legs toward her pubes; in fact, it was common to depict goddesses with serpents on their torsos, hips and thighs,[107] which symbolized the male-fertilizing aspect of the life principle.[108] In Mesopotamia as elsewhere in accordance with the archetype, the goddess (as *zoe*) has as her consort a son or brother god (as *bios*). Thus Langdon described their relationship: "He is a more concrete divinization of life than mother earth. She represents apparently the productive *powers* of the earth, the son represents rather *what* is pro-duced."[109] As such, each year he must die, descend to the underworld in the winter, and be resurrected. As a manifestation of his goddess-consort, or of the same underlying force or principle embodied in the goddess, the god also frequently took serpent form,[110] which, as discussed above, was typical for departed souls. In Mesopotamia this god was Tammuz, also known as Du-muzi, both meaning "true [or faithful] son"[111] (of the goddess).[112] His annual cycle replicated the behavior of serpents, which retreat underground (into Mother Earth, *zoe*) to hibernate in the winter and reemerge (as *bios*) in the

spring as plants come to life. The serpent was thus associated with the fundamental life force which revived each spring and gave new life to the earth.
The god's annual death and resurrection was famously told in the myth
known as *The Descent of Inanna,* in which he was consigned to spending half
of each year in the underworld. The annual revival of life was celebrated in
the sacred marriage ceremony in which Inanna and Dumuzi (and their earthly
representatives, in imitative magic) copulated and engendered life. The rite
took place in a sacred garden setting, symbolizing life and fecundity, and at
its culmination the pair would partake of the bounty of the plants. This idea is
captured elegantly in a cylinder seal from 2330-2150, in which the goddess
(probably Inanna), kneeling beneath a bent-over tree, receives the god (almost certainly Tammuz), who rises like a sprout from the base of the tree,
symbolizing the rebirth of vegetation (Fig. 38).

Tammuz's brother-in-law was another serpent god, Ningiszida. Originally portrayed as two serpents, over time he came to be represented anthropo-
morphically, his two serpents becoming stylized and merely protruding from
his shoulders to symbolize his ophidian nature.[113] He is famously depicted in
pure serpent form in the above-mentioned vase of King Gudea, as a double
serpent entwined around a pole or a tree, in caduceus form (Fig. 30). As an
incarnation of the sacred tree, he was known as "Lord of the tree of truth" or
"Lord of the steadfast tree," while his wife Gestinanna (sister of Tammuz)
was goddess of the vine and the underworld and was called "the lady who
renews the gardens."[114] He was venerated as "the wise serpent that produces
the harvest"; King Gudea, responsible for fertility in the land, claimed to be
his son.[115] The two serpents which are either Ningiszida alone or Ningiszida
with Gestinanna, like the pair Inanna and Tammuz and the serpents on
Hermes caduceus, represent the unity and balance of the male and female
aspects of the divine force.[116]

In Mesopotamia the entwined serpents eventually took a stylized and
simplified form as a kind of caduceus, in which only the upper parts and
heads of the two serpents appeared on either side of the top of the staff and so
were not actually depicted as being entwined, which was simply assumed.[117]
This staff was either held by hand (as Hermes did) or stood in the ground.

Egyptian Serpent Symbolism

Serpent symbolism in Egypt had a bewildering array of meanings and forms
of representation, some positive and others negative. But there is some
rhyme and reason to it. When the serpent is elongated and horizontal (i.e.,
crawling), it is normally portrayed in negative terms, representing darkness,
chaos, evil and death, whereas if it is upraised (particularly the cobra as
uraeus) it is uniformly positive and represents concepts such as guardianship,
protection, royalty, wisdom, strength, energy and regeneration.[118] This re-

calls the archetypal dualistic understanding of serpent power as symbiotic forces of creation and destruction discussed above. Thus, according to one Egyptian proverb, "One should welcome the *uraeus* and spit on Apep."[119] In between these poles lies the coiled serpent, which is mostly positive in that it represents, as described earlier, the fundamental latent energy or force of nature leading to creation and life, or creative wisdom.[120] Thus, as Osiris is reborn and rises, the serpent is straightened out (in some versions cut into pieces) as the life energy is released (Fig. 28).[121] Serpents were referred to as "Life of Forms," "Life of Spirits," and "Life of Earth."[122]

The upraised serpent from Egypt is important to serpent symbolism in ancient Palestine and in the Eden story. The Egyptian hieroglyph (determinative) for "goddess," the upraised cobra, seems to have originated in the Nile delta area, where cobras lived in abundance and were venerated even in predynastic times. The divine energy symbolized by the serpent was considered feminine and was represented by the goddesses Wadjet, Neith, and Hathor,[123] Isis, and her sister Nephthys. The cult of the serpent-goddess was centered in the city of Per-Wadjet (Buto to the Greeks), which was the ecclesiastical center of Lower Egypt at the time. As the city's patron deity, Wadjet had a temple there. She was usually portrayed with a papyrus staff (scepter), around which a cobra was entwined.

The upraised cobra is known as the *uraeus,* a Greek term derived from the Egyptian *iaret,* meaning "the rising goddess"; she was also called *nesret,* "the fiery goddess."[124] According to Clark, this imagery "is a sign of the uprightness of the universe" and "represents the cosmic force which lifts things."[125] Thus, for example, according to the Egyptian *Book of the Dead,* when someone died,[126] Wadjet in serpent form was thought to inhabit the body and make it the embodiment of *maat* (divine order and justice), rising up and protruding from the forehead,[127] at which point the soul is made perfect.[128] Thus, this serpent both protects the deceased from harm and enables him or her to be reborn (recreated).[129] The *uraeus* on the forehead, which protected its bearer and made him powerful, became a symbol of Egypt's king. Neith, also from the Nile delta, where she was patron deity of Sais, had a similar symbolism and Mother Goddess qualities. Like Wadjet she was represented as a rearing cobra, though not as consistently.[130]

The thinking behind the primeval serpent in the above-mentioned Atum myth came later, and is also reflected in J's story. As we have seen, in that Egyptian myth, at creation the power of the primeval serpent had to be curtailed and mastered by Atum using knowledge (though according to some versions he had gained it from the serpent), after which the serpent had to be kept at bay to maintain the orderly cosmos.[131] After creation, serpents dwelled in the underworld, still possessing magical powers. Thus, in the Middle Kingdom *Myth of the Heavenly Cow,* Atum, when departing the abyss for the sky after creation, instructs Geb (the earth god) to guard them lest they wreak chaos:

> Take care of the serpents which are in you [earth]. Behold, they showed respect for me while I was down there. But now you have learned their [real] nature. Proceed to the place where Father Nun [primeval waters] is, tell him to keep guard of the serpents, whether in the earth or in the water. Also you must write it down that it is your task to go wherever your serpents are and say: "See that you do no damage!" They must know that I am still here (in the world) and that I have put a seal upon them. Now their lot is to be in the world for ever. But beware of the magical spells which their mouths know, for Hikê is himself therein. But knowledge is in you. [132]

Their status is being degraded, as in the Eden story, and they must stay so. Accordingly, in one Pyramid Text, the serpent is admonished:

> *If you become dangerous to me I will step on you,*
> *but if you recognize me I will not tread upon you,*
> *for you are that mysterious and shapeless thing, of whom the gods foretold*
> *that you should have neither arms nor legs*
> *on which to go following your brother gods.* [133]

Clark astutely describes this passage as "strangely reminiscent of the serpent in the Garden of Eden which was doomed to go upon its belly," [134] but the similarity does not end there: The essential thinking in the story is later found in J. In this mythology the emphasis is on creation occurring not from a vague generative power as in the old Goddess religion, but via knowledge possessed by the High God (Atum or Yahweh). Rather than the serpent power itself (as the Goddess) creating the cosmos, the High God subdues and manipulates this power in the creation process. Creating an ordered cosmos out of primeval chaos is an exercise of intelligent direction. Mythologically this process is narrated in stories of overcoming the serpent in some manner, as in the Egyptian myths, or in vanquishing Tiamat or other sea serpent-monsters as we saw in Chapter 4. Egypt's Heliopolitan mythology likewise developed a sea monster myth, in which the sun god Ra battled a primordial serpent named Imy-Uhaf ("the Slippery One") for cosmic supremacy, fighting it with a harpoon (so it must have been a water monster). In its attempt to win the world from Ra, the serpent utilized the ruse of turning itself into a beautiful woman, a most dangerous form of the dragon of chaos that finds echoes in female creatures from Homer's Circe to Wagner's Venus in *Tannhäuser,* and, of course, Eve paired with the serpent. The process in the above myths entails order (opposites) superseding the serpent-chaos-totality, devising a means of preventing it from returning, and in some cases even stripping the serpent of divinity.

That is what Yahweh did to the serpent in Eden. Like Atum, Yahweh lays claim to knowledge at the expense of the serpent, consigns the serpent to the ground as opposed to letting it exist (or aspire to exist) in some divine capacity, and decides that the serpent shall suffer physically. J relegates the serpent to crawling on the ground, whereas the above Egyptian text says that serpents were *already* by divine design limbless and therefore are on the ground, but in both cases the idea is to portray the serpent as a lowly being rather than allow it to rival the High God. From the manner in which Atum creates through knowledge followed by his withdrawal from the earth to the sky, we also see the idea of divine transcendence in which God and his creations are distinct. [135]

Egyptian and archetypal concepts of the good serpent are well illustrated by the Middle Kingdom *Tale of the Shipwrecked Sailor.* In that story a traveler sets off on a ship to Egypt's mining region in Sinai but a storm destroys the ship. The sole survivor washes ashore on a paradisiacal island brimming with sycamore figs, grapes, animals, and other bounties. It is a Center where the cosmos meets the beyond. After eating his fill, he makes a burnt offering to the Gods, in response to which a huge serpent appears and rears upraised as the sailor prostrates himself before him. He is the supreme creator god (probably Ra), who through dialogue with the traveler gives him wisdom, on the basis of which he may return to his worldly existence and eventually properly meet his death. After four months of such initiation, a ship comes to take him home, after which the island dissolves into the (primeval) waters. [136]

Serpent veneration and symbolism in Syria-Palestine, which became prominent during the Middle Bronze Age, [137] owes much to Egypt, as a result of the combination of the Hyksos retreat from Egypt followed by renewed control of Syria-Palestine by the New Kingdom Egyptians [138] who brought their religion with them. Egyptian-style serpent symbolism and veneration was widespread in Ugarit and other cities along the Phoenician coast with which Egypt traded. These cities had tutelary goddesses who either were Egyptian goddesses or were modeled on them. Chief among them was Hathor, whose telltale coif appears in many Syro-Palestinian statues and plaques (Figs. 3 and 4). Temples were built to her there and she appeared in texts, as when she was invoked in numerous Amarna Letters written by the local vassal kings to the Pharaoh. The Egyptian goddess Qedesh/Qudshu (derived from Asherah) [139] was also associated with serpents, as evidenced by the many plaques and amulets showing her holding serpents at her side (Fig. 3). [140] Importantly, while much Syro-Palestinian serpent veneration and symbolism, including imagery of the bad serpent, came from Egypt, ophidian symbolism and cult objects relating to agricultural and human *fertility* derived primarily from Mesopotamia. [141] Let us now examine serpent symbolism and veneration in Palestine in detail.

Serpent Veneration and Symbolism in Palestine

The religion of ancient Palestine for centuries prior to J had featured veneration of serpents. Unfortunately, outside of the Bible no ancient Palestinian texts have been discovered that describe this serpent worship, but there is abundant archeological evidence of it beginning in the Middle Bronze Age and running through J's time and after. These finds come from some two dozen sites stretching from Dan in the north down to Timna in Sinai near the Gulf of Aqaba. This evidence points to numerous serpent cult centers in Palestine as of when Israel was formed.[142] In fact, the name of one of these cities, Beth-Shan, means "house of the serpent," derived from the Babylonian serpent goddess Sahan, goddess of health.[143] Rather than review the finds site-by-site or chronologically, we discuss them in a conceptual manner according to their categories and contexts, which better explains the symbolism.

One fundamental motif connects the divine powers of serpents with those of the Goddess, as already seen in Chapter 3 with the Qedesh/Qudshu (Asherah) goddess from Syria holding serpents. Similar representations have been found in Palestine right into the Iron Age. For example, in Gezer a clay plaque of the Qedesh/Qudshu type but dated to 1000 or later was found, which portrayed two upraised serpents on each side of a goddess, identified by Professor Charlesworth as Asherah.[144] A second plaque found there depicts the goddess with serpentine artwork (probably representing serpents) rising from her shoulders.[145] In Hazor a 14th-13th century silver plated bronze standard used in cult processions was found depicting a female figure, most likely a goddess, between two serpents rising on either side of her, which she may be holding as in the Qedesh/Qudshu models, and a moon crescent above (Fig. 40).[146] Shechem yielded a limestone plaque from the Middle Bronze Age showing a serpent rising upward from earth toward the pudenda of a female figure who is probably a goddess,[147] while a similar relief dated to the 1500s was discovered at Beit Mirsim, which the excavator (Albright) characterized as a serpent goddess.[148] Another piece, a large plaque from Beth-Shemesh dated about 1400, shows a Hathor-like goddess with a long serpent draped across her left shoulder and breast and running across her hip and resting its head on her left thigh.[149]

Whereas the above figures of upraised or rising serpents are in a non-Egyptian (Mesopotamian, possibly also Cretan) style, the quintessentially Egyptian figure of the upraised cobra *(uraeus)* also has been found all over Palestine. In Beth-Shan a number of faience pendants and amulets from the reign of Amenhotep III (ended mid-14th century) were found depicting the *uraeus,* some even with a human face similar to a sphinx.[150] At Gezer two Late Bronze copper/bronze cobras were found with upraised heads, one of them at a high place.[151] Eight other scarabs with *uraei* were found in Megiddo, dating from 900 forward,[152] while in Ekron, where the Philistines lived, a golden upraised cobra was found dating from the 600s.[153]

Uraei (or similarly upraised cobras) were often combined with female/ goddess imagery or that of sacred trees (which in turn often symbolizes the Goddess). Thus, at Beth-Shan a 15th century pottery cult object was found in the form of an upraised cobra with female breasts. Another pottery cult object from the late 1400s depicted an upraised cobra with female breasts beneath which was a receptacle intended to capture the milk. It was found together with a figure of Ashtoreth whose hands cup her breasts.[154] Two other contemporaneous clay cobras, head upraised, also had breasts, one of them with a cup, also probably meant to capture the milk.[155] A Middle Bronze IIB scarab from Jericho depicts a stylized tree flanked by four *uraei* whose tails connect with the tree so that they have the appearance of branches, possibly even as fruit on branches (Fig. 32).[156] In another Middle Bronze IIB scarab from Shechem, a stylized tree is flanked by two female figures whose pose replicates the profile of a *uraeus,* while above two *uraei* flank a head of a goddess (Fig. 41).[157] Late Bronze images of Hathor's head flanked by two *uraei* were found in Lachish and at other sites (Fig. 42).[158]

Serpents also appeared on cult stands. At least six 12th century cult stands were found in Beth-Shan, most with apertures and depicting serpents and doves.[159] The best example, from the mid-1100s, is cylindrical with a place on top for burning incense (Fig. 43). It has several triangular openings in which doves with breasts are perched (others perch on the two handles),[160] while four serpents crawl up the sides and toward the upper openings; their heads are next to the openings but do not enter them.[161] The doves represent a goddess, most likely Astarte/Ashtoreth since the dove is most typically her bird[162] and because she was the chief deity worshipped at the site and had her own temple there during both the Canaanite/Egyptian and Philistine occupa- tions.[163] The serpent is Tammuz,[164] who descends to the underworld in the winter, when Israelites wept for him before the Temple (Ezek. 8:14). Doves are generally harbingers of spring and are so characterized in the Bible (Song of Sol. 2:11-12; Jer. 8:7). The dove at the aperture thus represents the coming of spring in the form of an allegorical birth (particularly if the apertures represent the vulva), while the serpent could represent the force of life and/or Tammuz/vegetation that accompanies the Goddess as *bios.*[165] This fertility imagery is Mesopotamian rather than Egyptian in style and seems to derive from the pair Tammuz and Ishtar.[166] In fact, a mid-third millennium cult stand from the Ishtar temple in Assur similarly featured apertures (both trian- gular and square), serpents, and doves.[167] Another cult stand, from 11th century Beth-Shan, depicts a serpent crawling up between two square aper- tures toward the feet of a nude man standing above and holding two birds (Fig. 44),[168] and at its top is a place for burning incense.

These cult stands with apertures were probably filled with earth and planted with seeds or growing plants and watered to grow the plants, in a process of "sympathetic" or "imitative" magic intended to promote the growth and renewal of vegetation. [169] As such, they would be like the "Gardens of Adonis" [170] described by classical writers, [171] and explained by Frazer as follows:

> Perhaps the best proof that Adonis was a deity of vegetation, and especially of the corn, is furnished by the gardens of Adonis, as they were called. These were baskets or pots filled with earth, in which wheat, barley, lettuces, fennel, and various kinds of flowers were sown and tended for eight days, chiefly or exclusively by women. Fostered by the sun's heat, the plants shot up rapidly, but having no root they withered as rapidly away, and at the end of eight days were carried out with the images of the dead Adonis, and flung with them into the sea or into springs. These gardens of Adonis are most naturally interpreted as representatives of Adonis or manifestations of his power; they represented him, true to his original nature, in vegetable form, while the images of him, with which they were carried out and cast into the water, portrayed him in his later human shape. All these Adonis ceremonies, if I am right, were originally intended as charms to promote the growth or revival of vegetation; and the principle by which they were supposed to produce this effect was homoeopathic or imitative magic. For ignorant people suppose that by mimicking the effect which they desire to produce they actually help to produce it; thus by sprinkling water they make rain, by lighting a fire they make sunshine, and so on. Similarly, by mimicking the growth of crops they hope to ensure a good harvest. [172]

Such cult stands are condemned in Isaiah (17:10-11): [173]

> *For you have forgotten the God of your salvation*
> *And have not remembered the Rock of your refuge;*
> *therefore, though you plant pleasant plants*
> *and set out slips of an alien god,*
> *though you make them grow on the day that you plant them,*
> *and make them blossom in the morning that you sow;*
> *yet the harvest will flee away*
> *in a day of grief and incurable pain.*

The serpent also appeared on altars. The top of an altar found in Timna has a serpent crawling along its edge. [174] In Beer-Sheba on an ashlar at the bottom of a 4-horned altar dated to the 700s a serpent is engraved, its head pointing toward the earth, thus having some chthonic meaning. [175] The purpose of serpents on altars seems to have been to consecrate the offerings. [176] In the ancient Near East live serpents were kept at temples and used on altars, perhaps also on cult stands, for this purpose. Ovid thus wrote of a prayer addressed to Isis:

by your sistrum I pray, by the sacred head of Anubis—
so may Osiris love your holy rites forever,
and the slow serpent glide about your altar. [177]

Another common cult object was the serpent "house" or "box," often modeled as a temple. They contained small live (or maybe bronze) serpents, probably (since they lack holes to allow breathing) for transporting them for use in rituals. A beautiful example was found in Ugarit dating from the 15th century. [178] Two were found from Late Bronze II Hazor, at least one of them in a temple complex in which bronze serpents were also found (see below). [179] A 12th century serpent house from Dan appears to be modeled as a temple. [180]

Possibly related to the serpent houses are the many bronze votive serpents found throughout Palestine in cultic settings, as they were small enough to fit within the serpent houses, though it is also possible that they were used independently. At Hazor, two dating from the Late Bronze (1400-1200) were found at a temple complex. [181] Two more were discovered at Megiddo, one 18cm long with an upraised head dated to between 1650 and 1550, and the other 10cm long and dated Late Bronze IIB or Iron Age. [182] Another, this time probably a cobra with its head raised, dated to Late Bronze, was found at Gezer, [183] while two more were found at Shechem. [184] In Beth-Shan broken remains of bronze serpents were discovered. [185]

The most interesting metal serpent find, however, comes from Timna in the south and deserves special attention. Timna was located on the west side of Arabah in the Midian, where Yahweh worship seems to have originated. There Moses met the priest Jethro, married his daughter, and first encountered Yahweh at the burning bush, where his staff was turned into a serpent. This is also in the general area of the account in Numbers 21:4-9 of the attacks of fiery serpents, which Moses countered by erecting a bronze serpent on a pole. In the 1300s the Egyptians commenced large-scale copper mining and smelting operations at Timna, which were supervised by Egyptians using local Midianite and Amalekite labor. Eventually, as a result of earthquakes and the Bronze Age Collapse, in the early 12th century the Egyptians vacated the site and the Midianites occupied it until the end of the 1100s, when they too abandoned it. In Timna the Egyptians built a temple to Hathor, the patron goddess of miners and mining. After the Egyptians left, the Midianites built their own sanctuary there, consisting of a tent over the shrine. [186] (The biblical Tabernacle comes to mind.) Also, the Midianites erected along one side a row of pillars, [187] which were typical at high places in Palestine.

Within the temple complex the excavator, Beno Rothenberg, discovered a votive copper serpent similar to those discussed above, only more finely crafted (Fig. 45). Indeed, it has gold gilding on its head; originally the entire figure may have been gilded. Except for the missing gold leaf, it is in near-perfect condition. It is 12-13 centimeters long with seven graceful, even undulations, and since it was found in what had been Hathor's temple, it has often been interpreted in terms of this goddess.[188] Rothenberg, however, eventually dated the serpent to the post-Egyptian Midianite occupation of the site (i.e., 12th century). Since the Midianites defaced the site's Hathor images as well as the hieroglyphic inscriptions, the serpent could not be part of Hathor veneration.[189] The serpent was probably used in the veneration of another goddess who had functions similar to Hathor, as occurred to the north. Given that Asherah was a serpent goddess, was later venerated in nearby Kuntillet Ajrûd, and that the city of Elath just to the south may have been named after her, she is the best candidate.

Serpent symbolism also appeared in jewelry in the ancient Near East, including Palestine. Numerous examples have been found at Megiddo.[190] Serpents in circular form became popular as bracelets, rings and earrings, which evidence a popular understanding of the circular serpent representing totality and oneness as discussed above.[191] Presumably, in addition to symbolizing those qualities, these decorations also served as amulets to ward off illness and other misfortune.

A final serpent motif appears in pottery jars and bowls, which feature serpents on or near their rims or on the handles (or as the handles) (Fig. 46). These have been found dating as far back as 3300 at Tepe Gawra,[192] which Karen Joines concluded are early examples of the serpent symbolism that made its way from Mesopotamia to Palestine.[193] In most cases such objects were found in temples, stored with temple objects, or in tombs, and so were probably used in rituals. In Palestine such objects have been found in cultic settings at Dan, Hazor, Jericho, Megiddo, Munhata, Shechem, Ashkelon, Gibeon, Gaza, Beth Shemesh and Timna.[194] These serpents serve as guardians of the contents, and probably also to bless and consecrate them.[195]

Importantly, many of the objects discussed above appear to have been deliberately broken or defaced. At Beth-Shan the serpents with female breasts had their heads broken off, as did the Ashtoreth, the cult stands were fragmented, and other serpent figures had their heads missing or smashed.[196] The above-mentioned horned altar at Beer-Sheba was dismantled around the end of the 8th century.[197] These finds appear in archaeological contexts that fit the biblical description of Hezekiah destroying pagan sanctuaries and cult objects.[198] In that case, we would have concrete evidence of Yahwists eliminating serpent veneration in Israel, important when interpreting the Eden story.

This leads to a final important aspect of serpent symbolism in Palestine, Baal's connection with serpents. By J's time Baal had become associated with many of the meanings of serpents discussed above, qualities which J wanted Yahweh to possess instead, for example the role of physician-healer.[199] As we have seen, in the increasingly patriarchal biblical world, sky gods were viewed as fertilizing Mother Earth, enabling the plants to grow in the spring. For this purpose the god appropriated serpent symbolism. Thus, in the Canaanite cult (as in Mesopotamia) the serpent became an adjunct or aspect of the Goddess (perhaps associated with the son-god), a "helper"[200] in fulfilling her functions.[201] Baal assumed this role, the goddess being his consort Anat. But Baal's association with serpents and related creatures was somewhat schizophrenic, because he was also their killer. In the Ugaritic epic Baal fought and killed the sea serpent-dragon Yam, his enemy, and in another myth he and his consort Anat killed the dragon Tannin.[202] In iconography he was commonly depicted as smiting an ordinary snake, usually a horned viper.[203] This image served to associate him with the Egyptian god Seth, who before each dawn killed the chaos serpent Apep. In this form, Baal was known as Seth-Baal.[204] Yahweh coveted these roles of Baal, and J facilitated this. Some commentators have identified the serpent in Eden with Baal himself, in which case the Eden story would be at least in some part an allusion to Yahweh dethroning Baal.[205] In our view, in light of the evidence, the serpent's association with the Goddess must be primary, but it is indeed possible that J secondarily targeted Baal.

THE SERPENT IN THE BIBLE

Before turning to J's portrayal of the serpent in the Eden story, it is important to put it in the context of the other Hebrew Bible serpent stories authored by other proponents of Yahweh, because they held complimentary views. The first is the two related episodes about Yahweh turning Moses's staff into a serpent (Exod. 4:1-5, by E) and Aaron turning his staff into a serpent that defeats and swallows the serpent-staffs of the Egyptian magicians (Exod. 7:8-12, by P). The second is E's story in Numbers 21:4b-9 about the fiery serpents that Yahweh set upon the Hebrews (who had accused Yahweh and Moses of leading them into the desert to die), and (after the Hebrews repented) the bronze serpent on a pole that Yahweh had Moses make to heal people bitten by the fiery serpents. The third is the report in 2 Kings 18:4 that King Hezekiah destroyed, on grounds of being non-Yahwistic, this very same bronze serpent of Moses, which until then had stood before the Temple. Obviously there is some explaining to do. We need not undertake a full explication of these passages, but it is important to focus on the serpent symbolism and the possible reasons why the authors chose to use it. Finally we discuss serpent sites in Jerusalem: the "Serpent's Stone" by the En-Rogel spring (2 Sam. 17:17; 1 Kings 1:9) and the "Serpent's Pool" mentioned by Josephus.[206]

The Serpent Staffs of Moses and Aaron

When Yahweh reveals himself to Moses at the burning bush and explains to Moses his task and destiny, Moses doubts that the Hebrews will listen to him. In response, Yahweh tells Moses to cast his rod (staff) to the ground, where-upon it turns into a snake *(nāḥāš)*, but when Moses picks it up by the tail, it turns back into a wooden staff. Yahweh explains that this shall be a sign to the Hebrews of Yahweh's power so that they will believe Moses (Exod. 4:1-5, by E). Later, when Moses and Aaron arrive at Pharaoh's court to ask permission for the Hebrews to leave, per Yahweh's instructions to Moses, Aaron throws his staff to the floor and it turns into a serpent *(tannîn)*.[207] Pharaoh then summons his magicians, who perform the same feat. But then Aaron's serpent devours the magicians' serpents (Exod. 7:8-12, by P), which is meant to demonstrate the superiority of Yahweh to Egypt's gods and magic, and also to show that Yahweh is the source and master of serpent power.

This story draws on classic serpent symbolism. Wizards and magicians have been portrayed with magic staffs (or wands) from antiquity down to the present day (as in the case of Gandalf and Saruman in *Lord of the Rings* and characters in *Harry Potter)*. Moses wields his staff in a like manner, in order to part the Red Sea and later to draw water from a rock. A staff is also likened to a tree, which as we have seen mediates divine powers from other cosmic planes, as does the serpent. Consequently, we see serpents and staffs paired, with the serpent often entwined about the staff as in Mesopotamia, on the caduceus of Hermes and staff of Asklepios, and with Moses's own bronze serpent. In Egypt the quintessential staff, the *was* scepter, symbolized all power both human and divine, as well as strength and prosperity, and was wielded by kings and deities. This staff/serpent power was portrayed in Egyptian art, in some cases by depicting staffs with serpents twined about them, while in other cases the staffs themselves were erect serpents.[208] Egyptian magicians utilized these in the exercise of their powers, hence P's desire to challenge them.

The Bronze Serpent

This story is best explained by beginning with the bronze serpent on a pole that the Bible says stood before the Temple (2 Kings 18:4), because this seems to be historical and is consistent with the above archeological record. This cult object stood in front of the Temple together with the Asherah, both of which Hezekiah removed and destroyed at the same time. Scholars agree that the bronze serpent was a symbol adopted from Canaanite religion,[209] which is to say initially in Israelite religion, a conclusion corroborated by the above archeological evidence. It served the usual purposes of serpents in

Canaanite/Israelite religion discussed above: a means of connection with the Goddess's and male deity's serpent powers, as an agent of healing, and as a giver of life and fertility. Importantly, this serpent, twined on a pole, was in an "upraised" position so that worshippers would have to look up at it.

But the question remains, what was its exact origin, and when and how did it come to stand before the Temple? One intriguing explanation was advanced by H.H. Rowley.[210] He argued that, before David's capture of Jerusalem, Zadok was the local Jebusite priest (of the god Zadek), and that the bronze serpent, representing this Jebusite god, stood and was venerated at the Jebusite holy sanctuary.[211] When David arrived, in order to peacefully assimilate the local population and its religion, he compromised and not only made both the Yahwist Abiathar and the Jebusite Zadok his co-priests (2 Sam. 20:25), but also brought both the Jebusite bronze serpent and the Israelite Ark into the Tabernacle complex that he installed in the city. Thus, although the bronze serpent was originally non-Yahwistic, in a straightforward case of religious syncretism eventually it became so, with Yahweh appropriating the serpent powers of the Jebusite deity. Under this explanation, the bronze serpent would have remained there for a long time (as did the Asherah), and together with the Asherah would have been a longstanding part of official Yahwistic cult practice.

Oddly, between Numbers 21:9 and 2 Kings 18:4 (and thereafter) the Bible never mentions this bronze serpent. If it really was made by Moses at Yahweh's command, or even if it was Jebusite but approved and retained by David, one would expect it to be associated with the Tabernacle and the Temple and be mentioned at least someplace in Deuteronomy, Joshua, Judges or Samuel. For this reason, many scholars believe that the account of the bronze serpent in Numbers was invented by E as an etiological story to explain the origin of and legitimize this cult object that stood before the Temple.[212] And he did so in a way that further glorified his hero, Moses, at the expense of Aaron, by associating Moses with this holy object.[213]

The Bible never says when the bronze serpent appeared in Jerusalem, mentioning only that people were burning incense to it before Hezekiah removed it. Hezekiah ruled during the fall of Israel to the Assyrians in 722, which he and his priests attributed to Israel's apostasy, specifically its Canaanite cult practices and veneration of Canaanite deities. Further, even Yahwistic cult practice in Israel differed from that in Jerusalem and had many Canaanite traits. When Israel fell to Assyria and its Shiloh priests fled to Jerusalem, Hezekiah and his Aaronid priests, prophets like Isaiah (who advised Hezekiah), and perhaps P too, decided that the time was ripe to purify Judahite religion and purge it of its Canaanite elements, including the Asherah and the bronze serpent, lest Judah suffer Israel's fate. One can imagine the ensuing rivalry between the priesthoods.[214] The bronze serpent may have been a holy object from Shiloh brought by the Levite emigrées and venerated at the Temple for a short time before being removed. It is easier to eliminate something new and controversial than something old and venerable.

The more interesting question from the perspective of serpent symbolism is E's explanation of the origin of the bronze serpent. First, the original purpose of this cult object had to be consistent with its actual meaning and use at the Temple, hence E claimed its purpose was for healing. Second, in order to portray Moses as creating the bronze serpent, E set the event in Sinai. E needed something against which the bronze serpent could exercise healing powers. The word used by E for these serpents *(śārāp)*, means "fiery (or burning) serpent," which may refer to the burning feeling from its venomous bite.[215] Yahweh commanded Moses to make a bronze serpent on a pole as the antidote. This is another example of "sympathetic magic," which entails defeating (or encouraging) something using its exact image,[216] which was practiced widely in Egypt[217] and elsewhere in the biblical world.[218]

In this story E made the same point as J, portraying Yahweh as the source of the powers of the serpents and as controlling them.[219] The incident in Numbers 21:4-9 was the first time the Hebrews as a group had questioned and disobeyed Yahweh. Their doing so was associated with serpents that brought death, a palpable allusion to Genesis 3, when humans first questioned and disobeyed Yahweh. Looking up at Moses's bronze serpent implied venerating and obeying Yahweh as the embodiment of serpent power, in this case in order to protect life and facilitate healing. Worshippers would have recognized that the upraised serpent symbolized divine power, life, healing, and rejuvenation; E wanted to ensure that this power would be attributed to Yahweh.[220] Later, Hezekiah and his advisor Isaiah might not have disagreed with the above principle, but in practice the bronze serpent was being treated as an idol, so it had to go, in order that the focus would be on Yahweh himself as the healer. Indeed, when Hezekiah later fell sick, Yahweh appeared to Isaiah, instructing him to tell Hezekiah that "I [Yahweh] will heal you," which he did and added years to Hezekiah's life (2 Kings 20:5-11).

Other Serpent Symbols in Jerusalem

The bronze serpent was not the only example of serpent veneration in Jerusalem. Just to the south of Jerusalem's walls stood a sacred stone known as the "Serpent's Stone," right beside the spring En-Rogel (1 Kings 1:9), most likely the "Spring of the Serpent" mentioned in Nehemiah 2:13,[221] which was the site of religious rites and other ceremonies. In light of the possible local origin of the bronze serpent, it is relevant that the site was connected to Zadok. When Absalom revolted against David, the sons of both Zadok and Abiathar stationed themselves there (the priests themselves were at the central shrine in the city), awaiting news to convey to David (2 Sam. 17:17).

Later, when David was dying and his son Adonijah claimed the throne over his half-brother Solomon, he went to the Serpent's Stone with a retinue of leading officials to be crowned king, made sacrifices, and began to celebrate (1 Kings 1:9, 19, 25). Being proclaimed king at this sacred site would confirm his sovereignty in association with the fertility and well-being of the land, in line with usual serpent symbolism.[222] When Adonijah was informed that David had chosen Solomon, he relented (1 Kings 1:41-53). Clearly the Serpent's Stone was an ancient holy place long venerated by the local population.[223] Although we lack other reports of what serpent cult rituals were conducted there, presumably they resembled those elsewhere in Palestine.

The other important ophidian site in Jerusalem was the "Serpent's Pool."[224] It is so identified only by Josephus[225] rather than in the Bible, and only in a passing reference. Most likely this was the baths located at Bethesda,[226] a place of healing presided over by the god of health and healing, Eshmun/Asklepios, where patients had gathered for centuries before its destruction in 70 CE.[227] Those baths featured serpent imagery, as one would expect.[228] This is the same "pool" described in John 5 where Jesus performed healing miracles, using his own serpent healing powers without even needing the water of the pool. John in 3:14-15 (epigraph to this chapter) makes the same kind of point, attributing serpent powers to Christ while not actually claiming (as did the Ophites) that he was a serpent.[229] While descriptions of the Serpent's Pool date from Christ's time, the site is much older and the kinds of healing practices that took place there went back centuries, possibly to J's time.

Summary of Serpent Cults and Symbolism in Palestine

We have no texts describing the Canaanite/Israelite serpent cults, so we cannot know exactly what transpired at the rituals, but based on the archeological record, the Bible, and what we know about Palestinian deities, we have a good idea. Importantly, this serpent symbolism and cult practice is almost entirely positive,[230] and much of it is reflected (in negative terms) in the Eden story. Notably, of the many words for serpents used in the Hebrew Bible, the term used for the serpent in Eden *(nāḥāš)* is the one most connected with cult practice,[231] which is consistent with the idea that J was alluding in part to serpent veneration.

People in ancient Canaan/Palestine invoked and utilized serpents when they sought to evoke or influence the divine force, because serpents represented that force, which among other things generated plants and other life. As such, serpents were used in fertility rites to ensure a bountiful harvest, and also in connection with human and animal procreation. Serpents seem to have been associated with the "dying and rising god" (Tammuz, Adonis) and thus also with his goddess-consort, together symbolized as serpents and doves, representing complimentary aspects of the divine force. Serpents also played a role in sacred marriage rites[232] and other rituals that involved human and animal copulation. Serpents were also probably employed in rituals involving ecstatic flights by shamans, prophets, prophetesses, and priests. Live or man-made serpents would have been used at high places, and may have been connected with the trees, asherahs and pillars that stood there. Serpents were also held to have powers of healing, and were used in healing rites. They also seem to have played roles as guardians, particularly of life and anything sacred, including sacred trees.

Serpents, as symbols of the divine force, were aware, thinking, and wise beings that could communicate with humans, hence the popular practice of divination through serpents (ophiomancy). Indeed, the word for serpent in the Eden story, *nāḥāš*, connotes divination and giving omens.[233] Ophiomancy was common in Palestine, and it is possible that the prophesizer was naked (cf. 1 Sam. 19:23-24). So when the serpent in Eden, speaking by the oracular tree, opines on what will and will not happen to Eve if she eats the fruit,[234] its speaking to her could be expected, and its words carried weight. Serpents were also used as mediators or tools to manipulate magical power, as seen prominently in the case of the serpent rods of Moses and Aaron and the bronze serpent. With this in mind we can now better understand the references, discussed in Chapter 3, to "Yahweh and his Asherah" working wonders. As we have seen, Asherah too was associated with serpents. Yahweh could wield the power of the goddess, in the form of her asherah symbol, as a mediating agency of serpent power, much as the bronze serpent (which stood together with the Asherah before the Temple) was so utilized. In this manner she could remain an accepted part of official Yahwism except during Hezekiah's and Josiah's reforms.

Finally, the Goddess and the serpent were an inseparable pair in Palestinian religion. Since J considered Yahweh the sole legitimate repository of divinity, it was important that he advance Yahweh's claims over both members of this team. Yahweh's appropriation of Asherah's powers entailed usurping serpent power as well.

THE SERPENT OF EDEN

We may begin by considering why it is a serpent that appears in the Garden of Eden. Why not choose another kind of protagonist? Why did J write the story this way? The above discussion helps us understand why it had to be so.

The Eden story leads inexorably to the transgression, so J had to choose what would be its catalyst,[235] which had to be portrayed in a meaningful, symbolic way. It could not be a human since we are dealing with the first couple who are the objects of the trickery, but neither could it be a divine figure, as this would detract from Yahweh's own stature. Therefore, it had to be one of Yahweh's creatures.[236] By choosing the liminal figure of the serpent and combining its symbolism with that of the other elements of the garden, J could better discredit the religious beliefs and practices that he opposed.

More specifically, the serpent as a symbolic figure was right at home among the other symbols of the garden and would have been recognized by J's audience as fitting in. As we have seen, the serpent represents the fundamental force responsible for creation, and this story is about the consummation of the creation. The creation occurs at the Center, which is the garden. And in the Center grows the archetypal sacred tree which is the *axis mundi*. As we have seen, serpents are archetypally portrayed together with sacred trees and poles, as serpent power runs along this axis to cross the planes of the cosmos and have the desired effects. Veneration of trees (or asherahs) and serpents occurred together at Palestinian high places, to which J seems to have been analogizing the garden. As discussed in Chapter 6, the drama in the garden can be understood in part as a portrayal of what is wrong with high places and the rituals that were conducted at them, prefiguring the more explicit and detailed criticisms of later biblical authors.

This brings us to the second reason why J utilized a serpent. J must have been quite conscious of serpent veneration and serpent symbolism in Palestine, and probably also of that in Mesopotamia and Egypt.[237] He knew that the serpent was a respected and credible embodiment of wisdom and divine powers: those of creation, life, fertility, healing, and of renewal and possibly immortality. But he was equally aware of the negative symbolism of serpents, including in the creation myths involving the vanquishing of the serpent-dragon by the sky god. To him, paganism in Israel was a manifestation of chaos, and the serpent was its prime symbol. In order to elevate Yahweh, he had to discredit serpent veneration on the one hand while on the other hand attribute to Yahweh the positive qualities associated with serpents, a difficult balancing act. In order to do this, he utilized some negative characteristics of serpents to diminish the positive ones and portrayed Yahweh as in control, including as being able to determine the fate of the serpent itself. J thus wove the serpent into his story in a clever way that enabled him to focus maximum blame on the first humans (who must be seen to be consciously exercising their power of choice) rather than on an outside agency.[238] The result was a rich and complex mythological composition, some important details of which we can now explore.

According to J, Yahweh created all creatures, including the serpent (Gen. 3:1). This has crucial implications. Merely having the serpent appear in the story evokes its traditional associations with divinity,[239] but by making the serpent Yahweh's own creation J denies it any supernatural, divine, or magical nature or powers.[240] Yahweh stood anterior to any serpent, whereas in the

Mesopotamian and Egyptian myths the serpent had embodied the divine creative force of the cosmos and engendered even the first deities. Now J claimed that Yahweh embodied that force. J's message was that whatever "divine" powers Israelites may attribute to serpents are really powers of Yahweh. As we have seen, E and P later made similar points when writing about the bronze serpent and Moses's and Aaron's staffs/serpents. J and his successors wanted to strip serpents of any pretense to divine status, although it was acceptable (at least until Hezekiah) to symbolize Yahweh's powers in serpent form in order to convey this idea to people through a familiar symbol.

In the Eden story the serpent is a wild creature (Gen. 3:1). Adam was created and forbidden to eat from the tree of knowledge of good and evil before all animals (including serpents) were created. Animals were created with the idea of providing from among them a suitable companion for Adam, who named them. Therefore, the serpent must have been among the beasts that were created for this purpose, which should mean that humans are superior to serpents. This implies being superior in wisdom,[241] at least by the end of the story. If humans are superior to serpents, they do not deserve to be venerated by humans.

Nevertheless, the serpent could give humans trouble, in this case through its mental faculties. It was evidently superior to the other wild animals in important ways, for (according to J) it is the cleverest of the wild creatures (Gen. 3:1). It is able to converse with, reason with and even "beguile" (as Eve put it) a human. The appearance in the Eden story of a talking serpent arrests the modern reader's attention and may seem odd. But J's audience (and Eve) would have seen nothing remarkable about this. In ancient times the boundaries between humans and animals were not so precisely perceived as in modern consciousness.[242] This would be even more so the case in the primeval garden, evidenced by Yahweh thinking that one of the animals might be a suitable companion for Adam. Further, as discussed above, serpents were viewed as messengers charged with communicating important information to humans, and so were used as oracles for divination; an oracle must be able to communicate. We know of numerous stories from antiquity in which serpents whispered into the ears of kings and gods,[243] or in which other animals talk. The Egyptian *Tale of the Shipwrecked Sailor* consists mainly of a dialogue between the shipwrecked traveler and an upraised serpent (god) that offers sage advice.[244] In the Hebrew Bible itself, Numbers 22:30 even features a talking donkey, while in Judges 9:8-20 trees, vines and brambles talk to each other.

J's portrayal of the serpent draws on longstanding ancient Near Eastern traditions of a serpent embodying real wisdom on the one hand and mere craftiness (including in the service of evil) on the other. Scholars have long debated the precise meaning of the Hebrew word in question *(ārûm)* and its various English translations ("subtle," "clever," "crafty," "wise," "sly," "wily," "cunning," etc.). J would never attribute real wisdom to the serpent. Rather, he wanted to emphasize to his audience the simple cleverness or trickiness (bordering on deceptiveness) of the serpent, like Reynard the fox.[245] This is the quality which the serpent used delicately and masterfully to bring Eve to the point where she could essentially make her own decision, so that the humans (rather than an outside agency) could be held mainly responsible for the transgression. For such purpose, J could not portray the serpent as overbearing or an evil villain. Further, portraying the serpent one-sidedly in too bad a light could make it more difficult to transfer its powers to Yahweh. So J walked a fine line, as evidenced by his choice of a word *(ārûm)* that is fairly neutral and flexible to describe the serpent's mental qualities.[246] Its meaning in the Bible can range from "prudent" in a positive sense (in Proverbs 12:16, 23; 13:16; 14:8, 15, 18; 22:3; 27:12) to "crafty" in a pejorative sense (in Job 5:12; 15:5).[247]

J clearly considered the physical appearance and lifestyle of the serpent important, because Yahweh changed it at the end of the story, condemning the serpent to crawl on its belly and eat dust. It follows that this was not the case before then, when it was conversing with Eve, which suggests that its head was roughly at the level of Eve's. So the question arises, what physical form did the serpent originally have and why, in terms of its mythological significance?

Since originally the serpent was not crawling on its belly as ordinary snakes do, it was elevated in some manner, but how? There are three possibilities. First, the serpent could have had legs, perhaps even something of a body with arms, a neck and head. Second, the serpent could have been twined around the trunk or a lower branch of the tree, so that its head was at or even above Eve's (much as people looked up to the bronze serpent of Moses). Third, the serpent could have been legless but upraised, as characteristically depicted in the Mesopotamian and Egyptian iconography described above.[248]

The explanation that the serpent of the Garden had legs has been advanced by some commentators,[249] and sometimes it has been portrayed this way in Western art. We can consider this idea from the standpoints of the biblical text and terminology, the iconographic evidence, and conceptually in terms of usual serpent symbolism and J's own polemic in the story. First, the term used for the serpent, *nāḥāš,* is the usual term for an ordinary snake. There are no biblical examples of a *nāḥāš* with legs, nor is the term used to refer to any other kinds of legged natural or hybrid animals. J further describes the serpent as a *ḥayyâ śādê* ("animal [or creature] of the field [or open country]" (Gen. 3:1). This is a generic term that refers to any non-domesticated living creature including reptiles,[250] so it is not helpful in determining the serpent's appearance. Had J intended a hybrid or dragon-like beast with legs, presumably he would have used a more particular word for it, as did other biblical authors when they wanted to portray such creatures.[251] Second, there is no iconographic or other archaeological evidence in ancient Palestine for a serpent *(nāḥāš)* with appendages. As seen above, ordinary snakes fitting the description of a *nāḥāš* (living or metallic) were used in the serpent veneration rites that J was targeting.[252] The notion that a different kind of serpent appeared in the Eden story would demand a compelling explanation.[253] Third, a legged serpent would be inconsistent with the serpent symbolism discussed above and J's own arguments in the story. In order for J to criticize serpent veneration in Palestine he must envision the same kinds of serpents used in the serpent symbolism and rites discussed above, not some fantastic creature.[254] All of the serpent symbolism that is in play in the Eden story (wisdom, knowledge, cleverness, immortality or rejuvenation, messenger function, chthonic meaning, association with life force, etc.) is that associated with the legless serpent (especially if erect), whose very physical appearance accounts in part for these symbolic meanings. A fantastic creature having appendages would symbolize nothing in these terms. Such a creature does not slough its skin and is not associated with rejuvenation and immortality, nor does it live in the ground, hibernate, and emerge in the spring so as to represent rebirth. Nor are dragon-like monsters with legs thought of as wise, whereas ordinary serpents are. Depriving such a creature of its legs would convey no mythological meaning, and indeed would be without mythological precedent.[255] Therefore, the notion that the serpent of Eden originally had appendages which Yahweh cut off is only a mechanical explanation without explanatory power or any connection with J's arguments in the story.

The question then becomes where and in what position was the legless serpent. The idea that the serpent was twined around the tree, or possibly in its lower branches has some explanatory power but is weak in other ways. As we have seen, images of serpents twined around trees, poles and staffs were common in Mesopotamia, Egypt and in Palestine. (Many Western paintings also portray the serpent of Eden in this pose.[256]) Such an image makes mythological sense and carries explanatory power in line with the ideas that are at play in the Eden narrative. It would associate the serpent more closely with the sacred tree and the meanings that they carry in common. As we have seen, this imagery first and foremost represents the cosmic energy (symbolized as serpent power), most particularly the life force rising from the ground up the tree and into our world where things come to life. J was concerned with the continuing popularity of Canaanite religious practices. He therefore used serpent imagery to portray something both tempting and (in his view) wrong. The serpent, already symbolic of eternal life, implies to Eve that it knows and understands the sacred tree, has partaken of its fruit, and possesses the wisdom for which Eve yearns, thus lending credibility to its explanations; having both eternal life and wisdom, the serpent would appear to her as divine. The problem with an already legless serpent in the tree, however, is that in such case Yahweh's punishment of the serpent would only amount to eliminating its ability to climb trees, which would have little meaning. Further, such an interpretation contradicts reality (because in the real world serpents can climb trees), and so would have no etiological credibility.

The third possibility, that the serpent was on the ground but upraised (erect) makes the most mythological sense, and there is evidence for it.[257] Positioning the serpent at the base of the tree rather than as twined about it has a strong basis in the iconography and mythology of the ancient Near East. As we have seen, in Mesopotamia the serpent is normally portrayed (singly or entwined with another serpent) upraised, typically standing on its tail or nearly so, without legs or feet, with its head at human level rather than much lower as in real life even when upraised (Figs. 30, 37; 39).[258] In Egypt when a positive meaning is intended for the serpent, it is as the *uraeus*, a cobra rising up from its coils, in which position it can be a goddess (or god) or symbolize the king. Thus, in the *Shipwrecked Sailor,* while conveying its wisdom to the prostrate traveler-initiate the serpent-god was in an upraised, actually towering position. The Egyptians often depicted staffs in the form of erect serpents.[259] This notion is clearly reflected in the transformation of Moses's and Aaron's staffs into serpents and back into staffs, staffs which perform miracles. In all cases the fundamental meaning of this erectness is the same: the rising up of the divine energy. That is the meaning which J transferred to Yahweh by depriving the serpent of this power.

SUMMARY

We may now summarize much of what J intended the serpent to represent. As with serpent symbolism generally, the symbolism here is multivalent and no single meaning suffices. In light of this, it is helpful to begin with the literary framework that J constructed, namely that the serpent was portrayed as a tempter who leads humans astray, away from correct beliefs and from the proper relationship with Yahweh. The serpent served as a proxy for the broad range of Canaanite religious beliefs and practices (especially but not limited to serpent cults) which purported to confer life, fertility, health and wisdom to humans. J combated such ideas by showing Eve being tempted and deceived by these beliefs and practices. The serpent in the garden setting recalls the Canaanite high places and sacred groves, thus enabling J to criticize what took place at them, including serpent, sacred tree and Asherah veneration. Instead of the positive outcome claimed by Canaanite paganism, the humans face death, shame, toil, and expulsion from the garden. As for the serpent, it is dethroned, and any appearance and pretense by it to divinity is dissipated as it is brought from an upraised position down to being degraded below both domesticated and wild creatures, crawling on the ground and eating dust, making it literally the lowest kind of animal. Such a creature cannot be associated with life (particularly eternal life), fertility, health, or wisdom. Associating its diet with dust rather than the forbidden fruit that confers divine wisdom may also be intended to show that the serpent does not possess wisdom. Deprived of both eternal life and wisdom, it possesses neither prong of divinity. These only Yahweh has. In this regard, as the serpent was connected with Asherah and other goddesses, there is an important allusion to and polemic against Yahweh's wife. Finally, Yahweh's dispensing of the serpent may have been intended to evoke the Hebrew tradition of Yahweh vanquishing the sea monster during the creation. In both these traditional stories and the Eden story, the serpent represents primordial chaos (evil), and its defeat marks the point when the victorious god can set up the familiar orderly world in which we can live in earthly time.

But the above does not exhaust the symbolism of the serpent in the garden. Other aspects and questions remain, and until we resolve them we will not fully understand what is this serpent and all that it symbolizes in the story, and thereby in turn fully appreciate how its fate in Western civilization has played out. These questions include: What is the serpent's relationship to Eve? Are there sexual connotations in the scene of Eve and the serpent? In light of the association of serpents with fertility, how does J deal with this in connection with Eve becoming fertile? In order to answer these questions we must now focus on Eve.

Chapter Eight

Eve:
The Hidden Goddess
in the Garden

Fair as the first that fell of womankind,
When on that dread yet lovely serpent smiling,
Whose image then was stamped upon her mind—
But once beguiled—and evermore beguiling.

—Byron, *The Bride of Abydos*

From a woman sin had its beginning,
And because of her we all die. . . .
Much labor was created for every man
And a heavy yoke is upon the sons of Adam,
From the day they come forth from
their mother's womb
Till the day they return to the mother of all.

—Sirach 25:24; 40:1 [1]

We cannot understand the history of Eve without seeing her as a deposed Creator-Goddess.

—John Phillips [2]

In the beginning God fashioned a man and set him on the earth; after that he fashioned a woman. The two looked at each other and began to laugh, where-upon God sent them into the world.

—Tribal myth from West Africa [3]

Eve was the pivotal character at the climax of the story. She, not Adam, talked with the serpent, with which she was likened. She was the first to

215

transgress, and prevailed upon Adam to do likewise. She became the "mother of all the living," the prototype for all women. She entered the Western imagination and for centuries dominated our culture's flawed images of women and of the relations between the sexes. Over Christian history, if not so much in the story itself, she rather than Adam or the serpent was blamed for the human condition featuring evil, death, and alienation from God, which in turn provided the rationale for the life and sacrifice of Christ. As we shall see, not all of Eve's legacy was faithfully derived from the Eden story. In order to separate fact from imagination and understand what J intended, we must delve into the mythological past that enabled J to script the figure of Eve. Then we can understand why J gave Eve this role, as well as the various details in J's portrayal of her.

ADAM AND THE ANIMALS:
THE REASON FOR EVE'S CREATION

Initially Yahweh created a single human who at first lived alone in the garden, which he soon pronounced "not good" (Gen. 2:18). (In contrast, in P's Genesis 1, God created both male and female humans simultaneously and pronounced that good.) In the ancient Near East, to pronounce a new creation "not good" meant that it was dysfunctional, imperfect, incomplete, and there-fore not even fully in existence. Thus, Eve was essential to completing hu-manity's creation.

Yet Yahweh's first attempt to remedy Adam's loneliness was to create the beasts of the field and the birds and parade them before Adam as poten-tial mates, which to our modern minds may seem bizarre. Didn't Yahweh understand that the animals would be unsuitable? Why not create a woman immediately for this purpose (as in P's account) and create the animals separately? Why does Yahweh go through the trouble of creating Eve from Adam's rib rather than from the soil like Adam? Why these detours?[4]

The detours were used to illustrate how Eve is distinguished from the other candidates and portray her as perfectly matched with Adam and sharing a unique bond.[5] The animals and birds were created from the same ground *(ădāmâ)* as Adam, so while they share the same substance, no animal is distinctively suitable, hence the need for a more particular link between Adam and his future partner. This was illustrated through the naming pro-cess, because it was when he named the woman that he recognized her as his match: "This one at last: bone from my bones and flesh from my flesh." He called her *iššâ* ("woman") because she was "taken from man" *(îš)* (Gen. 2:23). The two are quite literally bosom companions. Her name corresponds to her source, just like *ādām* and *'ădāmâ*. Adam needed a mate for humanity to be complete just as the *'ădāmâ* needed a cultivator.[6] These two parallel correspondences run through the remainder of the Eden story and shape it.

Thus, the long naming exercise was essential as a test, in the ancient Near Eastern tradition of a name signifying something's nature, purpose and destiny, and in this case the names of the animals just didn't fit. It was important that Adam go through the experience of considering and rejecting each animal and feel it more personally and deeply when the right match appears.[7] The important wordplay between *'iš* and *'iššâ*[8] also signified the couple's strong natural bond, a point driven home in the very next verse, which explains that this is why "a man abandons his father and his mother, and clings to his wife, and they become one flesh" (Gen. 2:24). This is an affirmation of their natural bond, the strongest that humans can have, stronger even than that between parents and children.[9] In these passages Adam so enthusiastically desires the woman (not merely sexually) that this appears to be a set-up for Eve's later desire for Adam as part of her punishment for the transgression, which subjects her to his rule and mars their original near equality and ideal bond (Gen. 3:16).

THE MANNER OF EVE'S CREATION AND ITS MEANING

The imaginative manner in which Eve was created has provoked much controversy regarding its meaning. Why did J choose this way to create woman? Why was Adam "asleep" when it happened? Was Eve really created from Adam's "rib," or was it meant to be just flesh from his side, or (as some have argued) even his whole side? And what was the sex of the human (if any) before Eve was created? These questions can be usefully addressed from the perspective of the mythology of the time.

The episode begins when Yahweh puts Adam into a deep sleep before commencing his divine work. Some commentators argue that Adam was put to sleep because, being only human, he must not be permitted to observe the divinity creating.[10] This would be consistent with J's theme of humans not being allowed to access the divine, and so it is possible that J intended this meaning, but no such idea comes straight from the text. A simpler mechanical explanation accepted by many biblical scholars is that this was serious surgery during which the human simply could not be conscious.[11] But more fundamentally, this is a standard mythological motif. In myths, transformation typically occurs through a descent into the underworld, in a dark cave (similarly in initiation rituals), in a night journey (Muhammad), or during sleep, a dream (Jacob), or state of intoxication.[12] Likewise, magical sleep during which mystical events transpire followed by an awakening into a transformed existence is a widespread motif in sagas and folktales, as in *Sleeping Beauty, Snow White,* and the Valkyrie Brynhildr in the Norse

Völsunga Saga.[13] We shall discuss the meaning of this motif in the next section.

After putting Adam to sleep, Yahweh took "one of his ribs" and then closed the opening, after which he "built" the rib into a woman (Gen. 2:21-22). These are two separate operations. Our traditional image of this moment has been colored by the many paintings and reliefs depicting a fully-formed Eve emerging from Adam's side.[14] But nothing of the sort actually happened. Rather, Yahweh built Eve from the rib only after he had taken it out of Adam and closed up the wound.

There has been controversy over whether Yahweh took just a rib, a rib with some flesh on it, an even larger portion of Adam's side, or even whether Adam was divided in two. It is at least clear that a rib was involved, as this is the usual meaning of the Hebrew word that J chose *(ṣēlā)*; thus "rib" is the translation in the NRSV and in the translations of most Bible scholars.[15] Some commentators, however, point out that the word also can mean "side" and argue that this is the better translation in this case, meaning that Yahweh took an undesignated part of Adam's side (but including a rib) rather than a particular organ or bone.[16] One commentator, as part of an argument that Adam and Eve were created equal (from an androgyne human), claimed that this side was essentially one-half of Adam's body, so that male and female were created by a process of division.[17] This notion has not gained traction, but the idea that some flesh was attached to the rib (giving Yahweh flesh material to work from) is sensible. Indeed, this would naturally occur and corresponds to how Adam himself describes the result: "bone from my bones *and* flesh from my flesh" (Gen. 2:23). This combination of bone and flesh is actually a set expression that appears frequently in the Hebrew Bible when describing familial propinquity, indicating specifically parentage from the same bones and flesh.[18]

The origin of J's account of woman's creation remains a mystery. It is not paralleled in (and indeed is contradicted by) P's creation account, and unlike other aspects of the Eden story there is little known ancient Near Eastern mythology of a similar character.[19] In particular, there is no known ancient[20] precedent for the first woman being created from a man's rib, but one possible source of inspiration often mentioned by commentators[21] is the Sumerian myth known as *Enki and Ninhursag,* discussed earlier. In that story Enki's rib ails him and the goddess that Ninhursag sends to cure him is Ninti,[22] whose name means "Lady of the rib." But the Sumerian word *ti* as a verb also means "to make live," so Ninti also came to be known as the "Lady who makes live" or "Lady of life."[23] In the myth, therefore, there was wordplay on "rib" and "life." This recalls Eve (in Hebrew *ḥawwâ,* meaning "life") both being created from a rib and being given the epithet, "mother of all the living" (Gen. 3:20), which as we shall see was common to many goddesses. In Hebrew no such pun is possible, but this does not negate the possibility of the myth being one source of inspiration for J's account.[24] Be that as it may, J seems to have used the rib for his own wordplay, because the Hebrew word for rib *(ṣēlāʾ)* is virtually identical to that for "stumbling" or "misfortune" *(ṣela)*. Thus, although Eve had been designed as Adam's helper, J ironically portrayed her as his and humanity's stumbling block. On the other hand, as discussed below, Yahweh's use of bone to make Eve could involve further wordplay since the word for bone *(eṣem)* also means "strength," which could symbolize Eve becoming the strength or helper corresponding to Adam that Yahweh desired in Genesis 2:18.[25]

WHAT SEX WAS ADAM BEFORE EVE?

Many commentators, beginning with the Gnostics (borrowing from Plato) and into modern times, have debated whether the first human was initially an androgynous being containing both male and female potentialities, which split and became manifest when Eve was created.[26] The notion of the first human or humans being an androgynous, perfect unity has an intrinsic appeal in our modern age, carrying the notion of a perfect unity of opposites, especially of the masculine and feminine principles, and even of spiritual accord.[27] But we must confine our analysis to the text of the story and the mythology of that time and place, and not impose our world view or desires on the text.

J's text does not affirmatively advance any androgyne theme,[28] yet we cannot initially discount the notion. After all, J called Adam only the "human" (or "earthling") until Eve was created; only after that does the word "man" appear. Nevertheless the story's details provide no affirmative indication that J intended to characterize Adam as originally androgynous, nor is this supported by other mythology of the time.

It is best to start with the mythological background of androgyny, which in fact does not fit well with the Eden story. One aspect is *divine* androgyny (i.e., androgynous divinities), which is more prevalent, and the other is *human* androgyny.[29] Divine androgyny, through bodily symbolism, connotes totality, unity, and perfection in the cosmos through the union of opposites. In ancient mythology divine male and female pairs commonly symbolize this totality and unity by representing the opposites concretely in terms of gender.[30] An example discussed earlier was that of the Sumerian god An ("heaven") and goddess Ki ("earth") together comprising the entire cosmos ("an-ki"). The notion of human androgyny, modeled on the divine, similarly embodies the idea of perfection, in particular that the male and female principles are in balance, as with Shiva-Shakti and Yin-Yang.

In the ancient Near East, the notion of divine androgyny was not common, not appearing in Mesopotamia or Syro-Palestine and being restricted to certain deities in Egypt.[31] Further, the notion of the androgyne human had no place in the ancient Near East before or during J's time. Rather, the concept of androgyny seems to have originated with the Greeks, well after J wrote, and the notion in relation to Adam first appeared in medieval rabbinical writings.[32] Rather, in the case of divinities, in the ancient Near East the idea of unity and totality was conveyed not by androgyny but through divine male-female pairs who were consorts. In Syria-Palestine this originally included El and Asherah, and subsequently Yahweh and Asherah. Together a divine pair was complete and could express unity and totality. The sacred marriage expressed this in myth and ritual. Adam and Eve marrying and forming one flesh in marriage expressed the same kind of unity at the human level. This can explain why Yahweh considered existence of the sole human not good, which becomes for us a key to interpreting this aspect of the story. Given that Adam being alone was not good, the state of perfection in human creation was achieved only *after* both sexes existed as a matched pair of opposites, signified by Yahweh presenting her to Adam like the proud father of the bride followed by Adam's epiphany. As Adam and Eve become one flesh, they are complimentary and in balance. The facts that this culmination occurred only after Eve's creation and that the prior situation was "not good" indicates that, *in J's view,* no androgyne principle with its usual symbolism existed in the lone Adam.

Other details of the Eden story corroborate this conclusion. First, the fact that J has Adam searching for a mate among the animals, who are already male and female,[33] should be taken to mean that he was considering the females, which implies that Adam was already male. Second, Yahweh's removal of a rib is not the kind of operation that would alter Adam's sex (or lack thereof). If J had intended an androgyne dividing, presumably he would have used corresponding wording and imagery as is typically the case in androgyne myths, such as in the *Brihadaranyaka Upanishad* discussed in Chapter 4, in which the Self divided into man and woman. Third, in verse 23 the woman was named by the *'ādām* as having come "from man [*'îš*]," which indicates that Adam was already male.[34] Fourth, in J's usage there is no definitive transition from "human" to "man" after verse 23.[35] J continued using *'ādām* for this human even after he was clearly male, starting only two verses later when referring to "the man [*'ādām*] and his wife [*'iššâ*]" (Gen. 2:25).

For such reasons most modern commentators believe that physically Adam was male from the start,[36] which implies that Yahweh imparted the female element after the rib was extracted. But it is also important to recognize that before verse 2:22 J never stressed Adam's maleness. At that stage physical sexual distinctions were not important.[37] What was important was the mythological meaning of Adam's initial state of being, which was uroboric as he had not yet been made into opposites (male-female). As mentioned in the prior section, the episode occurred while Adam was unconscious, and transformations of consciousness occur through a descent into the unconscious. Such transformations require an encounter with the creative, transformative feminine principle (which inheres in the unconscious realm), so that what existed initially (in this case, Adam alone) can "die" and something new can emerge.[38] Here the plot is quite direct regarding this feminine principle, because here woman is first conceived of and created. As Adam wakes into consciousness, he recognizes, albeit dimly,[39] the first pair of opposites (male and female) that has emerged in the creation—*from himself*—and reacts to this, a key step which symbolizes the beginning of a transition to a somewhat higher level of consciousness. Eve's birth facilitated the emergence of male and female principles from the uroboros.[40] As we shall see in Chapter 9, the acquisition of the knowledge of good and evil was a greater (psychic) step that completed the transformation, in the context of *all* opposites. From the mythological and literary standpoints, the birth of Eve forms a prelude to that. Unfortunately, the debate over whether Adam initially was "androgynous" has focused on the *physiological* details of the story, a literalistic approach that is too often the case in interpretations of biblical stories. Such approach misses the important mythological and psychological point: Before Adam was transformed and Eve emerged, his psyche was *symbolically* "androgynous" in that he was unaware of man-woman or any other of pairs of opposites and so by definition a low level of consciousness. Appropriately, it was Yahweh who recognized that the situation of Adam being alone (i.e., without a corresponding opposite) was "not good" and brought about the change. Mythologically, "not good" meant that humankind needed to advance.

Back on the level of divine androgyny, as the idea of monotheism in the official religion took hold, all qualities tended to become centered in the one supreme deity, Yahweh. As Peter Ackroyd observed in this connection, "An eventual monotheism must by some process eventually move beyond male and female distinctions."[41] While this process in Israel led to the attempted assimilation of Asherah's functions into Yahweh and her elimination as his consort, Yahweh himself never became an androgyne. Rather, this idea seems to be reflected in his ineffable nature and the prohibition on portraying him, although he retained masculine features.

THE INITIAL NATURE OF WOMAN AND OF RELATIONS BETWEEN THE SEXES ACCORDING TO J

The nature and position of Eve, as a prototype for women, and her relationship with Adam, as a prototype for men, are treated twice in the Eden story, first when Eve is created (Gen. 2:18-24) and later in dealing with consequences of the transgression (Gen. 3:12-20). The pictures painted in these episodes differ, and they illustrate and implement the etiology that J sought to convey. It is therefore essential to have an accurate picture of the initial stage.

We can begin by considering the nature of the companionship that Adam needed and received (stated in Gen. 2:18, 20), which has been a controversial point. Much of the problem lies in the English translations from the original Hebrew, *'ēzer kĕnegdô,* translated in the RSV as "a helper fit for him." Arguably this implies that the man is primary and the woman is subordinate, a sidekick. The Hebrew phrase in question carries no such connotation, however. In fact, in most instances the word *'ēzer* is used to refer to Yahweh when describing his active intervention on behalf of humans;[42] it is better understood, scholars agree, as meaning "counterpart" or "companion"[43] or possibly even as a "strength."[44] Its complement *kĕnegdô* likewise does not imply inferiority but rather should be understood in the sense of "corresponding to," "vis-à-vis," or "partner."[45] In fact, this may help explain why Yahweh chose to build Eve from a bone of Adam. In Hebrew the word for bone *('eṣem)* also means "strength," so using a bone to make Eve appropriately answers Adam's need for a strength corresponding to him. Further, the Hebrew word for flesh *(bāsār)* can connote weakness (as in Isa. 31:3). Therefore, when Adam characterizes Eve as "bone of my bones and flesh of my flesh," this could be a merism connoting the full range of human weaknesses and strengths that they each have and making them necessary for each other, symbolizing the totality, unity, and complementarity of their relationship.[46] Thus, although a "helper" is created *for* the man, it is better to view such relationship not in terms of whatever minor degree of hierarchy may be implied but in terms of the pair being a perfect match and having an ideal bond, each completing the other. Perhaps the intent is that Eve will "help" most importantly in this sense, not just in helping to tend the garden, meeting Adam's sexual needs, or later (not yet in the picture) in reproduction.[47]

Another question is whether the sequence of Adam's and Eve's creations should be taken to imply that one or the other is primary. According to 1 Timothy 2:13, Adam's coming first accords him priority over Eve, and thus also men over women in general. Some commentators believe that Adam's being created first accords him higher status, while others claim that Eve's coming last makes her the crown of human creation and therefore of higher status.[48] Even in J's story, however, first does not seem to be the best or highest. Adam was derived from the soil, and the plants existed before him, but clearly Adam is deemed a higher entity than both.[49] And the animals are created after Adam and from the ground just like him, but no one would argue that the animals (which he names) are superior. Arguing here that later implies higher or better imposes our modern notions of progress that did not exist in J's world. Only after Darwinian evolution became popular in the late

19th century did people come to the general view that later in development implies higher in quality.[50] If J intended to convey male dominance in this episode, it would come not from the mere temporal sequence but more easily from the woman being derived from man and/or from Adam's naming of the woman, to which we now turn.

A further question related to the temporal sequence of Adam and Eve's creation is whether Eve being derived from Adam's flesh signifies a lower or higher status of Eve. The phrasing "taken from man [*îš*]" and corresponding choice of name *(iššâ)* arguably is intended in part to signify the woman's derivative and therefore lesser status. As we have seen, however, a principal concern of J in deriving Eve from Adam was to be able to use the wordplay on *îš* and *iššâ,* which he did in order to emphasize their bond and completeness together.[51] In this context, to press any implied hierarchy too hard (which J does not) would militate against this purpose.

Once Adam's companion was built, according to the ancient Near Eastern formula he (or Yahweh) *must* name her in order to complete her creation.[52] As we saw in Chapter 4, according to ancient Near Eastern thinking and practice the naming of something accords that thing its nature, purpose, and destiny, and also reflects the superiority, dominance and sovereignty of the namer over the thing named. The question is whether Adam's naming of the woman is intended as the traditional process that reflects the namer's dominion over the creation named, in this case man over woman. Most Bible scholars agree that this is the case when Adam names the animals created by Yahweh. But when it comes to the final candidate in the series, the woman, some commentators have resisted, using imaginative arguments worthy of the clever serpent himself in an attempt to get around the problem.[53] It is hard to imagine that J's audience would not hear echoes of the traditional meaning of the naming process, meaning that some precedence of Adam is inevitably present here. Nevertheless, it is more important to remember that J's main purpose in the naming sequence was to arrive at the *îš-iššâ* formula in order to emphasize the recognition of the man's and woman's common essence and the couple's initial tight bond.[54] As a literary matter, a complimentary, ideal and nearly equal relationship at the outset was necessary to set up and dramatize the later discord resulting from the transgression, in particular the subordination of women to men.[55] Therefore, it would indeed be counterproductive to be highlighting any hierarchical status normally implied by naming. Thus, while some degree of the usual implications of naming is unavoidable here,[56] J seems not to have pressed the point.

This brings us to an important point of perspective. While feminist interpretations of Genesis 2:18-24 have provided valuable corrective insights regarding Eve and her initial relationship with Adam insofar as they go, in order to understand this part of the story as a whole we must then step back and look at the broader perspective to see how this fits into the overall

mythological framework. Mythologically speaking, Genesis 2 is a continuation of the perfect, ideal creation through the forging of fundamental, harmonious bonds, not only that between man and woman but also between man
and the soil, man and the animals, and humans and God. This is a cosmic
phenomenon. Genesis 3 is then a turning point that describes how this initial
unity begins to break down in *all* of these respects.

MARRIED LIFE IN EDEN: DID THEY HAVE SEX?

Upon seeing the woman, Adam exclaims, "This one at last: bone from my
bones and flesh from my flesh" (Gen. 2:23). Verse 24 then describes man
and wife as becoming one flesh in marriage, and verse 25 portrays them as
being naked together, without shame. Bible scholars view verse 23 as a
covenant formula (used throughout the Hebrew Bible) that cements the pair's
marital relationship,[57] including sexual union,[58] while verse 24 elaborates on
the switch of primary loyalty as discussed above[59] and probably is meant to
include the prototypical humans Adam and Eve. Eve is called his "wife" four
more times in the Eden story (Gen 3:8, 17, 20, 21). Calling them spouses
implies that a sexual relationship exists. For such reasons, most modern
scholars take the view, as did Milton long ago,[60] that the couple were married
and had sex prior to the transgression,[61] although it is not clear that Eve was
already fertile (see below). Indeed, Adam and Eve were husband and wife
living in a world that signifies completeness and perfection; it would strain
credulity to suppose that the spouses were not making love. This picture
accords with ancient Near Eastern creation mythology, in which man's creation is not deemed complete (i.e., full humanity is not achieved) without
having human companionship and some elements of civilization. Mythologically speaking, marrying and consummating their marriage was a prerequi-
site for Adam and Eve becoming fully human.

   This conclusion is important because so many commentators, when discussing the nature of the knowledge of good and evil, have displayed a
Freud-like myopic fixation on sex, claiming that the knowledge in question
was sexual knowledge.[62] In fact, the primeval pair already had that. We
elaborate on the question of sexual knowledge in Chapter 9.

THE SIGNIFICANCE OF EVE'S NAME AND HER ROLE

After the transgression and after Yahweh announced his curses and meted
out his punishments, but before expelling the pair from the garden of Eden,
Adam gives his wife the proper name Eve *(ḥawwâ)*. Why did J choose
ḥawwâ? Adam (J) says that she was called *ḥawwâ* "because she was the
mother of all living [*ḥāy*]." Why this added epithet? What wordplay was J

engaging in here? As in the case of Adam's name, this is important because of the traditional link between name, function, and destiny. Here there are at least three layers of meaning to unravel.

Layer One: Eve as Mother and Representing Life

Adam gave his companion a second, proper name because her function and destiny had now changed somewhat and had to be made clear. Instead of living alone with Adam and helping him in the garden, it was now clear that her primary role would be to bear children and serve as a mother. Bible scholars agree that *ḥawwâ* signifies "life" and that J intended this symbolism, making Eve the prototypical mother. Indeed, the Septuagint's Greek transla-tion of Eve's name is *Zoe*,[63] which as discussed in Chapter 3 signifies time-less, infinite and transcendent life.

Scholars have struggled, however, to agree on a precise etymological derivation of *ḥawwâ*. The Hebrew verb for "to live" is *ḥāyyâ,* but it has no direct etymological connection to *ḥawwâ;*[64] J's wordplay here is again that of popular etymology based on assonance.[65] The origins of the word *ḥawwâ* are uncertain,[66] but both Ugaritic and Phoenician have a root *ḥyy/ḥwy* mean-ing to live/make live, which scholars consider to be the most likely etymo-logical derivation of *ḥawwâ*.[67] If so, *ḥawwâ* may indeed be a borrowed foreign word (or derived from one) or ancient traditional name,[68] which J would have used for purposes of wordplay in Genesis 3:20 and 4.1 and for its further symbolic-polemical utility (discussed below). It being of foreign deri-vation could also explain why it appears nowhere else in the Hebrew Bible.[69]

The Canaanite derivation of *ḥawwâ* leads us to Asherah. Beginning in the mid-1st millennium, a version of Asherah named Tannit emerged both in Phoenicia in the Levant[70] and in the Phoenician (Punic) empire in the west-ern Mediterranean, especially Carthage.[71] The name Tannit derives from the Canaanite/Hebrew word *tannîn,*[72] meaning 'serpent," which as seen in Chap-ter 3 is etymologically related to Tiamat and also appears in the Hebrew Bible (e.g., Exod. 7:10; Isa. 29:1, 51:9). Thus, Tannit means "the One/Lady of the Serpent," or simply "Serpent Lady."[73] One 3rd-2nd century Punic inscription refers to her by her epithets: "Lady Hawat [*ḥwt*], Elat."[74] The epithet Hawat is a feminine form derived from the above-mentioned Canaan-ite-Phoenician root *ḥwy* connoting life from which *ḥawwâ* is also derived.[75] Thus, Hawat, similarly to *ḥawwâ*, means something like "Lifegiver."[76] Tan-nit's other epithet, Elat, as we saw in Chapter 3, was a common Canaanite epithet of Asherah meaning "her Holiness."[77] "Tannit" itself is likely an epithet of Asherah.[78] The Tannit connection thus evidences a link between Eve and Asherah.[79]

Another theory of the origin of *ḥawwâ* deserves mention since it also leads us to a goddess, in this case the Hurrian/Hittite goddess Heba (also spelled Hepa, Hebat or Khebat), wife of the weather god Teshub. Some scholars have argued that *ḥawwâ* is traceable to Heba.[80] Heba fell squarely within the Mesopotamian/Anatolian mother goddess tradition. She was venerated in Syria as well as Palestine, as is evidenced in a series of Amarna Letters referring to and authored by a Jebusite king of Jerusalem named Abdi-Heba ("servant of Heba"), indicating that she was worshipped in Jerusalem at the time.[81] The name of one of David's key warriors from the Jerusalem-Hebron area, Elihaba, is most likely a theophoric name derived from Heba, possibly meaning "My Deity is Heba" (2 Sam. 23:32; 1 Chr. 11:33).[82] It thus seems that Heba had a particular connection with the Jerusalem area. In light of the strong Hittite/Hurrian presence and influence in Syria and Palestine, this additional possible allusion, if not derivation, remains an intriguing possibility that would coincide with J's effort to eliminate the Goddess.

Layer Two: Eve as Evoking Serpents and Serpent Goddesses

Numerous scholars from ancient times to the modern era have connected the figure of Eve and her name *ḥawwâ* with serpents and serpent goddesses. Some scholars have even proposed that in an earlier version of the story Eve and the serpent were the same.[83] Ancient commentaries argued that "Eve was so named because she had done the serpent's work in tempting Adam."[84] Early rabbinic works made a similar connection, one stating "the serpent is your [Eve's] serpent and you are Adam's serpent."[85] Numerous modern scholars on various grounds also accept a link between Eve and the serpent.[86]

The word *ḥawwâ* has been connected with serpents. We have already noted an indirect connection through Tannit via her epithet *ḥwt* meaning serpent. Charlesworth points out that *Ḥeva* is a name for a female snake in ancient (pre-biblical) Hebrew and suggests that it may be the source of *ḥawwâ*.[87] Similarities also abound in other nearby Semitic languages.[88] The word for serpent in Aramaic was *ḥewyā*, while in Syriac it was *ḥewyâ;* in Arabic *ḥayya* means snake.[89] In Persian *ḥaiyāt* indicates serpents.[90] While a strict etymological derivation of *ḥawwâ* from any of the above similar terms seems unlikely on technical grounds and the above-mentioned derivation from Canaanite *ḥwy* seems most probable,[91] this does not eliminate the possibility that their similarity of sounds with *ḥawwâ* could be used for popular wordplay alluding to serpents, much like J did with "life" in the case of the etymologically unrelated *ḥāy* and *ḥawwâ*.

Such a connection indeed plays out in the story. The serpent talks to and persuades Eve, and in turn Eve persuades Adam. Thus, when being interrogated by Yahweh, Adam effectively blames Eve, and Eve in turn blames the serpent, saying it beguiled her. Eve and the serpent thereby are cast in similar roles and as doing similar things. Then Yahweh establishes enmity between the serpent and the woman, which suggests that they were originally aligned in a close relationship with each other, as in fact serpents and goddesses (including Asherah) were aligned in the biblical world. Yahweh's putting enmity between the serpent and Eve (and all humanity) seems to be aimed against serpent veneration, in which women and goddesses were prominent, in the hope of discrediting and discouraging the practice. [92]

Layer Three: Eve Holding the Honorific Title of Goddesses

The appellation "mother of all living" is not simply a description of Eve's personal motherhood but rather an honorific title or epithet of goddesses. [93] The fact that she is given this honorific epithet suggests that a goddess is lurking in the background of Eve as a character. [94] Thus, Professor Kikawada concluded that "behind the character of Eve was probably hidden the figure of the creatress or the mother goddess." [95] Joseph Campbell similarly argued that Eve "must be recognized as the missing anthropomorphic aspect of the mother-goddess." [96]

It was usual in the ancient Near East for gods and goddesses (also kings) to have one or more descriptive epithets in addition to their proper names, [97] which highlight the main functions and aspects of these deities. Thus, El was called "father of the Gods" and "Father of Man," [98] while an epithet of Baal was "rider of the clouds," [99] which Yahweh also subsequently adopted since, like Baal, he claimed to bring rain. [100] Likewise, Eve's epithet gives us a further clue to her nature and symbolic meaning.

Assigning this epithet to Eve was a continuation of a long ancient Near Eastern tradition of assigning this or similar epithets to mother or earth goddesses. [101] As mentioned above, the Sumerian goddess Ninti who cured Enki's rib was known as "Lady of life." The Akkadian mother goddess Mami who created humans in *Atrahasis* in that myth was termed "creatress of mankind" and, after creating humans, was called "Mistress of All the Gods." [102] Siduri, whom Gilgamesh encountered on his journey and counseled him not to aspire to immortality and godliness, was known as the "genius of life." [103] And most importantly, within Canaan, Asherah was known as "Progenitress of the Gods" and as "Mother of the Gods." [104] The fact that Eve was given an epithet in common with a long line of goddesses, and in particular the Canaanite/Israelite Asherah, indicates that J intended to identify Eve with such goddesses and with Asherah in particular. [105] Leading Genesis scholars have suggested that behind Eve and her title lurks an earlier Canaanite/Israelite myth concerning the Goddess in her traditional role as the progenitress of all living things. [106]

J brought the goddess forth in the Eden story in order to demythologize and demote her. In fact, as Kikawada observed in connection with Eve, "the Bible completely demythologizes the function of the goddess," [107] while

Bledstein remarked, "Ironically, when the woman is least powerful she receives the title of the great goddess. The awesome mother of all living is
human; men need not fear her."[108] The fact that Eve receives her "honorific"
title immediately after the transgression but just before Yahweh confers the
power of fertility upon her (see below) indeed suggests that J intended this
title to be ironic, in two respects corresponding to these two events.

FIRST IRONY: THE FALLEN GODDESS

As we have seen, J associated the transgression with pagan beliefs and the
cult practices that took place at high places, in particular in the autumnal
New Year festival, which involved goddess worship and serpent veneration.
Giving Eve a title of the goddess immediately upon Yahweh pronouncing his
punishments for the transgression conveyed to his audience that veneration
of Asherah (and the related veneration of serpents and sacred trees) is the
wrong road.

This stance corresponds to other ancient myths of the fall of a goddess or
blaming goddesses for the troubles of mankind. The most illustrative is that
of Pandora. Pandora is most familiar to us as the first woman, who, like Eve,
brought evil to mankind. In fact, she was a dethroned goddess. As shown
both by vase paintings and literary texts, in pre-classical Greece Pandora was
the Earth Goddess (Gaia or Rhea) in her maiden *(kore)* aspect. In earlier
depictions she was typically portrayed as emerging from the earth through an
omphalos, summoned and welcomed by Hermes (serpent god and mediator
between earth and the underworld) and satyrs (representing primitive
man).[109] Because the Earth Goddess confers life and the earth's bounties, she
was also known as Anesidora ("she who sends up gifts," i.e., from within
earth).[110] The name Pandora ("all gifts") likewise originally meant that she
bestowed gifts on mankind necessary for life, for which she was venerated
and each year was bestowed the first fruits of the earth (like goddesses in the
ancient Near East).[111] Because of her chthonic nature, she was associated
with the first day of the annual Anthesteria festival in which the winged
spirits (ghosts) of ancestors flew out of the earth, communed with their
descendants (who venerated and placated them), and then returned to the
underworld.[112] In this process, the spirits emerged from and returned to a
large ceramic jar or urn *(pithos,* from which the name of that day of the
festival, Pithoigia, is derived), half buried in the ground, which symbolized
the womb of the Goddess.[113] The spirits were thus not just ancestors but
manifestations of the Goddess. They could be either harmful or beneficial,
and were viewed as the source of all good, and all evil, Pandora and Pandro-
sos.[114]

But the mythology changed with the rise of Zeus and the Olympian pantheon. Thus, Homer portrayed Zeus as possessing two *pithoi* in his Olympian palace, one containing good gifts and the other evil ones, and distributing them among humans;[115] now *he* rather than the Goddess controlled such things. Hesiod, our main source for the Olympian myth of Pandora, wrote that Zeus, offended by Prometheus when he stole fire (a divine prerogative) from Zeus through trickery and gave it to mankind, resolved upon revenge to punish mankind: "I'll give another gift to men, an evil thing for their delight."[116] So far, there had been no women; men lived in a near-paradise, "apart from sorrow and painful work, free from disease, which brings the Death-gods in."[117] Zeus and other Olympian deities created Pandora as the first mortal woman, out of clay. The Olympians gave her various gifts, and Hermes (whose presence was retained from the older myth) named her Pandora, "for the gifts which all the gods had given her, this ruin of mankind."[118] Among the qualities that she was given was a lying and deceitful character. Hermes put in her breast "lies and persuasive words and cunning ways";[119] she had "sly manners, and the morals of a bitch."[120]

To implement his scheme, Zeus through Hermes bestowed Pandora upon Prometheus's slow-witted brother Epimetheus (meaning "hindsight" or "afterthought") as his wife, who ignored Prometheus's earlier warning not to accept any gift from Zeus but to send it back lest it injure men.[121] Now on earth, Pandora could not resist the urge to know what was in her *pithos,*[122] and opened it. Out flew all the evils, diseases, pains and troubles of the world. In this story, there was no second *pithos* containing good.

The Olympian account of Pandora is thus a case of mythological inversion[123] similar to what happened in the case of Asherah and Eve. In both patriarchal myths the Goddess was no longer self-generated and earth born, but needed a creator. The goddess was dethroned, no longer divine but mortal.[124] Her curiosity and desire for knowledge led to evil and the hardships of mankind.[125] Until then men lived in paradise. Rather than representing life (or the entire cycle of life, death and rebirth), she was only a source of mortality and death. While Eve became a prototypical mother, she was mortal, so she was mother only to humans rather than being the divine source of life to all the world.[126] In the Pandora myth Hermes, a serpent god, played a mediating role similar to the serpent in the Eden story, helping to clarify this separation between humankind and the divine.[127] Pandora's name now connoted her receipt of gifts from the Olympians rather than the Goddess's own gifts to the world. According to J, now the Goddess-Eve too was reduced to receiving the ultimate gift, that of her own fertility, from Yahweh.

SECOND IRONY: THE INFERTILE GODDESS

The second irony relates to the powers of life and fertility that had traditionally been attributed to the Goddess. In the Eden story, the first thing that Eve
does after receiving her honorific title is to be expelled from the garden and
then conceive and give birth (Genesis 4:1), after which she disappears (in
name) from the Hebrew Bible. In this account there is an important twist to
the Mother Goddess role: Upon bearing her son Eve exclaims, "I have gotten
a man *with the help of* Yahweh."[128] In early ancient Near Eastern mythology,
the Goddess was responsible for life and fertility. J denies this, claiming that
Goddess-Eve was infertile until Yahweh conferred fertility on her.

   This indeed reflected the trend in the increasingly patriarchal mythology
in the ancient Near East, in which some level of participation and *help* by the
sky-father god was necessary for the woman (goddess) to produce life,[129] or
even to generate the Goddess herself. As seen in Chapter 3, the Goddess
originally was herself self-generated and also self-generated life, including
her own son-consort-lover, who returns to her to be reborn. As societies
became more patriarchal, the mythology changed so that anthropomorphic
goddesses in one way or another were accounted for as the offspring of gods.
Thus, in Olympian Greek mythology, Aphrodite arose from the genitals of
Uranus thrown into the sea by Cronus,[130] while Athena was described as
being born from the head of Zeus,[131] which episode Jane Harrison termed "a
desperate theological expedient to rid an earth-born Kore [maiden] of her
matriarchal conditions."[132] Thus, Aeschylus had Athena say:

> *There is no mother bore me for her child,*
> *I praise the Man in all things (save for marriage),*
> *Whole-hearted am I, strongly for the Father.*[133]

As for the Goddess's new inability to generate life on her own, we have
already seen the common motif reflecting of the earth (the goddess) becoming fertile only after having been inseminated by the sky-weather god's rain-
semen. But the perceived need of the goddess for a god to help create life
was not always sexual in nature. A good example comes from *Atrahasis*. In
that myth, when the mother (or birth) goddess Mami (there also called Nintu)
was summoned to create humans, she replied:

> *It is not proper for me to make him,*
> *The work is Enki's;*
> *He makes everything pure!*
> *If he gives me clay, then I will do it.*[134]

Enki then had the ringleader of the rebellious gods slaughtered, performed a
purification ritual, after which Nintu mixed the god's flesh and blood with

clay, spat upon the clay, and created humankind.[135] The gods then conferred upon her the epithet (i.e., function and destiny) "Mistress of All the Gods."[136] Another example is a Babylonian creation text reciting that "Aruru [Ishtar] together with him [Marduk] created the seed of mankind."[137] Professor Skinner termed that passage "strikingly similar" to Eve's exclamation in Genesis 4:1, which "certainly gains in significance if we suppose it to have survived from a more mythological phase of tradition, in which *Hawwah* was not a mortal wife and mother, but a creative deity taking part with the supreme god in the production of man."[138] Similarly, Speiser compared Eve's exclamation in Genesis 4:1 to the Akkadian expression, "With Bel [Marduk] there is life."[139] In line with this trend, in J's account the Goddess figure (like the serpent and sacred trees) is created by Yahweh, and from a man (thus reversing for this purpose the sex from which life is derived). The principal female function upon which Goddess veneration had been based was thus usurped.[140] In order for her to conceive her firstborn, she needs the help of Yahweh's creative power. Eve was but the first of a line of cases in the Hebrew Bible where Yahweh was credited with making barren women fertile.[141]

This interaction between Yahweh and Eve could also be an allusion to and rejection of the traditional sacred marriage, which initially was between the Goddess and her son-lover and later between the high god and his consort. In Canaan this occurred between El and Asherah[142] as well as Baal and Anat, while in Palestine in J's time presumably between Yahweh and Asherah. In all cases the marriage was reenacted by humans on earth at important festivals such as that of the New Year. Yahweh making Eve fertile seems to evoke this sacred marriage imagery,[143] but J turns it around to cut Asherah out of the picture and have Yahweh directly grant fertility to humans. Instead of a sacred marriage, we have a divine divorce.

In this connection Yahweh's punishment of Eve—that she will bear children in pain—is also relevant. This may be, among other things, a deliberate reversal of the Mesopotamian notion that goddesses bore painlessly.[144] For example, in the Sumerian myth *Enki and Ninhursag* discussed earlier, set in the paradise of Dilmun, the goddesses bore their young "like butter" (i.e., with ease).[145] As Kramer noted, "The birth of the goddesses without pain or travail illuminates the background of the curse against Eve that it shall be her lot to conceive and bear children in sorrow."[146] We must recall that Asherah was a patroness of mothers, offering protection to women in childbirth.[147] This punishment serves as a reminder that Eve is human and will give birth as humans do and that she has not become "like the gods" (or rather goddesses) in this respect,[148] and perhaps also that she should not aspire further to divine qualities lest she be punished more. It is sometimes claimed that Eve's punishment does not fit her crime, but if we view Eve as an allusion to the Goddess and the story as a demotion of the Goddess, then the punishment matches J's rhetorical purposes well. Indeed, given the recognized absence of any other clear connection between Eve's action and her punishment, this punishment in itself can be taken as evidence that J used Eve as a Goddess figure.

This process of dethronement of the Goddess as the source of fertility is also reflected in J's use of the garden setting itself, which he seems to be analogizing to a high place. As we have seen, originally in Mesopotamia and elsewhere, the sacred garden in the holy sanctuary was the province of the Goddess.[149] Over time, however, male deities assumed control over the garden sanctuaries as patriarchy advanced and the institution of kingship in large cities developed. Thus, in Eridu Enki presided over the temple and its garden, located over the deep *(apsu),* and Enki had Adapa tend the garden much as Yahweh decreed that Adam should tend his. Likewise, Enlil presided over his temple with a sacred garden in Nippur. Later, in Babylon, Marduk ruled over his temple complex and garden, a position he gained as told in *Enuma Elish.* Similarly, in the Eden story the sacred garden is Yahweh's. He creates it, he causes the flow to spring forth and water the garden, and he creates in it verdant and fruitful plants, and then animals. He also plants in it the sacred tree of life with which he is identified through his symbols. In the garden all human needs are satisfied, and even eternal life could be had thanks to Yahweh. Thus, by the end of the story, the Goddess has been ousted from her own traditional estate. J's message here was that she should likewise be ousted from the high places and other sanctuaries and from Israel itself.

In summary, the Eden story is an ironic inversion of the earlier mythological tradition of the Goddess as the sole source of all life.[150] The Goddess (Asherah), represented by Eve, is dethroned and by the power of Yahweh rendered merely human. She could not produce life until Yahweh conferred this power, thus showing that Yahweh is the ultimate source of life. As an etiological myth, it establishes as part of the divinely created order male precedence in Hebrew society, even as it preserves the older motif of humans returning to earth upon death. In fact, as discussed earlier, this process was inevitable in human development and therefore is seen universally in mythology. When consciousness and patriarchy emerge in tandem, the genetic and psychic principles of the matriarchal world are denied. The Father now becomes the source. This is reflected in Eve's emergence from Adam, J's deliberate reversal of the traditional mythology.[151]

J'S VIEW OF THE NATURE OF WOMAN AND RELATIONS BETWEEN THE SEXES

The above discussion provides a framework in which to asses J's views on the final nature and position of woman, as represented by Eve. We can anticipate the result in light of the above discussion outlining the dethronement of Asherah and Yahweh's assumption of her powers. The result can hardly be different on the human level, and J was clearly analogizing between the two. As above, so below.

The role into which women are put at creation is a sensitive issue to our modern minds, but in our present analysis we must put our own views aside and seek only to determine J's intent based on the text, the mythological background of the story, and on what we know about the society in which he lived. If we do not like what the author offers, we must avoid the temptation to make the story something that it is not. Rather, we can simply disagree with it[152] and learn a further lesson from whatever pernicious influence this aspect of the story has had over human history. Logically, the temptation to interpret the original story to suit our own views exists only to the extent one might consider the Eden story as authoritative scripture regarding the relations between the sexes. The alternative is just to treat J as we would any other author, doing our own thinking on the question and agreeing or disagreeing accordingly.

On the other hand, our views on this subject can be colored by traditional interpretations of the story not based solidly in the text and which therefore cannot be fairly attributed to J. For example, the degree to which Eve can be deemed responsible for the subsequent fate of humankind depends on whether one accepts the church doctrine that the transgression in the garden constituted "original sin" or the "fall of man."[153] If, as we argue in this book, the transgression is only the first in a long series of more serious offenses in the primeval history, then being free from these doctrines should eliminate much of any perceived need to engage in strained argumentation to rehabilitate Eve.

Our analysis of the text has shown that initially the degree of inequality between Adam and Eve was rather minimal and that, rather, J's main point at the moment of Eve's creation was to demonstrate the close, natural, and happy bond that existed between the spouses. This original situation of harmony set the stage for the discord and rupture in that bond that J portrayed as the result of the transgression. Adam blames Eve for giving him the fruit and even Yahweh for giving him the woman; Eve then ducks responsibility for her actions by blaming the serpent for "tricking" her.[154] Yahweh then faults Adam for listening to his wife, and punishes him for it. In a reversal of Adam's desire for Eve in Genesis 2:23-24, Yahweh decrees that Eve's desire shall be for her husband, and that he shall rule over her. In the end, the initial happy state in Genesis 2:23-24 is not entirely destroyed, but for reasons of etiology is made to accord with the realities in Israelite society. J may not necessarily have had anything against women; he may have just been ac- counting for how things came to be the way they are, but doing so in a rhetorical manner that enabled him to polemicize against Canaanite religion.

WHY IT WAS EVE WHO INITIATED THE TRANSGRESSION

In light of the above, we can profitably consider why the serpent chose to initiate dialogue with Eve rather than Adam, why Adam had to be passive and functionally absent[155] during that dialogue, and why the initial transgres- sion was committed by Eve rather than Adam. Mythologically, this process also shows how from the outset Eve is being set up as a transforming figure for primitive humankind. Historically and in myths up to when the Eden story was written, generally women were regarded as being in greater touch with the mysteries of life, were the bringers of life, and were at the core of primordial mysteries. They were the creative agents of transformation in numerous ways, including as the keepers of food, the originators of agricul- ture, the guardians and keepers of the fire and hearth, the transformation of food through cooking (including the creation and brewing of intoxicants), and the developers of medical remedies. She was the transformer of matter and life, and so too was regarded as transformer of spirit.[156] Modern psychol- ogy indeed affirms that it is by following the feminine principle (the anima) that humans are creative and attain self-knowledge.[157] Eve's role was thus natural, historical, and already traditional by the time J wrote.

This vision of the female's transformative role is evidenced in Mesopota- mian mythology, which depicted humans initially existing in a savage *(lullu)* primeval state until going through a transformation (catalyzed by deities or their earthly intermediaries) that elevates them to being fully human, func- tioning socially in civilization. The classic Mesopotamian portrayal of this process is contained in the *Epic of Gilgamesh*. In that story the prototypical primeval *lullu* man is Enkidu, who like Adam was created from clay, though by the mother goddess Aruru (Ishtar). At first Enkidu is a wild savage, little different from our images of cave men: He lives on the wild steppe, goes naked (like Adam), and has long, unruly hair. Like Adam, initially he does not know women; instead, he lives and eats with the animals, and possibly consorts with them.[158] When hunters encounter him, he thwarts their hunt and defends the animals. In order to remove Enkidu from the company of their prey, the hunters have Gilgamesh, king of Uruk, summon a temple priestess-prostitute to raise him to the fully human level. He had intercourse with her over six days and seven nights, as a result of which he and his world were transformed. His former companions, the animals, now shunned him and ran away. His body changed:

> *Startled was Enkidu, as his body became taut,*
> *His knees were motionless—for his wild beasts had gone.*
> *Enkidu had to slacken his pace—it was not as before.* [159]

And most importantly, like Adam and Eve, he gained knowledge and wisdom from his encounter with the divine:

> *But he now had wisdom, broader understanding.*
> *Returning, he sits at the feet of the harlot.*
> *He looks up at the fact of the harlot,*
> *His ears attentive, as the harlot speaks;*
> *The harlot says to him, to Enkidu:*
> *"Thou art wise, Enkidu, art become like a god!*
> *Why with the wild creatures dost thou roam over the steppe?*
> *Come, let me lead thee to ramparted Uruk,*
> *To the holy temple, abode of Anu and Ishtar, . . .* [160]

He then moved to live in civilization, in Uruk, as the best friend and companion of Gilgamesh, with whom he embarked on the heroic exploits recounted in the myth.

In *Gilgamesh* females (the courtesan and Siduri) play a mediating, transformational role in humankind reaching its potential and therefore in the definition of being human, and the Eden story is similar in this way. As part of this purpose, both stories portrayed man initially living among the animals, above whom humans must then be elevated for etiological purposes. In the Eden story, J went one step further in creating the serpent among the animals who in tandem with Eve served this mediating role in facilitating the transformation that occurred. [161] Yahweh's tortuous effort to provide a "helper" for Adam first from among the animals and finally by creating Eve thus has this ironic result, which indeed seems to be a literary device.

But J put a further slant on this already traditional role of women. Gerhard von Rad argued that Eve was the prime actor in the story because J understood "that the woman confronts the obscure allurements and mysteries that beset our limited life more directly than the man does. In the history of Yahweh-religion it has always been the women who have shown an inclination for obscure astrological cults." [162] As seen in Chapters 3, 6, and 7, women were most prominent in divination, goddess worship and serpent cults in Palestine, and the Hebrew Bible portrays women as such. It was women who made clothes for the Asherah in front of the Jerusalem Temple (2 Kings 23:7) and wept for Tammuz there (Ezek. 8:14). The many goddess figurines found throughout Palestine were used by women. The Hebrew Bible also portrays women as luring men into pagan worship, as in the cases of Solomon's wives and Jezebel.[163] J was thus in line with the later biblical authors in opposing such pagan practices and in portraying women as troublemakers. J wanted to discredit the women who venerated the goddess (and serpents) and introduced their menfolk to such religion.[164] Therefore, in the Eden story it served his purposes well to cast the woman in this role, making her and the serpent joint catalysts in the transgression. According to this logic, it was appropriate and necessary to subject women to men so that order could be preserved going forward.[165]

The above also explains Adam's functional absence from the temptation scene and the nature of his particular sin once he reenters the narrative. Where Adam erred, stresses Yahweh, was in listening to his wife when deciding whether to eat the forbidden fruit that she offered him. This is not simply an etiological element to establish male dominance as often supposed. Rather, given that Adam's sin occurs just before Eve is named and identified with the Goddess, the more important meaning is theological. The mere fact that Adam would listen to and follow Eve on this question of possibly attaining divine qualities is significant. It suggests that she symbolized the divine qualities of the Goddess,[166] and/or that the serpent (also traditionally deserving veneration and respect and associated with the Goddess) spoke through her. J had to quash such notions and substitute Yahweh as the sole divine authority. By having Adam listen to Eve and having Yahweh punish him for doing so, J seems to have been serving a warning on the people of Israel not to be misled by Goddess worship and serpent cults. As Campbell commented, "There is a historical rejection of the Mother Goddess implied in the story of the Garden of Eden."[167]

J's initially designating the woman as Adam's helper appears to set up a further irony connected with Eve's role in the transgression. As mentioned in Chapter 7, the Goddess often had a serpent as her adjunct "helper." Further, in ancient Near Eastern mythology, the serpent dragons that the high god vanquished typically had "helpers."[168] Thus, in *Enuma Elish* Tiamat's cohort marching at her side were called her "helpers,"[169] while in Ugaritic mythology, Anat defeated dragons associated with Leviathan, not merely the latter.[170] In the Hebrew Bible itself, Job 9:13 refers to the "helpers of Rahab" who bowed before Yahweh after his victory.[171] In the Eden story J too combined such roles, but with the goddess figure (Eve) functioning together with an ostensibly separate serpent. Thus, in her only action in the garden, in the most immediate sense she ends up as the serpent's rather than Adam's helper. Mythologically, this is indeed Eve's and the serpent's function, to mediate the transformation. Given that Yahweh surely knew that the humans would transgress his prohibition, in Chapter 9 we will consider whether ultimately the help that Eve rendered was to facilitate a necessary and inevitable transformation of human consciousness (as only the feminine principle can).

We can thus see how J combined the traditional ancient Near Eastern mythological elements of the sacred tree, the serpent, and the Goddess into a symbolic trinity that epitomized for his audience the nature, elements and dangers of Canaanite religion. This rhetorical symbolism is important to note because it has not yet fully been brought out either in the popular mind or in the scholarly literature. But ultimately this Canaanite angle of the story in itself is not the most important point, for the Canaanite religion that J parodied is just one example of chaos at work. J's main religious and sociological goal beginning with the Eden story and through the remainder of his book was more generally to show humans the key to preventing chaos (and hence evil) from dominating the world, and creating instead a good and stable society. We can now turn to J's idea of how to accomplish this.

Chapter Nine

The Transgression
and Our Transformation

Yet thou hast made him little less than God....

—Psalm 8:5

All men possess by nature a craving for knowledge.

—Aristotle[1]

The secret things belong to Yahweh, our God, and the things that are revealed belong to us and to our children forever, that we may do all the words of this law.

—Deuteronomy 29:29

God has given humans an instruction manual for life on planet Earth so they can partner with God in the management of chaos.

—Gregory Mobley[2]

It is now time to synthesize the various threads of the Eden story that we have explored so far. The ensemble of mythological symbols that we have discussed provides a fitting setting for the story's climax. The first humans, already experiencing existential angst, are in a holy garden sanctuary, a Center in which the creation occurs and interaction with the divine and a more profound understanding of reality is possible. There stand two sacred trees: one that acts as the conduit between the humans and the divine, enabling godlike wisdom, and another that can accord eternal life. Together they represent the two prongs of divinity: wisdom and immortality. The traditionally vital, cosmic serpent power is present, yet the serpent also represents the entry of chaos into the world. The presence of Asherah is felt through her symbols: sacred trees, the serpent, Eve, and the sacred garden precinct itself.

The traditional ancient Near Eastern (especially Canaanite) ways to experience the sacred and achieve an awakening are all in place. We can thus appreciate how these mythological motifs come together in the climax of the story and how J altered their traditional mythological meanings for his own purposes. To do so, we must review what place the Eden story occupies in the narrative arc of the Hebrew Bible, as well as J's overall agenda as revealed in that plot.

THE PRIMEVAL HISTORY

The Eden story is just the opening episode in J's long book. We can understand this episode better if we know what themes J stressed in the remainder of his account, because they line up with those in the Eden story. The Eden story's focus was not on the creation of the whole cosmos, but rather on the creation and original situation of humankind, in order to make key religious arguments and explain aspects of human etiology. J's goals, arguments, and selection of symbols and other material for the plot were driven by what he considered to be the pressing issues of his time.

In light of the importance that the Christian world has given to the Eden story, it is notable that the story is never mentioned again in the rest of the Hebrew Bible, except obliquely in the exilic Ezekiel 28:13.[3] Nor are Eve, the serpent, or the tree of knowledge of good and evil mentioned again. Adam is clearly mentioned again only in Genesis 5:3-5, a genealogy describing his descendants.[4] As Paul Ricoeur observed, Adam "remained a mute figure for practically all of the writers of the Old Testament."[5] It was St. Paul who resurrected the story in order to accord meaning to the death and resurrection of Christ and thereby provide the theoretical basis for Christianity itself (Rom. 5:12, 18; 1 Cor. 15:22), which idea was then taken up by St. Augustine and the Catholic Church to formulate the doctrine of original sin.[6] This fact suggests that, for the ancient Israelites, the Eden story had a fairly limited and precise purpose and function, and as such it did not cast a long shadow over their religious thought; it was never the kind of seminal event (a fall of man that lasted into their own day) portrayed in Western Christian theology. Therefore, in order to understand the story, first and foremost we must determine how it originally fit into the Hebrew Bible and Israelite thinking.

The Eden story is near the beginning of the self-contained initial literary unit of the Hebrew Bible known as the "primeval history," which reaches its climax with the flood story and ends with the tower of Babel story, after which the Hebrew Bible transitions to the appearance of Abraham, who founds the Hebrew nation. Except for P's creation account and some P material included in the flood story, the main *narrative* of the primeval history is almost entirely J's.[7] Into that narrative R (in Genesis 5) and later P and J (Genesis 10) added genealogies tracing the generations *(tôlēdôt)* of humankind from Adam through Noah and certain of his descendants, which serve as chronological and etiological rungs in the development of that history.[8]

An important example of how viewing the Eden story in the context of the overall primeval history can aid us is the flood story. As we saw in Chapter 4, following a long build-up of sin and violence, the flood and its aftermath represented a new creation, a wiping clean of essentially all[9] that had existed and transpired on earth before in order to make a fresh start.[10] At the outset of that new creation, Noah sacrificed to Yahweh (the first sacrifice in history),[11] in response to which Yahweh entered into a covenant with Noah and with the earth itself to govern a new relationship between Yahweh, mankind, and the earth and its living creatures, symbolized by his placing a rainbow in the sky.[12] Yahweh lifted the curse on the ground that he had imposed in the Eden story, promising, "I will never again curse the ground because of man . . . ; neither will I ever again destroy every living creature as I have done. While the earth remains, seedtime and harvest, cold and heat, summer and winter, day and night, shall not cease" (Gen. 8:21, by J). Yahweh then made the land fertile and yield its bounty without undue human toil, and so Noah became "the first tiller of the soil," planting a vineyard (Gen. 9:20, by J). This had been predicted at Noah's birth: "Out of the ground which Yahweh has cursed this one shall bring us relief from our work and from the toil of our hands" (Gen. 5:29, by J), namely the toil that had been imposed on Adam as punishment (Gen. 3:17). According to the text itself, Israelite theology based on this story, and mythological archetypes, no consequences of Adam and Eve's transgression (other than etiological consequences listed in Genesis 3:14-20) could have endured beyond this new creation.[13] The very reason for the flood was to cleanse and purify the earth. Any consequences of the transgression were literally washed away by the flood, much as baptism is said to wash away sins.[14] This is not a trite comparison. As Eliade explained:

> Immersion in water symbolizes a return to the pre-formal, a total regeneration, a new birth, for immersion means a dissolution of forms, a reintegration into the formlessness of pre-existence; and emerging from the water is a repetition of the act of creation in which form was first expressed. Every contact with water implies regeneration: first, because dissolution is succeeded by a "new birth," and then because immersion fertilizes, increases the potential of life and of creation.[15]

Understanding that the transgression's consequences were so removed explains why the Eden story did not need to be mentioned again in the rest of the Hebrew Bible. It also helps explain why there is no textual basis or need for any doctrine of original sin, as discussed below.

Preserving the Human vs. Divine Orders

Another important point of continuity between the Eden story and the rest of the primeval history is J's idea that, as part of the designed order of creation, there are strict boundaries between the human and the divine which humans should, but often fail, to respect. Humans inevitably aspire to and seek to experience the divine realm, and sometimes they succeed, as did Adam and Eve. This is an important point of departure for understanding their transgression.

The human trespass on divine prerogatives begins in the Eden story. The serpent tells Eve, "For God knows that when you eat of it your eyes will be opened, and you will be like God, knowing good and evil" (Gen 3:5), and indeed, after Adam and Eve acquire such knowledge, Yahweh concludes that "the man has become like one of us" (Gen. 3:22). Then, in Genesis 6:1-4, the "sons of the gods"[16] descend to earth and take as wives "the daughters of men" and produce offspring, mighty giants *(nephilim)*[17] who were "men of renown."[18] Apparently, as a result of such interbreeding, some element of the divine spirit entered humans that would have enabled them to share in the divine prerogative of immortality (or nearly so). This constituted an impermissible attempt to disrupt and reduce the boundary between the human and the divine, which brought further disorder (chaos) into humanity.[19] Yahweh therefore declared, "My spirit shall not forever be bottled up astray in man, for he is flesh."[20] Yahweh therefore stepped in to limit the human lifespan to 120 years,[21] thereby enforcing the mortality first imposed on humanity after Adam and Eve's transgression.[22] Nevertheless, apparently such interbreeding with divine beings had introduced further and irremediable corruption and wickedness in the human race and on earth in general (i.e., chaos).[23] For Yahweh this was the final straw. He regretted creating humanity and unleashed the flood to destroy it, save for Noah and his family.

J's final example of such improper human aspirations and trespass onto the divine in the primeval history was when humans, after the flood, started building the tower of Babel. The builders announced, "let us build for ourselves a city, and a tower with its top in the heavens, and let us make a name for ourselves, lest we be scattered abroad upon the face of the whole earth" (Gen. 11:4). Yahweh then descended to observe the goings on, after which he reported (apparently to his divine council), "this is only the beginning of what they will do; and nothing that they propose to do will now be impossible for them" (Gen. 11:6). Therefore, he proposed, "Let us go down and babble their language, that they may not understand one another's speech" (Gen. 11:7). As a result, the humans were unable to complete the project and scattered into their various nations with their own languages. Here too, humans were aspiring to more than their proper station (to reach the heavens and make a name[24] for themselves) on their own and for their own benefit.

(According to the Hebrew Bible, one earns a great name only through faithfulness to Yahweh, as in the case of David (1 Sam. 7:9, 26; 8:13), in which case it is conferred by Yahweh.) Here J was portraying a human intrusion into divine space and divine matters.[25] Thus, the narrative arc of the primeval history opens and closes in Mesopotamia, with the Babel problem being a recurrence of the Eden problem,[26] i.e., human nature.

The most basic, threshold nature of Adam and Eve's transgression was that they disobeyed Yahweh's command.[27] While that in itself can be considered a serious matter because Yahweh demands obedience, some scholars have viewed the prohibition as a mere peccadillo[28] and believe that J meant it as such, particularly since Adam and Eve were not yet equipped to understand it (see below). We must look beyond the mere fact of disobedience to the more important questions of what inspired it and what Adam and Eve hoped to gain (and did gain) by it. In composing his story J could have chosen any kind of prohibition and any kind of disobedience, and given any reasons therefor. But J chose the human aspiration toward the divine and in particular the desire for certain knowledge reserved for the gods (Gen. 3:22), which he called the knowledge of good and evil. Why did J choose this from among so many possibilities? And what exactly is the knowledge of good and evil? In order to answer these questions, it helps to refer again to what J wrote elsewhere in the primeval history.

The Importance of Evil

The most pervasive theme in the primeval history is that of growing evil on earth, which begins in the garden of Eden and then snowballs leading into Noah's flood, only to erupt anew after the flood.[29] Similarly to how the human drama of the Eden story began with Yahweh warning Adam about the forbidden tree, the very first episode following the Eden story begins with Yahweh warning Cain about committing sin, which is the first time sin is mentioned in the Hebrew Bible. But Cain still slays Abel. In the next episode, Cain's descendant Lemech kills a man for only wounding him, and a youth merely for striking (but apparently not injuring) him (Gen. 4:23), thus committing the sin of disproportionate punishment. Then, as recounted in Genesis 6:1-4, the "sons of the gods" intermarried with human women, which was regarded as human sin and degradation (even though it transpired at the initiative of deities).[30]

Originally humans were charged with caring for the earth, to maintain its perfection as created (Gen. 2:15). But as a consequence of cumulative human evildoing, the earth itself and all living things became thoroughly polluted and corrupt. Thus, J wrote that "Yahweh saw that the wickedness of man was great in the earth, and that every imagination of the thoughts of his heart was only evil continually" (Gen. 6:5). Similarly, P wrote, "God saw the earth, and behold, it was corrupt; for all flesh had corrupted their way upon the earth," and so God announced, "I have determined to make an end of all flesh; for the earth is filled with violence *through them"* (Gen. 6:12-13). And so Yahweh decided to "blot out man whom I have created from the face of the ground, man and beasts and creeping things and birds of the air, for I am sorry that I have made them."[31] Importantly, here we see not only the increasing evil of humans, but in parallel the magnification of Yahweh's initial curse on the ground resulting from Adam and Eve's transgression. The sins of humans had infected all of nature, an idea characteristic of Israelite thought. For example, this same theme was later taken up by Hosea (3:3), who lamented the consequences to Israel of not observing Yahweh's word:

> *Therefore the land mourns,*
> *and all who dwell in it languish,*
> *and also the beasts of the field,*
> *and the birds of the air;*
> *and even the fish of the sea are taken away.*

Although the flood had wiped all manifestations of evil from the earth, man by nature had not changed and was still capable of evil. To emphasize this, J has Yahweh observe after the flood, "The imagination of man's heart[32] is evil from his youth" (Gen. 8:21). It did not take long for evil to return. When Noah drank wine, became intoxicated and lay naked in his tent, his son Ham, the father of Canaan, saw Noah's nakedness. Instead of covering Noah, Ham reported this to his brothers Shem and Japeth, who duly proceeded to cover their father, taking pains not to see his nakedness by walking backwards when carrying the garment to cover him. The story considers that Ham did something immoral to his father.[33] In consequence, Noah curses Ham's son Canaan, declaring that he shall be a slave to his brothers. Canaan's descendants eventually populated the land of Palestine and Syria that accordingly became known as Canaan. This sin thus sets the stage and provides justification for the Hebrews' later conquest of Canaan, the population of which, in J's view, consisted of immoral, sexually perverted drunken sinners cavorting in vineyards. The episode of Noah's drunkenness has a number of parallels with the Eden story which J may have wanted to convey to his audience: that both Adam and Noah were men of the ground *(ădāmâ)* and tended plants; that their environments were similar (a garden and a vineyard) and that they consumed fruit[34] from them; that both incidents involve nakedness in a context of shame, in response to which nakedness is then covered; and that both incidents end with curses (on the ground and the snake in the Eden story, and on Canaan in the second).[35] In J's view, while the founding of a vineyard marked progress in civilization (a higher level of agriculture), humankind had not improved since Adam and Eve in terms of its ability to avoid perpetrating evil, as shown soon again in the tower of Babel episode. It was right after that when Abraham appeared on the scene (Gen. 12), through whom Yahweh began developing for humanity a path out of its depraved state.[36]

From the above it is evident that J was focused on the origin and spread of evil in the world. As we shall see, he saw this evil ultimately as the manifestation of chaos on earth, which he connected with the imagination and aspirations of the human heart, one example of which is improper aspirations to the divine. At the same time, J designed his stories so as to criticize Canaanite, Mesopotamian and Egyptian civilization and religious practices, which in his mind were themselves examples of this evil as a form of chaos.

J's focus on the origin and spread of evil suggests that his description of the forbidden knowledge as that of "good and evil" relates to that very theme. J seems to have meant literally what the words suggest.[37] We must apply Occam's razor and exercise caution when considering whether to read more adventurous meanings into the term. Let us now examine this hypothesis in more detail as well as the more creative alternative theories.

THE NATURE OF THE KNOWLEDGE OF GOOD AND EVIL

Commentators have debated for centuries what kind of knowledge Adam and Eve obtained when they ate the fruit of the tree of knowledge of good and evil, but they have never reached a consensus. As we just mentioned and will discuss below, this knowledge mainly concerns having the wisdom to discern between good and evil and act accordingly. But we must also consider other meanings that various commentators have favored (though as principal meanings),[38] especially since to some extent they complement the principal meaning. These are:

• Knowledge of the arts of civilization
• Sexual knowledge
• Some form of esoteric knowledge
• A merism meaning knowledge of "everything"

This diversity of inconsistent views comes from taking too narrow a view of the question and concentrating only on certain details. In our view, the fundamental meaning of the concept can be derived by appreciating how the underlying mythological understanding of the universe among the peoples of the ancient Near East (including in Palestine) bears on the story, which approach is largely not reflected in the above-mentioned alternatives. Before examining these alternatives, we must review that mythology, and before that review how the term "knowledge of good and evil" is used in the Eden story and elsewhere in the Hebrew Bible, as that sheds light on how Israelites—the audience of the story—would have understood the term.

The Knowledge of Good and Evil as Explained in the Bible

When Eve saw the tree of knowledge of good and evil, she recognized that it "was to be desired to make one wise" (Gen. 3:6), which was her principal interest in it.[39] Then, once she and Adam ate the forbidden fruit, "the eyes of both were opened and they knew" certain things (Gen. 3:7). Observing this, Yahweh remarked, "Behold, the man has become like one of us [gods], knowing good and evil" (Gen. 3:22). This means that such knowledge included wisdom and an ability to perceive, discern and distinguish. This interpretation is borne out by how the notion of knowing good and evil is described elsewhere in the Hebrew Bible. This usage appears most prominently in descriptions of the age at which men become mature and wise enough to take on adult responsibilities in life, most notably in the case of kings, as exemplified by David and Solomon.

The Hebrew Bible refers to men reaching an age of maturity at which they are deemed to "know good and evil" and therefore may assume adult roles and responsibilities. Isaiah 7:14-16 describes a stage in the growth of a child before "he knows how to refuse the evil and choose the good." Rules in Hebrew law similarly refer to the age of 20 as when men acquire certain rights and responsibilities (in essence, legal capacity[40]), such as performing military service, giving offerings to Yahweh, and obligations to pay taxes.[41] This concept is exemplified in the curse that Yahweh placed on the Hebrews in the wilderness as punishment for their sin of doubting and murmuring against Yahweh,[42] because it was imposed only on people 20 years of age and older (Num. 14:29-30), presumably because only they were old enough to be deemed capable of and responsible for sin.[43] Thus, Deuteronomy 1:39 refers to these same exempted young people as those who "have no knowledge of good or evil." That reference, in light of the above overall understanding of the term, clearly refers to that age of maturity at which one has the wisdom and discernment to tell right from wrong and therefore the ability to sin (or not), and correspondingly the responsibility not to sin and instead follow and obey Yahweh's commands.[44] Likewise, the Dead Sea Scrolls, in outlining the rules for a young man entering the congregation at Qumran, state that such entry shall occur when "he is 20 years of age when he knows good and evil."[45] Then he may be enrolled in the ranks and take his place among the men of his clan, join the holy congregation, and have intercourse with women and thus marry.

This concept grows in proportion and importance in the case of kings, who have the greatest responsibility of any humans as political/religious leaders, and therefore have the most need for such wisdom. David, who followed Yahweh's path, was described as a king able "like the angel of God to *discern good and evil*" (2 Sam. 14:17). He had "wisdom *like the wisdom of the angel of God* to know all things that are on the earth" (2 Sam. 14:20). This passage recognizes that this is a divine, godlike quality, as both Yahweh and the serpent recognized in the Eden story.[46] Later, when the pious Solomon became king, he prayed to Yahweh: "Give thy servant therefore an understanding mind to govern thy people, that I may *discern between good and evil*" (1 Kings 3:9). Yahweh's response (1 Kings 3:10-12) is instructive:

> It pleased Yahweh that Solomon had asked this. "Because you have asked for this, and have not asked for yourself long life or riches or the life of your enemies, but have asked for yourself *understanding to discern what is right,* behold, I now do according to your work. Behold, I give you *a wise and discerning mind,* so that none like you has been before you and none like you shall arise after you."

This wisdom was immediately brought to bear in the famous story of the two women who each claimed a child was hers. Solomon was able to resolve the dispute by proposing to cut the child in half because "the *wisdom of God* was in him, to render justice" (1 Kings 3:28). The text then explains, "God gave Solomon wisdom and understanding beyond measure, and largeness of mind like the sand on the seashore, so that Solomon's wisdom surpassed the wisdom of all the people of the east, and all the wisdom of Egypt. For he was wiser than all other men" (1 Kings 4:29-31). This episode provides a fitting culmination to the arc of the biblical narrative from the beginnings of man to the rise of the Israelite nation to its apogee, a story bookended by Adam and Eve's seeking knowledge not through Yahweh on the one end and Yahweh's own conferral of such wisdom upon Solomon on the other. Not being in the right relationship with Yahweh, Adam and Eve sought divine illumination directly in a manner reminiscent of Canaanite religious practices. In contrast, Solomon was a righteous man and king who followed Yahweh and realized that divine wisdom must only be granted by Yahweh in his grace, which approach respects the boundary between humans and the divine. So he prayed for and received it, to the greatest possible human degree. Knowing good and evil and choosing the good, Solomon could lead the nation to greatness. This interpretation is reinforced by the Hebrew Bible's later use of the word used in Genesis 3:6 to describe Eve's desire to be wise or insightful *(haśkēl).*[47] Jeremiah 3:15 says that Yahweh will provide Israel with kings having this quality of knowledge and understanding. The book of Proverbs (1:3), which claims to be from Solomon, says that the book was written to provide young men (that is, those still be endeavoring to attain the knowledge of good and evil) such insight into wise behavior.

These concepts are important for understanding the kind of knowledge that Adam and Eve gained from the forbidden fruit. It was originally and by nature a divine capacity, but in one way or another humans may—indeed must—acquire it to some sufficient degree. It is a form of wisdom that gives one the ability to identify and distinguish among alternatives,[48] which forms the basis for being able to make wise choices, especially as between good and evil. This implies that, prior to obtaining such knowledge, human understanding was undeveloped and humans could not be fully responsible for their actions, as specified in the biblical passages discussed above in reference to minors.

This conclusion has far-reaching implications. It means that before the transgression Adam and Eve were in the same position as youths under 20. That is, they lacked the essential capacity to distinguish good from evil, did not know what evil was because they had never experienced it, and could not have understood the true meaning of the name of the forbidden tree. Therefore, they could not understand the nature or weight of Yahweh's prohibition or the consequences of violating it. In such circumstances, it is difficult to consider the transgression a full sin in the usual biblical meaning of the word (indeed not used in the story), much less a seminal "fall of man." To the contrary, the transgression in an important sense results in the *elevation* of humans above their prior state (and above the rest of the created world), sharing to some extent in divine understanding, thereby becoming capable of following the divine instructions of Yahweh. It becomes the basis for a successful relationship with Yahweh, which basis could not exist before. Adam and Eve put their new knowledge to immediate use, as in recognizing that nakedness is uncivilized and shameful and in response performing their first creative act, the fashioning of rudimentary clothing.

Which brings us to the next fundamental question. Understanding the turning point at which humans acquire such knowledge is one thing, but understanding more precisely what wisdom the knowledge consists of is another. In order to do so, we must first understand the nature and meaning of the terms "good" and "evil" themselves, as well as together in the phrase "good and evil." We must consider this in terms of the mindset of J's audience, in which was reflected the ancient Near Eastern mythology concerning the creation and nature of the cosmos. Because J knew that his audience understood these mythological concepts and symbols, he did not have to explain their application in the Eden story (myths rarely provide such explanations), but that means we must do so here.

The Mythological Perspective: The Cosmic Nature of Good and Evil

In Chapter 4 we saw that according to ancient Near Eastern cosmogonies, including P's and J's accounts in the Hebrew Bible, the cosmos was not created from nothing. Rather, before the creator embarked on acts of "creation," there existed only an undifferentiated primordial substance, conceived of as a watery chaos. Creation consisted of giving form and order to this preexisting material, and the created cosmos was formed as an island or bubble within the surrounding primordial waters. The creation can be undone, as essentially occurred in Noah's flood, when the upper and lower waters converged to cover earth, returning things virtually to their pre-creation state, with only Noah's ark surviving within a kind of protective bubble.

According to this ancient Near Eastern paradigm, creation (order, form) is deemed good and indeed is initially perfect, whereas chaos is deemed bad or evil; it threatens and can destroy creation. This is the mythological import of the statements in P's creation account that the result of each step of creation was "good" (*tôb,* the same word used in the phrase "knowledge of good and evil") and the whole of creation "very good" (Gen. 1:31); J had the same idea in mind with the ideal garden of Eden. Importantly, this means that only the created cosmos ("heavens and earth") is good, not the surrounding chaos. But inevitably chaos tends to intrude into the perfect creation. What creator gods did was to wall off chaos in order to establish initial good form and order, and then endeavor to keep it walled off by various means, which differ from myth to myth and culture to culture. As Jon Levenson expressed this idea in respect of Yahweh and Israel,

> the confinement of chaos rather than its elimination is the essence of creation, and the survival of ordered reality hangs only upon God's vigilance in ensuring that those cosmic dikes do not fail . . . . That vigilance is simply a variant of God's covenantal pledge in Genesis 9 never to flood the world again. . . . The world is not inherently safe; it is inherently unsafe.[49]

Inevitably, over time there will be some degree of retreat from the initially perfect creation; chaos will to some extent pollute the earth. From the standpoint of mythology, this is the meaning of the many world myths portraying a decline of creation including humankind, often over a series of ages. The scheme of the Hebrew Bible's primeval history fits this pattern. The appearance of evil, including its human manifestation in sin, is an aspect of chaos, and as such is a natural part of the fabric of reality. As Professor Blenkinsopp observed in his study of the primeval history, "there can be no creation, however, good, without allowing for the possibility of disorder, deviance, and evil."[50] Thus, ancient Near Eastern creation by its nature presupposes that the cosmos as initially created will be compromised and can even be destroyed. In the primeval history, this is what began to happen in the garden of Eden; thus began J's lengthy etiological explanation of the degenerated state of mankind and the world.

In light of the above, we can see that *the content of the knowledge of good and evil consists of understanding how this divine cosmic dynamic of order (good) and chaos (evil) operates in the world and the role that humans play in this dynamic.* Originally divine knowledge, it affords a godlike "perspective." At first only God could have had this perspective since he was the creator that established the difference between cosmos and chaos (good and evil); but this knowledge needed to be conveyed to humans in some manner or other, hence the etiological aspects of the story.[51] That humans actually have such knowledge is hardly speculation; it is actually fundamental to being able to behave in the world according to Yahweh's will and avoid evil. Indeed, the biblical authors understood that they themselves had such knowledge, and accordingly used it to teach their audiences. This is what made it possible for Yahweh to warn Cain, in the first mention of sin in the Hebrew Bible: "If you do not do well, sin is couching at the door; its desire is for you, but you must master it" (Gen. 4:7). The presumed ability of Cain to understand and master sin assumes his knowledge of good and evil. Yahweh could not have said this to Adam and Eve, because they would not have understood it. But once humans acquired such knowledge they correspondingly acquired the power of choice and the responsibility to exercise that choice in favor of the good. Martin Buber expressed this succinctly: "The deed of the first humans belonged to the sphere of pre-evil, Kain's deed to that of evil, which only came into being as such through the act of knowledge."[52]

With this knowledge, humans likewise have the power to be creators (agents of order, good) or destroyers (agents of chaos, evil), to uphold and advance the creation or to compromise or even ruin it. Maintaining the order of creation is not only Yahweh's task. Humans must "walk together" with Yahweh in this effort, guided by Yahweh's commandments, which serve as rules for maintaining order and preventing the eruption of chaos into the world. As Gregory Mobley phrased it, "God has given humans an instruction manual for life on planet Earth so they can partner with God in the management of chaos."[53] The nature of this partnership helps us to understand, from a mythological perspective, the emergence of the biblical notion of covenant, which sets the framework for how Yahweh and humans must act together within and upon cosmic reality. True human wisdom consists of understanding this cosmic-human dynamic, which as we just saw is especially important for kings, who should serve as Yahweh's regents on earth to implement his will. That is why Yahweh granted Solomon a higher than normal degree of knowledge of good and evil. Adam too was cast somewhat in the role of a king,[54] being put in charge of the garden by Yahweh (Gen. 2:15), much like any ancient Near Eastern king was entrusted by the gods with a domain and charged with keeping order in it.[55] But Adam was not up to the task, not yet being equipped with the knowledge of how to do so.

This understanding of the nature of good and evil also explains how human actions can determine the fate of the rest of the world, including the animal kingdom and the earth itself. If evil is really a form of chaos rooted in the very fabric of reality, then human evil can literally "pollute" that reality, as J described in Genesis 6. That is why not just humanity but the rest of the earth and its life had to be cleansed by the flood. This power to pollute the cosmos is principally that of humans, because only they have acquired the divine knowledge of good and evil, so they can sin or not sin; animals do not have such knowledge and cannot consciously commit sin (just as Adam and Eve could not), though they can be its unwitting agents and still contribute to polluting the cosmos.

The above concept of how evil emerges in the world is crucial to understanding the nature of Adam and Eve's transgression and the subsequent sins of humankind. From this we see that Yahweh is not omnipotent. Chaos was present even before Yahweh's creative acts. Consequently, Yahweh is not ultimately responsible for evil's existence and the challenges that it brings. In his acts of creation, and also in his battles with the chaos monsters described elsewhere in the Hebrew Bible, Yahweh simply restrained it and caused the good order of creation to emerge (or be restored), but its hold is forever tentative. And just as Yahweh was able to control chaos to create and maintain the world, so too must humans, now that they have the knowledge of good and evil that equips them to do so.

In the ancient Near East, evil chaos was archetypically portrayed in the form of sea monsters (serpents, dragons) that had to be defeated in order to create (or restore) the cosmos, because water and particularly the sea itself was often understood as chaos (hence the notion of primordial waters), particularly its farthest reaches leading into the unknown. Such serpent imagery is not limited to the ancient Near East. In ancient Classical and medieval maps the limits of the known world were commonly depicted as the edge of the ocean surrounded by an uroboros serpent, which serpent partook of both the ocean and the unknown beyond, and so represented not only the boundary between cosmos and chaos but the means of connection between them.[56] Thus, J's choice of a serpent to appear as chaos in the perfect garden of Eden and be the interlocutor for the humans was therefore itself perfect. It represented the intrusion of chaos (and therefore evil) into the creation,[57] and also served (together with the sacred tree) as the mediator between the known and unknown, as the catalyst for the activation and extension of human consciousness, and the completion of the creation of humans.

Thus, when considering what was the essence of Eve's decision to eat the fruit, we must appreciate that the serpent's words were really externalizing the chaos (imagination, as J puts it) percolating in Eve's heart (mind), which chaos is also symbolized by the serpent's crafty nature.[58] Indeed, we must recall that Eve herself was a goddess symbol and that primeval goddesses (e.g., Tiamat) commonly took serpent form as representations of chaos. In these circumstances, the transgression was quite natural and indeed inevitable, because Eve and Adam did not yet possess the knowledge of good and evil that would equip them to recognize and control the element of chaos that was within themselves as a natural part of their being.

Possible Complimentary Meanings

The fact that the above mythological background framed the primary meaning of the knowledge of good and evil does not mean that J, like any talented writer having much to say, was not making ancillary, complimentary points. We can now consider the other above-mentioned possible meanings suggested by commentators, namely knowledge needed to build civilization, sexual knowledge, esoteric knowledge, and merism.

Knowledge of the Arts of Civilization

Some scholars believe that the knowledge which Adam and Eve acquired was knowledge necessary for them and their descendants to create civilization.[59] This idea derives from the fact that the Eden story is in part both an etiological and functionalist myth. Creation-related myths commonly portray humans acquiring from deities theretofore exclusively divine abilities and knowledge required to develop civilization.[60] Thus, in ancient Mesopotamia, the gods taught the newly created humans the arts of agriculture, tool making, city building, and so forth. In the *Gilgamesh* myth, the courtesan civilized Enkidu so he could go to Uruk (civilization) and befriend Gilgamesh.

Civilization motifs are also present in the Eden story. Adam is destined to till the ground, which he begins to do in the garden and presumably continues to do after the expulsion. Adam and Eve acquire from Yahweh the ability to procreate and thus populate the earth. The institution of marriage is established, with the husband ruling over the wife. Whereas at the outset Adam and Eve were helpless babes in the garden, at the end of the story they possess knowledge that equips them for life in the real world. Now they know how life is to be increased and mastered.[61] J continues this civilization theme in his genealogy of Cainites, where he explains the origins of both nomadic and sedentary life as well as of various professions and the establishment of cities (Gen. 4:17-22).

This civilizing motif is also probably one idea behind the nakedness vs. clothing imagery in the Eden story. When Adam and Eve first met they were not ashamed of their nakedness (Gen. 2:25). This referred not to some idyll or merely to their uroboric state, but also to the fact that, like small children, they did not know any better. (One need only observe small children playing naked to see this.) We recall from *Gilgamesh* how Enkidu ran naked before being civilized by the courtesan. Likewise, once Adam and Eve gained their knowledge from the forbidden fruit they immediately knew better (were ashamed) and sewed fig leaves to cover themselves (Gen 3:7). This was their first thought and action upon gaining the knowledge, even before they thought of or heard Yahweh. The knowledge and this realization were then explicitly linked by Yahweh when asking, "Who told you that you were naked? Have you eaten of the tree of which I commanded you not to eat?" (Gen. 3:11). Yahweh then covers them with proper clothes (Gen. 3:21). From the literary standpoint, having their "eyes opened" and at once *seeing* their nakedness works beautifully. Generally in the Hebrew Bible nakedness is considered shameful, as seen in the episode of Noah's drunkenness. In failing to cover his father's nakedness, Ham failed to act as Yahweh had in covering Adam and Eve; he did not apply that lesson. This represented a momentary unraveling of civilized life. Similarly, by setting the story in the context of a vineyard and of drinking wine to excess and having Yahweh curse Ham's son Canaan due to Ham's sin, J probably was also characterizing Canaanite civilization as coarse, uncivilized, and shameful, since its harvest festivals and rituals likewise featured drinking and nakedness. Indeed, Hosea (2:9-10), when criticizing these Canaanite festivals, likened Israel to a participant in them, regarding which Yahweh proclaimed,

> *Therefore I will take back my grain in its time,*
> *and my wine in its season;*
> *and I will take away my wool and my flax,*
> *which were to cover her nakedness.*
> *Now I will uncover her lewdness in the sight of her lovers,*
> *and no one shall rescue her out of my hand.*

Some commentators, however, have connected Adam and Eve's nakedness with a perceived sexual meaning of Eve's transgression, which we discuss next.

Sexual Knowledge

The Eden story certainly has sexual overtones, but less clear is in what connection. Some commentators have interpreted the acquisition of knowledge of good and evil as learning about sex,[62] but the weight of scholarly opinion rejects this interpretation as being inconsistent with the context of the story.[63] Such interpretation is also inconsistent with what we have already learned about Adam and Eve in prior chapters as well as with J's focus on good and evil in the primeval history. As already discussed, Adam and Eve were married and sexually active from the start, which excludes the knowledge of good and evil being about sex, and the attested biblical usage of the term knowing "good and evil" has nothing to do with sex.[64] Other reasons for rejecting the sexual explanation include:

- Yahweh issued the prohibition immediately upon Adam's creation, before Eve was created, in fact before Yahweh even realized that she needed to

be created. Without a woman, there is no logical sexual connection between the prohibition and the nature of the knowledge acquired by violating it.[65]

- J stressed that Eve ate the forbidden fruit in order to become wise like
  God. This is hardly a sexual achievement or the result of sexual activity,
  but rather is an elevation to (or conferral of) something divine.[66] J was
  dealing with higher concepts here.

- If the forbidden divine knowledge through which Adam and Eve became
  "like gods" were sexual in nature, this would imply that sexuality was a
  key aspect of the gods' character, but that is not how the Hebrew Bible
  portrays Yahweh. The idea of a sexual Yahweh was abhorrent to Yahwism,[67] which is one reason why Asherah had to go.

- The animals in the garden were in pairs and had to have mated in order to
  survive as a species,[68] and their knowledge about sex was obviously not
  divine in nature.[69] Since even animals knew this, surely so did Adam and
  Eve from the moment of their acquaintance. The fact that the knowledge
  of good and evil *distinguishes* us from animals suggests that it cannot be
  about sex.[70]

- It would make no sense for Yahweh to create humans (like the animals)
  with sexual organs but forbid them to have sexual activity.[71]

- Under Israelite law, punishments normally fit the crime, but Adam and
  Eve's punishments have nothing to do with sex. Indeed, it is hard to
  understand why gaining knowledge of sex would be prohibited as knowledge of the gods when even animals copulate. The punishment was simply
  that she would give birth in increased toil or pain, corresponding to
  Adam's toil in getting food from the land (see below).

The elements of the story which some think point toward a sexual meaning do not hold up under scrutiny. As seen in Chapter 7, the serpent is a
symbol of wisdom and divination, which meanings best fit the context of Eve
seeking wisdom and the serpent helping her to gain it. Thus, insofar as J's
serpent had a sexual connotation, this most likely alluded to Canaanite religious rites, which featured nakedness,[72] serpent veneration, and sex. We know
that in Canaan and early Israel diviners prophesized while naked (mentioned
even in the Hebrew Bible);[73] and as seen in Chapter 3, goddesses were
frequently depicted naked with serpents, so J could have been alluding to
veneration of goddesses in connection with serpents.[74] To the extent that in
the Eden story the serpent was linked with nakedness, the connection was
probably not that Eve herself had sex or learned about it at the tree of
knowing good and evil, but with the fact that the native religious cults which
J opposed featured nakedness together with serpents and sex.[75] In this connection, we must also recall that the Canaanite New Year's festival featured a
sacred marriage rite, which seems to have featured serpents as an aid to

fertility, and in which the participants emulated the sacred marriage of the deities both in leafy booths and in the open vineyards, so J could be alluding to such sexual rituals.[76] J would be motivated to make such an allusion because he sought to dissolve Yahweh's marriage with Asherah and to accord to Yahweh the divine power over procreation traditionally possessed by goddesses, which was understood and portrayed as an aspect of serpent power.

Although the divine knowledge in question cannot be simply of sex, it is still possible that such knowledge includes that of how the creative activity of procreation works. This is consistent with the aforementioned civilization motif, since humans must procreate and populate the earth in order to have civilization. A paramount Israelite value was the ability to procreate, as seen in the frequent exhortations in P passages that humans should be fruitful and multiply (e.g., Gen. 1:28; 9:1).[77] Adam and Eve could not be sent into the real world without this capacity. Indeed, it was at this stage that Eve was designated as "the mother of all the living" (Gen. 3:20) and conceived "with the help of Yahweh" (Gen. 4:1). As seen in Chapter 8, this amounted to Yahweh's usurpation of the power over procreation and birth traditionally held by a goddess, in this case his wife Asherah. In addition, as explained in Chapter 7, this may also have been a usurpation of serpent power, which was associated with the life force.

Esoteric Knowledge

Another possibility is that Adam and Eve received secret, esoteric knowledge, which may consist of key universal, secret principles attained by accessing the divine which provide essential wisdom for understanding the world, acting in it, and conducting one's spiritual life.[78] Outside the examples of the prophets (who were said to have a line to Yahweh) and isolated non-prophets such as Solomon upon whom Yahweh conferred wisdom on a need-to-know basis as a matter of grace, however, the notion of attaining esoteric knowledge through contact with the divine is absent from the Hebrew Bible's theology, and in particular that of J. Indeed, the idea that humans could directly and privately access and experience the divine was characteristic of the Canaanite religious practices that J was deriding.

According to the Hebrew Bible, the knowledge of good and evil, though originally a privilege of the divinity, is actually necessary for humans to avoid evil by following the Law; otherwise it would not be feasible to expect observance of the Law. In P's creation account, humans probably were created with this ability from the start. This knowledge is not esoteric: In Israelite thought, *all* adult humans must know and understand it and apply it in their daily lives. This is the import of Deuteronomy 29:29 in the epigraph to this Chapter: "The secret things belong to Yahweh, our God, and the things that are revealed belong to us and to our children forever, that we may do all the words of this law." This does not mean that some humans such as prophets or Solomon may not attain a higher degree of such knowledge that may border on the esoteric, but to do that they must first have proved themselves as upright people who follow Yahweh, who then grants it as a matter of grace. Adam and Eve, even upon acquiring such knowledge, were nowhere near that stage, so such higher levels of knowledge need not be considered when interpreting their story.

Knowledge of Everything (Merism)

Some scholars believe the phrase "knowledge of good and evil" is a merism meaning knowledge of everything (universal knowledge),[79] an attribute of divine beings. Similarly, the term "heaven(s) and earth" is sometimes a merism referring to the entire created cosmos, while "night and morning" can mean all hours of the diurnal round.[80] A literal merismic interpretation is not without some basis in the biblical text. The passage discussed above concerning David which said that he was like an "angel of God to discern good and evil" also said that he was able "to know all things that are on the earth" (2 Sam. 14:17, 20). Later, Proverbs 15:3 states:

> *The eyes of Yahweh are in every place,*
> *Keeping watch on the evil and the good.*

Professor Waltke termed this passage a "merism for all humanity."[81] Indeed, Yahweh is watching over all of creation. Further, to speak neither good nor evil probably means to say nothing (Gen. 31:24, 29; 2 Sam. 13:22), to do neither good nor evil probably means to do nothing (Zeph. 1:12), and being unable (as in one's youth (see above) or dotage) to discern what is good vs. bad (or evil) (2 Sam. 19:35) probably means that one cannot distinguish or understand anything at all.[82]

In our view, the accuracy and explanatory power of this merismic interpretation depends on whether it is understood in its proper mythological context. Since knowledge of good and evil was originally divine, a merismic meaning can help signify what the serpent implied: an extension of human capabilities and understanding beyond that established by Yahweh for humans at their creation.[83] On the other hand, we cannot make too much of the idea of good and evil signifying "everything." Although the forbidden fruit did expand human knowledge and capabilities and this capacity enabled humans to understand more than just literally human good and evil, to conclude that the universal knowledge of the gods about everything was downloaded into the primal pair would be unwarranted. Humans obviously do not have such vast knowledge and are nowhere near to the gods in this respect. As the story itself says, Adam and Eve became only "like" Yahweh, and only in knowing good and evil (Gen. 3:5, 22), which is far from connoting identity with the divinity.[84] As just seen, even the wisest of humans, King Solomon, needed to receive an extra dose of wisdom from Yahweh in order to rule wisely, meaning that ordinary humans do not have even that much.

Understanding the knowledge of good and evil as a merism dovetails with the cosmological mythology outlined above. As such, the term encompasses knowledge of chaos (evil) on the one extreme to knowledge of perfect order/ form (good) on the other, which amounts to knowledge of ultimate cosmic good vs. evil as well as their manifestation on the human level. Humans need only understand the essentials of this dynamic, not all the details, which can be known only by Yahweh. J was concerned only about that crucial portion of such understanding that can enable humans to behave properly in the world in accordance with Yahweh's commands and thereby avoid perpetrating evil. The merism concept thus extends, on the human level, to the entire spectrum of human good and evil conduct, as well as to the correspondence between that and, at the highest level, cosmic good and evil. As such, thinking of knowledge of good and evil as a merism elegantly embodies J's ideas and concerns, and can be depicted as in Diagram 9.1.

On the cosmic level in Diagram 9.1, the ideal good is represented as the initial creation, which is pure form and order, while evil is chaos. On the earthly human level, corresponding to cosmic good is Yahweh's Law,[85] which gives proper form and guidance to human existence (particularly Israel's); correspondingly, the human manifestation of cosmic chaos is sin. The

Cosmic Level

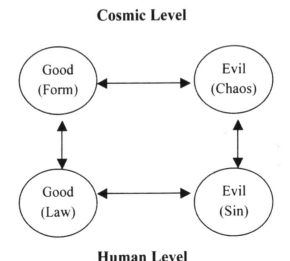

Human Level

Diagram 9.1. "Good and Evil" as Merism.

cosmic and human levels are not really separate because humans are part of the cosmos and have within them both cosmic chaos (evil) and cosmic order (good). The makeup of every existing thing, including humanity, falls somewhere along a spectrum having chaos at one extreme and the order of perfection on the other. Each thing in the universe by nature partakes of each of these opposites to a greater or lesser degree. This thinking echoes that of Heraclitus, who held that wisdom consists in understanding how the world works, *in terms of how opposites interrelate,* in which understanding only God can be completely wise.[86] In this understanding, seeing the world as in the above diagram is to see it from the perspective of God, which we believe is the sense in which Adam and Eve became "like" the gods upon gaining the knowledge of good and evil. This ability in itself can be viewed as a higher, holistic good, because it is not good simply as the opposite of evil but in the sense of a wholeness of perspective and being that comprehends and transcends the opposites. (We shall return to this theme in the Epilogue.) This model has affinities not only with Heraclitus but also with the Platonic ideal of the Good, which is the point where the whole of knowledge and of being is unified, which humans must endeavor to understand and then emulate on earth. As Plato expressed it in his Myth of the Sun, just as our eyes have a certain affinity with the sun that enables us to see things in the world illuminated by it, our minds can have the perspective that enables us to see all and align with the Good, to understand it and shape our lives by it,[87] just as J believed in the case of the knowledge of good (and evil). To have this knowledge is the key to knowing thyself and being able to live on the side of the good and the Law. Both J and Plato saw that in this essential way the world and humanity form an organic whole.

At the higher, cosmic level in Diagram 9.1 Yahweh and his host of other divine beings operate. Lower down the vertical axis of the above diagram, at the highest possible human level, would be a just king like Solomon applying the Law (see above), or leaders like Moses and Joshua. They create and maintain order on earth and operate closer to the cosmic level and to the divine than do ordinary humans. At the lowest level might be common criminals and, in J's view, Canaanites and devotees of Canaanite religion. Adam and Eve existed within this scheme too, but until they acquired the knowledge of good and evil they did not realize that such scheme even exists, much less where they fit into it. Adam and Eve learned about it the hard way, but the first time Yahweh explained anything about this to a human ahead of time (because he could understand it) was when he warned Cain about sin (Gen. 4:7).

This holistic principle is akin to another merism, the opposites Yin and Yang, which in classical Chinese thought similarly govern and explain the cosmos. As the two are commonly depicted (Diagram 9.2), in the middle of each there is a dot from the other to remind us that each of the two opposites (such as chaos and order) nevertheless contains an element of the other:

Thus, within chaos lies the germ of order, while ordered creation retains a residue of chaos. Humans and their actions are just one aspect of this dynamic whole, never separate from and always part of the cosmic aspects. Indeed, as seen in Chapter 4, the biblical narrative brings the cosmic aspects prominently into human and Israelite history (the flood, the crossing of the Reed Sea, the Conquest, the exile, etc.). This also explains why, as the primeval history relates, the evil actions of humans can pollute nature itself.

Based on the above, in summary we may understand the knowledge of good and evil as a key subset of the total divine knowledge of the gods. At the most fundamental level, it consists of knowing the fundamental workings of the cosmic geography, which is to say how the universe itself works in terms of the interplay of the opposites of order and chaos, an aspect of which is that of good and evil. As Martin Buber put it,

> "Knowledge of good and evil" means nothing else than: cognizance of the opposites which the early literature of mankind designated by these two terms; they still include the fortune and misfortune or the order and the disorder which is experienced by a person, as well as that which he causes. [88]

Such knowledge extends to understanding the workings of all pairs of opposites as well as other things necessary to establish and develop human civilization, which is ultimately a creative ability. Further, it constitutes a godlike perspective that *transcends* the particular opposites.

For Israelites, this knowledge includes in particular the knowledge necessary for building a righteous nation by attaining the correct relationship with Yahweh, namely that knowledge which enables humans to possess a mature, discerning mind so as to be able to understand what is good vs. evil and

Diagram 9.2. Yin-Yang as Merism.

choose how to act. This is a tool that enables humans to avoid practicing pagan religion and committing other sins by being able to understand and obey Yahweh's Law. Because everything is connected, if this question of good and evil is managed well at the human level, then affairs at the cosmic level also will tend to take care of themselves. [89]

So understood, the knowledge of good and evil is itself a form of order (to which the Law corresponds) which in the Eden story became implanted in the human mind as a necessary structure for attaining, stabilizing, maintaining, and developing further our higher existence in the world, what today we recognize as a higher degree of consciousness. As such, the acquisition of such knowledge was an event of creation in an etiological myth that transformed humans into their current state, resulting in a higher degree of order in the cosmos.

But the question then becomes, why did Yahweh seemingly not want humans to have such knowledge? Why didn't he (like P) create humans already stocked with such "software," given that it is necessary in order to fully understand Yahweh's commands and maintain the order of civilization? Why did J construct the story so that humans could obtain it only by disobeying Yahweh? What motivated Eve and then Adam to violate the prohibition? In order to address these questions we must look into the circumstances of the transgression.

THE NATURE OF THE TRANSGRESSION

Having arrived at an understanding of what the "knowledge of good and evil" means, we can now examine the nature of what transpired between Eve and the serpent under the tree and when she and Adam ate the forbidden fruit. We can begin by observing that the word "sin" never appears in the Eden story, nor does the Hebrew Bible ever later refer to what Adam and Eve did as a sin. And as noted, the story is virtually absent from the rest of the Hebrew Bible.

Bible scholars have long noted the logical problem of how Adam and Eve could be considered to have sinned, because like ignorant, immature children they did not yet have the knowledge and understanding necessary to recognize good from evil. [90] Scholars have found no clear answer to this question. Some have pointed, out, for example, that under Hebrew law certain kinds of serious sins do not require intent and can be committed by accident or even unknowingly. [91] Most such sins are in categories such as cultic mistakes which defile Yahweh's sanctuary, or involuntary actions which defile oneself. Adam and Eve mistakenly (by not yet knowing any better) following Canaanite religion in Yahweh's garden sanctuary arguably comes close to that category, but the transgression involves much more than a mistake. In order to understand the nature of the transgression better, we must examine the ultimate source of the temptation, how the temptation was aroused, how the transgression transpired, and its consequences in the form of Yahweh's punishments.

Why Adam and Eve Ate the Forbidden Fruit

The starting point for examining this question is the fact that, as we have seen, evil (as a form of chaos) is primordial in nature and a cosmic principle. According to the scheme of traditional ancient Near Eastern cosmogony and cosmology, it existed before and as of the time of creation, continues to exist, and intrudes into and is always a factor in the created world. The creation itself was simply a transformation of some (but far from all) of the preexisting chaotic substance into order. This means that Yahweh was not quite omnipotent. In the Ancient Near East, no deity—not Marduk, not any Egyptian god, not El—was able to eliminate (or initially create) the chaos which surrounded the created cosmos and threatened it. Yet the Hebrew Bible portrays Yahweh as able to control it, when he wants, at least when it penetrates and threatens his creations on earth. This is important to recognize because it means that evil did not originate with Adam and Eve's transgression. Rather, the germ of evil and potential for its expansion are woven into the fabric of nature, including in the nature of humans. It is thus important to appreciate the difference between the manifestation of evil in the world and its ultimate source and cause. A holy sanctuary, of course, is conceived of as pristine and untainted. Thus we can understand why, as part of the creation, Yahweh created the garden of Eden as a pristine Center and placed humans there, endeavoring to keep them in a primal state of perfection (and charging Adam with keeping it so), with them not even knowing what evil and sin are. But chaos was at the garden's gates, trying to get in, and inevitably did, just as it got into the human mind.

How was this elemental chaos manifested in humans? J was quite clear on this. He thought that the source of human evil lies in our "imagination,"[92] a form of chaos through which humans visualize things other than as they are in reality, spin out various wishes and desires, and then try to actualize them. Thus, in Genesis 6:5 J wrote that Yahweh saw that "every *imagination* of the thoughts of [man's] heart was only evil." Likewise, in Genesis 8:21, J described Yahweh's feelings after Noah had made a sacrifice to Yahweh after the flood: "I will never again curse the ground because of man, for the *imagination* of man's heart is evil *from his youth.*"[93] Thus, by the end of the flood if not before, Yahweh had come to understand that humans have an innate quality in their hearts that is the source of their sins.[94] Based on the above two J verses (and Genesis 4:7), later rabbinical writings developed the notion of the *yēṣer hara* ("the evil inclination"), which became the standard rabbinical teaching on the origin of sin.[95] This teaching postulated an inherent inclination in human nature to do evil, but held that it can be resisted and offset through conscious effort, the study and observance of the Torah, and prayer.[96]

Thus, the existence of this evil inclination or impulse within us counterpoised to the knowledge of good and evil acquired in the garden results in the existence of opposites within the human being—a chaotic, dark, shadow side and an orderly, higher, light side—and an interplay between them (see Diagram 9.1). Since this evil imagination lies in the human faculty of mind (heart), *correspondingly* it needs to be countered and controlled by an antithetical faculty of mind: the knowledge of good and evil, which was essential to enable humans to follow the Law and thus further order and the good. That is why Yahweh needed to bequeath the Law to humans. The Law was considered not an imposition but an enabling gift that can eliminate sin, yield happiness, and bring humans into the optimal relationship with Yahweh.[97] It was designed as a set of ordering principles to be used to control and counteract chaos: to bring order in the human mind and human activity, analogously to how Yahweh brought order to the chaotic primeval substance during the creation.[98] As such, bringing about the Law was a creative act that was the product of primordial Wisdom[99] and embodied absolute Good.

Since humans have a natural dark side, Yahweh decided that an extreme punishment such as the flood is excessive (Gen. 8:21; 9:15). Better to accept humans as they are but, rather than let them continue to act according to their natural impulses, control their nature and evil by establishing another kind of relationship with them, which soon enough becomes one of covenant and adherence to Yahweh's Law. Since human nature is not the fault of either humans or Yahweh, they should work together to limit its destructive effects.

These ideas play out in the Eden story and its aftermath. Adam was created from the earth of the chaotic desert wasteland, Eden, to which were applied the chaotic waters from the *tehôm* in order to form him. Having thus been made by ordering chaos, he was then placed in the garden and expected to behave perfectly and maintain the perfection of the garden—an expectation doomed from the start for such an imperfect creature, like a flawed tragic hero. Chaos can manifest itself in humans just as it does elsewhere in the cosmos: the sea, the weather, or on land (earthquakes, volcanic eruptions). It arises as a small kernel of unease within the human heart, in which the underlying chaos grows like a software virus and eventually manifests itself in full proportion as true evil and sin. This is shown in Eve's dialogue with the serpent.

There had been no hint of such imaginative stirrings in Eve's heart until the serpent appeared. Thus, from the literary and psychological standpoint, we may view the serpent's words as an externalization of Eve's inner discourse, but the serpent represents something more important than just that. It is metaphysical and cosmic: The serpent represents the manifestation of chaos (including as craftiness and rationalization) in Eve's heart, which leads to her decision.[100] Not yet having the knowledge of good and evil that would give her the presence of mind to control such turmoil, her transgression was inevitable. Indeed, noting that the word that J chose for "serpent" *(nāhāsh)* is associated with other Hebrew words connoting magic, divination, and bewitchment, Professor Blenkinsopp concluded, "We can readily understand that, confronted by such a formidable interlocutor, the woman had little chance of winning the verbal duel."[101] Thus, the serpent did not have to be, and was not, overbearing, ostensibly leaving Eve free to choose.[102] The reason why the outcome was a foregone conclusion was not because the serpent was overwhelming, but because, lacking the knowledge of good and evil, Eve was in no position to resist or make a rational and right decision, and thus was a pushover.

In this role, the serpent represented not just chaos as in the dragon fight myths discussed earlier. As seen in Chapter 7, in the minds of J's audience, the serpent also was associated with goddesses and was an object of veneration among the people, and J wanted to discredit it. Portraying the serpent as a clever deceiver served this purpose, as did putting some of the blame for the transgression (insofar as it was not purely human choice) on the serpent. Mythologically speaking, in such role the serpent fits into what is termed the "trickster motif,"[103] where in etiological myths and stories a trickster figure embodying disorder deprives early mankind of some desired quality or catalyzes something bad coming into the world.[104] In this way, onto the trickster (a kind of scapegoat) are projected the fears, failures, and unattained ideals of the society.[105] Earlier we saw an early example of such trickery in *Adapa,* when Enki tricked Adapa out of immortality. The Prometheus/Pandora mythology utilizes trickery throughout to explain the origin of evil in our world. In the Eden story the serpent embodied both negative and positive trickster qualities: While J used it to represent evil coming into the world, it also facilitated Adam and Eve gaining the very knowledge needed to combat evil. Indeed, a trickster can also catalyze order from chaos, teach humans the skills of civilization, and shape human culture into its familiar form, thus being a "culture bringer" defining human destiny.[106] In psychological terms, the trickster consolidates human consciousness,[107] symbolized in this myth by the coming of the knowledge of good and evil.

What, more precisely, was the content of Eve's imaginings and yearnings? J knew that his audience needed to understand this in order to recognize the issue within themselves. The possibilities run a full range, and scholarly opinion indeed spans a wide spectrum. Let us examine the two extremes as well as a middle ground.

At one end of the spectrum, some commentators argue that Eve was moved by simple curiosity or velleity.[108] Indeed, in J's account some simple, unsophisticated motivations did figure into Eve's thinking. She saw that "the tree was good for food, and that it was a delight to the eyes" (Gen. 3:6). Further, the mere existence of any prohibition, of course, can provoke special attention to the subject and temptation, rendering the transgression an instance of the "one forbidden thing" motif[109] where the one thing that is forbidden is inevitably done. It would be a bare violation of Yahweh's prohibition with hardly any meaningful intent, yet in terms of our model it is a yielding to an impulse (of chaos) that can lead to sin. This line of thinking has a long tradition in our religion. A famous maxim of St. Bernard was, "Curiosity is the beginning of all sin."[110] Milton similarly wrote of this wondering and wandering mind in *Paradise Lost,* presaging the transgression:

> *How fully hast thou satisfied me, pure*
> *Intelligence of Heav'n, angel serene,*
> *And freed from intricacies, taught to live*
> *The easiest way nor with perplexing thoughts*
> *To interrupt the sweet of life from which*
> *God hath bid dwell far off all anxious cares*
> *And not molest us, unless we ourselves*
> *Seek them with wand'ring thoughts and notions vain.*
> *But apt the mind or fancy is to rove*
> *Unchecked and of her roving is no end*
> *Till warned or by experience taught she learn*
> *That not to know at large of things remote*
> *From use, obscure and subtle, but to know*
> *That which before us lies in daily life*
> *Is the prime wisdom.* [111]

Yet this already hints at the opposite extreme, that of affirmative rebellion against God, against the human condition, striving to make ourselves like gods, the approach of Promethean or (more modernly) Nietzschean man. Adam and Eve's actions are often characterized as a kind of *hubris,* an immoderate, rebellious attempt to transcend humanity's assigned place in the world.[112] Such behavior would understandably offend a jealous god and necessitate punishment. There is indeed a basis in J's other writings for this interpretation: As we have seen, both his tower of Babel and "sons of the gods" stories are about humans improperly transgressing human limits into the divine, so this is indeed a human tendency on which J was focused. Yet unlike in other ancient Near Eastern myths in which divine aspirations were futile, Adam and Eve's endeavor to achieve a status closer to the divine was to crucial degree successful. The serpent was right about their becoming enlightened. So in the end the result should be looked upon not simply as an improper acquisition of divine prerogatives but also as an etiology, a giving of final form to humans as they now are, and indeed must be in order to be able to follow Yahweh's Law. In our view, in the story J actually goes quite light on the theme of hubris as such in the transgression, focusing rather on simply highlighting the difference between humans and God. None of the words, actions, or attributions of the humans in the story clearly indicate hubris or rebellion, although the serpent may have been guilty of that.[113] In fact, although the serpent tries to tempt Eve by saying she will become like God, such a particular desire is conspicuously absent from the reasons she gives for eating the fruit.[114] At most she wants wisdom, and surely Yahweh knows that she needs it. One would expect that a jealous god offended by human rebellion would have punished the humans in a more wrathful way that did more than fill in requirements of human etiology. This is understandable because Adam and Eve were not yet in a position to control their natural impulses.

Between these two extremes lies a middle ground, that of archetypical human yearnings toward the sacred and divine and seeking to understand and experience it, but not necessarily with rebellious intentions. Humans are not satisfied with a profane and seemingly absurd (and evil) world. They seek more, whether by aspiring to divinity (wisdom and immortality), experiencing the divine from time to time, or at least by gaining the wisdom to understand the nature of such things. In modern philosophy, existentialism, for example, confronts this issue head-on, offering both religious (e.g., Kierkegaard) and secular (e.g., Sartre, Camus) solutions. Indeed, modern psychology also holds that humans are naturally inclined to seek the divine and higher levels of consciousness.[115] In the pre-modern world, myths addressed such questions, in part by offering an explanation of why such yearnings cannot be satisfied, at least fully. As Paul Ricoeur astutely observed, "the man of myths is already an unhappy consciousness."[116] The peoples of the ancient Near East, and their mythological heroes such as Gilgamesh and Adapa, were indeed haunted by such questions. Ancient Near Eastern polytheistic religions, including Canaanite, sought to satisfy these needs through their own rituals and beliefs, which involved among other things veneration of the Goddess, sacred trees, and serpents. J knew very well that his audience had such feelings and engaged in such practices, and he needed to present to them a viable Yahwist alternative. Professor Soggin summarized these competing visions eloquently:

> What does the serpent propose in our story? He wants to make man like unto a god. According to Israel's belief, man is thus initiated into a sphere to which he is completely alien, but which the Canaanite religion must have considered noble and sublime. The Yahwist's evaluation of the role of the serpent is clearly negative, but in the primitive Canaanite story the judgement would have been positive, since the serpent helps man to attain certain powers that he lacked but which were his by right.[117]

Why Was a Transgression in the Story?

At this juncture we may ask why the Eden story goes through all this trouble. Why did the knowledge of good and evil have to be acquired by disobeying Yahweh? Why didn't Yahweh simply create humans with this necessary "software" already installed? Surely J had reasons for framing the story in this way, which we now address.

In P's creation account, all events unfold smoothly, and at the end everything in creation is pronounced good, including humans, so apparently they already had the knowledge of good and evil. The primordial waters preside before and at the beginning of the creation, but then are kept outside the created cosmos, and they are peaceful: The sea monsters were said to be created by God (Gen. 1:21; also Ps. 104:26), and so are docile under his control, and are even pronounced good. In this somewhat Panglossian vision, there is no hint of opposition, that chaos might enter this best of all worlds and become a problem. Curiously, however, there is no further P narrative in the primeval history until the flood story, where he writes that the world had already become corrupted by flesh and that it must be destroyed by the flood (Gen. 6:9-22). P never explains what happened in between, that is, what is the origin of evil. [118] J, however, confronted the issue.

But in doing so, didn't J risk running into a classic philosophical conundrum? Namely, given that there is evil and suffering in the world, then either (a) God, if good, is not omnipotent and thus unable to prevent evil, or (b) if God is omnipotent and thus is in a position to prevent evil, then he is not good (at least not entirely), for evil is part of what he created and he lets it continue, as eloquently portrayed in Dostoevsky's story of the Grand Inquisitor in *The Brothers Karamazov.* J wanted to portray Yahweh as being as powerful as possible, yet not blame him for what is wrong in the world. Fortunately, however, neither J nor his audience would have felt the above dilemma as acutely as our Western philosophers have. As seen above, in the ancient Near Eastern way of thinking, primeval chaos and therefore the potential for evil existed even before the creation and lay outside the creator and his powers. No ancient Near Eastern deity existed outside this paradigm, so no deity could be entirely omnipotent or necessarily be blamed for evil in the world. All preeminent gods had to contend with chaos (evil) in some manner, whether in creating the cosmos (as with Marduk in *Enuma Elish)* or in maintaining it (as in Baal's contest with Yam). J took the approach of bringing humans into this dynamic as a proactive force, once they had the knowledge of good and evil that enabled to them to play a role in maintaining order/good. After the flood, Yahweh provided a basic guarantee of the "playing field" through his covenant with Noah, by promising that the creation itself would not be undone again. Yahweh would control evil chaos to that extent, but within that framework human behavior would determine whether and to what degree lawlessness and violence vs. good would spread on earth. Yahweh did not necessarily have to step in at every instance to save humans from themselves; humans must learn how to do it, beginning with Israelites obeying the holy covenants and following the Law. In this way, order and good eventually can prevail. This process ultimately serves a *creative* purpose.[119]

But at the outset in the garden of Eden this dynamic could not yet operate. Yahweh took a chance on the humans (who knew no evil yet) being able to preserve a perfect world. If they could do so despite lacking understanding, then human evil would not develop and pollute the cosmos. In order for this to happen, the humans only needed to obey, as Milton phrased it, "one easy prohibition."[120] Presumably J's audience was not at all surprised that it was broken, and they would have understood why and how: That is how the world works, as anyone at that time possessing the knowledge of good and evil would know. Understanding this point of view does not come so easily to modern humans, who have not been raised to think of our world as underpinned by the cosmic opposition of chaos vs. order. (Over the last century we have, however, come to understand the relevant equivalent: the light (conscious) and dark (unconscious, Shadow) sides of our psyche, the roles of which we shall explore below.)

J recognized that humans in his day had the knowledge of good and evil and why it was so crucial. In his etiological myth, the only question was to explain how we came to possess it. For J, it was important that this knowledge not be downloaded to the couple at their creation, but be gained in the manner of learning a lesson the hard way (analogous to Adam first having to reject animals before recognizing Eve as his partner). It was important that J first highlight to his audience the natural operation of human nature, without having the knowledge that can control it, because this underscores for the audience the importance of this knowledge and the need to apply it to follow Yahweh's commands. By such example, J explains the knowledge as something that we can use to control our chaotic nature. By gaining the knowledge through first experiencing pure and uncontrolled chaos within themselves, Adam and Eve realized first-hand how the world works (including on a cosmic level), and therefore better understood the error of their ways and how to conduct themselves. In so constructing the story, J enabled his audience to experience and understand the same. Thus, on J's part it was an ingenious plot device to create humans initially without the knowledge, issue the prohibition (meaningless to Adam and Eve in the context) and show where human nature leads without such knowledge. Without it, humans were unable to venerate Yahweh, monotheism (or monolatry) was not possible, covenants could not be made or kept, and there was no point in having the Law yet because it could not be understood and followed. Once the consequences of initial human nature became apparent, however, the value and role of the knowledge of good and evil could be understood, a point that J quickly made in the scene where Yahweh explains to Cain his power to choose. Gaining the knowledge did not eliminate our natural chaotic impulse, but it added an element to our nature that, in J's view, should enable us to control it.

J was acutely aware of this dynamic playing out in his own time. If we are correct in our suggested dating of J, he would have witnessed how the now defunct Omride political power as well as its northern, Phoenician-influenced culture had dominated Judah and Jerusalem. Israelites worshipped other deities, including goddesses such as Yahweh's own wife, Asherah. The people venerated serpents and sacred trees at high places, all associated with Asherah. To J, these evils were all manifestations of chaos that would lead to worse evils and again corrupt the earth, so they had to be eliminated if the glory of Judah was to be rebuilt (or, as many historians now hold, established for the first time). His Eden story, which through its imagery reminded the audience of these practices, was designed to combat them. In order to achieve this goal at the level of human society and history, it was necessary to understand and confront the problem as a metaphysical cosmic phenomenon, a case of "as above, so below." As such, the story itself served a creative purpose.

YAHWEH'S PUNISHMENTS

The punishments meted out to Adam, Eve and the serpent illustrate and corroborate the points made above, showing what was and was not the nature of the transgression. Normally in Israelite law the punishment should fit the crime, meaning that it should be of the same nature as the offense and also in proportion to the offense (e.g., "an eye for an eye"). Applying this idea helps us understand what J considered to be the nature of Adam's and Eve's offenses, and also in what respects there may not have been a "sin."

After interrogating Adam and Eve, Yahweh first punishes the serpent, telling it that it shall henceforth crawl on its belly and eat dust; also, Yahweh tells Eve (not Adam) that henceforth there shall be enmity between serpents and women, and also men (Gen. 3:14-15). As discussed in Chapter 7, this is in part simply etiology (serpents do crawl, and there is indeed a measure of enmity between them and humans), but also it is polemic against Canaanite religion, an effort to dethrone the serpent as an object of veneration in Israel. Dethroning the serpent by implication also dethrones the Goddess,[121] while Yahweh's creating enmity between the serpent and women (and choosing to announce this to Eve alone) breaks the affinity between the serpent and the Goddess (divides and conquers them). We must bear in mind that when J likely wrote, Nehushtan stood before the Temple in Jerusalem, together with the image of Asherah.

Yahweh next turns to Eve. Unlike in the cases of the serpent and Adam, no offense is recited, and her punishment does not seem tied to anything she did. Yahweh simply foretells that she will bear children in increased toil (pain) and that her husband shall rule over her (Gen. 3:16). This too is etiology, as well as functionalist myth (to justify male dominance in the society), but it does not seem to fit as a punishment for her disobedience to Yahweh. (Only the above-mentioned enmity with serpents seems to relate to the offense.) It is as if as a woman she lacks legal capacity, so that Adam rather than she will mainly be held accountable, which seems borne out by what Yahweh now tells Adam.

Adam's offenses, Yahweh states, were that he listened to his wife (as if she were divine, a possible allusion to goddess veneration and to Yahweh's own wife Asherah[122]) and ate of the tree that Yahweh commanded him not to eat. But Adam himself was not punished directly. Rather, Yahweh cursed the ground, which in turn will make it hard for Adam and his descendants to develop agriculture, until the curse is lifted after the flood. Importantly, in stating that Eve will give birth in greater "pain" and that Adam will farm in "toil," J uses the same Hebrew word *(iṣṣābôn)* in both instances.[123] The English translations (e.g., RSV, NRSV) miss the fact that J chose the same word to show a parallelism and commonality in their punishments and fates in which he is emphasizing an overall hardship in life (and in bringing life) for which the examples of farming (what men do) and giving birth (what women do) are prime examples (both having to do with fertility).[124] Yahweh's cursing the ground and then removing the curse may, among other things, be one more way of asserting that the earth is Yahweh's province rather than that of the Goddess (Asherah) or serpents. Thus, Yahweh becomes the source of fertility, both in humans and in agriculture.

Another punishment in the story, of course, is that of death, although this is framed obliquely in the context of the actual expulsion, by barring access to the tree of life; Yahweh never speaks to the humans about it when punishing them. Earlier, when issuing the prohibition, Yahweh warned Adam that he would die "in the day" that he ate the forbidden fruit (Gen. 2:17), whereas the serpent assured Eve that this would not happen (Gen. 3:4). If Yahweh's warning is taken literally and directly, then the serpent was right, since they did not die on the day they ate the fruit but went on to live long lives. But surely J did not think the serpent was right. So what did he mean in these seemingly contradictory statements by Yahweh and the serpent? As we will discuss shortly below, the death in question may not be physical death but involve a type of initiation scenario whereby the original human is transformed ("dies") into the new human possessing the higher knowledge of good and evil. But this is only one possibility, and there are others which fall more into traditional scholarly discussion.

While no one has suggested that Yahweh was merely bluffing when warning Adam, a simple explanation that avoids linguistic gymnastics is that Yahweh, taking into account the circumstances of the transgression, relented as an act of grace and modified his penalty, as he did in other cases in the Hebrew Bible.[125] Other scholars hold that Yahweh did follow through, by interpreting the threat as meaning not that humans will die on that very day, but that as of that day they became destined to die (rather than live eternally in the garden).[126] Another proposal is that "in the day" is idiomatic and in this case really means something like "as surely as,"[127] which would avoid the apparent contradiction, because Yahweh then is not specifying when Adam will die. A final possibility, following a proposal of Othmar Keel, is that when relenting in such cases Yahweh is assuming a merciful aspect of the Goddess, because in some older myths it was goddesses such as Ishtar who stood up for humans against gods who wanted to destroy humanity.[128] In any of these cases, however, the result is the same, because the story goes on to say that, by being deprived of access to the tree of life, the humans will suffer death, which is to say that they are deprived of immortality (the second prong of divinity), just like the protagonists in other ancient Near Eastern myths. This settles the etiological aspects of the story such that humans may then be placed in the real world, and live and die in it.

The final "punishment," known as the expulsion, in terms of authorial intent was an etiology: a transfer of the humans from quasi-reality to full reality. As such, one way or another, and for whatever reason, Adam and Eve had to get out of the garden and into the real world as we know it, which one suspects was Yahweh's intention from the start;[129] he just needed to make his point first through the drama that transpired. Their transgression involved seeking knowledge on their own that made them more independent. In response, Yahweh makes them independent by expelling them from the garden, so that they will indeed fend for themselves. It is the biblical version of, "Be careful what you wish for, because you might get it." But is this really punishment? Mythologically speaking, it is less a punishment than etiology at work and a motif of inner transformation. Through the transgression the final touches were put on the creation of humans, which for them was a transformation similar to an initiation. Their old world had died for them, as had their former selves. Now clothed, having the ability to procreate, and possessing the knowledge of good and evil and of the means to create civilization, they were ready to face the real world.

Finally, any account of how human affairs came to be as they are in this world must explain the nature and origin of evil, which indeed was a focus of J. Interpretations of this aspect of the Eden story led eventually to the notions of the "fall of man" and original sin. We are now in a position to examine these ideas.

THE MYTHS OF "ORIGINAL SIN" AND THE "FALL OF MAN"

We can now consider two related conventional understandings that over time have developed from the story in the Christian world. The first is the idea that Adam and Eve's transgression fundamentally alienated humans from Yahweh, meaning that humanity's relationship with Yahweh had to be restored in some manner, which for Christians occurs through Christ. The second, is the doctrine of original sin, according to which Adam's and Eve's sin resulted in a taint on humanity which was passed on from generation to generation in a hereditary fashion, escape from which was made possible only through the life and sacrifice of Christ and is achieved by an individual through baptism and belief in Christ.[130]

We can begin by examining whether there is any basis for these ideas in the text of the story or elsewhere in the Hebrew Bible. In the story, J lays out the consequences of the transgression in detail, but the *acquisition* of a sinful nature is not among them. In fact, sin is never mentioned in the story.[131] The word first occurs in Genesis 4:7 in relation to Cain, where sin is likened to a ravenous beast lurking at the door which Cain can and should overcome (because he has knowledge of good and evil), but didn't. The reason why these texts do not, and cannot, mention any *acquisition* of a sinful nature after the creation of humans is apparent from our earlier discussion of chaos as a cosmic principle and of our "evil inclination" as its human manifestation. This defect was *already* in humans from their initial creation, even before they had a chance to act. It did not arise or attach within humans *by reason of* the transgression; it was the underlying *cause* of the transgression. Evil in the post-Eden world did not need to be explained to Israelites, and was not explained, as a transmission by hereditary means of a sinful nature acquired in the garden. Indeed, the notion of a sinful nature being acquired by sinning is circular: It still begs for an explanation of the first sin. J gave it. The ancient Near Eastern concept embraced by J provided this answer for both the transgression and all subsequent sins.

It is often claimed that Adam and Eve's disobedience marked an alienation of humanity from God.[132] Obviously, Yahweh was disappointed by what Adam and Eve did, but, given that the essential defect in humans was there from their creation, he (having perfect knowledge of good and evil) could not have been surprised, so we must be careful about drawing conclusions about the existence, nature, extent, or duration of any "alienation" arising specifically from the transgression. It is hard to postulate an original meaningful relationship where the humans do not know good and evil and therefore cannot understand Yahweh's commands. Indeed, the Eden story itself says nothing about any initial relationship between man and Yahweh while in the garden. As Professor John Goldingay observed:

> Sometimes people imagine them [Adam and Eve] living in close relationship with God, and only then falling. Maybe they did, but Genesis leaps straight from their creation to their failure and rather implies there was nothing in between. There was no honeymoon period. [133]

The first clear indication of a budding alienation of any human from God comes after the first true sin, by Cain, when Yahweh punishes him for his murder of Abel and Cain exclaims, "My punishment is greater than I can bear. Behold, you have driven me this day from the face of the ground, *and from your face I shall be hidden*" (Gen. 4:13-14). Any "alienation" in the Eden story can be better explained on another level, as Adam and Eve's coming into awareness of pairs of opposites, the key one for this purpose being the preexisting difference between humans and God, [134] a distinction that J himself insisted upon. So viewed, this distinction in itself has more cognitive than moral meaning, and rather than being a harmful result is actually a necessary means to achieving what J thought best: structuring a *relationship* with the divine (God) rather than experiencing the divine directly as did the Canaanites.

The other details of the story likewise do not suggest that whatever relationship that existed between humans and Yahweh was then broken, either temporarily or permanently. Yahweh does not abandon Adam and Eve even as he recognizes that they have decided to act somewhat independently. [135] He makes garments for them as they go into the world, and he makes Eve fertile so that humans can procreate. Yahweh supports the humans' movement toward civilization. This pattern continues afterwards even in reaction to full-fledged sins. In response to Cain killing Abel, the ground curses Cain, so that for him farming will be not merely difficult like for other humans but actually impossible, meaning that he must become a wanderer, making his living by means other than agriculture. But even so Yahweh equips him to survive by marking him with a sign, much as he had clothed Adam and Eve to survive after their expulsion from the garden, and Cain's descendants flourish and build civilization. A turning point of true alienation occurs only later, and *by Yahweh's own decision,* in the lead-up to the flood where he regrets creating humans (Gen. 6:5-6). But this alienation proves temporary. After the flood, Noah sacrifices to Yahweh, who makes peace with the human evil inclination (Gen. 8:21) and responds favorably. At that moment the world has been re-created, all prior sins have been expatiated, and Yahweh's relationship with humanity has been restored. Yahweh has given humans a fresh start. [136] Nothing like our concepts of "original sin" or the "fall of man" in the garden could have been intended by J even if the transgression were a true sin, because the effects would never have lasted beyond the flood. The transgression is better viewed as just the start of a gradual build-up of chaos (evil and sin) in the antediluvian world, and as being limited to it.

Israelite theology had to come up with a more practical and ongoing way of dealing with sin, which was by expatiating it each time it occurs. According to this theology, any rupture or alienation with Yahweh due to sin not only can but must be expatiated. This is done through the right combination of ritual acts and repentance followed by divine forgiveness, so as to put the sin in the past, eliminate its effects, and reestablish the right relationship with Yahweh.[137] This is important not just to an individual, but even more so for society. It was essential to the community that sins be cleansed, and promptly, because their effects must not be left to fester in and pollute the community, otherwise worse catastrophes will befall it.[138] That, in fact, is what happened in the primeval history leading up to the flood, because humans committed sins but did not expatiate them, so their pernicious effects snowballed in human society and in the cosmos as a whole. Yahweh therefore had to erase them himself through the flood.[139] For these reasons, any doctrine whereby anyone's sin (including Adam's and Eve's, if considered a sin) could be left to fester across post-deluvian generations and indefinitely into the future would have been entirely unacceptable to Israelite thinking. This is consistent with the traditional approach taken throughout the ancient Near East, as in the case of the New Year's festival where the tainted past was put behind and a new, pure world was established annually. The idea of original sin inaccurately diverts this original collective focus on how sins are expatiated to one of an individual's salvation.

As demonstrated above, Adam and Eve's transgression did not rise to the level of true sin in the first place. In that case, there was no sin to be expiated and therefore no possibility of any fundamental breach in the relationship (if any) with Yahweh. As shown above, in order for humans to be capable of sin, humans first must possess the knowledge of good and evil. Otherwise they are like minors lacking legal capacity. Adam and Eve were in that primitive state when they committed the transgression. The function of the Eden story, then, is as an etiological prelude: to illustrate human nature and then equip humanity to understand what sin is and thereafter be in a position to avoid it. Real sin then begins in the very next episode, with Cain, when Yahweh takes care to explain and warn him about it beforehand (Gen. 4:6-7). There would have been no point in explaining this to Adam and Eve because they would not have understood it.

These conclusions are supported by the text of the Eden story. For all of J's emphasis on "evil" and "sin" in the primeval history, such words and descriptions are conspicuously absent in his Eden story. If any taint of original sin existed, we would expect this to be mentioned in J's description of

Yahweh meting out his punishments. But nothing of the kind occurs. There is no curse on the humans or other stigma attached to them. Only the serpent and the ground are cursed. The only sanctions on the humans are the natural circumstances of human life and, for Eve, being ruled by her husband. The first curse and stigma placed on a human was that put on Cain, and the story gives no sign that Adam and Eve's actions had any influence on Cain's sin.[140] Nor does the Hebrew Bible later say that what occurred in the Eden story was a sin, although the term is used throughout the primeval history beginning with the Cain episode.

THE LESSONS OF THE GARDEN

We began this book with an epigraph from John A. Sanford, who had the distinction of being both an Episcopal priest and a Jungian analyst. From this insightful perspective, he saw the Eden story as a combination of myth (a product of human psychology) and J's conscious intentions, an approach that we embraced in the Introduction and have followed throughout this book. It is therefore fitting that we summarize the results of our investigation in terms of these two prongs of the analysis.

J's Conscious Purposes

J structured the Eden story as an etiological myth explaining how things came to be as they are, especially evil. He portrayed humans by nature as being inclined to sin, but he had the first humans emerge from the garden equipped to avoid it by virtue of having acquired the knowledge of good and evil. And by placing the emergence of sin and evil within the traditional ancient Near Eastern cosmic framework of chaos vs. order, J kept Yahweh blameless for evil.

J's more immediate religious and social concern, however, was to use the story as his opening argument for making Yahwism Israel's religion. So naturally Yahweh emerged from the Eden story victorious and in a favorable theological light.[141] He created and then established sole jurisdiction over the garden-Center, which formerly had been the province of the Goddess. He was shown to control the *tehôm*. Yahweh largely repelled human aspirations to divinity, thus protecting his prerogatives. He dethroned and divorced his Goddess-wife and assumed her powers. He humiliated and physically changed the serpent, put it under his control, and assumed its powers.[142] He created and was in control of sacred trees formerly associated with the Goddess. Here too he appropriated the powers of these objects of the people's veneration, which was symbolized by placing his cherubim and sword to guard the tree of life. The story also claimed to establish men as dominant over women. In the end, the Center and the world were Yahweh's, and humankind's only legitimate route to the sacred would be through him. This ideal became that of Israel, with the Jerusalem temple as the Center of the earth, which would become another garden of Eden, with the Israelites walking with Yahweh according to the Law by applying their knowledge of good and evil.

The Mythology of Eden

Beyond J's own conscious intentions lay the underlying, largely archetypal, meanings of the mythological material that he utilized. We can assume that J was only partially conscious of these mythological meanings, because we ourselves have developed an understanding of them only over the past century or so. It is therefore important to bring forth these insights here, as they have not fully made their way into the literature on the Eden story.

We saw above that what Christian tradition has labeled the "fall" was in important and essential ways a positive, transformative event in human development, and that J recognized this. Indeed, Cyrus Gordon observed that the Eden story "is not so much an account of the 'fall of man' but rather of the rise of man halfway to divinity,"[143] while David Wright concluded that "if there is a vertical movement in the story, it is not a 'Fall' but an 'Ascension,' toward the rank and species of deity."[144] Similarly, Bruce Naidoff wrote that "Genesis 2-3 reflects a *coming to a state of awareness* that, as it were, precedes sin."[145] Modern mythological studies and psychology not only agree with this understanding, but also help explain the underlying reasons why it is correct. Indeed, as Joseph Campbell stressed regarding the Eden story, "This story yields its meaning only to a psychological interpretation."[146] In the field of mythological studies, this line of thought concerning the story has been developed not only by Campbell but by other mythologist-thinkers such as Carl Jung, Erich Neumann, Marie-Louise von Franz, John Sanford, Ken Wilber, and Keiron Le Grice, among others. Their analyses dovetail well with our understanding of J's thinking as explained in this book.

As we have seen, J thought of human evil (sin) as a manifestation of an underlying natural chaos (a cosmic principle) that lies within the human mind that manifests itself in impulses (in later Jewish thought called the *yēṣer hara*). Today psychologists understand this as our Shadow, the unconscious dark side of our psyche in which resides, among other things, what one rejects as one's evil side.[147] Indeed, as explained in Chapter 4, the very notion of primordial chaos in creation myths is really a projection of our own chaotic unconscious, and the mythological motif of creation as a process of imposing order (especially pairs of opposites) reflects and projects the emergence of human ego consciousness. That is, in creation myths, humans effectively bring the outside world into being through an act of consciousness, a self-aware knowing of the outside world. [148] As Jung stressed, "cosmogonic myths are, at bottom, symbols for the coming of consciousness." [149] As such, Adam and Eve's eyes being opened upon gaining the knowledge of good and evil and being able to see opposites symbolize their transition from an archaic undifferentiated psychic unity (the uroboros) [150] to a higher level, that of ego consciousness. [151] Psychologically speaking, through this transformation humans became able to make subject-object distinctions, distinguish their selves in relation to the outside world, and perceive and understand the world in terms of opposites. [152] This means all opposites, not just good and evil, which as we have seen can be taken as a merism symbolizing the other opposites as well. [153] As discussed above, in J's terms this new awareness— the knowledge of good and evil—yields just such an understanding of the dynamic of chaos vs. order in the cosmos and in human affairs. Historically, gaining this psychic awareness was an evolutionary process, but in myths like the Eden story it gets dramatized as a singular epiphany.

Earlier we concluded that the *content* of the knowledge of good and evil is not esoteric, but noted that the *process* that Adam and Eve underwent has much in common with the initiations of protagonists in myths and in esoteric traditions, in which the initiate's entire mode of being is transformed. In an initiation, the candidate enters into sacred space, conceived of as being removed from the real world, in a mode of preexistence. [154] In the Eden story, where Adam and Eve are at the sacred Center and the tree of knowledge of good and evil is at the center of the Center, the scene is ready-made for such a transformation into a new mode of being. [155] An initiate's transformation to a higher stage of being is likened to death, because one's former state of being is said to die and be left behind. [156] Such transformations are typical of creation myths. As von Franz observed, "the creation myth forms an essential teaching in the ritual of initiation." [157] The reference to Adam and Eve's eyes being opened represents the coming of consciousness, enlightenment, and understanding (typically symbolized in myths by the eye and light), [158] while unconsciousness is darkness. This is why at the start of an initiation ritual the candidates often wear blindfolds, which are removed once they are enlightened and their old selves have died, and why the ritual begins in a dark chamber and ends with the enlightened being led out into the light. [159] This also explains why blinding is often the fate of failed heroes (e.g., Oedipus, Samson). [160]

In this connection, as seen in Chapter 6, eating fruit from a sacred tree facilitated both transformation during life and rebirth following death. Yahweh told Adam that if he ate the forbidden fruit he would die on that day (Gen. 2:17), yet surely Yahweh knew that the effect of eating the fruit would be to confer special knowledge that would raise humans' state of being so they would be capable of following Yahweh, for which purpose they, of course, must remain alive. In the uroboros, the opposites of life and death do not yet exist,[161] but inevitably they must appear in our world. Thus, one meaning that Yahweh may have intended is not bodily death or even becoming mortal, but the symbolic death of the virginal human and the transformation into one having a consciousness that can be aware of the opposites of life and death, which phenomenon indeed can be understood as the first appearance of death in the world (even though no one had died yet), and hence also as the first appearance of the desire for immortality.[162] Indeed, the serpent too, in telling Eve that she would not die by eating the fruit, was clearly distinguishing between bodily death on the one hand, which it knew would not happen, and enlightenment on the other, which it knew about and promised.

Inherent in this enlightenment motif is that of a special individual who initiates the transformation, where he and thereby all humans as a whole become (or can become) more independent, self-aware beings existing at a higher level of consciousness. As mentioned in the Introduction, in this archetypal myth, a courageous hero-figure, a man or god transgressing a taboo or other rule of the establishment, overturns the status quo by confronting and defeating a dragon, serpent or similar monster (a goddess or her male satellite) that represents the uroboric state and which sometimes guards the "treasure" (which is knowledge);[163] the defeated monster is then dismembered in some literal or figurative way (e.g., Tiamat's dismemberment), which is an ordering process.[164] The uroboros is associated with the Great Mother and so is feminine, which is why heroes are so often detained, and their quest threatened, at places (often a paradise) run by females.[165] (Mythologically, paradise is a feminine attraction.[166]) Correspondingly, psychologically this victory reflects identification with the Father God, together with the rise of patriarchy and of civilization and its rules. These story lines are apparent in the Eden story as well: The humans are protagonists who, unsatisfied with their lower state of being, violate a prohibition, overturn the status quo and thereby rise to a higher level of being, which lays the basis for order and civilization in the real world, including in religious life. In the story, the uroboros (idyllic garden, serpent as chaos, Goddess as chaos) is eliminated for the humans; the serpent is flattened and symbolically defeated. Here the humans play a heroic kind of role. Importantly, so too from this perspective does Yahweh, by appropriating the garden and other symbols of the Goddess and of the feminine and setting up the new patriarchal establishment. Only unlike in some later hero myths, here the feminine is not reintegrated (see Epilogue).

In the Eden story, an interesting difference from the usual hero motif is the initially leading role of Eve (rather than a male) in the transformation process, but this is not as unusual as it may first appear. In hero myths the male protagonist often has a female helper who aids him in realizing his quest. Examples include Isis helping Osiris, Andromeda helping Perseus,

Ariadne helping Theseus, both Hera and Medea helping Jason, Athena helping Odysseus (and even Zeus as his sidekick), and more recently in *The Lord
of the Rings,* Galadriel helping Frodo. From the way J wrote the story, we can
appreciate that Eve's sole role in the garden was to catalyze the transgression
and the resulting enlightenment. Mythologically speaking, this is how Eve
acted as Adam's and humankind's "helper." Once that happened, her role
receded, and Yahweh spoke only with Adam and held him principally to
account, his fault having been listening to her, and at the end the story
mentions expelling only "the man" *(hā́ādām)* from the garden,[167] as if Eve
had no legal capacity and didn't matter. Thus, J ultimately viewed the male
figure as primary.

Notwithstanding J's conscious views, however, mythologically there is an
important reason (in addition to those mentioned in Chapter 8) why a female
initiated the transformation and why it occurred in a sacred garden, which as
we saw earlier was traditionally associated with a presiding goddesses. As
discussed in Chapter 8 and the Epilogue, according to modern psychology, it
is by getting in touch with one's feminine principle (in man the anima) that
men are stimulated into creativity, self-knowledge, and higher consciousness. Mythologically, Eve represents this principle. The garden as Center can
be thought of in feminine terms, as a transformative vessel containing the
latent opposites that will become manifest during the course of the myth.[168]
Pandora's jar likewise had this function.

When ego consciousness arises, one develops a superego incorporating
the rules of the community (collective), a conscience that worries and keeps
track of whether one obeys these rules, and a persona, which is the ego's self-
image presented to the outside world. If we follow the rules, we feel pride;
when we violate them, we feel guilt and shame. But guilt and pride cannot
arise until the superego and conscience exist, which can exist only if ego
consciousness exists.[169] Thus, hubris is the inflation of an *already existing*
ego.[170] Therefore, in addition to the reasons mentioned above for why hubris
was not a feature of the transgression we have a mytho-psychological one: It
was impossible for Adam and Eve to have transgressed out of pride (hubris)
because they were incapable of experiencing that feeling until after they
acquired ego consciousness *as a result* of the transgression (although tradition found it easy to pin hubris on them centuries after the fact). This is seen
in Eve's internal dialogue, which consists of simple notions that do not
evidence developed ego consciousness, such as a conscience that would be
bothered if she ate the fruit; the story quite clearly attributes that quality to
the pair only after the transgression, when they fear Yahweh.

Once the victory over the uroboros has been achieved, however, a mythological protagonist is often haunted by guilt. Where he has violated a taboo in
crossing the threshold, his newfound conscience naturally feels guilt because
he has violated the rules of the patriarchal authority figure, which motif is

clearly present in the Eden story. But this is not the most fundamental guilt, for which reason it is sometimes called "surplus guilt."[171] According to some psychologists/mythologists, more fundamental is the "primordial guilt" naturally and inevitably resulting from the emergence of self-consciousness as an aspect of ego consciousness.[172] Thus, in Neumann's view, "With the emergence of the fully fledged ego, the paradisal situation is abolished," a fact which "is experienced as guilt, and moreover as original guilt, a fall."[173] Having cut itself off from the maternal uroboros (sensed as the separation from one's mother's body, the severance of the umbilical cord), the ego feels discord and loneliness.[174] Further:

> Ego consciousness not only brings a sense of loneliness; it also introduces suffering, toil, trouble, evil, sickness, and death into man's life as soon as these are perceived by an ego. By discovering itself, the lonely ego simultaneously perceives the negative and relates to it, so that it at once establishes a connection between these two facts, taking its own genesis as guilt, and suffering, sickness, and death as condign punishment. . . . This is as much as to say that for primitive man chance does not exist: everything negative comes from the infringement of a taboo.[175]

"In reality," Neumann argues, "the guilt experienced by the ego comes from the sufferings of the unconscious"[176] resulting from the ego's triumph over the unconscious. While humans really are proactively relinquishing the uroboros, the transition is experienced as a punitive expulsion.[177] It is important to recognize that, from the mythological perspective, Adam and Eve effectively grew up and walked out of the garden on their own.[178] That moment occurred within themselves once they recognized duality (opposites), at which point they were automatically "exiled."[179] And it occurred in their heads, as Campbell observed: "The Garden is a metaphor for the following: our minds."[180] The transgression is thus reminiscent of the famous scene in the film *The Matrix,* where the hero Neo is faced with a choice of taking two pills, a blue one that will enable him to resume his former uroboric, unaware life in the Matrix, or a red one that will make him aware and reveal the truth, from which there will be no turning back.[181] In selecting the red pill, Neo too got up and walked out of the uroboros. We can therefore see, in particular, that the closing scene in the story where Yahweh's sends Adam and Eve out from the garden and places the cherubim and flaming sword to guard against turning back is both a dramatization reflecting J's conscious purposes and a reflection of the underlying mythological structure.

Because the unconscious content that the ego has denied remains part of our overall psyche, the ego will continue to suffer until ways are found to realize its own true values and approve of its deed.[182] This typically involves some combination of repression, suppression, and sublimation. In myths and in real history, this often occurs through some honorific transformation, restoration, and absorption of feminine symbols in a less threatening, acceptable form,[183] including the Father-God's marriage with the formerly dominant goddess. In ancient Israel, for example, despite Yahweh's prominence and pretentions, Asherah still flourished as Yahweh's consort, the sacred tree became sublimated into the acceptable menorah, and the serpent lived on as the bronze serpent.

Other natural outgrowths of the establishment of ego consciousness were the solidification of patriarchy and the development of law.[184] In ancient Israel, observed Neumann, "patriarchal development brought about a revaluation of the feminine . . . in which all the maternal-chthonic characteristics of the primitive world of the Canaanites were devalued, reinterpreted, and replaced by the patriarchal Jehovah-valuation."[185] In the Eden story, this is reflected both in the treatment of Asherah and goddess symbols, and in the ending where women are subjected to men. The Law too was, among other things, a tool to achieve these ends.

Such is the mythological understanding of the emergence of good and evil, the knowledge of good and evil, and of the transgression. It remains for us to consider and summarize in the Epilogue some aspects of how the Eden story has affected our civilization, what lessons to draw from that, and how to use the story's meaning to improve our future.

Epilogue

Taking the Eden Story Personally:
Its Meaning for Us Today

The oldest myths, whether of the Fisher King or of the Fall, whether of Ulysses or of the Tower of Babel, are contemporary. Pattern is given to the welter and jungle of human society not by historical development but by myth. The locus of the soul is not in London or New York or Vienna but at the barred gate of Eden . . .

—Amos Wilder[1]

Know thyself.

—Socrates

This thing of darkness I acknowledge mine.

—Shakespeare, *The Tempest*[2]

Through this dream I understood that the self is the principle and archetype of orientation and meaning. Therein lies its healing function. For me, this insight signified an approach to the center and therefore to the goal. Out of it emerged a first inkling of my personal myth.

—Carl Jung[3]

Now that we understand the essential mythological aspects of the Eden story, we can reflect on how it may be relevant in our personal lives and for our society today. What parts still resonate with us, and which don't? What truths does it draw to our attention that can be valuable lessons for us? Conversely, are some parts of the story unsuitable in this day and age, which we should best leave aside? Because of the vast influence that this story has had and still has on our spiritual life and our culture, these questions are not academic but have tremendous practical and personal meaning and importance, so it is appropriate to examine them at the end of our study. As we have done throughout, we examine these questions from the standpoint of J's conscious authorial intent as well as from the underlying mythological perspective. The latter is especially important because that perspective and the lessons to be drawn from it are not well known or understood. We begin with the former, because those considerations help frame the mythological discussion.

APPROACHING J'S IDEAS TODAY

Human Nature as Good or Evil, and Our Power of Choice

J directly confronted the question, still with us after centuries, of whether humans are good or bad by nature.[4] As we have seen, J believed that we have within us an element of chaos that manifests itself as impulses and imaginings and eventually as evil and sin. (Today psychology equates this chaos with the workings of the unconscious.) The question then becomes how to prevent our nature from causing evil. According to J, the first part of the answer appeared in the garden when we acquired the knowledge of good and evil, which enables us to understand our nature and hopefully control it. Thus, as of the end of the Eden story, our nature was mixed, with the potential for our good side to prevail. One lesson of the Eden story was to show what happens when humans don't have (or don't apply) this knowledge and our more primitive impulses take their natural course. But in order for good to prevail, J believed, having the knowledge of good and evil is not enough, as depicted in the downward spiral of humanity in the primeval history from Cain to the tower of Babel. For good to prevail, we need Yahweh's guidance, in the form of his commands (laws), which our knowledge of good and evil enables us to understand and follow.

J thus believed that, even though there is an evil element to human nature, ultimately we, walking with Yahweh, have the power to choose to act on the side of the good, as defined by the Law. This power of choice must be an assumption in any ethical and legal system. The question then becomes how the good should be defined and what should be the source, nature, and content of our ethic. For J and the other authors of the Hebrew Bible, the answers to these questions were obvious: the good is what Yahweh declares it is, and it is to be achieved (and evil avoided) by following Yahweh's Law. In the mythological discussion below, we argue that J was right about some part of us containing "evil" (though our concept of the term differs from J's) and that we have a knowledge of good and evil that is essential to deal with it, but that trying to eliminate evil prophylactically through law and ethical strictures is not the fundamentally viable approach to resolving the problem.

The Quest for Knowledge

As we have seen, J considered the mere desire for knowledge to be a manifestation of chaos and of the inclination to evil. In light of history and what we know about human psychology, we can now appreciate that the desire for knowledge is separate from the problem of evil. Because J conceived Yahweh's commands (Law) as the embodiment of the good, we can understand how J feared that independent thinking and seeking of knowledge might undermine the human conformity to and realization of the good, so defined. History has shown, however, that increased education and knowledge, whether in science, social sciences, humanities, or in spirituality actually helps head off evil and increases the amount of good, well-being, and happiness. Indeed, over history keeping people in the dark has been a means of oppression, while freedom of inquiry, the availability of information and increased knowledge have proven essential to our freedoms and greater well-being.

Humans and the Environment

A valuable insight of J was his emphasis on humanity's close relationship with the earth, which resonates with today's concerns over the human impact on the environment. In the Eden story, Yahweh put the garden in Adam's hands to tend it, which was a conferral of responsibility to keep it well, to preserve the creation. In the case of P's creation account too, God conferred upon humans dominion over all of the earth and its animals (Gen. 1:26-30), which was a conferral of responsibility, not a license to exploit it without facing consequences. This biblical idea reminds us of our responsibilities as stewards of the earth's environment. As we saw in Chapters 4 and 9, J believed that human misbehavior could infect the world and set in motion further chaos in nature herself, thus polluting and spoiling the world, making it too a form and manifestation of evil, as occurred in the Bible during the lead-up to the flood. Our own actions can and have polluted the environment and are a cause of global warming, which in turn have had and will continue to have harmful effects on our health, the economy, and our well-being. J's and P's stories serve as reminders of the dangers and of our responsibilities.

The Role of Women, and of the Feminine

As we have seen, the Eden story affirms the subjugation of women and generally takes a negative view of them, a view that has been perpetuated in Western religion over the centuries and even to this day (e.g., the Catholic prohibition against female priests). Eve was the leading human agent of the transgression. Adam was faulted for having listened to her, as if she were divine. Yahweh punished Eve (and all women) not only with greater pain in pregnancy and childbearing, but by decreeing that her husband will rule over her. Further, the story polemicized against the goddess Asherah, Yahweh's wife, which is to say against the feminine principle. As seen in Chapter 8, the Eden story on balance cannot be "rehabilitated" so as to present a positive view of women or of the Goddess.

Insofar as the Eden story was an etiological statement about the position of women, it was functionalist mythology designed to reinforce the dominant position of males in that society. But the laws of a tribal god are social, local, and historic, not generally applicable to all of humanity.[5] What might have been understandable from that perspective for a primitive society almost 3,000 years ago should have no relevance or validity in modern society.

More subtle is the Eden story's treatment of the feminine principle in the form of the goddess Asherah, represented not only by Eve but also alluded to by the symbols of the sacred trees, the serpent, and the garden precinct itself. In the Eden story, J sought to suppress and eliminate it. Modern psychology teaches that this has pernicious effects. The feminine principle is an essential part of the psyche (in the form of the anima), just as is the male principle (the animus). In order for anyone to be psychologically and spiritually balanced and healthy, these principles cannot be suppressed or repressed but must be integrated into the personality. Likewise with our culture. We address this below in the mythological discussion.

The Devil/Satan

One enduring figure traditionally thought to be represented in the Eden story is that of the Devil, or Satan. In fact, however, J intended no such character. The Hebrew word *sātān* ("adversary," or, if appointed by God, a judge or prosecutor), does appear over 20 times in the Hebrew Bible,[6] but not in any texts by J; the texts in which the word appears are all from a later period. The figure of Satan or the Devil as a demonic figure that is the cause of evil developed in later Judaism and in Christianity.[7] Bible scholars overwhelmingly agree that the serpent in the garden of Eden was not Satan or the Devil.[8] To view J's serpent as such would be a misreading of the story that misses the symbolism that J was endeavoring to convey. In J's view, chaos preceded even the creation, and remained to some extent in the cosmos and therefore also in human nature (manifested as evil). Therefore, no outside agency such as the Devil was needed to introduce evil into the world. The transgression in the garden was just nature taking its course. Therefore, the serpent was not the *source* of evil but only a symbol for it, namely for the intrusion of chaos into the garden and its welling up in the human heart, which were the same thing. As we shall see below, modern psychology similarly views the Devil/Satan as a manifestation of our unconscious dark side.

Humans as Matter and Spirit, and Accessing the Divine

J considered humans to be of the same substance as the earth. This makes us one with the earth and with the rest of the cosmos, but as we have seen, J viewed the cosmos as inert material with no divinity in it, although Yahweh imparted the breath of life to creatures. In Western civilization[9] the notion that humans have some element of divinity within them (in the form of a soul) took hold in ancient Greece, and was adopted in Christianity only centuries after J wrote. This idea developed through a dualist distinction between matter vs. spirit (or the soul). In the West, the two were never happily fused; there has never been a satisfactory explanation of how they could co-exist or relate to each other.

Einstein discovered that matter is really energy. Everything in the universe, including ourselves, is made up of energies that developed into structured matter. Phenomena such as quantum entanglement and nonlocality show us that everything is connected, even across extraordinary distances and even while "violating" (getting around) the "speed limit" of light. Our "bodies" cause physical effects (and may indeed be considered to extend) beyond the surface of our skin, while other things "outside" in the cosmos penetrate and influence us all the time. As Einstein put it:

> A human being is part of the whole, called by us "Universe"; a part limited in time and space. He experiences himself, his thoughts and feelings as something separated from the rest—a kind of optical delusion of his consciousness. This delusion is a kind of prison for us . . . . Our task must be to free ourselves from this prison . . . .[10]

Physicists, neuroscientists, and neuropsychologists have begun to connect the phenomena of physics with the origins and functioning of the human psyche.[11] This body of study suggests that our psyche (Self) and body can and do connect in some way with the underlying energies in and around us, and that in this may lie what we can consider the nature and essence of divinity.

As we saw earlier, in the ancient Near East originally people generally believed that the divine pervaded all of creation, including humanity, so that humans could access and experience it and thereby gain spiritual knowledge. In Far Eastern religions from ancient times to this day, a similar concept has prevailed, whereby through yoga, meditation and similar spiritual practices people dissolve their everyday egos and the appearances of the material world, so that their inner self can connect with the fundamental forces and energies of the universe, which can be viewed as "divine." In such spiritual traditions, the everyday material world (in Buddhism called maya) is not denied as nonexistent; rather, it is just not the important, fundamental level of reality on which our spirituality should be based.

J, however, held that material humans and divinity are in separate realms and should remain that way, so the two cannot and should not connect. Instead, J advocated a *relationship* between humans and God, which relationship soon became mediated by a priesthood making the relationship with God less direct. Further, Yahweh was the sole avenue to any relationship with the divine; other deities, in particular the Goddess, were excluded. Other faiths, deities, and spiritual paths were not to be tolerated. Finally, Yahwist religion was aimed less at an individual's personal spirituality than at a social purpose, serving primarily the well-being of the community, namely the Israelite nation, while other peoples were regarded as the enemy.

For today's world, however, J's above position is problematic. We must recognize that there are many valid paths to divinity that can provide spiritual and psychic satisfaction, and be respectful and tolerant of them. Further, as we have learned, it is our ego that separates and orders things, including the opposites of the human and the divine, which is what results in seeing a need for *relationships* between them, as J advocated; the ego needs this for its own self-preservation, and we must recognize this phenomenon as just that. [12] But this separation prevents wholeness and is spiritually unsatisfying. As we shall see below, to address this problem modern psychology advocates connecting with our unconscious, where our sense of the divine comes from. Psychology thus has much in parallel with Christian and other mystical traditions and Eastern spiritual practices.

As discussed in Chapter 9, in traditional Christian interpretations, accessing and experiencing the divine directly as Adam and Eve did has been considered hubris in defiance of God. As we have seen, however, pride and hubris are the products of inflated ego consciousness, which Adam and Eve could not yet have. Thus, any spiritual practices that, through direct connection with the divine, seek to moderate the ego and integrate it with the rest of our psyche cannot be examples of pride or hubris. Practitioners of Eastern religions would be astonished at such a claim against them. In their practice, connecting directly with the divine actually necessitates *dissolving* the ego. Similarly, the Canaanites that J opposed (or likewise Dionysians) would be surprised to be told that in practicing their rites they were asserting their prideful egos and thereby diminishing any deity. Modern psychology recognizes that both the yearning for and conception of the divine are archetypal manifestations of our unconscious, not of our conscious ego. Thus, contrary to some interpretations of the Eden story, prideful desires and the yearning to experience the divine are inherently different, having different sources in our psyche and running in opposite directions, although our ego may seek to intertwine them.

THE MYTHOLOGY OF EDEN TODAY

Adam and Eve's gaining the knowledge of good and evil symbolized a transition into full ego consciousness from a primordial state (the uroboros) in which the human psyche had been dominated by impulses and instincts of the type that J highlighted and which caused the transgression. In this process, in mythological and psychological terms the uroboros (the Great Mother, in at least her dark aspects) was defeated, and the ego (which is masculine) took over. A result of this process was a transition in Israel and elsewhere that we described earlier as the Great Reversal: Sky-gods became dominant while Goddess religion declined, society became dominated by patriarchal authority, and law and a rigid ethic developed. The Reversal is often judged harshly today, but psychology recognizes that this was necessary at the time in order to firmly establish, stabilize and further develop human consciousness and thereby civilization,[13] which seems evidenced by the universal nature of this phenomenon. In particular, the separation of the opposites of good and evil developed our consciousness, because that made us more self-aware of our thoughts, feelings, and actions.[14]

But the problem is that the ego has never stopped and became hyperactive. Over history the ego has continued to suppress and repress both the feminine and the part of our psyche that contains what we consider evil (part of our Shadow), both in individuals and in communities. This occurs because the ego perceives these elements of our psyche as threats to itself and thus acts consciously (by suppression) or in a non-aware manner (by repression) to beat them back into submission. But they never submit. They remain and always will be part of our psyche, and they strive for a voice. Until a true equilibrium is attained through a higher authentic individuation of the personality (rather than using expedients), there is a dangerous split in the psyche; repressed contents will lead an active underground life and undermine consciousness.[15] In our psyches (though usually not in the outside world) we live a double life, like Dr. Jekyll and Mr. Hyde,[16] largely unaware of what both the ego and Shadow are doing; in many cases neurosis results. Analogous problems arise at the collective level. Below we examine this problem in two contexts that J focused on in the Eden story: evil[17] and the feminine. These are important because that is where in our Judeo-Christian tradition this pattern of suppression and repression began.

Evil

Our natural approach to our dark side (what J called our evil inclination) and the evil that it produces is to try to suppress it, on both the individual and collective levels. This is done by various measures, including strict ethical requirements and discipline, asceticism, and laws and punishments.[18] As we have seen, this was J's approach and that of the Hebrew Bible generally (except for asceticism). Such restraints on our natural behavior cause a certain amount of suffering, but it is felt that the result will be worth this price. The fact that this is undertaken proactively means that the evil content in question remains in contact with the ego, so that we are acknowledging its existence.[19] J at least confronted the issue squarely.

In Western European secular thought similar approaches were taken by Thomas Hobbes and Edmund Burke, who held similarly pessimistic views of human nature.[20] Thus, for J and such later thinkers, our knowledge of good and evil is to be used only to control our unalterable evil impulses. Perfection is realized and defined simply by suppressing (though in reality more often repressing) our negative qualities.[21] The definition of good becomes a limited one: that which is left at one end of the spectrum of opposites after our innate evil qualities have been suppressed or repressed.[22] But this is not a fundamental, holistic solution to the problem. It has not worked to master our destructive qualities,[23] as an understanding of history and a reading of our daily news headlines shows. Reverend Sanford thus counseled against such an approach:

> [T]here is an inevitable dark side to our nature that refuses to be assimilated into our lofty ideals of goodness, morality, and ideal human behavior. Indeed, if we strive to be too good we only engender the opposite reaction in the unconscious. If we try to live too much in the light, a corresponding amount of darkness accumulates within. . . . Psychology warns us against trying to be better than we are, and urges us to strive not so much for a forced "goodness" but for consciousness, and to live, not out of ideals we cannot keep, but from an inner Center which alone can keep the balance. . . . To try to be good, and disregard one's darkness, is to fall victim to the evil in ourselves whose existence we have denied. . . . So psychology suggests that we reject any pretense of being good that forces us to keep our evil hidden from ourselves. We thus follow the example of Jesus who, when he was addressed by the rich young man as "Good Master retorted, "Why do you call me good? No one is good but God alone."[24]

The incorrect and tragic assumption in the thinking behind the above model is that the human psyche is fixed and cannot develop higher. It is a static, prophylactic model that assumes that there can be no fundamental progress on the question of evil, and thus it becomes oppressive because it prevents real progress on the issue; further, such model can be and has been misused by the powerful in church and state to oppress people socially, politically, and religiously, which is an evil in itself. But the assumption behind this theory is outdated: Psychology has shown that our psyche has evolved over time, which means that it can evolve further.[25] This was shown by the Jean Gebser in his seminal work, *The Ever-Present Origin,* and the idea has been carried forward in the West by thinkers such as Ken Wilber and Allan Combs who describe paths to evolving to higher states of consciousness, and (independently) in the East by such figures as Sri Aurobindo. We got ourselves out of the uroboros (the garden) through a transformation of consciousness, so we can progress higher again. Our knowledge of good and evil (and here J's definition of it is apt) can and should be applied to develop in ourselves a higher level of consciousness and wholeness that will, among other things, deal with the problem of evil at its source, an approach which will treat the disease and not merely its symptoms. As this endeavor succeeds, the ethics and laws by which we live can be determined not by the ego, driven by its conscience and falsely perceived threats, but by the inner Voice of our whole Self (see below).[26] In this way, instead of fighting evil by imposing impossible absolute ethical requirements and prophylactic laws from the egocentric top down as J and his successors did, the problem of evil will naturally be addressed in a realistic and honest manner at its source.[27] The focus instead becomes one of *evolving and improving the human being,* so that the need for external restraints and suppression will lessen. The approach includes spiritual practices, psychology, and myth.

As we have seen in Chapter 9, the knowledge of good and evil as conceived by J enables us to recognize and understand the full nature and extent of opposites and the dynamic of their operation in the world, especially those of good and evil. In the Eden story, both the serpent and Yahweh describe this capability as being like the gods (Gen. 3:4, 22). From such a godlike perspective (rather than that of our ego) we are able to comprehend our *entire* Selves, both the good side and the evil side that J had identified.[28] J held that exercising this capability is essential for dealing with evil. Thus, we must understand the nature of our dark side and then deal with it in the most effective manner. In calling attention to this truth J did a great service, much as did Socrates whose maxim was, "Know thyself."

Modern psychology teaches essentially the same, only using different terminology and benefiting from our better understanding of the human psyche. In the view of modern psychology, we must first recognize the entire make-up of our individual and collective psyches, not just the ego, which is only the tip of the iceberg. This is the equivalent of using J's conception of the knowledge of good and evil, the godlike perspective. In psychological terms, this means operating (eventually) from the center of our psyche, which is the Self and incorporates both ego consciousness and the unconscious.[29] In psychological terms the Self is an archetype, but practically it is useful to think of it as a point or (godlike) perspective in one's own inner "space" that can be aware and enable us to view, recognize, understand, and process the components and workings of our psyche. It enables us to view, as if from the outside, ourselves and our way of thinking, behaving, and "being" in the world.

The alternative to the prophylactic approach thus actually begins where J began, by recognizing our dark side, but then departs from J and his successors by applying our knowledge of good and evil not simply to understand the nature of the Law and obey it, but to explore more deeply the human being and identify, confront, and assimilate that dark side of ourselves. This is necessary because there is much more to our dark side than the part that we admit to and proactively try to suppress. The more prevalent practice is to slide into repression of our dark side (not done so consciously).[30] Our ego has an ideal picture of ourselves that it strives to protect and uphold so that we can enjoy self-esteem, and this self-image becomes the persona that we project to the outside world. As a result, we reject all of our qualities that are inconsistent with this picture, because they threaten the ego.[31] The traits that we reject are driven into the unconscious where they coagulate into the Shadow and live an autonomous life,[32] usually below the surface (ego) but sometimes appearing, for example, in our dreams and in our sense of humor.[33] Our Shadow contents could have become part of our ego but did not, and thus represent an unlived part of our lives.[34] As a result, our psyche is divided rather than whole.

Our "evil" qualities are perhaps the most prominent among these repressed shadow contents, but they are far from the only ones. In fact, our notion of what is "evil" becomes somewhat subjective, because *anything* inconsistent with our self-image could end up being regarded as such. Insofar as people's individual ego ideals vary, so too correspondingly do their shadow personalities,[35] including the make-up of any "evil" content. For example, in the case of criminal gang members for whom aggressiveness and hostility is integral to their ego's self-image, their Shadow will embody their more gentle, loving, and socially acceptable traits.[36] Therefore, in order to address the problem of evil, the Shadow as a whole must be confronted.

In the normal case of repression when we consider ourselves better than we really are, instead of seeking and achieving true wholeness we compensate and discharge guilt by projecting the rejected and repressed elements "out there."[37] We see these instead in another person or group that is consequently regarded as the villain or enemy, who is to be fought and eradicated. Humans want evil to be "out there" because so too will be the solution: eliminating or reforming the "other."[38] We are reluctant to look for the demons within ourselves, whether as individuals or collectives, because that would demand that we (our ego) change.[39] As a result, in our conscious lives the Shadow is experienced externally and indirectly.[40] As Jung observed, this is a rift in the psychic system that "appears as a religious projection, in the form of a split between the powers of Light and Darkness."[41] Thus, for example, the Devil/Satan is a shadow figure,[42] and this same dynamic lies behind the various dualistic religious doctrines (e.g., Zoroastrianism, Manichaeism, Gnosticism). By contrast, Native Americans were perplexed by our notion of a satanic being, because they accepted that humans combined in themselves both good and evil, so there was no need to invoke the idea of an external devil.[43] Similarly, in Greek mythology, where no deity created the world and was responsible for it, the gods and goddesses each had both good and evil qualities, so there was no satanic figure embodying evil, and the "problem of evil" was not a large issue.[44] We would do well to move closer to such recognitions.

This externalization of evil and the Shadow is most visible on the collective level (tribes, nations, and other communities). As we saw in Chapter 2, J and other biblical writers took such externalization a step further by denying that Israelites are Canaanites and erecting a substitute mythology of Israelite origins and identity. This problem is not unique to the biblical world, however. Refusing to confront our own dark side and projecting it onto others lay behind the religious persecutions of the Church over history (witches, heretics, infidels), and continues to this day on both the individual and collective levels, as in the case of radical fundamentalist Islam (and the counterpoising opinion among many in the West regarding even mainstream Islam), and religious, political or social extremes of any kind. As a result of this split in our psyches and scapegoat mentality, the problem of evil is left fundamentally unaddressed and unresolved, a problem that has remained to this day with obviously disastrous consequences that continue to form our daily news headlines.

Along somewhat similar lines are short-term expedients that serve to transfer evil from ourselves to "out there," which in practice if not always in theory become exercises for temporarily externalizing and exorcizing evil rather than fully confronting it in ourselves. Thus, the Israelites practiced a scapegoat ritual and a sin offering.[45] Similarly, the sacrament of baptism, usually performed in infancy when we are not fully conscious beings, is defined as a form of exorcism that purports to remove the taint of original sin and drive out its instigator, the Devil.[46] According to traditional views of Christian churches, Christ and belief in him also serve to redeem us from our sins in life (again caused by the Devil), which is to say that in Christian doctrine the problem of evil is still externalized and personalized through outside figures of Dark and Light rather than being addressed directly by confronting it in our selves.[47]

Because our post-Eden psyche is split rather than whole, it is not easy to operate from the godlike perspective of the Self and one must learn by trying. Such transformation is a two-step process: recognition and comprehension followed by actual practice and realization[48] where we assimilate shadow contents into our personality.[49] Eventually our ego can mature by controlling its innate will toward self-preservation and fear of destruction, realizing that its existence is not necessarily threatened by these unconscious contents.[50] Here our ego must do the work; there is no one else to do it. The ego emerged and has always functioned as an organ for adapting to reality;[51] the reality has simply shifted as we face the dysfunctional consequences of suppression and repression together with the technological capacity to destroy ourselves and our environment, hence the objective and urgent need for further adaptation. The process is difficult and entails suffering when we honestly confront our dark side.[52] But if the process is seen through, matters will tend to resolve themselves. For example, the fearsome shadow figures of our nightmares terrify us, but through confronting and working with them we come to realize that they really are our friends.[53] Thus, the Shadow is a friend, because it is actually a guide that holds the key to our wholeness.[54]

The Feminine

With the above in mind we can turn to the question of the feminine in the male psyche and in our society. As we have seen, the Eden story devalued it: The Goddess was sent into oblivion and earthly women were subjected to rule by men. Here a similar kind of problem developed as with the Shadow.

The dismemberment of the serpent-dragon (chaotic/dark side of the Great Mother) can leave the higher feminine (symbolized by the Good Goddess) intact. In reality, the hero kills only the dark side of the female, freeing up the good, fruitful and joyous side so that he can join with her.[55] But in the Great Reversal (as seen in Yahweh's divorce from Asherah) this result was largely not realized, with much of the feminine being suppressed and repressed. When it is realized, the feminine part of the unconscious (the anima) is assimilated into masculine ego consciousness, a process called "the crystallization of the anima from the mother archetype."[56] In hero myths this is typically symbolized by the hero first killing the dragon that holds a female captive, which proves him worthy of her, and then marrying her, which symbolizes the assimilation of ego-hero with the anima.[57] When the feminine flows into the masculine ego, there is an irruption of creativity and the psyche becomes more whole.[58] Our creativity and spiritual transformation depend on the feminine unconscious, so we must access and nourish it.[59] We must not dethrone and put away the Goddess as J did, but resurrect and embrace her.[60] Studies show that the most developed personalities have a healthy balance of the masculine and feminine principles.[61] The individuation process yields a stable consciousness that can relate to the feminine in a stable, mature way, neither repressing it so that the ego can continue to dominate nor letting it overcome the ego (in which case one would regress back into the uroboros).[62]

The Synthesis

The result of this individuation process is to shift our self-identity and entire way of being from the ego into our Center, the Self.[63] It is the alchemical transformation from lead into gold.[64] The personality is then whole, where the opposites are unified as in the divine.[65] A psychologically satisfying and "true" spiritual world will have been built within the framework of the arche-type of the divine,[66] which perhaps is what Adam and Eve were seeking. Going into the details of how this process works would take us far beyond the purpose and scope of this book, and others are more qualified to describe it and have done so, in both West and East.[67] Also, what approaches and tools are best will vary from person to person and from community to community. Here we simply mention the more common examples of practices and policies which proponents of this individuation process consider impor-tant:

- Tending carefully and rigorously our dreams (on one's own and perhaps with the help of an analyst), because they are reservoirs of the unconscious where the Shadow lurks.[68] Native Americans thought that the Great Spirit sent humans dreams to keep the soul from falling into evil and wandering from the right path, so they should be heeded.[69] Dreams are compensa-tions endeavoring to reattune consciousness and the psyche as a whole.[70]
- Similarly to dreams, tending symbols that resonate with us, as they origi-nate in the unconscious and can mediate the achievement of wholeness (see below). Symbols representing the unity of opposites (e.g., mandalas, which Jung utilized for himself) are especially important.[71]
- As with symbols, appreciation (better yet, the practice) of art, music, and dance, which speak to us on many psychic levels[72]
- Attention to our sense of humor, because it is usually our shadow person-ality laughing[73]
- Meditation, which among other things enables us temporarily to escape from (dissolve) our egos and then come back the better for it[74]
- Developing collective myths oriented toward the planet and humanity as a whole (in books, film, theater),[75] together with our own personal myths (see below).
- Encouraging new cultural heroes who embody and forge this path, as models for the rest of us in our own lifelong process of individuation, as the hero's journey has always been a mythical representation of the indi-viduation process[76]
- Accessing and nourishing the unconscious feminine (anima) in ourselves (see above). This includes approaching sex as a psychic and spiritual experience.[77]
- Rethinking educational theory and institutions accordingly[78]

- For some people, undertaking therapy with a qualified analyst; for others, counseling with one's priest, pastor, or master.

While this process is difficult and takes one along a razor's edge, it is helped by the unconscious, an ally. In psychology there is a "law of compensation"[79] akin to Newton's Third Law (i.e., for every action there is an equal and opposite reaction). It holds that the unconscious functions as a compensatory mechanism that aims to restore psychic equilibrium and wholeness when the ego goes hyperactive; thus the unconscious not only threatens the ego with its instincts (when repressed) but also helps to correct and redeem it.[80] It wants to be welcomed rather than rejected and externalized. The Self too is an organ (archetype) of our collective unconscious that seeks wholeness,[81] and as such in psychological terms is where our religious impulse and sense of the divine (God-image) come from.[82] (Whether a real deity ultimately lies behind it cannot be objectively proved or disproved,[83] so is either a matter of faith or, as some maintain, direct albeit subjective experience.) As a result, here religion and psychology work in the same direction and can be complementary, as they both seek to relate a person's ego to the larger reality (God, Self).[84] A person must live a life that satisfies this yearning of the Self. If not, a person is psychically dried up, drained of psychic energy (libido), spiritually dead, and finds it difficult to effectively carry out even normal tasks in life; in the worst cases neurosis results.[85] On the other hand, people are energized and happy when they live according to an authentic inner purpose, whatever that may be. This explains why any religion or mythology can work (the various "Masks of God," as Campbell termed it), because they satisfy this same universal need and can be psychologically true.[86] To achieve this, using the Voice of the Self, one must formulate what both Jung and Campbell called one's personal myth,[87] which focuses one's purpose. Campbell called this exercise one of "Creative Mythology," because it is a mythology individually created by a person through one's Self by tapping the creative powers of the unconscious (especially the feminine).[88] This endeavor is not a regression but an advance to higher consciousness and is authentic, because it is self-aware and the ego is still present. And if done right one is living by Campbell's dictum, "Follow your bliss."

In the end we realize that the higher, ultimate Good is the wholeness of the Self in individuals and communities achieved through this never-ending process of "sharpening the saw." There the opposites are transcended. This individuated Self is similar to Plato's idea (form, archetype) of the Good, which constellates the other forms around itself, makes them visible and intelligible, and to some extent accords them further being (content):[89] "This reality, then, that gives their truth to the objects of knowledge and the power of knowing to the knower, you must say is the idea of good, and you must conceive it as being the cause of knowledge, and of truth in so far as known."[90] From the godlike perspective, we can measure what we should consider good and evil by the yardstick of wholeness.[91]

Part of this process should also involve unraveling J's conscious alterations of archetypal symbols in the Eden story in the service of his polemic. These symbols must be understood and nourished in their original, essential archetypal meaning (which we have endeavored to convey in this book) and restored to their proper roles in the service of our psychological and spiritual well-being. As Campbell observed specifically in regard to the Eden story,

> it is surely a bewilderment to the psyche to have to respond to images that say one thing to the heart and are presented to the mind as programming another, opposite meaning. This paradox produces a kind of schizoid situation, and undoubtedly one of the main reasons for the prosperity of psychoanalysts today is this tangling and short-circuiting of the symbolic imagery through which the conscious and unconscious systems of our minds were to have been held in touch.[92]

As we have seen, the same symbols re-emerge anyway in another form (e.g., sacred tree as menorah, Christmas tree, or Maypole; feminine/Goddess in Virgin Mary veneration), which testifies to our psychic unity with people even from J's time.[93]

As we attain higher individuation by applying the godlike perspective of our knowledge of good and evil, we come to realize that we are the creators of our own Selves, and also that we literally create our own world in which we live, for which we are solely responsible. The Center lies not in Eridu, Babylon, Jerusalem, or Eden, but within. We have our own internal high place with its sacred tree connecting us to the divine. We can access it, live there, and pluck and digest its fruit anytime, wherever we are. We can activate the serpent power and utilize it. The God and Goddess within us can live still happily married, in their kingdom there. And "out there" the "Canaanites" are really our friends, so we can befriend them and live together in harmony. In both its positive and negative ways, the mythology of Eden has led us to the threshold from which we may and must move ever higher from Eden. To do that we each must, proceeding from the Center that is our Self, create our own personal myth to guide us there.

Abbreviations Used in Citations

AASOR: *Annual of the American Schools of Oriental Research*

ABD: *The Anchor Bible Dictionary.* Edited by David L. Freedman. 6 vols. New York: Doubleday, 1992.

AfO: *Archiv für Orientforschung*

AJA: *American Journal of Archaeology*

AJSL: *American Journal of Semitic Languages and Literatures*

ANEP: *The Ancient Near East in Pictures Relating to the Old Testament.* Edited by James Pritchard. Princeton: Princeton University Press, 1954.

ANES: *The Ancient Near East Supplementary Texts and Pictures Relating to the Old Testament.* Edited by James Pritchard. Princeton: Princeton University Press, 1969.

ANET: *Ancient Near Eastern Texts Relating to the Old Testament.* Edited by James Pritchard. 2nd ed. Princeton: Princeton University Press, 1955.

ASOR: *American Schools of Oriental Research*

BA: *Biblical Archaeologist*

BAR: *Biblical Archaeology Review*

BASOR: *Bulletin of the American Schools of Oriental Research*

BD: The Egyptian Book of the Dead

BDB: Brown, F., S. R. Driver, and C. A. Briggs. *A Hebrew and English Lexicon of the Old Testament.* Oxford, 1907.

BSOAS: *Bulletin of the School of Oriental and African Studies*

BT: *The Bible Translator*

CAD: *The Assyrian Dictionary of the Oriental Institute of the University of Chicago.* Chicago, 1956-2010.

CBQ: *Catholic Biblical Quarterly*

CCC: *Catechism of the Catholic Church.* 2nd ed. New York: Doubleday, 1995.

CW: *The Collected Works of C.J. Jung.* 20 vols. Princeton: Princeton University Press (1954-1979). Dates given to cited material are to the dates of the CW volume in which they are reproduced rather then the date when the works originally appeared. Cites are to page numbers rather than the numbered paragraphs.

COS: *The Context of Scripture: Canonical Compositions from the Biblical World.* Edited by William Hallo. 3 vols. Leiden: Brill, 1997-2002.

CQ: *Classical Quarterly*

CT: The Egyptian Coffin Texts, in Faulkner 1973.

DCH: *Dictionary of Classical Hebrew.* 8 vols. Edited by David Clines. Sheffield: Sheffield Academic Press, 1993-2007.

DDD: *Dictionary of Deities and Demons in the Bible.* Edited by Karel van der Toorn, Bob Becking, and Pieter W. van der Horst. 2nd ed. Leiden: Brill, 1999.

DFML: *Funk & Wagnall's Standard Dictionary of Folklore, Mythology and Legend.* Edited by Maria Leach. New York: Harper & Row, 1972.

DSS: *The Dead Sea Scrolls.* Translated and edited by Michael Wise, Martin Abegg, Jr., and Edward Cook. San Francisco: HarperSanFrancisco, 1999.

EA: Moran, William, ed. and trans. *The Amarna Letters.* Baltimore: Johns Hopkins, 1992.

EDHL: *Etymological Dictionary of the Hebrew Language for Readers of English.* Edited by Ernest Klein. New York: MacMillan, 1987.

EL: *Merriam-Webster's Encyclopedia of Literature.* Kathleeen Kuiper, ed. Springfield, Massachusetts: Merriam-Webster, 1995.

EncJud: *Encyclopaedia Judaica.* 17 vols. Jerusalem: Keter Publishing House, 1972.

ER: *The Encyclopedia of Religion,* 16 vols. Mircea Eliade, ed. New York: Simon & Schuster Macmillan, 1995.

ERE: *Encyclopedia of Religion and Ethics.* Edited by J. Hastings. 13 vols. New York, 1908-1927.

HALOT: Koehler, Ludwig, Walter Baumgartner, and Johann Stamm, *The Hebrew and Aramaic Lexicon of the Old Testament.* Translated and edited under the supervision of M.E.J. Richardson. 4 vols. Leiden: Brill, 1994-1999.

HBD: *HarperCollins Bible Dictionary.* Edited by Paul Achtemier et al. 2nd ed. San Francisco: HarperSanFrancisco, 1996.

HR: *History of Religions*

HS: *Hebrew Studies*

HTR: *Harvard Theological Review*

IDB: *Interpreter's Dictionary of the Bible.* Edited by G.A. Buttrick. 4 vols. Nashville, 1962.

IDD: *Iconography of Deities and Demons in the Ancient Near East.* This is a companion to DDD, partially available through the University of Zurich in electronic pre-publication at www.religionsissenscharg .unizh.ch/idd

IEJ: *Israel Exploration Journal*

JANER: *Journal of Ancient Near Eastern Religion*

JANES: *Journal of the Ancient Near Eastern Society*

JAOS: *Journal of the American Oriental Society*

JARCE: *Journal of the American Research Center in Egypt*

JBL: *Journal of Biblical Literature*

JBQ: *Jewish Bible Quarterly*

JCS: *Journal of Cuneiform Studies*

JE: *The Jewish Encyclopedia.* I. Singer, ed. 12 vols. New York: Funk & Wagnalls, 1925.

JEA: *Journal of Egyptian Archaeology*

JETS: *Journal of the Evangelical Theological Society*

JHS: *Journal of Hellenic Studies*

JIAS: *Journal of the Institute of Asian Studies*

JNES: *Journal of Near Eastern Studies*

JNSL: *Journal of Northwest Semitic Languages*

JRAS: *Journal of the Royal Asiatic Society*

JSOT: *Journal for the Study of the Old Testament*

JSS: *Journal of Semitic Studies*

KJV: King James Version of the Bible

MIFL: Thompson 1955-1958.

NLEM: *New Larousse Encyclopedia of Mythology.* London: Prometheus, 1959.

NOAB: *New Oxford Annotated Bible.* Edited by Herbert May and Bruce Metzger. New York: Oxford University Press, 1977 (uses RSV translation).

NRSV: New Revised Standard Version of the Bible. 4th ed. Edited by Michael Coogan. Oxford: Oxford University Press, 2010.

OCD: *Oxford Classical Dictionary.* Edited by N. G. L. Hammond and H. H. Scullard. 2nd ed. Oxford, 1970.

OED: *The Oxford English Dictionary.*

OLP: *Orientalia lovaniensia periodica*

Or: *Orientalia*

PT: The Egyptian Pyramid Texts, in Faulkner 1969.

RB: *Revue biblique*

RSV: Revised Standard Version of the Bible

SJOT: *Scandinavian Journal of the Old Testament*

SJT: *Scottish Journal of Theology*

SR: *Studies in Religion*

SVTQ: *St. Vladimir's Theological Quarterly*

TA: *Tel Aviv*

TD: *Theology Digest*

TDOT: *Theological Dictionary of the Old Testament.* Edited by G. Kittel and G. Friedrich. 10 vols. Translated by J. T. Willis, G. W. Bromiley, and D. E. Green. Grand Rapids, 1964-1976.

ThTo: *Theology Today*

TS: *Theological Studies*

TWOT: Harris, Archer and Waltke 1980.

UF: *Ugarit-Forschungen*

UJEnc: *The Universal Jewish Encyclopedia.* I. Landman, ed. 10 vols. New York: Ktav Publishing House. 1939-43.

VT: *Vetus Testamentum*

ZA: *Zeitschrift für Assyriologie*

ZAW: *Zeitschrift für die alttestamentliche Wissenschaft*

Notes

PREFACE

1. Scholars usually use the neutral term "Hebrew Bible" to refer to the common Jewish and Christian canons from the period of the Old Testament, and we do so in this book. In this book references to the "Bible" are generally to the Hebrew Bible.

2. Langdon 1964, p. 183.

3. Most Westerners are not aware that the Adam and Eve story (or at least a number of details from it) is also contained in the Koran and thus is part of Islamic religious tradition. Since the Koran was written at least a millennium after the original biblical accounts of this story, however, it is of limited use for purposes of this book but we do include this material where relevant.

4. To be precise, this applies only to non-Orthodox Christianity, as Orthodox Christianity does not adhere to the doctrine of original sin.

INTRODUCTION

1. Sanford 1987, p. 116.

2. Berlin 1994, pp. 13, 20.

3. Campbell 2001, p. xvi.

4. The word originates from the Greek word *mythos*, meaning speech, thing said, or tale. *EL*, p. 794. The words "mythological" and "mythical" (also "mythic") are often considered synonyms, but here we generally use "mythological" when referring to the consideration or study of myths as a discipline, and "mythical" or "mythic" when referring to the qualities or characteristics of myths.

5. Segal 1999, p. 67; likewise Campbell 2001, pp. 7-9, 48.

6. Wismer 1983, p. 9; Sanford 1987, p. 116.

7. We use the term "ancient Near East" broadly to include Mesopotamia, the Arabian Peninsula, southern Anatolia, Syria-Palestine, the Sinai, and Egypt.

8. Jung, *CW* 6:474-75; see also Campbell 2001, pp. 7-9, 48.

9. Burrows 1946, p. 116.

10. Charlesworth 2010, p. 282.

11. Indeed, specialists in mythology perform research and teach classes about mythology (including Bible stories) in a variety of university departments, including anthropology, psychology, sociology, religion, history, literature (where Joseph Campbell taught), classics, philosophy, and single-nation or geographical region departments. In universities one hardly finds departments or program of mythology, or degrees in mythology awarded, and those which exist are always cross-disciplinary in content. Notable exceptions are Pacifica Graduate Institute in California, which offers Masters and Doctoral programs and degrees in mythology, and the University of Essex in England, offering BA and MA programs.

12. *NLEM,* p. vii.

13. Kirk 1973, p. 1.

14. Albertz 1994, p. 20.

15. See Evans 1980, and in it in particular Hallo 1980; Hayes 2005.

16. See, e.g., Hays 2005, pp. 34-45, in that case applying criteria to St. Paul's possible use of Hebrew Bible passages. But is recognized that these criteria can apply to extra-biblical texts as well, Carr 2012. Also see Hallo's Introduction in *COS* 1:xxv-xxviii.

17. Neumann 1954, p. 371.

18. In particular Eliade 1996; Eliade 1978. Regarding Eichhorn and biblical studies and his influence on Gunkel, see Ernest Nicholson, Foreword to Gunkel 1996, pp. 4-5.

19. As already noted, Biblical scholars have been influenced by and have applied this contextual or comparative (and contrastive) approach to the Bible. Hermann Gunkel is an early example, e.g., Gunkel 2006; Gunkel 2009. For later examples see Albertz 1994, pp. 2-12; Hallo 1980.

20. E.g., Goblet d'Alviella 1894.

21. The 20th century's most well-known mythologist, Joseph Campbell, was influenced by Bastian's theory. See Campbell 1990, pp. 93-94; Campbell 1959, pp. 32-33. Campbell was also well acquainted with Jung's approach, with which his own ideas were consistent. See his Editor's Introduction in *The Portable Jung* (New York: Penguin, 1983), pp. vii-xxxii. He later equated Bastian's elementary ideas with Jung's archetypes. Campbell 2001, p. 6. Jung was also influenced by Bastian's categories, likening them to the French anthropologist Lucien Lévy-Bruhl's concept of "représentations collectives," as well as to the theory of "categories of the imagination" propounded by the sociologists of comparative religion Henri Hubert and Marcel Mauss. Jung 1959, pp. 42-43; see Le Grice 2013, p. 14.

22. Segal 1999, p. 74.

23. Examples of archetypes include that of the mother, the father, the anima (the female aspect of male's unconscious), the animus (male aspect of a female's unconscious), the Shadow, divinity/deity, death-rebirth, the Great Mother, the Father, the Self. Le Grice 2013, p. 80; Jung 1959a, pp. 22-32; Jung 1959b, pp. 44-46; Jung 1959c; Jung 1959d; Jung, 1959e. Although the archetypes themselves are forms with no content, they become known to us consciously by reference to the common content that they each produce (the archetypal image). We can know the archetypes only obliquely and imperfectly based on the symbols that they generate. Segal 1999, p. 71.

24. Jung 1959, pp. 42-43.

25. Jung 1959, p. 44; Jung 1956, p. 158.

26. Jung 1989, p. 398. Jung 1969, pp. 31-32; Le Grice 2013, p. 221. See quotation from Jung regarding the God-image and the Self in the Epilogue, note 83.

27. Le Grice 2013, pp. 80, 153.

28. Jung 1960, p. 152.

29. See Segal 1999, pp. 68-69.

30. Neumann 1954, p. 349.

31. Segal 1999, p. 67.

32. Le Grice 2013, p. 7.

33. Le Grice 2013, p. 12.

34. Campbell 1949, p. 4.

35. Jung 1966, p. 69.

36. Segal 1999, p. 13.

37. Inevitably what follows is a simplified and somewhat composite description, as no single available mythical text contains all of the details.

38. Neumann 1954, p. xxiv.

39. Neumann 1954, pp. 5-38; Wilber 1996, pp. 25-40. Both Neumann and Wilber discuss this entire mythological cycle in great detail, to whom we refer readers for more information.

40. E.g., Dilmun in Sumerian mythology and the Golden Age in Greek mythology, discussed in Chapter 4.

41. Neumann 1954, pp. 15-16, 27-34, 43; Wilber 1996, pp. 127-30.

42. Neumann 1955, p. 90. For details see Combs 2009, pp. 21-34, 60-61, drawing on the work of both Jean Piaget (child developmental psychology and consciousness) and Jean Gebser (evolution of adult consciousness).

43. Neumann 1954, p. 42.

44. For this purpose, a hero means one who first tries out the next higher level of consciousness. Wilber 1996, p. 188. Whether man or god, the hero in the myths in question here represents the attainment of the same stage of emerging ego consciousness.

45. For example, in Mesopotamian myth (described in Chapter 3) Tiamat is dismembered and her parts are used to construct the cosmos; in Egyptian myth the chaos serpent Apep is cut up; and in the Eden story the serpent, previously erect in some manner (see Chapter 7), is flattened and made to crawl on the ground and eat dirt (Gen. 3:14).

46. Neumann 1954, pp. 41, 168, 432; Neumann 1955, pp. 43-44, 91; see examples in Eliade 1991b, pp. 37-42. Thus, we need not take a position on the controversial question whether there were once matriarchies in the sense of social, political, and religious dominance of women in any of the cultures that we describe in this book.

47. Wilber 1996, pp. 194, 237; Harrison 1927, p. 460; Neumann 1954, pp. 35, 131, 153, 245.

48. Neumann 1954, pp. 114-18, 347-48; Wilber 1996, pp. 306, 313. If the ego cannot overcome this guilt, it disintegrates and regresses back into the uroboros, as happens to Oedipus, when symbolized by his blinding himself (reversing the light and eye-opening of the enlightenment of the victory over the Sphinx-dragon and (albeit unknowingly—a literary technique) the Mother) and subsequently (in Sophocles's *Oedipus at Colonus*) by going into bowels of earth to meet death. Neumann 1954, p. 164; see also Bachofen 1967, pp. 181-82.

49. Neumann 1954, pp. 114, 122-23; Neumann 1955, pp. 66-67; Wilber 1996, p. 307.

50. Neumann 1954, pp. 131-32, 198, 354, 379.

51. Neumann 1954, pp. 187-88.

52. In contrast, in the separate creation account of Genesis 1 (written later), this motif lies in the background but the author reshapes it in a different way. There God is in the hero role and himself establishes the binary pairs of opposites from the outset (e.g., light and darkness, male and female, heaven and earth, upper and lower waters, sun and moon), which is to say that God creates humans already having ego consciousness. Before God undertook the creation there was as usual only the uroboric "formless void and darkness" (Gen. 1:2). The dragon fight is relegated to a special mention of God creating "the great sea monsters" (Gen. 1:21) in a peaceful process showing that God is in firm control and not threatened.

53. Malinowski 1984.

54. Malinowski 1944, p. 150.

55. Durkheim 1995.

56. Goldschmidt 1966.

57. See summary of the development of the ritual theory in Segal 2004, pp. 61-78, and Segal 1991, pp. 37-46.

58. Neumann 1954, p. 372. Neumann notes that some form of ritual usually will precede a developed myth, as the development of consciousness first manifests itself in actions, before cognitive and therefore spoken or written content develop. Neumann 1954, pp. 104, 126, 131. Whatever the exact order in any particular case, ritual and myth reinforce each other.

59. Lévi-Strauss 1955.

60. Kirk 1973, pp. 77-83.

61. Jung 1964, p. 59.

62. Jung, "Approaching the Unconscious," in Jung 1964, p. 89.

63. As Neumann explained, "Our retrospective psychological interpretation corresponds to no point of view consciously maintained in earlier times; it is the conscious elaboration of contents that were once extrapolated in mythological projects, unconsciously and symbolically." Neumann 1954, pp. 150-51.

64. Friedman 1997, p. 61.

65. Neumann 1954, p. 370.

66. Regarding this psychological impact of biblical scripture on its audience, see Kille 2001, pp. 2-3.

67. E.g., Leach 1961; Leach 1969; Leach and Aycock 1983.

68. In relation to the Eden story see Mettinger 2007, p. 76, and more generally, e.g., Kirk 1973, pp. 71, 77-83.

69. Kirk 1973, p. 81.

70. Neumann 1955, p. 50.

71. Campbell 2001, p. 42; Neumann 1955, p. 50.

72. Ellis 1968, p. 141. This is something of an overstatement but it does point to the necessary manner of analysis. Also, as we shall see, the author was talented and there was much more to the compositional process.

73. Ellis 1968, p. 143, citing McKenzie 1963, pp. 146-81.

74. McKenzie 1965, p. 599.

1. WHO WROTE THE EDEN STORY?

1. For a full comparison of the differences between St. Petersburg during Pushkin's and Dostoevsky's lives and the influence this had on their writings, see our history of the city entitled *St. Petersburg: The First Three Centuries* (Sutton Publishing, 2004), Chapter 9, entitled "Pushkin's St. Petersburg, Imperial St. Petersburg," and Chapter 10, "Dostoevsky's St. Petersburg." Professor Friedman used the example of Dostoevsky in making much the same point, Friedman 1997, p. 16, which inspired us to use this comparison from our own earlier work in relation to the biblical author.

2. Jung 1989.

3. In Christianity known as the Pentateuch (Greek for "five books") and in Judiaism as the Torah (Hebrew for "instruction," "teaching," or "law"). In this book, references to the "Law" are to the Torah, in particular its law codes.

4. Bible scholars often prefer to refer to the separate texts themselves, as "sources," rather than to their human authors/compilers. This allows for more than one contributor to a single "source," as well as for subsequent editing and earlier oral traditions. Nevertheless, commentators often do personalize them, as we do here.

5. The convention of using the siglum J comes from "Jahwe," the German spelling of Yahweh, because of the many German scholars who worked on parsing out the sources within the Pentateuch. The English word "Jehovah" (rather than "Yahweh") is actually a mistake originating with the translators of the KJV.

6. Many scholars believe that R was either Ezra or a scribe working with him. See Friedman 1999, pp. 7-31; Friedman 1997, pp. 117-49, 217-33.

7. For this purpose we refer readers to Friedman 2003, which sets out the texts of the various authors (sources) each by color and includes annotations, which among other things flag those few instances in which the authorship of passages is uncertain. The identification of sources by verse is also available in chart form in Hamilton 1990, p. 16; Friedman 1997, pp. 246-55; Friedman 1999, p. 12.

8. Baden 2012, pp. 16-20; Friedman 1997, pp. 18-24.

9. See Baden 2012, p. 16.

10. Exod. 19:11, 18, 20, 23; 34:2.

11. Exod. 24:16; 31:18; 34:29, 32; Lev. 7:38; 25:1; 26:46; 27:34.

12. Exod. 3:1; 17:6; 33:6.

13. Deut. 1:2, 6, 19; 4:10; 5:2; 9:8; 29:1 (28:69 in the Hebrew). See Friedman 2003, p. 309.

14. Exod. 2:18.

15. Exod. 3:1; 4:18; 18:1-2, 5-6, 9, 12, 27.

16. Gen. 7:8-9.

17. Gen. 7:2-3.

18. Gen. 7:12; 8:6, 8-12.

19. Gen. 7:24; 8:3b-5, 7, 13 (first sentence), 14-16. See Friedman 2003, pp. 44-45; Friedman 1997, pp. 53-60.

20. Gen. 8:7.

21. Gen. 8:8.

22. Gen. 37:26-27.

23. Gen. 37:21-22.

24. Gen. 37:28b; 39:1.

25. Gen. 37:28a, 36. For details and analysis see Baden 2012, pp. 1-12, 34-44.

26. See Friedman 1997, pp. 70-88.

27. That is, in that line of Levite priests said to be descended from Aaron, brother of Moses. Not all Levites were Aaronids, who were centered in Jerusalem rather than the northern kingdom of Israel.

28. According to Friedman, D wrote during the reign of Josiah (ruled 639-609) and composed/compiled most of Deuteronomy and the Deuteronomistic History. D appears to have been mainly a compiler of existing texts and may have authored little original material. The law code of Deuteronomy (an older work inserted as Deut. 12-26:15) is alleged in the Bible to have been from the hand of Moses and only discovered by Josiah's priest Hilkiah in the Temple library (2 Kings 22:8; 2 Chr. 32:1-23), but this story is regarded by most scholars as a fabrication. Except for the law code, the D material from prior to Josiah's death is known as Dtr[1], while that added after the king's death (probably by the same author D), apparently already during the exile since it reflects the fall of Judah, is known as Dtr[2]. Professor Friedman identifies D as Jeremiah's scribe Baruch, who expressed the prophet's ideas. See generally Friedman 1997, pp. 117-49.

29. Friedman 1997, p. 53.

30. In *The Epic of Gilgamesh*, the flood hero releases a dove, a raven, and a swallow. *ANET*, pp. 94-95.

31. Baden 2012, pp. 67-81 (most specifically in relation to the J source); also Van Seters 2006. The neo-Documentary Hypothesis focuses on the narrative claims made by each author/source (i.e., who did what, when, where and how; cause and effect) and the continuities running through each source that help resolve the reasons for the incoherencies (contradictions, repetitions, and discontinuities) in the Pentateuchal text. Compared to the classic Documentary Hypothesis, it relies only secondarily on particular vocabularies and writing styles to identify the sources, and it is not concerned with the dating of the four sources.

32. Schmid 2012, p. 27. See in particular Rendtorff 1990; Dozeman and Schmid 2006; Dozeman, Schmid, and Schwartz 201; Evans, Lohr, and Petersen 2012. For concise summaries of this scholarship see Westermann 1994, pp. 569-606 and the discussions in Baden 2012, especially pp. 53-67. Van Seters staunchly defends J as a discrete source while adhering to other aspects of the European approach. Van Seters 1992 and 2006.

33. Blum 2006, pp. 89-91.

34. Baden 2012. Other examples include Wynn-Williams 1997 and McEvenue 1994. Baden does, however, challenge the traditional view of the Documentary Hypothesis (noted below) that J and E were combined into a single text after the fall of Israel at the hands of Assyria after 722, Baden 2009, a view that has gained a substantial traction.

35. E.g., Schwartz 2013. As of this writing, a working group of Israeli, European and American scholars is working together and meeting periodically in Jerusalem in an attempt to resolve to the extent possible this "crisis" (as some term it) in Pentateuchal studies.

36. Schmid 2012, p. 27.

37. Schmid, for example, notes that J as a coherent work is detectable in Genesis, and that the problem of source attribution arises in the later books of the Pentateuch. Schmid 2006, p. 30.

38. Friedman 1999, p. 53.

39. What has traditionally been considered the entire J account (ending in Deuteronomy 34:1-6) can be read as a continuous text in Ellis 1968; Coote and Ord 1989; Bloom and Rosenberg 1990; Friedman 1999; and Campbell and O'Brien 1993 (also containing the complete continuous texts of P and E), each with their own translations. Professor Friedman, in a well-argued but controversial theory, contends that J's book extends through Joshua and Judges and makes up much of the rest of Deuteronomistic History (including what is known as the Court History) up through 1 Kings 2:46. Friedman 1999 (containing the entire extended text, sometimes called "Super-J"). This would take J's story through the accession of Solomon, marking the fulfillment of Yahweh's promises to Abraham when the people took responsibility for their land. Numerous other scholars have also proposed varying extensions of the J text beyond the Pentateuch. See discussion in *ABD* 6:1016. Our analysis is unaffected by whether the traditional or extended version of the J source is accepted.

40. Unless specified otherwise as in this case, in this book references to "Israelite" religion and "Israel" and its people include both the northern kingdom of Israel and the kingdom of Judah.

41. Friedman 1997, p. 87 (after 848 but leaving open a date as late as 722); Friedman 1999, p.51.

42. Friedman 1997, pp. 86-87.

43. See Friedman 1997, p. 87; Friedman 1999, p. 51; see also Friedman 2001, p. 95; Friedman 1992, pp. 613-14. Others too attribute this passage to J. Noth 1981, p. 29; Hamilton 1990, p. 16.

44. In the Hebrew Bible the name Ephriam became synonymous with the northern kingdom of Israel (e.g., in Hos. 14:8), whose initial capital (following Israel's split with Judah) was at Shechem in the hills of Ephriam. Some biblical passages link Ephriam specifically with Shechem (Josh. 20:7; 21:21; 1 Kings 12:25).

45. Friedman 1997, p. 66.

46. See Friedman 1997, pp. 74-75.

47. See Friedman 1997, pp. 70-83.

48. Friedman 1997, pp. 87-88.

49. See Baden 2009.

50. Below we refer to J and Yahweh's Law. What we mean by that is that J insisted on humans following Yahweh's commands, some of which J laid out, so as to produce order/good. Compared to elaborate law codes, produced by other authors of the Pentateuch, the Law as J conceived it was in its incipient stage, but nevertheless generally consistent with the ideas of the authors of the law codes, principally P and D.

51. Milgrom 1992, pp. 458-59.

52. Friedman 1997, p. 87.

53. P is considered to have written Chapters 1-16 and 27, whereas Chapters 17-26 are thought to have been compilations or redactions by him of earlier Aronid material known as the Holiness Code (or H for short). See Milgrom 1992; Friedman 1997, pp. 171-72, 214-15.

54. Genesis 1:1 says that God created the "heavens and the earth," whereas in the second sentence of Genesis 2.4 J says that God made "the earth and the heavens." We discuss this further in Chapter 4.

55. In quoted speech Elohim is used.

56. Actually, in J's narrative text "Yahweh Elohim" ("Yahweh God") appears rather than just "Yahweh." Most scholars consider that J's original text had only Yahweh and that Elohim was inserted later under the influence of P's opening account in order to smooth over the difference. Speiser 1964, p. 15 n. Translations that utilize Yahweh usually omit Elohim or its translation ("God"). E.g., Bloom and Rosenberg 1990; Friedman 1999; compare Speiser 1964, p. 14ff ("God Yahweh").

57. Of course, at the later redactional level (R or otherwise), editors thought that the two stories complemented one another, otherwise both accounts would not have been retained. But the differences between the two accounts that we have identified remain.

58. Burrows 1946, p. 117.

59. See Rad 76-77.

60. Ellis 1968.

61. Bloom and Rosenberg 1990.
62. Coote and Ord 1989.
63. Friedman 1999; see also Friedman 1997 and 2003.

2. HOW THE WORLD OF PALESTINE
LED TO EDEN

1. Albright 1944b, p. 148.
2. Coote and Ord 1989, p. 19.
3. Exod. 34:11-16. The Bible contains two other versions of the Ten Commandments in Exodus 20:1-17 (not easily attributable to one of the major sources and probably is a separate document inserted by R, Friedman 2003, p. 153), and in Deuteronomy 5:6-21 (written by D), which are nearly identical to each other except that they give different reasons for honoring the Sabbath. Traditionally the first version in Exodus 34:11-26 has been attributed entirely to J, but more recent scholarship persuasively argues that verses 18-26 (subsequent to those quoted here) are not J's but of later origin. E.g., Bar-On 1998. Nevertheless, the traditional attribution to J of verses 11-16 quoted here remains secure. See Baden 2012, pp. 78, 118, 134, 276 n. 126. See also endnote 5 to this Chapter.
4. Asherim (Hebrew plural) or asherahs are wooden poles or posts, sometimes carved with images, placed upright in the ground and symbolizing the goddess Asherah. The pillars in question are of stone, symbolize a connection between earth and heaven and evoke the presence of the male deity. These and other features of Canaanite religion are described in more detail below.
5. This is the RSV translation except for the substitution of "Yahweh" for "the Lord," Because D was especially opposed to the enumerated pagan cult items and constantly inveighed against them in similar language (e.g., Deut. 12:3 (using Deuteronomic law code)), some scholars have noted the similarity of this passage with D language, e.g., *DDD*, p. 102 ("thoroughly Deuteronomistic in style"), while others go further and consider that these verses are an interpolation by D, see Olyan 1988, p. 18, and sources cited therein; Hadley 2000, p. 56. Friedman argues that these are authentic J passages on the ground that they contain some phraseology unique to J. Friedman 1999, p. 328. Noth 1981, p. 31; Baden 2012, pp. 78 & n.126, 118, 134, 276 n. 126; Halpern 2009, p. 130; and Campbell and O'Brien 1993, p. 148, also attribute this language to J; see also Day 1986, p. 406 ("commonly ascribed to J"). For our purposes this authorship issue is not critical because the passage is still entirely consistent with J's expressed views, which affinity could explain why D could place it there as it would fit right in.
6. See Chapter 3, endnote 3.
7. The term "Hebrews" is usually used for the period before the Conquest of Canaan as described in Numbers and Joshua, while the term "Israelites" is used for the period after the Conquest and in genealogical terms refers to the descendants of Jacob. In this book, unless otherwise noted, "Israelites" refers to the peoples of both Judah and the northern kingdom of Israel, and "Israel" to both territories.
8. See Smith 2002, pp. 3-4.
9. Wallace 1985, p. 32; see also Smith 2002, pp. 19-31.
10. The quoted passage lies at the beginning of the Deuteronomic law code and is the first commandment of Yahweh in it. The Documentary Hypothesis considers this an old, independent document used by D. Friedman 2003, p. 330.
11. Finkelstein and Silberman 2001, pp. 99, 121.
12. Judg. 21:25. This is meant as a contrast to the set phrase in the Hebrew Bible, "in the eyes of Yahweh," whose judgment was the yardstick of whether people or nations were doing good or evil. Thus, for example, David did good in Yahweh's eyes (1 Kings 15:5), while others did evil in his eyes, e.g., 1 Kings 14:22 (Judah itself); 1 Kings 16:25 (Omri); 1 Kings 16:30 (Ahab); 2 Kings 8:18 (Joram); and 2 Kings 8:27 (Ahaziah).

13. See descriptions of these sites in Dever 2005, pp. 135-54.

14. For example, in the case of El we see "El-Olam" ("the everlasting god") in Beersheba (Gen. 21:33), "El-Bethel" in Bethel (Gen. 31:13; 35:7), "El-Elyon" ("god most high") in Jerusalem (as before in Ugarit) (Gen. 14:19, 22), "El-Roe" ("god of seeing") in the Negeb (Gen. 16:13). Later, in the case of Yahweh we see multiple versions of Yahweh (a phenomenon known as "poly-Yahwism") such as "Yahweh Sabaoth" ("Yahweh of the hosts") in Shiloh (1 Sam. 1:3), "Yahweh in Hebron" (2 Sam. 15:7), and, as we will see in Chapter 3, "Yahweh of Samaria" and "Yahweh of Teman" in the 8th century. See generally Albertz 1994, pp. 30, 83.

15. Albertz 1994, p. 85; Hadley 2000, p. 74; Ringgren 1966, p. 24.

16. In fact, the name Jerusalem, which David either adopted or preserved, means "founded by Shalem." Shalem was formerly the Canaanite patron god of the city. Solomon's name may be based on Shalem. Albertz 1994, p. 135; Miller and Hayes 2006, p. 169.

17. Albertz 1994, p. 130.

18. Albertz 1994, p. 129.

19. Albertz 1994, pp. 131, 135-36.

20. Albertz 1994, pp. 134-35.

21. 1 Kings 11:11-13. Chronicles does not say this, as the writer represented the interests of the Aaronid priesthood, which was indebted to Solomon because he had given authority at the Temple entirely to the Aaronid priest Zadok, removing the Shiloh priest Abiathar. D was written from the viewpoint of the Shiloh priesthood. Friedman 1997, pp. 211-12.

22. 1 Kings 14:25-26; 2 Chr. 12:9-10. Shishak's own account of his campaign as recorded on the wall of the temple of Amun-Ra at Karnak does not mention Jerusalem as among the Palestinian cities that he conquered. This discrepancy is sometimes explained by the apparent fact that Rehoboam paid tribute rather than meet Shishak in battle, see 2 Chr. 12:5-8; *HBD*, p. 1016, but the inscription makes no distinction between whether a city surrendered or was captured or destroyed, Miller and Hayes 2006, p. 262.

23. Bright 2000, p. 271.

24. According to the traditional Documentary Hypothesis, this led to J's and E's texts being combined to produce the composite text known as JE.

25. Friedman 1997, pp. 188-216.

26. Albertz 1994, p. 224.

27. Friedman 1997, pp. 119-20.

28. The very end of this history covers the period from the death of Josiah to the fall of Jerusalem to the Babylonians. Bible scholars designate this part as Dtr[2], the principal D then being designated as Dtr[1], even though the author may have been the same D. Friedman 1997, pp. 136-46.

29. Friedman 1997, pp. 111-14.

30. See Rad 1961, pp. 136-37.

31. Redford 1992, p. 257. There are exceptions but only after the establishment of the monarchy, such as Solomon's alleged marriage to the daughter of the Pharaoh, Jeroboam's flight to and return from Egypt (1 Kings 11:40) followed by Shishak's campaign in Judah, and in relation to diplomatic relations between Judah and Egypt in the 7th century.

32. See generally Redford 1992, which describes this history in detail; also Mazar 1992, pp. 232-37, 279-85. As reflected in Genesis commentaries see, e.g., Rad 1961, pp. 136-37.

33. EA 84, line 37; 139, line 8. See Albright 1967, p. 221.

34. Some specialists had thought that the Hyksos originated north of Syria, but the weight of the evidence now favors a homeland in Canaan and Syria proper. See Redford 1992, pp. 99-100. Whether the Hyksos takeover was a result of a military conquest as opposed to a gradual infiltration followed by takeover from within is still a matter of debate. Compare, e.g., Redford 1992, pp. 101-06 and Finkelstein and Silberman 2001, p. 55, both stressing a relatively peaceful takeover resulting from infiltration, with Wilkinson 2010, pp. 167-68, who points to invaders from Lebanon.

35. See Wilkinson 2010, pp. 170-72; Goldwasser 2010, p. 49.

36. Redford 1992, pp. 149, 198-99.

37. As translated in Shanks 1992, p. 17.

38. *HBD*, p. 467.

39. Cross 1989, p. 80. See further discussion in Chapter 3.

40. Wilkinson 2010, p. 161; Goldwasser 2010. The details of this process are set forth in Hamilton 2006. Up-to-date accounts by leading Semiticist epigraphers of how this script developed into Phoenician and Hebrew are in Rollston 2010 and Sanders 2009.

41. Goldwasser 2010, p. 49.

42. Rollston 2010, p. 42; Sáenz-Badillos 1993, p. 16 (Paleo-Hebrew script starting ca. 800); Sanders 2009, pp. 105-06; also Cross 1989, p. 89 (chart showing beginning of Old Hebrew script around 800).

43. This caravan trade is described in detail in Albright 1967, pp. 58-73.

44. Albright 1967, p. 65.

45. Many provisions of Israelite law (including "an eye for an eye and tooth for a tooth") derive from the law code of the Babylonian king Hammurabi. See Gunkel 2009, p. 26.

46. Moran 1992, pp. xviii-xix.

47. Gunkel 2009, p. 28.

48. Etymologically the name "Hebrew" may derive from the root *br* meaning "to cross over," which has been interpreted to refer to Abraham's crossing the Euphrates into Canaan to found the new religion (e.g., Dever 2003, p. 74), although it may also refer to the crossing of the sea in the Exodus or even the crossing of the Jordan river from the Transjordan at the outset of the Conquest.

49. Available in English translation in *ANET,* pp. 129-55 and *COS* 1.86:241-74, 102:333-43, 103:343-58.

50. Geus 1991.

51. From which word "Palestine" is derived.

52. "Moses" is actually an Egyptian name meaning "born" or "child," from the Egyptian noun *ms* ("child") and verb *msi* ("to give birth"). It is incorporated into the names of many Egyptian kings, such as Thutmose ("born/child of Thoth") and Rameses ("born/child of Ra"). Redford 1992, pp. 417-18. J's Hebrew derivation of the name (Exod. 2:10) makes no sense because, as noted, Hebrew did not exist at the time, and even if it did one can hardly expect an Egyptian princess to be adept at Hebrew wordplay. In Egypt it was common for Canaanite subordinates to take the names of their Egyptian masters. So when biblical authors conferred the name, it may have been intended to elevate his status by evidencing that he had a position in the Egyptian royal court. Names of key Levites are also Egyptian, such as Hophni ("tadpole") and Phineas ("the Southerner"). See Redford 1992, p. 419; Friedman 1997, p. 82.

53. In the ancient world the number of arms-bearing males was frequently given as the population. To get the total population, a multiplier of 6 is commonly used. See Chandler 1987, pp. 8-9, 93-100. Applying that to the Exodus example would yield a Hebrew population of over 3.6 million.

54. Redford 1992, p. 408; see also Miller and Hayes 2006, p. 72; Dever 2003, pp. 18-19. Even marching 10 abreast, the line of people would have been over 150 miles long and would have taken 8 or 9 days to pass through any fixed point, Miller and Hayes 2006, p. 72, which among other things would eliminate any possibility of the Hebrews crossing the parted Reed Sea in a single night (Exod. 14:21-24) before the waters engulfed their Egyptian pursuers. Surely such a large group constituting over half the population of the country would have left some evidence, including in written records.

55. Dever 2003, pp. 7-21; Finkelstein and Silberman 2001, pp. 48-71, 326-38; Halpern 1992, pp. 92-108.

56. Dever 2003, pp. 19-20; Finkelstein and Silberman 2001, p. 63.

57. Dever 2003, p. 19.

58. Finkelstein and Silberman 2001, pp. 76-79.

59. Finkelstein and Silberman, pp. 60, 78. The king of Jerusalem requested only 50 men to "protect the land," while the vassal king of Megiddo requested only 100 soldiers to guard the city from an attack by the king of Shechem. Finkelstein and Silberman 2001, p. 78.

60. Dever 2003, pp. 37-74; Finkelstein and Silberman 2001, pp. 72-96.

61. Finkelstein and Mazar 2007, pp. 81 (Finkelstein), 94 (Mazar). As we discuss in Chapter 3, however, this conclusion is not inconsistent with the possibility that some small foreign groups may have arrived from Sinai or even Egypt, that some such group may have been led by

a figure who became known as Moses, and that such group(s) brought this Midianite god Yahweh with them and introduced him to the natives.

62. Dever lists 31 of the most important of these cities and their status as of the time. Dever 2003, pp. 56-57.

63. Hazor, a city of some 20,000 inhabitants in the far north, was destroyed by fire in the mid to late 13th century. The cause of the fire, however, is not clear; notably, there are no signs of a battle (e.g., weapons).

64. Dever 2003, pp. 23-74, 228; Finkelstein and Silberman 2001, pp. 72-98.

65. Finkelstein and Silberman 2001, pp. 77, 81-82.

66. Dever 2003, p. 69; Finkelstein and Silberman 2001, p. 89.

67. Dever 2003, p. 157.

68. See figures in Dever 2003, p. 98.

69. These various theories and models are surveyed and evaluated in Dever 2003, pp. 176-89; Shanks 1992, pp. 4-14; and Finkelstein and Silberman 2001, pp. 329-39.

70. Finkelstein and Silberman 2001, pp. 337-38; Finkelstein and Mazar 2007, p. 77 (Finkelstein); also Dever 2003.

71. Finkelstein and Silberman 2001, pp. 104-05. Some material culture typical of the lowlands was found, but once archaeologists understood the settlements better it turned out that they were not from the initial settlement period but were from later when the Israelites had established trade and other contacts with the lowland settlements.

72. Finkelstein and Silberman 2001, p. 113.

73. Finkelstein and Mazar 2007, pp. 76-77, 81-82 (Finkelstein). The evidence suggests that most of these pastoralists were goat and sheep herders who prior to settling in the highlands permanently would spend part of the year in semi-arid steppe and the other part in greener areas suitable for farming (perhaps engaging in some farming themselves) rather than bedouin nomads from the desert, although as discussed in Chapter 3, the Shasu nomads from the eastern Sinai seem to have formed some element of the settlers.

74. Finkelstein and Silberman 2001, pp. 111-17.

75. Finkelstein and Silberman 2001, pp. 117-18.; Finkelstein and Mazar 2007, pp. 81-82 (Finkelstein).

76. Finkelstein and Silberman 2001, p. 118.

77. This was actually the third of three waves of highland settlement by pastoralists. The first was in the Early Bronze Age (3500-2200) and the second in the Middle Bronze Age (2000-1550), and in each case two distinct highland societies emerged in what would be the highlands of Israel and Judah. Finkelstein and Silberman 2001, p. 153.

78. Finkelstein and Silberman 2001, pp. 119, 130; Finkelstein and Silberman 2006, p. 68; Finkelstein and Mazar 2007, pp. 77, 98 (Finkelstein).

79. Smith 2002, pp. 21-22; also Vriezen 1967, p. 24. Excepted are the coastal Phoenician cities, which were closely linked to Mediterranean, Egyptian and Mesopotamian civilization and culture.

80. Smith 2002, pp. 19-20, 22-24.

81. Smith 2002, pp. 19-22.

82. A famous exception is the bronze statuette of a bull found at a high place sanctuary near Dothan in the hill country of Ephraim and Manasseh. See Dever 2005, pp. 135-36. The bull was both the symbol and pedestal (throne platform) of El as well as Baal.

83. Dever 2003, p. 128.

84. Smith 2002, p. 28; see above and Chapter 3.

85. Albertz 1994, p. 103; see also Chapter 3.

86. Dever 1992, pp. 52-53.

87. Finkelstein and Silberman 2001, p. 110. No weapons were found in the settlements. In only a few cases did they have any defense walls, and poorly constructed at that. Finkelstein and Mazar 2007, p. 87 (Mazar).

88. Dever 2003, pp. 120-21. This was evidenced by the almost complete absence of Philistine or other lowland pottery or other artifacts in the early strata of the settlements.

89. Dever 2003, p. 108.

90. Smith 2002, pp. 22-24.

91. See Cross 1973, especially pp. 112-94; see also Albright 1967, pp. 1-52, 217-64.

92. Smith 2002, pp. 56, 80-91.

93. Albright 1967, pp. 33, 45.

94. Bright 2000, p. 220.

95. Miller and Hayes 2006, p. 197.

96. Finkelstein and Silberman 2001, p. 131.

97. Finkelstein and Silberman 2001, pp. 133-34, 143, 158; Alpert and Alpert 2012, p. 55. Just earlier, in the 11th century, the "Jerusalem area" had a population of 2,200-4,500. Dever 2003, p. 97.

98. Miller and Hayes 2006, pp. 169-70; Finkelstein and Silberman 2001, pp. 132, 158.

99. Finkelstein and Silberman 2001, pp. 133-34.; Alpert and Alpert 2012, p. 55.

100. Alpert and Alpert 2012, p. 55; Finkelstein and Silberman 2001, pp. 130-32. Tenth century Judah could not have supported more than a few hundred soldiers. Finkelstein and Silberman 2006, p. 97.

101. Miller and Hayes 2006, pp. 186-87, 204-09.

102. Finkelstein and Silberman 2006, p. 97. We do not mean to say that the issues have been finally settled, for there remains a vigorous debate of the extent of David's and Solomon's domains and the sophistication of Judahite civilization at the time. While excavations in Jerusalem continue to be inconclusive, outside Jerusalem at the moment two key points of contention are (i) the recently discovered site of Khirbet Qeiyafa on the border between 10th century Judah and Philistine territory and (ii) whether Solomon or the Omrides built the six-chambered gates at Megiddo, Hazor and Gezer. A discussion of these issues is impossible here for reasons of space and scope. Regarding the gates, see the debate in *BASOR* 277 and 278 (1990). Regarding Khirbet Qeiyafa, there is not yet a consensus on its dating, who built it, and the language of the inscription found there, so as of the time of this writing we are not in a position to factor it into our analysis.

103. Davies 1994, p. 55 (actually saying this when challenging the Dan inscription discussed below). Other examples of such so-called "minimalist" views include Whitelam 1996 and Thompson 1992 and 1999.

104. Finkelstein and Silberman 2001, p. 128.

105. As translated in Finkelstein and Silberman 2001, p. 129. For simplicity, we have removed brackets around reconstructed words and letters.

106. According to some scholars, another 9th century inscription, that of Mesha, king of Moab, also refers to the house of David. But whether it really refers to David is a matter of debate, as the language in question must be reconstructed.

107. Finkelstein and Silberman 2001, pp. 161-62.

108. Kuan 1993, p. 231. Kuan points out that the root *'mr* occurs only in Omri in the Hebrew Bible, but is common in Phoenician and Punic. Kuan 1993, pp. 233-35.

109. Kuan 1993; Miller and Hayes 2006, p. 285. Further, John Gray suggests that the area around Samaria was in the Phoenician orbit and was given to Ahab as a dowry. Gray 1976, p. 385.

110. Finkelstein and Silberman 2001, p. 245.

111. Miller and Hayes 2006, p. 412.

112. Finkelstein and Silberman 2001, p. 243.

113. Finkelstein and Silberman 2001, p. 245.

114. Finkelstein and Silberman 2001, p. 245-46.

115. As suggested in Alpert and Alpert 2012, p. 62; see generally Finkelstein and Silberman 2001, pp. 169-95.

116. Indeed, as noted earlier, Professor Friedman believes that J's text continues beyond Numbers into 1 Kings up to where Solomon is made king and "the kingdom was secure in Solomon's hand." 1 Kings 2:46 (Friedman's translation); Friedman 1999, p. 291. For a summary of opinions on the issue of the "end of J," see *ABD* 6:1016.

117. Miller and Hayes 2006, p. 286.

118. Finkelstein and Silberman 2006, p. 103.

119. Miller and Hayes 2006, p. 286.

120. Discussed in Chapter 4, text accompanying notes 190-96.

121. Roux 1992, p. 289; Miller and Hayes 2006, p. 284. The relevant annal of the expedition is reproduced at *ANET,* pp. 275-76.

122. *ANET,* p. 281; Roux 1992, pp. 297-98.

123. *ANET,* p. 281; text also reproduced in part in Miller and Hayes 2006, p. 307, photograph of Obelisk at p. 330. The reference to Jehu being the "son of Omri" probably is not meant to state that Jehu was Omri's son, but may mean that Shalmaneser simply considered him to be of the same line of rulers. The Hebrew Bible contains a substantially different account of these events, claiming that it was not Hazel but Jehu and his men who chased down and killed both Joram and Ahaziah following their defeat (2 Kings 9). Jehu's ascension to the kingship is presented as the work of Yahweh through his prophet, Elisha, who arranged for Jehu to be anointed (2 Kings 9:1-13). Jehu himself is presented as a great king and (mostly) Yahwist religious reformer who reversed the pagan policies and practices of the Omrides, assassinated Jezebel and "wiped out Baal from Israel" (2 Kings 9:30-37; 10:28). Yet he allowed the golden calves to remain in Bethel and Dan and did not entirely follow Yahweh's law (2 Kings 10:28-31), so Yahweh allowed the disintegration of Israel to continue (2 Kings 10:32-33).

124. Professor Charlesworth astutely observed that J probably wrote because of some theological or political crisis, but stayed with the traditional dating (revolt of Israel). Charlesworth 2010, p. 288.

125. See Chapter 1, endnote 43 and accompanying text.

3. THE GENESIS OF YAHWEH AND HIS WIFE, AND THEIR DIVORCE

1. 1:438-46. Sion is Zion; the mountain is the Mount of Olives in Jerusalem; the uxorious King is Solomon.

2. Stone 1976, p. 1.

3. E.g., Wallace 1992c, p. 677 (Eve as allusion to the goddess Asherah; Canaanite fertility cult); Wallace 1985, pp. 154-72 (same); Cornelius 1988, pp. 62-63 (Canaanite cult in general and against Asherah in particular); Kikawada 1972 (Eve as dethroned Goddess); Blenkinsopp 1992, p. 66 (serpent representing Canaanite cults and women as "the occasion for adopting these cults"); Hvidberg 1960 (goddess, serpent, sacred trees, sacred waters); Wyatt 1981, pp. 18-21 (northern kingdom of Israel and Asherah cult); Soggin 1975, pp. 94-111 (Asherah and serpent (goddess) veneration); Park 1991, pp. 129-35 (priestesses in fertility rites using snakes; goddess veneration; association of Eve with both); Olyan 1988, pp. 70-71 (as to Asherah, Eve and the serpent).

4. See generally, e.g., B. Greene, *The Fabric of the Cosmos: Space, Time and the Texture of Reality* (New York: Vintage, 2004), and *idem., The Elegant Universe: Superstrings, Hidden Dimensions, and the Quest for the Ultimate Theory* (New York: Vintage, 1999).

5. See, e.g., Rosenblum, Bruce and Fred Kuttner, *Quantum Enigma: Physics Encounters Consciousness* (New York: Oxford University Press, 2006); see also Goswami, Amit *The Self-Aware Universe* (New York: Penguin, 1993); Walker, Evan Harris, *The Physics of Consciousness* (New York: Basic Books, 2000). This area of consciousness studies is in its early stages and as such is inherently speculative.

6. Campbell 1962, pp. 12-13.

7. James 1966, p. 246.

8. Neumann 1955, p. 56.

9. Marett 1914, p. 109.

10. Frankfort 1961, p. 27.

11. Frankfort 1961, p. 24; also Campbell 1962, p. 112.

12. CT, Spell 1130.

13. Dever 2005, pp. 3, 243; Wright 2000, pp. 85-88 (regarding Israelite religion); see also, in reference to Gen. 2:7 in which Adam becomes a living being, Westermann 1994, pp. 206-07; *NOAB* Gen.2:7 n. See discussion in Chapter 5 of whether Adam had a soul.

14. Xenophanes famously and astutely observed that if horses had gods, they would look like horses, which actually illustrates our point. That too would be valid if it enabled horses to better experience the divine.

15. Modern psychology does much to explain this process. The various corresponding gods and goddesses reflecting aspects of divinity are viewed as natural projections from the archetypes of the collective unconscious. Hillman 1981; Miller 1981. Our unconscious psyche projects these symbols when we confront the unknown, which is functional and healthy for our psychic and spiritual life. Jung 1959a, pp. 7-8; Franz 1995, pp. 2-3, 11.

16. Danielou 1991, p. 4. In reference to religion in ancient Israel, see Keel and Uehlinger 1998, pp. 7, 12-13.

17. Campbell 1962, p. 36.

18. The notion of an overall purpose or divine plan for the universe, humanity or a particular people, as well as the notion of progress, arose from our later concept of linear time (below) and from monotheism, where one deity is in supreme control can declare a purpose. For a discussion of this principle as applied in ancient Israel, see Van Seters 1997, pp. 239-41.

19. Hence, for example, the word *Upanishad* in Indian spiritual practice, which means "near-approach," as well as the term *yoga,* which means "yoking" oneself to or "uniting" with the divinity of the world.

20. Danielou 1991, p. 9.

21. Caesar, *The Conquest of Gaul*, VI.17, calling them only by their Roman names, "about whom they [the Gauls] have much the same ideas as other nations."

22. E.g., Van De Mieroop 2007, p. 138 (Hittite treaties with vassal states sworn before the deities of both sides).

23. Lucius Apuleius, *The Golden Ass* (Cambridge: Harvard University Press, 1915, 1965; trans. W. Adlington), pp. 545-47.

24. The word "matter" was originally applied to the inner wood of a tree and denoted the "matrix" or "mother" from which the tree's new growth came. The word "matrix" is from the same Latin root and originally referred to the womb.

25. Neumann 1955, p. 95, noting (as of when he wrote in the 1950s) that only 5 of the 55 Paleolithic statuettes discovered thus far were male.

26. Neumann 1955, pp. 95-96.

27. Wilber 1996, p. 127.

28. Not in the sense of being literally unconscious as in sleep, but in the sense of human ego consciousness not having developed yet, such that the transpersonal unconscious processes of the psyche, including instincts and impulses, dominated and determined humans' perception and understanding of the world.

29. Neumann 1954, pp. 5-38; Neumann 1955, p. 42; Wilber 1996, pp. 25-40.

30. Neumann 1954, pp. 5-38, 43.

31. We use the term "Great Mother" or simply "Goddess" to refer to the original, all-encompassing goddess, without emphasizing either her good or dark aspects, and specify when we mean one aspect or the other. The term "earth goddess" refers to the phase when her sphere had been relegated to earth.

32. That is, she was a goddess of heaven too; only in patriarchal times was she replaced there by sky gods and relegated to the earth and sometimes the underworld.

33. Neumann 1954, p. 52. An Egyptian example is Neith. Budge 1969, 1:462.

34. Neumann 1954, pp. 52, 133-35; Neumann 1955, pp. 267, 269.

35. Frazer 1963, 8.2:261-62.

36. Kerényi 1976, pp. xxxi-xxxvii.

37. Kerényi 1976, p. xxxv.

38. Neumann 1955, pp. 287-91.

39. The above processes are summarized in Neumann 1955, pp. 132-34, 282-91. In contrast, J credits Yahweh and men for founding civilization. Gen. 3:21 (clothing); 4:2, 17-22 (farming, cities, animal husbandry, music and instruments, and metallurgy).

40. For a review and criticism of these matriarchy theories see discussions in Eller 2000 and (as to the ancient Near East) Westenholz 1998.

41. Neumann 1954, pp. 41, 168, 432; Neumann 1955, pp. 43-44, 91; see examples in Eliade 1991b, pp. 37-42.

42. Campbell 1990, p. 51.

43. Analogously, our word "sacrifice" comes from the Latin compound *sacer facere,* ("to make whole/holy/sacred") which was understood to denote giving up one thing for another, of restoring something that has been lost in order to restore wholeness and allow life to continue.

44. Eliade 1996, p. 333.

45. Campbell 1959, p. 139.

46. Eliade 1996, pp. 332-33.

47. Eliade 1996, pp. 331-32.

48. See Baring and Cashford 1993, p. 147.

49. Baring and Cashford 1993, pp. 75, 141.

50. Baring and Cashford 1993, p. 497.

51. Baring and Cashford 1993, p. 207 (discussing in relation to Tammz myth in Mesopotamia, with Tammuz being date clusters).

52. A variant on this motif was for the Goddess to have a daughter who becomes the consort of a god representing the dying phase of the moon, and the mother rescues her daughter, as in the case of the Greek goddess Demeter rescuing Persephone from Hades.

53. For the association of the Goddess with various animals, see Johnson 1988. The most comprehensive treatment of the somewhat abstract designs, and the most far-reaching claims regarding them, are in Gimbutas 1989. These designs are claimed to include spirals, chevrons, lozenges, waves, net patterns, labyrinths, and meanders. Others question whether such images indeed represent any goddesses. See Eller 2000, pp. 118-33.

54. Hence, later among Christains the goat came to symbolize lust and represented the damned at the Last Judgment (Matt. 25:31-46). In ancient Greece too, the lustful Pan and Satyr had goat-like features. But since in Greek Pan's name means "all," he symbolized the totality of nature, not simply its sexual features.

55. Neumann 1955, p. 222.

56. Space considerations do not allow us to elaborate on this psychological aspect of water imagery in biblical and other ancient Near Eastern myths. For discussions, see Jung 1959, pp. 18-19; Hoffman 1999, pp. 144-45; Le Grice 2013, pp. 149, 180; Jung 1970, p. 272; Ronnberg 2010, p. 36.

57. Westenholz 1998, p. 76.

58. A more detailed account of these developments can be found in Baring and Cashford 1993, pp. 150-58.

59. Campbell 1974, pp. 72-74.

60. As to the Indo-Europeans and other Eurasians generally, see Mallory 1989, pp. 24-109.

61. Campbell 1964, p. 7; Neumann 1955, p. 155.

62. Beyond the historical factors mentioned in this immediate discussion, there may have been other causes for this psychic change that as a historical matter are hard to pinpoint, but presumably they would have varied from individual to individual and from community to community. At this stage of our study, we are concerned mainly with the results of this historical process, not its underlying psychological causes.

63. We must therefore defer our discussion of the psychological aspects of this change until we discuss the acquisition of knowledge of good and evil, in Chapter 9.

64. Campbell 1962, p. 36.

65. Wilber 1996.

66. Wilber 1996, pp. 194, 237; Harrison 1927, p. 460; Neumann 1954, pp. 35, 131, 153, 245. As explained by Gebser 1985, Combs 2009, and Wilber 1996, each subsequent stage in the development of human consciousness must build on and integrate all prior stages (which remain in our psyche); we should not attempt to suppress or repress them (as occurred in connection with the Great Reversal).

67. Campbell 1964, p. 24; see Wilber 1996, pp. 211-14; Le Grice 2013, p. 38.

68. Campbell 1962, p. 36; likewise Wilber 1996, pp. 304-07. See discussion in Chapter 9.

69. Wilber 1996, pp. 163-66, 178-84.

70. Eliade 1996, pp. 91-92.

71. As quoted in Eliade 1996, p. 76.

72. Kramer 1979, pp. 29-30.

73. Eliade 1996, p. 76.

74. Neumann 1954, pp. 68-69, 94, 323.

75. Neumann 1954, pp. 354, 379; Wilber 1996, p. 238.

76. Wilber 1996, pp. 126, 142.

77. Neumann 1954, p. 323.

78. Dever 2005, p. 167.

79. Eliade 1996, pp. 420-22.

80. Eliade 1996, p. 421.

81. Kramer 1972, p. 39.

82. Kramer 1972, p. 39 & n. 41.

83. Kramer 1963, p. 29.

84. This airspace was a substance called *lil*, which can be translated as air, atmosphere, wind, breath, or spirit (like the wind/spirit of God *(rûaḥ)* in Genesis 1:2). This is similar to the air god Shu in Egyptian mythology, who also separated heaven and earth, as well as P's creation account where God separated heaven and earth. Conceptually, such separation enabled light, the celestial bodies, and time to exist.

85. Kramer 1972, p. 37.

86. Kramer 1956, pp. 82-83; Kramer 1972, pp. 74-75.

87. Kramer 1963, p. 119.

88. A similarly nationalistic adaptation of this motif appears in the Hebrew Bible, where Moses receives the fundamental laws from Yahweh on tablets, the possession of which (as housed in the Ark) was thought to confer power and render the Israelites invincible before all foes.

89. The Biblical tower of Babel was such a ziggurat, condemned by J due to the humans' desire to be godlike, which was not the Sumerian idea at all.

90. Hoffman 1999, p. 102.

91. Hoffman 1999, p. 102. We elaborate on the process of sympathetic magic in Ch. 7, text accompanying notes 169-73.

92. The change to Ea seems to have come about as Sumerian civilization declined. In Sumerian the word "A" means both water and semen. Thus, his name means "temple of water," referring to the god's (formerly Enki's) temple in the *apsu*. Hoffman 1999, p. 96.

93. Kramer 1972, p. 77.

94. Kramer 1972, p. 38.

95. Kramer 1972, pp. 79-82.

96. Keel 1997, p. 48.

97. Keel 1997, pp. 47-48.

98. The name Tiamat is derived from *tamtum*, meaning "sea," Jacobsen 1968, p. 105, just as Nammu means sea. The Biblical name for "the deep" *(tehôm)*, discussed below, is at least etymologically related to (though not directly derived from) Tiamat, Day 1985, pp. 7, 50, while some claim a direct etymological link, Ringgren 1966, p. 107. A Mari text also evidences the etymological correlation between Tiamat and Yam, the Ugaritic sea dragon discussed below; a variation of *tamtum (tamtu)* also appears in an Ugaritic text meaning "the great Sea." Smith 2002, pp. 94-95.

99. The name Marduk can mean either "Son of the storm" or "Son of the sun." Although *Enuma Elish* uses solar imagery when Marduk was born, in the remainder of the epic storm imagery prevails and seems to reflect the primary understanding of Marduk's essence. Jacobsen 1968, pp. 104--06. Among other things, Marduk functioned as a storm god, like Baal and Yahweh.

100. Dalley 1989, p. 253. For ease of reading we have changed Dalley's "*imhullu*-wind" to "evil-wind," which is how Dalley (p. 251) translates it.

101. Dalley 1989, pp. 254-55.

102. Kramer 1972, p. 274.

103. Although Marduk was in part also appropriating the above-mentioned creation mythology of Enlil in which he likewise creates (separates) heaven and earth, Enlil subordinated the

Goddess by marrying rather than killing her. The theogony in *Enuma Elish* lists only the direct ancestors of Marduk, with each generation surpassing the other in wisdom, strength and personality. Enlil, who was so prominent in the earlier mythology as a creator, is conspicuously omitted.

104. Rig Veda, I.32.8-12.

105. Campbell 1964, p. 22.

106. Yam means "sea" and is etymologically related to Tiamat. Smith 2002, p. 95. As we have just seen, the serpent/dragon monster is often the son of the Goddess (her proxy), and Yam was Asherah's son. Asherah was known as "Asherah of the sea" (see below). Unlike *Enuma Elish* this tale is not on its face a cosmogonic myth, but in terms of the Myth of the Eternal Return discussed in Chapter 4 it can be seen as a reenactment of the creation. See Clifford 1984, arguing that the Baal myth is cosmogonic.

107. In both the crossing of the sea, in ending the flood, and subduing the monster, Yahweh, like Marduk, utilizes the wind to overcome the waters (or the serpent monster). See Gen. 8:2; Exod. 14:21; Job 26:12-13.

108. Westermann 1994, pp. 200-01.

109. Graves and Patai 1983, p. 31.

110. Gen. 49:25. The same formulation referring to the *tehôm* is used in the Blessing of Moses in Deuteronomy 33:13.

111. Smith 2002, pp. 48-52.

112. Maier 1986, p. 31; Keel and Uehlinger 1998, p. 74 (referencing in this regard Gen. 49:25).

113. Smith 2002, pp. 19-31.

114. This process is discussed in detail in Smith 2001, pp. 47-53.

115. As to Asherah, see Patai 1965, p. 38; Reed 1949, p. 77; Keel and Uehlinger 1998, p. 74 (also noting that she is called "womb").

116. This is the most direct origin of the biblical account in which El assigns each of his 70 god-sons as patron deities of the 70 nations of the earth. See Day 2002, pp. 22-24. In that account, Yahweh is a son of El and is assigned the Israelites. Deut. 32:8-9.

117. Day 2002, pp. 32-33.

118. See James 1966, p. 142.

119. Keel 1997, pp. 47-48; see also James 1966, p. 142.

120. Smith 2001, p. 137; the text can be found at *ANES*, p. 519.

121. Smith 2001, p. 137. Other epithets included El Elyon ("El Most High") and El Shaddai (often translated as "El Almighty" but more accurately as "El the Mountain one," derived from the word for "breast"). Day 2002, pp. 32-33.

122. In Ugarit he was thought of as a son of El, but may have had another lineage as he was also called the son of Dagon, a Mesopotamian god of grain and agriculture. Smith 2001, p. 136. Baal is a good example of the common Amorite heritage of Old Babylon, Mari and Ugarit. In Mari he was known as Addu or Adad, which in Ugarit became Hadad. Smith 2002, p. 95. That he was related to Marduk we know from *Enuma Elish,* where Addu is listed one of Marduk's many names, *ANET*, p. 72, and from another text stating that "Adad [is] Marduk of rain," Smith 2002, p. 97, which corresponds to Baal's main Canaanite/Israelite aspect as a weather (storm) god.

123. *DDD,* p. 110.

124. Olyan 1988, p. 10.

125. See generally Eliade 1996, pp. 96-99; Eliade 1987, pp. 125-27.

126. Cross 1973, pp. 190-91.

127. Day 2002, pp. 16-17; Albertz 1994, pp. 30-31.

128. Deut. 33:2-3; Judg. 5:4-5; Hab. 3:3, 7; Ps. 68:8-9; Zech. 9:14. The RSV translates "Teman" as "the south."

129. While the name Mt. Horeb is used occasionally in Exodus (E) and consistently in Deuteronomy, elsewhere in Exodus (P) Moses's holy mountain is called Mt. Sinai (Exod. 19:11), which has led most people to endeavor to locate it in Sinai to no avail. Scholarly opinion now tends to locate the mountain southeast of the Arabah (i.e., northwest Arabia). Day 2002, p. 15. Clifford observes that most uses of the name Horeb in the Bible do not refer to a

mountain at all and therefore suggests that Horeb is not just E's and D's equivalent of J's and P's Mt. Sinai, but is not a mountain at all but a region associated with a variety of events. Clifford 1972, pp. 121-22.

130. Cross 1973, p. 201; Mazar 1965, pp. 297-303. The excavations at Arad, however, show that its *fortress* was established only in the 10th century; prior to then the term referred to that region, probably derived from the name of a clan or tribe that had inhabited the area. Mazar 1965, p. 299.

131. Cross 1973, p. 201.

132. Albertz 1994, p. 51.

133. Day 2002, pp. 15-16; Smith 2002, pp. 32-33; Halpern 1992, pp. 105-07; McCarter 1992. This is known as the Kenite (or Midian-Kenite) hypothesis. Technically the term Midianites may be traceable to and taken to refer to descendants of Abraham through one of his sons, named Midian (Gen. 25:1-2). The Bible refers to Jethro as both a Kenite (Judg. 1:16) and a Midianite (Num. 10:29), as well as a "priest of Midian" (Exod. 3:1). Midianite came to refer to anyone from that region, whereas Kenite refers to a particular group, probably one clan/tribe of Midianites, Blenkinsopp 2008, p. 144 n. 43; Albertz 1994, p. 51, or possibly metalworkers in general. The most recent leading summary of the evidence for this hypothesis is gathered and analyzed in Blenkinsopp 2008.

134. Dever 2005, pp. 162-63. Scholars are not certain where in the south Teman should be located, but they agree that it appears to be a region somewhere in south Edom (which may include Kuntillet Ajrûd) rather than a particular site. See discussion in Hadley 2000, pp. 127-29; Day 2002, p. 49; Keel and Uehlinger 1998, p. 228; Zevit 2001, p. 650; Blenkinsopp 2008, p. 138.

135. "Kenite" comes from *qayin,* connoting "smith" or "metal-worker." Some relate this to Cain, whose descendant Lemech had three sons who established professions, one being the forging of copper and iron, founded by Tubal-Cain (Gen. 4:17-22). See Albright 1968, p. 98; BDB, p. 883; *HALOT* 3:1097.

136. Hathor was venerated by turquoise and copper miners in Sinai and Midian, and was associated with serpents (see Chapter 7). In Canaan she was identified with Asherah.

137. See Redford 1992, pp. 272-73 and sources cited therein; Blenkinsopp 2008, pp. 139-40; Dever 2003, pp. 128, 150-51, 236-37; Halpern 1992, p. 105; Albertz 1994, p. 5; Mazar 1977.

138. Redford 1992, pp. 273-75, 279-80; Levy, Adams, and Muniz 2004, pp. 63-89; Mazar 1977.

139. Redford 1992, pp. 279-80.

140. Note that this hypothesis only explains the origins of Yahweh, not that of most of the Israelites themselves, already discussed in Chapter 2. Any large migration of Kenites/Shasu/Midianites into Canaan would leave an archeological footprint, of which there is none, while smaller movements of nomads would not explain the rapid population growth in the central highlands in the 12th and 11th centuries. Even assuming the truth of this "Kenite hypothesis," it is still clear that the ancestry of most Israelites was Canaanite.

141. Friedman 1997, p. 82.

142. Albertz 1994, pp. 72-83.

143. Dijkstra 2000b, pp. 94-95.

144. Deut. 32:8-9; Ps. 82.1; 89:6-9.

145. Day 2002, p. 14; Smith 2002, pp. 32-33.

146. Day 2002, pp. 17-22; Smith 2002, pp. 35-37.

147. Smith 2002, p. 39.

148. Day 2002, p. 36.

149. See Chapter 4, text accompanying notes 36-48.

150. Smith 2002, p. 34.

151. Gen. 32:28 (E text), 35:10 (P text).

152. Smith 2002, pp. 41-42.

153. Adapted from RSV and Cross 1973, p. 5.

154. Smith 2001, p. 141; Smith 2002, p. 34.

155. Friedman 1997, p. 82.

156. The RSV capitalizes the word in reference to the Asherahs at the Jerusalem Temple and at Samaria even though the term is referring to the wooden cult object rather than the Goddess herself. In order to avoid confusion, we preserve the capitalization in reference to these two asherahs.

157. In Akkadian her name was Astartu. This became Athtart in Ugaritic and Ashtart (Astarte) in Phoenician. In the Hebrew Bible, the end of her name sometimes was deliberately corrupted by the authors so as to become Ashtoreth, in order to engage in word play on the word for "shame" or "abomination," *bosheth.* Day 2002, p. 128.

158. The Ugaritic goddess Anat did not survive well in Canaan and Israel into the time of J and is not mentioned as a goddess in the Hebrew Bible; evidence of her appears only as part of some personal (Shambar ben-Anat in Judges 3:31) and place names (Beth-Anat in Josh. 19:38 and Judg. 3:31; Anathoth in Benjamin, in numerous references starting in Josh. 21:18), evidencing some earlier importance. In Ugarit she had evolved into a war goddess, and these traits seem to have been appropriated by Yahweh. See Smith 2002, pp. 101-07, demonstrating close parallels between Ugaritic texts describing her exploits and biblical texts describing Yahweh's.

159. The Hebrew Bible exhibits confusion when identifying the goddesses in Canaan and Israel (e.g., in different places Ashtoreth and Asherah being identified with Baal), and scholars have had difficulty making sense of it. See Reed 1949, pp. 11-16; Baring and Cashford 1993, p. 458. Yahwists opposed the worship of both goddesses, but seem to have focused on Asherah as the greater threat, seemingly to the point of distorting identities. As mentioned, Astarte (Ashtoreth) was the chief goddess in Sidon during the monarchy, which seems to be corroborated by the Bible's statement that "Solomon went after Ashtoreth the goddess of the Sidonians" (1 Kings 11:5). But shortly after that passage the Bible says that king Ahab under the influence of his Sidonian queen Jezebel introduced the worship of *Asherah* (setting up an Asherah at Samaria) and maintained her prophets, who attended the contest at Mr. Carmel (1 Kings 16:31-33; 18:19). Many scholars believe that the reference to Asherah's prophets in 18:19 is an interpolation to the text, Smith 2002, p. 110, and its author may either have been mistaken about Astarte vs. Asherah, or deliberately misrepresented the goddess as Asherah and the prophets as hers. But even if so, this would still point to the popularity of the Asherah cult, so for our purposes whether this is an interpolation or the wrong goddess is not important. Further, it is not disputed that an asherah stood at Samaria. Therefore, in our discussion we utilize the biblical descriptions at face value.

160. Smith 2002, p. 127 (noting that she was "the only West Semitic goddess bearing this title during the Iron Age"); Dever 2005, p. 233. This epithet traces back originally to the Sumerian goddess Inanna and was assumed by Ishtar and then Astarte. Baring and Cashford 1993, p. 199. The main biblical description of her cult is by Jeremiah (7:17-18; 44:17-19).

161. Jer. 7:17-18; 44:17-19. See Albertz 1994, p. 194; Graves and Patai 1983, pp. 63-65.

162. Day 2002, p. 131-32; Baring and Cashford 1993, p. 460.

163. Smith 2002, pp. 126-27. This includes in association with Yahweh, possibly eventually replacing Asherah as his consort, see Albertz 1994, pp. 194, 211, or being identified or merging with her, or being seen as paired goddesses, see Halpern 2009, pp. 83-84.

164. In the Septuagint the Hebrew asherah was translated as *alsos* (plural *alse*), except in Isaiah 17:8 and 27:9 where *dendra* ("tree") was used, and in 2 Chronicles 15:16 and 24:18 where the translation was erroneously rendered as Astarte. Olyan 1988, pp. 2-3.

165. Jerome used *lucus* ("grove") in all instances except in Judges 6:12, 26 and 30, where he used *nemus* ("wood" or "grove") and in Judges 3:7 where he wrote "Ashteroth" (deciding that "Asheroth" was a reference to Ashtoreth; if he was convinced that Asherah meant "grove," he would not have had the choice of choosing between the two goddesses). Hadley 2000, p. 82; see also Dever 2005, p. 225.

166. The archeology of Palestine yields no asherahs or images of the goddess. According to the Bible the asherahs (and perhaps some actual images or idols of her) were destroyed by the reformist kings Hezekiah and Josiah, and in any event asherahs were wooden, so any that survived Josiah could not have lasted long. The Israelite aniconic tradition associated with Yahweh may not have allowed (or would have at least limited) public representations of the goddess Asherah in the first place: Since images of Yahweh were forbidden, perhaps the same

would apply for his consort, so that only symbols of her were allowed. See Hadley 2000, p. 153; Smith 2002, p. xxxiii.

167. Day 2002, p. 42.

168. See generally Wiggins 1993, pp. 132-50; Margalit 1990, pp. 270-71; Cross 1973, p. 57; see also Hadley 2000, pp. 44-45; Albright 1968, pp. 78, 178; Day 2002, p. 61; Patai 1965, p. 39; Van Buren 1933, pp. 16-17.

169. EA, pp. 218-221 (No. 137); *ANET,* pp. 483-44; see discussions in Wiggins 1993, pp. 147-48, and Wyatt 1999, p. 100.

170. Day 2002, p. 61. Because of the generic nature of the term, this epithet was not exclusive to Asherah and sometimes was used to refer to other goddesses such as Anat. Hadley 2000, p. 42; Smith 2002, p. 29. But it was most regularly used with Asherah. Most scholars once believed that her epithet etymologically means "she who treads on (or subdues) the sea (or dragon)," perhaps referring to her role in the Ugaritic Baal epic where she helped Baal defeat Yam the sea dragon. The weight of recent scholarship disfavors this view on technical grounds. See discussion in Day 2002, p. 61-62; also Margalit 1990. In Ugarit her proper name was Athirat, which became Asherah in Hebrew.

171. Margalit 1990, p. 272.

172. Olyan 1988, pp. 53-61; Oden 1977, pp. 92-93.

173. Smith 2002, pp. 29, 115; Hadley 2000, p. 42. This epithet was not exclusive to Asherah and sometimes was used to refer to other goddesses such as Anat, but it was most regularly used with Asherah. Similarly, our use of "Asherah" should be interpreted to allow for the possibility discussed below (text accompanying notes 247-49) that in Israel it was a generic title for any goddess (like Baal was for gods) and when used with Yahweh designated that goddess which was associated with Yahweh.

174. Patai 1965, p. 39.

175. Gen. 35:4. See Albright 1968, pp. 78-79; Smith 2002, p. 114.

176. Albright 1968, p. 79.

177. Albright 1968, pp. 78-79; see Albright 1967, pp. 190-91; Smith 2002, p. 114.

178. Smith 2002, pp. 114-15.

179. Day 2002, p. 47; Smith 2002, p. xxxii, stating that "most commentators believe that Asherah was a goddess in monarchic Israel."

180. Keel and Uehlinger 1998, p. 74. The figurine in Figure 2 is identified by Dever as Asherah. 2005, pp. 187-88. Keel and Uehlinger also agree this is possible. 1998, pp. 72-75.

181. Those equating Qedesh/Qudshu with Asherah include Cross 1973, pp. 33-35; Wallace 1985, pp. 155-56; Hadley 2000, pp. 46-49; Day 2002, p. 48; and Albright 1967, p. 121.

182. Translation from Wallace 1985, p. 155, except that we have Anglicized the transcriptions to get Qedesh and Elat. He rejects the idea that here Qedesh means sanctuary. Likewise Maier 1986, pp. 27-28.

183. See discussions of possibilities in Hadley 2000, pp. 49-53; Reed 1949, p. 91.

184. Day 2002, pp. 61-62; Reed 1949, pp. 16, 91; Lipinski 1972, pp. 114-16.

185. Reed 1949, p. 91; Skinner 1910, p. 388.

186. E.g., Day 2002, pp. 63-64.

187. See Gray 1964, p. 76; Reed 1949, p. 91.

188. See Wyatt 1999, p. 99; Albright 1968, pp. 77-78.

189. Margalit 1990.

190. Smith 2002, p. 111.

191. It seems that knowledge of and devotion to Asherah faded following the Babylonian conquest, when the religious infrastructure was broken up, leading citizens were dispersed, and other gods rose to prominence. This seems evident from the post-exilic text of Chronicles. See Hadley 2000, p. 209; Day 2002, p. 46.

192. Day 2002, pp. 42, 44, 47-48, 60; Smith 2002, p. 52; Albertz 1994, p. 85; see also Olyan 1988, pp. xiv, 38-61.

193. Dever 2005, p. 167; see also discussion in Albertz 1994, pp. 86-87.

194. Albright 1967, pp. 122-23; Albright 1944a, p. 18.

195. 2 Chr. 14:4; 34:4, 7; Isa. 17:8; 27:9. See Olyan 1988, p. 15. The word for incense altar, *hammanim,* leaves the meaning clear in Hebrew, but it is sometimes (e.g., 2 Chr. 14:4) translated simply as altar with no reference to incense. See Reed 1949, pp. 40-46, 51-52.

196. See Smith 2002, pp. 113-14. One translation of the biblical passage translates the word as "tunics" rather than simply hangings. See Reed 1949, p. 35.

197. Albertz 1994, p. 87.

198. Albertz 1994, p. 95.

199. Dever 2005, pp. 176-95; Hadley 2000, pp. 188-205. The figurines are discussed and illustrated at greater length in Kletter 1966 and Pritchard 1943. Not all specialists agree that these figurines represent Asherah, but space does not allow discussion of the arguments.

200. Hestrin 1991, p. 57; see Dever 2005, p. 179.

201. The excavators at Lachish also discovered the charred remnants of an olive wood pole in ashes next to a pillar and concluded that was "very probable" that it was an asherah. But since it was burned, there are other possible explanations for the object, and since excavation surrounding it was limited, specialists generally regard the find as inconclusive. Hadley 2000, p. 164; Zevit 2001, pp. 217-18.

202. Cross 1954, pp. 20-21; Hadley 2000, pp. 157-60; Dever 2005, p. 226; Smith 2002, p. 29; Day 2002, p. 56; Hestrin 1991, p. 54. Mattan was apparently the individual making the offering to Asherah. Hestrin 1991, p. 54; Cross 1954, p. 21.

203. Hestrin 1991, p. 54, noting, "it is no accident that the word Elat appears over the tree that represents Elat/Asherah."

204. Hestrin 1991, p. 56.

205. Albright 1944a, pp. 18-19; discussed in Wiggins 1993, p. 149. The letter probably dates to shortly after Thutmose III defeated Megiddo (in 1468) and left a garrison there, giving them control over nearby Taanach as well.

206. Wiggins 1993, p. 149.

207. Olyan 1988, pp. 13, 22, 33, 71-73; Patai 1990, p. 50.

208. Halpern 2009, pp. 57-97, argues that the campaign against Asherah in Deuteronomy and the Deuteronomistic History was part of a broader campaign against the host of heaven, which formerly seems to have been acceptable (including to J) as these deities were originally considered subordinate to Yahweh but were now demonized on grounds that they are foreign deities of other nations.

209. See Friedman 1997, pp. 118-24.

210. The reference is to "the Asheroth," a feminine plural for Asherah (rather than *asherim* referring to the asherah poles, having a masculine ending despite the noun being feminine, not uncommon in Hebrew). While most specialists accept this reference as being to Asherah, some believe that this is a scribal mistake and that Ashtoreth (Astarte) is intended. Some modern translations simply use "Asherah." For background see discussion in Hadley 2000, pp. 63-64.

211. See Graves and Patai 1983, pp. 39-41.

212. Patai 1965, pp. 51-52. Interestingly, even in Ezekiel's view the Asherah seems to be the least of the abominations. His list of sins against Yahweh proceeds in an ascending order of greater and greater sins, of which the Asherah is only the first. Worse (in ascending order) are the burning of incense; the presence of beasts and idols; women weeping for Tammuz; and worship of the sun. Ezek. 8:7-18.

213. See Patai 1990, p. 50. All four kings after Josiah were said to have done "what was evil in the sight of Yahweh, according to all that [their] fathers had done." 2 Kings 23:32, 37; 24:9, 19. This most likely includes restoration of the Asherah at the Temple.

214. Patai 1990, p. 50.

215. It is not clear what these vessels were, but since the Bible says they were burned, they must have been made of wood. Dever 2005, p. 216.

216. Olyan 1988, pp. 13, 22, 33, 71-73; Smith 2002, p. 109.

217. E.g., Patai 1965, p. 46; Dever 2005, p. 211.

218. Later, Hosea (early 8th century) and Amos (mid-8th century) also do not mention Asherah. Amos 8:14 contains a puzzling reference to the Ashimah ("guilt") of Samaria, but there is no scholarly consensus on what this means. See Hadley 2000, p. 77; Dever 2005, p. 150. Later Judahite prophets writing during or after the downfall of the northern kingdom of

Israel do mention and condemn the Asherah cult. See Isa. 17:8; 27:9 (mid to late 8th century); Mic. 5:13-14 (late 8th century, after Isaiah); and Jer. 17:2 (during the reign of Josiah and writing of Deuteronomy).

219. Olyan 1988, p. 17; see also Zevit 2001, p. 466.

220. Olyan 1988, pp. 6-8, 34-35; Zevit 2001, pp. 466, 651-52.

221. Hadley 2000, pp. 173, 175; Olyan 1988, p. 10.

222. Deut. 16:21. See Olyan 1988, p. 9.

223. Olyan 1988, p. 9.

224. See Olyan 1988, pp. 9, 33, 43.

225. Taken from Day 2002, p. 50. Other, essentially consistent translations can be found in Hadley 2000, p. 86, and Dever 2005, p. 132.

226. This is a "consensus" translation from Dever 2005, pp. 162-63. Scholars have argued vigorously over the details of the Khirbet el-Qom and Kuntillet Ajrûd translations, but these differences do not affect the analysis and conclusions here. For a detailed linguistic analysis of the possible alternative translations and some of the complexities involved, see Hadley 2000, pp. 84-136.

227. E.g., Hadley 2000, p. 153; Day 2002, p. 52 (the tree "probably illustrates the Asherah alluded to in the inscription").

228. Olyan 1988, p. 33.

229. E.g., Emerton 1982, pp. 13-19; Lemaire 1984; Keel and Uehlinger 1998, pp. 234-36; Tigay 1986.

230. Those considering this argument decisive include Lemaire 1984 and Day 2002, pp. 51-52. As Lemaire notes, however, this would not be a problem if the word were a title or sobriquet of the goddess, which as explained below is likely the case.

231. E.g., Keel and Uehlinger 1998, pp. 234-36, though arguing that the asherah had by then (8th century) lost its particular association with the goddess (but then regained it by the late 7th century!).

232. Hadley 2000, p. 99.

233. Olyan 1988, p. 32; Ackermann 2001, pp. 65-66. See also Ringgren 1966, p. 157 (the asherah symbolizes the goddess).

234. Regarding the potency of the Goddess down to Josiah and beyond, see James 1959, pp. 80-81.

235. Wiggins 1993, p. 180 ("the parallelism strikes us as unusual"); Hess 1991, p. 19 ("understanding a cult object in parallel with the divine name Yahweh "would upset the symmetry of ideas such as might be expected in prayers and blessings").

236. Margalit 1990, p. 276: "The most significant, indeed decisive, feature of the blessing formula in its bearing on the Asherah problem is that it is stereotyped. The formula *brk l-* never admits of anything but a divine persona or agency following the preposition."

237. Dever 2005, p. 204.

238. Olyan 1988, p. 32; Day 2002, p. 227; Dever 2005, p. 200; James 1966, p. 249 ("the symbol is regarded and treated in the same way as the spiritual entity it symbolizes"); Van Buren 1933, p. 22. Wyatt 1999, p. 103, notes that "the distinction between deity and cult object is ultimately not an ancient, but a modern one."

239. Olyan 1988, p. 32. Similarly, Halpern 2009, p. 68, explained specifically in reference to the Khirbet el-Qom asherah/Asherah, "Yet what is the icon except a representation (whether figurative or not) of the goddess, and thus what is the goddess herself but the idealization of the icon. In other words, Yhwh's asherah is indeed the goddess."

240. Hadley 2000, p. 72.

241. See discussion in Bonatz 2007, pp. 15-6, 18; Baring and Cashford 1993, pp. 120-22; Olyan 1988, pp. 31-32.

242. E.g., Dever 2005.

243. This argument is compelling if the drawings were made before or together with the inscription. If the drawing was later, then it was the artist who connected the inscription and the drawing.

244. Zevit 2001, p. 403; Hess 1991, pp. 15-16; see discussions of this point in Hadley 2000, pp. 97-99, and Day 2002, pp. 51-52. This ending is not attested in the Hebrew Bible.

245. See Wilson 2001, p. 113, who observed in connection with this inscription, "It is ever surprising that we continually encounter the expectation of text scholars that the ancients always used the perfect grammar and syntax that they have constructed for them hundreds of years later." Likewise is David N. Freedman: "I believe the way to approach a strange grammatical construction is not by invoking a rule that somebody invented in the nineteenth century that says it is impossible but rather by investigating the possible reasons for such an unusual arrangement." His suggested reason is that in the Hebrew Bible Asherah occurs in the plural as well as singular, so there are many of them possibly associated with different gods and/or locations, so the inscription designates the goddess associated with Yahweh. Freedman 1987, pp. 246-47.

246. See sources cited in Day 2002, p. 51.

247. Halpern 2009, pp. 65, 67-69 (quoted); Wyatt 1999, p. 101; Margalit 1990, pp. 276-77; Taylor 1994, p. 54; Meshel 1979, p. 31. The use of the title enables one to refer to the same goddess in her localized forms, or even to different goddesses. See Freedman 1987, pp. 246-47.

248. The same pattern occurs in the Bible when Baal is mentioned as a deity. As modern examples, in Christian usage "the Christ" and "the Messiah" clearly refer to Jesus and "the Lord" to the Christian God.

249. Margalit 1990, p. 269.

250. As Judith Hadley explained in her study of Asherah, "If you destroyed the cultic object of a deity, it could be said that the deity was vanquished as well." Hadley 2000, p. 72; see also Reed 1949, p. 95.

251. Wilson 2001, p. 112.

252. Space allows us to mention only the major discoveries here. For discussions of the other finds that may evidence Asherah or asherahs, see Hadley 2000, pp. 156-87.

253. Dever 2005, p. 171.

254. Dever 2005, pp. 174-75.

255. This association of the Goddess/female with pithoi dedicated to her strengthens the association of the Kuntillet Ajrûd pithoi inscriptions with the goddess Asherah. Interestingly, the clay used for the pithoi at Kuntillet Ajrûd was from the Ekron area, Hadley 2000, pp. 181-82; Wiggins 1993, p. 182 n. 106, so perhaps they too were made in that region.

256. Halpern 2008. p. 68-69; Wiggins 1993, p. 182; Smith 2001, p. 73 and cited works. Regarding the same views by the excavator, Seymour Gitin, see Gitin 1993, p. 252. See also general discussion in Hadley 2000, pp. 179-84.

257. Halpern 2009, p. 68.

258. Gitin 1993, p. 254 and fig. 5:b.

259. Detailed analyses of this stand are contained in the original treatment, Hestrin 1987a, as well as in Hadley 2000, pp. 169-76 and Zevit 2001, pp. 318-25.

260. Taylor 1994, pp. 53-54.

261. Taylor 1994, p. 61.

262. There is no consensus on whether it is a young bull (calf) or a horse. For those favoring a young bull, see Zevit 2001, p. 321; Hestrin 1987a, p. 67; for those favoring a horse, see Taylor 1994, p. 57; Hadley 2000, pp. 171-73; Day 2002, p. 153 (citing Taylor). A horse would be more consistent with the appearance of horses at the Temple in association with the sun in 2 Kings 23:11.

263. See Hadley 2000, p. 172 and sources cited; Dever 2005, pp. 219, 220; see Zevit 2001, p. 324; Hestrin 1987a, pp. 68-74.

264. See discussion in Hadley 2000, p. 174; Taylor 1994, p. 58.

265. Hadley 2000, p. 172; Taylor 1994, p. 55.

266. Taylor 1994; Day 2002, pp. 151-63. A sun cult is also evidenced by the place name Beth-Shemesh ("House of the Sun"), used for four cities, *HBD,* p. 119, as well as other place names containing the word for sun, Day 2002, p. 152.

267. Hadley 2000, pp. 172-73. Also, at Hazor a late 10th century terracotta head of an animal was found with a sun disk on its head between the ears, which the excavator, Yigael Yadin, thought might be either a bull or horse, and in the latter case "the figurine represented the sun cult, often associated with the chariot and horses." Yadin 1975, p. 189. Other specialists believe that the head is of a horse. See Taylor 1994, p. 58; Day 2002, p. 153.

268. Vriezen 2001, pp. 47-48.
269. Smith 2002, p. 148.
270. Hestrin 1987a, pp. 75-76.
271. Day 2002, pp. 157-58.
272. So interpreted in Taylor 1994, pp. 60-62; see discussion in Hadley 2000, pp. 173-74. In fact, another inscription from Kuntillet Ajrûd contains the verbal root for to "rise" used to describe the rising sun and used in the Bible for solar imagery. Smith 2002, p. 149.
273. Hadley 2000, p. 174.
274. See discussion in Hadley 2000, pp. 172-75; Dever 2005, p. 151; Zevit 2001, p. 324; Taylor 1994.
275. Hadley 2000, pp. 187, 208.

4. THE CREATION, THE GARDEN IN EDEN, AND ITS RESTORATION

1. Blok, Alexander, "O naznachenii poeta" ["The Poet's Mission"], in *Sobranie sochinenii* ["Complete Works"], 6:161 (Moscow: Khudozhestvennaya Literatura, 1962) (authors' translation from Russian).
2. *ANET,* p. 417.
3. These are properly recognized as three phases in the development of a generally consistent Egyptian understanding of the creation, not as competing theories as sometimes portrayed. See Allen 1988.
4. E.g., Currid 1997, p. 35, as to Egypt.
5. Clifford 1984, pp. 184-87, 197, 201.
6. For example, when Marduk made half of Tiamat into the heavens, he secured it with a bolt or bar so that the waters could not stream down. *ANET,* p. 67 (Tablet IV, lines 139-40); see also Gunkel 2006, p. 25.
7. The Hebrew word usually translated as "firmament" *(rāqî),* see Gen: 1:6-8, derives from a blacksmithing term for a hammered strip of metal. *HBD,* pp. 338-39; see Friedman 2003, p. 9; Speiser 1964, p. 6. Similarly, according to W. Max Müller, in later Egyptian times an iron dome *(benipet,* meaning "sky metal") held up the celestial waters, while the word for thunder *(khrubai)* meant "sound of the metal." Thunder apparently was conceived of as the beating or rattling of the sheet of metal that constituted the firmament. Müller 1964, p. 35.
8. In *Enuma Elish* this was when Marduk set up the zodiac, the moon and the sun to mark the days, months, and time of year. *ANET,* pp. 67-68 (Tablet V). In P's creation account this was when God created the sun and the moon to mark day and night, the appointed times and years. Gen. 1:14-18. The extant form of J's creation account does not address this.
9. In fact, our word "cosmos" comes from the Greek *kosmos,* connoting "order." Pythagoras is said to have first applied this word to the universe.
10. We may ask why creation myths the world over conceive of the creation as order emerging from chaos. Psychologists argue that this is a natural result of our psyche experiencing its own consciousness coming into being as a "world-becoming." That is, to our psyche, our becoming aware of the world and the world coming into existence are one and the same. (This process occurred not only when humans first developed ego consciousness but also occurs in any young child's development and in the life of adults, e.g., as we wake up in the morning.) Thus, the dawn of consciousness and the creation of the world are parallel and related processes which throw up the same symbolism. The dawn of our own consciousness projects itself in cosmic form, so that cosmogonic myths reflect the coming of consciousness through corresponding symbols. Our unconscious has no sense of space or time and therefore no sense of order; it is indeed chaotic and is experienced as such. Thus, the notion of primordial chaos is a natural projection of an archetypal image that helps make the unknown comprehensible. Only our conscious ego can put order (in space and time) to the initially chaotic content of our psyches, meaning that creation of the outside world can occur only when and as we cross the

border from unconsciousness into consciousness. A common symbol that humans have projected to mark the border between the existent and non-existent, the known and the unknown "beyond," whether inner or outer, is the uroboros (originally the Egyptian *mehen* serpent, Hornung 1982, p. 179), which for example often encircles drawings of the known cosmos and the edges of ancient maps of the known world. Franz 1995, pp. 2-4; Neumann 1954, pp. 6, 211-12, 278, 329; Jung 1969, p. 148. As we shall see in Chapter 9, a similar process may lie behind the acquisition of the knowledge of good and evil, opposites that are one aspect of chaos vs. order.

11. Walton 2006, pp. 180-81.

12. *ANET,* pp. 60-61.

13. By contrast, in the above quote from the later *Enuma Elish,* the freshwater primordial deep, Apsu (at this point in time thought of as male), is differentiated from the salt water primordial ocean, Mammu-Tiamat (female), and they commingle "as a single body." This sexual motif of generation departs from the earlier Sumerian concept of self-generation by the Mother Goddess.

14. See generally Allen 1988.

15. Roberts 1995, pp. 34-36.

16. Roberts 1995, pp. 9, 34-36. There are no examples of Maat and Hathor together on the prow of the bark in Roberts, but a good example is at the Edifice of Taharqa by the Sacred Lake at the Karnak Temple in Thebes. See drawing in Cooney 2000, p. 24.

17. Black and Green 2003, p. 130.

18. Walton 2006, pp. 196-99.

19. Walton 2006, pp. 113-14, 196-99; Batto 1992, pp. 27-28, 30. In *Atrahasis* the lesser gods revolt against the great gods because they have to labor (resulting in the creation of man to do the work instead), which in essence is an aspiration to full divine status. Batto 1992, pp. 27-28, 30.

20. Walton 2006, pp. 196-99; see Cross 1973, p. 120.

21. Roux 1992, pp. 133-35; also Moran 1991.

22. Moran 1991, pp. 126-27.

23. *ANET,* p. 78.

24. Frankfort 1978, pp. 51-52. In Mesopotamia, although the institution of kingship was divine in origin, the king himself was not (according to the original scheme) divine, whereas in Egypt both the institution and the king himself were divine. See generally Frankfort 1978.

25. Batto 1992, p. 87; see Gen. 6:5; 8:21. See discussion in Chapter 9.

26. See Talmon 1966, p. 55.

27. Hornung 1982, p. 179.

28. Hornung 1982, p. 179 (as to Egypt).

29. CT 1130, as translated in Quirke 2008, p. 78.

30. In fact, in many cultures a cyclical view of creation, in which the cosmos is periodically destroyed and recreated, is central to their mythology. Examples include ancient Hinduism and the Mayan religion.

31. Hornung 1982, p. 179; Pinch 2002, p. 65. As we shall see in Chapter 9, the evil that arose in the garden of Eden and during the rest of the primeval history carried the same connotation.

32. Eliade 1987, pp. 143-44; Eliade 1996, pp. 251-52.

33. Hornung 1982, p. 179.

34. Batto 1992, pp. 85-88.

35. Clifford 1984, p. 185.

36. This motif as it appears in the Hebrew Bible is discussed extensively in Day 1985; Batto 1992; and Gunkel 2006, pp. 21-77.

37. E.g., Job 7:12: "Am I the sea, or a sea monster, that thou settest a guard over me?" This is an allusion to the scene in *Enuma Elish* in which Marduk set a guard over the body of the vanquished Tiamat. *NOAB,* pp. 619-20; Gunkel 2006, p. 44; see *ANET,* p. 67.

38. Job 7:12; 9:8; 26:12; 38:7-11; Ps. 89:10; 93:1-4; Isa. 27:1; Nahum 1:4. This listing is according to Cross 1973, p. 135, but Isaiah 27.1 may be identifying Leviathan with Assyria and possibly other enemies, *NOAB,* p. 852n.

39. The Hebrew word is *rûah,* the same term used for the wind over the deep in Genesis 1:2. Many scholars think the wind in this passage of Job is an allusion to or modeled upon *Enuma Elish,* because of the critical part that Marduk's wind played in the battle with Tiamat (also Marduk piercing Tiamat with an arrow). Driver and Gray 1921, p. 224. For this reason, Gunkel 2006, pp. 24-25, goes so far as to translate not as "wind" but the "bolt" of heaven, saying it derives from when Marduk bolted heaven (one half of Tiamat) to make it secure, e.g., from water streaming down. In reference to the prior line, he also suggests that Yahweh's smiting Rahab through his "understanding" derives from Marduk, being the "cleverest" of gods, craftily capturing Tiamat in his net. Gunkel 2006, p. 24

40. Most scholars interpret this to refer to the defeat of the chaotic waters at creation and not to earthly "enemies" as discussed in the next paragraph. Day 1985, pp. 26-27.

41. Eliade 1987, pp. 29-30.

42. Hornung 1982, p. 180.

43. Hornung 1982, pp. 180-81.

44. Gunkel 2006, p. 22; Cross 1973, p. 120; see generally Batto 1992.

45. While as noted earlier the prophet Isaiah lived and wrote during the late 8th and early 7th century, Chapters 40-66 of Isaiah were written later during the captivity and are therefore known as Second Isaiah. See *NOAB,* p. 822.

46. This story was originally at the end of Daniel but it was not accepted as canonical, so it is now part of the Apocrypha. It is contained in *NOAB,* Apocrypha, pp. 216-18; NRSV, pp. 1552-54.

47. Bel like the name Baal (perhaps derived from Bel) simply means "Lord," but it was commonly used in reference to Marduk.

48. As explained in Chapter 3, in the ancient Near East it was a common practice to make cakes (from the harvest, the bounty of the fertility goddess (in Canaan/Israel especially Astarte)) and eat them ceremonially to partake of the body of the Goddess, and therefore of divinity. Thus, perhaps Daniel's story was meant to be ironic, in that the body of the Goddess destroyed a creature originally associated with her. The story also represents something of a reversal of the Eden story, because here it is the snake-dragon who eats the (false and poisonous) sacred food at the urging of the pious man and dies.

49. See Roux 1992, p. 101.

50. For the story see Lambert and Millard 1969. Our telling of the story follows the emphases in Batto 1992, pp. 27-33. A similar Mesopotamian flood myth is contained in Tablet XI of the *Epic of Gilgamesh,* which seems to be derived from *Atrahasis.* Lambert and Millard 1969, p. 11. We refer to it as well where relevant.

51. Oden 1981, pp. 206-07. Similarly, in *Enuma Elish* the earlier generation of gods raised a clamor and disturbed the rest and sleep of Apsu and Tiamat. *ANET,* p. 61 (Tablet I, lines 37-40).

52. Generally, in ancient mythology loud noises are an attribute of and within the province of the divine. Leach 1974, pp. 95-97. That is what the *igigi* gods did when raising a din. For humans to do the same signifies not simply rebellion but, by emulation, their aspiration to be godlike. Oden 1981, pp. 207, 209.

53. Oden 1981, p. 204; Batto 1992, pp. 29-31; Blenkinsopp 2011, p. 13. See text in Lambert and Millard 1969, pp. 101-05. Unfortunately, the tablets at this important stage of the narrative are damaged and most of the regulations are not known. According to Batto's analysis of the regulations, apparently the original "primitive" humans could either live forever or for an extraordinarily long time (as they had been created in part from the blood of the chief of the rebel lower gods), because under the new regulations the new ordinary humans *(nisu)* were now destined to die a natural death, signifying a diminishment of the divine spirit and with it the din that had denied Enlil his sleep. Batto 1992, p. 31. This conclusion appears to go beyond the extant text pertaining to the new regulations, but it is consistent with the mythological idea in the story. Blenkinsopp interprets the new measures as including celibacy of dedicated priestesses, infant mortality and probably also disease and pestilence. Blenkinsopp 2011, p. 13. In the *Gilgamesh* version of the flood myth, Enlil went further and reconciled himself with humankind, blessed the hero (there Utnapishtim) and his wife, and even granted them immortality. *ANET,* p. 95 (Tablet XI, lines 190ff). It is not clear whether Enlil went so far in *Atrahasis*

because a number of lines are missing at that point in the text, but at least he relented and reconciled himself to mankind as modified.

54. See Batto 1992, pp. 29-31.

55. These acts of measureless blood revenge in retaliation for slight wounds are interpreted as another expansion of human wickedness. Yahweh taught only proportional retribution (eye for an eye, wound for wound, etc.) (Exod. 21:23-24). Most translations spell the offender's name Lamech (due to a pausal Qamets in the word's first appearance), but the correct spelling from the Hebrew is Lemech.

56. The *tehôm* is thought of as both upper (above the firmament) and nether, perhaps derived from the upper and lower halves of Tiamat. See Wensinck 1916, pp. 7-8, 10.

57. Analogously, in *Gilgamesh*, during the flood "all of mankind had returned to clay." *ANET*, p. 94 (Tablet XI, line 133).

58. Similarly, in *Gilgamesh* Enlil blessed Utnapishtim after the flood.

59. This imagery probably comes from *Enuma Elish*, where it had the same meaning. After vanquishing Tiamat, Marduk retired to his palace to rest and set his bow in the sky (in that case as a constellation), affirming his control over the cosmos and protection from chaos. *ANET*, p. 69; see Batto 1992, pp. 35, 87-88.

60. Oden 1981, p. 215; Skinner 1910, p. 169.

61. Batto 1992, p. 31.

62. Kugel 1997, pp. 118-20.

63. See Eliade 1991b.

64. Eliade 1991b, pp. 51-62; Eliade 1987, pp. 78-80, 104-07.

65. Indeed, it is possible that *Enuma Elish* was compiled, in the form that has come down to us, specifically in order to be used in the New Year's holiday ritual (which goes back to earlier times) rather than to be merely read. See Dalley 1989, pp. 231-32.

66. Eliade 1991b, p. 56.

67. Roux 1992, p. 98.

68. *ANET*, p. 72 (Tablet VII, lines 132-34).

69. E.g., Gunkel 2009, pp. 41-44; Gunkel 2006, pp. 78-111.

70. Kugel 1997, pp. 53-58.

71. Smith 2001, p. 38.

72. See description in Kramer 1972, pp. 40-42. Similarly, P later says that God uses the wind (same word, *rûah,* as in Genesis 1:2) to drive back the chaotic waters of Noah's flood in a symbolic new creation. Gen. 8:1. God later uses the same wind *(rûah)* to part the sea so that the Hebrews can escape Pharaoh's pursuing chariots (Exod. 14:21), and which the following Song of the Sea likens to God's right hand. Exod. 15:1-18. See also the preceding Exod. 14:30.

73. Neither Enlil nor Elohim created all things by utterance. Marduk had shown in a test that he was capable of creation by utterance (*ANET*, p. 60 (Tablet IV, lines 21-26)), but in the creation following his defeat of Tiamat he actually never did so, instead creating through artful acts.

74. Brandon 1963, p. 122; likewise Skinner 1910, p. 51.

75. This opening clause follows the typical style used at the beginning of *Enuma Elish* (quoted above) and other Mesopotamian myths that describe a state of affairs prior to the action (creation or otherwise) in the story. Albright 1967, pp. 91-92; Wallace 1985, p. 67.

76. See, e.g., Albright 1967. p. 185; Bloom and Rosenberg 1990, pp. 30-31.

77. As noted earlier, the Sumerian god of heaven was An, while the goddess of earth was Ki, leading to the Sumerian word for "universe," "an-ki" ("heaven-earth"), personified by the deities.

78. Rendsburg 1986, p. 13.

79. Gen. 2:5. Eden was the larger territory in which the garden was located, not the garden itself.

80. Haldar 1950, p. 35; Walton 2006, pp. 88-89; Hornung 1982, p. 180; Wensenick 1968, p. 53; Batto 1992, pp. 47-48; Eliade 1991b, p. 9; Talmon 1966. Batto notes that the Hebrew Bible represents such dry wasteland and unformed ocean as the monsters Behemoth and Leviathan respectively, representing chaos on earth and as water. Batto 1992, pp. 47-48. Similarly, P wrote that in the beginning there was only a "formless void." Gen. 1:2. The Hebrew is *tōhû wā-*

bōhû. Tōhû, meaning "formless" or "without form," is etymologically related to *tehôm,* the primeval deep. The desert, like the primordial waters, is portrayed as the refuge of monsters and demons in both the Bible, Talmon 1966, p. 43, and in ancient Near Eastern myths generally, Haldar 1950, p. 36. The idea of the desert as the realm of nonexistence was similar in Egypt. Hornung 1982, pp. 179-80.

81. E.g., Hamilton 1990, p. 103.

82. Thompson 1971, p. 199.

83. The text does not explicitly state that Yahweh caused these waters to spring forth, but it is hard to believe that J would consider Yahweh not to be in full control of these events.

84. Eliade 1991b, p. 10.

85. Talmon 1966, pp. 37, 44-49.

86. Talmon 1966, pp. 37, 47-48, 54.

87. See Num. 14:29-30; Deut. 1:39. We discuss the meaning of this in Chapter 9.

88. *NOAB,* p. 12. See injunctions in Lev. 18:6-30.

89. Batto 1992, pp. 128-52.

90. As discussed earlier, such noise is the prerogative of divinities, so defeating Jericho with a shout signifies divine intervention; a mere human shout could not have such effect.

91. See Friedman 1999, p. 295. We elaborate on this connection below. If Friedman is indeed correct that J's text runs all the way to David's kingship and Solomon's coronation, then this is only one of several literary "bookends" between the Eden story and the culmination of J's work that would give further meaning to the Eden story. We discuss these possibilities in Chapter 9.

92. See Lundbom 1999, pp. 356-63, describing the passage as "Chaos Revisited."

93. This "waste and void" is the same *tōhû wa-bōhû* that preceded the creation in P's account (Gen. 1:2).

94. Allen 1988, p. 14.

95. Allen 1988, p. 13.

96. CT, Spell 1130.

97. *Brhadaranyaka Upanishad,* 1.2.1-4 (First Brāhmana); 1.4.1-5 (Second Brāhmana); see discussion of Second Brāhmana in Campbell 1962, pp. 9-11.

98. *Brhadaranyaka Upanishad,* 1.4.5, as translated in Campbell 1962, p. 10.

99. See Campbell 1962, p. 11.

100. Westermann 1994, p. 119.

101. Cassuto 1998, p. 8.

102. P, in contrast, does not mention God creating man from some other substance; he merely recites that God made man in his own image, Gen. 1:26-27. This is a more elevated conception of humankind than in J.

103. Phillips 1984, p. 13.

104. Compare the quote of Christ from the Gospel of Thomas, epigraph to Chapter 3.

105. Campbell 1962, p. 10.

106. Although these stories are relevant here, we defer to our discussion of these stories to Chapter 9, where we discuss this position of J in more detail.

107. See Campbell 1962, p. 11.

108. Wilber 1996, p. 5. As the biblical scholar Michael Cooghan (2008) explained, "the word 'covenant' in Hebrew, *berit,* really means contract. It's used in the Bible to describe all sorts of secular agreements. It's used for treaties between one king and another. It's used for marriage. It's used in debt slavery, in which someone would pay off a debt by agreeing to work for someone."

109. Eliade and Sullivan 1995; Eliade 1991b, pp. 12-17 and sources cited on p. 12; Campbell 1974, pp. 184-207.

110. E.g., Roux 1992, p. 105 (as to the Sumerians).

111. Eliade and Sullivan 1995, p. 166.

112. Eliade 1991b, p. 16, giving many examples.

113. Thus, the symbolism of the Center as it relates to the cosmogony is often expressed in terms of embryology. As described in the Midrash, "The Holy One created the world like an

embryo. As the embryo proceeds from the navel onward, and from there it spread out in different directions." Wensinck 1916, p. 19; Eliade 1991b, p. 16.

114. Eliade and Sullivan 1995, pp. 167, 170.

115. Eliade 1987, p. 42.

116. Eliade 1987, pp. 79-81; see Eliade 1996, p. 378.

117. Neumann 1954, p. 39.

118. See description in Graves 1960, pp. 35-37.

119. Centers are inevitably localized. The multiplicity of sanctuaries symbolizing the Center, even within one civilization, is not considered a contradiction because what is being represented is sacred space, not earthly geometrical space. Sacred space is existential and can be established in the earthly realm at any number of places to allow humans to experience it. See Kramer 1979, p. 57; Eliade and Sullivan 1995, p. 166.

120. Eliade 1996, pp. 379-80; Eliade and Sullivan 1995, p. 169; also Lewis-Williams and Pearce 2005, pp. 88-122.

121. See generally Eliade 1991b.

122. Sometimes these two motifs are combined so that the sacred tree stands atop the cosmic mountain, or on a hill. See Holmberg 1964, pp. 349-60. See also Figure 21 depicting a seven-branched menorah-like tree atop a cosmic mountain.

123. Mount Tabor is the Old Testament site of the battle between Barak and the army of Jabin (Judges 4), and later traditionally the site of the Transfiguration of Jesus. Judges 9:37 refers to Mount Gerzim as the "navel *(tabbûr)* of the earth." The name Tabor may also be an adaptation of *tabbûr* and thus also signify navel. Burrows 1935, p. 51; Eliade 1991b, pp. 13-14.

124. Clark 1959, pp. 37-39.

125. Clifford points out that the term "cosmic mountain" may be misleading in the case of Mesopotamia because Mesopotamians did not consistently describe the Center as such nor are the various Mesopotamian Centers located in mountain geography. Clifford 1972, pp. 9-12 ("mountains simply were not central to the experience of the Mesopotamians"). This may be true in terms of actual geography, but we are dealing with mythology here. Green later adduced numerous examples of Eridu and its apsu and other locations being described using cosmic mountain imagery. Green 1975, pp. 162-63, 170, 176, 209. And as we have seen, a ziggurat, the central point of the temple complex and sanctuary, was conceived of as a cosmic mountain. Because the mountain imagery is widely used in Mesopotamian texts and in the scholarly literature, the term is retained here.

126. Westermann 1994, p. 217; Clifford 1972, p. 101; Jung 1983, pp. 278-85; Chetwynd 1998, p. 287.

127. *Vishnu Purana*, Book 2, Chapter 2, 119ff.

128. Dakpa 2005, pp. 5-6.

129. *Rig Veda*, 9.74; see also 1.62.6.

130. Same as Mt. Meru, the prefix *su* giving it the meaning "Great (or Wonderful) Meru." "Meru" itself is an allusion to the spinal column (the *meru-danda),* which in yogic practice locks into the axis mundi. (See Chapter 6.) This is why in Buddhist symbolism the Buddha could not turn his head but had to rotate his entire body "like an elephant"; his spinal column was fixed as the axis of the universe. See Hoffman 1999, p. 132; Eliade 2009, pp. 235-36.

131. Sadakata 1997, pp. 26-27.

132. Sadakata 1997, pp. 30-35.

133. Kramer 1963, pp. 284-85; see Roux 1992, p. 146. The extant texts do not describe or locate the Center where the four corners of these lands meet; as we shall see later in this chapter, Mesopotamians admitted of many Centers.

134. Roux 1992, pp. 156 (Narâm Sin of Akkad example: "King of the Four Regions"), 169 (Shulgi of Ur: "Four Quarters"). The Assyrian kings Tiglath-Pileser I and Esarhaddon called themselves king of all four rims of the earth, *ANET,* pp. 274-75, 289, while Shalmaneser III claimed he was the only power within the four rims of the earth, *ANET,* p. 276. Arad-Nirari II (810-783) said that he made the princes of the four rims of the earth submit to him, *ANET,* p. 281. Frankfort 1978, p. 228, notes that this title originally was applied to certain gods.

135. Müller 1964, p. 105; James 1966, p. 41.

136. i.50; v.70ff.

137. Holmberg 1964, p. 359.
138. Sturluson 2005, p. 15.
139. Markman and Markman 1994, p. 129.
140. Markman and Markman 1994, p. 91.
141. James 1966, p. 13.
142. 1.3.
143. *DFML,* p. 797.
144. Lewis-Williams and Pearce 2005, p. 89.
145. Holmberg 1964, p. 359.
146. Holmberg 1964, pp. 350, 358.
147. Holmberg 1964, p. 350. Likewise, the sacred tree of the Mordvins has a spring at its roots.
148. Markman and Markman 1994, pp. 19, 299, 416.
149. E.g., Homer, *Odyssey,* 6.41.
150. Haynes 2009, pp. 74, 189.
151. Dalley 1989, p. 99; see also *ANET,* p. 89.
152. See Lewis-Williams and Pearce 2005, p. 257, using the example of quartz, and discussing same in Australia, American west and Newgrange, Ireland. The authors note that the presence of glistening stones and crystals in mythology may also derive from entoptic phenomena (crystals may also induce altered states), again involving an experience with a different reality. Lewis-Williams and Pearce 2005, p. 259.
153. Eliade 1996, p. 271. This tree is discussed further in Chapter 6.
154. Langdon 1914, p. 5. See discussion in Chapter 3.
155. See Eliade 1996, p. 101.
156. Baring and Cashford 1993, p. 186.
157. Albright 1920, p. 264.
158. West 1997, p. 464.
159. James 1966, p. 140.
160. Kramer 1972, pp. xiii, 28-29.
161. Langdon 1914, pp. 44-45.
162. Kur originally meant "mountain," as evidenced by its Sumerian ideogram representing a mountain. But the word eventually acquired several meanings, one of them being "land." Sumer itself was described as *kur-gal* ("the great land"). Kur also became the name for the underworld (netherworld), as well as for a dragon-like monster living where the underworld meets the primeval waters. Kramer 1972, p. 76.
163. According to *The Feats and Exploits of Ninurta,* discussed earlier, after Ninurta performed his heroic feat of building a heap of stones to divert the waters from the Kur to the hitherto barren Tigris valley, his mother Ninmah ventured into the dangerous Kur, where Ninurta lived, to congratulate him, and in honor of her visit he named the mound of stones *hursag* ("mountain") and renamed his mother *Nin-hursag* ("queen (or lady) of the mountain"). Kramer 1979, pp. 38-39.
164. Lewis-Williams and Pearce 2005, pp. 106-10.
165. Translation at *COS* 1.157:512 (line 18). See Clifford 1994, p. 31; Clifford 1972, p. 14; Frankfort 1978, p. 217.
166. In Sumerian *ka-dingir-ra,* Akkadian *bâb-ilâni.* Roux 1992, p. 184; see also Gelb 1994, pp. 266-67. In fact, this was a common appellation that several cities in Mesopotamia held at one time or another, each with its Center. Dalley 2005, pp. 25-50. As noted above, the ancients saw no contradiction in having multiple Centers.
167. See Keinast 1979, p. 247 ("forest of life"); also Lenorrmant 1883, p. 85; Goblet d'Alviella 1894, p. 153.
168. See descriptions in Green 1975, pp. 182-85.
169. See Lewis-Williams and Pearce 2005, pp. 190, 192.
170. *ANET,* p. 265.
171. *ANET,* p. 43.
172. Kramer 1972, pp. xiv, 107; see also version in *COS* 1.170:547-50; Kramer 1952.
173. Van Seters 1992, p. 190.

174. Actually, in that region there are no mountains, but Eridu was built on a rise in the marshy lowland of the Euphrates delta, where it was believed the *apsu* rose up. At the time, the location did fit the archetypal image of the cosmic mountain rising from the waters like an island, because originally a course of the Euphrates swung just south of the site of Eridu before rejoining the northerly branch downstream of Ur, Green 1975, pp. 4-5, thus making the area an island that fit the archetype.

175. James 1966, p. 13.

176. Kramer 1972, p. 70.

177. Widengren 1951, pp. 13-19; Yarden 1971, p. 35.

178. Widengren 1951, p. 19.

179. *ANET,* p. 101; Langdon 1932, p. 176.

180. It was not merely a mythological paradise, however, but, like Eridu, was a historical place mentioned in Mesopotamian sources, which eventually gained mythological status. While specialists have debated its location (Bahrain being the most popular), no ruins have yet been discovered by archeologists.

181. Reproduced and translated in *ANET,* 37-41; see discussion in Kramer 1972, pp. 54-59. This is the title that the translator, Samuel Noah Kramer, gave it; we do not know what the Sumerians called it.

182. Probably a bird whose cry is a mark of death and desolation. *ANET,* p. 38.

183. *ANET,* p. 38. Brackets indicate lacunae in the text on the original tablets, and words have been filled in by the translator where feasible.

184. Kramer 1972, p. 59.

185. Kramer 1956, p. 144; also Kramer 1963, p. 149.

186. *ANET,* p. 44. In the Babylonian version of the flood story contained in the *Epic of Gilgamesh,* Dilmun is not mentioned and the place is described only as being "far away, at the mouth of the rivers," presumably the Tigris and Euphrates. *ANET,* p. 95.

187. *ANET,* p. 95. See above regarding meaning of the mouth of the rivers as the Center. It is associated with Eridu rather than Dilmun.

188. *ANET,* pp. 93-97.

189. E.g., Westermann 1984, p. 210.

190. The Hebrew word translated here as Eden is *'eden,* whereas the garden is in *ēden.* The consonants are the same and the vowels may have been pointed differently to distinguish the two. BDB, p. 727.

191. Another biblical mention is Ezekiel 27:23, which refers to Eden as a place among others in Mesopotamia without giving a precise location, but this could be Beth Eden. *NOAB,* p. 27. J in Genesis 4:16 refers to Cain being banished to "the land of Nod, east of Eden," but Nod simply means "wandering" and so is not helpful in determining what Eden means.

192. Roux 1992, p. 272.

193. Roux 1992, pp. 289, 297; *ABD* 6:344-45; Robertson 1903, p. 255; *NOAB,* p. 1107 (note to Amos 1:5). The capital city itself was on the east bank of the Euphrates and was called Til Barsip (or Barsib) now known as Tell Ahmar, in which case and Bit-Adini would have referred to the surrounding region. See Roux 1992, p. 297; *ABD* 6:345.

194. In Hebrew *'awen* means "iniquity," "idolatry," "offense," "or nothingness" (cf. chaos).

195. Amos 1:5. Damascus was the chief Aramaean state at the time. Kir refers to Niniveh.

196. Cf. Holter 1990, pp. 108, who notes that Isaiah 14:29 utilizes a serpent as a metaphor for the threat from Assyria.

197. E.g., Albright 1922, p. 26; Speiser 1964, p. 16; Haldar 1950, p. 57; Roux 1992, p. 104; Gunkel 1997, p. 7; see discussion in Westermann 1994, p. 210, citing the many scholars who have supported this theory.

198. *CAD* 4:33; Giovino 2007, p. 16.

199. Albright 1922, p. 26; Speiser 1964, p. 16; Haldar 1950.

200. The noun "mesopotamia" means a flat land between two rivers, from which Mesopotamia derives its name. It comes from the Greek *mesos* ("middle") and *potamos* ("river").

201. Gunkel 1997, p. 7.

202. See *CAD* 4:33.

203. See examples in *CAD* 16:138-47.

204. Indeed, even after J's time the Assyrian king Ashurbanipal (668-627) boasted that he knew Sumerian, which he would have learned from his scribes. Van der Toorn 2007, pp. 54-55. In the ancient Near East, Sumerian enjoyed prestige as the archaic language understood by educated classes, much like Greek and Latin in post-classical Europe and in America.

205. Carr 2005, pp. 47-58.

206. E.g., Millard 1984, pp. 103-04; Wallace 1992d, p. 281; see Westermann 1994, p. 210.

207. See Stordalen 2000, p. 260; Cassuto 1998, pp. 107-08; Gen. 13:10.

208. Cassuto 1998, pp. 107-08, citing, e.g., Ps. 36:9.

209. Greenfield 2001, pp. 220-21, 224; Millard 1984, p. 105; Mikaya 1981.

210. Since the initial consonants of the two words differ, Eden beginning with an Ayin and *ēd* with an Alef, a strict etymological relationship is not possible.

211. *NOAB*, p. 3; Speiser 1964, p. 16; see also dictionary entries in *EDHL*, p. 283; *DCH*, 6:465.

212. E.g., Cassuto 1998, p. 107. See discussion of issue in Westermann 1994, p. 210.

213. E.g., Skinner 1910, p. 57 ("There is no probability that the proper name was actually coined in this sense [i.e., of delight]."); see also Robertson 1938, p. 24 ("the use of the preposition 'in' seems definitely to rule out such theorizing" of Eden meaning "bliss").

214. A good, up-to-date scholarly summary of the various attempts can be found in Cline 2007, pp. 1-15.

215. E.g., Day 2002, pp. 29-30.

216. Thus, Westermann 1994, p. 216, who comments, "all attempts to explain or locate the sources of the four rivers geographically are ruled out," and Gunkel 1997, p. 9, who comments: "The geographical concepts behind these details are so immature that it is entirely improper to attempt to reconcile this system of rivers with actual geography. . . . The author's world view rests only partially in reality and partially in traditions whose origins cannot be sought at any rate, in actual geographical circumstances."

217. James 1966, p. 74.

218. Quoted in Cline 2007, p. 15.

219. Le Grice 2013, p. 6.

220. Campbell 2001, p. 50.

221. Westermann 1994, p. 216.

222. Although all of Genesis 2 is usually attributed to J, many commentators consider verses 10-14 an unnatural deviation from the main line of the story and thus the work of a later author or part of some other ancient text inserted by a later redactor, although it could have been a text at hand to J who inserted it (with edits). See Cassuto 1998, p. 114, and discussions of this issue in Westermann 1994, pp. 215-16. Professor Friedman believes that the passage is an authentic J text because it contains vocabulary and wordplay typical of J. See Friedman 2003, p. 36. For the reasons explained in Chapter 1, we use the text of the story as given, and our references to J here should be understood accordingly. Nevertheless, if verses 10-14 are an insertion by a later writer or editor who wanted to make the story less mythological, then J's original text can be seen as more purely mythological in the manner that we have described above.

223. This is the RSV translation except that in the first line we have substituted professor Speiser's "river rises in" for the RSV's "river flowed out." Speiser points out that the RSV gives the wrong tense, and that in this instance the river cannot flow out of Eden because the garden itself is in Eden. Speiser 1964, p. 14. As detailed below, this translation also fits the mythological symbolism.

224. Nevertheless, it is worth touching upon one point often debated by commentators. Given Eridu's status as perhaps the original Center in Mesopotamia located over the *apsu,* that location is sometimes mentioned as the prototype for the garden of Eden. Logically this may not seem to make sense, because the four rivers of Eden are said to originate in the garden there and we know that rivers flow from their sources downstream to the sea (the Tigris and Euphrates toward the Persian Gulf), which is why many investigators have sought to locate Eden in Turkey/Armenia at the headwaters of the Tigris and Euphrates. As explained by Professor Kramer and others, however, according to the understanding of the ancient Mesopotamians, it was the deep at the confluence of the Tigris, Euphrates and Persian Gulf which, with Enki's mediation, fed the Tigris and Euphrates and made the land fertile. The tidal waters from the

Gulf would regularly reverse the rivers' flow, as a result of which the Babylonians called the Gulf "the bitter river" (as opposed to "sweet" freshwater). Kramer 1944, p. 28; see also Clifford 1972, pp. 50-51, 100.

225. *NOAB,* pp. 3-4 nn. to Gen. 2:10-14; also Wallace 1985, p. 74, noting that most commentators agree that verse 10 is a further development of the motif of verse 6 rather than something different.

226. Clifford 1972, p. 100; Wallace 1985, p. 74; *NOAB,* pp. 3-4 (note to Gen. 2:10). Even if this water originated in Eden outside of the Garden, this body of water's symbolizing the Center is not lost, because it is still within the Garden where it divides into four, which junction in itself symbolizes the Center as in the many other examples discussed earlier in this chapter.

227. Speiser 1964, p. 16; *NOAB,* p. 3 (note to Gen. 2:6); Wallace 1985, p. 74. Scholars have long debated whether this water wet the ground by flowing over it or by rising into the air and falling down as mist, rain or entirely near the surface like a water sprinkler. This controversy derives in part from the unclear meaning of the Hebrew term in question (*ēd,* discussed in the next paragraph), which has been translated variously as "mist," "flow," "flood," "stream," "river," etc. See summary of the viewpoints in Westermann 1994, pp. 200-01. The water being a flow rather than a mist works better mythologically because this better renders the site as a Center, as in the Mesopotamian myths in which the Center was located above the *apsu* from which the water flowed onto the earth.

228. Westermann 1994, p. 201; Speiser 1967b; Speiser 1964, p. 16. Regarding *edû* see Gunkel 1997, pp. 5-6; Speiser 1964, p. 16 (saying is Sumerian loanword); *CAD* 4:35-36 (also saying is a Sumerian loanword).

229. Brandon 1963, p. 123 (Assyrian); Westermann 1994, p. 200 (Babylonian); Cassuto 1998, p. 104.

230. Speiser 1967b, p. 22.

231. Westermann 1994, p. 201; Wallace 1985, pp. 73-74; Albright 1967, pp. 92-95; Clifford 1972, pp. 100, 159; Cassuto 1998, p. 104. A text describing the river god's cosmogonic role, known as *An Address to the River of Creation,* together with commentary is set forth in King 1902, 1:128-29, 200-01.

232. *ANET,* p. 38.

233. Kramer 1963, pp. 284-85.

234. West 1997, p. 422.

235. Dalley 1989, p. 190.

236. Widengren 1951, p. 18.

237. See further descriptions in Wallace 1985, pp. 75-76; Albright 1967, pp. 95-96.

238. Wallace 1985, pp. 70-71.

239. Wallace 1985, p. 71.

240. Clifford 1972, p. 101. Thus, occasionally commentators will go further to argue that the creative author intended that Eden be nowhere. Radday 1982, p. 31 (noting the names Havila and Kush are "intentionally ambiguous, each being equally applicable to two countries lying at opposite ends of the ancient world").

241. Friedman 2003, p. 36.

242. Space prohibits a discussion of the Mesopotamian mythology describing assaults on the holy sanctuary by demons from the desert. They are described in Haldar 1950. There is biblical imagery of the same, described in Talmon 1966, pp. 42-44. E.g., Isa. 13:21-22; 34:11-14.

243. In Exodus 34:12, quoted at the beginning of Chapter 2, J portrayed Canaan and its inhabitants as a "snare" for the Hebrews to beware of and avoid.

244. See Clifford 1972, p. 102.

245. *ANET,* p. 133-41.

246. As Professor Charlesworth notes, this clashes with verse 29 only a few lines later setting Yahweh's temple (dwelling place) in Jerusalem. Apparently the author was eager to portray Yahweh as supplanting Baal on the mountain, much as in an earlier Canaanite myth Baal had acquired the place upon defeating Bashan. Charlesworth 2010, p. 430.

247. Stager 2000, p. 37.

248. See Skinner 1910, p. 328. Both the land of that episode (Gen. 22:2) and the Temple Mount (2 Chr. 3:1) are called Moriah. It is now generally agreed the Abraham and Isaac

episode probably occurred elsewhere. *ABD* 4:905. Most likely the name of the original location was suppressed in favor of Moriah so as to associate the episode with the Temple Mount. *ABD* 4:905; see Skinner 1910, pp. 328-29.

249. Clifford 1972, pp. 183-87. Not all such references are in the full mythological sense of a place linked to heaven, however.

250. Wallace 1985, p. 74; Clifford 1972, p. 160.

251. Eliade 1996, p. 377; Eliade 1991b, p. 15; Eliade 1987, p. 41.

252. See Clifford 1972, p. 179; Albright 1968, p. 149.

253. *ABD* 6:359-60 (entry for Temple, Jerusalem).

254. This same archetypical scheme was later adopted in Christian cathedrals. Their heights seemingly reached up to heaven and ceiling paintings portrayed heavenly scenes, while below the floors were crypts and often springs or wells evoking the netherworld. And much as the Temple was built above the Gihon spring, many cathedrals were built on top of springs or wells that were sacred in pagan times.

255. *ABD* 6:360 (entry for Temple, Jerusalem); Patai 1967, p. 132.

256. The concept was that, since the sanctuary had to represent the cosmos as a whole, the ziggurat or temple represented the mountain while the basin represented the *apsu*, thus uniting the three tiers. See Albright 1968, pp. 148-50; Kraus 1965, p. 187; see also Clifford 1972, p. 179. The Bronze Sea's basin was supported by four groups of oxen, which probably represented the four directions of the compass and the four seasons, Albright 1968, p. 150, which as discussed also is Center imagery.

257. Van Buren 1933, p. 10; Albright 1968, pp. 148-49; Kraus 1965, p. 187. Albright also mentions the temple's lavers as having this association. Albright 1968, p. 148.

258. See Wallace 1985, p. 74 regarding some elements.

259. See generally Stager 2000; Stordalen 2008.

260. In the mountainous region northeast of the Sea of Galilee now known as the Golan Heights.

261. Eliade 1991b, pp. 16-17; Eliade 1996, p. 375.

262. Neumann 1955, p. 253.

263. This of course recalls the Mesopotamians ascending the (usually) seven levels of the ziggurat in order to encounter the gods at the heavenly level, and also the gate of An's heavenly palace being guarded by the two tree gods Dumuzi and Ningizzida in the Adapa myth.

5. THE CREATION OF ADAM

1. We address the question whether this human was a man or an androgyne in Chapter 8.

2. Phipps 1976, pp. 271-72.

3. Hamilton 1990, p. 159; Ellington 1979, p. 202.

4. Westermann 1994, p. 338. The word appears twice in P's Genesis 1 creation account, but it is always translated simply as "man," in the sense of "mankind" or "humans/humanity" rather than a single individual, and it expressly includes women (Gen. 1:27-28).

5. E.g., Speiser 1964, pp. 14-15, 21-23 (not at all); Westermann 1994, pp. 181-83 (not at all); Friedman 2001 (not at all). In the original Hebrew text the word *ādām* appears 24 times in the Eden story (16 times in Genesis 2 and 8 in Genesis 3). Of these, the KJV translates it as the proper name Adam 10 times (6 times in Genesis 2 and 4 times in 3), while the RSV does so only once, in Genesis 3:1 (NRSV never translates as the proper name). Verses 2:20 and 3:17, 21 are the only cases in the story where the definite article is (apparently in the Masoretic Text) absent, in which case the proper name would be intended. Hamilton 1990, pp. 174, 194-95, 204, 208, thus consistently translates as "Adam" where the article appears and as "the man" where it does not. But it is possible that the Masoretic Text is simply not correct. *BHS* suggests "the man (or human)," and Westermann 1994, p. 264, says to read with the article. Speiser 1964, p. 18, says that the disappearance of the article in the Masoretic Text is an "anachronism." The Septuagint uses the definite article in all 3 instances. In our view, translating as "the man" or "the human" throughout is preferable because it is consistent with J's other usage in

the story. There is no apparent reason for the author to shift to a proper name and then resume with the definite article before the word.

6. Friedman 2001, p. 17. Technically the masculine noun *ādām* and the feminine *ădāmâ* are not etymologically related, so the wordplay is based simply on assonance (having a similar sound), as was so often the case with J. Plaut 1981, p. 29.

7. Earth and earthling do share common etymologies, so that the wordplay is not based simply on assonance as in J's usage. Homo and humus do not appear to be etymologically related.

8. Wallace 1992a, p. 62. The Hebrew word comes from the Semitic root *'dm*, which for example appears in both Ugaritic and Phoenician.

9. Wallace 1992a, p. 62.

10. Eliade 1978, pp. 9-11. This seems not to have been practiced in Israelite burials, which coincides with their not having a concept of afterlife or rebirth.

11. Wallace 1992a, p. 62.

12. Adam is also the name of a town by the east bank of the Jordan, just north of where Joshua and the Israelites were said to cross into Canaan (Josh. 3:16, probably also in Hos. 6:7 ("at Adam they transgressed the covenant; there they dealt faithlessly with me"), now Damia in Jordan. A town called Adamah, supposedly fortified, was located just east of the Sea of Chinnereth (later Galilee) (Josh. 19:36). Another town called Admah, located near the Dead Sea (Gen. 10:19; 14:28), was said to be destroyed by Yahweh along with Sodom and Gomorrah for the same sins, its land then becoming infertile. Deut. 29:22; Hos. 11:8; *ABD* 1:73. No one has been able to trace the origins and meanings of these town names or to link them with the Eden story. In Hosea 6:7 *ādām* cannot refer to the first human Adam because he did not stand in a covenant relationship with Yahweh. Interpreting it to refer as a collective to humans in general as transgressors would make more sense (e.g., "as people are wont they trans-gressed . . .") , but the word appears to be the antecedent to the following locative "there," in which case it should have a geographical meaning. However, nowhere in the Hebrew Bible does any transgression occur in the town of Adam. As a result of problems with all alternatives, the meaning is unresolved. At least the appearances of such names show that *ādām* was current in biblical Palestine.

13. Gelb 1954, pp. 210-11, 222; see Hamilton 1990, p. 253, also p. 160. One meaning of *adamu* is an important, noble person. *CAD* 1:95.

14. Regarding this kingly role in relation to the creation generally, see Ricoeur 1967, pp. 191-98.

15. There is also a possible Phoenician connection. Albright suggests that Adam could be derived from the Phoenician name for Adonis at Byblos, *Damu,* noting that the god was paired with a goddess named *Hut,* whose name is associated with life. Albright 1920, pp. 282, 284.

16. Brandon 1963, p. 124; Eliade 1978, p. 165.

17. Cassuto 1998, p. 106; Brandon 1963, p. 124 (also illustration p. 61). Khnum used four different types of clay or mud: from Egypt, the Mediterranean coast of Africa west of Egypt, the mountainous desert east of the Nile, and Africa south of Egypt, accounting for four different peoples of those regions.

18. Speiser 1964, pp. 14, 16.

19. E.g., 2 Sam. 17:28; Isa. 29:16 and Jer. 18:2, 4, 11; see Hamilton 1990, p. 156; Skinner 1910, p. 56.

20. Skinner 1910, p. 56; see Green 1975, pp. 170-74.

21. Gunkel 1997, pp. 6, 23; Campbell 1964, p. 29.

22. Eliade 1996, p. 248.

23. Eliade 1996, p. 247; *OCD,* "Gaea," p. 452.

24. Eliade 1987, pp. 141-44.

25. Eliade 1987, p. 143.

26. Westermann 1994, pp. 203-04. See the many examples described in Frazer 1923, pp. 3-11, 14.

27. Werner 1994, pp. 81-82.

28. See also generally Plato, *Menexenus,* 237a-238b.

29. Pausanias, *Description of Greece,* 8.1.4; see Graves 1960, p. 27.

30. Homer, *Iliad.*, IV.8. This story, like that of Eden, is an example of patriarchal mythology that is still derivative of Mother Goddess mythology. In it, Alalcomeneus is said to have been born before the moon (i.e., to antedate the Goddess, the Moon and moon goddess being later creations of Zeus), to have been the tutor of Athena (meaning that the goddess is incapable of wisdom without male tutoring), and then marries a woman named Athenais (obviously a distorted name of the goddess) much like Zeus did to absorb the Goddess's functions. See Graves 1960, p. 37; Kerényi 1951, pp. 122, 209, 211-12.

31. Hesiod, *Works and Days*, 109-119.

32. Interestingly, Cadmus was said to be from Canaan (Phoenicia). Herodotus, *Hist.*, 2.49. He was the son of Agenor the king of Tyre, and was sent to Greece by his parents to find and escort home his sister Europa after she had been abducted from Phoenicia by Zeus.

33. Hyginus, *Fabulae*, 178; Apollodorus, *Library*, 3.4.1; Pausanias, *Description of Greece*, 9.10.1; Ovid, *Metamorphoses*, III, 1-137; IV, 563-603.

34. Graves 1960, p. 34.

35. Graves 1960, p. 34.

36. Clifford 1994, p. 28. Significantly, in the later *Atrahasis* flood myth, before resorting to sending a flood Enlil sends a drought to make the earth barren in part by not letting the water flow up from the deep any more. *ANET*, pp. 104-06. This essentially reverses the creation process in which the waters of the deep had fertilized the previously barren land. In the Bible flood story, Yahweh wreaks his punishment directly by the flood, which is brought on not only by rain but by opening up the fountains of the deep, and is ended by shutting them. Gen. 7:11; 8:2.

37. Clifford 1994, pp. 14-16, 22-32.

38. Clifford 1994, pp. 29-30.

39. Clifford 1994, pp. 30-22.

40. Kramer 1972, p. 70.

41. Kramer 1972, pp. 69-72.

42. The story of creation of humans is sometimes separated from the flood portion of *Atrahasis* and considered a separate myth, as indeed it appears to have been simply appended and has no close relationship to the rest of the story. See *ANET* pp. 99-10 vs. 104-06 where they are separated. But other scholarly works treat the creation as part of the story, e.g., Clifford 1994, pp. 74-82, and that approach is taken here as well as it reflects our approach to J's story: The Mesopotamian mythmaking process usually involves piecing together portions of earlier myths in new ways to suit the author's purposes, a tradition that J followed as well.

43. Dalley 1989, p. 15.

44. Dalley 1989, p. 15.

45. *ANET*, pp. 74, 94.

46. Gunkel 1997, p. 6.

47. P, on the other hand, apparently following the above Akkadian tradition, considers blood the animating force of life. See Gen. 9:4-6; Westermann 1994, p. 207.

48. Frankfort 1961, p. 22.

49. Parkinson 1997, p. 39.

50. Kramer 1979, pp. 41-42; see also Kramer 1972, pp. 72-73.

51. Wright 2000, pp. 85-88; Westermann 1994, pp. 206-07; Vaux 1997, p. 56; Eliade 1978, p. 165 n. 6.

52. Vaux 1997, p. 56; e.g., Num. 6.6; Lev. 21:11.

53. Brandon 1963, p. 124.

54. Westermann 1994, p. 228.

55. See *ANET*, p. 44; *COS* 1.158:515.

56. *ANET*, p. 96 (Tablet XI, line 279).

57. Wright 2000, p. 85.

58. This distinction between the Egyptian and Semitic views is noted in Frankfort 1978, p. 65. Egyptian thought and mythology on the divine aspects of humans is elaborate. Each individual has various aspects of divinity, including the *ka, ba,* and *akh,* the first existing in both life and death and the latter two arising only at death. A full discussion of these concepts is beyond the scope of this book, but a useful discussion is at Frankfort 1978, pp. 61-78. That

living humans have an element of divinity in them is implied from the myth that they were created from the tears of Ra (see, e.g., CT 1130), meaning that they were literally formed from and partake of divinity. See Quirke 2008.

59. *NOAB,* p. 3 (note to Gen. 2:7); Wright 2000, pp. 87-88, 191; Ricoeur 1967, pp. 279-305. Even in Greece, however, the concept of *psyche* did not match the later European concept of a soul. See Bremmer 1983; Snell 1953. Space limitations preclude a detailed discussion of the evolution of the concept of the soul in the ancient Near East and Western Civilization.

60. See Wright 2000, pp. 86-87.

61. Brandon 1963, pp. 121-22.

62. We discuss this issue in relation to Eve in Chapter 8.

63. P in his creation story painted arguably a happier picture. There Elohim blessed the first humans (male and female) upon their creation and told them to be fruitful and multiply. Humans may fill all of the earth and have dominion over it and its creatures. And almost as if to contradict and correct J, P stressed that humans may eat any plant: "Behold, I have given you every plant yielding seed which is upon the face of all the earth, and every tree with seed in its fruit; you shall have them for food." (Gen 1:29) Elohim imposes no prohibitions.

64. Wallace 1985, pp. 69-70.

65. Dalley 1989, p. 9.

66. Dalley 1989, pp. 10-13.

67. The Anunnaki were a group of 50 higher gods created by An said to have descended from heaven to earth (including the underworld). Initially they performed labor there, and later became involved in human affairs.

68. Kramer 1972, p. 53.

69. The Dulkug was their birthplace and residence, in heaven atop their cosmic mountain.

70. Kramer 1972, p. 73.

71. Baring and Cashford 1993, pp. 198-99.

72. The Sumerian King List says that his father was a gardener. His autobiographical Legend of Sargon says that his mother was a priestess and that he did not know his father. *ANET,* p. 119; *COS* 1.133:461. Since children of priestesses were deemed virgin-born, Baring and Cashford 1993, p. 697, this may explain his claim not to know his father and also his famous story of being cast into the river in a basket like Moses.

73. *ANET,* p. 119; *COS* 1.133:461.

74. *ANET,* p. 40.

75. Campbell 1962, pp. 6-7.

76. Batto 1992, pp. 49-53.

77. Batto 1992, pp. 50-52.

78. Batto 1992, p. 50.

79. The question of Yahweh having cursed the ground (which at first may seems incompatible with humans being destined for agriculture) is taken up in Chapter 9. In short, humans brought that curse upon themselves and it was their burden to bear until after the flood, when it was lifted (Gen. 8:21 (J)).

80. Westermann 1994, pp. 220-21.

81. Batto 1992, pp. 202-03.

82. Cf. Eliade 1987, p. 31.

83. Gen. 5:29, as translated in Friedman 2003, p. 41.

84. As we have seen, in the *Atrahasis* myth the gods imposed consequences to the humans' revolt, but the revolt was not simply about seeking divine knowledge but was broader, amounting to a strike.

85. Wright 2000, p. 85.

6. THE SACRED TREES, THE CHERUBIM,
AND THE FLAMING SWORD

1. 10.81.4.
2. II.1.
3. Jung 1983, pp. 287-88.
4. Eliade 1987, p. 148.
5. Goblet d'Alviella 1894, pp. 171.
6. Goblet d'Alviella 1894, pp. 170-71.
7. See generally James 1966, pp. 32-33; Eliade 1987, pp. 34-36; Butterworth 1970, p. 37. It is 1 Peter 2:24 that equates the cross and the tree.
8. J's text refers to only one tree being in the middle of the garden, which has led to confusion over which of the trees is intended and to much discussion among commentators. If one views the symbolism from the mythological perspective, however, we see that this is a somewhat misplaced question because the symbolism of the Center requires both to be at or near the middle of the garden, so they would be in close proximity to each other and it does not matter which is closer to the exact center. Further, in any event, as discussed below, the two trees ultimately are aspects of the one Cosmic Tree. When understood from this perspective, we can understand why J (and redactors) did not need to be precise.
9. Philpot 1897, p. 142.
10. Eliade 1991a, p. 44. For an expanded discussion see Eliade 1996, pp. 269-78.
11. Crossley-Holland 1980, pp. xx-xxiii.
12. E.g., the *Etana* myth and Nonnos's tree of Tyre, both discussed below.
13. Holmberg 1964, pp. 333-35 (examples from Siberian and Central Asian peoples); Lewis-Williams and Pearce 2005, p. 63 (Navajos with eagle at top of pole representing World Tree, around which the Sun Dance was performed).
14. Butterworth 1970, pp. 3, 4, 6, 17, 57, 70-72; see also Cook 1988, p. 9.
15. Haynes 2009, p. 66.
16. Philpot 1897, pp. 110, 117.
17. For an Egyptian example, see BD, vignette to Chapter 64.
18. Haynes 2009, pp. 66, 71.
19. The Proto-Indo-European word for "oak" was *dorw,* which also meant "firm," "strong," or "enduring." That is also the source of our words "tree," "truth," "trust," as well as "Druid" (which means "seer of oaks"). In Sanskrit, which like English is derived from Proto-Indo-European, the word for "tree" (derived from *dorw*) was *daru,* while the word for the Pole Star was the related word *dhruva,* which like *dorw* means "the abiding, the firm, or fixed one." The descendants of this word for oak are prominently represented in Indo-European languages from Europe to India. Powell 1982, p. 67-69.
20. Philpot 1897, p. 128. Columns always support something, whereas pillars may either do the same or be freestanding like obelisks (which carry a similar meaning).
21. E.g., PT Utterance 217.
22. 1.52-54.
23. See likewise Job 9:6 (Yahweh makes pillars of earth tremble); Job 26:11 (pillars of heaven quake in response to Yahweh); Psalm 75:3 (when earth and its people quake, Yahweh holds its pillars firm).
24. In their original form, pillars, whether free standing or as supports in buildings, were wooden; stone was used once humans learned how to fashion them in stone. Evans 1901, p. 88; James 1966, pp. 32, 34.
25. Evans 1901, p. 88.
26. Burrows 1935, p. 48.
27. As explained in Chapter 4, in Mesopotamia temples were conceived of as standing over the *apsu* and therefore were connected to the underworld. Similarly, temples or other holy sanctuaries elsewhere (and later Christian cathedrals) were often located on or by sacred springs, clefts, other entry points underground such as at Delphi and Dodona, or on points thought to be of telluric significance which afforded a connection to the underworld, such as

Chartres Cathedral, which was built on the site of a Druid sanctuary. Charpentier 1972, pp. 34-35.

28. This symbolism was continued in Christian cathedrals and churches, both by their height and through depictions of heavenly scenes on their ceilings.

29. Clifford 1972, p. 179; Albright 1968, pp. 144-48.

30. See examples in Giovino 2007, Figs. 51-54.

31. Meehan 1995, pp. 37-41.

32. Wright 1970, p. 80.

33. Butterworth 1970, pp. 3, 48; Eliade 1992, p. 269; Holmberg 1964, p. 349.

34. Butterworth 1970, p. 48. An image similar to Fig. 21 is in Frankfort 1965, pl. 17.h.

35. Philpot 1897, p. 130.

36. Butterworth 1970, p. 36.

37. Butterworth 1970, pp. 26, 33, 37. Thus, accounts of out-of-body or near-death experiences often describe the person, while in the altered state, as being connected to one's earthly body by a silver-colored or luminescent string or rope linked to (usually) the navel, as an umbilical.

38. Butterworth 1970, p. 37.

39. Philpot 1897, p. 77.

40. See, e.g., the photographs of ancient coins from Tyre, Cyprus, Byblos, Emesa, and Seleucia Pieria in Butterworth 1970, plates II and III.

41. *Pythian Ode* 4.74. Actually, it is not entirely clear that Pindar was referring to the Delphic oracle in particular, Butterworth 1970, p. 35, but the point applies regardless of which sanctuary's *omphalos* is in question.

42. Holmberg 1964, p. 350; Haynes 2009, pp. 71-72.

43. Crossley-Holland 1980, p. xxiii.

44. Quoted in Holmberg 1964, p. 350.

45. James 1966, pp. 29-30.

46. Philpot 1897, p. 93.

47. Apollonios Rhodios, *Argonautica,* I.526-27, IV.582-83; see Jones 1995, p. 428.

48. Sturlson 2005, p. 24.

49. See generally Eliade 1992, pp. 184-89.

50. Eliade 1992, pp. 125-27.

51. Powell 1982, p. 76; Eliade 1992, pp. 123-26; Eliade 1994, p. 17.

52. *Taittirīya Samhīta,* I.7.9 and VI.6.4.2 (quoted in Eliade 1991a, p. 45).

53. 616B.

54. Gen. 28:10-22, using translation in Friedman 2003, p. 77 but spelling out "Yahweh" rather than using YHWH.

55. James 1966, p. 83.

56. Butterworth 1970, p. 4.

57. Eliade 1992, pp. 482-84.

58. Haynes 2009, p. 74; Wensinck 1921, pp. 3, 8. As discussed in Chapter 4, in association with the sacred tree as the essential feature of the Center.

59. Wensinck 1921, p. 3 (as to life); Biedermann 1994, pp. 204-06 (divinity, spirit, and additional meanings).

60. Neumann 1954, p. 6; see generally Cassirer 1955, pp. 94-104.

61. Exod. 13:21-22, 24; Num. 14:14. Notably, all such references are in J passages. See Friedman 2003.

62. Yarden 1971.

63. Both *benu* and *benben* are related to the Egyptian verb *weben,* "to shine."

64. See generally Clark 1959, pp. 245-49; Quirke 1992, pp. 26-27; Wilkinson 1992, pp. 90-91, 99.

65. Nonnos, *Dionysiaca,* XL:468-500. See discussion in Butterworth 1970, pp. 85-86. As similar example, perhaps inspired by the Tyrian tree, appears in the sacred golden olive tree of Pygmalion (legendary king of Tyre and brother of Dido) growing in the temple of Heracles at Gades (Cadiz) near the pillars of Heracles, as described in Philostratus's *Life of Apollonius of*

Tyana,(5.5), which has fruit of emerald. Here the Mesopotamian imagery of sacred trees has spread beyond the Levant to the Atlantic. Wensinck 1921, p. 19.

66. Govinda 1969, p. 216.

67. Elijah fits the classical description of a shaman, and at his earthly end he did what shamans do, ascend to heaven (2 Kings 2:11).

68. The word "yoga" is derived from the Sanskrit root *"yuj,"* which means to "yoke" or "unite." Flood 1996, p. 94. Our English words yoke and yoga come from the same root.

69. Quoted in Eliade 1991a, p. 45 (emphasis added).

70. Coleridge 1972, p. 71.

71. Butterworth 1970, pp. 80-82.

72. VIII.713-29.

73. Cook 1988, pp. 13-16; James 1966, pp. 30-31; Hall 1974, p. 307. See also discussion of goddesses and trees in Chapter 3.

74. Holmberg 1964, p. 359; see also Butterworth 1970, p. 12.

75. Later examples are in St. Mark's in Venice (Philpot 1897, frontispiece) and Celtic art, where the tree grows from a pot symbolizing the womb. The pot was often shaped from two triangles (cf. Star of David) symbolizing the unity of heaven and earth, and of the male and female principles. Meehan 1995, pp. 39, 73ff.

76. Eliade 1992, p. 272.

77. James 1966, p. 98. See examples in Frankfort 1965, pl. xx.b, g, k; pl. xxv.c, d; pl. xxxi.c; pl. xliii.c.

78. James 1966, p. 30.

79. Butterworth 1970, pl. XXII(b).

80. Pausanias, *Description of Greece,* 1.27.2.

81. Image at Philpot 1897, p. 88, and Goblet d'Alviella 1894, pp. 143-44. The inscription does not indicate which goddess, and it is not possible to determine this from the tree image.

82. The image apparently is that described in Pausanias, *Description of Greece,* 8.13.2; see also. 3.22.12.

83. 9.22.2.

84. Ovid, *Metamorphoses,* 13.634-35 (mentioning only Apollo, but Artemis was his twin so it must incorporate both). Other ancient sources have her clasping or leaning on one palm tree while giving birth to them.

85. As in Plutarch's *Life of Romulus.*

86. Dodona means "dove," which symbolizes the Goddess. The three priestesses who attended and interpreted the oracle were known as doves. The oak was cut down by Christians ca. 391 CE.

87. The name of the original goddess associated with the holy site predates Greek history and is not known to us, but in Greek times the goddess Dione (meaning simply "Goddess") was essentially the same as the earth goddess Rhea, and was associated with it. Later Aphrodite, the daughter of Zeus and Dione, was associated with the oracle.

88. Harrison 1991, p. 333. Actually it is not clear whether Zeus married the Pelasgian goddess who then became known as Dione, or whether Dione was already his wife and she was substituted for the Pelasgian goddess.

89. In some accounts her father, further reflecting Olympianization.

90. As later told in Ovid, *Metamorphoses,* 1.556-57.

91. James 1966, pp. 129-30; Clark 1959, p. 67.

92. See Keel 1997, pp. 191-92; Frankfort 1970, p. 318. The god is probably either the sun-god Ra being born from a lotus blossom or Horus being born in the marshes. The latter seems more likely as Horus had been hidden in the marshes by Isis to protect him from his enemies, whereas guardian figures in the birth of Ra (the creator god at the creation) would be out of context. See Frankfort 1970, p. 318 & n. 155.

93. Quirke 1992, pp. 48-50.

94. PT, Utterance 470 (§ 916), p. 159.

95. James 1966, p. 40.

96. Malek 1999, pp. 102, 217, 357.

97. Faulkner 1962, p. 55.

98. Wilkinson 1992, p. 117.

99. Wilkinson 1992, p. 117.

100. The details of the ceremony are described in James 1966, pp. 39-40.

101. James 1966, p. 40.

102. Budge 1973, 2:199-200; see BD, Ch. 155; PT, Utterance 321.

103. PT, Utterance 321.

104. Cook 1988, p. 14. See hieroglyph for *djed* meaning "stable, enduring" in Faulkner 1962, p. 325.

105. The Egyptian word for sycamore, *nehat,* which was also a general word for tree, connotes shelter and protection. Faulkner 1962, p. 135; Quirke 1992, p. 50.

106. PT, Utterance 470 (§ 916), p. 159.

107. BD, Chapter 109; see Lurker 1974, p. 119.

108. Wensinck 1921, p. 5.

109. See examples in Parpola 1993, pp. 162, 200-02.

110. Parpola 1993, pp. 165-68.

111. Respectively the sun god Shamash and Dumuzi/Tammuz, thus symbolizing the sky and underworld to which the sacred tree is a connection.

112. Widengren 1951, pp. 5-6, except last line from Green 1975, p. 188. For a discussion of the Sumerian vs. the Akkadian versions and the translation issues, see Langdon 1928.

113. As translated in Sayce 1897, p. 238. Parentheses have been removed for simplicity.

114. James 1966, p. 13; Sayce 1987, p. 238 n. 4.

115. Widengren 1951, p. 6; James 1966, p. 13.

116. James 1966, p. 13.

117. Sayce 1897, p. 238 n. 1, 240 n. 1.

118. Widengren 1951, p. 9.

119. Widengren 1951, pp. 9-10.

120. Widengren 1951, p. 10.

121. See the discussions in Chapters 3 and 4. Regarding Inanna's sacred garden see Widengren 1951, p. 9 n. 2, p. 10 n. 3.

122. *ANET,* p. 91 (Tablet X(i), line 49; X(iii), line 7).

123. *ANET,* p. 88 (Tablet IX(i), lines 6-7; (iii), lines 3-5). At this point in the story Gilgamesh does not know about the flood story, which we later learn was known only to the gods and Utnapishtim; Gilgamesh knows only that Utnapishtim has achieved immortality.

124. As translated in Albright 1920, p. 259. Compare translation in *ANET,* p. 89 (Tablet IX(v), lines 48-51):

> *The carnelian bears its fruit;*
> *It is hung with vines good to look at.*
> *The lapis bears foliage;*
> *It, too, bears fruit lush to behold.*

125. Wensinck 1921, pp. 3-4.

126. *ANET,* p. 90 (Tablet X(ii), lines 1-14). These lines are remarkably similar to those in Ecclesiastes 9:7-10 and seem to have formed the basis for them. Seow 1997, pp. 305-06; Hooke 1963, pp. 53-54.

127. *ANET,* p. 96 (Tablet XI, lines 269-76).

128. *ANET,* p. 96 (Tablet XI, line 296).

129. See text in *COS* 1.131:453-57; Dalley 1989, pp. 189-202, and description in Hooke 1963, pp. 59-60.

130. Widengren 1951, p. 33 (his translation). The key term is translated variously as "plant of life" by Widengren, "grass of life" in Jacobsen 1976, p. 59, or simply "food of life" in *ANET,* pp. 54-56; Kramer 1972, p. 86; Wolkstein and Kramer 1983, p. 54. In all cases is clear enough that a plant is being eaten.

131. See text in *ANET,* pp. 37-41 and descriptions in Kramer 1972, pp. 54-59, and James 1966, pp. 69-70.

132. Dalley 1989, p. 182.

133. Dalley 1989, pp. 184-87.

134. Evans 1901, pp. 7-8, 44 (Fig. 25), 84-87 (Figs. 56-57, 59). Evans notes that in the Druid religion sacred trees and the menhir stone pillars were similarly associated.

135. Betancourt 1977, pp. 17-22. Regarding Mycenae see Persson 1942, pp. 131-32; see also examples in Evans 1901, p. 41 (Fig. 23), 56-57 (Figs. 32-33). In Egypt such pillars were found not in the building's structure but in painted depictions of columns. Betancourt 1977, p. 19. Variations also appeared in Assyria. See Giovino 2007, Figs. 67-68, 69b, 70 and compare Figs. 85-86.

136. Betancourt 1977, pp. 17-18, 21.

137. Betancourt 1977, pp. 39-40. As discussed in Chapter 2, however, the biblical vision of Solomon's splendor may have been appropriated from that of the Omrides.

138. Keel and Uehlinger 1998, pp. 26-31; Negbi 1976, nos. 1661, 1664, 1685, 1688, 1691, 1692; Hestrin 1987b, pp. 216-18.

139. It was not essential that the high place be at the top of the hill or mountain; it is sufficient to be close by. Thus, for example, Shechem (like Delphi) is situated in a mountain pass, by Mt. Gerizim, deemed by Canaanites and early Israelites a cosmic mountain and the center of the earth. A slightly lower elevation also facilitates a location near to a spring or other water source representing the waters of life, and is more practical for the people of the town to access. Still, many biblical passages refer to the high places being on hills and mountains, e.g., Deut. 12:2; 1 Kings 11:7; 14:23; 2 Kings 16:4; 17:10; 2 Chr. 28:4; Isa. 30:25; 57:7; Jer. 2:20; 3:6; 17:2-3; Ezek. 7:13; 20:28; Hos. 4:13.

140. See Wright 1970, pp. 76-79.

141. 1 Sam. 9:19-22 (feasting in hall at high place); 1 Kings 12:31 ("houses"); 13:18-22 (house, at which Yahweh appears). A number of references to "shrines" at high places (2 Kings 17:29, 32; 23:19) may refer to buildings, but this is not certain.

142. Albertz 1994, p. 85; Hadley 2000, p. 74; Ringgren 1966, p. 24.

143. Moreh means "oracle giver," "teacher" or "instruction," *HBD,* p. 703, so the tree is the "Oak of Oracles."

144. In those days it was acceptable to worship Yahweh at the high places because Jerusalem was not the capital and there was no Temple or priesthood. Later, under Hezekiah and then Josiah, the high places became objectionable on the separate ground that Yahweh should be worshipped only in Jerusalem at the Temple, which required destroying all high places. In J's time there was no such centralization, so for him the location of worship in itself was not a problem. Thus, in Exodus 34:11-16 discussed at the outset of Chapter 2, J makes no mention of high places. Rather, J's concern was doctrinal: It was the other deities, cult practices, and cult objects of other deities at the high places that were objectionable.

145. The asherah, of course, in itself presents a problem because by definition it embodies only Asherah. J opposed asherahs and their veneration since they would detract from Yahweh being the sole legitimate repository of divinity. A compromise solution discussed in Chapter 3 seems to have been to accept asherahs as mediating Yahweh's divinity. Although such compromise essentially was an appropriation by Yahweh of Asherah's powers, this would not have been good enough for J, who called for asherahs to be entirely eliminated.

146. For example, Abraham set up altars by trees at Shechem (Gen. 12:6-7) and Hebron (13:18), Jacob at Bethel (Gen. 35:7, presumably by the pillar), and Gideon by the oak at Ophrah (Judg. 6:24, 26).

147. E.g., Deut. 7:5; 12:3; 16:21; Judg. 6:25-30; the passages in Kings and Chronicles describing the reigns of Hezekiah and Josiah, and the writings of various prophets including Isaiah, Jeremiah, Ezekiel and Hosea.

148. Deut. 12:2-3; 1 Kings 14:23; 2 Kings 16:4; 17:10; 2 Chr. 28:4; Isa. 57:5; Jer. 2:20; 3:6, 13; 17:2; Ezek. 6:13; 17:24; 20:28.

149. Deut 12:2; 1 Kings. 14:15; 23; 15:13; 16:33; 18:19; 2 Kings 13:6; 17:10, 16; 18:4; 21:3, 7; 23:4, 6-7, 14-15; 2 Chr. 14:3; 15:6; 17:6; 19:3; 24:18; 31:1; 33:3, 19; 34:3-4, 7; Isa. 17:8; 27:9; Jer. 17:2; Mic. 5:14.

150. 1 Kings 14:23; 2 Kings 17:10; Jer. 17:2.

151. 2 Kings 17:10.

152. Deut. 12; 2; 1 Kings 14:23; 2 Kings 17:10; 23:14; 2 Chr. 14:3; 31:1; Jer. 2:27.

153. Deut. 16:22.

154. 2 Chr. 24:18; 33:19; 34:3-4.
155. Isa. 57:4-7; Jer. 3:6, 9, 13.
156. Isa. 57:4-5.
157. Jer. 2:20; 3:6, 9, 13.
158. Hos. 14:12; Hab. 2:19; see Smith 2002, p. 116.
159. Mic. 5:11-13.
160. 2 Kings 16:4; 2 Chr. 28:4; Ezek. 16:13; 20:28.
161. Hos. 4:13 ("make offerings upon the hills, under oak, poplar, and terebinth"); Ezek. 20:28 (drink offerings).
162. 2 Chr. 28:4; Ezek. 20:28; Hos. 4:13 ("sacrifice on the tops of mountains"). These are apparently animal rather than child sacrifices, as child sacrifice is not mentioned in connection with the sacred trees or high places, and when it is mentioned it is at other places, such as under clefts of rocks. Isa. 57:5.
163. Amos 8:14.
164. In the case of J, Exod. 34:13 as discussed in Chapter 2. Other verses demanding this include Deut. 7:5; 12:3; Judg. 2:2. To like effect are 1 Kings 19:10; 2 Kings 11:18; 2 Chr. 14:3, 5; 30:14; 31:1; 32:12; 33:15; 34:4-5, 7; Isa. 27:9; 36:7; Ezek. 6:4, 6; Hos. 10:2; 12:11; Amos 3:14.
165. Asherahs: (Deut. 16:21; Judg. 6:25, 28, 30); sacred trees: (Josh. 24:26-27) (sacred oak in sanctuary, where altar must have stood).
166. Deut. 16:21. Sometimes an asherah is said to stand next to an altar of Baal. Judg. 6:25-30. Since Baal's consort was Anat, here there is perhaps a simple confusion of the deities, or else a purposeful attempt to associate Asherah with Baal, both to discredit her generally and as a way to disassociate her from Yahweh.
167. See examples discussed in Dever 2005, pp. 135-67 (at Dan, Hazor, Shechem and other sites). For further details regarding Shechem, see Wright 1964; regarding Dan, see Biran 1994.
168. Greenberg 1983, p. 168 (translating it as the "statue of outrage"); Patai 1985, pp. 51-52.
169. Widengren 1951, pp. 20-32.
170. Pedersen 1991, 2:421-22, 737-42. The booths made of leafy branches were not particular to the Israelite festival but were characteristics of similar festivals in ancient Greece, Ptolemaic Egypt, and Rome. Pedersen 1991, 2:740-41. See also Snaith 1947, p. 12.
171. James 1958, p. 68; Pedersen 1991, 2:421, 737-38; Moor 1972, 1:28-29; Hooke 1938, pp. 57-58; Vaux 1997, p. 501.
172. Pedersen 1991, 2:418-19; see generally Moor 1972.
173. See generally Heskett and Butler 2012, pp. 17-77; McGovern 2003, pp. 210-38.
174. *HBD*, pp. 1193-94.
175. Moor 1972, 1:29.
176. Heskett and Butler 2012, p. 11, also p. 7; Skinner 1910, p. 183.
177. Moor 1972, 1:6, 14-15. Such right was obviously incompatible with Yahwism, but it is likely that the sons of the priest Eli, Hophni and Pinehas, oversaw this ceremony. Moor 1972, 1:15.
178. Pedersen 1991, 2:416-17, 420-21.
179. Moor 1972, 1:29.
180. See generally Gaster 1961, pp. 34-41 and discussion in Chapter 4.
181. Gaster 1961, p. 34; Vaux 1997, pp. 508-09; Wright 1992, p. 73; Hooke 1938, pp. 51-54.
182. Eliade 1978, p. 159; Vaux 1978, p. 150; see also Hooke 1938, p. 55, and Hooke 1961, p. 36, suggesting that Psalm 104, which among other things celebrates Yahweh gaining control over the primeval waters of chaos, was sung at this festival. It generally celebrates the fertility bestowed on the land by Yahweh, including "wine to gladden the heard of man." 104:15.
183. E.g., Hooke 1961, p. 36.
184. E.g., Walton 2009, pp. 87-92.
185. It is possible that Cain and Abel's offerings were on the occasion of this new year, which again reflects J's awareness of the centrality of this holiday. Snaith 1947, pp. 12-13.
186. Num. 13:17-24. The name Eschol may be that of a wine god. Heskett and Butler 2012, pp. 28-29.

187. Many scholars consider the text to be confused and believe that Canaan himself was the original figure.

188. Discussed in Chapter 9.

189. Skinner 1910, pp. 183, 185; Ellis 1968, pp. 140-41, 168, 199.

190. Hiebert 1996, p. 48.

191. E.g., Isa. 28-30; also Judg. 9:27.

192. See survey of opinions on this point in Mettinger 2007, pp. 5-11.

193. Engnell 1955, p. 110.

194. Pedersen 1969; Joines 1975, pp. 5-7; Joines 1974, pp. 22-23.

195. Gunkel 1997, p. 8; Wensinck 1921, p. 14; Mettinger 2007, p. 5; Walton 2012, p. 2. See generally Pedersen 1969.

196. Gunkel 1997, p. 8.

197. *ANET*, p. 75.

198. Gunkel 1997, p. 8; Cirlot 1971, pp. 348-49. Childs 1962, p. 695, says that "Tree of Truth" should be abandoned as mistranslation, but without explaining why or proposing an alternative, but be that as it may we still will have an example of paired sacred trees with different names and meanings. Our point is not that "truth" here is somehow equated with "knowledge"; the idea in the Mesopotamian example is that the god represented by the tree is loyal and faithful (i.e., truthful).

199. Wensinck 1921, pp. 14-15, Figs. 14, 18.

200. BD, Chapter 109.

201. See Eliade 1992, p. 271 for summary of various religious ideas implied in the symbolism of the World Tree.

202. Cook 1988, p. 24. In this example the duality is a pair of opposites (life and death) rather than complimentary aspects of divinity as in Eden, but this still illustrates duality represented by two trees or two parts of the same tree. Moreover, J also casts the two trees respectively as images of life vs. death.

203. Cirlot 1971, pp. 347-49.

204. The apple emerged as the most typical fruit of the transgression, but in older traditions each Christian nation chose its own kind of plant to represent the tree and fruit, generally in line with local flora. Thus Greece chose the fig and orange trees, Burgundy and Champagne chose the grape vine, and Ile de France chose the cherry tree. The eventually dominant tradition of the apple tree originated in Picardy. Goblet d'Alviella 1894, p. 134.

205. Charlesworth 2010, p. 308.

206. Jones 1995, p. 19.

207. Yarden 1971, p. 40; Philo, *Moses II,* 186.

208. Philo, *Moses II,* 181.

209. Yarden 1971, p. 41.

210. Yarden 1971, pp. 40-41. Yarden mentions that this symbolism of life and immortality "explains the word's subsequent use in Aramaic, where Luz stands for both the almond and the 'indestructible' bone in the spinal column (*os coccyx*) which, as was believed, will serve as the nucleus for the resurrection of the body (*os resurrectionis*)." Yarden 1971, p. 41.

211. Yarden 1971, pp. 40-41.

212. Only the word *lûz* refers to almond trees, and only in Gen. 30:37.

213. Gunkel 1997, p. 38 and sources cited.

214. Skinner 1910, p. 59. This assumes, however, that J wanted to be faithful to the geography, which may not be the case because he was most concerned with religious practices in Palestine.

215. Goblet d'Alviella 1894, p. 154.

216. Dever 2005, p. 148. Dever also discusses similar pomegranate scepter heads from Phoenicia, through which they could have entered Palestine.

217. 36:2, 40:1, 3, 41:2, in Charlesworth 1983, 2:272, 274

218. Exod. 27:20; Lev. 24:2.

219. Such uses combined with their ability to grow in the local terrain is one reason why, as seen in Chapter 2, the olive and olive oil industry became important in Israel and eventually

Judah as well, with the result that olive trees were ubiquitous. There was scarcely a part of life in Palestine that they did not touch. *HBD,* p. 782.

220. Thus demonstrating that the tree was living and excluding the possibility that it was dead debris of the flood. Westermann 1994, pp. 448-49; Gunkel 1997, p. 65.

221. E.g., 2 Kings 19:29; Isa. 37:30, 65:21; Song of Sol. 8:11-12; Hos. 10:1; Zech. 8:12.

222. McGovern 2003, p. 212, citing Lutz 1922, who makes this argument at p. 25. The Hebrew word in question, *debaš,* can mean both bee honey and grape syrup or even date syrup. *HALOT* 1:212-13; BDB, p. 185; Holladay 1988, p. 68. Most wines from Syria and Palestine were sweet and thus like syrup. Lutz 1922, p. 26. Also, wine was also fortified with honey, since sugar was unknown there at the time.

223. Heskett and Butler 2012, pp. 7, 11.

224. See 3:6 through 4:17, in Charlesworth 1983, 1:666-68.

225. Goblet d'Alviella 1894, p. 134.

226. See Wensinck 1921, pp. 3-4, 23; Goblet d'Alviella 1894, p. 141.

227. Hamilton 1990, p. 210; Patai 1990, p. 69; Westermann 1994, p. 274; Albright 1920, p. 282.

228. Patai 1990, p. 69; Westerrnann 1994, p. 274; Speiser 1964, p. 24.

229. Barton 1934, p. 144.

230. Skinner 1910, p. 90; Albright 1920, p. 282.

231. E.g., 2 Sam. 22:11; Ps. 18:9-10; also Ezek. 10:18-19.

232. Westermann 1994, p. 274 (Mesopotamia); Gunkel 1997, p. 24 (Egypt, Persia, Mesopotamia, Greece); Cross 1973, pp. 35-36 (Mediterranean); Frankfort 1965, p. 205 (Mesopotamia, Persia, Palestine, Syria).

233. E.g., in Ps. 80:2; 99:1; see Cross 1973, p. 69.

234. The cherubim on the Ark apparently had a single face, whereas Ezekiel's temple cherubim had two faces (Ezek. 41:18) and those in his vision had four (10:14). The nature of the faces ranged from human to bovine, aquiline and leonine; sometimes it is a quadruped, sometimes a biped. See *HBD,* p. 175.

235. See Westermann 1994, p. 275. Indeed, Professor Westermann observed that since expulsion of the couple from the Garden was in itself definitive, the cherubim are rather linked to the tree of life itself, in order to associate it with Yahweh. The narrative of the expulsion is really complete with verse 23. Verse 24 containing the reference to the cherubim at its beginning duplicates the action in verse 23 of Yahweh in driving the couple from the Garden, leading some commentators to regard these as doublets reflecting independent sources that J melded together. Westermann 1994, p. 274; Skinner 1910, pp. 88-89.

236. Friedman 1997, pp. 43, 47, 72-73; Keel 1978, pp. 167-70; Frese 2012.

237. Vaux 1997, pp. 299-300; Frese 2012.

238. Here meaning the northern kingdom of Israel. See Chapter 1, note 44.

239. The Hebrew text has "him" rather than "you." The RSV translates as "you" apparently because Yahweh is addressing Israel (Ephraim).

240. Arguably this is an allusion to Eve's transgression, since the Hebrew noun used for the rib from which she was created *(ṭēlā)* is virtually identical to that for "stumbling" *(ṭelā),* wordplay which J used in the Eden story. Hosea, however, uses the verb *kāšal.*

241. Day 1980, p. 314 (and sources cited).

242. Day 1980.

243. Just as in English the word "fruit" may connote the consequences of human actions, the Hebrew word *perî* does likewise. BDB, p. 826; *HALOT* 3:968. Thus, a double meaning may be intended.

244. See discussions in Hadley 2000, pp. 75-76 and sources cited, and in Day 1980, pp. 314-15. Scholars who have favored such or a similar emended translation include Graham and May 1936, p. 112 ("I am his Anath and his Asherah") and Cornelius 1988, pp. 46, 63 ("I am his goddess and his asherah").

245. Day 1980, p. 315.

246. Hadley 2000, p. 76.

247. Butterworth 1970, p. 13.

248. See Friedman 1997, pp. 46-48, 70-74. See generally discussion in Propp 2006, pp. 574-83.
249. E.g., Westermann 1994, p. 274; Skinner 1910, p. 89.
250. Gunkel 1997, pp. 24-25.
251. Hadley 2000, p. 175.
252. Albright 1920, p. 282.
253. Albright 1920, p. 283.
254. Rad 1961, p. 95; Gunkel 1997, p. 25; Westermann 1994, p. 275; Skinner 1910, p. 89.
255. E.g., Exod. 9:23-24; 19:16; 20:18; 2 Sam. 22:13-15; Job 36:30, 32; 37:3, 11.
256. Biedermann 1994, p. 336.
257. See Cirlot 1971, p. 324.
258. See generally Cirlot 1971, pp. 324-25; Chetwynd 1998, p. 388; Ronnberg 2010, p. 492.
259. See generally Yarden 1971; Widengren 1951, pp. 64-67; Butterworth 1970, pp. 41-42; Cook 1988, p. 20; Wensinck 1921, p. 29; see also Gunkel 2006, p. 191.
260. Yarden 1971, p. 40.
261. Yarden 1971, pp. 39-40.

7. THE SERPENT WHOSE POWERS YAHWEH USURPED

1. Soggin 1975, pp. 95, 99; Charlesworth 2010, p. 70.
2. Soggin 1975, p. 99.
3. MacCulloch 1962, p. 403.
4. Charlesworth 2010, pp. 196-268, 299.
5. See also Fromm 1951, pp. 15-18, who similarly argues that symbols become universal when they connect with common emotional experiences in our minds, creating an intrinsic relationship between the symbol and the feeling or idea it represents.
6. See Neumann 1954, pp. 320-35.
7. Fromm 1951, p. 19; Campbell 1988, pp. 51-52. See also discussion and sources cited in Introduction.
8. Neumann 1954, p. 323.
9. Charlesworth 2010, p. 328.
10. Charlesworth 2010, pp. 234-35; Cirlot 1971, p. 285; Clark 1959, pp. 240-45.
11. Daniélou 1991, pp. 150-51.
12. Dimmitt and van Buitenen 1978, p. 17.
13. *Vishnu Purana* 2.5.1-27, in Dimmitt and Van Buitenen 1978, p. 49.
14. Spell 321, 14-17, quoted in Clark 1959, p. 51; for another translation, see Faulkner 1973, p. 249.
15. Utterance 510 (Section 1146), as quoted and translated in Clark 1959, p. 50; for another translation, see Faulkner 1969, p. 186.
16. Dimmitt and van Buitenen 1978, p. 26.
17. Dimmitt and van Buitenen 1978, p. 61.
18. *Codex Laud,* folio 8.
19. Clark 1959, pp. 50-52; Neumann 1954, p. 238..
20. Charlesworth 2010, p. 235; Joines 1974, p. 20. The symbolism of being drawn through Apep's body may represent the sloughing of the serpent's skin, which symbolizes renewal, occurring at dawn.
21. Clark 1959, pp. 167-71.
22. Lurker 1974, p. 108.
23. Clark 1959, p. 55.
24. Some commentators identify her as Nammu, whereas others believe that is not possible to determine which goddess this is or suggest Nintu, the birth goddess. Mundkur 1983, p. 185. Similarly, some identify the heads as those of serpents, but others only call them more general-

ly reptilian. See Mundkur 1983, pp. 185-86. Mythologically, however, no reptile but a serpent would seem to fit. Other reptiles such as lizards are obscure in Mesopotamian mythology (and iconography), Mundkur 1983, p. 187, whereas the archeological context of these statues being found in graves fits the scheme of a chthonic goddess taking back the deceased's spirit in the form of a serpent while at the same time suggesting a later rebirth, particularly if the goddess is Nintu.

25. Frothingham 1916, pp. 197-98; Ward 1910, p. 377 (Figs. 18a-18c; goddess identified as Ishtar).

26. Clark 1959, pp. 239, 259.

27. Cooper 1992, p. 215.

28. Campbell 2001, p. 18.

29. Anthes 1961, p. 30.

30. As translated in Charlesworth 2010, p. 139.

31. This idea is encouraged by the serpent's linear form lacking limbs, ears, eyelids, or other protrubances, and simple sleek appearance, suggesting a primeval simplicity, before the appearance of multiplicity during the creation.

32. Regarding such symbolism of the circle see Cirlot 1971, pp. 46-48; Biedermann 1994, pp. 69-71. In ancient Egypt the symbol (and hieroglyph) for totality/eternity was a string/rope tied to form a circle. Clark 1959, p. 258; Biederman 1994, p. 70. Called a shen ring, the symbol was used in jewelry as an amulet to ward off illness and other misfortune.

33. Clark 1959, p. 258; Biedermann 1994, p. 70; Wilkinson 1992, p. 193.

34. Charlesworth 2010, p. 241.

35. Crossley-Holland 1980, pp. xxi, 33, 193; Biedermann 1994, p. 310.

36. Campbell 1988, p. 37.

37. Campbell 1989, p. 254.

38. This symbolism is reinforced by typically depicting Nuwa holding a compass (representing the circle and heaven derived from the sun and moon disks) and Fu Xi a square (representing the geometric square and the earth). Similar is William Blake's painting *The Ancient of Days*, depicting God with a compass drawing a circle on the face of the deep as in Proverbs 8:25.

39. Van Buren 1945, p. 40. Chetwynd believes that one or two serpents twined on a pole represents the union of the male-female opposites, the pole being male and the serpent female. Chetwynd 1998, p. 366.

40. See Frothingham 1916 and the many illustrations therein, most of which were taken from in Ward 1910.

41. Frothingham 1916. Some scholars, however, believe that it derives from Egypt. E.g., Joines 1974, p. 86.

42. Chetwynd 1998, p. 366.

43. Pinch 2002, p. 58.

44. Merism is the expression of totality by reference to two opposites or extreme poles, by implication including everything in between, such as in the expressions "A to Z" or "the alpha and omega."

45. Liesegang 1955, p. 229.

46. Liesegang 1955, pp. 228-29. Charlesworth 2010 contains the most extensive analysis yet of Christ being portrayed as a serpent in this manner, this being the main theme of the book.

47. Pinch 2002, pp. 89-90.

48. Liesegang 1955, pp. 221-22.

49. Harrison 1991, pp. 6-7.

50. Charlesworth 2010, pp. 247-48.

51. Hermes is the source of the word "hermaphrodite." The name of the son of Hermes and Aphrodite is Hermaphroditus, a combination of his parents' names.

52. Harrison 1927, p. 297; Frothingham 1916, p. 179.

53. See Baring and Cashford 1993, p. 497.

54. Albright 1920, p. 279.

55. Wolkstein and Kramer 1983, pp. 6-8.

56. Wolkstein and Kramer 1983, p. 9.

57. Dalley 1989, p. 191; *ANET,* pp. 114-15.

58. Howey 1955, pp. 109-11.

59. Charlesworth 2010, p. 97; Murison 1905, p. 113; Jung 1956, p. 259.

60. Charlesworth 2010, p. 229.

61. Charlesworth 2010, pp. 69, 97-100, 111-12, 120.

62. Cooper 1992, p. 214 (using Greek example).

63. Charlesworth 2010, p. 242.

64. Murison 1905, p. 113.

65. The idea is that the deceased must have a material body, which according to ancient thinking meant an animal body so as to retain some element of life. It was natural to view serpents, being chthonic creatures, as the conduit (dwelling place) of the departed soul. Murison 1905, p. 113.

66. Biedermann 1994, p. 311; Cooper 1992, p. 214. Thus, the Greek Erinyes were spirits of the dead who remained about the house to avenge any injury or insult. Murison 1905, p. 114.

67. Harrison 1927, p. 424.

68. Harrison 1927, pp. 396-406.

69. *ANET,* p. 96.

70. Charlesworth 2010, pp. 49-50.

71. Charlesworth 2010, p. 225.

72. There is no evidence, at least in Palestine, of serpents having a direct phallic significance, so directly equating serpents and the phallus would be unwarranted. Joines 1968, p. 250; Albright 1920, p. 277; Coote 1972, p. 108. See also generally Mundkur 1983, pp. 172-208. The association in question is focused more on the fertility/life aspect than on the phallus itself or copulation. See Neumann 1955, pp. 143-45.

73. Mundkur 1983, pp. 172-208.

74. Apollodorus, *Library,* III.4.1.

75. Cook 1988, p. 115, Documentary Illustration 55.

76. Charlesworth 2010, p. 222; Coote 1972; Young 1977; Pardee 1978.

77. Coote 1972, p. 91.

78. Wilson 2001, p. 52. In this text the word for serpent is *nāḥāš,* the same as in the Eden story. The word for "marriage price" *(itnn)* in the text later developed into the Hebrew word used to mean "harlot's wage" in reference to cultic prostitution *('etnan).* The use of the two words together in this text illustrates *ittn's* and most likely *'etnan's* original association with serpent symbolism. Wilson 2001, pp. 53, 58-60.

79. Murison 1905, p. 114. Castiglioni 1942, p. 1164; Joines 1974, p. 86; Wilson 2001, p. 75 ("Present here [in Num. 21:6-9] is the ancient notion of the multiple potentialities of the deity, namely, that incurring death, life and healing are mutually inclusive powers."); Soggin 1975, p. 99.

80. Meaning "health" and from whom our word "hygiene" is derived.

81. Harrison 1991, p. 342.

82. Kerényi 1959, p. 50.

83. Harrison 1991, pp. 19, 341. In the culminating book of Ovid's *Metamorphoses* (15:660-62), Asclepius (Roman spelling of the god) changes himself into a serpent.

84. In the Hebrew Bible, when people experience such ecstatic flights and prophesize, it is said that the Spirit of God comes upon the person. E.g., 1 Sam. 19:23 (Saul's ecstatic flight in which he prophesized, naked).

85. We discuss the connection of serpents and divination in Israel and in the Eden story below.

86. Graves 1960, p. 625.

87. Graves 1960, pp. 233, 372, 456.

88. Charlesworth 2010, pp. 246-47.

89. See generally the discussion in Charlesworth 2010, pp. 197-218, on which the short summary below is based.

90. Speiser 1935, pls. LVII, 26, 27, LVIII, 32, 33, 38.

91. Goff 1963, p. 129 and fig. 514; see also Speiser 1935, pl. LVIII, 41 (serpents rising from and descending to earth on each side of copulating couple).

92. Goff 1963, p. 37 and fig. 197.
93. Goff 1963, p. 143 and fig. 321; Speiser 1935, pls. LXXV.208, LXXVI.7, 12, 13.
94. Charlesworth 2010, pp. 69, 97, 111-12, 120.
95. Speiser 1935, pp. 111-12, pl. L.2, 14; Speiser 1929, pp. 36, 94 fig. 133.
96. Discussed in Mundkur 1983, pp. 188-89.
97. For other examples, see Babylonian clay tablet ca. 2000 depicted in Charlesworth 2010, p. 273, and Goff, fig. 703.
98. Cf. Langdon 1914, pp. 3-4, 116.
99. Langdon 1914, pp. 114-22; Albright 1920, p. 273.
100. E.g., Frankfort 1965, pls. 12.c, 26.c., 27.j; Frothingham 1916, figs. 10-13.
101. Ward 1910, p. 138 (fig. 388).
102. E.g., Smith 1880, pp. 88-89.
103. Campbell 1964, p. 14; Ward 1910, p. 138.
104. See Elizabeth Williams-Forte's annotation to the seal in Wolkstein and Kramer 1983, p. 178.
105. Langdon 1914, p. 9.
106. Langdon 1914, pp. 87, 114-22.
107. E.g., Mundkur 1983, p. 186-87 & fig. 86.c, (Ishtar); Grant 1929b, fig. 3 (figure of Hathor-like goddess with serpent draped over shoulder, hop and thigh); Johnson 1988, p. 139 (figure of Canaanite goddess holding 2 serpents draped around her body, ca. 1200); Mundkur 1983, p. 21 (figurine from Eneolithic Maikop in southern Russia depicting a serpent draped across the front of a female figure from her shoulder to her hip) and 23 (depicting a statue from 3rd millennium Turkmenia showing a serpent crawling on the front of a woman's thigh and hip up to her navel); and Charlesworth 2010, p. 81 (showing 1st century CE Carmel Aphrodite with a serpent on Aphrodite's thigh). See also Figure 4.
108. Neumann 1955, pp. 143-45.
109. Langdon 1914, p. 5. Thus, Jacobsen notes that originally Dumuzi was "little more than the élan vital of new life in nature, vegetable and animal, a will and power in it that brings it about," and in describing Inanna's early role as "Lady of the date clusters," observes that Inanna embodied the power (numen) of the date storehouse itself, whereas her consort represents the date harvest stored within it. Jacobsen 1976, pp. 26, 36, 135.
110. Langdon 1914, pp. 114-20.
111. Frankfort 1965, p. 111; Langdon 1914, pp. 2, 9.
112. Langdon 1914, p. 5.
113. Frothingham 1916, pp. 183-87. We do not mean to say that the symbol of entwined serpents is exclusively linked with Ningiszida or any other deity. This was an older symbol that appeared in objects long before king Gudea. Van Buren 1945, pp. 40-41. As such, it is a general symbol that was adopted in association with Ningiszida.
114. Joines 1974, p. 115; Langdon 1914, pp. 7-8.
115. Joines 1974, p. 115.
116. Frothingham 1916, pp. 187-88.
117. Frothingham 1916.
118. Joines 1974, p. 47; Howley 1955, p. 29; see also Budge 1969, 2:377.
119. Pinch 2002, p. 199. For consistency we retain the Egyptian term Apep rather than the Greek Apophis.
120. Joines 1974, p. 46 (as to creative wisdom).
121. See Clark 1959, pp. 169-71.
122. Joines 1974, p. 112.
123. Clark 1959, p. 242; Budge 1969, 2:376.
124. Quirke 1992, p. 32; see also Clark 1959, p. 242. Similarly, likewise, according to Langdon, the serpent god in Sumer was a fire god. Langdon 1914, p. 120.
125. Clark 1959, p. 242.
126. The "Book of the Dead" is the term coined in the 19th century for a collection of spells known to the Egyptians as "Spells for Going Forth by Day." Pinch 2002, p. 26. Egyptologists generally regard these texts as spells designed to enable the elite dead to achieve and maintain a full afterlife, but other commentators have observed that the principles at work here could

apply in the context of initiation scenarios in which the candidate symbolically dies and is "reborn" as a new, enlightened human being.

127. In many spiritual traditions, this spot is known as the third eye, an opening to and center of the divine force.

128. Budge 1969, 1:443-44.

129. Budge 1969, 2:377.

130. E.g., Johnson 1988, p. 133 (showing example from Tutankhamen's tomb).

131. Clark 1959, p. 243.

132. Quoted in Clark 1959, pp. 243-44. Hike is the primeval power from which magic is derived, manifested as the god of magic. Clark 1959, p. 281.

133. PT Utterance 378 (§ 664), as quoted in Clark 1959, p. 243.

134. Clark 1959, p. 243.

135. Clark 1959, pp. 244-45.

136. Parkinson 1997, pp. 92-98. For a thoughtful interpretation of the story as being more than a folk tale but as involving mythical elements and the conferral of esoteric knowledge, see Baines 1990.

137. Joines 1974, p. 99.

138. Charlesworth 2010, pp. 72-73.

139. See the discussion of Qedesh/Qudshu in Chapter 3.

140. Space does not allow us to describe this interesting goddess. There may indeed have been some cross-influence between Crete and Syro-Palestine in connection with the goddesses. The similar way in which both the Cretan snake goddess and Qedesh/Qudshu hold serpents at their sides is particularly intriguing. For a general description of the Cretan goddess, see Baring and Cashford 1993, pp. 106-44.

141. Joines 1974, pp. 95, 99. This Mesopotamian or Western Asian influence includes that of the Hyksos, who originated there.

142. Charlesworth 2010, p. 70; Macalister 1912, p. 399.

143. Joines 1974, p. 121; Bodenheimer 1960, p. 186 (calling her Shanan); see also Charlesworth 2010, p. 74 (not specifying her by name); Albright 1920, p. 274 (saying she could be Sagan or Serag).

144. Charlesworth 2010, p. 68; Macalister 1912, pl. 221.9.

145. Charlesworth 2010, p. 68; Macalister 1912, pl. 221.10. This item unfortunately cannot be accurately dated because it was found in nonstratified waste. Joines 1968, p. 247, and Pritchard 1943, p. 7 (no. 11), conclude that serpents are represented, partly because the same motif is on the cult standard from Hazor discussed immediately below, which clearly depicts serpents; Charlesworth 2010, p. 68, is not so sure.

146. Charlesworth 2010, pp. 69-70.

147. Charlesworth 2010, pp. 65, 501; Pritchard 1943, p. 27 (no. 240).

148. Albright 1938, pp. 42-43, 117-18 (pls. 21-22); Albright 1928, pp. 3 (illustration), 6; Pritchard 1943, p. 27 (no. 238) and fig. 22; Charlesworth 2010, pp. 65, 501.

149. Grant 1929a, p. 216 & Registry 444; Grant 1929b, pp. 2, 10 (fig 3); see Joines 1974, p. 66; Joines 1968, p. 247; Charlesworth 2010, p. 121.

150. Rowe 1940, pls. 33:7; 34:42, 61, 62; Charlesworth 2010, p. 74; see also similar Early Bronze IV finds in Oren 1973, figs. 41:31, 51:9, 25.

151. Charlesworth 2010, p. 67.

152. Charlesworth 2010, p. 66.

153. Charlesworth 2010, p. 79.

154. Rowe 1940, plate 45A:5; Charlesworth 2010, p. 74.

155. Rowe 1940, plate 42A:5; Charlesworth 2010, p. 74. These date from the reign of Amenhotep III, early to mid 14th century.

156. Keel and Uehlinger 1998, p. 30 (illustration 15c).

157. Keel and Uehlinger 1998, p. 30 (illustration 14a).

158. Keel and Uehlinger 1998, pp. 68-69 (illustrations 74, 75a-b).

159. Charlesworth 2010, p. 73.

160. Some specialists including the excavator think the triangular openings represent the female pubic triangle (i.e., life, fertility). Joines 1974, p. 120. As described in Chapter 3, pubic

triangles associated with the Goddess appear on pottery (such as the Lachish goblet) and in gold amulets, themselves often triangular in shape and having the same symbolism. See Keel and Uehlinger 1998, p. 55. On the Hazor cult standard mentioned above, the goddess herself is wearing a triangular necklace. Joines 1968, p. 247. In such cases the triangle naturalistically points downward, whereas in the case of this cult stand the triangles point upward, which arguably casts doubt on the idea. Similar contemporary cylinder stands from Egypt depicted in Rowe 1940, p. 53, however, have triangular apertures on a single stand pointing both up and down, while other stands depict female figures with their triangles prominently displayed. See likewise stands from Tepe Gawra depicted in Speiser 1935, pls. XXVIII.a.4; XXX; LXXIV, figs. 200, 205.

161. In light of the interpretation below, it is possible that the intent is to represent the serpents as they rise inside and are about to emerge from the apertures, like the doves.

162. Bodenheimer 1960, p. 213; Rowe 1940, pp. 53. Astarte/Ashtoreth was also known in Beth-Shan as Antit, and like other Canaanite/Palestinian goddesses was invoked as "the queen of heaven, the mistress of all the gods." Rowe 1940, p. 34.

163. Rowe 1940, pp. 31, 34, 53; Joines 1974, pp. 119-20.

164. Joines 1974, p. 120.

165. Joines 1974, p. 120.

166. Joines 1974, p. 120.

167. Joines 1968, pp. 249-50. It is pictured in *ANEP*, pp. 195, 320 (no. 591).

168. *ANEP*, pp. 195, 320 (no. 590); Rowe 1940, pl. 17, no. 1.

169. Rowe 1940, p. 52.

170. Adonis was the Phoenician dying and rising god equivalent to Tammuz. He later became a Greek god.

171. See Rowe 1940, p. 52.

172. Frazer 1963, 5: 236-37.

173. Rowe 1940, p. 52.

174. Rothenberg 1972b, p. 154; Charlesworth 2010, pp. 71-73; see also Rothenberg 1988, p. 302 and fig. 16.1-3 (3 different objects).

175. Aharoni 1974; Charlesworth 2010, pp. 79-80.

176. Howey 1955, p. 14.

177. *Amores*, 2.13.

178. Charlesworth 2010, pp. 70-71.

179. Charlesworth 2010, pp. 70-71.

180. Biran 1994, pp. 152-53; Charlesworth 2010, p. 77.

181. Charlesworth 2010, p. 68.

182. Charlesworth 2010, p. 65

183. Macalister 1912, p. 399 (fig. 488); Charlesworth 2010, p. 67.

184. Joines 1974, p. 246, noting that she personally examined one of them, but apparently they remain unpublished. Charlesworth does not mention them.

185. Charlesworth 2010, p. 74.

186. Rothenberg 1972a, p. 151. The tent shrine is depicted on page 152.

187. Rothenberg 1972a, pp. 150-51.

188. E.g., Charlesworth 2010, p. 72.

189. Rothenberg 1972a, p. 152. A Midianite rather than Egyptian origin and use for this serpent is reinforced by the fact that the ophidian pottery found at Timna (see below) is Midianite. Rothenberg 1988, p. 93, figs 16.2-3. Further, as already mentioned, there is no evidence of bronze serpents being used in Egyptian cult practice. This conclusion fits with the biblical associations of bronze serpents and Midianites with Moses and the Hebrews.

190. Charlesworth 2010, pp. 66,

191. Charlesworth 2010, p. 241 and illustrations on pp. 101-04.

192. See examples in Goff 1963, p. 143 and fig. 321; Speiser 1935, pls. LXXV, 208; LXXVI, 7, 12, 13.

193. Joines 1974, pp. 109-10.

194. Regarding Dan see Biran 1994, pp. 166-67; Charlesworth 2010, pp. 76-77 (Iron Age (1000-800), perhaps from the reign of Jeroboam I). Hazor: Charlesworth 2010, pp. 68-70

(Middle Bronze II). Jericho: Charlesworth 2010, pp. 63-64, and Joines 1968, p. 249 (Middle Bronze IIB). Megiddo: Charlesworth 2010, pp. 65-66, and Joines 1968, pp. 248-49 (Middle Bronze II). Munhata: Charlesworth 2010, p. 61 (5th millennium). Shechem: Charlesworth 2010, p. 65, and Joines 1968, p. 249 (Middle Bronze – Hyksos period). Ashkelon: Charlesworth 2010, pp. 64-65 (Middle Bronze IIB). Gibeon: Joines 1968, p. 249 (Middle Bronze – Hyksos period). Gaza: Joines 1968, p. 249 (Middle Bronze). Beth Shemesh: Joines 1968, p. 249 (Middle Bronze II). Timna: Rothenberg 1988, p. 302 and figs. 16.2 and 16.3 (from Midianite occupation).

195. Charlesworth 2010, pp. 69, 97-100, 111-12, 120; see Howey 1955, p. 14. The same symbol has been found in Ugarit (Middle Bronze II). Joines 1968, p. 249.

196. Charlesworth 2010, p. 75.

197. Aharoni 1974, p. 6; Charlesworth 2010, p. 80.

198. See Charlesworth 2010, p. 75; Aharoni 1974, p. 6 (as to Beer-Sheba altar).

199. Hvidberg 1960, p. 287.

200. J may have been playing upon these roles, with the serpent "helping" Eve (a goddess figure) to transgress, and Eve being created after Adam to be his helper, likewise in connection with the transgression since that is her only action in the story. See Chapter 8.

201. Hvidberg 1960, p. 287.

202. See Charlesworth 2010, pp. 429, 434.

203. Lambert 1985, pp. 443-44.

204. Keel and Uehlinger 1998, pp. 42-43, 76-79, 114-16. Baal was also depicted as slaying crocodiles and lions.

205. E.g., Hvidberg 1960, p. 289; Ringgren 1966, p. 110 (citing Hvidberg).

206. *Jewish War*, 5.108.

207. Exod. 7:10, by P. Note the differences in the names for the snakes due to the two different authors, E and P. Whereas Moses's staff in E's story turns into a *nāḥāš*, an ordinary snake as in the Eden story, Aaron's in P's story turns into a *tannîn*, the word used for the sea serpents that according to P Elohim created on the fifth day of creation and which, as noted earlier, is etymologically related to Tiamat. P thus intended something more impressive to serve the polemical purposes of his story.

208. Joines 1974, p. 85; see Neumann 1955, p. 328.

209. Hvidberg 1960, p. 288; Joines 1974, pp. 73-74; Joines 1968, p. 255 (referring simply to it symbolizing Yahweh's "agricultural" powers); Charlesworth 2010, p. 344; Rowley 1939, p. 137.

210. Rowley 1939.

211. Rowley 1939, pp. 130-31; Skinner 1910, pp. 267-68; see Vriezen 1967, p. 86. At the time of Joshua the king of Jerusalem was Adoni-zedek (Josh. 10:1-3), which is probably a theophoric name meaning "Zedek is lord," while in the time of Abraham the priest (and possibly chieftain) of Jerusalem was Melchizedek ("Zedek is king") (Gen. 14:18). Rowley 1939, p. 131; Cooke 1918, p. 84.

212. Gray 1965, p. 275; Rowley 1939, p. 132; Ringgren 1966, p. 165.

213. According to Friedman, E came from the circle of priests in Shiloh, in the Northern Kingdom, who glorified Moses over Aaron and were rivals to Jerusalem's Aaronid priesthood. Thus, E never mentions the Ark, which was associated with the Aaronid priesthood in Jerusalem, and instead discusses the bronze serpent, never mentioned by P. The removal of Nehushtan and the reform as a whole was a blow to E's Shiloh priesthood in Israel. See Friedman 1997, pp. 126, 210-11; Friedman 2003, p. 278.

214. See Friedman 1997, pp. 210-11.

215. Charlesworth 2010, pp. 329-30, 443.

216. E referred to the bronze serpent that Moses made as a *nāḥāš*, a synonym of *śārāp* and an ordinary word for serpent (used by J for the serpent in the Garden of Eden), probably because that was the term used for the serpent in front of the Temple. This is apparent from the words of Hezekiah. *Nāḥāš* sounds similar to the (unrelated) word for bronze *(neḥōšet)*, so it is likely that D was punning in having Hezekiah call the serpent Nehushtan, a mere "bronze thing" rather than a serpent with powers. Charlesworth 2010, p. 348. The question arises whether there is really a discrepancy or intentional meaningful distinction in E's use of both *śārāp* and *nāḥāš*.

Charlesworth reads nothing significant into it, concluding that the words are sufficiently close synonyms and that did this for literary variety rather than conceptual distinction. Charlesworth 2010, p. 333. Some scholars have pointed out that seraphs are often winged and even have feet, including in Isaiah 14:29 and 30:6, but in such cases the word is qualified with appropriate adjectives such as "winged" or "flying." Charlesworth 2010, pp. 332, 443, 575. It seems that E did not visualize a *śārāp* as being physiologically distinct from a *nāḥāš*, otherwise (i) the requirements of sympathetic magic would not have been met, which would require the serpent on the pole to match the fiery serpents, and (ii) Moses would be disobeying Yahweh's instructions.

217. Pinch 1994, p. 32, who states, "One of the basic principles of Egyptian magic was that like should be fought with like." See also Joines 1974, pp. 87-89; Joines 1968, pp. 251-52; Budge 1969, 2:377. For example, in Egypt a serpentine amulet was placed on mummies to prevent attacks by serpents of the underworld. Joines 1974, p. 87.

218. A biblical example of sympathetic magic was when Yahweh brought plagues of mice and tumors upon the Philistines after they seized the Ark. To eliminate the plagues, they made five golden images of mice and images of their tumors, and placed them in the Ark when returning it to the Israelites (1 Sam. 6:4-11).

219. Cf. Vriezen 1967, pp. 131-32, noting that starting with the wilderness period the biblical texts emphasize Yahweh as an ineluctable power or force that "electrifies his environment."

220. Charlesworth 2010, pp. 336-37.

221. See Joines 1974, p. 92; Charlesworth 2010, p. 78. "Spring of the Serpent" is Joines's translation (1974, p. 96). Charlesworth uses "Dragon's Well" (see also KJV) and only suggests that it may be the same site as En-Rogel. Charlesworth 2010, p. 78. There were only 2 springs by Jerusalem's walls, En-Rogel and Gihon, however, so there is no logical alternative. Joines 1974, p. 92.

222. Joines 1974, pp. 92-93.

223. Charlesworth 2010, p. 78.

224. Charlesworth 2010, p. 78.

225. *Jewish War*, 5.108

226. Meaning in Hebrew "house of grace" or "house of mercy," appropriate for a place where healing is conferred.

227. Charlesworth 2010, pp. 108, 376.

228. Charlesworth 2010, pp. 108-16.

229. Charlesworth 2010, p. 421.

230. Charlesworth 2010, p. 119; Soggin 1975, pp. 95-99.

231. Wilson 2001, pp. 53, 65-67.

232. Coote 1972; Young 1977.

233. Charlesworth 2010, pp. 248, 438; Murison 1905, p. 117; Hamilton 1990, p. 187; see also Wilson 2001, pp. 66-70, 85, 178. The noun for snake is *nāḥāš*, while the verb *nāḥaš* means to practice divination or observe signs. See Charlesworth 2010, p. 438.

234. The word *nāḥāš* can also connote the notion of offering, toasting, or libation, Wilson 2001, pp. 70, 85, 178, which fits the story's image of the serpent virtually offering the fruit to Eve.

235. Rad 1961, p. 85.

236. Westermann 1994, p. 236.

237. Murison 1905, p. 127 n. 35.

238. Rad 1961, p. 85; Soggin 1975, p. 94.

239. See Skinner 1910, pp. 71-72.

240. Hamilton 1990, p. 188; Soggin 1975, p. 94.

241. Joines 1975, p. 7.

242. Gunkel 1997, p. 15; Neumann 1955, p. 269; see generally Cooper 1992, p. ix.

243. Charlesworth 2010, p. 114.

244. In Parkinson 1997, pp. 89-101.

245. This very allusion appears in Titian's *Adam and Eve*, depicting a fox sitting between Eve and the tree.

246. The word, *ārûm*, also sounds similar to the word for "naked" *(ărôm)*, so the word also could have been chosen to facilitate wordplay in reference to the naked pair. Hamilton 1990, p. 187. As will be discussed in Chapter 9, J could also be alluding to the fact that serpent veneration, ecstatic flights and other forms of pagan rituals were conducted while naked, which could partly explain why he had Adam and Eve become ashamed of their nakedness once they acquired the knowledge of good and evil.

247. Hamilton 1990, p. 187.

248. As advocated by Skinner 1910, pp. 78-79.

249. E.g., Charlesworth 2010, pp. 87-88, 311-12.

250. BDB, p. 312. It can even refer to creatures of all sizes living in water (Ps. 104:25) or hybrid creatures (Ezek. 1:5). It would also include all categories of animals mentioned by P in Genesis 1:24.

251. For example, in Isaiah 6:2 *śārāp* is used to describe a hybrid creature with wings and legs or feet.

252. There is also the iconography of Baal in a smiting posture, in which he is sometimes depicted as killing a serpent, which never has legs. See, e.g., Keel and Uehlinger 1998, pp. 77, 155-57.

253. At best one can point only to the fact that in Mesopotamia and Egypt "serpents," and in Mesopotamia "dragons," sometimes have legs, arms and torsos with necks and heads. E.g., late papyrus in Charlesworth 2010, p. 87. The Egyptian serpent Apep is sometimes described as having appendages which are cut off when he is killed, for example as portrayed in the Books of Overthrowing Apep. See Müller 1964, pp. 127-28, 490 n. 38; Budge 1969, 1:324-27. However, such texts describe his annihilation in so many other ways (spearing him, cutting off his hide, blinding his eyes, cutting off his ears and tongue, cutting him into pieces, burning him, etc.) that cutting off his arms and legs has no particular meaning. Apep is generally portrayed horizontally, not as being upraised in any manner.

254. In the story the serpent ends up in the form associated with its positive symbolic qualities except that it is not erect. This is not problematic for our interpretation, however, because in the story itself the serpent was flattened from an erect posture, which J says transformed the serpent into the lowliest of animals.

255. Outside Palestine there is a mythological motif of dismembering a monster or dragon (e.g., Tiamat), but only if it is first killed, which is not what happens here.

256. For example, Michelangelo's portrayal on the Sistine Chapel ceiling; Titian's *Adam and Eve;* Raphael's *Adam and Eve;* Brueghel's and Rubens's *Paradise and the Fall of Man;* Jacopo Pontormo's *The Expulsion from Earthly Paradise;* and Masolino's *Temptation of Adam and Eve.* Interestingly in this regard, in Jacopo della Quercia's *Temptation* the serpent's body is depicted as actually passing through the trunk of the tree in addition to being twined around it.

257. Interpretation supported, e.g., by Skinner 1910, pp. 78-79.

258. See also examples in Frankfort 1965, pls. 4.a, 27.c, 34.g, and 44.m; Goff 1963, fig. 699.

259. Joines 1974, p. 85.

8. EVE:
THE HIDDEN GODDESS
IN THE GARDEN

1. Note here, nevertheless, the holdover from Goddess religion in which the dead return to the Earth Mother, not simply to dust as J states.

2. Phillips 1984, p. 3, relying on Kikawada 1972.

3. Frazer 1923, p. 11.

4. These detours echo ancient Mesopotamian myths describing how the gods at first did not make perfect humans and how primeval humans were not fully human. In the myth known as *Enki and Ninmah*, for example, Enki and Ninmah each make several defective humans

before succeeding in making fully functional humans. See Kramer 1972, pp. 70-72; Clifford 1994, p. 42.

5. At the same time this enabled J to show how, in contrast, the serpent was created by Yahweh as an ordinary animal that Adam both named and rejected as a partner corresponding to him, thus confirming human superiority over it and making it unworthy of human veneration.

6. Robbins 2012, pp. 29, 34.

7. Robbins 2012, p. 30. Similarly, as we shall see in Chapter 9, it was important that Adam and Eve not be born already possessing the knowledge of good and evil, but first experience how their chaotic minds work in its absence, resulting in the transgression.

8. Here again, J's wordplay is based on assonance rather than etymology, unlike the English "man" and "woman," which do share the same etymology. See Speiser 1964, p. 18; Hamilton 1990, p. 180.

9. Bible scholars have struggled to identify an Israelite marriage institution that matches the pattern described in verse 24, but to no avail. It seems clear that this passage is intended simply to affirm the couple's natural affinity and bond and the psychological transformation entailed by their switch in primary loyalties. See Hamilton 1992, p. 568; Hamilton 1990, pp. 180-81; Rad 1961, pp. 82-83; Lawton 1986, p. 98; Tosato 1990, pp. 399-400. The connection signified by these terms is not merely one of blood but one of a bond of covenant and loyalty in marriage. Hamilton 1992, p. 568; Bruggemann 1970; Robbins 2012, p. 31.

10. Skinner 1910, p. 68; Rad 1961, p. 81; Gunkel 1997, p. 12.

11. Cassuto 1998, pp. 133-34.

12. Neumann 1955, pp. 292, 299-300.

13. In the Norse saga, Brynhildr had to judge a fight between two kings, and decided in favor of the one that the god Odin opposed. In retaliation, Odin rendered her mortal and imprisoned her in a castle behind a wall of shields on a remote Alpine mountaintop, where she must sleep within a ring of fire until a man rescues and marries her. The hero Sigurd Sigmundson awoke her, removed her helmet and cut off her chainmail, fell in love with her on the spot, and proposed to her with the magic ring Andvaranaut.

14. Examples in paintings include Michelangelo's *Creation of Eve* on the Sistine Chapel ceiling; see also William Blake's drawing, *The Creation of Eve*. Examples in reliefs include on the west front of Notre Dame Cathedral, Paris; Lorenzo Mitanni's *Creation of Eve* at Oriento Cathedral; Jacopo della Quercia's *Creation of Eve* at San Petronio, Bologna; and Wiligelmo's *Creation of Eve* at the Duomo, Modena.

15. E.g., Friedman 2003, p. 36; Speiser 1964, p. 15; Westermann 1994, p. 182.

16. E.g., Hamilton 1990, p. 178.

17. Reisenberger 2001, p. 448. Contra is Trible 1978, p. 95, who translates as rib.

18. Cassuto 1998, pp. 135-36. See, e.g., Gen. 29:14 ("Surely you are my bone and my flesh."); Judg. 9:2 ("Remember also that I am your bone and your flesh."); 2 Sam. 5:1; 19:12-13; 1 Chr. 11:1. Notably, in the extended version of the J text proposed by professor Friedman, he attributes all of these references to J, except of course that in Chronicles.

19. In the Egyptian *Tale of the Two Brothers,* the creator god Khnum "builds" for the younger brother a woman companion who had the quality of a goddess, as (like Adam) he had been living in isolation in a valley of a sacred tree, in which his soul resided atop its highest blossom, but presumably she was built from clay on Khnum's potter's wheel; still, however, having the same substance as a man. (Like Eve, she eventually transgresses and brings death.)

20. Frazer recounted that the Karens of Burma believe that God created man from earth and then took a rib from the man to create the woman, and also that the Bedel Tartars of Siberia believed that man was first created alone, but then while he slept the devil touched his breast, a bone grew out of one of his ribs, fell to the ground, and then grew into the first woman. Frazer 1923, p. 6. However, it has not been possible to assign an ancient, pre-biblical date to these stories; rather, they appear to be adaptations of the biblical (or Islamic) story which reached them later. The Karens were influenced by Christian missionaries centuries ago, while the Tatars are not an ancient people. See Marshall, H. "The Karen People of Burma," *Ohio State University Bulletin* 26: 210-18 (1922).

21. E.g., Hooke 1963, p. 115; Kramer 1963, p. 149.

22. *ANET,* p. 41.

23. Kramer 1963, p. 149.

24. See Kapelrud 1980, pp. 258-59.

25. See also discussions in Bruggemann 1970; Hamilton 1992, p. 568.

26. Graves and Patai 1983, p. 67.

27. See generally Cirlot 1971, pp. 147-47; Chetwynd 1998, p. 197; Biedermann 1994, p. 11.

28. Skinner 1910, p. 68.

29. See generally discussion of the two types in Eliade 1996, pp. 420-25.

30. Eliade 1996, p. 422.

31. In Egypt, androgyny was generally restricted to the original self-generating creator god, who was undifferentiated sexually and in all ways, and produced the first sexually differentiated divine couple, Shu and Tefnut, who in turn conceived other male-female couples and thus initiate the process of procreation and birth. Akhenaten regarded his god Aten as mother-father, and thus envisaged himself in the same way, resulting in Akhenaten's own uniqueness. See Horning 1982, p. 171.

32. The principal rabbinical text in this regard is the *Genesis Rabbah,* which states: "Adam and Eve were made back to back, attached at their shoulders; then God separated them with an axe, or cut them in two. Others have a different picture: the first man, Adam, was a man on his right side, a woman on his left; but God split him into two halves." As quoted in Eliade 1996, p. 423.

33. The existence of separate male and female animals is not specifically stated but can be presumed. There is no account of the separation of any other living beings from one being into male and female. In P's account male and female birds and water creatures are created at the same time without explicitly mentioning male and female, but Elohim tells them to be fruitful and multiply. Gen. 1:20-23. The creation of land animals is likewise, only without the command to multiply, Gen. 1:24-25, but the existence of male and female can be presumed.

34. Hess 1990, p. 1; Stratton 1995, p. 103.

35. Stratton 1995, pp. 103-04; Clines 1990, p. 40.

36. See Robbins 2012, p. 18 & n. 9 and sources cited. Likewise among older commentators, e.g., Skinner 1910, p. 68. Examples arguing for androgyny include Trible 1978, pp. 80, 94-99; Bal 1987, pp. 112-19; and Reisenberger 1993; see also summary of feminist commentators holding this view in Abraham 2002, pp. 57-59.

37. Friedman 2001, p. 20.

38. Neumann 1955, pp. 291-92.

39. Adam and Eve did not yet clearly think of male and female as opposites. Campbell 1988, p. 48. This is evident from the words of Adam's exclamation in verse 23 stressing only their similarity and common origin, as well as the fact that they were not ashamed of their nakedness.

40. Wilber 1996, p. 243.

41. Ackroyd 1983, p. 249.

42. Wallace 1992c, p. 677; Hamilton 1990, pp. 175-76 (citing relevant biblical passages); Speiser 1964, p. 17; Westermann 1994, p. 227.

43. Wallace 1992c, p. 677; Speiser 1964, p. 17; Gunkel 1996, p. 11; Hamilton 1992, p. 568.

44. Friedman 2001, p. 19.

45. See Hamilton 1990, p. 175; Westermann 1994, p. 227. The NRSV uses "partner" here.

46. Brueggemann 1970, p. 533; Hamilton 1992, p. 568.

47. These other alternatives and their proponents are discussed in Stratton 1995, pp. 97-98; see also Robbins 2012, pp. 29, 34. Below we develop additional possible senses in which Eve helps.

48. Phipps 1976, p. 269.

49. Gardner 1990, pp. 6-7; Robbins 2012, p. 30; Trible 1978, p. 101.

50. Phipps 1976, p. 269.

51. Gardner 1990, p. 9.

52. Gunkel 1997, p. 12.

53. For example, Trible (1978, pp. 99-10) claims that no naming occurs in the case of the woman, arguing that for this to occur a rigid naming formula must be used (the verb for "call"

(qārāh) in conjunction with the noun for "name" *(šēm)*), which she views as absent in Genesis 2:23. Later commentary, however, has shown that no such rigid formula is needed for naming to occur and that verse 2:23 should be regarded as an instance of naming. Ramsey 1988.

54. Robbins 2012, pp. 23-35; Beeston 1986, p. 115.
55. Cf. Niditch 1993, p. 40; Jobling 1986, pp. 34-35, 38.
56. Clines 1990, pp. 38-39.
57. Brueggemann 1970; Hamilton 1990, pp. 179-80.
58. E.g., Wallace 1985, p. 163; Williams 1977, p. 373; see also Hamilton 1990, p. 181.
59. Hamilton 1992, p. 568; Hamilton 1990, pp. 180-81; Brueggemann 1970, p. 540.
60. *Paradise Lost,* IV.739-75.
61. E.g., Barr 2012, pp. 67-69; Wallace 1985, p. 163; Buber 1952, pp. 82-83; Bledstein 1977, p. 195.
62. E.g., Glenn 1977.
63. That is, in Gen. 3:20, apparently to highlight the wordplay on "mother of all the living." In Genesis 4:1 *ḥawwâ* is simply transliterated into Greek letters. See Layton 1997, p. 28.
64. Wallace 1992c, p. 676.
65. Williams 1977, p. 368; Wallace 1985, p. 150.
66. Wallace 1992c, p. 676; Gunkel 1997, p. 23.
67. Layton 1997; Kapelrud 1980. There are further similarities in other nearby languages, though a derivation from any of them is less likely. In later Aramaic the adjective for life was *ḥay,* the noun *ḥayyîn,* and the verb for "to live" *ḥāyā* or *ḥāyî.* Wallace 1985, p. 150. In Arabic the adjective *ḥayy* denotes "living" and the noun *ḥayāh* means "life." Charlesworth 2010, p. 250; Wallace 1985, p. 150-51. In Ethiopic the verb *ḥaywa* means "to live" and the noun *ḥeywat* means "life." Wallace 1985, p. 151. In Persian *ḥayāt* denotes "life." Charlesworth 2010, p. 250. In Syriac *ḥayyê* signifies "life." Charlesworth 2010, p. 250.
68. Wallace 1992c, p. 676; Kapelrud 1980, p. 258. Alternatively, *ḥawwâ* could be ancient and traditional in Hebrew (but still derived from Canaanite), but already archaic. Some commentators have posited that it might be ancient/traditional. Wallace 1992c, p. 676.; Wallace 1985, pp. 147, 150-52; Skinner 1910, p. 86. Gunkel apparently stood in between, calling *ḥawwâ* "an old tradition, although not of Hebrew origins." Gunkel 1997, p. 23.
69. Layton 1997, p. 26, notes that the above mentioned roots appear in Hebrew names in nonbiblical material, so they are attested in Hebrew as well.
70. Tannit is commonly thought of as a Punic goddess, but Maier has demonstrated that she was also a Semitic goddess known as such in Syro-Palestine. Maier 1986, pp. 96-99.
71. Scholars identifying Tannit with Asherah include Dever 2005, pp. 218, 221-22, 232; Maier 1986, pp. 96-118, 121; Wallace 1985, pp. 152-58; Olyan 1988, pp. 53-61; and Cross 1973, pp. 28-34. The reasons for equating Tannit with Asherah mentioned by these authors include: the increasingly confident identification of Tannit's consort Baal Hamon with El, Asherah's consort; their common associations with the sea, serpents, fish, doves, life, and motherhood; their common epithets Elat and Lady; and the similarity of Tannit's symbol with the images in the Qudesh plaques (which many scholars believe depict Asherah). There seems to be not much dispute regarding this identification, but there is a possibility of a partial identification or blending with Astarte. See Day 1986, pp. 396-97; Wiggins 1991, pp. 389-92; Maier 1986, p. 98 (possible blending in Sarepta).
72. Maier 1986, p. 100; Cross 1973, pp. 32-33.
73. Maier 1986, pp. 100, 115; Cross 1973, p. 34.
74. Layton 1997, p. 30; Wallace 1985, p. 152.
75. Layton 1997, p. 30; Wallace 1985, pp. 152-53
76. Layton 1997, p. 31.
77. See, e.g., Olyan 1988, p. 71 n.4.
78. Olyan 1988, p. 60; Wallace 1985, p. 157; Cross 1967.
79. Wallace 1985, pp. 157-58; Wallace 1992c, p. 677.
80. See discussions in Wallace 1985, pp. 149-50; Hess 2009, pp. 19-20; Graves and Patai 1983, pp. 12, 69, 150. The derivation of *ḥawwâ* from the Hurrian word for Heba was challenged by Speiser on technical linguistic grounds, but only to conclude that the derivation was probably the other way around, from Semitic to Hurrian! Speiser 1940-41, p. 41 and n. 91. His

argument, made in a book on Hurrian grammar, was only that *ḥawwâ* did not technically derive from the *Hurrian* word Hebat, and to say that the reverse process is actually "probable." He did not address whether *ḥawwâ* could have derived from *Hittite,* or whether J's use of *ḥawwâ* might simply be popular etymology. As we have seen, most of J's wordplay is based on assonance rather than technical etymological connections, so a precise etymological connection is not necessary here.

81. EA Nos. 280, 285-88, 290; see Redford 1992, p. 270.
82. Van der Toorn 1999, p. 392; see also *HALOT* 4:55.
83. See discussion in Wallace 1985, p. 148. This would mean, of course, that that Adam and a woman named Eve originally did not belong together.
84. Skinner 1910, p. 85, citing Phlio and Clement of Alexandria.
85. *Genesis Rabbba,* 20, as quoted in Wallace 1985, p. 148.
86. Gunkel 1997, p. 23, and Skinner 1910, pp. 85-86, seemed to accept this idea. See historical summary in Wallace 1985, p. 148; Kapelrud 1980, pp. 257-58. More modern commentators who see such reasonable link include Wallace 1985, pp. 155-61; Albright 1920, p. 284; Friedman 2003, p. 36.
87. Charlesworth 2010, pp. 449-50, 557 n. 368.
88. See generally the discussions in Charlesworth 2010, p. 250; Wallace 1985, pp. 147-52; also Skinner 1910, pp. 85-86; Albright 1920, p. 284.
89. Charlesworth 2010, p. 250; see also Wallace 1985, pp. 150-51.
90. Charlesworth 2010, p. 250.
91. Layton 1997, pp. 27-30; Kapelrud 1980, pp. 257-58.
92. Stratton 1995, p. 57.
93. Rad 1961, p. 93; Kikawada 1972, pp. 33-34; Plaut 1981, p. 36 n. 20; Wallace 1992c, p. 677; see Westermann 1994, pp. 268-69; Bledstein 1977, p. 199.
94. See Wallace 1992c, pp. 676-77.
95. Kikawada 1972, pp. 34-35.
96. Campbell 1964, p. 30. To like effect see Phillips 1984, p. 3 (quoted in epigraph to this chapter); Bledstein 1977, pp. 198-99.
97. Kikawada 1972, p. 34.
98. E.g., in the Keret legend, *ANET,* p. 143-44.
99. E.g., in the Baal epic, *ANET,* pp. 130, 132, 134, 136-38, 142. See Smith 1990, p. 81.
100. E.g., Ps. 68:4; 104:3; see Day 1985, p. 32; Smith 1990, pp. 81-82.
101. See Wallace 1985, pp. 149-58; Wallace 1992c, pp. 676-77; Westermann 1994, p. 268.
102. Lambert 1969, pp. 57, 61; see also Dalley 1989, pp. 15-16.
103. Albright 1920, p. 260. According to Speiser, "Siduri" was actually a Hurrian epithet for Heba meaning "young woman," much like the meaning of her Greek name, Hebe ("youthful beauty" (i.e., goddess as maiden, or kore)). *ANET,* p. 89.
104. Keel and Uehlinger 1998, p. 74 (noting that she was also called "womb"); Patai 1965, p. 38.
105. Wallace 1992c, p. 677. Kikawada 1972, p. 34, advocates the association with the mother goddess but suggests Mami in particular. See also discussions in Westermann 1994, pp. 268-69.
106. E.g., Brandon 1963, p. 138; Skinner 1910, p. 86; Westermann 1994, pp. 268-69; Wallace 1992c, p. 677; Wallace 1985, pp. 149-58.
107. Kikawada 1972, p. 35.
108. Bledstein 1977, p. 199.
109. Harrison 1991, pp. 277-81; Kerényi 1951, p. 219; see also Graves 1960, pp. 148-49, 714.
110. Harrison 1991, p. 281.
111. Harrison 1991, pp. 281, 283-84.
112. Harrison 1900, pp. 101-02.
113. Phillips 1984, p. 20.
114. Harrison 1900, p. 108.
115. Homer, *Iliad,* 24:526-27.
116. Hesiod, *Works and Days,* 56-57.

117. Hesiod, *Works and Days,* 91-92.
118. Hesiod, *Works and Days,* 81-82.
119. Hesiod, *Works and Days,* 78-79.
120. Hesiod, *Works and Days,* 70.
121. Hesiod, *Works and Days,* 85-88.
122. In Western tradition originating with Erasmus, the vessel has been known as "Pandora's box," but in the Olympian myth it was still the pithos as in the original myth.
123. See Harrison 1991, pp. 284-85.
124. Bledstein 1977, p. 198.
125. Similarly, in Apuleius's account of Cupid and Psyche, Psyche is given a sealed pixis, which she is to deliver to Hades, but curiosity gets the best of her and she opens it.
126. The Great Mother had been considered the source of all life, not just human life, which is why she was often portrayed from the earliest times together with animals. Neumann 1955, p. 96.
127. Kerényi 1951, p. 218.
128. The meaning of this phrase has been debated for centuries. Space does not permit a detailed discussion of the various possibilities that have been considered, but see the summary of interpretations in Westermann 1994, p. 291. It is well accepted that the preposition 'et can mean not merely "with" but in certain contexts connote accompaniment for the purpose of providing help, and Gen. 4:1 is typically used as a prime example. See, e.g., Waltke and O'Connor 1990, p. 195; Arnold and Choi 2003, p. 101; Williams 2007, p. 129.
129. See Skinner 1910, pp. 102-03; Westermann 1994, pp. 291-92.
130. Hesiod, *Theogony,* 189-200.
131. Hesiod, *Theogony,* 890-925.
132. Harrison 1991, p. 302.
133. *The Eumenides,* 736.
134. Dalley 1989, p. 15; see also Lambert and Millard 1969, p. 57.
135. Dalley 1989, pp. 15-16; Lambert and Millard 1969, pp. 57-59.
136. Dalley 1989, p. 16.
137. Westermann 1994, p. 291, excerpted in Skinner 1910, p. 47.
138. Skinner 1910, pp. 102-03.
139. Speiser 1964, p. 30, analogizing the Hebrew 'et to the Akkadian *itti* also translated as "with."
140. Gardner 1990, p. 7.
141. E.g., Gen. 18:9-21:2 (Sarah); Gen. 30:22-23 (Rachel); 1 Sam. 2:21 (Hannah).
142. See Hooke 1963, p. 93.
143. We are not suggesting any sexual activity between Yahweh and Eve in the Eden story, but rather the opposite. In the Hebrew Bible, Yahweh never had a sexual nature. Portraying him as such would have undermined J's purpose of eliminating the Goddess and appropriating her powers, a step on the road toward monotheism.
144. Bledstein 1977, p. 198. Painless birth by goddesses is described in Kramer 1963, p. 149; Kramer 1961, p. 101.
145. See Kramer 1972, p. 56; *ANET,* p. 39.
146. Kramer 1963, p. 149.
147. Lerner 1986, p. 159; Dever 2005, pp. 187-88, 194.
148. Stratton 1995, p. 94.
149. Chapter 4; see also Graves and Patai 1983, p. 80.
150. Wallace 1985, pp. 158-59; Campbell 1964, p. 30.
151. Neumann 1955, p. 58.
152. E.g., Stratton 1995, pp. 67, 85-108; Daly 1973.
153. We touched on these doctrines in Chapter 4 and will consider them in more detail in Chapter 9. Stratton notes, for example, that even Trible feels compelled to accept a traditional interpretation of Gen. 3:16 (men ruling over women) because she is working within the constraint of considering it a result of the "fall," and doesn't want to implicate God in patriarchy. Stratton 1995, pp. 61, 107.

154. Although the serpent initially misstates Yahweh's prohibition in order to draw Eve into conversation, she corrects the misstatement so is not deceived, and ultimately the serpent commits no fraud. What it says is true, and its predictions come to fruition: Adam and Eve's eyes are opened and come to know good an evil; they do not die anytime soon; and they do to some extent become like gods. In our view, J seems to be arguing that veneration of serpents itself is deception because they are false divinities, which women were prone to embrace.

155. The Hebrew text of Gen. 3:6 makes clear that Adam was physically present then, as it specifies that Eve gave the fruit to her husband "who was with her," but some English translations miss this phrase (e.g., RSV, corrected in NRSV).

156. Neumann 1955, pp. 181-91.

157. Le Grice 2013, p. 204; Neumann 1955, pp. 330-31; Neumann 1954, p. 212.

158. Some commentators have raised the sensitive question whether Adam (like perhaps Enkidu) was consorting with animals as part of this evolutionary process, e.g., Barton 1934, p. 141; Reik 1960, pp. 32-38, but this is not apparent from the text and would add no meaning, Skinner 1910, pp. 67, 91.

159. *ANET,* p. 75.

160. *ANET,* p. 75.

161. See Jobling 1986, pp. 34-35, 38.

162. Rad 1961, p. 88. Astrology is beside the point, and we take von Rad to be referring to any Canaanite religious cults in which women were prominent.

163. Gardner 1990, p. 15.

164. Gardner 1990, p. 14; Stratton 1995, p. 94; see also von Rad discussed immediately above.

165. Gardner 1990, p. 15.

166. Bledstein 1977, p. 198.

167. Campbell 1988, p. 48.

168. See discussion in Day 1985, pp. 24-25.

169. *ANET,* p. 67 (Tablet IV, line 107).

170. Day 1985, pp. 24-25.

171. Here the word "helpers" is a participle from the verb *'āzar,* related to *'ēzer.*

9. THE TRANSGRESSION
AND OUR TRANSFORMATION

1. *Metaphysics,* I.980a21 (the first line of the book).

2. Mobley 2012, pp. 1, 34.

3. Blenkinsopp 2011, p. 3; Barr 1988, p. 69; Shattuck 1996, p. 50.

4. Blenkinsopp 2011, p. 3, who also notes that a possible exception may be Job 31:33, where the phrase (in RSV) referring to concealing transgressions "from men" could be rendered as "like Adam," but Adam did not do that (there were no other men!). See also *NOAB,* p. 32.

5. Ricoeur 1967, p. 6; see also pp. 237-38.

6. For the Catholic Church's doctrine of original sin, see *CCC,* 396-421.

7. Gunkel 1997, p. 1; Friedman 2003, pp. 38-50. The P material interspersed in the flood story has been identified as Gen. 6:9-22; 7:8-9, 11, 13-16a, 21, 24; 8:1-2a, 3b-5, 7, 13a, 14-19, and 19:1-17, the remainder being J. The J and P texts of the flood story can be seen combined in Friedman 2003, pp. 42-47, and in Friedman 1997, pp. 54-59. There is some other minor P material later in the primeval history, namely Gen. 10:1b-7, 20, 22-23, 31-32, and 11:27b-31. See Friedman 1997, p. 247.

8. The genealogies in the primeval history are in Gen. 5:1-32; 9:28-29; 10:1; 11:10-26. For a general description of the narrative and genealogical pattern of the primeval history, see Kikawada 1992, p. 462-63. The genealogical structure extends beyond the primeval history, and more generally is known as the "*tôlēdôt* structure" of Genesis.

9. The exception was Noah and his entourage occupying the ark. Noah was a pure and righteous man whom Yahweh had graced (Gen. 6:8-9), so he could be allowed to survive as the link between the old and new worlds without tainting the new. Another example of the same was when the generation of Hebrews that had left Egypt with Moses was punished for its sins by not being allowed to live to see the Promised Land, but Joshua and Caleb were exempted, "for they have wholly followed Yahweh" (Num. 32:12; also 14:24).

10. Blenkinsopp 2011, p. 19.

11. This according to J (Gen. 8:20-22). There is no sacrifice in P's flood account because he claimed that making sacrifices was the prerogative of the priesthood, so according to him the practice originated at Sinai with the establishment of the priesthood and the Tabernacle (Exodus 40). This is why in P's account Noah needed to take only two of each species aboard the ark; J, however, said that Noah took aboard seven pairs of pure (sacrificeable) animals, because he looked forward to their being sacrificed immediately after the flood. See Friedman 2003, pp. 43, 46.

12. This description of the covenant (Gen. 9:1-17) is a P text, but it is consistent with the surrounding J text, which in 8:21 describes the lifting of the curse on the ground so that it will become fertile and in which Yahweh promises never again to destroy life on earth. P simply amplifies the result into formal covenant language and legalities.

13. Certain etiological consequences which J selected (e.g., women giving birth in increased pain) by definition must survive since they form part of real human life, but their survival does not contradict the central mythological aspects of the flood story.

14. Ricoeur 1967, p. 262 n. 14.

15. Eliade 1996, pp. 188-89.

16. This is the only instance in which J uses the term *elōhîm* in narrative. Friedman 2003, p. 42. Although *elōhîm* standing alone can be either singular ("god") or plural ("gods") depending on the context, here it is preceded by the definite article *ha,* which grammatically renders the expression plural ("the gods"), meaning that this reference is not to the one god (Yahweh) but to a plurality of gods. Fisher 2011, pp. 1-2, 54. A second reason why this reference cannot be to Yahweh is that in narrative J never uses *elōhîm* to refer to Yahweh; as discussed in Chapter 1,only his characters use it in direct speech. Thus, the reference must be not to Yahweh but to lesser deities in Yahweh's divine council, and/or to their sons. By attributing these improper actions to such other deities, J shields Yahweh from blame for the evil and enables him to be the one to step in and take corrective action.

17. The term literally means "the fallen ones," from the verb *nāfal,* meaning "to fall."

18. J's account in Genesis 6:1-4 is an abbreviated version of older stories. Subsequent variations include the Book of Giants found in the Dead Sea Scrolls (see DSS, pp. 246-250) and the Book of the Watchers in the apocryphal 1 Enoch (Chapters 1-36). In the Book of the Watchers, angels similarly descend to earth and father giants with human women; further, they transfer to humans both practical skills and knowledge as well as secret knowledge that was supposed to have been preserved in heaven but which humans were striving to learn. All this was said to lead to corruption of the human race which brought on the flood. In a vision, Enoch sees in heaven the Tree of Wisdom, identified with the Tree of Knowledge of Good and Evil, from which heavenly angels eat and gain wisdom. In the Book of Giants, angels similarly descend to earth and father giants with human women, and apparently disclose divine secrets to humans. That Book mentions the Mesopotamian hero Gilgamesh, who apparently is one of the semi-divine giants. Enoch is also mentioned, which seems to connect the story to that in 1 Enoch.

19. Blenkinsopp 2011, p. 122; *DDD,* p. 618; Walton 2012, p. 2 (focusing on aspect of causing disorder).

20. Gen. 6:3 (author's translation). The infinitive construct form of the verb here, key for our purposes but often left untranslated, is *šāgag,* meaning to go astray, be in error (inadvertently), or sin inadvertently. BDB, pp. 992-93; *HALOT* 4:1412; *ABD* 6:35; see, e.g., Lev. 4-5; 22:14; Num. 15:22-29. Thus, J means that the divine spirit does not belong in humans but at the time was waywardly bottled up in them. As for the translation "bottled up," which helps convey this meaning, see Fisher 2011, p. 54.

21. The majority of scholars appear to view this as a restriction on the human lifespan, e.g., Blenkinsopp 2011, p. 122, and indeed this view is most consistent with the idea that a divine spirit (not merely the breath of life) entered some humans (who were killed in the flood) and that Yahweh's response should correspond to the trespass. Other scholars stress, however, that Noah and several patriarchs lived far beyond 120 years, and therefore argue that the 120-year term probably referred instead to the period remaining for humans to live before they would perish in the flood, Hamilton 1990, p. 269, or was perhaps a probationary period after which humanity would perish if they would not reform, Speiser 1964, p. 46. The question should be what J meant since this is his text, and in J no human lives longer than 120 years; the references to subsequent longer lifespans are from the Book of Records (Gen: 9:29; 11:10-26, 32), not J's writings. This supports the traditional conclusion that J meant that Yahweh was restricting the human lifespan to 120 years; Moses died at exactly 120 (Deut. 34:7, by J). See Friedman 2003, p. 42.

22. Westermann 1994, p. 374 ("the restraining judgment of God is aimed at an intolerable attempt to prolong life").

23. Skinner 1910, pp. 139-40.

24. The people in question were descendants of Noah's son Shem who settled and populated Mesopotamia and Arabia. In Hebrew Shem's name means "name," "reputation," or "renown."

25. Blenkinsopp 2011, pp. 166-67.

26. See Walton 2012, p. 3.

27. Reicke 1956, p. 195.

28. Naidoff 1978, p. 2 (noting that Humbert had called it a "peccadillo").

29. Engnell 1955, p. 116; Ringgren 1966, p. 139.

30. In Israelite theology not all sins need be intentional. An alternative way to look at this episode is not so much as a human sin but as a simple violation of the natural (perfect) created order that unnaturally altered humans, creating disorder, so that the natural order had to be restored by action towards humans even if they were not at fault.

31. Gen. 6:7, by J. Likewise P: "I will destroy them with the earth" (Gen. 6:13).

32. Throughout the ancient Near East, the heart was considered the organ of human thought.

33. The only details that the story reports are that Ham saw his father naked and did not cover him, so it is possible that the sin lay in merely seeing his father naked, though more probably it was that he did not immediately cover him and instead told his brothers, which revelation is itself an offense. Westermann 1994, p. 488; see also Hamilton 1990, pp. 322-23. Some scholars, however, speculate that something more occurred, i.e., some sexual act with Noah or with his wife (with Canaan as the progeny). See discussion in Hamilton 1990, pp. 322-23. The precise nature of the sin, other than that it was something immoral, is not important for our purposes.

34. As seen in Chapter 6, the forbidden fruit may indeed have been a grape.

35. Blenkinsopp 2011, p. 154.

36. Baden 2012, p. 69.

37. As to the literal meaning, we note that the Hebrew word in question *(ra)* most commonly translated as "evil" in this phrase (e.g., RSV; KJV) can also have the more general, amoral meaning, as an adjective, of simply "bad" or merely disagreeable or displeasing, and as a noun misery, distress, injury, or misery. See BDB, pp. 948-49; *HALOT* 3:1250-53. Some translations of this word as it appears in the Eden story indeed translate it as "bad." E.g., Speiser 1964, p. 14; Friedman 2003, pp. 36-38. As so translated, the term can be read to connote not merely human (moral) evil/sin but anything else in the world that is bad or disagreeable. If the term is so understood, this would lend credence to the interpretation of "good and evil" as a merism (discussed below). In light of J's aforementioned focus on human evil which he said causes other bad things on earth, however, we prefer the traditional translation of "evil" as being more in line with J's polemics in the story and the primeval history as a whole.

38. For a summary of the opinions, see Westermann 1994, pp. 242-45.

39. Blenkinsopp 2011, p. 76.

40. In law, legal capacity refers to the ability (through age, sound mind, and other criteria) to understand the nature and effects of one's acts such that one is deemed capable of assuming

legal obligations and being legally responsible for one's actions. See, e.g., *Black's Law Dictionary.* 5th ed. St. Paul: West Publishing, p. 188.

41. Buchanan 1956, p. 115. The military service obligation commencing at 20 years is found throughout Numbers (1:2, 20, 22, 24, 26, 28, 30, 32, 34, 36, 38, 40, 42, 45; 26:2 (the census of the people to determine who is able to go to war); and 32:11), and also in 1 Chronicles 27:23 and 2 Chronicles 25:5. The obligation to make an offering to Yahweh beginning at age 20 is specified in Exodus 30:14 and 39:26. The tax obligation applicable for men 20 years of age and older (until 60) is contained in Leviticus 27:3.

42. This occurred after the spies that Moses sent to Canaan reported back that it was inhabited by fearsome giants.

43. Their punishment was that they would not live to see the Hebrews' entry into the Promised Land. As noted earlier, Joshua and Caleb, though older than 20 years, were exempted because they were righteous and untainted by the sin, much as the righteous Noah was graced and selected to survive the flood.

44. See Buchanan 1956, p. 116; Stern 1958, p. 415; Blenkinsopp 2011, p. 75.

45. Buchanan 1956, p. 114, whose translation is adopted here. The scroll in question is 1QSa, known as the Rule of the Congregation, which can be found at Wise, Abegg and Cook 1996, p. 145, which translates the key phrase instead as "knows right from wrong" (the Hebrew word is still the same that J uses for "evil," namely *ra*), which supports our interpretation of the phrase below.

46. Gen. 3:5, 22; see Blenkinsopp 2011, p. 75.

47. Harris, Archer and Waltke 1980, p. 877.

48. Thus, for example, the spies that Moses sends to scout out the land of Canaan are charged with discerning between alternatives, all phrased in terms of opposites (merisms): "whether the people who live in it are strong or weak, whether they are few or many, and whether the land they live in is good or bad" (Num. 13:18-19). Likewise, priests are charged with discerning whether animals brought for offerings and consecrated houses are good or bad (Lev. 27:12, 14).

49. Levenson 1988, p. 17.

50. Blenkinsopp 2011, p. 18.

51. In P's creation account, humans did not become like gods in the course of the account, but were created in the image of God, and the entire creation (including humans) was deemed "very good," so it seems that humans possessed the knowledge of good and evil from the start. No transgression was needed, an idea that P seems to have rejected.

52. Buber 1953, p. 82.

53. Mobley 2012, pp. 1, 34.

54. See generally Ricoeur 1967, pp. 191-98.

55. Thus, in Egypt, kings were supposed to establish and preserve cosmic order *(maat)* on earth, the opposite of chaos *(nesfet),* which was evil. Pinch 2002, p. 65. Similarly, in Mesopotamia, much as Marduk earned kingship over the other gods by subduing chaos and creating order, the human king was appointed by the gods and charged to do the same on earth. See Frankfort 1978, pp. 234-36.

56. Franz 1995, p. 2. This appears to be a result of universal human psychology. When known reality stops and our consciousness encounters the unknown, we project an archetypal image. Medieval depictions of the constellations and zodiac likewise depict the uroboros at the limits. Franz 1995, p. 2. For an extended discussion of this point, see Neumann 1954, pp. 5-38.

57. Walton 2012, p. 2; Cassuto 1998, p. 142; see discussion in Chapter 7.

58. Blenkinsopp 2011, p. 10; Cassuto 1998, pp. 142-43.

59. See, e.g., Reicke 1956, pp. 198-99.

60. E.g., the knowledge bestowed on Adapa, who undertook civilizing activities, Dalley 1989, p. 184, and Enki helping to set up agriculture in *Enki and Ninhursag, ANET,* p. 38.

61. Reicke 1956, p. 201.

62. E.g., Gordis 1936, pp. 90-94; see list of such commentators set forth in Wright 1996, p. 313 n. 30.

63. E.g., Wallace 1985, p. 146 and sources in n. 6 ("no consistent interpretation of Gen. 2-3 in their present form can be developed with sexual relations or fertility as the central point"),

163; Engnell 1955, pp. 115-16; Childs 1962, p. 696. As noted in Chapter 8, most scholars now agree that Adam and Eve had sex from the start. E.g., Bailey 1970, p. 145; Wallace 1985, p. 163; Barr 2012, pp. 67-69; Buber 1952, pp. 82-83; Bledstein 1977, p. 195.

64. Wallace 1985, p. 163.

65. Stern 1958, pp. 406-07.

66. Stern 1958, pp. 407-08; Wright 1996, pp. 317-18.

67. Kuyper 1947, p. 491.

68. They would not have had access to the tree of life so had to reproduce. Also, Yahweh's clothing the humans in skins in verse 3:21 would result in extinction of the species in question unless they were already reproducing. As we have seen, J was aware of such a extinction issue because he had Noah take extra pairs of sacrificial animals onto the ark so that sacrifices could be made without the species going extinct (Gen. 7:2).

69. Wright 1996, p. 315.

70. Robbins 2012, p. 93.

71. Stern 1958, p. 407; Robbins 2012, p. 93.

72. Thus, it is not surprising to see J engaging in wordplay between the word "naked" and that for "cunning" in reference to the serpent. The Hebrew adjective for "naked" in Gen. 2:25 (and subsequently in Gen. 3) is *'ărôm* (there in the plural form *'ărûmmîm*), and that used for "cunning" in the very next verse (3:1) is *'ārûm*.

73. 1 Sam. 19:24 (Saul prophesizing while naked).

74. Joines 1974, p. 111.

75. Engnell 1955, pp. 117-18; Wallace 1985, pp. 161-64.

76. Engnell 1955, pp. 117-18; Wallace 1985, p. 162.

77. Pedersen 1991, 1:204-06; Stern 1958, p. 408.

78. See generally discussion of aspects of "forbidden knowledge," including esoteric knowledge, in Shattuck 1996, pp. 327-37.

79. Rad 1961, pp. 79, 86-87; Gordon 1960, p. 36; see Soggin 1975, pp. 103-04.

80. Honeyman 1952, p. 16.

81. Waltke 2004, p. 614.

82. Rad 1961, p. 86.

83. Rad 1961, p. 87.

84. Wisner 1983, p. 178.

85. As mentioned in Chapter 1, note 50, in J the Law is only incipient (in the form of commandments) rather than being a fully developed law code as in D and P. We only mean to say that J set the direction in terms of humans taking their commands from Yahweh. The point is that Yahweh is to give structure to human activity so as to steer us clear of chaos and evil.

86. Kirk, Raven, and Schofield 2007, pp. 202-03.

87. Plato, *Republic,* 507-511. See Jones 1969, p. 135.

88. Buber 1953, p. 73.

89. In contrast, the Catholic Church treats physical evil in the world as God's doing and plan; humans are responsible only for their own moral evil. *CCC,* 310-11.

90. E.g., Wallace 1992d, p. 657; Stern 1958, pp. 409-10; see also Childs 1962, p. 696 (questioning "how there could have been real disobedience without a prior sense of right and wrong").

91. See discussion of inadvertent sins in Cover 1992, pp. 34-36.

92. Stern 1958, p. 417.

93. Likewise, in J's Tower of Babel story, where Yahweh concludes that if he does not stop the project, then (in the KJV translation) "nothing will be restrained from them which they have imagined to do" (Gen. 11:6). See Shattuck 1996, pp. 17-18. While the Hebrew word in 11:6 (lexical form *zāmam*), more commonly translated as to "devise" or "plan evil" (BDB, p. 273; *HALOT* 1:273) differs from that in Genesis 6:5 and 8:21 *(yēṣer),* such scheming also presumably arose from chaotic human imagination.

94. Although J wrote that the source of such temptation lies in human nature, he stopped short of holding the creator, Yahweh, responsible. The closest J came to this was when Yahweh regretted creating man, and therefore unleashed the flood (Gen. 6:7). Compare, for example,

Egyptian Coffin Text Spell 1130, in which the creator states, "I did not command that they do evil, it is their hearts that destroy what I have said." Allen 1988, p. 79.

95. Wismer 1983, pp. 29-31. Regarding the doctrine generally, see *EncJud,* "Inclination, Good and Evil"; *JE,* "Yeẓer ha-Ra"; *UJEnc,* "Evil Inclination"; Porter 1901. It originated in the Hebrew Bible as a cosmic principle as we have discussed but in rabbinical writings it shifted from the original metaphysical meaning to a psychological principle. *EncJud,* "Inclination, Good and Evil."

96. *EncJud,* "Inclination, Good and Evil"; *JE,* "Yeẓer ha-Ra."

97. See, e.g., Ps. 19:7-14. Based on the allusions in this passage, it seems to be contending that the Law is more perfect than the knowledge of good and evil attained in the transgression, Clines 1974, but the very fact that such an argument is made actually affirms the kind of integral relationship between such knowledge and the Law that we are postulating.

98. In contrast, Catholic doctrine does not recognize the cosmic context of human evil and therefore traces the human tendency toward evil solely to humans themselves, a quality that it calls "concupiscence." *CCC,* 1264, 1426. Rather than this being a trait of human nature from the beginning as understood in the Hebrew Bible, i.e., as sin's cause, the Catholic Church argues that it became part of our nature only as a result of Adam's original sin. *CCC,* 404-405.

99. Ricoeur 1967, p. 127.

100. See Cassuto 1998, p. 142.

101. Blenkinsopp 2011, p. 73.

102. See Rad 1961, p. 85; Soggin 1975, p. 94.

103. Vawter 1977, p. 77; Wismer 1983, p. 168.

104. Wismer 1983, pp. 168-69; Hendel 2012.

105. *The New Encyclopædia Britannica (Micropaedia),* 15th ed., s.v. "trickster tale."

106. Sullivan 1987, p. 45; Wismer 1983, p. 168.

107. Franz 1995, p. 95.

108. E.g., Gunkel 1997, pp. 16-17 ("harmless and childish desire").

109. Campbell 1988, p. 51.

110. Shattuck 1996, p. 70.

111. VIII, 180-94.

112. E.g., Hauser 1982.

113. Wismer 1983, p. 179.

114. Wismer 1983, pp. 159-60.

115. Sanford 1981, p. 11.

116. Ricoeur 1967, p. 167.

117. Soggin 1975, pp. 99-100.

118. While it is possible that the extant P text leaves out original material, we might have expected R to include what P had to say about the origin and nature of evil if he indeed wrote about it.

119. Levenson 1988, p. 22.

120. *Paradise Lost,* IV.433.

121. Cf. Bledstein 1977, p. 198.

122. Cf. Bledstein 1977, p. 198.

123. Prior to saying that Eve will give birth in toil *(iṣṣābôn),* Yahweh says that he will multiply the pain *(eṣeb)* of her pregnancies. The word *eṣeb* has been understood to be wordplay on the forbidden tree *('eṣ)* which caused the trouble. Cassuto 1998, p. 165.

124. Wallace 1985, pp. 145-46; see also Robbins 2012, pp. 60-61.

125. E.g., Skinner 1910, p. 67; Gunkel 1997, p. 10; Westermann 1994, p. 225; Rad 1961, p. 92; see also Friedman 2001, p. 19. In another instance, for example, God said he would kill Abimelech (Gen. 20:3) but allowed him to live. And later on in the context of the flood story Yahweh does indeed change his mind about humanity. In the Eden story, Yahweh decided to help out the couple by providing clothes for them, and later made Eve fertile.

126. E.g., Cassuto 1998, p. 125; Speiser 1964, pp. 15, 17.

127. Hamilton 1990, p. 172 ("for as surely as you eat of it you shall die"). He gives other biblical examples in which the literal phrase "in the day" cannot have the literal meaning

because the action in question could not possibly be carried out in a single day (e.g., 1 Kings 2:37, 42; also Exod. 10:28).

128. Keel 1989.

129. Campbell 2001, p. 50.

130. For the full official Catholic discussion of the doctrine, see *CCC*, 385-421. See also Tenant 1903; Blocher 1997.

131. Naidoff 1978, p. 3.

132. E.g., Hauser 1982.

133. Goldingay 2010, p. 46.

134. See Le Grice 2013, p. 34; Campbell 2001, pp. 50-51; and below.

135. Blenkinsopp 2011, p. 79.

136. Rad 1961, p. 118.

137. See Cover 1992, p. 39.

138. Cover 1992, p. 36.

139. Kugel 1997, pp. 118-20.

140. Wismer 1983, p. 29.

141. Soggin 1975, p. 111.

142. Soggin 1975, p. 94.

143. Gordon 1960, p. 37.

144. Wright 1996, p. 320.

145. Naidoff 1978, p. 11 (emphasis ours).

146. Campbell 2001, p. 50. Here he has left aside the aspect of J's conscious intent, but his focus in the context was on the contemporary meaning of the story to us today, not what J was arguing to his own audience.

147. Sanford 1981; Neumann 1990; Le Grice 2013, p. 57.

148. See Franz 1995, p. 5; Le Grice, pp. 41, 43.

149. "The Fish in Alchemy," in Jung 1969a, p. 148. Likewise is Neumann 1954, pp. 5, 329.

150. The initial uroboric state was not literally unconsciousness as in sleep, but rather was a primitive "chaotic" psychic state in which instincts and impulses were dominant (much as J described, and also illustrated by Enkidu in *Gilgamesh*) and humans did not clearly perceive subject-object distinctions (including between their selves and the outside world) and therefore any opposites.

151. Campbell 2001, pp. 50-51; Campbell 1988, p. 48; Le Grice 2013, pp. 34-35, 204; Wilber 1996, p. 309; Neumann 1954, p. 178; Neumann 1955, p. 328.

152. Le Grice 2013, pp. 34-35.

153. See Campbell 1988, p. 66.

154. Eliade and Sullivan 1995, p. 167.

155. In physical and topographical terms, the Eden story is a journey from outside the Center (chaos) into the Center where transformation occurs (death to one's former self), and then a return to a world that for the initiates has changed, much as in hero's journey motif. On the way toward the Center Adam is administered the prohibition and Eve is created, while on the way out of the garden there is the confrontation with Yahweh and Yahweh's decrees.

156. Eliade and Sullivan 1995, pp. 170-71.

157. Franz 1995, p. 1.

158. See Neumann 1954, p. 114; Cirlot 1971, p. 99. Eyes on the wings of angels and cherubim symbolize their knowledge. Becker 1992, p. 106.

159. Neumann 1954, p. 161.

160. Neumann 1954, pp. 159-60; Wilber 1996, p. 253.

161. Neumann 1954, p. 12.

162. Cf. Wilber 1996, p. 208 (regarding the desire for immortality).

163. Neumann 1954, p. 123.

164. Neumann 1954, pp. 317-18.

165. E.g., in *The Odyssey* Calypso's island, and similarly the episode with the Sirens, which Campbell 1964, p. 172, called "symbolic of the allure of the beatitude of paradise"; in the myth of Jason and the Argonauts, the island of Lemnos populated solely by women, who detained them, and also the Sirens on the return; and Dido's kingdom in *The Aeneid*. Similarly (without

a physical place), Gilgamesh's temptation by Ishtar, whom he rejects, whereas Samson succumbs to the wiles of the Goddess figure Delilah.

166. Le Grice 2013, pp. 204-05.

167. Hess points out that, although *hāādām* can be a collective term to mean humanity in general, in this context it more likely refers to the single male. Hess 1990, p. 2 & n. 6 (citing sources in agreement).

168. Neumann 1955, p. 327.

169. See Wilber 1996, p. 276.

170. Neumann 1990, p. 43.

171. Wilber 1996, pp. 306-07.

172. Wilber 1996, p. 306; Neumann 1954, p. 347.

173. Neumann 1954, p. 114.

174. Neumann 1954, p. 117.

175. Neumann 1954, p. 115.

176. Neumann 1954, pp. 347-48.

177. Neumann 1954, p. 118.

178. Campbell 1988, p. 48; Wilber 1996, p. 314.

179. Campbell 2001, p, 50; Campbell 1988, p. 107.

180. Campbell 2001, p. 50.

181. Cf. Le Grice 2013, pp. 142-43.

182. Neumann 1954, p. 348.

183. Neumann 1954, p. 348.

184. Wilber 1996, pp. 287-89; Neumann 1954, pp. 141-44; Neumann 1990, p. 63-64.

185. Neumann 1954, p. 433 n. 8.

EPILOGUE

1. Wilder 1952, p, 212.

2. V.1.275.

3. Jung 1989, p. 199.

4. While we discuss dealing with our evil side below, a discussion of whether according to modern views humans are essentially good or evil would take us far beyond the scope of our purpose here. We note, however, that this has been the subject of much modern psychological research. For a good summary of the current findings that emphasizes the cooperative (good) side of our nature, see Nowak 2012; for a more negative view, see Pinker 2002. The trend of the research shows that both our good/cooperative and "evil" or hostile qualities are products of human evolution, each of which historically had a useful function and survival value. The cooperative aspects had evolutionary value within our close circles of family and communities, while hostile qualities were defensive in nature and enabled humans to deal with nature, animal threats, and humans outside their circles of cooperation. Our modern challenge is that the hostile aspects of our nature that served us well long ago did not evolve (so as to recede) at the pace at which civilization (which requires cooperation) progressed, and so are now dysfunctional and dangerous in our contemporary complex, technologically-armed society. Nowadays, we face the challenge of understanding those aspects of our nature, preventing them from doing harm, and evolving further. This is still much the challenge that J faced and described.

5. Campbell 2001, p. 41.

6. Num. 22:22, 32; 1 Sam. 29:4; 2 Sam. 19:22; 1 Kings 5:4, 11:14, 23, 25; 1 Chr. 21:1; Job 1-2 (10 times); Ps. 109:6; Zech. 3:1-2 (4 times). In most cases, the word appears without the definite article and as such is a general word for an adversary that must be translated as such. In Job and Zechariah the word appears with the definite article and as such could be considered either a title or proper noun.

7. Ringgren 1966, p. 139.

8. Westermann 1994, p. 237 (theory that the serpent is Satan has been "abandoned in modern exegesis"); Rad 1961, p. 85 ("In the narrator's mind it is scarcely an embodiment of a

"demonic" power and certainly not of Satan."); Skinner 1910, p. 73 (the notion that the serpent is Satan is "foreign to the thought of the writer [J]"); Ringgren 1966, p. 139.

9. As noted earlier, the ancient Egyptians recognized an element of divinity in humans.

10. As quoted in Gowan 1975, p. 1. This was from a 1950 letter of Einstein first quoted in this manner in the *New York Times,* Mar. 29, 1972, but in another version, after the second sentence it differs though the idea is almost the same: "The striving to free oneself from this delusion is the one issue of true religion. Not to nourish it but to try to overcome it is the way to reach the attainable measure of peace of mind."

11. For a psychological perspective on many of these issues that is both scholarly and up-to-date, see Kelly et al 2007. For discussions from the perspective of physics, see sources cited in Chapter 3, note 5.

12. Neumann 1954, p. 116.

13. Neumann 1954, p. 245; Wilber 1996, pp. 194, 237; Harrison 1927, p. 460.

14. Le Grice 2013, pp. 42, 45.

15. Wilber 1996, p. 241; Neumann 1990, pp. 34-35.

16. See Sanford 1981, pp. 85-111; Neumann 1990, p. 138.

17. We wish to be clear that we do not purport to deal with the "problem of evil" comprehensively, but are focusing only on J's position that evil is part of human nature and, in such case, how best to deal with that.

18. Neumann 1990, p. 34.

19. Neumann 1990, p. 34.

20. Wilber 1996, p. 354. See generally the discussion in Neumann 1990, pp. 33-58 of the traditional "old ethic" which views perfection as being realized by eliminating negative qualities.

21. Neumann 1990, pp. 33-35.

22. Wilber 1996, p. 354.

23. Neumann 1990, p. 26.

24. Sanford 1981, pp. 23-24.

25. Gebser 1985; Stevens 1993; Wilber 1996; Combs 2009. For example, Gebser identified 5 stages of the evolution of consciousness: archaic; magical; mythical; mental; and integral. Wilber essentially builds on that framework to add higher levels of evolution.

26. Neumann 1990, p. 142; Neumann 1954, p. 127.

27. Sanford 1981, p. 23, 39.

28. Cf. Sanford 1981, pp. 9-10.

29. Sanford 1981, p. 9, 11.

30. Neumann 1990, p. 35.

31. Sanford 1981, p. 50.

32. Sanford 50-51; Neumann 1990, p. 35.

33. Sanford 1981, pp. 50, 53, 61.

34. Sanford 1981, pp. 50-51.

35. Sanford 1981, p. 53.

36. Sanford 1981, pp. 53-54.

37. Neumann 1981, p. 50.

38. Sanford 1981, p. 15.

39. Sanford 1981, p. 15.

40. Neumann 1990, p. 138.

41. As translated by Eugene Rolfe in Neumann 1990, p. 138. As translated by R. F. C. Hull in *CW,* it reads, "is projected, and appears in the form of a metaphysical split between the powers of light and the powers of darkness." Jung 1967, p. 243.

42. Neumann 1990, p. 138.

43. Sanford 1981, p. 21.

44. Sanford 1981, p. 18.

45. The scapegoat ritual and sin offering rituals are described in Leviticus 16. A goat onto which the sins of the people are projected is driven out of the community (order) into the wilderness (chaos). See Talmon 1966, p. 44.

46. The Catechism of the Catholic Church holds that children are "Borne with a fallen human nature and tainted by original sin" (1250). Accordingly, "Since Baptism signifies liberation from sin and from its instigator the devil, one or more *exorcisms* are pronounced over the candidate" (1237). The Roman Rite of Baptism of Children (86) thus asks God to "cast out the power of Satan, spirit of evil, to rescue man from the kingdom of darkness and bring him into the splendour of your kingdom of light. We pray for this child: set him (her) free from original sin."

47. As Reverend Sanford has pointed out, however, Christ's own teachings were geared not toward eliminating the Devil or evil as such, but toward the development of our consciousness and fulfillment of our personality. Sanford 1981, pp. 38-39, 69, 80-81; more comprehensively see Sanford, John, *The Kingdom Within: The Inner Meaning of Jesus' Sayings.* Rev. ed. New York: HarperCollins (1987).

48. Wilber 1996, p. 345; Neumann 1990, p. 145.

49. Sanford 1981, pp. 136-37, 144-45; Wilber 2001, pp. 80-93; Wilber 1996, p. 345; Neumann 1990, p. 145.

50. Neumann 1954, pp. 358-59.

51. Neumann 1954, p. 341.

52. Sanford 1981, p. 40; Neumann 1990, p. 142.

53. Aizenstat 2011, pp. 61-88.

54. Sanford 1981, p. 79; Neumann 1954, p. 353; Neumann 1990, pp. 140, 143-44; Wilber 1996, p. 292.

55. Neumann 1954, p. 199.

56. Neumann 1954, pp. 198-99, 204, 218-19; Le Grice 2013, p. 218.

57. Neumann 1954, pp. 163, 198-200, 212-13.

58. Neumann 1954, p. 212.

59. Neumann 1955, pp. 330-31.

60. Neumann 1955, pp. 331-36.

61. Wilber 1996, p. 239.

62. Le Grice 2013, p. 218.

63. "The self is not only the centre but also the whole circumference with embraces both conscious and unconscious; it is the centre of this totality, just as the ego is the centre of the conscious mind." Jung 1953, p. 41.

64. Neumann 1990, p. 147.

65. Neumann 1990, p. 147.

66. Neumann 1954, pp. 358-59.

67. See, e.g., Wilber 1996 and his many subsequent writings on what he terms integral psychology; Combs 2009; Neumann 1954 and 1990. For the Western perspective the works of Jung are fundamental. For an example of the Eastern perspective, see the works of Sri Aurobindo, especially 1996.

68. Sanford 1981, pp. 22, 31. The process of tending our dreams is explained well in Aizenstat 2011.

69. Sanford 1981, p. 22.

70. Neumann 1954, pp. 372-73.

71. Neumann 1954, pp. 361, 367, 389-91, 413-14; Jung 1976; see Campbell 2004, p. 93.

72. Neumann 1954, p. 376.

73. Sanford 1981, p. 53.

74. Wilber 1996, p. 340.

75. Campbell 1988, p. 32.

76. Le Grice 2013, p. xvii; Neumann 1954, pp. 376-77.

77. Wilber 1996, p. 346.

78. Wilber 1996, p. 346.

79. Neumann 1990, p. 28; Neumann 1955, p. 330.

80. Jung, Forward to Neumann 1990, p. 17; Neumann 1955, p. 331.

81. Sanford 1981, p. 31; see Jung 1969, pp. 31-32.

82. Le Grice 2013, p. 221.

83. As Jung put it, "It is only through the psyche that we can establish that God acts upon us, but we are unable to distinguish whether these actions emanate from God or from the unconscious. We cannot tell whether God and the unconscious are two different entities. Both are border-line concepts for transcendental contents. But empirically it can be established, with a sufficient degree of probability, that there is in the unconscious an archetype of wholeness which manifests itself spontaneously in dreams, etc., and a tendency, independent of the conscious will, to relate other archetypes to this centre. Consequently, it does not seem improbable that the archetype of wholeness occupies as such a central position which approximates it to the God-image. The similarity is further borne out by the peculiar fact that the archetype produces a symbolism which has always characterized and expressed the Deity . . . . Strictly speaking, the God-image does not coincide with the unconscious as such, but with a special content of it, namely the archetype of the self. It is this archetype from which we can no longer distinguish the God-image empirically." Jung 1969c, pp. 468-69. Thus, "One can, then, explain the God-image . . . as a reflection of the self, or, conversely, explain the self as an imago Dei in man." Jung 1969b, p. 190.

84. Sanford 1981, p. 8.

85. Franz 1995, p. 11; Neumann 1954, pp. xv-xvi (citing Jung).

86. Thus, we can understand why having a religious impulse and sense of the divine has evolutionary value. As such, the religious impulse is an objective phenomenon natural to us and is by no means a weakness.

87. Jung 1989, pp. 171, 199; Campbell 2004, pp. 85-108; Le Grice 2013, pp. 8-9.

88. Campbell 1968.

89. *Republic,* 508b-509a.

90. *Republic,* 508d-e.

91. Sanford 1981, p. 141.

92. Campbell 2001, p. 42.

93. See Neumann 1990, p. 96.

Cited Works and Bibliography

Abraham, Joseph. 2002. *Eve: Accused or Acquitted?* Carlisle, UK: Paternoster.

Ackerman, Susan. 2001. *Under Every Green Tree: Popular Religion in Sixth-Century Judah.* Winona Lake, Indiana: Eisenbrauns.

Ackroyd, Peter. 1983. "Goddesses, Women and Jezebel," in Averil Cameron and Amélie Kuhrt, eds. *Images of Women in Antiquity.* Detroit: Wayne State University Press, pp. 245-59.

Aharoni, Yohanan. 1974. "The Horned Altar of Beer-sheba," *BA* 37:2-6.

Ahlström, Göstra. 1986. *Who Were the Israelites?* Winona Lake, Indiana: Eisenbrauns.

Aizenstat, Stephen. 2011. *Dream Tending: Awakening the Healing Power of Dreams.* New Orleans: Spring Journal.

Albertz, Rainer. 1994. *A History of Israelite Religion in the Old Testament Period: Volume I: From the Beginnings to the End of the Monarchy.* Louisville: Westminster/John Knox Press.

Albright, William Foxwell. 1919. "The Mouth of the Rivers," *AJSL* 35:161-95.

———. 1920. "The Goddess of Life and Wisdom," *AJSL* 36:258-94.

———. 1922. "The Location of the Garden of Eden," *AJSL* 39:15-31.

———. 1938. "The Excavation of Tell Beit Mirsim. Vol. II: The Bronze Age," *AASOR* 17: xi-141.

———. 1939. "An Aramaean Magical Text in Hebrew from the Seventh Century B.C.," *BASOR* 76:5-11.

———. 1943. "Two Little Understood Amarna Letters from the Middle Jordan Valley," *BASOR* 89:7-17.

———. 1944a. "A Prince of Taanach in the Fifteenth Century B.C.," *BASOR* 94:12-27.

———. 1944b. Review of S. Kramer, *Sumerian Mythology. JAOS* 64:146-48.

———. 1967. *Yahweh and the Gods of Canaan.* Winona Lake, Indiana: Eisenbrauns.

———. 1968. *Archeology and the Religion of Israel.* 5th ed. Louisville: Johns Hopkins.

Allen, Charles. 1991. *A Mountain in Tibet: The Search for Mount Kailas and the Sources of the Great Rivers of Asia.* London: Warner.

Allen, James. 1988. *Genesis in Egypt: The Philosophy of Ancient Egyptian Creation Accounts.* New Haven: Yale.

Alpert, Bernard, and Fran Alpert. 2012. *Archaeology and the Biblical Record.* Lanham, Maryland: Hamilton Books.

Anderson, Bernhard. 1957. "The Place of Shechem in the Bible," *BA* 20:10-11.

———. 1978. "From Analysis to Synthesis: The Interpretation of Genesis 1-11," *JBL* 97:23-39.

Anthes, Rudolf. 1961. "Mythology in Ancient Egypt," in Kramer 1961, pp. 15-92.

Arnold, Bill, and John Choi. 2003. *A Guide to Biblical Hebrew Syntax.* Cambridge: Cambridge University Press.

Astour, Michael. 1968. "Two Ugaritic Serpent Charms," *JNES* 27: 13-36.

Aurobindo, Sri. 1996. *The Synthesis of Yoga.*Twin Lakes, Wisconsin: Lotus Press.

Bachofen, J. J. 1967. *Myth, Religion, and Mother Right: Selected Writings of J. J. Bachofen.* Princeton: Princeton University Press.

Baden, Joel. 2009. *J, E, and the Redaction of the Pentateuch.* Tübingen: Mohr Siebeck.

———. 2012. *The Composition of the Pentateuch: Renewing the Documentary Hypothesis.* New Haven: Yale University Press.

Bailey, John. 1970. "Initiation and the Primal Woman in Gilgamesh and Genesis 2-3," *JBL* 89:137-50.

Baines, John. 1990. "Interpreting the Story of the Shipwrecked Sailor," *JEA* 76:55-72.

Bal, Mieke. 1987. *Lethal Love: Feminist Literary Readings of Biblical Love Stories.* Bloomington: Indiana University Press.

Bar-On, Shimon. 1998. "The Festival Calendars in Exodus XXIII 14-19 and XXX 18-26," *VT* 48:161-95.

Baring, Anne, and Jules Cashford. 1993. *The Myth of the Goddess:Evolution of an Image.* London: Penguin.

Barr, James. 1988. "The Authority of Scripture: The Book of Genesis and the Origin of Evil in Jewish and Christian Tradition," in Gillian Evans, ed. *Christian Authority: Essays in Honour of Henry Chadwick.* Oxford: Clarendon Press, pp. 59-75.

———. 1992. *The Garden of Eden and the Hope of Immortality.* London: SCM Press

Barton, George. 1934. *Semitic and Hamitic Origins—Social and Religious.* Philadelphia: University of Pennsylvania Press.

Batto, Bernard. 1992. *Slaying the Dragon: Mythmaking in the Biblical Tradition.* Louisville: Westminster/John Knox Press.

Beck, Pirhiya. 1982. "The Drawings from Ḥorvat Teiman (Kuntillet ʿAjrûd)," *TA* 9:3-68.

Becker, Udo. 1992. *The Continuum Encyclopedia of Symbols.* New York: Continuum.

Becking, Bob, Miendert Dijkstra, Marjo C. A. Korpel, and Karel J. H. Vriezen. 2001. *Only One God? Monotheism in Ancient Israel and The Veneration of the Goddess Asherah.* London/ New York: Sheffield Academic Press.

Beeston, A. 1986. "One Flesh," *VT* 36:115-17.

Berlin, Adele. 1994. *Poetics and Interpretation of Biblical Narrative.* Winona Lake, Indiana: Eisenbrauns.

Betancourt, Philip. 1977. *The Aeolic Style in Architecture: A Survey of its Development in Palestine, the Halikarnassos Peninsula, and Greece, 1000-500 B.C.* Princeton: Princeton University Press.

Betlyon, John. 1985. "The Cult of Asherah/Elat at Sidon," *JNES* 44:53-56.

Biedermann, Hans. 1994. *Dictionary of Symbolism: Cultural Icons and the Meanings behind Them.* New York: Meridian.

Billing, Nils. 2002. *Nut: The Goddess of Life in Text and Iconography.* Uppsala: Akademitryck.

Binger, Tilde. 1997. *Asherah: Goddesses in Ugarit, Israel and the Old Testament.* Sheffield: Sheffield Academic Press.

Biran, Avraham. 1994. *Biblical Dan.* Jerusalem: Hebrew Union College.

Bird, Phyllis. 1994. "Bone of My Bone and Flesh of My Flesh," *ThTo* 50:521-34.

Black, Jeremy and Anthony Green. 2003. *Gods, Demons and Symbols of Ancient Mesopotamia: An Illustrated Dictionary.* Austin, Texas: University of Texas Press.

Bledstein, Adrien. 1977. "The Genesis of Humans: The Garden of Eden Revisited," *Judaism* 26:187-200.

Blenkinsopp, Joseph. 1992. *The Pentateuch.* New Haven: Yale University Press.

———. 2004. *Treasures Old and New: Essays in the Theology of the Pentateuch.* Grand Rapids, Michigan: Eerdmans.

———. 2008. "The Midianite-Kenite Hypothesis Revisited and the Origins of Judah," *JSOT* 33:131-53.

————. 2011. *Creation, Un-Creation, Re-Creation: A Discursive Commentary on Genesis 1-11.* London: T&T Clark International.

Blocher, Henri. 1997. *Original Sin: Illuminating the Riddle.* Downers Grove, Illinois: InterVarsity Press.

Bloom, Harold, and David Rosenberg. 1990. *The Book of J.* New York: Grove Press.

Blum, Erhard. 2006. "The Literary Connection between the Books of Genesis and Exodus and the End of the Book of Joshua," in Dozeman and Schmid 2006, pp. 89-106.

Bodenheimer, F.S. 1960. *Animal and Man in Bible Lands.* Leiden: E.J. Brill.

Bonatz, Dominik. 2007. "The Iconography of Religion in the Hittite, Luwian and Aramaean Kingdoms," *IDD,* pp. 15-16, 18

Brandon, S. G. F. 1963. *Creation Legends of the Ancient Near East.* London: Hodder and Stoughton.

Bremmer, Jan. 1983. *The Early Greek Conception of the Soul.* Princeton: Princeton University Press.

Bright, John. 2000. *A History of Israel.* 4th ed. Louisville: Westminster/John Knox Press.

Broshi, Magen. 1992. "The Serpent's Pool and Herod's Monument—A Reconsideration," *Maarav* 8:213-22.

Brueggemann, Walter. 1970. "Of the Same Flesh and Bone (GN 2,23a)," *CBQ* 32:532-42.

Buber, Martin. 1953. *Good and Evil: Two Interpretations.* New York: Charles Scribner's Sons.

Buchanan, Briggs. 1971. "A Snake Goddess and Her Companions," *Iraq* 33:1-18.

Buchanan, George. 1956. "The Old Testament Meaning of the Knowledge of Good and Evil," *JBL* 75:114-20.

Budge, E. A. Wallis. 1969. *The Gods of the Egyptians.* 2 vols. New York: Dover Publications.

————. 1973. *Osiris & the Egyptian Resurrection.* 2 vols. New York: Dover Publications.

————. 1989. *The Book of the Dead.* Arkana: Penguin.

Burrows, Eric. 1935. "Some Cosmological Patterns in Babylonian Religion," in Hooke 1935, pp. 45-70.

Burrows, Millar. 1946. *An Outline of Biblical Theology.* Philadelphia: Westminster Press.

Butterworth, Edric. 1970. *The Tree at the Navel of the Earth.* Berlin: Walter de Gruyter & Co.

Campbell, Antony, and Mark O'Brien. 1993. *Sources of the Pentateuch: Texts, Introductions, Annotations.* Minneapolis: Fortress Press.

Campbell, Joseph. 1949. *The Hero with a Thousand Faces.* New York: MJF Books.

————. 1959. *The Masks of God: Primitive Mythology.* New York: Penguin.

————. 1962. *The Masks of God: Oriental Mythology.* New York: Penguin.

————. 1964. *The Masks of God: Occidental Mythology.* New York: Penguin.

————. 1968. *The Masks of God: Creative Mythology.* New York: Penguin.

————. 1974. *The Mythic Image.* New York: MJF Books

————. 1989. *Historical Atlas of World Mythology: The Way of the Seeded Earth, part 3.* New York: Harper & Row.

————. 1990. *Transformations of Myth Through Time.* New York: Harper & Row.

————. 2001. *Thou Art That.* Novato, California: New World Library.

————. 2004. *Pathways to Bliss: Mythology and Personal Transformation.* Novato, California: New World Library.

Campbell, Joseph, with Bill Moyers. 1988. *The Power of Myth.* New York: Doubleday

Carr, David. 1993. "The Politics of Textual Subversion: A Diachronic Perspective on the Garden of Eden Story," *JBL* 112:589-91.

————. 2005. *Writing on the Tablet of the Heart: Origins of Scripture and Literature.* New York: Oxford University Press.

————. 2012. Method in Determining the Dependence of Biblical on Non-Biblical Texts. Paper presented at the annual meeting of SBL. Chicago, Ill.

Carus, Paul. 1996. *The History of the Devil and the Idea of Evil.* New York: Gramercy Books.

Cassirer, Ernst. 1955. *The Philosophy of Symbolic Forms: Mythical Thought.* New Haven: Yale University Press.

Cassuto, Umberto. 1998. *A Commentary on the Book of Genesis, Part I: From Adam to Noah.* Jerusalem: The Magnes Press, The Hebrew University.

Castiglioni, Arturo. 1942. "The Serpent as Healing God in Antiquity," *Ciba Symposia* 3:1158-67.

Chandler, Tertius. 1987. *Four Thousand Years of Urban Growth: An Historical Census.* Lewiston: St. David's University Press.

Charlesworth, James, ed. 1983. *The Old Testament Pseudepigrapha.* 2 vols. Peabody, Massachusetts: Hendrickson Publishers.

————. 2010. *The Good and Evil Serpent: How a Universal Symbol Became Christanized.* New Haven, Yale University Press.

Charpentier, Louis. 1972. *The Mysteries of Chartres Cathedral.* New York: Avon Books.

Chetwynd, Tom. 1998. *Dictionary of Symbols.* London: Thorsons.

Childs, Brevard. 1962. *Myth and Reality in the Old Testament.* Eugene, Oregon: WIPF & Stock.

————. 1962. "Tree of Knowledge, Tree of Life," *IDB* 4:695-97.

Cirlot, J.E. 1971. *A Dictionary of Symbols.* 2nd ed. New York: Philosophical Library.

Clark, R. T. Rundle. 1959. *Myth and Symbol in Ancient Egypt.* London: Thames and Hudson.

Clifford, Richard. 1972. *The Cosmic Mountain and the Old Testament.* Cambridge: Harvard University Press.

————. 1984. "Cosmogonies in the Ugaritic Texts and in the Bible," *Or* 53:183-201.

————. 1994. *Creation Accounts in the Ancient Near East and in the Bible.* Washington, D.C.: Catholic Biblical Association of America.

Cline, Eric. 2007. *From Eden to Exile.* Washington, D.C.: National Geographic.

Clines, David. 1974. "The Tree of Knowledge and the Law of Yahweh," *VT* 24:8-14.

Clines, David. 1976. "Theme in Genesis 1-11," CBQ 38:483-507.

————. 1990. *What Does Eve Do to Help? and Other Readerly Questions to the Old Testament.* Sheffield, United Kingdom: Sheffield Academic Press.

Cohen, Jeremy. 1980. "Original Sin as the Evil Inclination," *HTR* 73:495-520.

Coleridge, Samuel Taylor. 1972. *Lay Sermons.* Vol. 6 of *The Collected Works of Samuel Taylor Coleridge.* Edited by R. J. White. Princeton: Routledge & Kegan Paul.

Combs, Allan. 2009. *Consciousness Explained Better: Toward an Integral Understanding of the Multi-faceted Nature of Consciousness.* St. Paul: Paragon House.

Cooghan, Michael. 2008. "The Bible's Buried Secrets." PBS interview for NOVA documentary. Online: http://www.pbs.org/wgbh/nova/ancient/writers-bible.html

Cook, Roger. 1988. *The Tree of Life: Image for the Cosmos.* New York: Thames & Hudson.

Cooney, Kathlyn. 2000. "The Edifice of Taharqa by the Sacred Lake: Ritual Function and the Role of the King," *JARCE* 37:15-47.

Cooper, J. C. 1992. *Dictionary of Symbolic & Mythological Animals.* London: Thorsons.

Coote, Robert. 1972. "The Serpent and Sacred Marriage in Northwest Semitic Tradition." Ph.D. diss., Harvard University.

Coote, Robert, and David Ord. 1989. *The Bible's First History.* Philadelphia: Fortress Press.

Cornelius, Izak. 1988. "Paradise Motifs in the 'Eschatology' of the Minor Prophets and the Iconography of the Ancient Near East. The Concepts of Fertility, Water, Trees and 'Tieffrieden' and Gen-2-3," *JNSL* 14:41-83.

————. 2004. *The Many Faces of the Goddess: The Iconography of the Syro-Palestinian Goddesses Anat, Astarte, Qedeshet, and Asherah c. 1500-1000 BCE.* Fribourg: Editions Universitaires.

Cover, Robin. 1992. "Sin, Sinners (Old Testament)," *ABD* 6:31-40.

Cross, Frank Moore. 1954. "The Evolution of the Proto-Canaanite Alphabet," *BASOR* 134:15-24.

————. 1967. "The Origin and Early Evolution of the Alphabet," *EI* 8:8-24.

————. 1973. *Canaanite Myth and Hebrew Epic.* Cambridge: Harvard University Press.

————. 1989. "The Invention and Development of the Alphabet," in *The Origins of Writing* (ed. Wayne Senner; Lincoln: University of Nebraska Press), pp. 77-90.

Crossley-Holland, Kevin. 1980. *The Penguin Book of Norse Myths.* London: Penguin.

Currid, John. 1997. *Ancient Egypt and the Old Testament.* Grand Rapids, Michigan: Baker Books.

Dakpa, Nyima. 2005. *Opening the Door to Bon.* Ithaca: Snow Lion Publications.

Dalley, Stephanie, ed. and trans. 1989. *Myths from Mesopotamia*. New York: Oxford.

―――. 2005. "Babylon as a Name for Other Cities Including Ninveh," in *Proceedings of the 51st Rencontre Assyriologique Internationale* (Chicago: Chicago: Oriental Institute SAOC), pp. 25-34.

Daly, Mary. 1973. *Beyond God the Father: Toward a Philosophy of Women's Liberation*. Boston: Beacon Press.

Daniélou, Alain. 1991. *The Myths and Gods of India*. Rochester, Vermont: Inner Traditions International.

Davies, Philip. 1994. "'House of David' Built on Sand: The Sins of the Biblical Maximizers," *BAR* 20.3:54-55.

Day, John. 1980. "A Case of Inner Scriptural Interpretation," *JTS* 31:309-19.

―――. 1985. *God's Conflict with the Dragon and the Sea: Echoes of a Canaanite myth in the Old Testament*. Cambridge: Cambridge University Press.

―――. 1986. "Asherah in the Bible and Northwest Semitic Literature," *JBL* 105:385-408.

―――. 2002. *Yahweh and the Gods and Goddesses of Canaan*. London: Sheffield Academic Press.

Decharme, Paul. 1886. *Mythologie de la Grèce Antique*. Paris: Librairie Garnier Frères.

Dever, William. 1992. "How to Tell a Canaanite from an Israelite," in Shanks et al 1992, pp. 26-60.

―――. 2001. *What Did the Biblical Writers Know & When Did They Know It? What Archeology Can Tell Us About the Reality of Ancient Israel*. Grand Rapids, Michigan: Eerdmans.

―――. 2003. *Who Were the Early Israelites and Where Did they Come From?* Grand Rapids, Michigan: Eerdmans.

―――. 2005. *Did God Have a Wife? Archaeology and Folk Religion in Ancient Israel*. Grand Rapids, Michigan: Eerdmans.

Dijkstra, Meindert. 2001a. "I have Blessed you by Yhwh of Samaria and his Asherah: Texts with Religious Elements from the Soil Archive of Ancient Israel," in Becking 2001, pp. 17-44.

―――. 2001b. "El, the God of Israel—Israel, the People of Yhwh: On the Origins of Ancient Israelite Yahwism," in Becking 2001, pp. 81-126.

Dimmitt, Cornelia and J. A. B. van Buitenen, eds. 1978. *Classical Hindu Mythology: A Reader in the Sanskrit Puranas*. Philadelphia: Temple University Press.

Dozeman, Thomas and Konrad Schmid, eds. 2006. *Farewell to the Yahwist? The Composition of the Pentateuch in Recent European Interpretation*. Atlanta: Society of Biblical Literature.

Dozeman, Thomas, Konrad Schmid, and Baruch Schwartz, eds. 201. *The Pentateuch: International Perspectives on Current Research*. Tübingen: Mohr Siebeck.

Driver, Samuel and George Gray. 1921. *A Critical and Exegetical Commentary on the Book of Job*. Edinburgh: T&T Clark.

Durkheim, Emile. 1995. *The Elementary Forms of Religious Life*. New York: The Free Press.

Edwards, I. 1955. "A Relief of Qudshu-Astarte-Anath in the Winchester College Collection," *JNES* 14:49-51.

Eliade, Mircea. 1978. *A History of Religious Ideas*. vol. 1. Chicago: University of Chicago Press.

―――. 1987. *The Sacred and the Profane*. Orlando, Florida: Harcourt.

―――. 1991a. *Images and Symbols: Studies in Religious Symbolism*. Princeton: Princeton University Press.

―――. 1991b. *The Myth of the Eternal Return*. Princeton: Princeton University Press.

―――. 1992. *Shamanism: Archaic Techniques of Ecstasy*. Princeton: Princeton University Press.

―――. 1994. *Rites and Symbols of Initiation*. Rev. ed. Putnam, Connecticut: Spring Publications.

―――. 1996. *Patterns in Comparative Religion*. Lincoln, Nebraska: University of Nebraska Press.

―――. 2009. *Yoga: Immortality and Freedom*. Princeton: Princeton University Press.

Eliade, Mircea, and Lawrence Sullivan. 1995. "Center of the World," in *ER* 3:166-71.

Eller, Cynthia. 2000. *The Myth of Matriarchal Prehistory: Why an Invented Past Won't Give Women a Future.* Boston: Beacon Press.

Ellington, John. 1979. "Man and Adam in Genesis 1-5," *BT* 30:201-05.

Ellis, Peter. 1968. *The Yahwist: The Bible's First Theologian.* Notre Dame, Indiana: Fides.

Emerton, J. A. 1982. "New Light on Israelite Religion: The Implications of the Inscriptions from Kuntillet'Ajrud," *ZAW* 94:2-20.

Engnell, I. 1955. "'Knowledge' and 'Life' in the Creation Story," in M. Noth and W. Thomas, eds. *Wisdom in Israel and in the Ancient Near East.* vol. 3. Leiden: Brill, pp. 103-119.

Evans, Arthur. 1901. *The Mycenaean Tree and Pillar Cult and its Mediterranean Relations.* London: Macmillan.

Evans, Carl. 1980. *Scripture in Context: Essays on the Comparative Method.* Pittsburgh: Pickwick Press.

Evans, Craig, Joel Lohr, and David Petersen, eds. 2012. *The Book of Genesis: Composition, Reception, and Interpretation.* Leiden: Brill.

Faulkner, Raymond. 1962. *A Concise Dictionary of Middle Egyptian.* Oxford: Griffith Institute.
———. 1969. *The Pyramid Texts.* Oxford: Clarendon Press.
———. 1973. *The Ancient Egyptian Coffin Texts.* Oxford: Aris & Phillips.

Finkelstein, Israel and Neil Silberman. 2001. *The Bible Unearthed: Archaeology's New Vision of Ancient Israel and the Origin of its Sacred Texts.* New York: Simon & Schuster.
———. 2006. *David and Solomon.* New York: Free Press.

Finkelstein, Israel and Amihai Mazar. 2007. *The Quest for the Historical Israel: Debating Archaeology and the History of Early Israel.* Edited by Brian B. Schmidt. Atlanta: Society of Biblical Literature. Each co-author wrote part of each chapter under his own name, so citations indicate in parentheses the co-author being cited.

Finkelstein, J. J. 1966. "The Genealogy of the Hammurapi Dynasty," *JCS* 20:95-118.

Finkelstein, J. J. and Moshe Greenberg, eds. 1967. *Oriental and Biblical Studies: Collected Writings of E. A. Speiser.* Philadelphia: University of Pennsylvania Press.

Fisher, Loren. 2011. *Genesis: A Royal Epic.* Eugene, Oregon: Cascade Books.

Flood, Gavin. 1996. *An Introduction to Hinduism.* New York: Cambridge University Press.

Frankfort, Henri. 1961. *Ancient Egyptian Religion.* New York: Harper and Brothers.
———. 1965. *Cylinder Seals: A Documentary Essay on the Art and Religion of the Ancient Near East.* Reprint, London: The Gregg Press.
———. 1970. *The Art and Architecture of the Ancient Orient.* 4th ed. New Haven: Yale University Press.
———. 1978. *Kingship and the Gods.* Chicago: University of Chicago Press.

Franz, Marie-Louise von. 1995. *Creation Myths.* Rev. ed. Boston: Shambhala.

Frazer, James George. 1923. *Folklore in the Old Testament: Studies in Comparative Religion Legend and Law.* London: Macmillan.
———. 1963. *The Golden Bough.* 3rd ed. 13 vols. New York: Macmillan.

Freedman, David Noel. 1987. "Yahweh of Samaria and his Asherah," *BA* 50:241-49.

Frese, Daniel. 2012. The Ark and the Cherubim. Paper presented at the annual meeting of SBL. Chicago, Ill.

Friedman, Richard Elliot. 1992. "Torah (Pentateuch)," *ABD* 6:605-22.
———. 1997. *Who Wrote the Bible?* 2nd ed. New York: Harper Collins.
———. 1999. *The Hidden Book of the Bible.* San Francisco: HarperCollins.
———. 2001. *Commentary on the Torah.* New York: HarperCollins.
———. 2003. *The Bible with Sources Revealed.* New York: HarperCollins.

Fromm, Erich. 1951. *The Forgotten Language: An Introduction to the Understanding of Dreams, Fairy Tales, and Myths.* New York: Rinehart.

Frothingham, A. L. 1916. "Babylonian Origin of Hermes the Snake-God, and of the Caduceus I," *AJA* 20:175-211.

Frymer-Kensky, Tikva. 1977. "The Atrahasis Epic and Its Significance for our Understanding of Genesis 1-9," *BA* 40:147-55.

Gardner, Anne. 1990. "Genesis 2.4b-3: A Mythological Paradigm of Sexuality or of the Religious History of Pre-exilic Israel?," *SJT* 43:1-18.

Gaster, Theodor. 1961. *Thespis: Ritual, Myth, and Drama in the Ancient Near East.* New York: W.W. Norton and Company.

Gebser, Jean. 1985. *The Ever-Present Origin.* Trans. N. Barstad and A. Mickunas. Athens, Ohio: Ohio University Press.

Gelb, Ignace. 1955. "The Name of Babylon," *JIAS* 1:1-4.

Geus, C. H. J. de. 1991. "The Material Culture of Phoenicia and Israel," in *Phoenicia and the Bible: Proceedings of the Conference held at the University of Leuven on the 15th and 16th of March 1990* (ed. Edward Lipinski; Leuven: Uitgeverih Peeters), pp. 11-16.

Gimbutas, Marija. 1989. *The Language of the Goddess.* New York: Harper & Row.

Giovino, Mariana. 2007. *The Assyrian Sacred Tree: A History of Interpretations.* Fribourg, Switzerland: Academic Press Fribourg.

Gitin, Seymour. 1990. "Ekron of the Philistines, Part II: Olive Suppliers to the World," *BAR* 16.2:32-42, 59.

———. 1993. "Seventh Century B.C.E. Cultic Elements at Ekron," in *Biblical Archaeology Today 1990: Proceedings of the Second International Congress on Biblical Archaeology: Jerusalem, June-July 1990* (ed. Avraham Biran and Joseph Aviram; Jerusalem: Israel Exploration Society), pp. 248-58.

Glenn, Justin. 1977. "Pandora and Eve: Sex as the Root of All Evil," *The Classical World* 71:179-85.

Goblet d'Alviella, Eugène. 1894. *The Migration of Symbols.* Westminster: Archibald Constable.

Goff, Beatrice Laura. 1963. *Symbols of Prehistoric Mesopotamia.* New Haven: Yale University Press.

Goldingay, John. 2010. *Genesis for Everyone, Part One: Chapters 1-16.* Louisville: Westminster John Knox Press.

Goldschmidt, Walter. 1966. *Comparative Functionalism: An Essay in Anthropological Theory.* Berkeley: University of California Press.

Goldwasser, Orly. 2010. "How the Alphabet Was Born from Hieroglyphs," *BAR* 36.2:36-50, 74.

Goodenough, Erwin. 1953. *Jewish Symbols in the Greco-Roman Period.* 13 vols. New York: Pantheon Books.

Goodison, Lucy and Christine Morris, eds. 1998. *Ancient Goddesses: The Myths and the Evidence.* Madison, Wisconsin: University of Wisconsin Press.

Gordis, Robert. 1936. "The Significance of the Paradise Myth," *AJSL* 52:86-94.

———. 1957. "The Knowledge of Good and Evil in the Old Testament and the Qumran Scrolls," *JBL* 76:123-38.

Gordon, Cyrus. 1960. *The World of the Old Testament.* London: Phoenix House.

Gorelick, Leonard and Elizabeth Williams-Forte. 1983. *Ancient Seals and the Bible.* Malibu, California: Undena Publications.

Govinda, Anagarika. 1969. *The Foundations of Tibetan Mysticism.* Boston: Weiser Books.

Gowan, Donald. 1988. *When Man Becomes God: Humanism and Hybris in the Old Testament.* Pittsburgh: Pickwick.

Gowan, John. 1975. *Trance, Art and Creativity.* Buffalo: Creative Education Foundation.

Graham, M. Patrick, William Brown, and Jeffrey Kuan, eds. 1993. *History and Interpretation: Essays in Honour of John H. Hayes.* Sheffield: JSOT Press.

Graham, William, and Herbert May. 1936. *Culture and Conscience: An Archaeological Study of the New Religious Past in Ancient Palestine.* Chicago: University of Chicago Press.

Grant, Elihu. 1929a. *Beth Shemesh.* Haverford, Pennsylvania: Biblical and Kindred Studies.

———. 1929b. "Beth Shemesh, 1928," *AASOR* 9:1-15.

Graves, Robert. 1960. *The Greek Myths.* London: Penguin.

Graves, Robert and Raphael Patai. 1983. *Hebrew Myths: The Book of Genesis.* New York: Greenwich House.

Gray, George. 1965. *A Critical and Exegetical Commentary on Numbers.* Edinburgh: T&T Clark.

Gray, John. 1964. *The Canaanites.* New York: Praeger.

———. 1976. *I & II Kings,* 3rd ed. London: Westminster Press.

Green, Margaret. 1975. "Eridu in Sumerian Literature." Ph.D. diss., University of Chicago.

Greenberg, Moshe. 1983. *Ezekiel 1-20: A New Translation with Introduction and Commentary.* Garden City, New York: Doubleday and Company.

Gunkel, Hermann. 1964. *The Legends of Genesis.* New York: Schocken Books.

———. 1997. *Genesis.* Macon, Georgia: Mercer University Press.

———. 2006. *Creation and Chaos in the Primeval Era and the Eschaton: A Religio-Historical Study of Genesis 1 and Revelation 12.* Grand Rapids: Eerdmans.

———. 2009. *Israel and Babylon: The Babylonian Influence on Israelite Religion.* Eugene Oregon: Cascade Books.

Hadley, Judith. 2000. *The Cult of Asherah in Ancient Israel and Judah: Evidence for a Hebrew Goddess.* Cambridge, UK: Cambridge University Press.

Haldar, Alfred. 1950. *The Notion of the Desert in Sumero-Accadian and West Semitic Religions.* Uppsala: Almqvist & Wiksells Boktryckeri.

Hall, James. 1974. *Hall's Dictionary of Subjects & Symbols in Art.* London: John Murray.

Hallo, William. 1980. "Biblical History in its Near Eastern Setting: The Contextual Approach," in Evans 1980, pp. 1-26.

Halpern, Baruch. 1992. "The Exodus from Egypt: Myth or Reality?," in Shanks et al 1992, pp. 86-113.

———. 2009. *From Gods to God: The Dynamics of Iron Age Cosmologies.* Tübingen: Mohr Siebeck.

Hamilton, Gordon. 2006. *The Origins of the West Semitic Alphabet in Egyptian Scripts.* Washington, D.C.: Catholic Biblical Association of America.

Hamilton, Victor. 1990. *The Book of Genesis: Chapters 1-17.* Grand Rapids: Eerdmans.

———. 1992. "Marriage: Old Testament and Ancient Near East," *ABD* 4:559-69.

Haran, Menahem. 1981. "Temples and Cultic Open Areas as Reflected in the Bible," in *Temples and High Places in Biblical Times.* Jerusalem: Nelson Glueck School of Biblical Archaeology of Hebrew Union College—Jewish Institute of Religion.

Harris, R. Laird, Gleason L. Archer, Jr., and Bruce K. Waltke. 1980. *Theological Workbook of the Old Testament.* Chicago: Moody.

Harrison, Jane. 1927. *Themis: A Study of the Social Origins of Greek Religion.* Rev. ed. Cleveland: World.

———. 1991. *Prolegomena to the Study of Greek Religion.* 3rd ed. Cambridge: Cambridge University Press. Repr., Princeton: Princeton University Press.

———. 1900. "Pandora's Box," *JHS* 20:19-114.

Hasel, Michael. 1998. *Domination & Resistance: Egyptian Military Activity in the Southern Levant, 1300-1185 BC.* Leiden: Brill.

Hauser, Alan. 1982. "Genesis 2-3: The Theme of Intimacy and Alienation," in *Art and Meaning: Rhetoric in Biblical Literature.* David J. A. Clines, D. M. Gunn, and Alan J. Hauser, eds. Sheffield: JSOT Press, pp. 20-36.

Haynes, Gregory. 2009. *Tree of Life, Mythical Archetype: Revelations from the Symbols of Ancient Troy.* San Francisco: Symbolon Press.

Hays, Richard. 2005. *The Conversion of the Imagination: Paul as Interpreter of Israel's Scripture.* Grand Rapids: Eerdmans.

Hedlam, Walter. 1934. "Prometheus and the Garden of Eden," *CQ* 28:63-67.

Hendel, Ronald. 1985. "The Flame of the Whirling Sword: A Note on Genesis 3:24," *JBL* 104: 671-74.

———. 1987. "Of Demigods and the Deluge: Toward an Interpretation of Genesis 6:1-4," *JBL* 106:13-26.

———. 2012. "Was the Snake in the Garden of Eden Satan," Huffington Post, Sept. 23, 2012, www.huffingtonpost.com/ronald-hendel/was-the-snake-in-the-garden-of-eden-satan_b_1900973.html.

Heskett, Randall, and Joel Butler. 2012. *Divine Vintage: Following the Wine Trail from Genesis to the Modern Age.* New York: Palgrave McMillan.

Hess, Richard. 1990. "Splitting the Adam: The Usage of 'Ādām in Genesis I-IV," in, *Studies in the Pentateuch* (ed. J. A. Emerton; Leiden: Brill), pp. 1-15.

————. 1991. "Yahweh and His Asherah? Epigraphic Evidence for Religious Pluralism in Old Testament Times," in *One God, One Lord in a World of Religious Pluralism* (ed. Andrew Clarke and Bruce Winter; Cambridge: Tyndale House), pp. 5-33.

————. 2009. *Studies in the Personal Names of Genesis 1-11*. Winona Lake, Indiana: Eisenbrauns.

Hess, Richard and David Tsumura, eds. 1994. *I Studied Inscriptions from before the Flood: Ancient Near Eastern, Literary, and Linguistic Approaches to Genesis 1-11*. Winona Lake, Indiana: Eisenbrauns.

Hestrin, Ruth. 1987a. "The Cult Stand from Taanach and its Religious Background," in Lipinski, Edward, ed., *Studia Phoenicia V: Phoenicia and the East Mediterranean in the First Millenium B.C.* Leuven: Uitgeverij Peeters.

————. 1987b. "The Lachish Ewer and the Asherah," *IEJ* 37:212-23.

————. 1991. "Understanding Asherah: Exploring Semitic Iconography," *BAR* 17.5:50-59.

Hiebert, Theodore. 1996. *The Yahwist's Landscape: Nature and Religion in Early Israel.* Minneapolis: Fortress Press.

Hillman, James. 1981. "Psychology: Monotheistic or Polytheistic," in Miller 1981, pp. 109-42.

Hodder, Ian. 2006. *The Leopard's Tale: Revealing the Mysteries of Catalhöyük.* London: Thames & Hudson.

Hoffman, Curtiss. 1999. *The Seven Story Tower.* Cambridge, Massachusetts: Perseus Publishing.

Holmberg, Uno. 1964. *The Mythology of All Races, vol. 4: Finno-Ugric Siberian.* New York: Cooper Square Publishers.

Holter, Knut. 1990. "The Serpent in Eden as a Symbol of Israel's Political Enemies: A Yahwistic Criticism of the Solomonic Foreign Policy?," *SJOT* 1:106-12.

Honeyman, A. M. 1952. *"Merismus* in Biblical Hebrew," *JBL* 71:11-18.

Hooke, Samuel, ed. 1935. *The Labyrinth.* New York: The Macmillan Company.

————. 1938. *The Origins of Early Semitic Ritual.* London: The British Academy.

————. 1961. *In the Beginning.* Westport, Connecticut: Greenwood Press.

————. 1963. *Middle Eastern Mythology.* Mineola, New York: Dover Publications, Inc.

Hornung, Erik. 1982. *Conceptions of God in Ancient Egypt: The One and the Many.* Ithaca: Cornell University Press.

Howey, M. Oldfield. 1955. *The Encircled Serpent: A Study of Serpent Symbolism in All Countries and Ages.* New York: Arthur Richmond Company.

Hvidberg, Flemming. 1960. "The Canaanitic Background of Gen. I-III," *VT* 10:285-94.

Jacobsen, Thorkild. 1968. "The Battle Between Marduk and Tiamat," *JAOS* 88:104-08.

————. 1976. *The Treasures of Darkness: A History of Mesopotamian Religion.* New Haven: Yale University Press.

James, Edwin. 1958. *Myth and Ritual in the Ancient Near East: An Archeological and Documentary Study.* New York: Frederick A. Praeger.

————. 1959. *The Cult of the Mother-Goddess: An Archaeological and Documentary Study.* London: Thames and Hudson.

————. 1966. *The Tree of Life: An Archeological Study.* Leiden: Brill.

James, Frances, Patrick McGovern, and Anne Bonn. 1993. *The Late Bronze Egyptian Garrison at Beth Shan,* 2 vols. Philadelphia: University of Pennsylvania Museum.

Johnson, Buffie. 1988. *Lady of the Beasts: Ancient Images of the Goddess and Her Sacred Animals.* New York: HarperSanFrancisco.

Joines, Karen Randolph. 1968. "The Bronze Serpent in the Israelite Cult," *JBL* 87:245-56.

————. 1974. *Serpent Symbolism in the Old Testament: A Linguistic, Archaeological, and Literary Study.* Haddonfield, New Jersey: Haddonfield House.

————. 1975. "The Serpent in Gen 3," *ZAW* 87:1-11.

Jones, Alison. 1995. *Larousse Dictionary of World Folklore.* Edinburgh: Larousse.

Jones, W. T. 1969. *A History of Western Philosophy: The Classical Mind.* 2nd ed. New York: Harcourt Brace & World.

Josephus (1999). *The New Complete Works of Josephus.* Grand Rapids: Kregel Publications.

Jung, Carl. 1953. *Psychology and Alchemy. CW,* vol. 12.

————. 1956. *Symbols of Transformation, CW,* vol. 5.

————. 1959a. "The Archetypes and the Collective Unconscious," *CW*, vol. 9.1, pp. 3-41.

————. 1959b. "The Concept of the Collective Unconscious," *CW*, vol. 9, part 1, pp. 42-53.

————. 1959c. "Concerning the Archetypes, with Special Reference to the Anima Concept," *CW*, vol. 9.1, pp. 54-72.

————. 1959d. "Psychological Aspects of the Mother Archetype," *CW*, vol. 9.1, pp. 73-110.

————. 1959e. "Concerning Rebirth," *CW*, vol. 9.1, pp. 111-47.

————. 1960. "The Structure of the Psyche," *CW*, vol. 8, pp. 139-58.

————, ed. 1964. *Man and His Symbols*. New York: Doubleday.

————. 1966. "On the Psychology of the Unconscious," *CW*, vol. 7, pp. 3-119.

————. 1967. "The Spirit Mercurius," *CW*, vol. 11, pp. 193-250.

————. 1969a. *Aion: Researches into the Phenomenology of the Self. CW*, vol. 9.2.

————. 1969b. "A Psychological Approach to the Dogma of the Trinity," *CW*, vol. 11, pp. 109-200.

————. 1969c. "Answer to Job," *CW*, vol. 11, pp. 365-470.

————. 1970. *Mysterium Coniunctionis.* 2nd ed. *CW*, vol. 14.

————. 1976. "The Symbolic Life," *CW*, vol. 20, pp. 267-90.

————. 1983. "The Philosophical Tree," *CW*, vol. 13, pp. 251-349.

————. 1989. *Memories, Dreams, Reflections.* New York: Vintage Books.

Kapelrud, A.S. 1980. "*chavvāh*," *TDOT* 4:257-60.

Keel, Othmar. 1989. "Yahweh as Mother Goddess," *TD* 36:233-36.

————. 1997. *The Symbolism of the Biblical World.* Winona Lake, Indiana: Eisenbrauns.

————. 1998. *Goddesses and Trees, New Moon and Yahweh: Ancient Near Eastern Art and the Hebrew Bible.* Sheffield: Sheffield Academic Press.

Keel, Othmar and Christoph Uehlinger. 1998. *Gods, Goddesses, and Images of God in Ancient Israel.* Minneapolis: Fortress Press.

Kelly, Edward, Emily Kelly, Adam Crabtree, Alan Gauld, Michael Grosso and Bruce Greyson. 2007. *Irreducibile Mind: Toward a Psychology for the 21st Century.* Lanham, Maryland: Rowman & Littlefield.

Kenyon, Kathleen. 1965. *Excavations at Jericho.* 5 vols. Jerusalem: British School of Archaeology in Jerusalem.

Kerényi, Carl. 1951. *The Gods of the Greeks.* London: Thames & Hudson.

————. 1959. *Asklepios: Archetypal Image of the Physician's Existence.* New York: Pantheon Books.

————. 1976. *Dionysos: Archetypal Image of Indestructible Life.* Princeton: Princeton University Press.

Kienast, Burkhart. 1979. "The Name of the City of Babylon," *Sumer* 35:246-48.

Kikawada, Isaac. 1972. "Two Notes on Eve," *JBL* 91:33-37.

————. 1992. "Primeval History," *ABD* 5:461-66.

Kille, Andrew. 2001. *Psychological Biblical Criticism.* Minneapolis: Fortress Press.

King, Leonard, ed. 1902. *The Seven Tablets of Creation.* 2 vols. London: Luzac.

Kirk, G. S. 1973. *Myth: Its Meaning and Functions in Ancient and Other Cultures.* Berkeley and Los Angeles: University of California Press.

Kirk, G. S., J. E. Raven, and M. Schofield. 2007. *The Presocratic Philosophers.* 2nd ed. Cambridge: Cambridge University Press.

Kletter, Raz. 1966. *The Judean Pillar-Figurines and the Archaeology of Asherah.* Oxford: Tempvs Reparatvm.

Kraeling, Emil. 1947. "The Significance and Origin of Gen 6:1-4," *JNES* 6:193-208.

Kramer, Samuel Noah. 1944. "Dilmun: The Land of the Living," *BASOR* 96:18-28.

————. 1952. *Enmerkar and the Lord of Aratta: A Sumerian Epic Tale of Iraq and Iran.* Philadelphia: University of Pennsylvania Press.

————. 1956. *History Begins at Sumer.* Philadelphia: University of Pennsylvania Press.

————, ed. 1961. *Mythologies of the Ancient World.* Garden City, New York: Anchor Books.

————. 1963. *The Sumerians: Their History, Culture, and Character.* Chicago: University of Chicago Press.

————. 1969. *The Sacred Marriage Rite: Aspects of Faith, Myth, and Ritual in Ancient Sumer.* Bloomington, Indiana: Indiana University Press.

————. 1972. *Sumerian Mythology,* rev. ed. Philadelphia: University of Pennsylvania Press.

————. 1979. *From the Poetry of Sumer.* Berkeley: University of California Press.

Kraus, Hans-Joachim. 1965. *Worship in Israel: A Cultic History of the Old Testament.* Richmond, Virginia: John Knox Press.

Kuan, Jeffrey. 1993. "Was Omri a Phoenician?," in Graham, Brown, and Kuan 1993, pp. 231-244.

Kugel, James. 1997. *The Bible As It Was.* Cambridge, Massachusetts: Belknap Press of Harvard University Press.

Kuyper, Lester. 1947). "'To Know Good and Evil,'" *Interpretation* 1:490-92.

Lambert, W. G. (1985). "Trees, Snakes and Gods in Ancient Syria and Anatolia," *BSOAS* 48, 435-51.

Lambert, W. G. and A. R. Millard. 1969. *Atra-Hasis: The Babylonian Story of the Flood.* Oxford: Clarendon Press.

Langdon, Stephen. 1914. *Tammuz and Ishtar: A Monograph upon Babylonian Religion and Theology.* Oxford: Clarendon Press.

————. 1928. "The Legend of the kiskanu," *JRAS* 4:843-48.

————. 1964. *The Mythology of All Races, vol. 5: Semitic Mythology.* New York: Cooper Square Publishers.

Lawton, Robert. 1986. "Genesis 2:24: Trite or Tragic?," *JBL* 105:97-98.

Layton, Scott. 1997. "Remarks on the Canaanite Origin of Eve," *CBQ* 59:22-32.

Le Grice, Keiron. 2013. *The Rebirth of the Hero: Mythology as a Guide to Spiritual Transformation.* London: Muswell Hill Press.

Leach, Edmund. 1961. "Lévi-Strauss in the Garden of Eden: An Examination of Some Recent Developments in the Analysis of Myth," Transactions of the New York Academy of Sciences (Series 2), 13:386-96.

————. 1969. *Genesis as Myth and Other Essays.* London: Jonathan Cape.

————. 1974. *Claude Levi-Strauss.* New York: Viking Press.

Leach, Edmund and D. Alan Aycock. 1983. *Structuralist Interpretations of Biblical Myth.* Cambridge: Cambridge University Press.

Leeming, David and Margaret Leeming. 1994. *A Dictionary of Creation Myths.* New York: Oxford University Press.

Leisegang, Hans. 1955. "The Mystery of the Serpent," in *The Mysteries: Papers from the Eranos Yearbooks* (ed. Joseph Campbell; Princeton: Princeton University Press), pp. 194-260.

Lemaire, André. 1984. "Who or What Was Yahweh's Asherah?," *BAR* 10.6:42-51.

Lenormant, François. 1883. *The Beginnings of History According to the Bible and the Traditions of Oriental Peoples from the Creation of Man to the Deluge.* New York: Charles Scribner's Sons.

Lerner, Gerda. 1986. *The Creation of Patriarchy.* New York: Oxford University Press.

Levenson, Jon. 1988. *Creation and the Persistence of Evil: The Jewish Drama of Divine Omnipotence.* Princeton: Princeton University Press.

Lévi-Strauss, Claude. 1955. "The Structural Study of Myth," *Journal of American Folklore* 86:428-44.

Levy, Thomas, Russell Adams, and Adolvo Muniz. 2004. "Archaeology and the Shasu Nomads: Recent Excavations in the Jabal Hamrat Fidan, Jordan," in Friedman and Propp 2004, pp. 63-89.

Lewis-Williams, David and David Pearce. 2005. *Inside the Neolithic Mind.* London: Thames & Hudson.

Lipinski, Edward. 1972. "The Goddess Atirat in Ancient Arabia, in Babylon, and in Ugarit—Her Relation to the Moon-God and Sun Goddess," *OLP* 3:101-19.

————. 1986. "The Syro-Palestinian Iconography of Woman and Goddess," *IEJ* 36:87-96.

Lloyd-Russell, Vincent. 1938. *The Serpent as the Prime Symbol of Immortality Has Its Origin in the Semitic-Sumerian Culture.* Ph.D. diss., University of Southern California.

Lundbom, Jack. 1999. *The Anchor Bible: Jeremiah 1-20.* New York: Doubleday.

Lurker, Manfred. 1974. *An Illustrated Dictionary of the Gods and Symbols of Ancient Egypt.* New York: Thames & Hudson.

Lutz, H. F. 1922. *Viticulture and Brewing in the Ancient Orient.* New York: Stechert.

Mabbett, I.W. 1983. "The Symbolism of Mt. Meru," *HR* 23:64-83.

Macalister, A. Stewart. 1912. *The Excavation of Gezer,* 3 vols. London: John Murray.

MacCulloch, J. A. 1962. "Serpent-Worship: Introduction," *ERE* 11:399-411.

Maier, Walter. 1986. *'Ašerah: Extrabiblical Evidence.* Atlanta: Scholars Press.

Malek, Jaromir. 1999. *Egyptian Art.* London: Phaidon Press.

Marett, Robert. 1914. *The Threshold of Religion.* New York: Macmillan.

Malinowski, Bronislaw. 1944. *A Scientific Theory of Culture and Other Essays.* Chapel Hill: University of North Carolina Press.

————. 1984. *Magic, Science and Religion and Other Essays.* Westport, Connecticut: Green-wood Press.

Mallory, J. P. 1989. *In Search of the Indo-Europeans: Language, Archaeology and Myth.* London: Thames & Hudson.

Margalit, Baruch. 1990. "The Meaning and Significance of Asherah," *VT* 40:264-97.

Markman, Roberta and Peter Markman. 1994. *The Flayed God: Mesoamerican Mythological Tradition.* New York: HarperCollins.

Mazar, Amihai. 1992. *Archaeology of the Land of the Bible, 10,000-586 B.C.E.* New Haven: Yale University Press.

Mazar, Benjamin. 1965. "The Sanctuary of Arad and the Family of Hobab the Kenite," *JNES* 24:297-303.

————. 1977. "Yahweh Came out of Sinai," in *Temples and High Places in Biblical Times: Proceedings of the Colloquium in Honor of the Centennial of Hebrew Union College-Jewish Institute of Religion* (Jerusalem: Hebrew Union College-Jewish Institute of Religion), pp. 5-9.

McCarter, Jr., P. Kyle. 1992. "The Origins of Israelite Religion," in Shanks 1992, pp. 119-36.

McEvenue, Sean. 1994. "A Return to Sources in Genesis 28, 10-22?," *ZAW* 106:375-89.

McGovern, Patrick. 2003. *Ancient Wine: The Search for the Origins of Viniculture.* Princeton: Princeton University Press.

McKenzie, John. 1963. *Myths and Realities: Studies in Biblical Theology.* Milwaukee: Bruce Publishing.

————. 1965. *Dictionary of the Bible.* Milwaukee: Bruce Publishing.

Meehan, Aidan. 1995. *The Tree of Life.* New York: Thames & Hudson.

Mettinger, Tryggve. 2007. *The Eden Narrative: A Literary and Religio-historical Study of Genesis 2-3.* Winona Lake, Indiana: Eisenbrauns.

Mikaya, Adam. 1981. "Earliest Aramaic Inscription Uncovered in Syria," *BAR* 4.4:52-53.

Milgrom, Jacob. 1992. "Priestly ("P") Source," *ABD* 5:454-61.

Millard, A. R. 1984. "The Etymology of Eden," *VT* 34:103-06.

Miller, Maxwell and John Hayes. 2006. *A History of Ancient Israel and Judah.* 2nd ed. Louis-ville: Westminster John Knox Press.

Milton, John. 2005. *Paradise Lost.* New York: Norton & Company.

Mobley, Gregory. 2012. *The Return of the Chaos Monsters—and Other Backstories of the Bible.* Grand Rapids, Michigan: Eerdmans Publishing Company.

Moor, Johannes C. de. 1972. *New Year with Canaanites and Israelites.* 2 vols. The Nether-lands: Kamper Cahiers.

Moran, William. 1970. "The Creation of Man in Atrahasis I 192-248," *BASOR* 200:48-56.

————. 1991. "Ovid's *Blanda Voluptas* and the Humanization of Enkidu," *JNES* 50:121-27.

————, ed. and trans. 1992. *The Amarna Letters.* Baltimore: Johns Hopkins (cited as EA when referring to particular Amarna Letters).

Müller, Max. 1964. *The Mythology of All Races, vol. 7: Egyptian.* New York: Cooper Square Press.

Mundkur, Balaji. 1983. *The Cult of the Serpent: An Interdisciplinary Survey of its Manifesta-tions and Origins.* Albany: State University of New York Press.

Murison, Ross. 1905. "The Serpent in the Old Testament," *AJSL* 21:115-30.

Naidoff, Bruce. 1978. "A Man to Work the Soil: A New Interpretation of Genesis 2-3," *JSOT* 5:2-14.

Negbi, Ora. 1976. *Canaanite Gods in Metal: An Archaeological Study of Ancient Syro-Palestinian Figurines.* Tel Aviv: Tel Aviv Institute of Archaeology.

Neumann, Erich. 1954. *The Origins and History of Consciousness.* Princeton: Princeton University Press.

———. 1955. *The Great Mother: An Analysis of the Archetype.* Repr. Princeton: Princeton University Press, 1983.

———. 1990. *Depth Psychology and a New Ethic.* Rev ed. Boston: Shambhala.

Niditch, Susan. 1985. *Chaos to Cosmos: Studies in Biblical Patterns of Creation.* Atlanta: Scholars Press.

———. 1993. *Folklore and the Hebrew Bible.* Minneapolis: Fortress Press.

Noth, Martin. 1981. *A History of Pentateuchal Traditions.* Atlanta: Scholars Press.

Nowak, Martin. 2012. "Why We Help," *Scientific American,* July 2012, pp. 34-39.

Obbink, Herman. 1928. "The Tree of Life in Eden," *ZAW* 46:105-12.

Oden, Robert. 1977. *Studies in Lucian's* De Syria Dea. Missoula, Montana: Scholar's Press.

———. 1981. "Divine Aspirations in Atrahasis and in Genesis 1-11," *ZAW* 93:197-216.

Olyan, Saul. 1988. *Asherah and the Cult of Yahweh in Israel.* Atlanta: Scholars Press.

Oren, Eliezer. 1973. *The Northern Cemetery of Beth Shan.* Leiden: Brill.

Pardee, Dennis. 1978. "A Philological and Prosodic Analysis of the Ugaritic Serpent Incantation UT 607," *JANES* 10:73-108.

Park, William. 1991. "Why Eve?," *SVTQ* 35:127-35.

Parkinson, R. B., ed. 1997. *The Tale of Sinuhe and Other Ancient Egyptian Poems 1940-1640 BC.* New York: Oxford University Press.

Parpola, Simo. 1993. "The Assyrian Tree of Life: Tracing the Origins of Jewish Monotheism and Greek Philosophy," *JNES* 52:161-208.

Patai, Raphael. 1967. *Man and Temple in Ancient Jewish Myth and Ritual.* 2nd ed. New York: Ktav Publishing House.

———. 1985. "The Goddess Asherah," *JNES* 24:37-52.

———. 1990. *The Hebrew Goddess,* 3rd ed. Detroit: Wayne State University Press.

Pedersen, Johannes. 1991. *Israel: Its Life and Culture.* 2 vols. Atlanta: Scholars Press.

———. 1969. "Wisdom and Immortality," in *Wisdom in Israel and in the Ancient Near East* (ed. M. Noth and D. Winton Thomas; Leiden: Brill), pp. 238-46.

Persson, Axel. 1942. *New Tombs at Dendra Near Midea.* Lund: C. W. K. Gleerup.

Pettey, Richard. 1990. *Asherah: Goddess of Israel.* New York: Peter Lang Publishing.

Phillips, John. 1984. *Eve: The History of an Idea.* San Francisco: Harper & Row.

Philpot, J. H. 1897. *The Sacred Tree in Religion and Myth.* London: Macmillan.

Phipps, William. 1976. "Adam's Rib: Bone of Contention," *ThTo* 33:263-73.

Piankoff, Alexandre. 1954. *The Tomb of Rameses VI.* Vol. 1. New York: Pantheon Books.

Pinch, Geraldine. 1994. *Magic in Ancient Egypt.* Austin: University of Texas Press.

———. 2002. *Egyptian Mythology.* New York: Oxford University Press.

Pinker, Steven. 2002. *The Blank Slate: The Modern Denial of Human Nature.* New York: Penguin.

Plaut, W. Gunther. 1981. *The Torah: A Modern Commentary.* New York: Union of American Hebrew Congregations.

Porter, Frank. 1901. "The Yeçer Hara: A Study in the Jewish Doctrine of Sin," in *Biblical and Semitic Studies: Critical and Historical Essays by the Members of the Semitic and Biblical Faculty of Yale University.* (New York: Charles Scribner's Sons), pp. 93-156.

Powell, James. 1982. *The Tao of Symbols.* New York: Quill.

Pritchard, James. 1943. *Palestinian Figurines in Relation to Certain Goddesses Known Through Literature.* New Haven, American Oriental Society.

———, ed. 1954. *The Ancient Near East in Pictures Relating to the Old Testament.* Princeton: Princeton University Press, 1954 (cited as *ANEP*).

———, ed. 1955. *Ancient Near Eastern Texts Relating to the Old Testament,* 2nd ed. Princeton: Princeton University Press (cited as *ANET*).

———, ed. 1969. *The Ancient Near East Supplementary Texts and Pictures Relating to the Old Testament.* Princeton: Princeton University Press (cited as *ANES*).

Propp, William. 2006. *Exodus 19-40: A New Translation with Introduction and Commentary*. New York: Doubleday.

Quirke, Stephen. 1992. *Ancient Egyptian Religion*. London: British Museum Press.

———. 2008. "Creation Stories in Ancient Egypt," in *Imagining Creation* (ed. Markham J. Geller and Mineke Schipper; Leiden: Brill), pp. 61-86.

Rad, Gerhard von. 1961. *Genesis: A Commentary*. Philadelphia: Westminster Press.

Radday, Yehuda. 1982. "The Four Rivers of Paradise," *HS* 23:23-31.

Ramsey, G.W. 1988. "Is Name Giving and Act of Domination in Gen 2:23 and Elsewhere?," *CBQ* 50:24:35.

Ratner, Robert. 1989. "'Garments of Skin' (Genesis 3:21)," *JBQ* 18:74-80.

Reed, William. 1949. *The Asherah in the Old Testament*. Fort Worth, Texas: Texas Christian University Press.

Redford, Donald. 1992. *Egypt, Canaan and Israel in Ancient Times*. Princeton: Princeton University Press.

Reicke, Bo. 1956. "The Knowledge Hidden in the Tree of Paradise," *JSS* 1:193-201.

Reik, Theodor. 1960. *The Creation of Woman: A Psychoanalytic Inquiry into the Myth of Eve*. New York: George Braziller, Inc.

Reisenberger, Azila. 1993. "The Creation of Adam as Hermaphrodite—and its Implications for Feminist Theology," *Judaism* 42:447-52.

Renckens, Henricus. 1964. *Israel's Concept of the Beginning: The Theology of Genesis 1-3*. New York: Herder and Herder.

Rendsburg, Gary. 1986. *The Redaction of Genesis*. Winona Lake, Indiana: Eisenbrauns.

Rendtorf, Rolf. 1990. *The Problem of the Process of Transmission in the Pentateuch*. Sheffield: JSOT Press.

Ricoeur, Paul. 1967. *The Symbolism of Evil*. Boston: Beacon Press.

Ringgren, Helmer. 1966. *Israelite Religion*. Philadelphia: Fortress Press.

Robbins, Ellen. 2012. *The Storyteller and the Garden of Eden*. Eugene, Oregon: Pickwick.

Roberts, Alison. 1995. *Hathor Rising: The Serpent Power of Ancient Egypt*. Rottingdean: Northgate Publishers.

Robertson, Edward. 1912. "Where Was Eden?," *AJSL* 28:254-73.

———. 1938. "The Paradise Narrative in Genesis 2, 3," *Journal of the Manchester University Egyptian and Oriental Society* 22:21-35.

Rollston, Christopher. 2010. *Writing and Literacy in the World of Ancient Israel*. Atlanta: Society of Biblical Literature.

Ronnberg, Ami, ed. 2010. *The Book of Symbols*. Cologne, Germany: Taschen.

Rosenberg, David and Harold Bloom. 1990. *The Book of J*. New York: Grove Press.

Rothenberg, Beno. 1972a. *Timna: Valley of the Biblical Copper Mines*. London: Thames and Hudson.

———. 1972b. *Were these King Solomon's Mines? Excavations in the Timna Valley*. New York: Stein & Day.

———. 1988. *The Egyptian Mining Temple at Timna*. London: Institute for Archaeo-Metallurgical Studies.

Roux, Georges. 1992. *Ancient Iraq*. 3rd ed. London: Penguin.

Rowe, Alan. 1929. "A Comparison of Egyptian and Babylonian Civilizations and their Influence on Palestine," Proceedings of the American Philosophical Society 68:313-19.

———. 1930. *The Topography and History of Beth-Shan with Details of the Egyptian and other Inscriptions found on the Site*. Philadelphia: University of Pennsylvania Press.

———. 1940. *The Four Canaanite Temples at Beth-Shan*. Philadelphia: University of Pennsylvania Press.

Rowley, Harold. 1939. "Zadok and Nehushtan," *JBL* 58:113-41.

Sadakata, Akira. 1997. *Buddhist Cosmology: Philosophy and Origins*. Tokyo: Kōsei Publishing Co.

Sáenz-Badillos, Angel. 1993. *A History of the Hebrew Language*. Cambridge: Cambridge University Press.

Sanders, Seth. 2009. *The Invention of Hebrew*. Urbana, Chicago and Springfield: University of Illinois Press.

Sanford, John. 1981. *Evil: The Shadow Side of Reality.* New York: Crossroad.

———. 1987. *The Man Who Wrestled with God: Light from the Old Testament on the Psychology of Individuation.* New York: Paulist.

Sayce, Archibald. 1897. *Lectures on the Origin and Growth of Religion as Illustrated by the Religion of the Ancient Babylonians.* 4th ed. London: Williams and Norgate.

Schmid, Konrad. 2006. "The So-Called Yahwist and the Literary Gap between Genesis and Exodus," in Dozeman and Schmid 2006, pp. 29-50.

———. 2012. *The Old Testament: A Literary History.* Minneapolis: Fortress Press.

Schwartz, Baruch. 2013. Divergence in Contemporary Pentateuchal Theory: Impressions of the Great Divide. Paper presented at the annual meeting of SBL. Baltimore, Md.

Segal, Robert. 1999. *Theorizing about Myth.* Amherst: University of Massachusetts Press.

———. 2004. *Myth: A Very Short Introduction.* Oxford: Oxford University Press.

Seow, C.L. 1997. *Ecclesiastes: A New Translation with Introduction and Commentary.* New York: Doubleday.

Seri, Andrea. 2012. "The Role of Creation in *Enuma Eliš,*" *JANER* 12:4-29.

Shanks, Hershel. 1992. "Defining the Problems: Where We Are in the Debate," in Shanks 1992, pp. 1-23.

Shanks, Hershel, William Dever, Baruch Halpern, and P. Kyle McCarter, Jr. 1992. *The Rise of Ancient Israel.* Washington, D.C.: Biblical Archeology Society.

Shattuck, Roger. 1996. *Forbidden Knowledge.* New York: Harcourt Brace & Company.

Skinner, John. 1910. *A Critical and Exegetical Commentary on Genesis.* New York: Charles Scribner's Sons.

Smith, George. 1880. *The Chaldean Account of Genesis.* London: Sampson Low, Marston, Searle and Rivington.

Smith, Mark. 2001. *The Origins of Biblical Monotheism: Israel's Polytheistic Background and the Ugaritic Texts.* New York: Oxford University Press.

———. 2002. *The Early History of God.* 2nd ed. Grand Rapids: Eerdmans.

Snaith, Norman. 1947. *The Jewish New Year Festival.* London: Society for Promoting Christian Knowledge.

Snell, Bruno. 2011. *The Discovery of the Mind in Greek Philosophy and Literature.* New York: Dover Publications.

Soggin, J. Alberto. 1975. "The Fall of Man in the Third Chapter of Genesis," in *Old Testament and Oriental Studies,* vol. 29 of Biblica et Orientalia Series. Rome: Biblical Institute Press, pp. 88-111.

Speiser, Ephriam. 1929. "Preliminary Excavations at Tepe Gawra," *AASOR* 9:17-57.

———. 1935. *Excavations at Tepe Gawra.* 2 vols. Philadelphia: University of Pennsylvania Press.

———. 1941. "Introduction to Hurrian," AASOR 20.

———. 1964. *The Anchor Bible: Genesis.* New York: Doubleday.

———. 1967a. "The Rivers of Paradise," in Finkelstein and Greenberg 1967, pp. 23-34.

———. 1967b "'ED in The Story of Creation," in Finkelstein and Greenberg 1967, pp. 19-22. Originally published in *BASOR* 140: 9-11 (1955).

Stager, L. E. 2000. "Jerusalem as Eden," *BAR* 26.3:36-47, 66.

Stern, Herold. 1958. "'The Knowledge of Good and Evil,'" *VT* 8:405-18.

Stone, Merlin. 1976. *When God Was a Woman.* Orlando, Florida: Harcourt Brace.

Stordalen, Terje. 1992a. "Genesis 2.4: Restudying a Locus Classicus," *ZAW* 104:163-77.

———.1992b. "Ma, Soil, Garden: Basic Plot in Genesis 2-3 Reconsidered," *JSOT* 53:3-26.

———. 2000. *Echoes of Eden: Genesis 2-3 and Symbolism of the Eden Garden in Biblical Hebrew Literature.* Leuven, Belgium: Peeters.

———. 2008. "Heaven on Earth—Or Not? Jerusalem as Eden in Biblical Literature," in *Beyond Eden: The Biblical Story of Paradise (Genesis 2-3) and Its Reception History* (eds. Konrad Schmid and Christoph Riedweg; Tübingen: Mohr Siebeck), pp. 28-57.

Stratton, Beverly. 1995. *Out of Eden: Reading, Rhetoric and Ideology in Genesis 2-3.* Sheffield: Sheffield Academic.

Stevens, Anthony. 1993. *The Two Million-Year-Old Self.* College Station, Texas: Texas A&M University Press.

Sturluson, Snorri. 2005. *The Prose Edda.* London: Penguin.

Sullivan, Lawrence. 1987. "Tricksters," *ER* 15:45-46.

Talmon, Shemaryahu. 1966. "The 'Desert Motif' in the Bible and in Qumran Literature," in *Biblical Motifs: Origins and Transformations* (ed. Alexander Altman; Cambridge: Harvard University Press), pp. 31-63.

Taylor, J. G. 1994. "Was Yahweh Worshipped as the Sun?," *BAR* 20.3:52-61, 90-91.

Tennant, Frederick. 1903. *The Sources of the Doctrines of the Fall and Original Sin.* Cambridge: Cambridge University Press.

Thompson, P.E.S. 1971. "The Yahwist Creation Story," *VT* 21:197-208.

Thompson, Stith. 1955-58. *The Motif-Index of Folk Literature.* 6 vols. Bloomington, Indiana: University of Indiana Press.

Thompson, Thomas. 1992. *Early History of the Israelite People from the Written and Archaeological Sources.* Leiden: Brill.

———. 1999. *The Mythic Past: Biblical Archaeology and the Myth of Israel.* New York: Basic Books.

Tigay, Jeffery. 1975. "An Empirical Basis for the Documentary Hypothesis," *JBL* 94:329-342.

———. 1986. *You Shall Have No Other Gods: Israelite Religion in the Light of Hebrew Inscriptions.* Atlanta: Scholars Press.

Tosato, Angelo. 1990. "On Genesis 2:24," *CBQ* 52:389-409.

Trible, Phyllis. 1973. "Depatriarchalizing in Biblical Interpretation," *JAAR* 41:30-48.

———. 1978. *God and the Rhetoric of Sexuality.* Philadelphia: Fortress Press.

Van Buren, E. Douglas. 1933. *The Flowing Vase and the God with Streams.* Berlin: Hans Schoetz.

———. 1935-36. "Entwined Serpents," *AfO* 10:53-65.

———. 1945. *Symbols of the Gods in Mesopotamian Art.* Rome: Pontificium Institutum Biblicum.

Van De Mieroop, Marc. 2007. *A History of the Ancient Near East.* 2nd ed. Malden, Mass.: Blackwell.

Van der Toorn, Karel. 1996. *Family Religion in Babylonia, Syria and Israel.* Leiden: Brill.

———. 1999. "Hebat," *DDD,* pp. 391-92.

———. 2007. *Scribal Culture and the Making of the Hebrew Bible.* Cambridge: Harvard University Press.

Van Goudoever, Jan. 1961. *Biblical Calendars.* 2nd ed. Leiden: Brill.

Van Seters, John. 1992. *Prologue to History: The Yahwist as Historian in Genesis.* Louisville: John Knox Press.

———. 1997. *In Search of History: Historiography in the Ancient World and the Origins of Biblical History.* Winona Lake, Indiana: Eisenbrauns.

———. 2006. "The Report of the Yahwist's Demise has been Greatly Exaggerated!," in Dozeman and Schmid 2006, pp. 143-57.

Vaughn, Andrew and Ann Killebrew, eds. 2003. *Jerusalem in Bible and Archaeology: The First Temple Period.* Atlanta: Society for Biblical Literature.

Vaux, Roland de. 1978. *The Early History of Israel.* Philadelphia: The Westminster Press.

———. 1997. *Ancient Israel: Its Life and Institutions.* London: Longman & Todd. Grand Rapids: Eerdmans.

Vawter, Bruce. 1977. *On Genesis: A New Reading.* Garden City, N.Y.: Doubleday.

Vriezen, Karel. 2001. "Archaeological Traces of Cult in Ancient Israel," in Becking 2001, pp. 45-80.

———. 1967. *The Religion of Ancient Israel.* Philadelphia: Westminster Press.

Wallace, Howard. 1992a "Adam," *ABD* 1:62-64.

———. 1992b. "Eden, Garden of," *ABD* 2:281-83.

———. 1992c. "Eve," *ABD* 2:676-77.

———. 1992d. "Tree of Knowledge and Tree of Life," *ABD* 6:656-60.

———. 1985. *The Eden Narrative.* Atlanta: Scholars Press.

Walsh, Jerome. 1977. "Genesis 2:4b-3:24: A Synchronic Approach," *JBL* 96:161-77.

Waltke, Bruce. 2004. *The Book of Proverbs.* Grand Rapids: Eerdmans.

———. 1990. *An Introduction to Biblical Hebrew Syntax.* Winona Lake, Indiana: Eisenbrauns.

Walton, John. 2006. *Ancient Near Eastern Thought and the Old Testament: Introducing the Conceptual World of the Hebrew Bible.* Grand Rapids, Michigan: Baker Academic.

———. 2009. *The Lost World of Genesis One.* Downers Grove, Illinois: InterVarsity Press.

———. 2012. The Tower of Babel and the Covenant: Rhetorical Strategy in Genesis Based on Theological and Comparative Analysis. Paper presented at the annual meeting of SBL. Chicago, Ill.

Ward, William Hayes. 1910. *The Seal Cylinders of Western Asia.* Washington, D.C.: Carnegie Institution.

Wellhausen, Julius. 1885. *Prolegomena to the History of Israel.* Edinburgh: Adam & Charles Black.

Wenham, Gordon. 1994. "Sanctuary Symbolism in the Garden of Eden Story," in Hess and Tsumura 1994, pp. 399-404.

Wensinck, Arent. 1916. *The Ideas of the Western Semites Concerning the Navel of the Earth.* Amsterdam: Johannes Müller.

———. 1918. *The Ocean in the Literature of the Western Semites.* Amsterdam: Johannes Müller.

———. 1921. *Tree and Bird as Cosmological Symbols in Western Asia.* Amsterdam: Johannes Müller.

Werner, E. T. C. 1994. *Myths and Legends of China.* New York: Dover Publications.

West, M. L. 1997. *The East Face of Helicon.* New York: Oxford University Press.

Westenholz, Joan. 1998. "Goddesses of the Ancient Near East 3000-1000 BC," in Goodison, and Morris 1998, pp. 63-82.

Westermann, Claus. 1974. *Creation.* Philadelphia: Fortress Press.

———. 1994. *Genesis 1-11.* Minneapolis: Fortress Press.

Whitelam, Keith. 1996. *The Invention of Ancient Israel: The Silencing of Palestinian History.* London: Routledge.

Whybray, R. N. 1996. "The Immorality of God," *JSOT* 72:89-120.

Widengren, Geo. 1951. *The King and the Tree of Life in Ancient Near Eastern Religion.* Uppsala: B. Lundequistska Bokhandeln.

———. 1967. "The Principle of Evil in the Eastern Religions," in Carl Kerényi et al, *Evil.* Evanston: Northwestern University Press, pp. 19-55.

Wiggins, Steve. 1991. "The Myth of Asherah: Lion Lady and Serpent Goddess," *UF* 23:383-94.

———. 1993. *A Reassessment of 'Asherah': A Study According to the Textual Sources of the First Two Millennia B.C.E.* Darmstadt: Neukirchen-Vluyn/Verlag Butzon & Bercker Kevelaer.

Wilber, Ken. 1996. *Up from Eden: A Transpersonal View of Human Evolution.* Wheaton Illinois: Quest Books.

———. 2001. *No Boundary: Eastern and Western Approaches to Spiritual Growth.* Boston: Shambhala.

Wilder, Amos. 1952. *Modern Poetry and the Christian Tradition: A Study of the Relation of Christianity to Culture.* New York: Charles Scribner's Sons

Wilkinson, Richard. 1992. *Reading Egyptian Art.* New York: Thames & Hudson.

Wilkinson, Toby. 2010. *The Rise and Fall of Ancient Egypt.* New York: Random House.

Williams, A. 1977. "The Relationship of Genesis 3.20 to the Serpent," *ZAW* 89:357-74.

Williams, Ronald. 2007. *Williams' Hebrew Syntax.* 3rd ed. Toronto: University of Toronto Press.

Williams-Forte, Elizabeth. 1983. "The Snake and the Tree in the Iconography and Texts of Syria During the Bronze Age," in Gorelick and Williams-Forte 1983, pp. 18-43.

Wilson, Leslie. 2001. *The Serpent Symbol in the Ancient Near East.* New York: University Press of America.

Winter, B. 1983. *Frau und Göttin: Exegetische und ikonographische Studien zum weiblichen Gottesbild im Alten Israel in dessen Umwelt.* Göttingen: Vandenhoek & Ruprecht.

Wise, Michael, Martin Abegg, Jr., and Edward Cook, eds. and trans. 1996. *The Dead Sea Scrolls.* San Francisco: HarperSanFrancisco.

Wismer, P. L. 1983. "The Myth of Original Sin: A Hermeneutic Theology Based on Genesis 2-3." Ph.D. diss., University of Chicago.

Wolkstein, Diane and Samuel Noah Kramer. 1983. *Inanna: Queen of Heaven and Earth.* New York: Harper & Row.

Wright, David. 1992, "Day of Atonement," *ABD* 2:73.

———. 1996. "Holiness, Sex, and Death in the Garden of Eden," *Biblica* 77:305-29.

Wright, G. Ernest. 1964. *Shechem: The Biography of a Biblical City.* London: Gerald Duckworth & Co. Ltd.

Wright, G. R. H. 1970. "The Mythology of Pre-Israelite Shechem," *VT* 20: 75-82.

Wright, J. Edward. 2000. *The Early History of Heaven.* New York: Oxford University Press.

Wyatt, Nicolas. 1981. "Interpreting the Creation and Fall Story in Genesis 2-3," *ZAW* 93:10-21.

———. 1999. "Asherah," *DDD,* pp. 99-105.

Wynn-Williams, Damian J. 1997. *The State of the Pentateuch: A Comparison of the Approaches of M. Noth and E. Blum.* Berlin: Walter de Gruyter.

Yadin, Yigael. 1975. *Hazor: The Rediscovery of a Great Citadel of the Bible.* New York: Random House.

Yamashita, Tadanori. 1963. "The Goddess Asherah." Ph.D. diss., Yale University.

Yarden, Leon. 1971. *Tree of Light: A Study of the Menorah.* Ithaca: Cornell University Press.

Young, Dwight. 1977. "With Snakes and Dates: A Sacred Marriage Drama at Ugarit," *UF* 9:291-314.

Zevit, Ziony. 2001. *The Religions of Ancient Israel: A Synthesis of Parallactic Approaches.* London: Continium.

General Index

Aaronid priests, 3, 7, 19–20, 204, 305n27, 308n21, 351n213

Abdi-Heba, 25, 226

Adam: androgyny and, 219–221; breath of life, 130–133; creation from earth, 127–130, 244; gardener role, 113, 116, 126, 129, 133–136; kingly role, 126, 334n14; meaning of name, 125–126, 244; naming power, 133; offense as consisting of listening to Eve, 269; proper name Adam being in story or not, 125–126; soul, and whether Adam had one, 130–133

Adapa and *Adapa* myth, 112, 116, 133, 134, 156, 166, 232, 263, 265, 333n263, 362n60

Adonis, 334n15; as dying and rising god, 51, 350n170; association with serpents, 206; association with trees, 149; Gardens of, 199

Ahab, 19, 33, 35, 73–74, 307n12, 311n109, 318n159

Amun/Amun-Ra, Egyptian god, 43, 82, 130, 184

An-Ki, 57, 83–85, 108–109, 326n77

Apep (or Apophis), Egyptian serpent of chaos, 88, 151, 182, 184, 194, 202, 303n45, 345n20, 348n119, 353n253

Aphrodite, 51, 143, 170, 230, 339n87, 346n51, 348n107

Apollo, 61, 149, 187, 190, 339n84

Arad, 17, 317n130; role in formation of Israel, 64; temple at, 77

Archetypes: collective unconscious and, xvi; definition and origin of, xvi; god-image as archetype, xvi; Jung and, xvi; myths and, xvi–xvii; Self as archetype, xvi; wholeness as archetype, xvi

Asherah (also Athirat), goddess, 68–80; archaeological evidence for in biblical Israel, 71–80; as Israelite goddess generally, 71–73; as Yahweh's consort or wife, xxiii; epithet of *elat*, 69, 71; meaning of name, 70; origins of, 69; Qedesh/Qudshu as. See Qedesh and Qudshu; Tannit as variation or epithet of. *See* Tannit. *See also* Khirbet el-Qom inscription; Kuntillet Ajrûd; Figures 2, 3, 4, 5, 6, 7, 8, 9, and 23

asherahs and asherim (cult object): archaeological discovery of, 69, 74, 318n166, 322n252; at Samaria, 17, 73–74, 318n156, 318n159; standing before Jerusalem Temple, 17, 67, 71, 72–73; characteristics and nature of, 17, 70, 140, 307n4, 318n166; condemnations of, 14–15, 67, 160, 172; destruction of (commandments to destroy and actual destruction), 14–15, 21, 67, 72, 77, 161, 341n145; location and setting at high places, 17, 67, 70–71, 74, 142, 158, 161, 207; meaning

389

Index of Authors

Index of Biblical Citations

Index of Citations to Apocrypha and Qumran Material

Index of Classical Sources

67893691R00274

Made in the USA
Middletown, DE
26 March 2018